Landscape Plants for Dry Regions

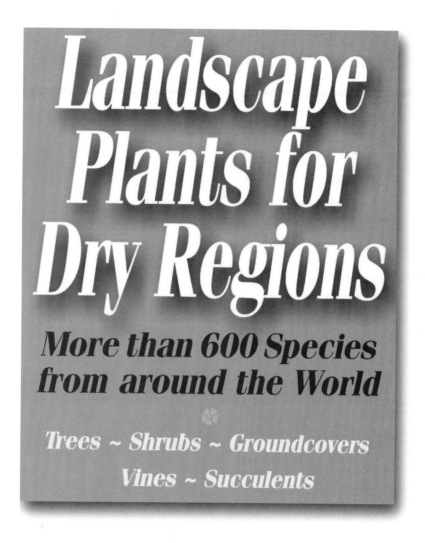

Landscape Plants for Dry Regions

More than 600 Species from around the World

Trees ~ Shrubs ~ Groundcovers
Vines ~ Succulents

By Warren Jones and Charles Sacamano

FISHER BOOKS™

Publishers: Howard W. Fisher, Helen V. Fisher
Managing Editor: Sarah Trotta
Editors: Melanie Mallon, Scott Millard
Production Manager: Randy Schultz
Interior Design: Randy Schultz, B. Josh Young
Page Layout: Nancy Taylor, Anne Olson
Cover Design: B. Josh Young
Indexer: Michelle B. Graye

Published by Fisher Books, LLC
5225 W. Massingale Road
Tucson, Arizona 85743-8416
(520) 744-6110
www.fisherbooks.com

Printed in U.S.A.
5 4 3 2 1

Library of Congress
Cataloging-in-Publication Data

Jones, Warren D.
Landscape plants for dry regions : more than 600 species from around the world / by Warren Jones and Charles Sacamano.
p. cm.
ISBN 1-55561-190-7
1. Arid regions plants. 2. Landscape plants. 3. Arid regions plants—Pictorial works. 4. Landscape plants—Pictorial works. I. Sacamano, Charles M. II. Title.

SB427.5 .J66 2000
635.9'525—dc21 00-028767

Note: The information in this book is true and complete to the best of our knowledge. This book is intended only as an informative guide for those wishing to know more about dry region landscape plants. The information in this book is offered with no guarantees on the part of the author or Fisher Books. The author and publisher disclaim all liability in connection with the use of this book.

PHOTOGRAPHY CREDITS

The authors and publisher would like to thank Arizona-Sonora Desert Museum, Boyce Thompson Southwest Arboretum, Mountain States Wholesale Nursery and Tucson Botanical Gardens for the many slides that feature their plantings. Photos not listed here were contributed by the authors.

Ted Bundy: *Acacia farnesiana (p. 10, top); Buddleia marrubifolia (p. 71, right); Caesalpinia gilliesii (p. 75, right, back cover); Erythrina bidwillii (p. 138, right); Fallugia paradoxa (p. 156, left); Gazania rigens (p. 171, top); Justicia spicigera (p. 192, right); Larrea divaricata tridentata (p. 196, right); Melampodium leucanthum (p. 215); Mimosa dysocarpa (p. 219, bottom right); Pennisetum setaceum 'Cupreum' (p. 245. right); Rhus ovata (p. 284, bottom); Ruellia californica pink form (p. 288, bottom right); Ruellia peninsularis (p. 289, right); Senna artemisioides filifolia (p. 302, right); Senna artemisioides petiolaris (p. 303, left)*
Allison Caronna: *Teucrium fruticans (p. 323, both)*
C. D. Crosswhite: *Guaiacum angustifolium (p. 176, right)*
Dr. M. Frederickson: *Atriplex barclayana (p. 52); Ipomea pes-caprae (p. 184, bottom left)*
Kelley Green Trees: *Juniperus erythrocarpa (p.190); Quercus buckleyi (p. 276, left); Quercus turbinellia (p. 279)*
Matthew B. Johnson: *Bursera microphylla (p. 74); Senna atomaria (p. 304)*
Scott Millard: *Malephora crocea (p. 210)*
Janet Rademacher: *Chitalpa (p. 105, left); Chrysactinia mexicana (p. 107, both--also on cover); Hymenoxys acaulis*
Greg Starr: *Aniscanthus thurberi (p. 44, right); Lantana horrida (p. 194, right); Penstemon pseudospectabilis (248); Prosopis pubescens (p. 271, right); Salvia leucophylla (p. 295)*
Kim Stone: *Santolina virens (p. 296)*
Walt Disney Horticulture Program, Chris Hassell, Program Specialist: *Bauhinia punctata (p. 59, bottom left)*
B. Josh Young: *Acacia eburnea (p. 9, left); Plumbago scandens (p. 264, right)*

CONTENTS

ACKNOWLEDGMENTS

Over the past thirty years, a number of highly motivated individuals have been exploring the world's semiarid regions and various deserts in search of potential low-water-use landscape plants. Many of the plants in this work have been evaluated as potential landscape plants at test sites in California and Arizona desert regions. It now seems appropriate to bring together and report on the results of these investigations.

Much of the testing and evaluation of new water-efficient landscape plants has taken place on the campus of the University of Arizona in Tucson. The campus is situated in an intermediate desert climate at an elevation of 2500 feet (760 m). A major goal of this project has been to identify more water-efficient substitutes for the common water-demanding urban plants generally used in city landscapes. The densely built university campus is ideal for this work because it presents a wide range of urban-type planting situations and microclimates.

The success of the University of Arizona project has been due in large measure to the cooperation and support of Superintendent of Grounds Charles Raetzman and his university grounds and labor department. Without the considerable help of this group, the project could not have succeeded.

William Kinnison, professor of horticulture at Central Arizona College, Coolidge, has been active in this study since the mid-1970s. The test plantings on the Central Arizona College campus provided a milder and lower-elevation test site. In addition, this campus furnished varied topographical situations, from rocky bajadas to flat agricultural land. As a result, the plantings of the Central Arizona College campus location, under the watchful eye of Professor Kinnison, have played an important role in the screening and evaluation of low-water-use candidates for landscape lists. Nearly mature plantings, some arranged in regional natural associations and others planted in a more urban landscape context, are found here.

Founded in the 1920s, the Boyce Thompson Southwest Arboretum at Superior, Arizona (elevation 2500 ft./760 m) is dedicated to the introduction and study of arid-land plants. The arboretum contains a historic plant collection from arid regions of the world begun by Colonel William Boyce Thompson after World War I. The colonel was ahead of his time in recognizing the need for arid-adapted plants to modify the rigors of living in desert climates. He contributed much effort and personal funds in establishing this great collection. The arboretum has developed a large demonstration garden that shows many different themes using only arid-desert plants. It has also been a valuable test site.

Significant work has been accomplished here, especially with low-water-use groundcovers. The arboretum has also contributed many useful additions to the water-efficient plant palette from its rich collection. Many of these additions were a result of recognizing the landscape potential of overlooked plants that had been a part of the collection for a long time.

The Arizona-Sonora Desert Museum west of Tucson has long been recognized as a pioneer institution in the testing and study of desert plants for landscape use. The museum's demonstration garden, which was originally cosponsored by *Sunset Magazine*, has tested and presented desert plants in a landscape setting for more than thirty years. For many years the museum's plant collection was primarily limited to species native to the Sonoran Desert. Recently, a few species from other deserts have been added. Nevertheless the museum's grounds graphically present the considerable landscape potential of desert plants to visiting researchers, nursery professionals and home gardeners alike. The designer, Landscape Architect Guy S. Green, *Sunset Magazine*, and Dr. M. Dimmitt, head of the museum's plant department, are to be congratulated.

For many years the Desert Botanical Garden at Phoenix, Arizona, has been a center for the study of desert plants. It is located in the Salt River Valley, a low-desert location. This garden has contributed to the list of rediscovered landscape plants and long-overlooked plants in their collection.

More recently, the Tucson Botanical Garden has developed extensive plantings of desert plants, including a demonstration garden featuring the irrigation principle of *hydrozoning*.

Low-desert plant-testing sites include the Desert Botanical Garden and the state capitol grounds at Phoenix, Arizona (elevation 800 ft./240 m), the University of Arizona station and farm at Yuma, Arizona (elevation 10 ft./3 m), and the Living Desert Museum at Palm Desert, California (elevation 500 ft./150 m). These locations have also contributed greatly to this body of information. Special appreciation is extended to Dr. and Mrs. Reck of Palm Desert, who agreed to the use of their spacious desert homesite as a testing location. In addition to dedicating most of the property to the project, Dr. Reck installed an irrigation system and maintained the test plants on a year-round basis. The residential setting of this site provided a useful frame of reference for evaluating new plants. In addition to the low-desert climate and residential scale, the site had very sandy soil, adding another dimension to the plant-testing data.

The ongoing collecting and testing of desert species of the family Fabaceae (Leguminosae) being carried on under the leadership of Mathew Johnson and the Desert Legume Program of the University of Arizona and the Boyce Thompson Arboretum continually adds to the list of exciting new species for landscape use. Testing is ongoing at the arboretum and the Campbell Avenue farm at the University of Arizona, but especially at the test plots on the University of Arizona farm on the Yuma, Arizona, mesa. Here much has been learned about cold-tender plants that researchers were unable to grow at other test sites. Mathew Johnson has been an avid collector in his own right.

The Raymond Ortega residence, also in Yuma, Arizona, has served as another valuable test location, especially for observing frost-tender plants that cannot tolerate the colder temperatures of higher elevations. This Yuma location has deep valley soil, which provided opportunities to observe the effect maximum root development has on the ultimate size of plants.

Many other investigators and collaborators, including Dr. William Feldman, Mr. Eric A. Johnson, Mr. Ralph DeLeon, Dr. David Palzkill and Mr. Greg Starr, have been pursuing and continue to pursue various phases of investigation relating to this work. The efforts of these individuals have contributed much to our knowledge of water-efficient plants.

Desert plants can be collected and evaluated for their landscape value indefinitely. However, until they are known and available for use by the landscape industry and home gardener, little progress can be made. Arizona nurseryman Ron Gass, owner of Mountain States Wholesale Nursery in Glendale, has accomplished much in this regard. Mr. Gass has been a catalyst and a leader in the introduction of little-known desert plants to the landscape industry for many years. His success has been achieved at no small economic risk: A new plant must be propagated, grown to salable size and promoted to a clientele largely unfamiliar with its landscape potential. There is no automatic guarantee that such efforts will result in acceptance of a new low-water-use landscape species. In addition to these achievements, Mr. Gass has collected extensively in the Sonoran and Chihauhuan Deserts and evaluated the landscape performance of candidate species in his own testing program. It is the authors' opinion that Mr. Gass stands alone as a leader and pacesetter in the water-efficient landscape-plant arena. To a large degree the increasingly diverse palette of low-water-use plants available in nurseries today is traceable to his efforts.

The authors also want to recognize the contributions of the late Dr. Rodney Engard, Director of the Tucson Botanical Garden. He explored and collected widely in search of new arid-landscape species. As a result of his work, especially in the Chihuahuan Desert of Mexico, we now enjoy a number of worthwhile plants in our arid landscapes.

ABOUT THE AUTHORS

Warren Jones, FASLA, educated two generations of landscape architects at the University of Arizona, before his promotion to Professor Emeritus. Jones currently serves on the advisory board of the Boyce Thompson Southwest Arboretum in Superior, Arizona, and as a consultant in arid regions throughout the world. He is also a fellow of the American Society of Landscape Architecture and a recipient of the Lifetime Award given by the University of Arizona. The Arizona Green Industry offers a scholarship to landscape-architecture students in his name. Warren Jones is the coauthor of *Plants for Dry Climates*, Fisher Books, 1998.

Charles Sacamano, Ph.D., earned his graduate degrees in Horticulture at the University of Missouri. His career as a landscape horticulture specialist for cooperative extension began at the University of Missouri followed by almost twenty years in the same position at the University of Arizona. In Arizona he also taught courses, directed graduate research and hosted *Sacamano's Gardens*, a TV series on gardening in the desert Southwest. Two television documentaries, "Jewels of the Jungle" and "Secrets of the Selva," relate to his plant exploration work in Mexico. Following retirement, he was awarded the title of Professor Emeritus of Plant Sciences and then settled in Puerto Vallarta, Mexico, where he consults on a broad range of tropical landscape and ecological projects along the Pacific Coast.

WEB UPDATES

For updated information on dry region landscape plants, including new plant listings, just visit our website at www.fisherbooks.com and register the purchase of your book in the "Feedback" section (under the "Fisher Books" pull down tab). Select "Desert Gardening" as your area of interest and follow the instructions.

Oenothera berlanderi

INTRODUCTION

The plants we describe in this book are native to warm deserts and bordering semiarid regions around the world. A number of them are available in nurseries and are commonly used in our landscapes. Others are not generally known but have considerable potential because of their low water requirements. Also included in this text are plants with greater water needs that are appropriate for an oasis-type treatment. These plants tolerate heat and dry air but require more water. Obviously, it is necessary to understand the climate preferences and limitations of each plant. With this understanding, we are able to select species that can be counted on to succeed in assorted and varied arid habitats.

Expanding the knowledge and available palette of low-water-demanding landscape plants is what this book is about. An additional goal is to list plants valuable for revegetation of disturbed sites. This has become a serious problem in the U.S. Southwest—restoring retired former farmlands to native plant cover. Many of these plants may have little value in a planned landscape but are useful for revegetation projects.

Other species are in this book because of their value in breeding and hybridizing projects to develop superior plants. Others may have little immediate application for our current landscapes but will satisfy new and different requirements in the future.

Note that we have included plants that can be invasive in certain situations, are toxic or have other negative characteristics. These plants have value if properly used. Take care to learn when to avoid them and when their unique qualities are useful by reading both the Landscape Value and Possible Problems sections of each chart.

Water-efficient shrubs and trees for the landscape may include non-native succulents—cacti, aloes, agaves and yuccas—as well as trees and shrubs from other arid regions. Although not a part of the native flora of your area, these non-natives convey a similar feeling and appearance and grow with similar care. Certain introduced plants are so well-adapted that they have naturalized in various arid locales, which can be either invasive or a wonderful way to add variety to the landscape. Others have been used so long in a particular region that they seem to be a part of the local flora.

Nurseries carry more and more species of arid-tolerant landscape plants. New species and varieties become available each year as interest in water-efficient plants accelerates. A prime goal of this book is to describe a wide range of water-efficient plants. These include many plants that are *potentially* interesting but are not currently available in the nursery industry, as well as plants that are common. We hope that describing plants not currently available will lead to further evaluation of these plants so that they have a chance to prove their worth before they are forgotten by the landscape world. Plants are often popular for a period of time then, due to a swing in public taste, disappear from the nursery trade because of lack of demand. Later they fill a unique landscape need and are rediscovered.

HOW THIS BOOK IS ORGANIZED

The plant charts that follow are not all-inclusive. However, in the authors' opinion, they include some of the most useful landscape species as well as some interesting newly collected plants.

Be aware that most plant characteristics and needs are influenced by factors related to soil, climate, water and nutritional status. The mature height and spread of a plant species as well as the size of its leaves, flowers and fruit can be estimated but not guaranteed. Landscape maintenance practices such as pruning may also have an effect on plant characteristics. As a result, it is difficult to place precise and absolute limits on the size and appearance of plants and their organs.

In the plant descriptions that make up the bulk of this book, measurements of height and spread of plants are average estimates based on repeat observations. Numerical values expressed in English units are converted to the metric system and *then rounded off.* Metric units are within parentheses. Temperature units are expressed as degrees Fahrenheit as well as degrees Celsius (which are in parentheses).

1 ***Acacia tortilis***
2 Umbrella thorn
3 Fabaceae (Leguminosae) family

4 

COLD HARDINESS 5
Low and intermediate zones. Nursery stock seems to be vulnerable to cold damage in the intermediate zone until well established in a landscape.

LANDSCAPE VALUE 6
Excellent umbrella-form shade tree that tolerates tough conditions.

CULTURAL REQUIREMENTS 7
- **Exposure:** Full or reflected sun.
- **Water:** Drought tolerant but thoroughly soak the root zone once or twice during the summer for good growth and to develop its potential.
- **Soil:** Accepts most soil types.
- **Propagation:** Seed. Scarify or soak in hot water to aid germination (see page xxiv.)
- **Maintenance:** Generally undemanding but good growing conditions speed its growth and ensure acceptable appearance.

POSSIBLE PROBLEMS 8
None observed.

More than 20 feet (6 m) high (reputed to get much taller in its native Africa under optimum conditions), spreading to 30 feet (9 m). Moderate growth. A promising new arrival from Africa and the Mideast that has the characteristic flat-top form associated with the acacias of the African big game country. Usually single-trunked, form is low-branching unless pruned up. Small feathery leaves line the thorny twigs. Tiny fragrant cream or white puffball flowers appear midsummer (not showy). They are followed by curious pods that roll up into a tight coil like a spring. Bark on mature trees is dark gray, rough and deeply fissured. Evergreen. 9

The Plant Chart

Above is a sample of the charts you will find throughout the book with a brief explanation of what you can expect to find in each subsection.

1. **Scientific Name:** The charts are alphabetized by their current scientific name, starting with genus and species. Some plants have been (or still are) known by different scientific names. When this occurs, the alternative name is listed in parentheses next to the most current scientific name.

2. **Common Name(s):** Under the scientific name, you will find one or more common names. These names may vary from location to location, so you may know a particular plant by another name not listed here. It is impractical (if not impossible) to list every possible common name used around the world. Ask for a plant by its scientific name because this will be more consistent from nursery to nursery.

3. **Family Name:** Beneath the common names is the name of the family the plant belongs to. Understanding the general growth characteristics and culture of a family provides a better understanding of the specific plant.

4. **Photo(s):** Photos show the average appearance of the plant plus additional characteristics, such as bloom, seasonal change, seeds, differing colors of varieties and other important features.

5. **Cold Hardiness:** Before reading more about a particular plant, you'll want to determine if it will grow successfully in your zone. (To determine your zone, read the descriptions on pages xiv and xv.) In this section, you will find information about where the plant will grow successfully (low, intermediate or high zone). This section may also include additional information on the effects of frost on the plant as well as in what zones it might grow successfully under certain circumstances.

6. **Landscape Value:** Each plant has greater chances of success in certain kinds of landscapes (such as medians, parks or patios). Within these landscapes, plants also have a number of possible uses (such as a barrier, privacy screen or accent). In this section, you will find information about the best ways to use each plant in the landscape. See also page xxxi for a pictorial guide to some different landscape design elements.

7. **Cultural Requirements:** Although all the plants in this book grow in arid regions, they don't share the same exposure, water and soil needs. This section lists the plant's typical exposure, water and soil requirements, in addition to the best propagation method (such as seed, cutting or division) and any particular maintenance requirements. Additional information on how to care for the plant will be listed in an optional miscellaneous section. Note that not all plants will have a miscellaneous entry.

   Keep in mind that these requirements are based on the average needs of the plant. If the plant is to thrive, you must evaluate these in light of your own unique circumstances. For more information about other factors to consider, see Planting Procedures, page xxv.

8. **Possible Problems:** This lists potential problems you should be aware of when selecting and growing each plant. This section includes problems that do not affect every plant of the species but that affect enough to warrant a watchful eye. Typical problems include vulnerability to certain pests and diseases, invasiveness, toxicity and troublesome physical traits, such as thorns. This section will also list aesthetic problems that are troublesome in certain landscapes: A tree that produces a lot of seed litter, for example, would not be a good choice next to a swimming pool, but that same tree might be terrific in a park setting.

9. **Description:** This section provides basic information about the plant, such as its native regions, physical characteristics (foliage, bloom, stems), size and growth rate, plus interesting or useful history or details that will help you get to know the character of the plant. Note: all metric measurements are rounded off.

Heteromeles arbutifolia

CLIMATE

Desert and semiarid climates stretch from the tropics to the arctic, representing a wide temperature spread. The plants presented here belong to the middle regions that lie between the two extremes: neither truly tropical nor cold desert. Frost is possible in all of these regions. The warmest regions will have some nearly frost-free areas within their boundaries while the coldest will experience a considerable number of below-freezing winter nights each year. All three *zones*—low, intermediate and high (the coldest)—can exist in close proximity as a result of changes in elevation. However, distance from the equator is the main factor to consider, with the coolest climate being farthest away from the equator.

Low Zone: Adenium obesum

Intermediate Zone: Tagetes lucida

The minimum temperature experienced in a zone is generally the primary limitation as to which plants will succeed there. However, sometimes major cold events are so infrequent that plants can recover between such occurrences. In these areas one must look at the *average minimum* winter temperature to determine if a plant will grow successfully in that particular zone.

Because of the importance of low-temperature tolerance in each zone, each plant chart includes a Cold Hardiness section near the top. The information in this section indicates, to the best of our knowledge, which zones (low, intermediate or high) the plant will flourish in. This data may be incomplete for some of the recent additions to the arid landscape, plants whose landscape potential and hardiness to cold are still untested.

High Zone: Prunus serotina capuli

UNDERSTANDING YOUR CLIMATE

Regional climates (*macroclimates*), wet or dry, are influenced by the following five basic factors:

1. Distance from equator (latitude)
2. Elevation
3. Oceans, seas and other large bodies of water
4. Continental air-mass effects
5. Regional topography

1. Distance from equator (latitude). This dictates how long and how cold winters will be, and the variation in day length from summer to winter. Day length has a controlling effect on growth rate, flowering and so forth.

2. Elevation. The higher elevations (and therefore higher zones) have colder winters and cooler nighttime temperatures all year than will be recorded in the lower elevations (lower zones). For example, the Saltillo area in the state of Coahilla, Mexico, is a dry part of the Chihuahuan Desert but enjoys cool summers because of its high elevation. In fact, it has become something of a summer resort for lower-elevation dwellers wishing to escape the summer heat. In general, low elevation zones become progressively cooler as you move north or south from the equator, although this is not always the case. In Arizona, Yuma and Phoenix are farther from the equator and lower in elevation than Tucson, but they are both distinctly warmer.

3. Oceans, seas and other large bodies of water. In some deserts that border the sea, humidity is higher than it is in inland deserts, although rainfall is scarce. Deserts next to warm oceans will be the most humid—almost tropical but arid. Examples include the Saudi Arabian lands bordering the Persian Gulf and the Red Sea, and the east coast of Baja, California, next to the Gulf of California. These areas also have high temperatures in summer.

In contrast, arid regions that border oceans with *cold* currents will have cool and foggy summers. The cold waters of the Pacific off the west coast of Baja, California, produce this type of foggy desert. Other similar deserts exist off the west coast of South America, from Peru to Chile, and the west coast of South Africa.

Average heat, or the lack of it, as well as maximum cold experienced limit what will grow in a given location. These factors influence how much irrigation will be necessary for a given plant to succeed. Plants require much less irrigation in cool summer deserts than in hot summer deserts. The presence of humidity in either region will definitely make the irrigation water go further.

Rainfall, though scant, can occur during both summer and winter seasons in arid regions adjoining warm bodies of water, although summer rain is more common. Regions fronting cold waters tend to receive a limited amount of precipitation in winter. Summer is usually rainless but is the most foggy season.

Top: Yucca aloifolia; Bottom: Cocos nucifera

4. **Continental air-mass effects.** The climate of arid regions located in the interior of a large land mass will not be greatly influenced by an ocean or sea. These places are subject to sudden short-term temperature changes brought on by movement of the *continental air mass:* an enormous body of air that maintains, as it travels, almost uniform temperature and humidity conditions. These short-term temperature changes occur mostly in winter.

   The low humidity of inland arid regions also permits a dramatic daily temperature swing, sometimes a difference of 40 to 50°F (22 to 28°C) between morning lows and afternoon highs. Rain in the form of localized thunderstorms is more common in the heat of the summer and precipitation can be considerable at the storm's center. Northern and western Sonora, Mexico, and southeastern Arizona are examples of regions that have this climate type. The interior of the Arabian Peninsula experiences extremely hot summers. Rain occurs only in winter here, so there is no moisture to provide even temporary relief from the searing summer heat. Landscape plants for cities like Riyadh, Saudi Arabia, have to be the toughest to tolerate such a stressful environment. Irrigation for landscape plantings is demanding and critical therefore. The failure of an irrigation system in summer can mean the loss of mature plantings in a matter of weeks.

5. **Regional topography.** Mountain ranges and hills modify climate by blocking marine air and channeling the passage of continental air masses across a region. In fact, most arid regions and deserts are the result of high mountains blocking out moisture-laden storms. The number and ruggedness of local hills, including the angle and orientation of slopes, the depth and breadth of valleys, plus the size and density of cities create local *mesoclimates* (see definition, following). South- and west-facing slopes and mountain foothills that are warmer than the regional average are called *thermal belts.* Northern slopes, canyons and valley bottoms tend to be colder than thermal belts because cold air, which is heavier than warm air, flows downhill and settles in low spots.

   Large arid-climate cities like Phoenix, Arizona, absorb much heat during the day. This heat is radiated back into the atmosphere after dark, elevating night temperatures (as well as increasing day temperatures). Cities of this kind are described as *heat islands.* They are significantly warmer than the surrounding countryside both day and night.

Pinus edulis in natural habitat

Ailanthus altissima in a microclimate created by a University of Arizona building.

MESO- AND MICROCLIMATES

Mesoclimates, such as the thermal belts and heat islands described above, fail to maintain increases in temperatures when a major cold continental air mass moves in. Temperatures fall and remain much lower for a longer period of time than is normal. This type of weather event, though rare, can be very destructive. Plantings not hardy to such low temperatures can be destroyed or critically damaged, depending on the duration of the cold. Plants in coastal deserts are less susceptible to continental cold waves because of the warming effects of the nearby water and the increased humidity it produces.

Microclimates, on a smaller scale, are produced by the spaces around manmade structures as well as natural structures, such as boulders, rows of trees and so on. Topography and ground-surface treatment, structural design, construction materials and even color are factors. Building orientation and existing landscape plantings also greatly influence high and low temperatures, air movement, day length and light intensity of small spaces in the landscape. Microclimates can create many unique opportunities and challenges for landscape planting.

ZONES

In this book, we use *zones* to indicate the cold tolerance of each plant. The zones reflect different climates (which are created by the factors described previously): *Low zone* is basically the warmest zone, *high zone* the coldest, and the *intermediate zone* falls in between. Although many other climate zones exist in the world, only these three zones are relevant to dry-climate plants. The bottom line that determines long-term success or failure of a plant is whether the plant will tolerate the minimum temperature of a zone or, if damaged, can recover quickly (and without irreparable damage) from temperatures expected in the coldest years of that zone.

Low zone. Low-elevation zones range from valleys below sea level to 2000 feet (610 m) above sea level. Near the tropics, this zone often extends to somewhat higher elevations because of these regions' proximity to the equator (see page xii). Most parts of the low zone will experience some light frost every winter, although practically frost-free areas do exist in this zone. They are the result of the unique orientation of local topography, proximity to a shoreline, or mesoclimates created by large urban areas (heat islands). In general, the *growing season* (days between killing frosts) may be all year in coastal arid regions such as Guaymas, Sonora, Mexico, on the Gulf of California. In Phoenix, Arizona, which is situated in an inland desert isolated from any ocean effects, the growing season lasts an average of 302 days.

The average winter minimum temperature may be only 36 to 37°F (2°C). However, temperatures as low as 20°F (-7°C) and even lower can occur in the coldest locations of the low zone. 102°F (39°C) is an average summer maximum but highs of up to 120°F (49°C) are not unheard of. Summer nights remain very warm in this zone: Minimums of 80°F (27°C) and above are the normal nighttime temperatures during the summer months.

Annual rainfall may be as much as 10 inches (255 mm) but often is less than 5 inches (130 mm). The wide seasonal swings in temperature plus the variations between night and day temperature extremes exclude growing some tropical plants. But the warm, more humid coastal zones permit use of a surprising number of tropical species if irrigated properly.

The arrival of cooler weather in fall signals the start of the real gardening season in the low zone. This is the time to plant winter annuals and vegetables and new plants in general. Such plants are generally hardy to the light winter frosts experienced in this zone.

Intermediate zone. Intermediate-elevation regions occur at an average of 2500 feet (760 m) and range to higher-elevation deserts in latitudes closer to the equator (see page xii). The higher elevation creates a more definite and shorter growing season, with an average of 220 to 240 frost-free days. However, this does *not* change the start of the main gardening season from early fall to spring. Most winter annuals, cool-season vegetables and general plantings are not damaged by the average low temperatures of this zone. These plants essentially go into a holding pattern during the coldest spells, continuing growth and flowering after the cold passes. *It is important to plant early enough in the fall to get good growth and development before cold early winter nighttime temperatures slow the plant's growth rate.* Some years, temperatures as low as 18°F (-8°C) and even lower in some locations have been recorded, but average winter frosts are much milder. Even so, subtropicals, such as bougainvillea, have to be considered marginal and must be planted in protected microclimates to thrive.

Maximum temperatures are generally 5°F (3°C) lower than highs recorded in the low zone. Summer night temperatures might drop to the low 70s F (around 22°C), making the summers at this elevation less stressful for people and plants. These cooler average temperatures coupled with a slightly earlier onset of fall enable more cool-weather plants to succeed here than in the lowest zone. This is especially true for regions in the intermediate zone that receive some summer rain.

Intermediate-zone regions that do experience summer rain generally receive more annual precipitation than any region within the low zone. Many areas in the intermediate zone may experience a summer rainy season and a short winter rainy season. The total annual precipitation may appear ample enough to make the arid-region classification seem questionable. However, the high temperature and evaporation rate plus long periods of dry weather between the two rainy seasons prevent accumulation of soil moisture from one season to the next. Annual rainfall averaging 10 inches (255 mm) or more is not unusual in regions with *two* rainy seasons. In intermediate arid regions with only one season, 5 to 7 inches (130 to 180 mm) of rain is average.

High zone. This is often referred to as the *high desert,* but in reality it includes high arid valleys where rainfall averages remain so low that irrigation is necessary to support any landscaping. The elevation ranges from 3300 to around 5000 feet (1000 to 1525 m) above sea level, varying somewhat higher or lower with latitude.

The growing season is 200 to 220 days, but locations in low latitudes may have a longer growing season; the last frost of spring occurs at an earlier date. Winter night temperatures hover at about 32°F (0°C) and it's not uncommon in colder winters for temperatures to drop to 15°F (-9°C). The average clear winter night near-freezing temperatures provide the chilling needed for many landscape plants and fruit trees that will not perform in the lower zones. Because of these chilling temperatures, many intermediate-zone plants become part of the high-zone landscape palette.

High summer daytime temperatures permit the use of an assortment of showy desert plants in the landscape. Many—such as yuccas, agaves and cacti—are native to these elevations. Rainfall is also higher at such elevations, and often these regions are adjacent to mountain ranges that can increase precipitation even more. The transition zone between the high zone and the mountainous areas has proved to be a rich area to find drought-resistant broad-leafed evergreens that also perform well in the more stressful lower-zone climates. Texas mountain laurel (*Sophora secundiflora*) and Arizona rosewood (*Vauquelinia californica*) are just two examples.

Arid grassland savannas. These often border deserts, but they don't qualify as a zone based on temperature because they may have the same temperature range as any of the above three zones. Precipitation may be less than in other zones, but the intensity and frequency of individual storms are enough to permit a grassy cover to develop during the short growing season. The constraints on landscape plants are about the same as in desert regions (usually in the low zone) because the long rainless periods are usually accompanied by high summer temperatures.

Dasylirion wheeleri, native to arid grasslands

Calotropis procera

DRY CLIMATE EFFECTS ON PLANT GROWTH

Arid regions throughout warm parts of the world have yielded a rich and diverse palette of landscape trees, shrubs and succulents. In the wild, broad-leafed evergreen and deciduous plants often grow together in varied and complex combinations. In addition, *ephemeral* plants (annuals and grasses) spring up in many regions during the limited wet periods. One group may appear during a summer rainy season, while another may depend on winter rains to trigger its growth. Some regions have both summer and winter rainy seasons with a distinctly different palette of ephemerals active each season. Many of these annuals and some perennials are attractive additions to the water-efficient landscape.

Frost-free periods in the world's subtropical arid regions vary from several months to year-round. As a result, arid landscape plants may be quite cold-hardy or very frost-tender, depending on the climate of their native habitat. Choosing plants whose cold and heat tolerance matches local conditions is critical.

We can't stress enough that plants differ greatly in their tolerance of frost and freezing air temperatures. Many species survive light frost or temperatures a few degrees below freezing without injury. These same plants are killed or severely damaged by intense cold. The extent of injury depends on a number of factors related to weather and to the plant itself.

A sudden drop in air temperature causes more damage than a gradual decline; likewise, rapid thawing of frozen plant tissue does more harm than a gradual thaw. In general, the longer the interval of below-freezing temperatures, the greater the damage to plants. Unseasonal cold snaps in fall or spring, or cold that follows a midwinter warm period, are also destructive. Plants are less conditioned or "hardened" to cold under these circumstances.

Most tropical plants never develop a tolerance of seasonal frost and freezing temperatures, but plants native to cold (or cool) winter regions undergo natural internal changes that make them more resistant to cold. This process is called *hardening off.*

Hardening off is gradual, beginning in late summer or early fall. It can continue well into winter in some species. Plants that are vigorous and healthy going into fall are less vulnerable to low temperatures than those weakened by lack of water or nutrients, or pest problems. Mature plants are more cold hardy than young plants. Likewise, nonactive plant organs (flower and leaf buds, twigs and branches) are more resistant to cold than tender, actively growing plant parts.

You can encourage hardening by withholding nitrogen fertilizers and reducing frequency of irrigation in late summer. Also avoid pruning in late summer, which can stimulate unseasonable new growth in fall. In addition to locating marginally cold- or frost-hardy plants in warm-winter microclimates, valuable cold-sensitive plants can be protected from frost and freezing temperatures. Frost-protection measures include creating a cover over the plant to reduce heat loss and, in some cases, adding a heat source, such as a light bulb or string of lights, to maintain temperatures within an acceptable range.

Typical late spring and early summer weather in most low- and mid-elevation locations (sea level to 3000 feet 910m) consists of a succession of clear sunny days with low humidity. Maximum temperatures hover near 100°F (38°C) or higher. Rainless spells of 40 to 90 days or more are not unusual. This combination of high temperatures, low humidity and dry soil forces many plants into a semidormant state or greatly reduces their growth.

In some arid regions, sporadic summer rains begin any time from late spring and last until the end of summer, or sometimes early fall. Although the humidity increases, temperatures may drop only slightly for a few hours or days during cloudy, rainy weather. Summer rains are often brief, intense and limited to small areas. Many annuals and grasses spring up at this time and, along with the rain-refreshed trees and shrubs, briefly give arid regions a lush green appearance. By early fall, the rains have usually ended and hot, dry weather returns.

A noticeable trend to cooler weather gradually comes on by mid- or late fall. Mild sunny days follow and generally last well into winter. Many arid regions have winter rains only. These develop any time in late fall and can continue sporadically into spring. These rains are usually gentle, unlike their summer counterparts, and soak into the soil. They also fall over a much wider area than summer rains do. A steady warming trend begins in early spring and ushers in the spring wildflower season. Flowers may be profuse or scarce, depending on the amount and timing of winter rains. Many arid-land shrubs, trees, cacti and other succulents bloom from midspring through summer, depending on species and location. Some species native to nearly or completely frost-free areas tend to bloom in winter rather than in spring or summer.

DRY CLIMATE SOIL

Soils in arid regions vary considerably. They tend to be shallow, coarse and rocky in foothills and on mountain slopes; coarse and well-drained on the open plains; deep and fine-textured in flood plains and almost pure sand in washes, arroyos and *wadis* (see Glossary). Flat open plains may have dense, poorly drained clay soils.

Naturally occurring organic matter is practically nonexistent in most arid-region soils. Soluble mineral salts may be present in large amounts, partly because there is not enough rain to leach them out of the upper soil layers. A layer of calcium carbonate called *caliche* is common in some regions, being found at the soil surface or slightly below. Caliche varies in depth from a few inches to several feet. This material may form a cementlike soil layer so compact that plant roots cannot grow into it. In the landscape, holes must be dug through this layer, sometimes at considerable effort, to provide critical drainage.

THE BEAUTY AND IMPORTANCE OF WATER-EFFICIENT LANDSCAPING

Water-efficient plants play an increasingly important role in landscapes throughout the world's arid and semiarid regions. There are several well-known and compelling reasons for this. Desert and arid regions are found on every continental land mass and exist in almost half the nations of the world. By some estimates, more than 30 percent of the land on the earth's surface is affected by aridity. Rapid population growth in many of these areas has placed a heavy demand on limited water resources. Studies have shown that in many communities, up to 50 percent of the water used by single-family residences is applied outdoors. The substantial increase in the demand for water has created a corresponding increase in its cost. Strong economic and ecological incentives now exist, creating a need for more efficient, conservative use of the water required to sustain landscapes.

In some areas, mandatory water-conservation programs and zoning ordinances place significant restraints on landscape irrigation. This encourages the trend away from landscape styles (and high-water-use plants) that evolved in regions with more abundant, cheaper water. In many water-scarce regions of the world it seems certain that future landscapes must be designed and maintained with much less water than in the past.

However, more positive factors contribute to the new emphasis on low-water-use landscapes and compatible plants. In the United States Southwest in particular, a shift in landscape tastes has led more and more people to appreciate the arresting beauty and unique character of arid-land plants. Landscapes where these plants predominate can have a dramatic quality, express an awareness of the natural environment and foster a definite "sense of place." The unique quality of a locale gives a landscape its distinctive character and charm.

Fortunately, the old image of the water-efficient landscape as a barren, sterile pile of rocks sprinkled with cacti, driftwood and an occasional wagon wheel has largely been laid to rest. Today, excellent examples of colorful, functional water-efficient landscapes are common in most communities.

Fouquieria columnaris, before and after winter rain

A few years ago, in these water-short regions, designing landscapes to conserve water was largely a local community-by-community effort and there was little communication or exchange of ideas between areas with similar problems. This "design in a vacuum" persisted for some time, until the introduction of the Xeriscape™ concept. *Xeriscape* provides a unifying vehicle for exchange of information and a design concept that could be applied in any water-short area regardless of climate variations.

Xeriscape (pronounced "zer-i-scape") is a word coined from the Greek word "Xeros," meaning *dry*, combined with a shortened version of the word *landscape*. The Denver Water Authority developed Xeriscape to identify and describe a water-efficient-landscape concept to replace traditional water-wasting landscape practices.

Lobelia laxiflora at the Boyce Thompson Southwest Arboretum

Today, Xeriscape has developed into a nationally recognized concept that has launched effective water-conserving landscaping practices across the United States, from California to Florida. Most regional members (cities or counties) prepare lists of plants considered water-efficient in their particular regions. Some even require that landscape practitioners designing civic and commercial projects limit their choices exclusively to plants from these lists.

Other countries with many water-scarce regions, such as Mexico and Australia, have expressed interest in the Xeriscape concept. But inquiries from the eastern United States and Canadian temperate zones are even more surprising.

Xeriscape subscribes to the following seven basic water-saving principles of landscaping, with minor variations:

1. Water-conserving design
2. Restricted use of lawn grass
3. Use of drought-tolerant or water-efficient plants
4. Water-harvesting techniques
5. Appropriate irrigation methods
6. Use of mulches
7. Proper maintenance practices

1. **Water-conserving design.** A water-efficient garden design follows the same principles that apply to any other kind of landscape design. First, you prepare a plot plan of the site to scale. This plan should show all existing structures, significant plants, paved areas and any other existing site features, even though they may not remain in the final plan. The plan must accommodate the day-to-day activities, special needs and interests of those who will use the site, so note these at the start. You must include in your plan such basics as climate control, circulation, outdoor spaces for assorted uses, entry courts, outdoor living areas, recreation, service and how much lawn, if any. Also note physical and environmental site characteristics such as topography, exposure to sun and wind, views (those to accentuate and those to hide) and location of utilities. With this information plotted and noted, you can develop a landscape plan that will be similar to a floor plan for a building. Except for early decisions to limit lawn, such a planning approach could be the basis for landscape design in any climate, wet or dry.

2. **Restricted use of lawn.** This second principle of Xeriscape probably conserves more water, but it is more difficult for most people to accept than any of the other principles. The wall-to-wall lawn—viewed as the ideal landscape—is a concept deeply rooted in the minds of people with northern North American and European backgrounds. Restriction doesn't mean *elimination*, however, and the Xeriscape minioasis concept often includes a small lawn area. People are finding that a limited area of lawn satisfies their need for a cool green retreat from aridity just as well as the traditional wall-to-wall lawn treatment. It also supplies a place for children and pets to play and creates a focal point for the rest of the landscape.

3. **Use of drought-tolerant or water-efficient plants.** Low-water-use plants can satisfy functional needs and carry out the goals of the design as well as the more thirsty plants did in the past. They can

- Define or enclose space
- Reduce the heat and glare of the sun
- Provide privacy and shelter from the wind
- Control the movement of people, animals or vehicles
- Add interest and enrichment to outdoor areas

Plants are a kind of *building material* that can be used along with other materials, such as walls, fences and overhead shelters, to shape outdoor spaces and make them more livable and pleasant.

4. **Water-harvesting techniques.** These techniques have only recently become a part of basic landscape planning. The concept was inherited from the practice in cooler and wetter climes, where the goal was just the opposite: gather and channel all storm runoff out of the site as quickly as possible. Wasting this valuable resource in water-short regions is a real crime, especially because surface runoff from rainfall contains far less salt than domestic water, which is often loaded with salts.

Water harvesting is actually a simple task, especially in the planning stage. First, design all roof and paved areas to drain into planted areas. These areas in turn must be graded to eventually drain the water from the site, but only after the water passes across the landscaped areas, slowly enough so that the water (or most of it) can be absorbed into the soil. In arid regions, you can't depend on storm runoff, but when it happens, plant roots are thoroughly soaked and leached of accumulated salts left from irrigation water. Large established desert trees, such as mesquite, will develop and often can be maintained with the runoff from a medium-size roof area.

Many extensive and sophisticated water-harvesting projects are being installed in the U.S. Southwest, involving temporary retention or holding areas. In some cases, tanks and underground cisterns are constructed to store water and later deliver that water to the plantings as needed.

Retention basins are required in many communities with large developments that produce considerable amounts of storm runoff from their parking lots and roof areas. Industrial plants, shopping centers and housing complexes fall into this category. The objective is not to save water but to reduce street flooding during heavy downpours. In most cases, they are required to hold the water only temporarily, with a constricted weir at the low end that permits a slow, controlled outflow. (A *weir* is a kind of dam, often used to catch fish, that, using gravity, allows water through at a slower rate.) Some basins permanently impound the runoff on the site where it must remain until it soaks in or evaporates. Both of these types ofwater-impounding areas offer special landscaping opportunities.

The temporary holding ponds are the most useable because they can be developed into an oasis-like green spot. Because of this, they are often placed in the center of the landscape. There is little inconvenience when the area floods because the flooding usually lasts only a short time. The moisture remains long enough, however, to permit a deep wetting of the soil and a valuable leaching of the unwanted salts left from irrigation. These holding ponds also save considerable water costs over the year, even though these spaces often have a system (equipped with soil-moisture sensors to trigger the irrigation system) designed to operate during the dry

interim periods. Smaller retention basins are often installed in more remote areas of the landscape to create sanctuaries for birds and other wildlife.

Holding ponds without a *gravity outlet* (such as a weir) are less useful because they may remain flooded until the water sinks in or evaporates, which may take a week or more. These basins are usually placed in perimeter locations and can be used to irrigate sports fields and playgrounds. The longer periods of flooding can damage or kill trees because most cannot tolerate standing water against their trunks. Grasses are more tolerant of the inundation and trees and shrubs do grow well at the edges, where the drainage is better.

It may be surprising to learn that many water-efficient plants thrive on short-term flooding. Many of the most useful of these plants are found in nature along desert washes and wadis, which may experience flooding only once or twice a year or remain dry for even longer periods. The plants typical of these places—acacias, mesquites and palo verdes, to name a few—have the ability to go into a holding pattern for long periods of time without water and show no particular stress. When the floods do come, these plants take advantage of the very wet condition, rapidly leafing out, flowering and putting out new growth at an incredible rate. The infrequent but heavy saturation of the root zone is a normal part of their natural environment.

5. **Appropriate irrigation methods.** One approach common to most water-efficient landscape design concepts is called *hydrozoning irrigation*. The landscape is divided into a pattern of varying widths, grading from the wettest to the driest, the width depending on the needs of each landscape design. This means designing the irrigation in zones to supply the needs of a small lush area grading out through more spacious transition areas to the driest at the perimeters. This small lush area, or *minioasis*, may include lawn or other high-water-use landscape treatments. Of course, this area is popular with users of the site, so it is usually located next to intensive-use areas, such as a structure, patio, swimming-pool area or in an entry court. These are places where the greater water expenditures will be most appreciated. Lawn and other high-water-use plantings should be no larger than is functionally necessary to satisfy user needs. Such petite lush spots, though quite small, supply the same amenities for outdoor comfort and pleasure as former water-squandering designs did, but using much less water. This is also the place to have fruit trees or bedding-plant displays, to indulge in hobby gardening or to have a small play lawn for children and pets. These special treatments, though conservative in scale, provide great value for those using the site.

   Beyond the small high-water-use area will be zones of plants that require substantially less water. They may include a transitional zone adjoining the minioasis and a zone of low-water-use plants near the perimeter. A goal of the low-water zone is to include plants that might perform well with little or no supplemental irrigation once established. These low-water-demanding plants can produce shade, shelter, privacy and beauty without sacrificing the desired design effect.

   The final zone uses the least amount of water and is usually around the perimeter of the site. It may also be the largest in area and is populated with the most drought resistant plants. Plants in this area should be watered more often when they are young to stimulate growth. After they achieve the size desired for the landscape design, gradually reduce the water to the point where the plants survive with infrequent irrigation. You might need to water some plants a bit more often to maintain an acceptable appearance.

   Occasionally, designers fill an area in the forefront with assorted cacti and other succulents with striking forms, such as aloes, yucca and agave. This kind of planting cannot be considered functional or in the true spirit of Xeriscape design. Succulent plants are showy, often spectacular, but because of their bold form, they tend to create an unfocused, jumbled effect and should be used with restraint. Cacti and other succulents are most effective as dramatic accent plants, judiciously placed at entrances, path intersections or for a silhouette against blank walls.

6. **Use of mulches.** Mulches include bark chips, compost, decomposed granite or water-worn rock. You apply them at the base of the plant. They improve the soil by

   - Controlling erosion
   - Reducing compaction
   - Reducing salt buildup
   - Retaining moisture
   - Controlling weeds

7. **Proper maintenance practices.** Plants that require little to no water usually require little maintenance. You'll still need to remove weeds periodically because they soak up precious water as well as fertilizer. Check your irrigation system for damage and leaks on a regular basis.

   Opt for a slow-release fertilizer, if you need to fertilize the plant at all, and be careful not to overdo it. In lawns, enhance quality and prevent insect and disease problems by dethatching and aerating annually.

   Finally, follow the pruning instructions for individual plants. Some may need no pruning at all, but many need occasional grooming, especially if you are trying to achieve a particular plant appearance. Also, if you live in a colder arid region or experience unusual frosts, take care to remove cold-damaged parts so that the plant has a chance to recover.

Landscape Design Tips

SAVE AND NURTURE EXISTING NATIVE PLANTS.

Why? Healthy plants that are growing onsite are attractive and require the least amount of water and effort. Plan to save existing trees or shrubs in the initial planning stage of your design. These plants often have dramatic forms or interesting character, so they are well worth incorporating into the new landscape. In some cases they can become the key elements around which you plan the rest of the landscape. Existing native plants, even if located near more lush plantings, can soften the transition from oasis-type areas to the more water-efficient plantings beyond.

KEEP IT SIMPLE.

The most successful water-efficient landscapes are simple and uncluttered. Select a few kinds of plants that meet the basic needs of the project and will grow with the soil, water and care that you can *realistically* provide. Look to landscapes in nature for ideas on grouping plants in interesting and attractive ways.

DON'T MIX PLANTS WITH DIFFERENT NEEDS.

Avoid the common mistake of randomly mixing low-water-demanding arid-region trees and shrubs with luxuriant vegetation that requires rich soils, heavy fertilization and large amounts of water. Such mixed plantings lack aesthetic appeal and are almost impossible to maintain properly. Keep in mind that plant combinations that are ecologically valid generally look great together. The plants that grow together usually go together.

KEEP YOUR ROCKS "NATIVE," TOO.

Rocks and boulders are popular and right at home in the water-efficient landscape design. The kind, size and arrangement of rocks should suggest natural formations, especially those found locally. If they are not placed in relationship to one another as they might appear in nature, scattered rocks and boulders only contribute a cluttered look and lose much of their landscape value.

AVOID UNUSUAL COLORS AND BIZARRE SHAPES AND TEXTURES WHEN CHOOSING ROCKS.

Use a few large boulders to create at least one key feature. Group smaller secondary rocks of varying sizes to help integrate the boulders into a composition.

MANY SMALL ROCKS LOOK FUSSY, ESPECIALLY IF THEY ARE EVENLY SPACED.

A frequent mistake is to surround each tree and shrub in the landscape with a circle of stones or place them in rows along walks so they resemble the teeth of a giant prehistoric reptile. Eight or ten well-chosen, well-placed boulders produce a much more dramatic effect than dozens of small rocks in unnatural formations.

CREATE ROCK MULCHES THAT BLEND.

Rock mulches are especially useful and make an attractive non-water-demanding groundcover. This is a recommended alternative to organic mulches in the Xeriscape concept. Choose natural-appearing rock: For example, water-worn pebbles are more attractive than a crushed or brightly colored gravel, which will appear out of character with nature. If you use boulders or large stones as a part of the landscape, select a rock mulch that appears to be of the same or compatible geological formation.

ROCK MULCHES ARE *NOT* A SHORTCUT.

Except for saving water, do not consider rock mulches as a shortcut to low-maintenance gardening. Weeds often grow better in a mulched area than in bare ground. They can be controlled by pre-emergence herbicides that kill only the germinating weed seeds and do not affect the established landscape plants.

Keep your rocks "native," too.

Keep it simple.

Create rock mulches that blend.

Save and nurture existing native plants.

Assorted *Leucophyllum*

WHERE TO FIND PLANTS

NURSERY-GROWN PLANTS

In general, buying and planting nursery-grown plants is a better option than gathering plants of the same species in the wild. Plants dug from their native habitat (except for succulents) suffer severe shock and are much less likely to survive transplanting. Also, native plants are protected by law in many areas.

Nursery-grown arid-region plants often look different than mature specimens of the same species in the wild because they have been grown under optimum conditions. Container-grown water-efficient plants often seem to lack the dense, full growth of the traditional water-thirsty species carried in the nursery and therefore lack customer appeal. In fact, young arid-region trees and shrubs do tend to be a bit more open and rangy in the juvenile stage. This should not discourage their use because they generally attain their classic natural form and texture within a year or two after being planted.

Erythrina flabelliformis; seed or softwood cuttings

HARVESTING AND PROPAGATING FROM THE WILD

Harvesting

Most native succulents—cacti, agaves, yuccas and so forth—are easy to transplant from the wild. However, this practice is strictly controlled by laws in the United States, as well as in most other countries. Many native trees and shrubs are difficult to move successfully, even as small plants, because most have deep and extensive water-searching roots that are lost in transplanting.

In recent years, however, techniques for transplanting mature plants have been developed, a task formerly thought to be impossible. This process begins with *trenching* to cut the side roots, *side boxing* (enclosing root ball with a wooden box with no bottom) and leaving roots at the base of the rootball intact for several months before the plant is moved. The rootball soil in the box is kept moist, and some growth is thinned from the top to lessen shock and the plant's demand for water. Several months later, the roots at the base of the rootball (or growing below the level of the box or depth of the trench) are cut and the bottom is put on the box. By this time, the previously cut side roots have resprouted in the box and are better able to support the needs of the tree. Even large desert trees are now being salvaged in this manner.

Propagating

As a practical alternative to harvesting wild plants, most species can be grown easily from seed, although this takes more time, so growers must plan accordingly. Seeds can be gathered in the wild or purchased from collectors who grow plants not commonly found in the nursery trade. In addition, seeds are often available from botanical gardens and arboretums or can be gathered with permission from specimens growing in public places. Many species can be propagated vegetatively when fresh cutting wood is available and growers are familiar with proper propagation techniques for the species.

Transplanting is not a problem, even for hard-to-transplant types, when the plants have been started from seed and grown in a pot or container for a period of time. For example, a mesquite or palo verde that is planted in a one-gallon container can develop into a small tree in just three years if watered properly.

The seeds of many arid-region trees and shrubs, especially those in the legume family, are covered with a hard seed coat that is impervious to water. This protective outer shell prevents germination until conditions are favorable for the plant to succeed. To activate the germination process, the seeds must be *scarified* (scratched to break through the seed coat) or soaked in hot water to soften the seed coat and allow water to enter. Unless this is done, the seeds germinate very slowly or not at all.

An ordinary metal file or two pieces of sandpaper work well to cut through the seed coat. You'll notice a distinct color change once you have filed through the outer shell to the seed tissue within. Only a small break at one point in the seed coat is necessary for water entry. Practically any seed that has a hard thick coat will germinate faster if scarified. Immersing the seed briefly (until you see a color change) in hot water (just below boiling temperature) will achieve the same effect. Other propagation recommendations for individual species are included in the Cultural Requirements section of the individual plant charts.

Gardening Terms

aeration. Exchange of gases between the soil and the atmosphere. Loosen the soil to improve aeration with hand tools, various machines designed for this purpose and, in some cases, with soil amendments.

backfill. Soil placed in the planting hole after the plant is set in place. Backfill is usually the same soil removed in digging the planting hole.

bare-root. Plants with all soil removed from roots. Most nursery stock is sold in containers, but some succulents are still sold this way.

heading back. Cutting a shoot back to a side bud or branch or removing it at the point of origin for more dense, compact growth.

mulches. A protective covering over soil made of loose material, such as bark, saw dust, rocks, leaves or straw that often serves aesthetic as well as maintenance purposes.

organic materials. Substances, such as a chemical or fertilizer, that come from a source that was once or still is alive.

pinching. Removing a shoot tip by actually pinching it off. Encourages bushy growth.

rootball. Clump of roots and the surrounding soil when plant is removed from a container.

thinning. Removing individual stems to open the interior of the plant to more sunlight or to allow freer air movement through the canopy.

Zauschneria californica latifolia

PLANTING PROCEDURES

Many arid-landscape plants survive and look attractive with little attention once established. However, all require proper planting and diligent care when they are young if they are to succeed.

WHEN TO PLANT

When grown in containers, most trees and shrubs (as well as cacti and other succulents) can be planted year-round in arid climates. However, when succulent plants are dug and delivered bare root, the warm season is the best planting time, preferably midspring rather than fall. Early fall through winter and early spring are excellent times to set out most container-grown plants. During these periods, cooler air and soil temperatures reduce heat- and water-stress. Frost-tender species are best planted in spring after the weather has settled into a consistently warm pattern and danger of frost has passed. Summer transplanting gives especially good results with most cacti, agaves, aloes, palms and yuccas.

HOW TO PLANT

Landscape planting procedures change over time as research and field experience develop more effective techniques. Much emphasis is now being placed on creating root zone soils that are well aerated and well drained beyond the confines of a planting hole. The hole itself should be adequate but not too big to accommodate the size of the rootball. Typically, this root environment is created by digging the soil in an area around the installed plant that is several times the diameter of and about the same depth as the planting hole.

Organic materials are not generally recommended as an ingredient of *backfill soil* (see page xxiv). However, an organic mulch provides important benefits when applied over the planting area and is strongly recommended for this use.

Remove nursery stakes when young trees are placed in the landscape. If the newly planted tree requires staking because it can't stay upright on its own, the stakes must be removed as soon as the tree gains sufficient strength.

In some suburban and rural areas, rabbits and rodents pose a serious threat to arid-landscape plants, sometimes for several years after they are set out. Use wire poultry netting to make a 20- to 30-inch (51- to 76-cm) cylinder around vulnerable plants (most young plants are vulnerable) until they are large enough to resist or tolerate such injury.

WATERING

In the beginning. Newly planted trees and shrubs need regular watering to encourage rapid establishment and good growth. The first four to six weeks are most critical for plants set out in spring or summer. Those set out in cool fall or winter weather require less frequent irrigation during the establishment period.

No single watering schedule can be applied to all recently planted nursery stock. Irrigation is determined by the nature of the soil, the weather, site microclimate and the water needs of the individual plants. During the early stages of establishment in the landscape, the idea is to keep the rootball and backfill soil moist at all times. The goal is to supply moisture to the existing root system (rootball) and encourage roots to spread into the surrounding backfill soil.

New trees and shrubs may require watering at one- to four-day intervals for the first three to four weeks following a warm-weather transplant. As new roots develop and extend outward, plants draw on a greater volume of soil for moisture. At that point, irrigate less frequently, but apply more water when you do irrigate.

Bare-root planting. Arid landscape trees and shrubs, except for succulents, roses and certain fruit trees, are seldom planted bare root. In the few cases when this is appropriate, bare-root plants must be watered regularly to ensure establishment after planting. After planting is completed, water thoroughly to eliminate air pockets from the backfill soil.

Container-grown plants. Container-grown plants are often produced under ideal nursery conditions. This sometimes causes top growth to develop that is proportionately larger than the root system confined in the container. Until these plants develop new roots outside the original rootball, give extra attention to watering. Such trees and shrubs are not likely to survive if the soil around their roots dries out before the plant can extend its roots beyond those in the nursery's container.

Overwatering. Too much water poses a special threat to young arid-landscape trees such as mesquite and acacia. Abundant water causes top growth to become so lush and thick that the developing root system cannot keep up. Often, the roots are unable to securely anchor and support the plant and the tree blows over easily in strong winds. Years of careful pruning and staking may be necessary to develop sturdy well-anchored trees from these blown-over specimens.

The importance of balanced irrigation. In one sense, irrigation is a powerful growth regulator of water-efficient landscape trees. Too little water and they are stressed or stunted. Too much water and they may overgrow their natural character or be damaged or killed by diseases or blown over by high winds. With the right amount of water, top and root growth of trees are strong, vigorous and well-balanced.

How to determine water needs. A number of sophisticated instruments and techniques are available or are being developed for determining plant water use and irrigation requirements. In addition, many advances have been made in the various components of drip, bubbler and sprinkler irrigation systems. As new technology is developed for landscape irrigation, scheduling will become easier and even more precise. If other methods are unavailable, the age-old practices remain useful. Experienced gardeners still estimate the moisture content of the soil by rolling it in a ball between the fingers. They also watch plants for the first early symptoms of wilt to provide an indication of when to irrigate. Of course, these same gardeners have learned the basics of their climate and the specific needs of each plant.

FERTILIZING

A light application of fertilizer four to six weeks after planting will encourage good growth and foliage color for trees and shrubs set out in spring or summer. Those planted in fall or winter can be fertilized in late winter or early spring. The nutrient most likely to be in short supply is nitrogen. Plant-available phosphorus and iron are also deficient in some arid-land soils. To satisfy plant needs for nitrogen, a nitrogen-containing fertilizer, whether organic or inorganic, will be satisfactory if applied in moderation. Most lawn and garden fertilizers are effective if applied at label-recommended rates for new transplants. Plants set out in fall, winter or early spring may be fertilized a second time in midsummer at the same rate. Be careful not to exceed recommended doses. This will often result in plant injury, or at best, weak, uncharacteristic growth that is easily damaged by wind, temperature extremes, insect pests or diseases.

PRUNING

At planting time, keep pruning to a minimum. Light pruning, which removes no more than a quarter of the potential leaf area, may be necessary to correct obvious growth defects. Severe pruning removes too much leaf area and may do more harm than good.

Trees. Light thinning and pinching back throughout the first growing season helps determine the permanent branching structure and character of the mature plant. Some trees, such as mesquite, produce limber trunks that may require staking for a time. Select strong branches that are well spaced around the trunk for the permanent framework. For a shade tree, permanent above-head-height branches should be 6 inches (15 cm) or more apart vertically on the main stem. They should be well spaced in a horizontal plane around the trunk to prevent weak, crowded growth. This not only applies to mesquite but to many species of acacia, palo verde and other small to medium-size arid-land trees.

Small branches that are already present or appear on the lower trunk of young trees may be shortened to 6 or 8 inches (15 or 20.5 cm) in length. However, they should be allowed to remain for two or three years because they contribute to faster, stronger trunk development and growth.

Shrubs. Shrubs can be made more dense and compact by cutting back extra-long branches. If an open tracery of branches is desired, thin out the interior of the shrub, leaving those branches that have the most interesting form and character.

The maintenance of a palm

CARE OF ESTABLISHED PLANTS

WATERING

Trees and shrubs that grow naturally in the warmest and driest regions are usually widely spaced by nature so they can survive and grow. Because plants in a landscape setting are closer together than those in nature, they require extra irrigation or grading to facilitate water harvesting. Local climate, including precipitation and temperature ranges, is also an important determining factor.

Examples of plants in this broad category (that is, native to the warmest and driest regions) are the U.S. Southwest arid-land acacias (*Acacia* species [spp.]), palo verdes (*Cercidium* and *Parkinsonia* spp.), hop bush (*Dodonaea viscosa*), jojoba (*Simmondsia chinensis*), creosote bush (*Larrea* spp.), Texas ranger (*Leucophyllum* spp.) and willow pittosporum (*Pittosporum phillyraeoides*).

Acacia farnesiana

These plants can endure long dry periods and look near death but recover quickly with rain or supplemental irrigation. However, in very hot, very dry places (such as Yuma, Arizona), just three or more thorough soakings of the root zone during the period from midspring through early fall greatly improves their growth rate, foliage color and flowering. If the objective is to produce vigorous growth and a mature landscape in as few years as possible, these plants should be watered regularly during the growing season. Established trees and shrubs of this group need little irrigation during the winter months except in prolonged droughts. Excess soil moisture during winter can kill some arid-landscape plants, especially succulents. If there is little or no rain during winter, one or two slow applications of water will be adequate.

Tecoma alata

A second group of plants, those found in moister situations or at slightly higher elevations bordering the desert (appropriate for minioasis areas) depends on regular watering to survive the hot summer areas of low- and intermediate-zone arid valleys. Representative plants include Arizona rosewood (*Vauquelinia* spp.), red and yellow bird of paradise (*Caesalpinia* spp.), sugarbush and other sumac species (*Rhus* spp.), yellow trumpet bush (*Tecoma* spp.), certain species of arid-land palms (*Chamaerops*, *Butia* and *Washingtonia* spp.) and some of the acacias.

These should also be watered during the winter, and especially as spring approaches, because their growing season begins quite early. Irrigation frequency depends on weather and soil characteristics, but additional moisture is usually necessary in the summer. Drought-tolerant conifers, including some pines (*Pinus* spp.), junipers (*Juniperus* spp.) and cypress (*Cupressus* spp.) as well as certain oaks (*Quercus* spp.), differ from the above in

Quercus bucklei

Fraxinus velutina in fall

that they will prosper on less frequent but deep irrigation. The riparian or watercourse trees of this zone, such as ash (*Fraxinus* spp.), have little drought tolerance and must be kept relatively moist at all times.

Irrigation schedules. Variations in microclimates, plant-related factors and soil characteristics are so great that it is impractical to specify precise irrigation schedules for the plants described in this book. We believe a more useful approach is to suggest a range of irrigation intervals, basing the final decision about established-plant irrigation on these site-specific considerations:

- Plant growth and appearance
- Feel of the soil (for moisture content)
- Current weather conditions
- Estimates of plant evapotranspiration (see Glossary)
- Data provided by soil-moisture-sensing devices such as tensiometers, electrical resistance blocks and capacitance sensors.

Thorough watering in this text means completely soaking the root zone to make up any water deficit that exists. If soluble salt levels in the soil are unacceptably high or if the irrigation water is salty, additional water must be applied to leach salts down and away from roots.

FERTILIZING

Most trees, shrubs and vines respond to increased soil fertility with more vigorous growth, better foliage color and improved flowering. Nitrogen is usually the key fertilizer element. Plants respond to other essential nutrients according to the soil conditions at the planting site. For information on specific characteristics of local soils and plant nutrient needs, consult landscape-industry professionals, universities or appropriate government agencies.

Arid-landscape plants respond well to most commercial fertilizers that contain nitrogen. Use complete lawn and garden fertilizers (those containing nitrogen, phosphorus and potassium) at the rate recommended on the package for trees and shrubs. Spread the material evenly on the soil surface from near the base of the trunk or stems out slightly beyond the spread of the branches. After applying fertilizer, irrigate thoroughly to move it down into the root-zone soil. One fertilizer application in late winter may be sufficient. If plants show a need for it, apply a second application in early summer. Fertilizer injectors combined with state-of-the-art irrigation systems are even more effective and efficient in satisfying plant nutrient needs.

PRUNING

The natural growth habit of native plants is usually far more attractive than anything people may impose on them by pruning. Therefore, the basic goal of pruning should be to reveal and display the inherent beauty of the *natural* plant form. This usually involves little more than routine removal of poorly placed growth, crossing or interfering branches and dead or diseased stems. With young, fast-growing trees, heading back some branch tips to a lateral twig or side bud may be necessary to develop a strong symmetrical-branch framework. When established native trees and large shrubs are saved and incorporated into the landscape, it may be desirable to remove a few of the lowest branches to help define the structural beauty of the trunks and main branch framework. This pruning should not drastically change the shape or height of the plant, but simply open up and emphasize its natural character. Some trees, such as acacias, mesquites and palo verdes, can be trained into shade trees by gradually removing lower side branches and watering regularly. Do *not* use power tools such as hedge clippers on desert plants unless you are designing a formal hedge. Many plants in commercial and public landscapes have been ruined by untrained workers using this tool without care or knowledge of how to prune or trim.

Cercidium praecox (trunk)

CACTI AND OTHER SUCCULENTS

SELECTION AND USE

Succulents, including cacti, yuccas, agaves and aloes, make a unique contribution to the arid landscape. Their tolerance of difficult conditions and their low maintenance requirements are also unique and require a separate discussion. Because of their striking forms and flower colors, they are most appropriate as dramatic specimen, container or accent plants. They can also function in other ways if properly selected and placed in the landscape. For example, they may be used as groundcover or bankcover, space definer or for screening and traffic control.

CULTURE

Cacti and other succulents have a popular image as tough low-water-use plants, superbly adapted to intense sun, heat and water stress. This reputation is well deserved by a number of species that manage to grow under some of the harshest conditions found on earth. However, succulents are native to a broad range of habitats that vary from hot to cool, dry to moderately moist and sunny to shady. Consider the following basic points when selecting and caring for succulents in the landscape.

Temperature

Some cacti and succulents tolerate snow and temperatures well below freezing. Others cannot survive even a light frost. The landscape potential of the latter group is limited to low-elevation, frost-free locations or to warm microclimates in transitional areas where only a few frosty nights occur each winter. Experience also tells us that the long, hot summers of low-desert regions can be harmful or fatal to cacti and other succulents native to coastal or cool high-elevation habitats. Natives of the hottest regions fail to develop satisfactorily where summers are cool, even though the region is arid. Knowing the preferred temperature range of particular succulents is essential to grow them successfully.

Sun exposure

A planting site in full sun is ideal for many, but not all, succulents. Some kinds are not well adapted to intense sunlight, especially in low- and mid-elevation desert regions. Types that orginate in cooler or less-arid climates, those that grow naturally in the shade of taller trees and shrubs or those from cliffs or hillsides shaded from the afternoon sun are best suited to locations that offer filtered or morning sun only.

Soil

Many succulents grow in a broad range of soil types, but good drainage is essential for *all* species. A heavy soil that remains wet and soggy after irrigation or rain is almost certain to spell disaster. The sandy or gravelly soils of many arid regions are satisfactory for most succulent plants because many grow naturally in such soil types. The root system of succulents is shallow to make the most of light, infrequent rains, so great soil depth is not necessary for most species, including the cacti.

Fertilization

Succulents that are native to your region often grow quite well in soils without supplemental fertilization. However, the growth and appearance of many exotic (non-native) *agaves, yuccas* and *aloes* may be improved by a light application of a nitrogen-containing fertilizer. The best time to do this is just before the beginning of the primary growing season, which is spring or summer for most species.

Opuntia ficus-indica

Irrigation

Succulents vary considerably in their water requirements. Some require no supplemental irrigation once established, while others benefit from occasional watering during long dry spells. Species that originate in areas of abundant rainfall or on soils of greater water-holding capacity may require irrigation on an infrequent basis. Climate and microclimate influence water requirements. The sunnier and hotter the planting site, the more water succulents need.

As with most plants, succulents respond to a little extra water by producing more rapid growth and more abundant flowering. However, the very fact that the plant has evolved water-holding tissue in leaves or stems is an indication that intermittent drying of the root zone is necessary. Excessive irrigation results in exaggerated growth that is brittle and prone to wind damage as well as making the plant more susceptible to various rot organisms.

Pruning

Succulents may require occasional shaping to develop or maintain the plant form desired or to remove broken, dead, diseased or insect-infested plant parts. Use sharp clean tools and make cuts at base of the stem or at the base of individual leaves.

Some *Agave* and *Aloe* species produce offset plants that form a clump at the base of the original specimen. Aloes can grow into a spreading colony that becomes quite large, even invasive at times. It may be necessary to reduce the size of these plant groups to preserve the desired landscape effect, or to limit maintenance.

PLANTING SUCCULENTS

Container-grown succulent nursery stock can be planted throughout the year, although it's best to plant marginally cold-hardy species in spring or summer. Plant dealers supply some succulents bare root. Plant these when the ground is warm—late spring to early fall.

Succulents growing in the filtered light of a greenhouse may be injured if suddenly moved to a planting site in full sun. This happens even during the short days of winter and is true for sun-tolerant species as well as for other types. To prevent such damage, gradually move plants into a high-light environment over a period of several weeks. Follow the same procedure with tender seedlings of most succulent species.

The planting hole for succulents should be slightly larger than the diameter of the plant rootball. Soil alteration with amendments or conditioners is not necessary before planting native succulents. Be careful not to plant succulents too deep. In most cases the top of the rootball should be just below the soil surface. Large upright and columnar specimens may be planted several inches deep and rootless cuttings can be planted at whatever depth necessary to hold them upright until roots develop. This reduces the danger of the plant being blown over before it becomes established.

Once the plant is in the ground, irrigate thoroughly to moisten the rootball and backfill soil. Some cacti, especially native species, may establish and grow with no further supplemental watering. Most newly planted agaves, aloes and non-native yuccas will benefit from irrigation at one- to two-week intervals for at least the first six to eight weeks after planting.

PICTORIAL GUIDE TO LANDSCAPE DESIGN ELEMENTS

Accent

Accents have bold forms and are used to emphasize points in a garden, to dramatize entrances or intersections. The yucca and palm clans offer many choices, but cacti and certain agaves run a close second. Even conifers, such as columnar Italian cypress and certain junipers, can be used.

Border

Border plantings include narrow planting strips along walks or wider beds in a garden, often using perennial borders or flower borders in general for special displays.

Background

Background plants are taller, denser shrubs at the back of a landscape design. They are nonattention-getting plants. They serve as screening and provide a foil for more showy and colorful plants in the foreground.

Buffer zones

Buffer-zone plantings act as a buffer between undesirable conditions of climate and site use and the more protected landscape garden area. Plants have the ability to withstand the negative conditions and modify them for the area that needs protection.

Banks

Plants for banks must have special qualities in order to grow on steep slopes. Similar to erosion-control plants, they must spread and root deeply into the soil to hold it in place. Also they must endure more wind exposure and drying conditions because of water runoff.

Close-up viewing

Plants filling this category are those with interesting details that get lost at a distance. These plants belong near sitting areas, outdoor patios and any living space where they can be enjoyed at close range.

Barrier/hedge

Barrier or hedge plants are those that will effectively restrict the passage of humans or animals as well as define property.

Color

Warm arid regions offer many opportunities for color in the landscape. Probably the most spectacular is Bougainvillea, *but other spectacular choices include* Nerium oleander, Delonix regia *and* Bauhinia variegata.

Containers

Plants in containers of varying sizes are useful in furnishing outdoor sitting places to offer close-range color and other effects. They offer an opportunity to change the effect at different times of year and grow plants more cold tender because you can move them into protected areas during the cold season.

Contrast

Contrast involves combining flowers or foliage color to achieve a sharp impact of different but complementary colors. Contrast also includes grouping bold and different plant forms to create interest and dramatic effect, as with cacti and other succulents.

Desert effects

Desert effects can be easily achieved by arranging interesting groups of cacti, yuccas and desert trees, such as palo verde, in a composition with rocks and pebble groundcovers. A planting concept useful in both small and large areas that requires very little maintenance.

Erosion control

Erosion-control plants include those that are suitable to counteract runoff or drainage problems, especially on disturbed sites and after regrading.

Espalier

Espalier involves specially training shrubs or small trees to grow flat on a wall. It is a high-maintenance procedure but useful and attractive for narrow planting spaces between walks and against blank walls. This technique was originally developed in Europe to grow fruit trees against walls and is even possible in open orchards.

Foreground

Foreground plants are low plants placed in the front of a large planting as part of the design.

Foundation

Foundation planting is similar to foreground planting—it relates to planting at the base of structures. This planting is important in relating the structure to the site and surrounding areas.

Groundcover

Groundcover can be achieved by pebbles or gravel, but it is generally assumed to be a low-growing type of planting that carpets various areas, large or small. Examples include ice plant or low-growing junipers.

Medians or parking islands

Medians and parking islands call for plants with special qualifications: They are generally low, spreading to cover the planting area. They must tolerate wind, heat, sun and pollution exposure. In the wider medians, larger plants, even trees, are appropriate, but they too must tolerate these same stressors.

Revegetation

Revegetation plants are those that are able to grow and restore cover to denuded land, a problem in the desert Southwest where there is considerable agricultural land being retired because of water shortage.

Minioasis

Minioasis *is a term in the Xeriscape™ design concept that allows small areas where more lush plants or even a small lawn can be planted. This area is usually placed adjoining outdoor sitting areas or entrances where the majority of the people using the site will have a chance to enjoy it.*

Roadside

Plants well-adapted to roadside planting must endure the stress of narrow streetside planting as well as more spacious situations along country roads and freeways. All must endure wind, pollution and, in many cases, little care.

Parks/Plazas/ Urban areas

Plants appropriate to busy, more populated places will perform well in paved areas adjoining traffic. They will endure reflected heat, pollution and wind channeled by urban structures.

Rock garden

Rock gardens can take advantage of a natural rock outcrop or involve tastefully composed rock formations. They present opportunities to use and display certain plants that revel in such situations. Rock in constructed gardens should all be from the same geological formation. Do not mix rocks.

Patio

Patios are the extension of the house into an outdoor living space. Scale is important. Patio trees are trees that can be trained to develop an umbrella-type cover as well as other plantings that are interesting at close range.

Screen

Screening plants, similar to background plants, are for privacy and also for wind and dust control. Large shrubs or even rows of taller trees make excellent screens.

Shade

While shade is often achieved with a manmade shade structure, there are many dry land trees that can produce the same shade plus the pleasure of dappled light and shadow, the cooling effect of the leaves and the sound of rustling foliage. Ficus, mesquite and ash are all good shade producers.

Transition zone

A transition zone *is an area between two different design concepts in a landscape, such as a space between a more lush garden treatment and a dry landscape. Plants chosen for such sitautions need to blend well with both concepts.*

Silhouette

A silhouette plant is one that has a dramatic see-through pattern when viewed against a plain wall or the sky. Taller trees at sunset can be especially striking. Palms and certain species of Eucalyptus *fit this category.*

Tropical effects

Design featuring lush-appearing, bold-form plants such as palms, less deserty yuccas, plus an assortment of leafy broadleaf evergreen trees and shrubs, especially those with colorful flowers, such as Bauhinia, Jacaranda *and* Bougainvillea.

Space definer

Space definers are plants that are useful to articulate divisions of use areas and spaces in the design. They include low hedges or taller plants, trimmed or informal.

Understory

Understory *refers to shrubs or trees that look appropriate and thrive under taller plantings. Trees can be understory when used in a forest planting that includes taller trees, such as African sumac in a eucalyptus grove.*

Specimen

Specimen plants are single plants generally used for unusual or dramatic form or color. In other words, it is used almost as a piece of scultpure in the landscape.

Woodsy landscape

Woodsy effects are achieved by planting canopy-type trees in groups close together and at varying distances from each other, revealing intermeshed overhead branches. These trees are allowed to grow informally.

LANDSCAPE PLANTS A TO Z

Abutilon palmeri

Sonoran flowering maple, Desert abutilon
Malvaceae family

COLD HARDINESS
Low zone. Plants sustain frost damage in intermediate-zone winters, although they recover rapidly in spring.

LANDSCAPE VALUE
- Shrub has a herbaceous* quality under optimum conditions, when its velvety foliage and mallowlike flowers can lend an almost tropical quality to plant composition.
- Foreground groupings, patios and other close-up viewing situations.

CULTURAL REQUIREMENTS
- **Exposure:** Full, even reflected, sun to part shade.
- **Water:** Tolerates hot, dry situations, but soak the root zone every week or so in summer to maintain an acceptable appearance. Much less water in the cool part of the year ensures acceptable growth and appearance.
- **Soil:** Will grow in most desert soils.
- **Propagation:** Seed or cuttings.
- **Maintenance:** Groom after heavy bloom. Remove frost damaged stems and foliage in early spring.

POSSIBLE PROBLEMS
Foliage and stems often die back from colder winters.

Grows 3 to 6 feet (1 to 2 m) high, spreading 2 to 4 feet (61 cm to 1 m). Rapid growth with regular irrigation, but slow with drought. A small upright shrub with pubescent leaves and stems that give a grayish cast to the green and an overall velvety quality to the plant. Produces attractive orange-yellow flowers in panicles*. Sometimes a few solitary flowers bloom in the leaf axils*. Bloom can occur any time during the warm season with rain or supplemental water. Native to Sonora.

** See Glossary*

ACACIA

The genus *Acacia* has contributed more trees, shrubs and groundcovers to the Xeriscape™ plant palette than any other genus. Numerous species grow in the Americas, from the southwestern United States to Argentina and Chile. They are also found in warmer parts of the Old World deserts and throughout the African continent. The subcontinent of Australia is probably the largest contributor to our plant list. All three hardiness regions (see page xiv) are represented in the following charts. Many more *Acacias* continue to be tested and evaluated for landscape use.

Acacia albida

Winter thorn, Apple-ring acacia

Fabaceae (Leguminosae) family

COLD HARDINESS

Adapted to low zone and warm-winter areas of the intermediate zone. Requires mostly frost-free winters. Tree-to-tree variations in cold hardiness limit dependable landscape use of winter thorn, but the specimen growing on the University of Arizona campus in Tucson has been surprisingly hardy.

LANDSCAPE VALUE

- In sunny, warm-winter areas, winter thorn has potential as a shade tree or for skyline or background effects.
- Its winter foliage creates interesting but challenging opportunities for contrast in landscape compositions.

CULTURAL REQUIREMENTS

- **Exposure:** Full sun.
- **Water:** Water every week or two until well established, then thoroughly every month or two during the dry season.
- **Soil:** Fast-draining soil.
- **Propagation:** Seed.
- **Maintenance:** Little maintenance required except gradual removal of lower branches when developing a canopy tree.

POSSIBLE PROBLEMS

A tree that's green in winter and bare in summer may be difficult to adjust to and challenging to use in a landscape composition.

To 90 feet (27.5 m) high, spreading 60 to 80 feet (18 to 24 m). Rapid growth when climate and soil satisfy its requirements. This deciduous African tree has a unique seasonal appearance—covered in green foliage in winter and bare in summer—a dramatic contrast to its companion trees, which are green in summer. *A. albida* becomes a large tree in tropical habitats, often with a flat-topped crown. Light-colored shoots bear blue-green bipinnately* compound leaves and pairs of straight spines about 1 inch (2.5 cm) long. The cream-colored flowers adorn long spikes. Curiously twisted oblong seed pods are 4 inches (10 cm) long.

Acacia aneura

Mulga

Fabaceae (Leguminosae) family

COLD HARDINESS

Low zone and mild microclimates of the intermediate zone. Moderately frost tolerant.

LANDSCAPE VALUE

- Tough and attractive evergreen screen, background or informal hedge.
- Small specimen, accent or patio tree.
- Useful in medians, buffer zone plantings and parking islands.

CULTURAL REQUIREMENTS

- **Exposure**: Full to reflected sun and heat, or part shade.
- **Water:** Drought tolerant. Performs well with water every month or two in most locations.
- **Soil:** Adapts to many soil types, from sandy loam to clay.
- **Propagation:** Seed.
- **Maintenance:** A clean low-maintenance acacia.

POSSIBLE PROBLEMS

None observed.

Grows to 20 feet (6 m) or higher, spreading to 10 feet (3 m) or more. Slow to moderate growth. Evergreen shrub or small tree from Australia. Tree and leaf forms vary but this acacia commonly produces many ascending thornless branches in a dense pyramidal to rounded shape. Dull gray-green to silvery phyllodes* are leathery, narrow, linear and grow up to 3 inches (7.5 cm) long. Tiny rod-shaped golden yellow flowers open in spikes to 3/4 inch (2 cm) long, mostly in spring. Flat oblong seed pods with blunt tips grow to 1 1/2 inches (4 cm) long when mature.

* *See Glossary*

Acacia angustissima 'Hirta'

Fern acacia, Hirta

Fabaceae (Leguminosae) family

COLD HARDINESS

All zones, except varieties from warmer zones. Will freeze to the ground each winter in colder zones and therefore won't become a woody shrub.

LANDSCAPE VALUE

The attractive summer flower display and delicate foliage character of this fern acacia make it at home in shrub borders and roadway plantings, as well as for erosion control on disturbed sites.

CULTURAL REQUIREMENTS

- **Exposure:** Full sun to light shade.
- **Water:** Soak the root zone every month or two in summer, less or not at all in winter.
- **Soil:** Adapted to most well-drained soils.
- **Propagation:** Seed, and probably vegetative cuttings.
- **Maintenance:** No maintenance required except to remove frost-damaged wood in colder areas.

POSSIBLE PROBLEMS

Fern acacia has a wide geographic range. The species includes varieties that differ in height as well as stem and foliage characteristics. Make sure you take seed or other propagative material from plants that have the attributes you desire.

To 5 feet (1.5 m) high, with equal spread. Moderate to rapid growth. A rounded, shrubby deciduous acacia. Deeply grooved, bristly stems are herbaceous* for most of their length, becoming woody only at the base of the plant. The fine-textured pinnate* foliage is divided twice into tiny oblong leaflets less than 1/4 inch (0.5 cm) long. Flower heads are round, 1/2 inch (1 cm) in diameter, displaying a compact mass of one hundred or more white stamens lightly tinged with pink or lavender. Flowering can occur any time from late spring into late summer. Seed pods with pointed tips may be as long as 4 inches (10 cm). This species is widely distributed from the southern United States through Mexico and as far south as Costa Rica. *A. angustissima* 'Angustissima' from Sonora, Mexico, develops into a medium shrub.

Acacia berlandieri

Guajillo, Berlandier's acacia

Fabaceae (Leguminosae) family

COLD HARDINESS

Low and intermediate zones. Probably hardy in the high zone as well.

LANDSCAPE VALUE

- Graceful specimen shrub or small tree.
- Space definer or background plant.
- Street and highway median or buffer zone plant.

CULTURAL REQUIREMENTS

- **Exposure:** Full sun to part shade.
- **Water:** Survives on natural rainfall of 5 to 6 inches (130 to 150 mm) per year. Grows faster and looks best at maturity with thorough soakings of the root zone two to three times a month during the hot season.
- **Soil:** Any soil with good drainage.
- **Propagation**: Seed.
- **Maintenance:** Little maintenance other than occasional raking of seed-pod litter and careful pruning and training of young plants if you wish to create the tree form.

POSSIBLE PROBLEMS

None observed.

Grows 10 to 15 feet (3 to 4.5 m) high, with equal spread. Moderate growth rate. Guajillo, a native of southern Texas and adjacent Mexico, develops into a large evergreen shrub or small multistemmed tree. Its broad, rounded form, arching branches and feathery bipinnately* compound foliage give this acacia a delicate symmetrical appearance. In midspring, clusters of creamy white flower heads at the branch tips add seasonal color and interest. Seed pods are velvety and up to 6 inches (15 cm) long when ripe. Small curved thorns develop on the young branchlets of some plants.

** See Glossary*

Acacia caffra

Kaffir thorn

Fabaceae (Leguminosae) family

COLD HARDINESS

Low and intermediate zones.

LANDSCAPE VALUE

- Medium street tree to patio-sized tree.
- Lush foliage looks tropical in summer.
- Adds fragrance when in bloom.

CULTURAL REQUIREMENTS

- **Exposure:** Reflected sun to part shade.
- **Water:** Drought resistant. Soak the root zone every week or two for good growth and bloom and attractive foliage.
- **Soil:** Native to rocky slopes, so good drainage is important; otherwise not particular about soil.
- **Propagation:** Grows readily from seed but best to plant several seeds directly in small containers, then thin to one good plant; seedlings don't transplant well when roots are disturbed.
- **Maintenance:** Thin canopy occasionally prior to windy seasons to let wind through and help prevent storm damage.

POSSIBLE PROBLEMS

- Susceptible to root-rot fungi.
- Thorns may be a problem on low-hanging branches.
- Hooked spines make pruning and training unpleasant.
- Heavy pod production can create garden litter.
- Wide-spreading tree canopy often outgrows the root system, making it vulnerable to blowing over when young.

To 38 feet (11.5 m) high, shorter in dry situations, spreading to 38 feet (11.5 m). Moderate to rapid growth under optimum conditions. An irregular but interestingly shaped thorny tree from South Africa with large green featherlike leaves. Fragrant, creamy white to pale yellow flower spikes appear in late spring followed by chocolate brown pods. Tends to develop low branches but can be trained to become a single-trunk tree. Said to be deciduous in South Africa, but it is nearly evergreen with regular moisture.

Acacia caven

Espino-caven

Fabaceae (Leguminosae) family

COLD HARDINESS

Low and intermediate zones.

LANDSCAPE VALUE

- An attractive specimen or accent tree that provides spring color and fragrance.
- Planted in groups and trained to a low-branching growth habit, this species also makes an effective thorny barrier or hedge.

CULTURAL REQUIREMENTS

- **Exposure:** Full sun, reflected heat.
- **Water:** Water every month or two to ensure survival, but soak the root zone every two weeks to maintain acceptable appearance of mature trees.
- **Soil:** A desert-tough and especially salt-tolerant acacia, able to withstand poor soil.
- **Propagation:** Seed.
- **Maintenance:** Prune to establish and maintain the desired growth form.

POSSIBLE PROBLEMS

- Fallen seed pods require cleanup in intensive-use areas.
- Thorny twigs and branches may be hazardous to those passing near low-branching trees.
- Subject to Texas root rot*.
- Has been short-lived in some Arizona plantings.

Grows 15 to 20 feet (4.5 to 6 m) high, spreading 10 to 20 feet (3 to 6 m). Moderate growth rate with adequate water. This small, thorny semideciduous acacia with feathery compound leaves is native to Chile. It may be trained as a single- or multistemmed tree. The dense, lacy foliage crown tends to be oval in young trees, becoming more irregular as specimens mature. A heavy crop of fragrant orange-yellow flowers appears in spring. Thick, dark brown seed pods ripen and fall to the ground in summer.

** See Glossary*

Acacia cochliacantha (A. cymbispina)

Boat-spine acacia

Fabaceae (Leguminosae) family

Grows 10 to 20 feet (3 to 6 m) high, with equal spread. Rapid growth when moisture is available. Does not grow in drought conditions. Fast-growing, thorny, scrublike evergreen tree that is taking over disturbed land in northwestern Mexico. Quite spiny in youth but thorns become less numerous in mature trees. These showy spines are shaped like a boat at the base, tapering to a point at the tip. The light-colored spines are sometimes used in dry flower arrangements. The feathery foliage is an attractive green with regular irrigation. Flowers are small yellow balls, about $1/4$ inch (0.75 cm) in diameter, not spectacular but attractive nonetheless. Resembles *A. farnesiana,* although leaves are larger and form is a little more open. Native to Sonora.

COLD HARDINESS

Low zone and warm microclimates of the intermediate zone.

LANDSCAPE VALUE

- Large barrier plant.
- Can be trained into a small patio-size tree.

CULTURAL REQUIREMENTS

- **Exposure:** Full sun. Withstands heat and wind.
- **Water:** Quite drought resistant but soak the root zone every month or two, especially in summer, for good landscape appearance.
- **Soil:** Undemanding of soil.
- **Propagation:** Seed.
- **Maintenance:** Prune and stake to develop it into a tree but little care otherwise.

POSSIBLE PROBLEMS

- Extremely thorny in youth, which makes early training and shaping difficult.
- Reseeds readily. Could become invasive in frost-free climates with summer rain.

Acacia constricta

White-thorn acacia, Mescat acacia

Fabaceae (Leguminosae) family

Grows 6 to 20 feet (2 to 6 m) high, with equal spread. Slow to moderate growth. As with so many other acacias, the mature size is largely determined by soil moisture. A shrub on dry sites, it becomes a small low-branched tree in moister locations. This deciduous acacia is native to the Sonoran Desert, throughout Texas, southern New Mexico and Mexico. It is usually multistemmed with a rounded, spreading crown of fernlike foliage. Plants are often thorny during juvenile stages but as trees mature, the conspicuous white thorns frequently dissipate. The yellow puffball flowers come in clusters and are pleasantly fragrant. The main bloom period is mid- to late spring, but flowering may continue intermittently into late summer, depending on summer rain or supplemental irrigation. Mature seed pods are slender, reddish brown, 2 to 4 inches (5 cm to 10 cm) long and constricted between the seeds.

COLD HARDINESS

All three zones.

LANDSCAPE VALUE

- Revegetation.
- In groups: effective barrier planting, large informal hedge for partial screening or wind and dust control, buffer zone plantings.
- A small multitrunked flowering tree.

CULTURAL REQUIREMENTS

- **Exposure:** Full sun.
- **Water:** Rainfall may be adequate for established trees but soak the root zone during long dry spells to improve appearance, shorten leafless period and increase flowering.
- **Soil**: Tolerates most soils. Found in gravelly washes and in heavy clay soils.
- **Propagation:** Seed.
- **Maintenance**: This tough desert acacia endures adverse conditions and requires little care once established. When your goal is a small tree, prune to limit the number of trunks and to gradually raise the height of the foliage canopy.

POSSIBLE PROBLEMS

- In intensive-use areas, seed pods create considerable litter.
- Use only where thorns will not injure passersby.
- If totally dependent on rainfall, it may remain dormant and leafless for four to six months following a dry winter.
- Mistletoe may infest plants in outlying areas where the tree is native.

* *See Glossary*

Acacia coulteri

Coulter's acacia

Fabaceae (Leguminosae) family

COLD HARDINESS

Low and intermediate zones. Not damaged by cold in the intermediate zone, where it has been growing for the last fifteen years, during which temperatures have dropped into the low-20s F (-5°C) several times.

LANDSCAPE VALUE

- Produces a lush green tropical mood.
- Large background shrub or small patio-size tree.

CULTURAL REQUIREMENTS

- **Exposure:** Prefers full sun but withstands some shade.
- **Water:** Thoroughly soak the root zone every week or two to every month or two depending on your location. Test the soil for moisture and check general plant health and vigor as a guide.
- **Soil:** Any soil with good drainage.
- **Propagation:** Seed.
- **Maintenance:** Undemanding. Gradually remove lower branches if using as a patio tree.

POSSIBLE PROBLEMS

None observed.

Grows 10 to 20 feet (3 to 6 m) high, spreading 15 to 20 feet (4.5 to 6 m). Slow to moderate growth. To date, there is limited information on Coulter's acacia, but it appears to have good potential as a patio tree. Its spreading, rounded evergreen canopy has a ferny tropical appearance. Rod-shaped, cream-colored flowers are not spectacular but brighten up the tree in spring. Foliage persists through the winter and the tree does not look sparse like many evergreen acacias. Does not produce an abundant crop of seed pods. Native to Mexico.

Acacia crassifolia

Butterfly-leaf acacia

Fabaceae (Leguminosae) family

COLD HARDINESS

All three zones.

LANDSCAPE VALUE

- Has the potential to become an interesting multistem patio tree because of its size and interesting foliage.
- Blossoms are not showy but are somewhat attractive at close range.
- Tolerance of severe desert conditions adds to its value as a landscape plant.

CULTURAL REQUIREMENTS

- **Exposure:** Best in full sun but can grow as an understory tree in part shade.
- **Water:** Drought resistant, but soak the root zone every week or two during the warm season to speed up the growth rate and maintain a satisfactory appearance.
- **Soil:** Tolerates a wide variety of desert soils and long periods of drought.
- **Propagation:** Seed.
- **Maintenance:** Requires little maintenance except to remove heavy set of seed pods for aesthetic reasons.

POSSIBLE PROBLEMS

None observed, except slow growth rate. Encourage faster growth with regular water.

Grows 10 to 15 feet (3 to 4.5 m) high, with equal spread. Slow to moderate growth. A small, shrubby evergreen tree from Mexico's Chihuahuan Desert. Its medium-green leaves are unique in the *Acacia* genus: They are arranged on the stem like a butterfly with two roundish wings. Because of this, the species has been confused with those of *Bauhinia*, the orchid tree genus, which it resembles at a glance. Ball-shaped flowers arranged in racemes* are not a strong feature because of their cream or off-white color. This acacia also bears medium-size woody brown pods, but not heavily.

* *See Glossary*

Acacia craspedocarpa

Waxleaf acacia, Leatherleaf acacia

Fabaceae (Leguminosae) family

COLD HARDINESS

Low and intermediate zones.

LANDSCAPE VALUE

- Privacy screen.
- Shrub background.
- Windbreak.
- Space definer.

CULTURAL REQUIREMENTS

- **Exposure:** Full sun to part shade.
- **Water:** Soak the root zone every month or two once plant is established or achieves functional size, more often while young.
- **Soil:** Tolerates most arid-climate soil types.
- **Propagation:** Seed.
- **Maintenance:** Requires little maintenance.

POSSIBLE PROBLEMS

None observed.

Grows 10 to 15 feet (3 to 4.5 m) high, with equal spread. Slow to moderate growth. This evergreen shrub acacia from Australia has thick, rounded gray-green leaves that form a dense foliage canopy. Bloom is seldom heavy at any one time, occurring intermittently from spring into late summer. The yellow, compact rod-shaped flower clusters are followed by large seed pods.

Acacia cultiformis

Knife acacia

Fabaceae (Leguminosae) family

COLD HARDINESS

Low and intermediate zones.

LANDSCAPE VALUE

- Sprawling bank cover.
- Wide screen.
- Interesting small gnarled tree when pruned up.

CULTURAL REQUIREMENTS

- **Exposure:** Reflected sun to part shade.
- **Water:** Soak the root zone every month or two. Water more often in extreme heat and in late winter to spring for improved growth in early stages.
- **Soil:** Well-drained.
- **Propagation:** Seed.
- **Maintenance:** Prune for tree form.

POSSIBLE PROBLEMS

Somewhat rangy growth habit, difficult to train and control.

Grows 10 to 15 feet (3 to 4.5 m) high, with equal spread. Moderate to rapid growth. Large shrub to small multistem tree with pruning. Silvery gray knife-shaped leaves form an unusual pattern on stems. Spring flowers cover the shrub with clouds of creamy yellow puffball blooms. Evergreen. Native to southwestern Mexico and United States.

Acacia eburnea

Arabian acacia

Fabaceae (Leguminosae) family

COLD HARDINESS

Arid regions of the low and intermediate zones.

LANDSCAPE VALUE

- Effective barrier or flowering specimen tree.
- Long silvery thorns add winter interest.

CULTURAL REQUIREMENTS

- **Exposure:** Full sun.
- **Water:** Thoroughly soak the root zone once or twice a season for basic growth; plant becomes more lush with regular watering.
- **Soil:** Most soils, even strongly alkaline.
- **Propagation:** Seed.
- **Maintenance:** Prune to remove lower branches that occasionally grow into the path of pedestrians or vehicles, and to maintain symmetrical growth.

POSSIBLE PROBLEMS

Sharp spines may present a safety hazard.

Grows 18 to 25 feet (5.5 to 7.5 m) high, spreading 15 to 20 feet (4.5 to 6 m). Moderate to rapid growth with regular moisture. Deciduous acacia with a spreading, rounded crown of feathery compound leaves. Toothpicklike white thorns to 2 inches (5 cm) long are conspicuous on twigs and branches. Fragrant yellow puffball flower clusters up to 1/2 inch (1 cm) in diameter bloom in late spring. With adequate water, flowers repeat at intervals throughout the summer. Mature seed pods may be as long as 6 inches (15 cm). Arabian acacia is native throughout the Middle East and India.

Landscape Design Example

A natural garden with plenty of *Ambrosia dumosa*.

* See Glossary

Acacia farnesiana (A. smallii, A. minuta)

Southwestern sweet acacia

Fabaceae (Leguminosae) family

COLD HARDINESS

Hardy types will grow anywhere in the intermediate zone, but seed from more tropical populations will grow only in the most protected areas of this zone. All types can be planted throughout low-zone arid regions.

LANDSCAPE VALUE

- Specimen or accent.
- Patio tree.
- Street or roadside tree.
- Large privacy screen, barrier or space divider.

CULTURAL REQUIREMENTS

- **Exposure:** Full sun; endures reflected heat.
- **Water:** Soak the root zone every week or two to every month or two, depending on your circumstances. Needs moisture to develop and grow in the warm season.
- **Soil:** Any soil with good drainage.
- **Propagation:** Seed.
- **Maintenance:** Prune to maintain good branching pattern and to remove frost-damaged wood.

POSSIBLE PROBLEMS

- Trees grown from seed of a frost-tender strain may experience considerable branch die-back* following cold winters.
- Hardy and tender strains have become mixed in the nursery trade, making it difficult to determine survivability and flowering tendencies.

Grows 15 to 25 feet (4.5 to 7.5 m) high, with equal spread. Moderate growth rate. A thorny, vase-shaped spreading tree. Lacy compound leaves are evergreen in mild winters but semideciduous following a hard frost. For a while, only the species native to the southern end of Florida and the Keys, the West Indies, southern Mexico and northern South America was classed *A. farnesiana.* A more cold-hardy, spring-blooming type native along the Mexican border of the southwestern United States was given species status first as *A. smallii,* which was later changed to *A. minuta.* At this writing, taxonomists have returned *A. smallii* and *A. minuta* to *A. farnesiana.*

Regardless of the nomenclature, it is important to secure seed or plants from the hardier, more spring-blooming strain for landscaping in the intermediate zone and colder areas. Plants grown from seed of the southern populations will freeze back in cold winters. In addition, the flowering of the fall- and winter-blooming type will be canceled by even the light frosts of mild winters. Intensely fragrant yellow puffball flowers, 1/4 to 1/2 inch (0.5 to 1 cm) across, open over a long period from late fall into spring. Most hardy forms open in spring only. Light winter frosts sometimes bring flowering to a halt even in the low zones. Dark brown bean pods to 2 1/2 inches (6.5 cm) long ripen and fall to the ground in summer. Sweet acacia has naturalized along the Mediterranean in southern Europe, Africa, tropical Asia and Australia.

* See Glossary

Acacia gerrardii

Gray-thorn acacia, Wadi acacia

Fabaceae (Leguminosae) family

COLD HARDINESS

Low and intermediate zones—to our knowledge, not tested in the high zone.

LANDSCAPE VALUE

- Usually a small patio-size tree but can become a spreading shade tree under optimum conditions.
- Its toughness under dry conditions makes it valuable for revegetation, medians, and parking and street shade.

CULTURAL REQUIREMENTS

- **Exposure:** Full sun, reflected heat.
- **Water:** Drought resistant but needs moisture to grow and develop into tree stature.
- **Soil:** Most any soil, but a native to gravelly wadis*. Appreciates soil depth.
- **Propagation:** Seed in containers, during the warm season.
- **Maintenance:** To train as a small tree, stake and prune and add more water. Requires little maintenance otherwise.

POSSIBLE PROBLEMS

None observed other than thorns on twigs and bark in early stages of plant development.

To 30 feet (9 m) high, depending on available moisture, spreading 20 to 30 feet (6 to 9 m). Rapid growth if moisture is present. A large round-headed evergreen tree with featherlike leaves and tan bark, thorny when young. As the tree reaches maturity, these thorns fall off with flakes of bark and are no longer present or replaced. This drought-resistant tree from the Middle Eastern deserts and wadis can be any size—large shrub or spreading tree—depending on available moisture. Produces light shade and fragrant yellow puffball blooms.

Acacia greggii

Cat-claw acacia

Fabaceae (Leguminosae) family

COLD HARDINESS

Arid regions in all zones.

LANDSCAPE VALUE

- Interesting small specimen tree with regular water.
- Low-water-use barrier plant.
- In combination with other plant types, revegetates and prevents soil erosion in disturbed areas.

CULTURAL REQUIREMENTS

- **Exposure:** Full to reflected sun.
- **Water:** Survives with just rainfall in the Sonoran Desert but soak the root zone once or twice a season during long dry periods to improve appearance.
- **Soil:** Tolerant of most soils.
- **Propagation:** Seed. Scratch seeds to break coat and promote germination.
- **Maintenance:** This tough, cold-hardy shrub or small tree is well adapted to the desert and requires little care. Prune occasionally to maintain form and branching structure.

POSSIBLE PROBLEMS

- Curved cat-claw–like thorns on twigs and branches make pruning difficult and limit use in pedestrian-traffic areas.
- May need to prune out parasitic mistletoe from tree in outlying areas where the tree is part of the native flora.

Grows 4 to 15 feet (1 to 4.5 m) high, spreading 6 to 20 feet (2 to 6 m). Slow to moderate growth. Cat-claw acacia survives the tough, dry conditions in its native southwestern United States and northern Mexico as a straggly shrub that grows 4 to 6 feet (1 to 2 m) tall. With plentiful water, however, it grows into a small semideciduous tree with a spreading, often irregular, crown. Twigs and branches are armed with short cat-claw–like curved thorns. The foliage is gray-green and finely divided. In spring, drooping, rod-shaped cream-colored flower spikes $1\frac{1}{2}$ to 2 inches (4 to 5 cm) long and $\frac{1}{2}$ inch (1 cm) in diameter add a pleasant fragrance to the landscape. Flowering is heaviest after abundant winter rainfall or irrigation.

* *See Glossary*

Acacia jennerae

Coonavitta wattle

Fabaceae (Leguminosae) family

Grows rapidly to 60 feet (18 m) high and 30 feet (9 m) wide, but usually smaller. A small, vigorous evergreen tree with medium-green, sometimes grayish, willowlike leaves. The 4- to 6-inch (10- to 15-cm) long leaves (called *phyllodes**) have a leathery texture. Blossoms are the typical small yellow puffballs of the *Acacia* clan. These are produced throughout the winter and followed by brown pods. This tough little tree from the Australian desert produces a clump of trunks at maturity, creating a little bosque* from root sprouts. The general trunk and branch structure is strongly vertical, but there are forms that produce pendulous side branches, creating an attractive weeping effect.

COLD HARDINESS

Low and intermediate zones and probably warmer areas of the high zone, although not tested as of this writing.

LANDSCAPE VALUE

- Screen and background planting (where space permits its clumping characteristics).
- Hillside erosion stabilization and control.
- Revegetation of disturbed areas.
- Roadside and highway plantings.
- Small tree for patios and paved areas in general, where the root sprouting is limited to the opening in the hard surface.

CULTURAL REQUIREMENTS

- **Exposure:** Full sun, including reflected heat.
- **Water:** Drought resistant, but performs best with weekly soakings of the root zone in the warm season, less in the cool season.
- **Soil:** Well-drained.
- **Propagation:** Seed, but propagate from root sprouts when you want a particular (weeping or nonweeping) growth habit.
- **Maintenance:** Little pruning required unless growing as a small tree in a paved area. In these locations, remove low branches and pull out root sprouts as they emerge.

POSSIBLE PROBLEMS

Sprouting roots can be invasive when planted in the wrong location.

Acacia karroo

Karroo thorn

Fabaceae (Leguminosae) family

Grows 6 to 12 feet (2 to 3.5 m) high, with equal spread. Moderate to rapid growth when supplied with regular water. Slow growth with just rainfall in most areas. Twigs and branches of this South African evergreen acacia are defended by white sharp-pointed spines to 3 inches (7.5 cm) long. Typically grows as a shrub but may become an attractive small tree under favorable conditions. Leaflets of the bipinnately* compound foliage are about 1/4 inch (0.5 cm) long. Fragrant yellow flowers open in clustered heads in late spring. The narrow seed pods, as long as 5 inches (13 cm), may be straight or curved.

COLD HARDINESS

Low zone and protected microclimates of the intermediate zone.

LANDSCAPE VALUE

- Thorny informal hedge, buffer or barrier.
- A tough erosion-control plant on disturbed sites.
- The patio-size tree is well worth the effort to train it. Once the canopy is developed above head height, thorniness is not a problem.

CULTURAL REQUIREMENTS

- **Exposure:** Full sun to partial shade.
- **Water:** Once established, soak the root zone every month or two during prolonged dry spells.
- **Soil:** Tolerant of a wide range of arid-climate soil conditions.
- **Propagation:** Seed.
- **Maintenance:** To train as a patio tree, stake tree and gradually remove side branches until all are above head height.

POSSIBLE PROBLEMS

- Reseeds readily. Can be invasive in moist areas.
- Thorniness makes it difficult to work with in its juvenile stages. Use with discretion in close-up situations.
- Prone to frost damage in colder regions of the intermediate zone, requiring frequent spring pruning of frost-damaged wood.

* *See Glossary*

Acacia longifolia

Sydney golden wattle

Fabaceae (Leguminosae) family

COLD HARDINESS

Low zone and warm-winter locations of the intermediate zone.

LANDSCAPE VALUE

- The rounded, dense form of this evergreen acacia makes it an excellent choice for massing in large screen plantings, buffer zones, along roadways and in informal shrub borders and background plantings. Needs plenty of space to accommodate its mature size.
- An effective erosion-control plant.
- Because of its salt-resistance, useful in seashore landscapes.
- Small tree, either single- or multitrunked, if trained.

CULTURAL REQUIREMENTS

- **Exposure:** Full to reflected sun. Tolerates heat.
- **Water:** Can tolerate month-long droughts, but soak the root zone every month or two during spring and into summer to promote good growth and flowering.
- **Soil:** Tolerates a wide range of soil types, including fast-draining sandy soils.
- **Propagation:** Seed.
- **Maintenance:** Shape and trim if using as a patio tree. Otherwise little maintenance required when planted with enough room to spread.

POSSIBLE PROBLEMS

Like many fast-growing plants, Sydney golden wattle is short-lived. Expect a life span of twenty to thirty years under average growing conditions.

To 20 feet (6 m) high, with equal spread. Rapid growth. True to its species name, the smooth green leaves of this large shrub *Acacia* are long: 3 to 6 inches (7.5 to 15 cm). Leaves are 1/2 inch (1 cm) wide and rounded at the tip. During late winter and early spring, a lavish display of bright yellow flowers in slender 2 1/2-inch (6.5-cm) long spikes appear along the branches. Native to Australia.

Acacia notabilis

Notable acacia

Fabaceae (Leguminosae) family

COLD HARDINESS

Low and intermediate zones.

LANDSCAPE VALUE

- Foliage color contrast in any arid-plant combination.
- Accent.
- Unclipped hedge.
- Screen or background plant.
- Roadside or highway median planting.
- Residential property plant.

CULTURAL REQUIREMENTS

- **Exposure:** Full or reflected sun to part shade.
- **Water:** Soak the root zone once or twice each growing season to maintain satisfactory appearance and growth of established plants.
- **Soil:** Well-drained.
- **Propagation:** Seed.
- **Maintenance:** May require occasional pruning during the first several years to attain desired form and branching structure. Minimum maintenance as a mature plant.

POSSIBLE PROBLEMS

None observed.

Grows 6 to 8 feet (2 to 2.5 m) high, spreading 6 to 10 feet (2 to 3 m). Moderate to rapid growth. A large, nonthorny evergreen shrub from Australia. It has a graceful spreading form and dense canopy of slender blue-green leaves. Puts on a showy spring flower display of bright yellow puffballs. Plant has sharp clean lines in the landscape.

* See Glossary

Acacia pendula

Weeping acacia, Weeping myall
Fabaceae (Leguminosae) family

COLD HARDINESS
Low and intermediate zones.

LANDSCAPE VALUE
A stately and graceful specimen or accent tree, especially noteworthy for its attractive weeping appearance and elegant gray foliage.

CULTURAL REQUIREMENTS
- **Exposure:** Full or reflected sun to open shade.
- **Water:** Soak the root zone every week or two to every month or two, depending on your situation. Use soil moisture and general plant health and vigor as your guide.
- **Soil:** Prefers good drainage.
- **Propagation:** Seed.
- **Maintenance:** Prune as needed to enhance the cascading form of the tree. Trim occasionally to allow winds to pass through canopy.

POSSIBLE PROBLEMS
- Susceptible to Texas root rot*.
- Heavy winds can break branches.

To 40 feet (12 m) high, spreading to 25 feet (7.5 m). Slow growth. A small evergreen tree with a rounded crown of drooping branches and striking pendulous silvery gray foliage. The narrow lance-shaped leaves (called *phyllodes**) are straight or curved and 1¾ to 4 inches (4.5 to 10 cm) long. The lemon yellow puffball flower clusters of this Australian native are rarely produced in arid landscapes.

Acacia pennatula

Sierra Madre acacia, Feather acacia
Fabaceae (Leguminosae) family

COLD HARDINESS
Low zone and protected microclimates of intermediate zone.

LANDSCAPE VALUE
Specimen or patio tree in locations that experience only mild frosts.

CULTURAL REQUIREMENTS
- **Exposure:** Full sun, withstands reflected heat. Part shade in warm-winter microclimates.
- **Water:** Soak the root zone weekly for good appearance during the warm season. Tolerant of some periods of drought, especially in winter.
- **Soil:** Any soil with good drainage.
- **Propagation:** Seed.
- **Maintenance:** Little care required except to remove frost-damaged wood. Remove lower branches to develop an overhead shade tree.

POSSIBLE PROBLEMS
Expect substantial cold injury in locations experiencing frost, requiring spring pruning.

Grows 10 to 24 feet (3 to 7.5 m) high, spreading 10 to 12 feet (3 to 3.5 m). Rapid growth. Bold, feathery leaves give this small round-headed acacia a distinctly tropical look. Native to the foothills of the lower Sonoran Desert and south into Mexico. This is a somewhat frost-tender species whose leaves turn a bronze color after a cool winter. Fragrant yellow puffball flower heads emerge in spring.

* *See Glossary*

Acacia peuce

Waddywood

Fabaceae (Leguminosae) family

COLD HARDINESS

Low and intermediate zones.

LANDSCAPE VALUE

Background shrub or a dramatic silver accent in a mixed shrubbery grouping, space definer or hedging.

CULTURAL REQUIREMENTS

- **Exposure:** Full sun, including reflected sun.
- **Water:** Soak the root zone every week to ten days to speed up growth. Providing moisture in winter and spring is probably more important than in late summer, judging from its native habitat.
- **Soil:** Any soil with good drainage.
- **Propagation:** Seed.
- **Maintenance:** Little maintenance required. Best to let it determine its own form. Avoid formal clipping, which detracts from the handsome finely cut leaves.

POSSIBLE PROBLEMS

None observed other than slow growth.

To 20 feet (6 m) high, spreading to 15 feet (4.5 m). Slow growth. This acacia is considered a remarkable tree in its native Australia, surviving the rigors of an especially dry interior desert region. It is reputed to be long-lived, in contrast to most of the Australian *Acacia* clan that are generally short-lived. The unusual silver-gray, soft-appearing, finely cut foliage is actually quite stiff. Specimens have been slow growing in Arizona, but the handsome silvery mass of foliage is worth the wait. This is a dense shrub or small tree, although it maintains branches and foliage clear to the ground, even as a tree. Typical yellow puffball blossom clusters are not particularly showy against the silver leaves.

Acacia redolens

Prostrate acacia, Desert Carpet™, Ongerup wattle

Fabaceae (Leguminosae) family

COLD HARDINESS

Low zone and all but the coldest microclimates of the intermediate zone. Frost tolerant and wind resistant.

LANDSCAPE VALUE

A neat low-maintenance plant for coastal as well as inland environments. Mounding groundcover for

- Exposed slopes and embankments.
- Street and highway medians.
- Buffer zones.

Also can be used as

- Foundation plant.
- Space divider.
- Low background or screen.

CULTURAL REQUIREMENTS

- **Exposure:** Full to reflected sun to part shade. Accepts heat.
- **Water:** Drought tolerant after established. Soak root zone every month or two to maintain satisfactory growth and appearance.
- **Soil:** Most well-drained soils are satisfactory.
- **Propagation:** Seed or cuttings.
- **Maintenance:** Prune occasionally for height control and form.

POSSIBLE PROBLEMS

None observed.

Grows 2 to 5 feet (61 cm to 1.5 m) high, spreading 6 to 12 feet (2 to 3.5 m). Rapid growth with adequate irrigation. Evergreen shrub from Australia that forms a dense spreading mound. Leathery spatulate leaves to 3 inches (7.5 cm) long are dull gray to olive green. Tiny globular yellow flower heads open in late winter and early spring. Lower growing, more prostrate selections of this plant, such as Desert Carpet™, are now available in the nursery industry. Other introductions are likely to follow.

* See Glossary

Acacia rigidula
Black-brush acacia, Chaparro prieto
Fabaceae (Leguminosae) family

COLD HARDINESS
Low and intermediate zones; borderline in high zone.

LANDSCAPE VALUE
- Barriers and screening.
- Can become an attractive 15-foot (4.5-m) patio tree with pruning and staking.

CULTURAL REQUIREMENTS
- **Exposure:** Full sun. Withstands wind and heat.
- **Water:** Tolerates long intervals between irrigation, but water every week or two speeds its development. Soak the root zone of mature plantings every month or two to maintain attractive appearance. Will survive with no supplemental irrigation in southwestern United States once established. Will tolerate lawn irrigation although this is not a preferred situation.
- **Soil:** Any soil.
- **Propagation:** Seed.
- **Maintenance:** Prune to thicken growth of shrub forms when young. Stake and train if you desire a patio tree.

POSSIBLE PROBLEMS
Extremely thorny, making training and pruning more of a chore.

Grows 10 to 15 feet (3 to 4.5 m) high, spreading 7 to 9 feet (2 to 3 m). Slow to moderate growth. Attractive small evergreen tree or large shrub from the Chihuahuan Desert. Leaves are small, glossy, dark green and closely spaced on spiny twigs. The plant is open and rangy at first but becomes quite dense with maturity. Creamy white rod-shaped flower clusters cover the branches in midspring.

Acacia salicina
Willow acacia
Fabaceae (Leguminosae) family

COLD HARDINESS
Low and intermediate zones.

LANDSCAPE VALUE
- Shade, specimen or street tree.
- Small spaces, entry gardens and patios.
- Golf courses and parking-lot islands.

CULTURAL REQUIREMENTS
- **Exposure:** Full sun.
- **Water:** Soak the root zone thoroughly every month or two. Tolerates brackish water. Irrigation and fertilization should be adequate to promote vigorous growth, but excessive watering results in a top-heavy tree easily blown over by wind. If you use a drip-irrigation system, place several emitters per tree to promote a wider and more uniform root distribution and a more wind-resistant tree.
- **Soil:** Most arid soils with good drainage. Tolerates saline soils.
- **Propagation:** Seed.
- **Maintenance:** Prune to thin the dense foliage crown to offer less wind resistance, so winds blow through the canopy.

POSSIBLE PROBLEMS
Improper irrigation causes weak, poorly developed root systems, making trees vulnerable to blow over.

Grows 20 to 40 feet (6 to 12 m) high, spreading 10 to 20 feet (3 to 6 m). Rapid growth. This willowy evergreen acacia from Australia has a graceful canopy of drooping gray-green foliage and branchlets. Faintly fragrant, creamy white flower balls 3/8 to 1/2 inch (1 cm) across appear in pairs or clusters of eight or more. The tree may bloom intermittently throughout the year, but most reliably from late summer through early winter.

* *See Glossary*

Acacia saligna

Weeping wattle

Fabaceae (Leguminosae) family

COLD HARDINESS
Low zone and warm microclimates in intermediate zone. Moderately frost tolerant.

LANDSCAPE VALUE
- Elegant colorful specimen or patio tree.
- Effective in groves or row plantings for privacy screening, and dust and wind control.
- Golf courses and medians.

CULTURAL REQUIREMENTS
- **Exposure:** Full sun.
- **Water:** Soaking the root zone from every week to once or twice a season, depending greatly on your situation. Test soil moisture and consider plant health and vigor to determine irrigation frequency.
- **Soil:** Accepts most well-drained soils.
- **Propagation:** Seed.
- **Maintenance:** Needs little care other than pruning and staking to develop a single- or multistemmed tree form. Prune gradually to avoid heavy suckering.

POSSIBLE PROBLEMS
Sometimes blown over by wind if watered excessively or with a single drip emitter close to the trunk. Rapid growth of young plants a particular cause of blow over.

Grows 15 to 25 feet (4.5 to 7.5 m) high, spreading 10 to 20 feet (3 to 6 m). Rapid growth. A small leafy evergreen tree from western Australia. It develops as a rounded single- or multitrunked specimen with gracefully arching branches and attractive linear leaves that grow up to 8 inches (20.5 cm) long. In spring, the branch tips are decorated with showy clusters of forty or more large bright yellow flower heads, each 1/2 inch (1 cm) in diameter.

Acacia schaffneri

Twisted acacia, Schaffner acacia

Fabaceae (Leguminosae) family

COLD HARDINESS
Low and intermediate zones. Foliage may drop as a result of drought or freezing temperatures, but wood is much hardier to cold.

LANDSCAPE VALUE
- Patio-size tree with a unique branching structure and foliage effect. It makes an arresting silhouette or specimen.
- Satisfactory screen, thorny barrier or buffer zone plant.
- Young nursery stock may look rangy in the container, but the tree develops real value and character as it matures in the landscape.

CULTURAL REQUIREMENTS
- **Exposure:** Full to reflected sun and heat.
- **Water:** Tolerates considerable drought stress. Established trees perform well with water every month or two.
- **Soil:** Accepts most arid-region soils if well drained.
- **Propagation:** Seed.
- **Maintenance:** Selective pruning necessary in the early years to establish the desired growth habit.

POSSIBLE PROBLEMS
- Mature form is variable: Not all seedlings develop that unique branching structure.
- Young plants often appear rangy.

To 20 feet (6 m) high, spreading to 25 feet (7.5 m). Moderate growth rate. Small tree with a picturesque silhouette. A spreading acacia native to Mexico and southern Texas. Deciduous to evergreen in mild winters. Finely divided leaves grow in a whorled pattern around long curving stems that are armed with short thorns. Fragrant yellow puffball flower heads appear along branch terminals* in spring. Seed pods are brown and velvety.

* See Glossary

Acacia stenophylla

Shoestring acacia

Fabaceae (Leguminosae) family

COLD HARDINESS

Low zone and warm microclimates in intermediate zone.

LANDSCAPE VALUE

- Young specimens present a stark appearance but become arresting specimen, accent or silhouette trees as they mature.
- The texture and form produce a unique effect in a grove planting. Plant five to ten trees (unevenly spaced) for a small grove effect.
- A good tree for the transition zone between areas of low- and high-water-use plants.
- Useful for roadway, median and parking-island planting.

CULTURAL REQUIREMENTS

- **Exposure:** Full to reflected sun.
- **Water:** Established trees are drought tolerant. Water every month or two for good appearance.
- **Soil:** Tolerates poor soil but fertile soil types improve performance.
- **Propagation:** Seed.
- **Maintenance:** Staking may be necessary for a year or two to promote a sturdy, well-proportioned trunk. Otherwise requires little care.

POSSIBLE PROBLEMS

- Occasional cases of Texas root rot* have been reported.
- Suckers* sometimes sprout from roots.

To 30 feet (9 m) high, spreading to 20 feet (6 m). Moderate to rapid growth. Evergreen thornless acacia from Australia. Ascending primary branches give rise to an open framework of arching secondary branches that display maroon-colored bark when young. The tree's common name derives from the drooping threadlike leaves (called *phyllodes**) that form a sparse foliage canopy. Leaves grow to 12 inches (30.5 cm) long. Clusters of pale yellow powderpuff flower heads, 1/2 inch (1 cm) across, bloom from fall into spring.

Acacia tortillis

Umbrella thorn

Fabaceae (Leguminosae) family

COLD HARDINESS

Low and intermediate zones. Nursery stock seems to be vulnerable to cold damage in the intermediate zone until well established in a landscape.

LANDSCAPE VALUE

Excellent umbrella-form shade tree that tolerates tough conditions.

CULTURAL REQUIREMENTS

- **Exposure:** Full or reflected sun.
- **Water:** Drought tolerant but thoroughly soak the root zone once or twice during the summer for good growth and to develop its potential.
- **Soil:** Accepts most soil types.
- **Propagation:** Seed. Scarify or soak in hot water to aid germination (see page xxiv).
- **Maintenance:** Generally undemanding but good growing conditions speed its growth and ensure acceptable appearance.

POSSIBLE PROBLEMS

None observed.

More than 20 feet (6 m) high (reputed to get much taller in its native Africa under optimum conditions), spreading to 30 feet (9 m). Moderate growth. A promising new arrival from Africa and the Middle East that has the characteristic flat-top form associated with the acacias of the African big game country. Usually single-trunked, form is low-branching unless pruned up. Small feathery leaves line the thorny twigs. Tiny fragrant cream or white puffball flowers appear midsummer (not showy). They are followed by curious pods that roll up into a tight coil like a spring. Bark on mature trees is dark gray, rough and deeply fissured. Evergreen.

* See Glossary

Acacia visco (A. abyssinica)

Visco, Abyssinian acacia

Fabaceae (Leguminosae) family

Note: This *Acacia* has long been misidentified as *Acacia abyssinica.* Based on certain taxonomic features, botanist Matthew Johnson determined that it is *Acacia visco,* native to South America, not Africa. It grows in Argentina and Bolivia, on the dry edge of the tropical deciduous forest.

COLD HARDINESS

Low and intermediate zones, except for occasional browning of leaves during colder winters of the intermediate zone.

LANDSCAPE VALUE

- Garden, large patio or street.
- In a grove, the proximity of other trees causes high branching and the development of an intermeshed canopy, making a desirable park tree.
- Often planted in plazas and other public spaces.

CULTURAL REQUIREMENTS

- **Exposure:** Full sun.
- **Water:** Water mature plants thoroughly every two to six weeks, depending on your situation. Water more often when grown on shallow soils underlaid with hard pan, but be careful not to create a waterlogged condition.
- **Soil:** Well-drained soil with some depth.
- **Propagation:** Seed.
- **Maintenance:** Needs little care. Remove low branches and stake trees in the early stages of development.

POSSIBLE PROBLEMS

- Tree is limber and withstands wind well but sheds small branches during storms.
- Some litter when blossoms drop in spring, followed by the pods.

To 40 feet (12 m) high (even taller in favored locations), spreading 20 to 25 feet (6 to 7.5 m). Moderate growth rate. Grows faster with fertilization. Beautiful spreading tree with large featherlike leaves. Evergreen in milder areas but becomes deciduous when winter temperatures drop into the mid-20s F (-4°C). Large yellow puffball blossom heads decorate the lush foliage in late spring. Handsome shade tree. Can be grown either as a single- or multitrunk specimen.

Acacia willardiana

Palo blanco, Willard's acacia

Fabaceae (Leguminosae) family

COLD HARDINESS

Nearly frost-free areas of low arid zone and protected microclimates of intermediate zone.

LANDSCAPE VALUE

- Striking accent or specimen for a hot sunny location.
- Weeping branching habit makes it useful as a patio tree and in entry gardens and small spaces.

CULTURAL REQUIREMENTS

- **Exposure:** Tolerant of full sun and great heat.
- **Water:** Drought tolerant. Rainfall or soaking of the root zone once or twice a season during long dry periods are all it needs.
- **Soil:** Tolerates even thin rocky soil.
- **Propagation:** Seed.
- **Maintenance:** A tough desert tree. No special care required once established except removal of frost-damaged wood in spring following a cold winter.

POSSIBLE PROBLEMS

None observed.

Grows 10 to 20 feet (3 to 6 m) high, spreading 5 to 10 feet (1.5 to 3 m). Moderate growth rate. The unique, almost stark, beauty of this slender, thornless acacia from Mexico's Sonoran Desert lies in the open airy crown of threadlike foliage and peeling silvery white bark on weeping stems and trunks. Quickly sheds four to five pairs of tiny leaflets under dry conditions, leaving behind a slender petiole*, 2½ to 12 inches (6.5 to 30.5 cm) long. Short creamy white flower catkins, 1¼ to 2½ inches (3 to 6.5 cm) long, appear in late spring.

* See Glossary

Acacia xanthophloea

Fever tree

Fabaceae (Leguminosae) family

COLD HARDINESS

Low zone; best in regions that receive only light frost. Can be grown in warmer areas of intermediate zone where it recovers rapidly from frost damage.

LANDSCAPE VALUE

- Undemanding, fast-growing shade tree with exotic look.
- Smooth light-colored bark adds special interest to the landscape.
- A barrier plant if planted closely in a hedge, leaving low branches intact instead of trimming them up.

CULTURAL REQUIREMENTS

- **Exposure:** Full sun, reflected heat.
- **Water:** Drought resistant, but to achieve good growth rate when young and acceptable landscape appearance when mature, water the root zone thoroughly every week or two during the warm season. Reduce applications in winter.
- **Soil:** Any soil.
- **Propagation:** Seed.
- **Maintenance:** Train on a regular basis when plant is young by pinching and pruning to shape for ultimate function (shade tree or barrier hedge). This avoids the need to go back later to reshape thorny branches that grew out of hand. Once the lowest branches are above head height, little pruning is necessary, except to remove frost-damaged wood after a cold winter.

POSSIBLE PROBLEMS

Thorny twigs and branches make it unsuitable for some locations. Thorns complicate pruning in general.

Grows 35 to 40 feet (11 to 12 m) high, sometimes taller, with equal spread, sometimes wider than height. Rapid growth. Interesting spreading semi-evergreen tree that develops the flat-topped look associated with trees of the African plains. Smooth cream-colored bark with a greenish cast is a special feature. Heavy thorns on branches are visually attractive and part of the African look, but they are certainly a deterrent when training or pruning. Feathery gray-green leaves clothe the rather open branch structure, providing a nice see-through silhouette. Flowers are yellow to white and not particularly showy. Although it has been drought resistant in Arizona test plantings, it is often found growing near swampy areas in its native South African habitat. Early settlers there thought the tree, rather than the malaria mosquito, was carrying the fever, thus the undeserved common name "fever tree."

Acoelorraphe wrightii (Paurotis wrightii)

Everglade palm, Saw cabbage palm

Arecaceae family

COLD HARDINESS

Low zone and mild-winter microclimates in the intermediate zone.

LANDSCAPE VALUE

- Minioasis settings as a strong accent or central feature, as well as for background and framing.
- Container plants.
- Tolerates coastal conditions.
- Surprisingly, it has done well in urban situations.
- Performs well as an understory plant beneath taller trees.

CULTURAL REQUIREMENTS

- **Exposure:** Full sun to part shade.
- **Water:** Water thoroughly every week or two during the hot season for satisfactory appearance. Tolerates wider intervals between irrigation at maturity and during the cool season.
- **Soil:** Prefers fertile soil. Adapted to wet locations, but accepts dry locations as well. Tolerates alkaline, sandy soils although growth is slower.
- **Propagation:** Seed.
- **Maintenance:** For a neater appearance, remove lower dead leaves and old fruiting stalks as they appear.

POSSIBLE PROBLEMS

- Reportedly slow growing on the U.S. Pacific coast.
- Resistance to pests and diseases yet to be evaluated.

To 25 feet (7.5 m) high, spreading to 15 feet (4.5 m). Slow to moderate growth. The native range of this round-topped, multistemmed fan palm extends from the Florida Everglades to Cuba, the Bahamas, West Indies and Mexico south into Central America. Several slender trunks, 4 to 5 inches (10 to 13 cm) in diameter, covered with a matting of fibers and persistent leaf bases grow in a clump with a dense stand of suckers* below. Fan-shaped leaves are 2 to 3 feet (61 cm to 1 m) across, often silvery beneath and divided into stiff segments. Sharp orange-colored teeth develop along the leaf petioles*. In early summer, long branching clusters of inconspicuous flowers appear within and above the foliage canopy. The shiny black round fruits are about 1/4 inch (0.5 cm) in diameter and appear after summer and fall.

Adansonia digitata

Baobab tree

Bombacaceae family

COLD HARDINESS

Warm locations in the low zone (will withstand some frost).

LANDSCAPE VALUE

- A dramatic presence in any landscape, the trunk and branching structure are like a piece of abstract sculpture.
- Size makes it suitable only for a park or large urban space with plenty of room.

CULTURAL REQUIREMENTS

- **Exposure:** Full sun, reflected heat.
- **Water:** Water every week or two during warm season for good growth. It has proved to be a survivor even during periods of drought, but little growth occurs when moisture is lacking.
- **Soil:** Any soil.
- **Propagation:** Seed or cuttings.
- **Maintenance**: Remove frost damage and twigs in borderline zones. No other pruning is necessary.

POSSIBLE PROBLEMS

- The ultimate trunk size, which may be as wide as the height of the tree, may be a problem in a small place. Some trunks get so large they are hollowed out for storage or even shelter.
- Occasional frost damage may occur in cold winters.

Grows 20 to 50 feet (6 to 15 m) high (highest in tropics), spreading to 40 feet (12 m). Slow to moderate growth. Probably no other tree so symbolizes Africa: The baobab tree ranges from the edge of the Sahara to South Africa. Other *Adansonia* species are also found in Madagascar. Mature specimens are broader than they are tall, with a massive trunk. Its more or less flat-topped canopy is covered with bright green edible leaves. It survives the marching desertification* now taking place in its native habitat and adapts to periods of drought. Large white flowers among the leaves add interest at close range. Deciduous.

* *See Glossary*

Adenium obesum and *Adenium* hybrid (*A. obesum* X *A. swazicum*)

Desert rose, Hybrid desert rose, Crimson star, Crimson sunset

Apocynaceae family

COLD HARDINESS

Use is limited to containers (to allow mobility to frost-free locations) except in the warmest areas of the low zone. Tolerates no frost or even prolonged chilling.

LANDSCAPE VALUE

A container plant *par excellence* for the summer patio or deck. It not only thrives in heat but tolerates the high soil temperatures that rule out many container plants in hot regions.

CULTURAL REQUIREMENTS

- **Exposure:** Reflected sun to open, shaded areas.
- **Water:** Water every week or two throughout the warm season. Water container plants once or twice in winter, but don't water at all when planted outside in the ground where hardy.
- **Soil:** Requires well-drained soil. Cannot tolerate cold, wet soil conditions.
- **Propagation:** Seed or cuttings, when available; propagate during warm season only. Plant directly in the ground in frost-free areas only. Plant in containers and move inside for protection against cold in other areas. Plants will continue to bloom indoors into winter when placed in a sunny window area.
- **Maintenance:** After spring heat begins, fertilize lightly.

POSSIBLE PROBLEMS

None observed.

Grows 6 feet or higher (2 m), spreading to 13 feet (4 m). Moderate growth rate. Interesting thick, twisted stems rising from an enlarged bulbous base create a unique silhouette. Sparse dark green leaves have rounded ends. Evergreen but sometimes completely deciduous. Deep pink funnel-shaped blossoms spread to 2 inches (5 cm) at the top and are produced in clusters throughout the spring and summer. The foliage thickens and becomes more lush over summer but not so dense it obscures the open silhouette.

The hybrid is similar but the blossoms are larger and a bright crimson red. Both types are real attention-getters during the heat of summer and the striking branch pattern is not a let-down in winter. Native to Central Africa and certain areas of the Middle East.

* See Glossary

AGAVE

Agaves encompass a host of dramatic succulent accent plants for the low-water-demand plant palette. *Agaves*, with a few exceptions, are drought resistant—able to endure hot and stressful situations. One drawback is that when they bloom, they die and, unless replaced, leave a void in the landscape. Maturity and onset of flowering varies among species, from ten to more than thirty years. Little information exists on this time element. Often, a plant is several years old by the time it is purchased for use in a landscape. Some species, however, produce offset plants before they bloom, which helps ensure the longevity of the planting design. They are native to the Southwest United States, throughout Mexico, and into northern South America. Therefore, hardiness varies from species to species, ranging from the edge of the cool intermediate zone into the tropics. Agave snout-nosed weevil is a problem with some species, causing growth damage and often death.

Agave americana

Century plant, Maguey

Agavaceae family

COLD HARDINESS

All three zones. Severe frost damage to leaves can disfigure plant and is slow to disappear.

LANDSCAPE VALUE

- Bold sculptural form.
- The flower stalks are often allowed to remain to create accent and emphasis after the plant dies.
- Effective as a tub plant for large containers and planters. The smaller-scale variegated forms are excellent container plants. Because of their size, they are even more appropriate in garden situations.

CULTURAL REQUIREMENTS

- **Exposure**: Tolerates reflected sun and heat. Also performs well in part shade.
- **Water:** Rainfall only may be adequate at higher elevations, but in the low desert, water every month or two to maintain acceptable plant appearance.
- **Soil:** Adapted to desert soil conditions.
- **Propagation:** Offsets* or seed.
- **Maintenance:** Easy to grow. If necessary, remove dead lower leaves. Prune unwanted offsets to maintain plant appearance.

POSSIBLE PROBLEMS

- Agave weevil* and scale.
- Plant dies after blooming and cannot be kept alive by cutting the stalk.
- Some people are allergic to the plant sap.
- Removal of plant after it dies can be a major project.
- Do not plant where growing space is inadequate for the mature plant (less than twelve feet apart from centers of plants) or where terminal* spines create a hazard to passersby.

Grows 5 to 7 feet (1.5 to 2 m) high, spreading 8 to 12 feet (2.5 to 3.5 m). Rapid growth with occasional irrigation. A large evergreen succulent with thick, fleshy gray-green leaves that grow in a basal rosette*. Leaves may be straight or gracefully curved inward; all have hooked spines along the margins and a stiff, sharp spine at the tip. Plants generally flower when ten or more years old. The massive single flower stalk elongates rapidly to a height of 15 to 30 feet (4.5 to 9 m), early to midsummer, and produces a spike of bright yellow flowers. After flowering and fruiting, the plant dies, but the dramatic dry bloom stalk may remain upright for several years. Originally from Mexican highlands, but now widely naturalized worldwide in desert and Mediterranean climates. There are several variegated forms with yellow or white stripes down the leaves. These are typically smaller than the average species size. See Variegated forms, following, for more information.

Variegated forms: *Agave americana* 'Marginata,' variegated century plant, is similar but slightly more refined and smaller in scale than the usual century plant. Its narrower leaf blades are gray-green with a yellow stripe down each margin. This agave looks nice in the garden as a contrast in color and form to other plants. It also blends well in desert or tropical groupings and is an attractive container plant. Moderate water is acceptable, with occasional deep soakings. It survives without any irrigation in areas with 10 inches (255 mm) or more annual rainfall. Like *A. americana,* it is well armed with spines and should not be placed near walkways.

Another variegated *Agave* thought to be a variety of *A. americana* 'Media Picta' is often sold as *A. picta.* It grows to 3 feet (1 m) tall and has gray-green leaves with wide, distinctly white stripes. It also has well-armed edges and tips on its leaves. Produces abundant offsets and, because of its petite size, is a favorite for containers. Cultural requirements are the same as for *A. americana* in general, but 'Media Picta' seems a little more sensitive to reflected sun. Tolerates full shade and survives in garden conditions as long as drainage is adequate.

* See Glossary

Agave attenuata

Nova, Century plant

Agavaceae family

COLD HARDINESS

Low zone only for landscape plantings. Even light frost will damage leaves. Protected microclimates or containers in intermediate zone.

LANDSCAPE VALUE

- The most tropical in appearance of the *Agave* genus with long, unarmed, soft gray-green leaves.
- Makes a dramatic clump of rosettes* on branched stems in cool-summer, frost-free arid regions.
- Excellent container plant in areas protected from frost.

CULTURAL REQUIREMENTS

- **Exposure:** Partial sun to open shade in hot-summer areas. Full sun in cool-summer regions.
- **Water:** Grows well with water every month or two. Water more often in summer for a satisfactory appearance; water container-grown plants every week to keep them attractive. This species is much more drought resistant in arid regions that have cool summers.
- **Soil:** Any soil with good drainage.
- **Propagation:** Cuttings.
- **Maintenance:** Remove old leaves and dry bloom stalks.

POSSIBLE PROBLEMS

- Top-heavy plant tends to tip over with the weight of the rosettes. Staking looks odd with this type of plant. You can cut off rosettes and reroot when the plant gets ungainly and top heavy. The cut stump will resprout new heads.
- Survives light frost but regrowth is slow to cover damage.

Develops stems 3 to 5 feet (1 to 1.5 m) long, an individual head 3 feet (1 m) across and branched clumps 4 to 5 feet (1 to 1.5 m) across in frost-free places. Moderate to slow growth. This agave has a soft, lush rosette of thornless leaves that are a cool, slightly gray-green. It forms multistemmed clumps of these heads that continue on after blooming. Some heads will die but other branches of the same plant usually maintain the life of the clump. Develops stout stems, unusual in size for the *Agave* clan. Native to high elevations in southeast Mexico and Central America.

Agave bovicornuta

Cow's horn agave, Lechuguilla verde

Agavaceae family

COLD HARDINESS

Low zone and warmer spots in the intermediate zone, where it will sustain frost damage in cold years. Frost damage is slow to disappear.

LANDSCAPE VALUE

- A stunning, bold accent plant in gardenlike settings.
- Looks at home even with tropical-effects plants. Does not belong in a desert setting of rocks, chollas and similar plants.
- Performs well in large containers.

CULTURAL REQUIREMENTS

- **Exposure:** Filtered sun to shade. Does not hold color or look attractive in reflected-heat situations.
- **Water:** Drought resistant but looks best with water every week or two during the warm season.
- **Soil:** Most soils, but avoid high alkalinity.
- **Propagation:** Seed and offsets*.
- **Maintenance:** Little maintenance required other than removal of dead plant after it blooms. After a cold winter in the intermediate zone, you may have to remove frost-damaged leaves.

POSSIBLE PROBLEMS

Sturdy leaf-tip spikes make it unsuitable near pedestrian-traffic areas.

Grows 3 feet (1 m) high, with equal spread. Moderate growth rate with regular irrigation, slower with irrigation at wide intervals. A lush bright green rosette* of broad paddlelike leaves that are 3 feet (1 m) wide at the base, up to 6 inches (15 cm) wide in the center, then quickly tapering to the end. They are edged with a dark saw-toothed armament along the margins, ending with a stout spike at the leaf tips. Bloom spike rises 8 to 10 feet (2.5 to 3 m). It produces few pups, offsets or bulbils*. This medium-sized *Agave*, one of the showiest of the genus, comes from Mexico and is of tropical highland origin.

* See Glossary

Agave bracteosa

Squid agave

Agavaceae family

COLD HARDINESS

All three zones.

LANDSCAPE VALUE

- One of the most attractive of the smaller agaves. Develops offsets, forming clumps.
- Rocky desert settings or mixed in with tropical-effect plants.
- Definitely a foreground plant.
- With its beautiful down-curving leaves and moderate size, this is one of the best agaves for pots and containers.

CULTURAL REQUIREMENTS

- **Exposure:** Withstands full sun but looks best in part shade.
- **Water:** Very drought resistant, but more attractive with water every week or two, especially in containers.
- **Soil:** Undemanding of soil and tolerates being pot-bound.
- **Propagation:** Offsets*.
- **Maintenance:** Remove dead plants after they bloom.

POSSIBLE PROBLEMS

None observed.

Grows 24 to 30 inches (61 to 76 cm) high, with equal spread. Slow to moderate growth. A rather open rosette* of slender, recurving* medium-green leaves. They are not armed and have no points or teeth. Graceful plant with an almost spidery effect. Short 3-foot (1-m) bloom stalk with white-orange flowers gives it an aloelike appearance. Plants go many years before blooming. Some plants remain single, while others produce an abundance of offsets or pups. Native to limestone ledges of the states of Coahuila and Nuevo León, Mexico. Apparently a long-lived agave—plants collected twenty years ago have not yet bloomed in cultivation.

Agave colorata

Mescal ceniza

Agavaceae family

COLD HARDINESS

Low to intermediate zones and probably high zone. Endures a wide range of heat and cold.

LANDSCAPE VALUE

- Bold texture of this noninvasive agave makes it an interesting accent plant.
- A good choice for locations where other agaves may grow too large, such as confined spaces and small properties.

CULTURAL REQUIREMENTS

- **Exposure:** Part shade; full to reflected sun.
- **Water:** Water once or twice a season under drought conditions.
- **Soil:** Any soil with good drainage.
- **Propagation:** Offsets* and seed.
- **Maintenance:** Little maintenance required except to remove dead plant after it blooms. Trim sharp terminal spike if planted near pedestrian traffic.

POSSIBLE PROBLEMS

None known except occasional attacks by the agave weevil*.

Grows 3 feet (1 m) high, with equal spread. Slow growth. An agave of striking appearance from Mexico. The flat, broad leaves grow to 2 feet (61 cm) long and are sometimes banded and tinged red with relatively few leaves to the rosette*. Each leaf is protected by teeth along the margin and a sharp 2-inch (5 cm) terminal* spine. A stalk to 10 feet (3 m) tall bears a spike of reddish orange to yellow flowers.

** See Glossary*

COLD HARDINESS
All three zones.

LANDSCAPE VALUE
- Rock gardens.
- Banks and slopes.
- Containers.
- Handles the harshest desert conditions.
- If used in clumps or colonies, the younger plants will mask the mature plant when it blooms and dies, therefore not leaving a hole in the landscape composition.

CULTURAL REQUIREMENTS
- **Exposure:** Full sun to part shade.
- **Water:** Tolerates no supplemental irrigation but appreciates some water once or twice a season.
- **Soil:** Generally found in rocky, well-drained soil. Accepts improved soil.
- **Propagation:** Offsets* and seed.
- **Maintenance:** Little maintenance required except to remove dead plants after they bloom. Dry bloom stalk is still an interesting form, which you can leave until it falls over. May need to replant young offsets in vacancies left by death of mature plants.

POSSIBLE PROBLEMS
Few known. Some are probably lost to agave weevil* damage and, like all agaves, the plant eventually dies after blooming.

Grows 18 to 20 inches (46 to 51 cm) high, flower stalks 6 to 15 feet (2 to 4.5 m) high. Spreads 18 to 20 inches (46 to 51 cm). Moderate to slow growth. A small clumping gray-leaved plant that has the typical agave rosette*: eighteen to thirty leaves that are broad at the base and toothed at the margins, with a strong terminal* spine. Found alone and in large colonies in low-desert foothills. More tolerant of heat and drought extremes than any other agave. Yellow flowers appear late spring into summer. They are arranged on side branches at the top of slender 5- to 15-foot (1.5- to 4.5-m) stalks. Native to low desert of eastern California into western Arizona and northern Baja California.

Agave deserti
Desert agave
Agavaceae family

COLD HARDINESS
Hardy in low zone and protected microclimates in intermediate zone. Suffers leaf damage in the mid-20s F (-7°C) but recovers rapidly in spring.

LANDSCAPE VALUE
- An attractive addition to the landscape.
- For tropical-effect compositions, place among boulders and at the base of palms and other tropical plants.
- Excellent container plant for sun or shade, even in colder regions, where it can be moved to protected locations during periods of low temperatures. Sometimes even grown as a house plant.

CULTURAL REQUIREMENTS
- **Exposure:** Full sun, including reflected sun to open shade.
- **Water:** Drought resistant, but when planted in hot sunny locations or grown as a container plant, will need supplemental water every week or two during the warm season.
- **Soil:** Any soil with good drainage.
- **Propagation:** Seed (produces no offsets*).
- **Maintenance:** May require treatment for agave weevil*.

POSSIBLE PROBLEMS
- Tender to frost, which somewhat limits its outdoor use in intermediate and high zones.
- Sharp spine-tipped leaves can be a hazard at close range.
- Like all agaves, it eventually blooms, dies and must be replaced.

To 3 feet (1 m) high, with equal spread. Moderate to rapid growth. A new agave on the scene with a form that is quite different from the typical agave. *A. geminiflora* is a solitary, short-stemmed plant that forms dense, symmetrical rosettes* of narrow dark green leaves. The slender leaves measure 2 feet (61 cm) long and 3/8 inch (1 cm) across. They are toothless along the margin, however, and sometimes have fine white marginal fibers. Because plants are all grown from seed, there is some variation in the amount of fibers along the leaf edge. Some plants may have none. The flower stalk is a narrow spike 15 to 18 feet (4.5 to 5.5 m) tall. The species name *geminiflora* is derived from the fact that there are two flowers at each bract* along the spike. The flowers are greenish near the base, flushed with red or purple above. As with all *Agave* species, this plant blooms only once and then dies. Because it is a solitary type, meaning it produces no offsets, it needs to be replaced after flowering. Native to west-central Mexico.

Agave geminiflora
Twin-flowered agave
Agavaceae family

* *See Glossary*

Agave lechuguilla
Lechuguilla
Agavaceae family

Grows 1½ to 2 feet (46 to 61 cm) high, with equal spread. Unbranched bloom stalks rise 6½ to 10 feet (2 to 3 m). Moderate growth rate that can speed up under optimum conditions and slow down in regions with low rainfall. A small green to light green species with lightly toothed margins on the rather upright, sharp-tipped, spinelike leaves. Forms large clumps, or colonies, which are difficult to walk through. Probably the most spreading and clumping of the entire *Agave* clan. Yellow blooms are sometimes tinged with red or purple. Native to the Chihuahuan Desert in the southwestern United States and into northern Mexico.

COLD HARDINESS
All three zones.

LANDSCAPE VALUE
- Good agave for naturalizing along banks and in open spaces.
- Although it dies after blooming, large colonies bloom every year without leaving holes in the planting because of the mass of plants of all ages.
- Could be used as a container or rock-garden plant, but because of its vigorous spreading habit, it might be too invasive in a rock garden.
- A good choice for semi- or completely shady areas.

CULTURAL REQUIREMENTS
- **Exposure:** Grows well in any exposure, from full sun to open shade, although plant color may look bleached in the hottest locations.
- **Water:** Drought resistant, needing no supplemental water except in extremely low-rainfall and high-heat areas. In such regions, water every month or two to maintain a presentable appearance.
- **Soil:** Any soil with good drainage.
- **Propagation:** Offsets*.
- **Maintenance:** Little maintenance required.

POSSIBLE PROBLEMS
- Not a plant for well-groomed areas.
- Dense clumps are sometimes difficult to get into when you want to remove dead or dying plants.

Agave lophantha (A. univitata)
Holly agave
Agavaceae family

COLD HARDINESS
Low and intermediate zones.

LANDSCAPE VALUE
- The dense rosette* of rich green leaves produced by this agave make it a colorful accent.
- Also appropriate for more lush well-watered situations.
- Individual plants are pleasingly symmetrical in form.
- Growth of offsets* create picturesque clumps.

CULTURAL REQUIREMENTS
- **Exposure:** Full to reflected sun or part shade.
- **Water:** Well-adapted to arid conditions. Water once or twice a season throughout the year to maintain acceptable appearance. With more water, plants grow faster and larger.
- **Soil:** Most soils with good drainage.
- **Propagation:** Offsets and seed.
- **Maintenance:** Offsets are noninvasive and you can control clump size by removing them when they are small.

POSSIBLE PROBLEMS
Subject to attack by agave weevil*, but less vulnerable than *Agave americana*.

To 3 feet (1 m) high, spreading 3 to 6 feet (1 to 2 m) in irregular colonies. Slow to moderate growth. Handsome cluster-forming agave native to Mexico. Stiff, glossy dark green leaves have a lighter green stripe along the midrib. Each leaf in the rosette is 2 inches (5 cm) wide, 1 to 2 feet (30.5 to 61 cm) long and sword-shaped. Sharp spines occur along leaf margins and at the tip. Pale green flowers are borne on a spike 6 to 10 feet (2 to 3 m) high.

* See Glossary

Agave murpheyi
Murphey's agave
Agavaceae family

COLD HARDINESS
Low and intermediate zones.

LANDSCAPE VALUE
- Distinctive specimen or accent.
- Smaller scale than species like *Agave americana*, so it's more versatile in the landscape.
- Combines well with other succulents and many arid-region trees and shrubs.
- Container plant.
- Develops offsets, ultimately forming clumps so that younger plants fill gaps after mature plants die.

CULTURAL REQUIREMENTS
- **Exposure:** Full to reflected sun and open shade.
- **Water:** Water established plants only once or twice a season during long dry periods. Younger plants require a little more water.
- **Soil:** Any soil with good drainage.
- **Propagation:** Offsets*, aerial plants or seed.
- **Maintenance:** Minimum maintenance. Occasionally remove dead leaves at the base of the plant and eventually the entire plant after it blooms and dies.

POSSIBLE PROBLEMS
- Agave weevil*.
- Sap causes allergic reactions in some people.
- Sharp terminal* leaf spines limit use in pedestrian-traffic situations.
- Plant dies after blossoming and must be removed.

To 3 feet (1 m) high, spreading 2 to 3 feet (61 cm to 1 m). Slow to moderate growth. Bluish to yellow-green linear, spine-tipped leaves develop in a basal rosette*. Leaf margins are edged with small spines. The bloom stalk grows to 12 feet (3.5 m) or more and produces a terminal cluster of waxy pale-green flowers. Small bulbils* or plantlets form on the bloom stalk after the flowers drop. Native to Arizona and Sonora, Mexico. Domesticated by Native Americans and cultivated for high sugar content in the heart at time of blooming. Cultivation ceased after Europeans settled in the region.

Agave ocahui
Ocahui agave
Agavaceae family

COLD HARDINESS
All three zones.

LANDSCAPE VALUE
- Niches among rocks and boulders.
- Compositions with other large-scale succulents.
- Tolerates range of locations, from very hot and exposed to open shade.
- Containers.
- Useful in agave clumps of different ages so all don't bloom and die at the same time.

CULTURAL REQUIREMENTS
- **Exposure:** Found in reflected-heat situations, but tolerates part shade, where it develops a somewhat larger rosette*.
- **Water:** Drought resistant. No irrigation except every month or two during the hot season.
- **Soil:** Any soil with good drainage.
- **Propagation:** Bulbils* or plantlets on blossom stalk, or seed.
- **Maintenance:** No maintenance except to remove and replace plants after they bloom and die.

POSSIBLE PROBLEMS
- Pointy leaves can be a hazard in pedestrian-traffic areas.
- No knowledge of attack by the agave weevil*.

Grows 18 to 30 inches (46 to 76 cm) high, with equal spread. Moderate growth rate. Striking dark green yuccalike leaves with reddish brown margins form a single dense rosette that seldom develops pups or offsets*. Single nonbranching flower stalks rise 8 feet (2.5 m) or more, cloaked tightly with small yellow flowers. Occasionally small plantlets will form on bloom stalks after flowers are pollinated and fade. Found on rocky slopes at elevations of 1,500 to 4,500 feet (450 to 1400 m) in the state of Sonora, Mexico.

* See Glossary

Agave palmeri
Palmer's agave
Agavaceae family

Grows 3 to 4 feet (1 m) high, with equal spread. Moderate growth rate. Medium-size agave with bright bluish or slightly gray-green leaves, arranged in a rosette* with red-tinged toothed margins and a stout terminal* spike. Rosettes of leaves develop into dramatic 3-foot (1-m) clumps. Bloom stalks branch at the top and are on average 15 feet (4.5 m) tall. The dry stalks add interest for several years. Flowers are yellow green to waxy white. Plants grow as a single rosette, eventually creating clumps. Native to dry oak woodlands and the desert edge of the southwestern United States into northern Mexico.

COLD HARDINESS
All three zones. More cold hardy than most medium-size agaves, an advantage in colder zones.

LANDSCAPE VALUE
- Medium-size accent plant.
- Among rocks and boulders.
- Containers.
- A pleasing shade of green. Its clump-forming characteristics make it useful for bank plantings.

CULTURAL REQUIREMENTS
- **Exposure:** Tolerates any exposure from reflected sun to full shade. Open shade to morning sun probably produces the best-looking clumps.
- **Water:** None needed, but more presentable with monthly watering.
- **Soil:** Almost any soil with reasonable drainage.
- **Propagation**: Offsets* or seed.
- **Maintenance:** No maintenance required except to remove dead plants and replace with young.

POSSIBLE PROBLEMS
None are known except removing dead plants from among live clumps after blooming. Dry bloom stalks have an attractive form but eventually need to be removed.

Agave palmeri chrysantha (A. chrysantha)
Golden-flowered agave, Pinal agave
Agavaceae family

To 2 feet (61 cm) high, spreading 3 to 4 feet (1 m). Slow to moderate growth. The gray-green sword-shaped leaves of this agave form a dense rosette* at ground level. Hooked spines to 3/8 inch (1 cm) long guard the margins of the leaves. Each leaf is tipped with a hard, sharp spine. Tightly packed clusters of one hundred to three hundred bright yellow flowers open late spring and early summer. They appear on short ascending branches along the high section of a stalk 13 to 24 feet (4 to 7.5 m) tall. Native to Arizona, Pinal County in particular.

COLD HARDINESS
All three zones. Native to elevations from 2,000 to 6,000 feet (610 to 1829 m), so it is quite cold hardy.

LANDSCAPE VALUE
- Robust form and foliage texture are enhanced by the dazzling floral display that unfolds on its tall stem.
- Strong accent or specimen, either as a single plant or in groups.

CULTURAL REQUIREMENTS
- **Exposure:** Well adapted to the intense sunlight, heat and aridity of the desert environment.
- **Water:** Water every month or two during establishment and then a few times a season to maintain landscape appearance during long dry periods.
- **Soil:** Any soil with good drainage.
- **Propagation:** Seed, or offsets* if available.
- **Maintenance:** Plant different ages to ensure continuous replenishment of the colony as older plants bloom and die.

POSSIBLE PROBLEMS
- Agave weevil*.
- Place with care near living areas because of spines.
- Some people are allergic to the sap.
- Unlike many *Agaves*, this species does not reproduce abundant offsets. As a result, when a mature plant flowers and dies, you may need to plant a replacement for landscape continuity.

** See Glossary*

Agave parryi huachucensis

Huachuca agave

Agavaceae family

COLD HARDINESS

All three zones.

LANDSCAPE VALUE

- Interesting rosettes* are smaller than average for agaves.
- Most at home in desertlike plant compositions.
- Good foreground plant, especially fine in rock gardens.

CULTURAL REQUIREMENTS

- **Exposure:** Full sun to light shade.
- **Water:** Water once or twice a season for healthy appearance in low-rainfall areas, especially during the hot season.
- **Soil:** Any soil with good drainage.
- **Propagation:** Offsets* or seed.
- **Maintenance:** Little maintenance except to remove and replace dead plant after it blooms. Dry bloom stalk is attractive and can remain as long as it stands.

POSSIBLE PROBLEMS

The agave weevil* is a potential pest, but infestations are rare. Otherwise no known problems.

Grows 1½ to 2 feet (46 to 61 cm) high, spreading 2 to 2½ feet (61 to 76 cm). Slow growth. A handsome clump-forming succulent with a dense rosette of short gray leaves. Leaf edges bear dark thorns and stout spikes at the tip. Rosettes are often broader than they are tall and offset plants crowd against the parent plant. Bloom stalk ranges from 12 to 18 feet (3.5 to 5.5 m) tall and is branched at the tip. Flower buds are pink, opening to pure yellow in late spring or early summer. Native to southeast Arizona and northern Mexico.

Agave parryi truncata

Gentry's agave

Agavaceae family

COLD HARDINESS

All three zones.

LANDSCAPE VALUE

- A small-scale plant for rock gardens.
- Lush character looks great in less desertlike plant combinations; however, this does not mean it *can't* be used in desert plantings.

CULTURAL REQUIREMENTS

- **Exposure:** Reflected sun to part shade.
- **Water:** Drought resistant, but soak the root zone once or twice a season during long dry periods to maintain satisfactory appearance.
- **Soil:** Any soil with good drainage.
- **Propagation:** Could be propagated by seed, but usually by offsets*.
- **Maintenance:** Little maintenance except to remove and replace dead plant after it blooms. Dry bloom stalk is attractive and can remain as long as it stands.

POSSIBLE PROBLEMS

No problems observed. Agave weevil* could attack, but is not a real threat.

Grows 2 to 3 feet (61 cm to 1 m) high, with equal spread or even broader. Slow growth. Grows in a dense rosette* of gray-green leaves that resembles an artichoke, with clumps formed by offsets. Similar to *A. parryi huachucensis* except the leaf tips curve back over the rosette. In addition, the leaves are broader and the plant has a more lush appearance. Blossom stalk rises 12 to 18 feet (3.5 to 5.5 m). Produces offsets that are tightly arranged around the parent plant. Reputed to be the favorite species of Dr. Howard Gentry, the world authority on agaves; hence the common name "Gentry's agave." Native to southern Chihuahua and northern Durango, Mexico.

* *See Glossary*

Agave salmiana

Pulque agave, Salm's agave

Agavaceae family

COLD HARDINESS

Low to intermediate zones. No information available on hardiness in high zone, but possibly hardy there also.

LANDSCAPE VALUE

An agave for large spaces and for making a bold statement in a landscape—it has little competition from other large agaves, even *A. americana*. Probably the most outstanding large agave for landscape use. A dramatic accent plant *par excellence*.

CULTURAL REQUIREMENTS

- **Exposure:** Under trees or in open, reflected sun.
- **Water:** Drought resistant, but water once or twice during warm season.
- **Soil:** Any soil.
- **Propagation:** Offsets*.
- **Maintenance:** Little maintenance except to remove and replace dead plant after it blooms. Dry bloom stalk is attractive and can remain as long as it stands. Mature size makes removal quite a project.

POSSIBLE PROBLEMS

None observed.

Grows 3 to 4 feet (1 m) high, with equal spread. Moderate growth rate. An impressive large agave with dark green leaves that have a bluish cast. The big leaves make it a real "chunk" of a plant in the landscape. The 4-foot (1-m) leaves have smooth margins with a single stout point at the tip. Most plants produce offsets and develop into clumps. The massive bloom stalks rise 20 to 25 feet (6 to 7.5 m), making a dramatic silhouette against the sky. Red buds open to flowers with yellow above and green below. Native to tropical highlands of Mexico. Grown in central Mexican plantations for the production of *pulque* (an alcoholic beverage), which is made from juice harvested from the plant just before it blooms.

Agave victoriae-reginae

Queen Victoria agave, Royal agave

Agavaceae family

COLD HARDINESS

Low and intermediate zones and probably high zone.

LANDSCAPE VALUE

- Striking container plant.
- Small specimen or accent.

CULTURAL REQUIREMENTS

- **Exposure:** Full sun to shade.
- **Water:** Water every month or two.
- **Soil:** Most soils with good drainage.
- **Propagation:** Seed or offsets* (when they occur).
- **Maintenance:** Fertilize occasionally to maintain best color and growth; transplants readily. Remove dead plants after they bloom, including the bloom stalk.

POSSIBLE PROBLEMS

- Agave weevil*.
- Plant dies after flowering.

To 1 foot (30.5 cm) high, spreading 1 to 2 feet (30.5 to 61 cm). Slow growth. Forms a tightly compressed rosette* of stiff dark green leaves that grow to 6 inches (15 cm) long. Leaves are beautifully marked with white lines along the margins and tipped with a small sharp spine. Flowers are pale green, to 2 inches (5 cm) long, borne on a stalk that reaches 3 to 4 feet (1 m). Offsets are seldom produced. Native to Mexico.

* *See Glossary*

Agave vilmoriniana

Octopus agave

Agavaceae family

COLD HARDINESS
Low and intermediate zones, but cold winters cause some tip burning.

LANDSCAPE VALUE
- The unique appeal of this agave is the sculptural effect created by the long, slender curving leaves.
- Specimen or accent, alone or in groups.
- Attractive tub or container plant, especially when young.

CULTURAL REQUIREMENTS
- **Exposure:** Full sun to part shade; no reflected sun.
- **Water:** Water every month or two during the warm season.
- **Soil:** Most soils with good drainage.
- **Propagation:** Propagate from the abundant bulbils* produced on the blossom stalk.
- **Maintenance:** Remove dead plant after it blooms. Bloom stalks are festooned with bulbils* and can remain. Best to plant replacement before plant dies so young plant can achieve some size.

POSSIBLE PROBLEMS
- Agave weevil*.
- Plant is short-lived and dies after flowering, leaving an empty space in the landscape unless placed next to a younger one.

Grows 3 to 4 feet (1 m) high, spreading 5 to 6 feet (1.5 to 2 m). Slow growth. Gracefully recurved* gray-green leaves to 3½ feet (1 m) long grow in a large open rosette* with a form that resembles an octopus. Margins of the fleshy leaves are smooth and spineless. Plants at least six to eight years old may bear yellow flowers on a stalk up to 15 feet (4.5 m) high in spring. These are followed by a heavy set of aerial plants (bulbils), which becomes the next generation. Does not produce offsets*. Native to northwest Mexico.

Agave weberii

Weber's agave

Agavaceae family

COLD HARDINESS
Low and intermediate zones and probably warmer locations in the high zone.

LANDSCAPE VALUE
- Bold statement in the landscape.
- Large containers.

CULTURAL REQUIREMENTS
- **Exposure:** Full sun to part shade.
- **Water:** Water every month or two.
- **Soil:** Any soil with good drainage.
- **Propagation:** Offsets* or seed.
- **Maintenance:** Little maintenance except to remove and replace dead plant after it blooms. Dry bloom stalk is attractive and can remain as long as it stands.

POSSIBLE PROBLEMS
- Like all agaves, it eventually blooms and dies, leaving a big hole in the landscape composition. Plan ahead and nurture young plants close by to replace old.
- The agave weevil* is a potential threat.

To 6 feet (2 m) high, with equal spread. Slow to moderate growth. One of the larger agaves for landscape use, bluish green and neater than *A. americana*, with more slender leaves. Teeth arming the leaves are less conspicuous, often with a spine at the tip only. Bloom stalks rise 18 to 24 feet (5.5 to 7.5 m); flowers are yellow and appear for the grand finale before the plant dies in late spring. Native to east central Mexico.

** See Glossary*

Ageratum corymbosum

Desert ageratum

Asteraceae (Compositae) family

COLD HARDINESS

All three zones. Dies back to ground in winter, but roots are not affected. The plant quickly regrows from the roots in spring.

LANDSCAPE VALUE

- Cool green low-growing plant for oasis situations.
- Bedding plant in a not-too-refined garden.
- Underplanting in a woodsy setting.

CULTURAL REQUIREMENTS

- **Exposure:** Full sun to part shade.
- **Water:** Tolerates periods of drought, especially in winter, but needs water every week or two during the warm season for healthy foliage and blossoms.
- **Soil:** Tolerates most desert soils but appreciates improved garden soil.
- **Propagation:** Divisions or seed.
- **Maintenance:** Cut back in winter.

POSSIBLE PROBLEMS

Looks drab in winter because dormant.

To 1 foot (30.5 cm) high, spreading 3 feet (1 m). Moderate growth rate. Light green, lush-appearing perennial with leaves that are usually round and heart-shaped at the base. Fringy clusters of light blue flowers are abundant throughout the warm season. Goes dormant in winter and looks drab, but can be cut back. New growth resumes in the spring. Sometimes compared to *Eupatorium greggii*, a native to southern Arizona that is more shrubby but not as good a bloomer. Desert ageratum is native to northeast Mexico, found in moist spots in that part of the Chihuahuan Desert and further south.

Ailanthus altissima

Tree of heaven

Simaroubaceae family

COLD HARDINESS

All three zones, even beyond the coldest.

LANDSCAPE VALUE

- City tree, often in planters in paved plazas or parking areas.
- Lawns where regular mowing prevents new seedlings from establishing.
- Tolerant of air pollution in inner cities.

CULTURAL REQUIREMENTS

- **Exposure:** Full sun and reflected heat.
- **Water:** Soak the root zone every month or two for adequate growth, but it even thrives in a high-water-use lawn situation.
- **Soil:** Any soil.
- **Propagation:** Seed.
- **Maintenance:** Undemanding.

POSSIBLE PROBLEMS

- Self-seeding—invades other plantings and areas of the landscape where it may not be wanted. Will not spread into dry areas.
- Late to leaf out in spring, leaving outdoor areas without shade the first hot days of the season.

To 50 feet (15 m) high, spreading to 30 feet (9 m) or more. Very rapid growth with regular moisture. Deciduous tree from China. When young, it is an unbranched single-trunk tree with large compound leaves, thirteen to twenty-five leaflets arranged on a midrib about 3 feet (1 m) long, much smaller on mature trees. Flowers are greenish and inconspicuous, but the clusters of red-brown winged fruit, which appear in late summer and fall, are quite showy and handsome. Reseeds freely and is often seen in clumps and thickets, but when maintained as a single-trunked tree, it will grow into a large impressive specimen. Considered an undesirable weed tree because of its original escape into the western Sierra Nevada foothills of California after planting by the '49ers. Tree of heaven has also naturalized in many other regions and has spread in the wetter temperate zones of the United States. However, it should be recognized for its ability to develop shade and beauty under adverse conditions.

Albizia julibrissin

Silk tree, Mimosa

Fabaceae (Leguminosae) family

COLD HARDINESS

All three zones.

LANDSCAPE VALUE

- Casts light-filtered shade that allows lawn and many garden plants enough sun to grow beneath its canopy.
- An appealing patio tree.
- Handsome color specimen or background tree.

CULTURAL REQUIREMENTS

- **Exposure:** Full sun and intense heat.
- **Water:** Well-established trees are moderately drought tolerant but stressed trees grow slowly and look blanched. Soak the root zone every week or two during the growing season.
- **Soil:** Tolerant of alkaline soils but needs good drainage.
- **Propagation:** Seed or cuttings.
- **Maintenance:** Prune to establish tree shape and landscape function. Stake and gradually remove lower branches for a walk-under shade tree. For a shrubby, more natural lower branching pattern, keep pruning to a minimum.

POSSIBLE PROBLEMS

- Short-lived.
- Weak, brittle wood makes silk tree vulnerable to storm damage.
- Heavy crop of seed pods hang on after leaf drop, which is unattractive to some.
- Leaves, flowers and seed pods generate considerable litter. Avoid placement near swimming pools.

Grows 20 to 40 feet (6 to 12 m) high, spreading to over 40 feet (12 m). Rapid growth. This deciduous tree has a flat-topped to rounded, spreading crown. It grows with one or more trunks, several of them often leaning. Left to grow naturally, horizontal branches tend to develop too close to the ground. Bipinnately compound leaves up to 10 inches (25.5 cm) long are feathery and fine-textured. In spring and into summer, large globular flower clusters with conspicuous pink stamens* open well above the ferny foliage canopy. A heavy crop of tan bean-pod–like fruits 4 to 6 inches (10 to 15 cm) long and $1/2$ inch (1 cm) wide persist on the tree into the leafless dormant winter period. The cultivar* 'Rosea' is more cold hardy and has a deeper pink flower color. Native from Iran to Japan.

Albizia lebbeck

Woman's tongue tree, Lebbek silk tree

Fabaceae (Leguminosae) family

COLD HARDINESS

Warm, almost frost-free low zone. Has been grown in warm microclimates of the intermediate zone. Tolerates light frost without wood damage.

LANDSCAPE VALUE

- Neat, attractive foliage and handsome floral display make this a useful shade tree, street tree or flowering specimen where winters are mild.
- When in leaf, the tree adds a lush green note to the arid landscape.

CULTURAL REQUIREMENTS

- **Exposure:** Full sun to reflected heat.
- **Water:** Reasonably drought tolerant but soak the root zone every month or two for good foliage and flowers.
- **Soil:** Any soil.
- **Propagation:** Seed.
- **Maintenance:** Fertilize at two- to three-year intervals for best appearance and flowering. Selectively prune to develop and maintain a strong, balanced branch framework.

POSSIBLE PROBLEMS

- Heavy crop of seed—not particularly attractive in winter.
- Leaves shed in light frost.
- Severe freezing temperatures can cause damage to structural branches, creating an unbalanced tree form.

To 50 feet (15 m) high, spreading 40 feet (12 m). Rapid growth. Semideciduous tropical tree with a vase-shaped foliage crown, native to tropical Asia. Compound leaves are composed of leaflets up to $1\frac{3}{4}$ inches (4.5 cm) long. Delicate greenish yellow flowers have powder-puff heads. Straw-colored bean pods 6 to 12 inches (15 to 30.5 cm) long and 2 inches (5 cm) wide stay on the tree after leaves have dropped and rattle in the wind, thus the common name "woman's tongue tree."

* *See Glossary*

Albizia sinaloensis

Sinaloan albizia

Fabaceae (Leguminosae) family

COLD HARDINESS

Low zones and warmer positions in the intermediate zones. Severe damage can occur when planted in low-lying areas that commonly receive cold air drainage from surrounding higher areas.

LANDSCAPE VALUE

- Large canopy tree—an intriguing prospect for tropical effects.
- Feathery foliage resembles that of *Jacaranda*.
- Should be tried in a variety of situations to verify its apparent hardiness to warm parts of the intermediate zone, which suggests it is completely hardy in low zones.
- Creamy puffball blossoms displayed among the feathery leaves add interest in summer.

CULTURAL REQUIREMENTS

- **Exposure:** Full sun.
- **Water:** Intermittent deep irrigation, especially in the hot season; little water in the cool season. Seems to tolerate thorough soaking of the root zone every month or two (judging from its native desert wash* habitat) to ample water (lawn situation at the University of Arizona campus).
- **Soil:** Collected from a desert-edge wash, which suggests it needs soil with enough depth for proper root development.
- **Propagation:** Seed.
- **Maintenance:** Little maintenance other than some pruning to improve shape of young developing tree.

POSSIBLE PROBLEMS

None observed.

Grows 40 to 60 feet (12 to 18 m) high in favored locations, spreading to 30 feet (9 m). Moderate to rapid growth in favored locations. Tall round-headed tree (in the wild) with 9-inch (23-cm) feathery leaves. Evergreen tree native to gravelly washes on the southern edges of the Sonoran Desert. Not much is known about this tree in cultivation. Judging from the handsome specimen on the University of Arizona campus, it develops into a magnificent tall tree with attractive feathery foliage. It has never shown frost damage. Great potential for the arid landscape. Along with exceptionally handsome foliage and a striking physical structure, it produces white blossoms borne in round heads.

* *See Glossary*

ALOE

The genus *Aloe* includes a number of dramatic forms that are useful as accents and container plants for the low-water-use plant palette. Native to Africa and the Middle East, *Aloes* are generally smaller in scale than their American counterparts, the *Agaves*. Shrubby and treelike species of *Aloe* are available and can be quite dramatic in a plant composition. However, the arborescent species are only hardy in the warmer zones. *Aloes* in general lack the hardiness of *Agaves*, but they don't die after their annual bloom. The flowering of the *Aloes* is a special event when their dramatic tubular flowers, ranging from yellow-orange to red, bloom 2 to 4 feet (1 m) above the plant.

Note: Aloe mite (see Glossary) causes deformed growth and can be a problem with some species.

Aloe dawei

Dawe's Aloe

Liliaceae family

COLD HARDINESS

Low zone and warm areas of the intermediate zone. Tolerates light frost but because flowers bloom in midwinter, they are more vulnerable to frost damage.

LANDSCAPE VALUE

- Effective combined with other desert succulents.
- Rock gardens.
- Tropical-effect compositions.
- Especially attractive in containers and large pots.

CULTURAL REQUIREMENTS

- **Exposure:** Full sun to open shade.
- **Water:** Being a succulent, it tolerates periods of drought, yet watering every week or two will produce a more luxurious plant.
- **Soil:** Most soils with good drainage.
- **Propagation:** Seed or cuttings taken during the warm season.
- **Maintenance:** Little maintenance except to remove spent bloom stalks.

POSSIBLE PROBLEMS

None observed at this point. Little experience to date with this new addition to the plant palette.

To 3 feet (1 m) high, with equal spread. Moderate growth. Vertical, multistem aloe with toothed, down-curving light green leaves arranged in whorls on tips of rigid stems. Orange blossom spikes that fade to yellow appear in winter, high above the leaves. Plants in bloom present an especially striking silhouette when displayed against a plain background. Native to higher elevations of central Africa (Kenya and surrounding areas). A new introduction to the Southwest that looks very promising.

Aloe ferox

Cape aloe

Liliaceae family

COLD HARDINESS

Low zone and protected microclimates of intermediate zone.

LANDSCAPE VALUE

Bold form and foliage of this treelike succulent make it an impressive accent plant with a colorful display of flowers in season.

CULTURAL REQUIREMENTS

- **Exposure:** Full or reflected sun to part shade.
- **Water:** Established plants survive if watered only during long dry periods, but irrigation every month or two yields a better-looking plant.
- **Soil:** Well-drained soil.
- **Propagation:** Seed. The occasional side branch can also be cut off and rooted.
- **Maintenance:** Little maintenance except to remove spent bloom stalks. Some prefer to remove dry leaves as well to expose the trunk.

POSSIBLE PROBLEMS

- Early spring bloom sometimes damaged by frost.
- Too large for many residential landscapes.

To 15 feet (4.5 m) high, spreading 2 to 3 feet (61 cm to 1 m). Slow growth. More rapid with irrigation. This evergreen succulent from South Africa develops a tall, usually unbranched, stem covered with dried and shriveled leaves. A dense clump of 3-foot (1-m) long, dull green succulent leaves, pointed and edged with brown-red teeth, crowns this aloe. Eye-catching candelabra-branched flower stalk up to 6 feet (2 m) tall produces a cluster of orange-red blooms during spring and into summer. Does not produce basal* offsets*, but it will occasionally grow a side branch from the trunk.

* *See Glossary*

Aloe saponaria

African aloe, Zebra aloe

Liliaceae family

COLD HARDINESS

Low and intermediate zones. Frost will damage leaf tips.

LANDSCAPE VALUE

- Valued for form, foliage and color in the arid landscape.
- A showy accent, tough groundcover or easy-care container plant.
- Profuse blooming adds color in spring and sporadically in other seasons.

CULTURAL REQUIREMENTS

- **Exposure:** Full or reflected sun to part shade.
- **Water:** Tolerant of long dry periods but appearance is improved by water once or twice a season during the dry, warmer months.
- **Soil:** Most soils with good drainage.
- **Propagation:** Easy to propagate with offsets*.
- **Maintenance:** Remove offsets to control size of planting. Clumps become overgrown, requiring thinning or digging and replanting. Old bloom stalks are unsightly and need to be removed. Remove mite-deformed blossoms for better appearance.

POSSIBLE PROBLEMS

- Aloe mite* can severely distort blooms and plant.
- Leaf tips sometimes damaged by hard freeze but new spring growth soon masks the injury.
- First bloom of season may be damaged by frost in intermediate zone.
- Tends to invade adjoining areas and take over.
- Sap can irritate the skin. This plant is easily confused with *Aloe vera*—do not use sap to treat skin ailments.

To 12 inches (30.5 cm) high, spreading 8 to 12 feet (2.5 to 3.5 m). Rapid growth. Evergreen succulent from South Africa grows as a clump-forming rosette*. Upright lance-shaped leaves are green with a reddish cast and have white spots on high surfaces. Leaf tips are typically brown and shriveled, armed with hard sharp teeth along the margins. Reddish or pinkish orange tubular flowers bloom on branching stalks up to 3 feet (1 m) tall. Flowers often appear in two or more bloom cycles from late winter through summer. Offsets spread to form a solid cover in a few years.

Aloe striata

Coral aloe

Liliaceae family

COLD HARDINESS

Low zone and mild-winter microclimates in intermediate zone. Seems to withstand more cold than *A. saponaria*, but late winter flowers may be damaged by frost.

LANDSCAPE VALUE

- The combination of textured foliage, bold exotic markings and a brilliant seasonal flower display make this an excellent specimen and accent plant.
- Unique and handsome container subjects.
- One of its best flowering displays comes in late winter when few plants are in bloom.

CULTURAL REQUIREMENTS

- **Exposure:** Filtered or afternoon shade to prevent sunburn in hot desert regions. Avoid reflected sun and heat.
- **Water:** Water every month or two, less often in winter, to maintain established plants.
- **Soil:** Tolerates most soils with good drainage.
- **Propagation:** Seed or offsets*.
- **Maintenance:** Requires little maintenance other than removal of spent flower stalks.

POSSIBLE PROBLEMS

The plant can be disfigured or killed by hard frost.

To 2 feet (61 cm) high, spreading to 2½ feet (76 cm). Slow to moderate growth. This large South African succulent grows as a rosette* of closely packed, pale gray fleshy leaves 20 to 24 inches (51 to 61 cm) long, broad at the base and tapering gradually to a point. The leaves are further distinguished by fine longitudinal lines and pink spineless margins. Old specimens may develop a short leaning trunk on which dead leaves remain for a considerable time. Clusters of coral red to orange flowers to 1½ inches (3 cm) long open on an upright stem as much as 3 feet (1 m) above the foliage in winter or spring.

* *See Glossary*

Aloe vera (A. barbadensis)

Aloe vera, Medicinal aloe

Liliaceae family

COLD HARDINESS

Low zone and protected microclimates of intermediate zone. Leaf tips and sometimes early flowers are damaged by frost.

LANDSCAPE VALUE

- A small accent or specimen succulent suitable for desert or tropical effects.
- Very much in character nestled among boulders or under an old mesquite or other desert tree or palm.
- Groundcover (no foot traffic)
- Attractive container plant.
- Often planted in medians for form, manageable size and color interest.

CULTURAL REQUIREMENTS

- **Exposure:** Part shade to full sun. Afternoon shade for best appearance in low-elevation, hot-desert locations.
- **Water:** Tolerates drought but looks better and grows faster with water once or twice a season.
- **Soil:** Sandy or other well-drained soil.
- **Propagation:** Easy to propagate with offsets*.
- **Maintenance:** Remove offsets or dig and reset plants and pups to reduce clump size. Remove spent flower stalks.

POSSIBLE PROBLEMS

Aloe mites* distort plant leaves and flower stalks, but this species does not seem as susceptible as *A. saponaria.*

Grows 1 to 2 feet (30.5 to 61 cm) high, spreading 3 feet (1 m) or more. Slow to moderate growth. Tight rosette* of fleshy gray-green leaves are narrow, pointed and erect, with soft pale spines along the margins. A spike of yellow tubular flowers (orange-colored blooms are probably hybrids) bloom on a 2- to 3-foot (61 cm to 1 m) stalk any time from late winter to summer, but most often in spring. Spreads by offsets to form dense clumps several feet or more in diameter. The clear viscous liquid extracted from the leaves is used to treat burns, abrasions and other ailments. Native to Mediterranean region and Africa.

Aloysia lycioides

White bush

Verbanaceae family

COLD HARDINESS

Low and intermediate zones and probably high zone.

LANDSCAPE VALUE

- Handsome shrub with attractive form and fragrant flowers.
- Screening and background.
- Space definition.
- Buffer zone.

CULTURAL REQUIREMENTS

- **Exposure:** Full sun to part shade.
- **Water:** Soak the root zone every month or two to maintain a good landscape appearance.
- **Soil:** Most desert soils.
- **Propagation:** Seed or cuttings.
- **Maintenance:** Low maintenance.

POSSIBLE PROBLEMS

None observed.

Grows 6 to 9 feet (2 to 3 m) high, with equal spread. Moderate growth. Large semievergreen shrub with slender gray branches and twigs that are often spiny near the tips. Undersides of tiny leaves are densely covered with fine hairs. Flower spikes that vary from less than 1 inch (2.5 cm) to almost 3 inches (7.5 cm) long are numerous on the stems. Each spike is crowded with small white flowers that are sometimes tinged violet. The spring-blooming flowers produce a strong vanilla-like fragrance. Native to New Mexico, Texas and Mexico.

* See Glossary

Aloysia wrightii

Wright's bee bush

Verbenaceae family

COLD HARDINESS
Low and intermediate zones. Frost hardy.

LANDSCAPE VALUE
- A handsome graceful shrub, even during its winter-dormant leafless period.
- Showy floral display is also appreciated by bees, making this a good honey plant.
- Space definer.
- Foundation plant.
- Background.
- Useful in transition or oasis zones.

CULTURAL REQUIREMENTS
- **Exposure:** Full sun to part shade.
- **Water:** Established plants need little water, but soak the root zone every month or two to keep them looking attractive.
- **Soil:** Any soil with good drainage.
- **Propagation:** Seed or cuttings.
- **Maintenance:** May need occasional pruning to maintain symmetrical form.

POSSIBLE PROBLEMS
None observed.

Grows 6 feet (2 m) high, with equal spread. Moderate growth. Deciduous spreading shrub, native in Southern California and Nevada through Arizona, New Mexico, Texas and Mexico. Has slender four-angled twigs and small, oval aromatic leaves, which are winter-deciduous. Slender flower spikes 1 to 3 inches (2.5 to 7.5 cm) long are produced in pairs at the leaf axils*. Each spike is densely covered with small white flowers in spring.

Ambrosia deltoidea (Franseri deltoidea)

Bursage, Rabbit bush, Triangle-leaf bursage

Asteraceae (Compositae) family

COLD HARDINESS
All three zones.

LANDSCAPE VALUE
- Low-growing shrubby groundcover for erosion control and revegetation in hot desert environments.
- Reliable cover with minimal irrigation.
- Understory shrub that integrates larger shrubs and trees in an arid landscape.

CULTURAL REQUIREMENTS
- **Exposure:** Tolerates heat, drought and full to reflected sun to open shade.
- **Water:** Water once or twice a season during long dry spells for better plant appearance, but supplemental water is not necessary for survival.
- **Soil:** Occurs naturally on rocky rather than sandy soils. Tolerates alkaline soil.
- **Propagation:** Seed.
- **Maintenance:** Maintenance-free except reseeding bare areas.

POSSIBLE PROBLEMS
- Pollen causes allergic reaction in many people.
- Tends to be short-lived but reseeds easily.
- Burs cling to socks and pets.

Grows 1 to 2 feet (30.5 to 61 cm) high, spreading 1 to 3 feet (30 .5 cm to 1 m). Moderate to rapid growth. This shrubby perennial* is evergreen, rounded and densely branched. Bursage has slender brittle stems and triangular resinous leaves up to 1 or more inches (2.5 cm) long. Undersides of leaves are covered with a dense mat of short hairs. Young green leaves gradually become more gray with age or increasing drought stress.

Inconspicuous flowers of both sexes are borne on the same bloom spike midwinter through midspring. Male flowers are borne near the tip; female flowers closer to the base, where they produce prickly burlike fruits. Native to southern Arizona, Baja California and Sonora, Mexico.

** See Glossary*

Ambrosia dumosa (Franseria dumosa)

White bursage, Burro weed

Asteraceae (compositae) family

COLD HARDINESS

Low and intermediate zones.

LANDSCAPE VALUE

- A tough shrubby plant that offers a delicate but full and bushy form and unusual whitish gray color. Adds an interesting gray foliage color in the planned landscape.
- Prevents soil erosion under harsh desert conditions.

CULTURAL REQUIREMENTS

- **Exposure:** Native to hot, dry sunny areas.
- **Water:** Tolerant of extreme drought. Even dry, apparently lifeless plants revive quickly after rain or irrigation.
- **Soil:** Native soils range from silky clays to pure sand.
- **Propagation:** Seed.
- **Maintenance:** Little maintenance except to reseed bare areas.

POSSIBLE PROBLEMS

- Some people may be allergic to pollen.
- Spiny seed attaches to socks and pets.

Grows 2 to 3 feet (61 cm to 1 m) high, with equal spread. Rapid growth with occasional irrigation. Compact, rounded shrublike perennial* that is native to the U.S. Southwest and Sonora and Baja California, Mexico. Densely branched from its base with slender, somewhat spiny stems and lacy divided leaves. Both stems and leaves are covered with short white hairs that give the plant a gray color. Spikes of crowded, inconspicuous flowers at the stem tips may appear over most of the year, producing spiny fruits. Most older foliage dies in late spring, but clusters of younger leaves may survive at the stem tips.

Anisacanthus andersonii

Magdalena palm canyon honeysuckle, Anderson's honeysuckle bush

Acanthaceae family

COLD HARDINESS

Low and intermediate zones.

LANDSCAPE VALUE

Best used as a color plant sandwiched in with plants that are more presentable year-round.

CULTURAL REQUIREMENTS

- **Exposure:** Full sun to part shade.
- **Water:** Drought resistant, but soak the root zone thoroughly every week or two for good growth and flowering during the warm season.
- **Soil:** Any soil with good drainage.
- **Propagation:** Seed or cuttings.
- **Maintenance:** Cut back after flowering to improve general appearance and possibly trigger more blooms. Prune and pinch overly long shoots to control ranginess.

POSSIBLE PROBLEMS

You will need to groom occasionally to compensate for its periodic shagginess.

To 8 feet (2.5 m) high, spreading 6 feet (2 m). Rapid growth. Large, rangy, usually evergreen, shrub. Produces a surprising display of showy spikes of orange-pink tubular flowers. May bloom several times during the warm season depending on available moisture. Varies from a spectacular color show to nondescript shrub after bloom. Native to Sonora, Mexico.

* *See Glossary*

Anisacanthus puperulus (A. insignis)

Red Chihuahuan honeysuckle

Acanthaceae family

COLD HARDINESS

All three zones.

LANDSCAPE VALUE

- Sporadic color plant during warm season. Flowering is triggered by summer rain in its natural habitat.
- Foundation planting or in combination with other shrubs in a border.

CULTURAL REQUIREMENTS

- **Exposure:** Full sun.
- **Water:** Drought resistant but water every week or two during warm season for good landscape appearance.
- **Soil:** Any soil with good drainage.
- **Propagation:** Seed or cuttings.
- **Maintenance:** Prune lightly as needed to stimulate new growth and control wayward branches.

POSSIBLE PROBLEMS

Not a good year-round appearance.

Grows 3 feet (1 m) high, sometimes taller, spreading 3 to 4 feet (1 m). Moderate to rapid growth with regular moisture. A fairly compact shrub for an *Aniscanthus*. Mostly evergreen with firecracker red tubular flowers in summer. Native to northeast Mexico and southern Texas.

Anisacanthus quadrifidus wrightii

Flame anisacanthus

Acanthaceae family

COLD HARDINESS

All three zones. This is a cold hardy species of *Aniscanthus.*

LANDSCAPE VALUE

- A radiant splash of flower color appears over a long season.
- Serves admirably as a point of emphasis or color plant in shrub borders and foundation plantings.
- Attracts hummingbirds and butterflies when in bloom.

CULTURAL REQUIREMENTS

- **Exposure:** Full sun promotes profuse flowering. Plants grow well in part shade but flowering is diminished.
- **Water:** Water every week or two from spring into late fall for best flower display.
- **Soil:** Good drainage.
- **Propagation:** Seed or cuttings.
- **Maintenance:** Prune back severely in late winter to promote new growth, which causes plant to flower more heavily.

POSSIBLE PROBLEMS

Not attractive in the winter landscape. Plants look better only after spring growth is well developed.

Grows 3 to 4 feet (1 m) high, with equal spread. Moderate to rapid growth. Orange-red tubular flowers 1½ inches (4 cm) long and four-lobed near the tip appear midsummer into late fall. Mounding deciduous shrub with bright green leaves that are also 1½ inches (4 cm) long. Native to southern Texas and northern Mexico.

Anisacanthus thurberi

Desert honeysuckle
Acanthaceae family

COLD HARDINESS

Native to low and intermediate zones and sometimes high zone, where it usually freezes to the ground in coldest locations.

LANDSCAPE VALUE

- A somewhat rangy shrub that is best treated as a perennial.
- Good color plant to sandwich between evergreen shrubs that will have good appearance all year.

CULTURAL REQUIREMENTS

- **Exposure:** Full sun.
- **Water:** Drought resistant but water whenever soil is dry during growing season to encourage flowering and maintain a good landscape appearance.
- **Soil:** Any soil with depth for its deep roots.
- **Propagation:** Seed or cuttings.
- **Maintenance:** Cut back to almost ground level each winter to produce more flowers and thicker growth the following spring.

POSSIBLE PROBLEMS

Looks straggly from late fall to early spring. Regular pruning in winter will help the problem.

Grows 3 to 5 feet (1 to 1.5 m) high, spreading to 4 feet (1 m). Rapid growth when moisture is available. Generally an evergreen shrub, but in cold areas it dies to the ground and behaves like a perennial. Spikes of yellow-orange tubular flowers that resemble honeysuckle blossoms contribute considerable color from winter and spring into summer, depending on the elevation. Bloom starts later in colder areas. Native to New Mexico, Texas, Arizona and northern Mexico.

Landscape Design Example

Atriplex space definers at the University of Arizona experimental research lab.

* See Glossary

Antigonon leptopus

Coral vine, Queen's wreath

Polygonaceae family

COLD HARDINESS

All three zones as a root-hardy* perennial. Top growth is frost sensitive but roots are hardier.

LANDSCAPE VALUE

- A spectacular color vine during its bloom season.
- Effective for temporary, informal summer shade and screening.
- Grows well against hot south or west walls.
- Supply with supports on which tendrils can twine: for example an arbor, trellis or fence.
- Elegant flower display is adequate reward for growing the plant.

CULTURAL REQUIREMENTS

- **Exposure:** Full to reflected sun and heat.
- **Water:** Established vines are drought tolerant. Soak the root zone every month or two in most landscape situations. More frequent watering yields a faster growing, larger flowering plant.
- **Soil:** Most soils with good drainage.
- **Propagation:** Seed.
- **Maintenance:** Prune frost-damaged plants back to ground level. Plants that survive warm winters more or less intact may be pruned lightly to encourage earlier bloom. Pruning may be necessary during the growing season to direct rampant growth and control plant size. Where hard freezes are common, protect roots with a winter mulch.

POSSIBLE PROBLEMS

- Not evergreen when temperatures drop below freezing.
- Winter freezes cause unsightly die-back* of leaves and stems.
- Flowers attract bees.
- Aggressive growth habit may overwhelm other plants nearby.

Grows 30 to 40 feet (9 to 12 m) high, with equal spread. Rapid growth. Evergreen vine that self-climbs by means of tendrils. Grows native from Mexico south into Central and South America. Heart-shaped leaves 2 to 6 inches (5 to 15 cm) long are thin with wavy margins and coarse-textured surfaces. Flowers 1/2 inch (1 cm) long have five sepals instead of petals. These grow in slender trailing clusters that resemble delicate chains of pink hearts, each cluster tipped with a sturdy curling tendril. A white-flowered form, 'Album,' is rarely seen; more common is the brilliant scarlet selection 'Baja Red' from Baja California. Red color is more intense in late summer. Flowering is heaviest from mid or late summer into fall. In warm subtropical regions, flowers are sporadic the rest of the year. Where winters are colder, the vine dies back to the ground when temperatures fall below freezing. Rapid regrowth in spring originates from large storage roots.

* See Glossary

Aptenia cordifolia (Mesembryanthemum cordifolia)

Hearts and flowers, Baby sun rose

Aizoaceae family

COLD HARDINESS

Low zone and protected microclimates in the intermediate zone and occasionally in the high zone.

LANDSCAPE VALUE

- The dense foliage is shiny and bright green, an uncommon characteristic in the succulent ice-plant family.
- Although individual flowers are not large, their color is lively and appealing.
- Useful groundcover (but no foot traffic) for hot arid regions.
- At home in seascapes because of its salt tolerance.
- Well-adapted to large planters and containers.
- Attractive as a hanging plant.

CULTURAL REQUIREMENTS

- **Exposure:** Full sun to light shade. Salt-resistant.
- **Water:** Requires more water for satisfactory performance than many arid-landscape plants, but allow the soil to dry between waterings.
- **Soil:** Excellent drainage is essential. Tolerant of infertile sandy soils. More lush and vigorous growth in better quality soils.
- **Propagation:** Quickly and easily propagated by stem cuttings.
- **Maintenance:** Prune back tip growth to encourage density.

POSSIBLE PROBLEMS

- Plantings may die due to rot problems if overwatered, especially during hot humid weather.
- Hard frost results in severe die-back* or death of plants.
- Tolerates little or no foot traffic.

To 4 inches (10 cm) high, spreading 2 feet (61 cm). Moderate to rapid growth. The fleshy heart-shaped or oval leaves of this low-growing herbaceous* perennial grow in pairs on branching succulent stems. Tiny glandlike protuberances on the leaf surfaces give the foliage a glossy appearance. Over a long period in summer, the plant bears small, solitary raspberry red flowers with many stamens*. 'Variegata' leaves have a white margin. The native range is in coastal-desert regions of South Africa.

Argemone platyceras

Prickly poppy, Chicalote

Papaveraceae family

COLD HARDINESS

Low and intermediate zones. Frost tender but often grown as an annual in cold-winter areas.

LANDSCAPE VALUE

- Showy display of flowers lends color and bright touches to the water-conserving landscape.
- Tuck in among boulders or a group of plants to create a color accent.
- Useful in a revegetation seed mix. Will naturalize once plants are established.

CULTURAL REQUIREMENTS

- **Exposure:** Full to reflected sun.
- **Water:** Highly drought resistant but blooms better with water once or twice a season in dry weather.
- **Soil:** Requires excellent soil drainage.
- **Propagation:** Grows easily from seed.
- **Maintenance:** A rugged plant that requires little or no maintenance.

POSSIBLE PROBLEMS

Sharp thistlelike spines on stems and foliage discourage any contact and can cause injury.

Grows 1½ to 3 feet (46 cm to 1 m) high, spreading 1 to 2 feet (30.5 to 61 cm). Moderate growth. Erect spiny annual or biennial with prickly stems and leaves. Large 2-to 4-inch (5- to 10-cm) diameter white flowers with a cluster of orange stamens* at the center of each are striking. Long bloom period, but flowers are most abundant from late spring into summer. Native to southwestern United States and northern Mexico.

* See Glossary

Aristolochia fimbriata

Prostrate Dutchman's pipe

Aristolochiaceae family

To 1 foot (30.5 cm) or higher, spreading 3 to 4 feet (1 m). Moderate to rapid growth in spring, but slows to no growth (dormancy) during summer. Sprawling herbaceous* groundcover, native to Argentina but naturalized in many warm regions. Deciduous or evergreen, depending on winter temperatures and available moisture. Lush, slightly gray-green heart-shaped leaves with light gray veins are decorative. Inconspicuous flowers are composed of a greenish brown calyx* tube outside and purple veins inside, with a curved, inflated base typical of the Dutchman's pipe family. *A. fimbriata* is a preferred host plant for swallowtail butterfly larvae, which may account for its appearance in so many warm-region gardens among butterfly enthusiasts. It has a fleshy root system that helps ensure its drought survival.

COLD HARDINESS

All three zones, but will go completely dormant in colder areas.

LANDSCAPE VALUE

- Groundcover with a lush appearance for protected garden situations in both sun and shade.
- Can be located outside a high-irrigation zone, such as a minioasis. Its fleshy underground root system stores moisture to tide it over through short-term droughts. This root system also ensures its return season after season.
- It reseeds in unexpected places in the garden and will trail over the edge of planters and larger pots, adding attractive surprise touches.
- Easy to control and is not considered invasive.

CULTURAL REQUIREMENTS

- **Exposure:** Accepts full sun, but probably looks best with part shade. Tolerates full shade without becoming stringy.
- **Water:** Drought resistant, surviving moderate periods of dryness. Water every week or two during the hot season to maintain a lush foliage look.
- **Soil:** Most soils, but amending the soil with organic matter improves growth, and plants produce more lush foliage.
- **Propagation:** Seed.
- **Maintenance:** For a solid groundcover, space 30 inches (76 cm) or less apart on center (measuring from center of one plant to center of the next). Will climb supports, but is best sprawling over the ground in combination with other plants.

POSSIBLE PROBLEMS

- Foliage has a strong smell that is not particularly pleasant. Avoid using it near outdoor living areas.
- Sometimes growth is spotty; other times plant goes completely dormant, making it undependable as a year-round groundcover.

Arundo donax

Giant reed, Carrizo

Poaceae (Gramineae) family

COLD HARDINESS

Low and intermediate zones. Grows in high zone, where it may freeze back in winter, recovering rapidly in spring.

LANDSCAPE VALUE

- Resembles a coarse-leaved bamboo; useful as a quick screen or windbreak.
- Erosion control.
- In character near ponds, streams and other water features.
- Not appropriate for refined landscape settings.

CULTURAL REQUIREMENTS

- **Exposure:** Full sun to part shade.
- **Water:** Looks and performs best with water every week or two but capable of surviving long dry periods.
- **Soil:** Tolerant of most soils. Grows best with improved soil.
- **Propagation:** Plant pieces of rhizome* or place mature canes horizontally in a 6-inch (15-cm) deep trench.
- **Maintenance:** Prune old stems, which die after several years' growth. Dig and remove rhizomes to control clump size. Remove cold-damaged leaves or stems. In certain areas, you can install underground barriers to control the spread of rhizomes.

POSSIBLE PROBLEMS

- Invasive nature may make this plant a pest in some moist situations, especially adjoining water features.
- Goes dormant in cold winters.

Grows 8 to 21 feet (2.5 to 6.5 m) high, spreading indefinitely. Spread must be controlled or plant will become invasive. Rapid growth with abundant water. A tall bamboolike evergreen reed that spreads by thick rhizomes to form clumps. Linear leaves are 2 to 3 inches (5 to 7.5cm) to 2 feet (61 cm) long and appear in pairs along the woody stems. Greenish purple plumelike inflorescenses* open at stem tips, mostly during summer. Native to Africa and Asia, naturalized in warm weather regions of the United States and Mexico.

* *See Glossary*

Asclepias linaria

Pineleaf milkweed, Threadleaf milkweed

Asclepidaceae family

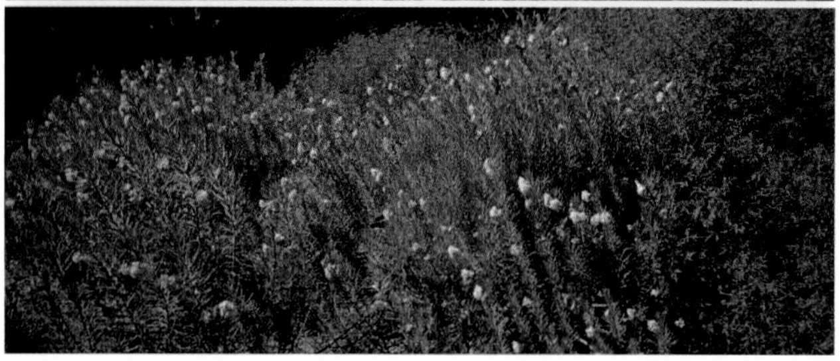

To 3 feet (1 m) high, with equal spread. Moderate growth. A shrubby member of the milkweed family, pineleaf milkweed grows as a native in southern Arizona and throughout most of Mexico. Mostly herbaceous*, it becomes woody at the base, with stems that are covered with fine white hairs. The needlelike evergreen leaves are linear, $\frac{3}{4}$ to $2\frac{1}{4}$ inches (2 to 6 cm) long and almost cylindrical in cross section. Leaves are arranged in a spiral along stems, tufted near the tips. Greenish or white flowers open in flat-topped 2-inch (5-cm) wide clusters from spring into fall. The papery seed pod is pointed at the tip and splits down one side at maturity. Flattened seeds with a terminal* tuft of silky hairs float away on air currents.

COLD HARDINESS

Low and intermediate zones and probably high zone.

LANDSCAPE VALUE

- Bright green fine-textured foliage provides accent and contrast in the low-water-use landscape.
- Planted in groups, it is effective in street-median plantings; as a transition plant in confined spaces, instead of larger species; in rock gardens and on small properties.
- Decorative flowers and seed pods make an attractive display over a long period.

CULTURAL REQUIREMENTS

- **Exposure:** Full sun.
- **Water:** Drought tolerant once established, but water every month to every week (depending on your location) from late spring into fall for good landscape appearance.
- **Soil:** Most soils with good drainage.
- **Propagation:** Seed.
- **Maintenance:** Low maintenance. Cut back after heavy set of pods, if unsightly.

POSSIBLE PROBLEMS

Wind-dispersed seeds may produce volunteer plants where they are not wanted.

Asclepias subulata

Desert milkweed

Asclepidaceae family

Grows 3 to 4 feet (1 m) high, spreading 2 to 4 feet (61 cm to 1 m). Moderate growth. Many slender herbaceous* stems, leafless and erect or ascending, grow in a dense cluster from this milkweed's woody base. Young stems produce linear willowy leaves to $1\frac{3}{4}$ inches (4.5 cm) long, but they are shed quickly. Clusters of five to fifteen pale yellow or cream-colored flowers with five petals open at intervals from spring into fall. The dry spindle-shaped seed pods, 2 to 4 inches (5 to 10 cm) long, split open along their length in summer or early fall, releasing seeds tipped with a tuft of silvery white hairs $\frac{3}{4}$ to $1\frac{1}{4}$ inches (2 to 3 cm) long. The milky sap that oozes from any break in the stem surface contains a significant amount of rubber. Native to Arizona, Nevada and California in the United States, and Sonora, Sinaloa and Baja California in Mexico.

COLD HARDINESS

Low and intermediate zones.

LANDSCAPE VALUE

- Interesting accent plant with strong vertical lines for arid and transition zones.
- Useful in revegetation seed mixes.
- Flowers attract butterflies.

CULTURAL REQUIREMENTS

- **Exposure:** Full sun; endures reflected heat.
- **Water:** Established plants generally grow well without supplemental irrigation. In hot dry locations or during prolonged droughts, water once or twice a season to ensure acceptable landscape appearance.
- **Soil:** Adapted to most well-drained soils.
- **Propagation:** Seed.
- **Maintenance:** After plants are well-established and are declining, cut back severely in winter. New growth will appear in spring, renewing plant vigor and appearance.

POSSIBLE PROBLEMS

None observed.

* *See Glossary*

Asparagus densiflorus 'Myers' (*A. myeri*)

Myer's asparagus, Asparagus fern

Liliaceae family

COLD HARDINESS

Low zone and warm areas of intermediate zone. Tolerates light frost, but plumes will be browned by 28°F (-2°C) or lower. Recovers rapidly in spring.

LANDSCAPE VALUE

- Fernlike effect with other evergreen perennials.
- Foreground foundation plant.
- Especially attractive in planters and containers.

CULTURAL REQUIREMENTS

- **Exposure:** Full sun to shade but no reflected sun. Prefers part shade.
- **Water:** Surprisingly drought tolerant because of abundant water-storing bulblets* on the roots. Water weekly for best landscape appearance, more often in containers.
- **Soil:** Not demanding, but responds with more lush growth when planted in well-drained, prepared garden soil.
- **Propagation:** Seed or divisions.
- **Maintenance:** Renew frost-damaged or tired plants by cutting back in late winter. Prune dead stems as needed.

POSSIBLE PROBLEMS

Stems are slightly prickly and therefore unpleasant when pruning or grooming the plant.

To 2 feet (61 cm) high, spreading to 3 feet (1 m). Moderate to rapid growth. A fluffy, fernlike evergreen perennial that sends up clumping 2-foot or higher (61 cm) upright plumelike stems that are clothed with bright green needlelike leaves. New stems grow in plumes from the center. Older ones spread outward, eventually touching the ground, creating a ferny mound or cascading over the edge when planted in a container. Native to South Africa.

Asparagus densiflorus 'Sprengeri'

Sprenger asparagus, Asparagus fern

Liliaceae family

COLD HARDINESS

Low zone and protected microclimates in the intermediate zone. Hardy to around 24°F (-4°C). Recovers from cold damage quickly in spring.

LANDSCAPE VALUE

- Mixed plantings with other perennials.
- Billowy groundcover.
- Foreground planting.
- Outstanding in planters and containers. Particularly attractive in hanging pots, especially in hot, dry climates where many other hanging plants do not succeed.
- Bright green foliage, decorated with little vivid red berries, is a noteworthy contrast with other greens. Develops a thick mass of roots with bulblets*.

CULTURAL REQUIREMENTS

- **Exposure:** Full sun to open shade. Tolerates salt mist in oceanside landscapes.
- **Water:** Drought tolerant on a short-term basis; containers can completely dry out. Plumy foliage will show no drought damage. Moisture is sustained by the bulblets* in the root mass. However, to achieve new growth and good landscape appearance, water every week or two.
- **Soil:** Surprisingly tolerant of varied soil types. Best appearance in improved garden soil.
- **Propagation:** Seed or divisions.
- **Maintenance:** Cut back frost-damaged or tired plants in late winter to early spring to renew them.

POSSIBLE PROBLEMS

- Trouble-free except removal of prickly stems that die from frost damage.
- Long-lived as a container plant but can develop a heavy bulblet root mass known to create enough root pressure to actually crack the container.

To 2 feet (61 cm) high, spreading 3 feet (1 m), give or take. Rapid growth after a rather slow initial seedling stage. Evergreen perennial with arching stems that sprawl across the ground or cascade downward over the edge of planter walls and containers. Stems are clothed in ferny, bright green needlelike leaves. Waxy white flowers are inconspicuous. Small numbers of bright red berries appear among the leaves after a sporadic flowering period. Native to South Africa.

** See Glossary*

Asparagus falcatus

Sickle thorn asparagus
Liliaceae family

COLD HARDINESS

Low zone and warmer areas of intermediate zone. Will freeze back in mid-20s F (-4°C), but regrows rapidly in spring. Freeze damage in cold locations can cause unsightly appearance.

LANDSCAPE VALUE

- An excellent vine to cover fences and trellises.
- Sprawls in large planters, with some pruning.
- Performs well as a large potted plant and tolerates a lot of heat. The fleshy roots tide it through occasional periods of neglect.

CULTURAL REQUIREMENTS

- **Exposure:** Best in full sun, even reflected heat. Also grows in shade, but becomes "leggy" as it tries to reach the sun.
- **Water:** Water every week or two to maintain good appearance, more often as it becomes established. Container plants need water every week or two, but occasional drying out does not set it back unless it is in a new growth phase.
- **Soil:** Tolerant of a wide variety of soils, but responds best to average garden soil with good drainage.
- **Propagation:** Seed.
- **Maintenance:** Needs fair amount of space, so do not use in confined areas.

POSSIBLE PROBLEMS

- Sharp thorns can be a problem when pruning or when in planters.
- It has been known to reseed and establish in adjoining irrigated areas, such as citrus groves, where it is definitely not wanted.

Can climb to 40 feet (12 m), but usually to 10 feet (3 m) in dry areas. As a groundcover, it can spread to 10 feet (3 m). Rapid growth with average maintenance, slow in low-water situations. This rapid-climbing vine has sickle thorns on its stems that assist it in climbing. New growth also twines around support wire or lattice, if allowed. Two to three elongated leaves in clusters of three to five at ends of branches cover plant densely. Small, fragrant white flowers are followed by uninteresting brown berries. Develops a mass of fleshy roots that store water to tide it over during dry periods. Of tropical origin from Ceylon to Africa.

Asteriscus maritimus

Mediterranean beach daisy
Asteraceae (Compositae) family

COLD HARDINESS

Low and intermediate zones.

LANDSCAPE VALUE

- Neat compact form makes it effective as a low mounding border, space definer or groundcover.
- Rich spring display of yellow flowers makes it an excellent color accent in mass plantings.

CULTURAL REQUIREMENTS

- **Exposure:** Afternoon shade at low elevations. Avoid locations in the intermediate zone where severe freezes are common.
- **Water:** Water every week or two.
- **Soil:** Provide good soil drainage. Responds to improved garden soils and occasional fertilization.
- **Propagation:** Seeds or cuttings.
- **Maintenance:** When old plants die, refurbish bare spots with new plants in spring.

POSSIBLE PROBLEMS

Tends to decline when exposed to extremes of cold, sun or heat.

To 1 foot (30.5 cm) high, spreading 1 to 1½ feet (30.5 to 46 cm). Slow to moderate growth. Low-mounding perennial herb from the Mediterranean region, best treated as an annual or biennial. Leaves are dense, gray-green and hairy. They grow up to 2 inches (5 cm) long and 1½ inches (4 cm) wide. Bright yellow composite flowers cover the plant late winter into late spring.

ATRIPLEX

The genus *Atriplex* represents a group of shrubs and groundcovers that are not particularly showy and often quite drab, yet very useful for many difficult, arid landscape situations. They are tough against heat, cold, wind, alkalinity and salinity. In fact, some species can be irrigated with seawater! *Atriplex* species are native to most arid regions throughout the world. More species could be included here but the following plant charts give some varied choices for a range of design functions.

Atriplex barclayana sonorae

Beach carpet saltbush
Chenopodiaceae family

COLD HARDINESS

Low zone. Suffers frost damage and dies back in cold winters of the intermediate zone.

LANDSCAPE VALUE

- Good groundcover for oceanfronts and erosion control.
- Can also be used inland when you need a plant to help cope with high-alkaline soil conditions.
- Not a groundcover for refined situations.

CULTURAL REQUIREMENTS

- **Exposure:** Full sun. Tolerates oceanfront areas and salt spray. Seems to have its flattest, best-looking form in such situations.
- **Water:** Drought resistant, but water every month or two to keep it presentable.
- **Soil:** Any soil. Found growing in sand or clay adjoining brackish marshes in its native habitat.
- **Propagation:** Seed or cutting.
- **Maintenance:** Little maintenance except to replace dead plants.

POSSIBLE PROBLEMS

- Probably short-lived.
- Rabbits are fond of this saltbush. Protect plants with wire cages.

Grows 3 to 6 inches (7.5 to 15 cm) high, spreading 3 feet (1 m) or more. Moderate to rapid growth. This low mat-forming shrub with small whitish gray leaves is often found on oceanfronts or along estuary edges where it may be inundated by storm tides. Some selections are extremely prostrate, producing a dense circular mat of grayish leaves. Cuttings from a low-growing individual do not always produce a ground-hugging form when grown farther inland. Flowering does not seem to contribute to a weedy appearance, which does occur with some saltbush species. Native to Baja California.

Atriplex canescens

Four-wing saltbush, Cenizo, Chamiso
Chenopodiaceae family

COLD HARDINESS

All three zones.

LANDSCAPE VALUE

- This tenacious, deep-rooted shrub is of value for erosion control and revegetation.
- Good fire-retardant characteristics.
- In more refined settings—a space definer or background shrub that produces a noteworthy fruiting display.
- May be clipped to form a hedge.

CULTURAL REQUIREMENTS

- **Exposure:** Full to reflected sun and heat. Cold and heat tolerant.
- **Water:** Water every month or two in dry weather for acceptable landscape appearance; thrives on brackish water.
- **Soil:** Any soil. Exceptional ability to withstand salty, highly alkaline soils.
- **Propagation:** Seed or cuttings.
- **Maintenance:** Established plants require little maintenance.

POSSIBLE PROBLEMS

None observed.

Grows 4 to 8 feet (1 to 2.5 m) high, with equal spread. Moderate to rapid growth with irrigation. Dense evergreen shrub with a rounded to irregular growth habit. Slender leaves, 1/2 to 2 inches (1 to 5 cm) long, are covered with a gray mealy coating. Flower clusters open at stem terminals*. Plants are male or female: Females fruit heavily, each fruit enclosed by bracts* that form four conspicuous wings. Native from South Dakota to Oregon and Kansas, Washington and Arizona in the United States; Baja California, Sinaloa, Sonora and Zacatecas in Mexico.

** See Glossary*

Atriplex lentiformis breweri

Lens-scale, Brewer's saltbush

Chenopodiaceae family

COLD HARDINESS

All three zones.

LANDSCAPE VALUE

- An excellent hedge or screen, sheared or unsheared.
- Background, privacy or windscreen where space is adequate for mature plants.

CULTURAL REQUIREMENTS

- **Exposure:** Full to reflected sun; tolerates exposed windy locations.
- **Water:** Drought resistant but water every month or two for best landscape appearance. Thrives on brackish water.
- **Soil:** Will survive on salty, alkaline soils.
- **Propagation:** Seed or cuttings.
- **Maintenance:** Little care required. Prune to maintain form and improve open woody habit. Remove somewhat unsightly seed clusters.

POSSIBLE PROBLEMS

Can look unkempt if seed clusters are not removed.

Grows 6 to 10 feet (2 to 3 m) high, spreading 8 to 15 feet (2.5 to 4.5 m). Slow to moderate growth. Large evergreen shrub with a dense rounded canopy of blue-gray mealy leaves to 2 inches (5 cm) long and almost as wide. Showy clusters of light yellow flowers and tan-colored fruit appear at the end of twigs in summer. Native to Southern California, Utah, Arizona (Mojave and Sonoran Deserts) in the United States; Sonora and Baja California in Mexico.

Atriplex nummularia

Australian saltbush, Chamisa

Chenopodiaceae family

COLD HARDINESS

All three zones.

LANDSCAPE VALUE

- Large background plantings and hedges.
- Accepts trimming well.
- Formal hedging and low windbreaks.
- Especially useful in areas of high salinity or in seaside locations exposed to salt spray.

CULTURAL REQUIREMENTS

- **Exposure:** Full sun, including reflected sun to open shade.
- **Water:** Drought resistant, but needs some supplemental water to maintain developing growth and an acceptable appearance. Thrives on brackish water.
- **Soil:** Any soil. Tolerates salinity and alkalinity.
- **Propagation:** Seed or cuttings.
- **Maintenance:** May need some grooming to remove seed capsules after they fade.

POSSIBLE PROBLEMS

Can look shaggy and unkempt after blossoms and seed bracts* dry up.

Grows 6 to 9 feet (2 to 3 m) high, with equal spread. Moderate to rapid growth, depending on available moisture. Large evergreen shrub with thick gray-green foliage. Plant produces a dense leaf mass that completely hides the stems and woody branches. Greenish flower clusters bloom at tips of branches. Plants are male or female. Consequently, the heavy crop of winged bracts* enclosing the seed will occur only on the female. Bracts add some interest in spring. Native to Australia.

* *See Glossary*

Atriplex polycarpa

Desert saltbush, Cattle spinach

Chenopodiaceae family

COLD HARDINESS

All three zones.

LANDSCAPE VALUE

- Important plant for revegetation and erosion control in extremely arid or alkaline situations.
- An important forage plant for cattle on the open range.

CULTURAL REQUIREMENTS

- **Exposure:** Full sun, including reflected sun.
- **Water:** Drought resistant but tolerates sites that occasionally become wet and poorly drained.
- **Soil:** Any soil, including poorly drained alkaline soils.
- **Propagation:** Seed or cuttings.
- **Maintenance:** No maintenance except reseeding to maintain cover.

POSSIBLE PROBLEMS

None observed.

To 3 feet (1 m) high, spreading 6 feet (2 m). Slow to moderate growth, depending on soil moisture. Mounding gray shrub with tiny leaves. This sprawling plant of the Southwest deserts of the United States and northern Mexico is found mostly on the alkaline flats, but sometimes grows on higher ground as spaced mounds among creosote bushes. It is the chief forage plant for the hottest and driest deserts. Flowers and fruit clusters are smaller and less conspicuous than those of the rest of the *Atriplex* clan. Local people often refer to it as sage, although it has no relation to the true sage family.

Atriplex semibacata

Australian saltbush

Chenopodiaceae family

COLD HARDINESS

Low and intermediate zones. Moderately frost tolerant.

LANDSCAPE VALUE

- An untreadable groundcover, drought tolerant and fire resistant.
- Useful for revegetation of disturbed areas and erosion control in parks, on roadsides and similar landscape applications.
- Decorative fruit display in autumn and winter.

CULTURAL REQUIREMENTS

- **Exposure:** Full or reflected sun to part shade.
- **Water:** Drought tolerant, but water every month or two for good appearance.
- **Soil:** Most soils with good drainage.
- **Propagation:** Seed or cuttings.
- **Maintenance:** Remove dead plants and those damaged by severe cold; replant resulting bare spots. Established plantings reseed easily. Thin out if too dense.

POSSIBLE PROBLEMS

- Difficult to maintain a dense uniform cover on large areas because individual plants are not long-lived in the landscape.
- Plants are brittle and do not tolerate foot traffic.

Grow 6 to 12 inches (15 to 30.5 cm) high, spreading to 6 feet (2 m). Rapid growth with regular water. Low mat-forming evergreen perennial, introduced into the United States from Australia, now naturalized from Central to Southern California and Arizona. Trailing stems, $\frac{1}{2}$ to $1\frac{1}{2}$ inches (1 to 4 cm), bear long gray-green leaves. Inconspicuous flowers bloom from April through September. Tiny bright red fruits ripen in fall and winter. Reseeds and spreads if moisture is adequate. Superior selections, such as 'Corto' with lusher foliage, are available.

Baccharis hybrid 'Centennial' (*B. pilularis* X *B. sarothroides*)

Centennial coyote bush, Desert broom hybrid

Asteraceae (Compositae) family

COLD HARDINESS

Low and intermediate zones and probably hardy in high zone. Not tested over a long enough time to expose it to the record lows high-zone regions can experience.

LANDSCAPE VALUE

- One of the best groundcovers in arid regions with hot summers.
- Rapid, wide-spreading and suited to moderate slopes and areas where low-mounding cover is desirable.
- The bright green color it inherits from its desert broom parentage adds a cheerful note to the arid landscape.

CULTURAL REQUIREMENTS

- **Exposure:** Full sun to light shade; withstands heat and wind.
- **Water:** Tolerates irrigation every month or two. Individual plants are drought resistant. When planted in mass, water more frequently to maintain a fresh, bright appearance throughout the hottest months.
- **Soil:** Any soil with depth and good drainage. Does not thrive on rocky soils or where caliche* lies near the surface.
- **Propagation:** Cuttings.
- **Maintenance:** Regular light pruning or topping of maturing plants will keep them fresh and vigorous.

POSSIBLE PROBLEMS

- Can become rangy and woody when mature.
- Not particularly long-lived.
- Female plant but not a heavy bloomer.
- Spider mites sometimes attack plants.

Grows 1 to 3 feet (30.5 cm to 1 m) high, spreading 6 to 8 feet (2 to 2.5 m), sometimes more. Rapid growth. This groundcover plant is a selection from Dr. Anson Thompson's hybrids, created by crossing dwarf coyote bush *(B. pilularis)* with the ubiquitous desert broom *(B. sarothroides)*. 'Centennial' was chosen from the numerous progeny of this cross for its broad spreading growth habit and bright green color. These characteristics make it an ideal groundcover for the hot low and intermediate zones (and, with some reservations, the high zone). Dwarf coyote bush, a popular groundcover in cool-summer arid regions, has a short life in hot-summer areas. This hybrid carries the heat tolerance of the desert broom and the attractive mounding and spreading qualities of the dwarf coyote bush.

Baccharis pilularis

Dwarf coyote bush, Chaparral broom

Asteraceae (Compositae) family

COLD HARDINESS

All three zones but often short-lived in low and intermediate zones. Cold hardy but not well-adapted to low elevation and intermediate desert regions with hot summers, especially if watered heavily during periods of high heat.

LANDSCAPE VALUE

- Excellent year-round appearance.
- Fire-retardant, untreadable groundcover for erosion control on slopes and steep banks.
- Rock gardens.
- Trailing over the sides of raised planters.

CULTURAL REQUIREMENTS

- **Exposure:** Full sun to part shade.
- **Water:** Drought tolerant but looks best if irrigated every week or two, more frequently during cooler months because its most rapid growth occurs during winter and spring.
- **Soil:** Withstands rocky, sandy or heavy soil types if they are well drained.
- **Propagation:** Cuttings.
- **Maintenance:** Can be maintained at 8 inches (20.5 cm) high by periodic pruning. Renew overgrown woody plants by cutting them back every one to three years.

POSSIBLE PROBLEMS

- Spider mites.
- Damping-off* diseases under hot moist conditions.
- Cottony seed heads of female plants blow around and collect to produce litter.

Grows 1 to 2 feet (30.5 cm to 61 cm) high, spreading 3 to 6 feet (1 to 2 m). Moderate to rapid growth. Prostrate evergreen shrub from coastal California that has a dense mounding form and fine-textured foliage. Plants are male or female: Both sexes have insignificant flowers. Nurseries usually propagate male selections because the fluffy white seed heads of female plants create litter. 'Twin Peaks #2' is a male selection with slightly larger dark green leaves and lower, more uniform growth than that of the parent species. 'Pigeon Point' grows larger and faster than the parent species or its varieties. It also has larger light green leaves.

* *See Glossary*

Baccharis sarothroides

Desert broom

Asteraceae (Compositae) family

Grows 3 to 9 feet (1 to 3 m) high, with equal spread. Rapid growth with occasional irrigation. Rounded evergreen shrub, native to Southern California, Arizona and New Mexico in the United States; northern Sonora and Baja California in Mexico. Slender green branchlets are grouped on stems to form broomlike clusters. Thin linear leaves to 1 inch (2.5 cm) long are present only on young, fast-growing stems. Plants are male or female. Flowers have no particular decorative value. Female plants produce dense terminal* clusters of white cottony seed heads in fall and winter. When mature seeds are released, they float away on air currents.

COLD HARDINESS

All three zones. Native stands in Arizona high desert (high zone) have frozen back in record cold winters but recovered rapidly in spring.

LANDSCAPE VALUE

- Erosion control and revegetation of disturbed land.
- Screens and hedges.
- Space definer.
- Street and highway medians.
- Bright green stems add color to the arid landscape even during drought.

CULTURAL REQUIREMENTS

- **Exposure:** Full or reflected sun, becoming sparse and open in heavy shade.
- **Water:** Survives with just rainfall if there is some runoff accumulation but can die out during long periods of drought without irrigation. It readily adapts to water once or twice a season or even every week or two.
- **Soil:** Tolerates a wide range of soils.
- **Propagation:** Seed or cuttings. Male plants can be grown from cuttings to avoid nuisance of fluffy seed litter.
- **Maintenance:** Tall leggy plants can be cut back to near ground level; abundant regrowth from the base results in a full dense plant.

POSSIBLE PROBLEMS

Cottony seeds of female plants can be a significant litter problem and volunteer seedlings are difficult to eradicate because of the deep tap root produced by plants. Prevent these problems by selecting nursery-grown male plants produced from cuttings. Don't plant female plants near a swimming pool.

Baileya multiradiata

Desert marigold

Asteraceae (Compositae) family

To 1 foot (30.5 cm) high or higher, with equal spread. Moderate to rapid growth with abundant water. Evergreen perennial native from Southern California into Texas, southern Utah and northern Mexico. Forms a 6-inch (15-cm) high clump of soft, woolly gray leaves, pinnately* parted at ground level, becoming entire along the lower stems. Solitary bright yellow daisylike flowers 1 to 2 inches (2.5 to 5 cm) in diameter on slender erect stems to 1 foot (30.5 cm) tall or taller appear from spring into fall. Plants may bloom year-round in low-elevation locations where soil moisture is adequate.

COLD HARDINESS

Low and intermediate zones and warm microclimates of high zone. Moderately frost hardy but cold will stop blooming for a period.

LANDSCAPE VALUE

- Undemanding perennial of rugged character for hot, sunny, exposed situations.
- Has the potential to flower over a long period.
- Wildflower, desert and rock gardens.
- Revegetation of disturbed sites.

CULTURAL REQUIREMENTS

- **Exposure:** Full to reflected sun and heat.
- **Water:** Drought tolerant. Blooms more freely and longer and reseeds more heavily if given extra water during extended dry spells.
- **Soil:** Most soils with good drainage.
- **Propagation:** Seed.
- **Maintenance:** Readily naturalized in the landscape; minimum maintenance. Cut back tired basal* growth in winter to renew plants.

POSSIBLE PROBLEMS

Short-lived but reseeds so easily there are always new plants to replace the dead plants.

* See Glossary

BAUHINIA

The *Bauhinia* genus, or orchid tree genus, possess this common name because of their showy orchidlike blooms, which suggest a fragile plant in need of protection and special care. *Bauhinia*, however, are tough and tolerate high heat and infrequent irrigation. Some species are tender to frost, so they are best used in the warmer low zone. *Bauhinia* that are native to the Chihuahuan Desert are hardy in all three zones. They also have attractive butterfly-shaped leaves that are unique to this genus.

Bauhinia blakeana

Hong Kong orchid tree

Fabaceae (Leguminosae) family

COLD HARDINESS

Almost frost-free areas of the low zone.

LANDSCAPE VALUE

- Stunning tropical-effects beauty when at the peak of its bloom season.
- One of the showiest flowering specimen or accent trees for the oasis zone of mild-winter landscapes.

CULTURAL REQUIREMENTS

- **Exposure:** Full sun to part shade. Avoid planting sites exposed to hot drying winds.
- **Water:** Water every week or two throughout the year.
- **Soil:** Grows in most well-drained soils except highly alkaline or saline types.
- **Propagation:** Cuttings and air layering*.
- **Maintenance:** Selectively trim young trees for best form and appearance.

POSSIBLE PROBLEMS

- Frosty temperatures may eliminate the flower crop. More intense cold disfigures branches and causes die-back*.
- Chlorosis* can be severe in highly alkaline, salty or poorly drained soils.

Grows 15 to 30 feet (4.5 to 9 m) high, with equal spread. Moderate to rapid growth. This umbrella-shaped subtropical tree traces its ancestry to a single specimen discovered in Guango (Canton), China. The canopy of alternately arranged gray-green two-lobed leaves 6 to 8 inches (15 to 20.5 cm) across is partly deciduous during the fall-winter flowering period. This lack of leaves makes the flowers on the bare branches that much more showy. Five-petaled flowers to 6 inches (15 cm) across range in color from pink to purple and maroon. The tree is a sterile hybrid and no seed is produced.

Bauhinia lunarioides (B. conjesta)

Chihuahuan orchid shrub

Fabaceae (Leguminosae) family

COLD HARDINESS

Low and intermediate zones and probably high zone, although not yet fully tested there.

LANDSCAPE VALUE

- Background shrub.
- Fine-textured spring and summer color plant.

CULTURAL REQUIREMENTS

- **Exposure:** Reflected sun to part shade.
- **Water:** Tolerates complete drought, but for dependable bloom and good appearance soak the root zone every month.
- **Soil:** Most soils.
- **Propagation:** Seed.
- **Maintenance:** May need a little pruning to improve shape.

POSSIBLE PROBLEMS

None noted to date. Must be grown from seed, so flower color is variable and can't be guaranteed.

Grows 6 to 8 feet (2 to 2.5 m) high, spreading 5 to 6 feet (1.5 to 2 m). Slow to moderate growth, depending on amount of irrigation. Hardy evergreen desert shrub from Mexico's Chihuahuan Desert. Green leaves that are slightly gray and shaped like small green-winged butterflies identify its kinship with other *Bauhinias*. Tiny, delicate orchid-shaped flowers in shades of pink and sometimes white cover plants from spring into summer. Blooms can appear as late as fall if triggered by rains. An abundant crop of small bean pods follows blooming.

Note: This species has been mistakenly sold as *B. unguigularis*, which is a totally different plant not commercially introduced as of 1997.

* *See Glossary*

Bauhinia macranthera

Chihuahuan orchid tree

Fabaceae (Leguminosae) family

COLD HARDINESS

Low and intermediate zones.

LANDSCAPE VALUE

- Small flowering tropical-effects tree.
- A patio-size shade tree with training.

CULTURAL REQUIREMENTS

- **Exposure:** Full sun or part shade.
- **Water:** Quite drought resistant, but soak the root zone every week or two for good flowering and appearance.
- **Soil:** Most soils, but prefers good soil with some depth.
- **Propagation:** Seed.
- **Maintenance:** Little maintenance required unless training as a patio-size tree.

POSSIBLE PROBLEMS

Larger leaves and flowers can wilt in heat and low humidity, even when not drought-stressed.

To 20 feet (6 m) high, spreading to 15 feet (4.5 m). Moderate growth rate. A transition-zone orchid tree native to the eastern edge of the Chihuahuan Desert. Large leaves and flowers make this species look less deserty than its relative *B. lunarioides*. Lavender-pink flowers 2 to 3 inches (5 to 7.5 cm) across appear on top of downward-arching branches in late spring and early summer. Very showy.

Bauhinia punctata (B. galpinii)

Red bauhinia, Red orchid shrub

Fabaceae (Leguminosae) family

COLD HARDINESS

Low zone and warm microclimates of intermediate zone.

LANDSCAPE VALUE

- Tropical effects and color plant.
- Excellent espalier on hot walls.
- Large mounding, spreading shrub.

CULTURAL REQUIREMENTS

- **Exposure:** Warm, sunny locations. Thrives in heat.
- **Water:** Water every week or two during hot season for good bloom and appearance. Tolerates water every month or two, especially during winter.
- **Soil:** Any soil with good drainage.
- **Propagation:** Seed.
- **Maintenance:** Tolerates training to espalier and shaping.

POSSIBLE PROBLEMS

- Produces large crop of brown pods.
- Frost tender. Can look ragged at end of winter, even when temperatures stay above freezing.

To 15 feet (4.5 m) high, with equal spread. Rapid growth with regular water and care. Sprawling African shrub that is half-climbing with large butterfly-shaped leaves. Showy orange-red orchid-like flowers produce a color display that is similar to that of bougainvillea. Plant is usually evergreen but can become semideciduous with drought or cold.

* *See Glossary*

Bauhinia variegata and *B. variegata candida*

Purple orchid tree, White orchid tree

Fabaceae (Leguminosae) family

COLD HARDINESS

Low zone and warm-winter areas of intermediate zone.

LANDSCAPE VALUE

- When clothed with a heavy mantle of exquisite purple or white flowers, the orchid tree is an unforgettable sight.
- A single or multi-trunked accent, specimen or focal point in a minioasis.
- Shrub borders, roadway plantings, street tree.

CULTURAL REQUIREMENTS

- **Exposure:** Full or reflected sun to part shade. Best in locations sheltered from strong drying winds.
- **Water:** Water every week or two throughout the year. Mature plants have shown some drought tolerance in the southwestern desert. Some plants have naturalized in the Indio–Palm Springs area, where they survive on irrigation runoff.
- **Soil:** Most soils with good drainage, free of high pH and soluble salt problems.
- **Propagation:** Seed.
- **Maintenance:** Prune lightly following flowering to remove numerous pods and to speed the start of summer foliage regrowth.

POSSIBLE PROBLEMS

- Heavy bean-pod crop is unsightly for a short period in early summer before new leaves begin to grow.
- Limited frost tolerance. Subject to unsightly winter-kill damage near the limits of its cold-hardiness range. This in turn can reduce spring flowering because blooms appear on the previous summer's twigs, which are the most vulnerable to freeze damage.

Grows 15 to 25 feet (4.5 to 7.5 m) high, with equal spread. Moderate to rapid growth. Subtropical and partly deciduous, this *Bauhinia* species is native to India and China. The thin, leathery twin-lobed leaves 4 to 6 inches (11 to 15 cm) across grow to become a dense spreading crown. The tree is well-named: Its 2- to 3-inch (5- to 7.5-cm) pale lavender to purple flowers, with broad overlapping petals, resemble those of some *Cattleya* orchids. Flowers bloom midwinter into spring, sometimes into early summer. A crop of new leaves emerges toward the end of the flowering season. The brown seed pods, to 1 foot (30.5 cm) long, have sharp-pointed tips. *B. variegata candida* is almost identical to the species in general, except its flowers are snowy white.

* See Glossary

Berberis haematocarpa *(Mahonia haematocarpa)*

Red mahonia, Pink-fruited barberry

Berberidaceae family

COLD HARDINESS
All three zones.

LANDSCAPE VALUE
- Space definer, barrier plant, hedge.
- Foundation plant.
- Gray foliage and seasonal display of yellow blossoms, followed by colorful fruit, add color interest.

CULTURAL REQUIREMENTS
- **Exposure:** Full sun to part shade.
- **Water:** Water every week or two in summer. Soak the root zone every month or two when plant is mature, but more often when young to speed growth.
- **Soil:** Improved well-drained soil, with an occasional light application of fertilizer to speed up growth.
- **Propagation:** Seed or cuttings.
- **Maintenance:** Some pinching or nipping back at first to thicken the plant while in the juvenile stage.

POSSIBLE PROBLEMS
Plant away from paths and patio areas because of spiny leaflets, which also make pruning less than pleasant.

Grows 6 to 8 feet (2 to 2.5 m) high, spreading to 6 feet (2 m). Slow growth. This rather open gray-leaved evergreen shrub is from the edges of the Chihuahuan Desert. Compound leaf with leathery hollylike leaflets add close-range interest. The abundant tiny fragrant yellow flowers borne in clusters put on a show in spring. They are followed by a crop of small bright pink to red berries. Colorful contrast to the bluish gray of the foliage. Berries are also edible and make a good jelly if you have the patience to gather them from among the prickly leaves.

Berberis harrisoniana *(Mahonia harrisoniana)*

Harrison barberry, Kofa mountain barberry

Berberidaceae family

COLD HARDINESS
All three zones.

LANDSCAPE VALUE
- Decorative foliage and small mature size make this a useful foundation plant, informal space-definer or shrub mass.
- Flowers and fruit add seasonal interest.

CULTURAL REQUIREMENTS
- **Exposure:** Full sun to part shade.
- **Water:** Water every week or two during the hot season and every month or two during the cool season to promote growth and attractive appearance.
- **Soil:** Adapted to well-drained rocky soils that are not highly alkaline.
- **Propagation:** Seed or cuttings.
- **Maintenance:** Other than occasional pruning for shape, this shrub requires little care.

POSSIBLE PROBLEMS
None observed.

Grows 1 to 3 feet (30.5 cm to 1 m) high, with equal spread. Slow to moderate growth. Small, rounded evergreen shrub native to the lower Sonoran Desert and southwestern Arizona. Noteworthy for its handsome hollylike foliage; the rich green trifoliate leaves are thick and leathery. Each 1¼- to 2-inch (3- to 5-cm) long leaflet is distinctly cleft and armed with five strong spines. In late winter, clusters of bright yellow flowers open at the branch tips. They are followed by blue-black fruit covered with a fine powdery-gray coating.

** See Glossary*

Berberis trifoliata (Mahonia trifoliata)

Algerita

Berberidaceae family

COLD HARDINESS

All three zones.

LANDSCAPE VALUE

- Space definer, background shrub, barrier plant with interesting foliage.
- Spring flowers add sprinkling of yellow throughout foliage.

CULTURAL REQUIREMENTS

- **Exposure:** Full sun to part shade.
- **Water:** Water every week or two during summer when plant is mature, more often when young to speed growth.
- **Soil:** Improved well-drained soil, with an occasional light application of fertilizer to speed up growth.
- **Propagation:** Seed or cuttings.
- **Maintenance:** Some pinching or light trimming to thicken plant.

POSSIBLE PROBLEMS

- Plant away from paths because of spiny leaflets.
- Algerita is a secondary host to black-stem rust, which could restrict its use in grain-producing areas.

Grows 6 to 8 feet (2 to 2.5 m) high, with equal spread. Slow to moderate growth. Spreading deciduous shrub with green, spiny compound leaves. Tends to be rangy when young but fills in with maturity.

Bocconia arborea

Pigeon flower, Giant poppy, Tears of blood

Papaveraceae family

COLD HARDINESS

Low zone and warm-winter microclimates of intermediate zone. Foliage damaged at about 28°F (-2°C).

LANDSCAPE VALUE

- Can be a gnarled small tree in protected areas of the intermediate zone and generally withstands light frost in the lower zone.
- The large and dramatic leaves evoke a tropical effect.
- Worth planting in intermediate zone because it recovers quickly in spring from winter frosts to produce summer foliage. Plant only if the unattractive appearance after winter cold is not objectionable.

CULTURAL REQUIREMENTS

- **Exposure:** Full sun to part shade.
- **Water:** Monthly thorough irrigation but needs weekly moisture in the hot season for good landscape appearance.
- **Soil:** Any soil with good drainage.
- **Propagation:** Seed.
- **Maintenance:** Prune annually to remove frost-damaged wood and to facilitate interesting trunk development. Remove dead leaves and wayward branches for best appearance during the year.

POSSIBLE PROBLEMS

- Sporadic growth spurts require pruning to control.
- Need to remove cold-damaged wood.

Grows 8 to 12 feet (2.5 to 3.5 m) high, usually lower, with equal spread. Rapid growth with regular water and warm temperatures. Evergreen but may go drought-deciduous during dry periods. Soft-wooded large shrub to small tree. Large gray leaves, almost white beneath, are pinnately* lobed. The unique size, two-toned color, texture, and configuration of the foliage is the striking part of the plant while the tiny flowers on panicles* are not showy. The seed heads add some interest. One of its common names, "tears of blood," is an English translation of the Mexican name. It was so named because of the red sap that seeps out when bark is injured.

* *See Glossary*

BOUGAINVILLEA

Bougainvillea, that most brilliant and exuberant of all flowering vines, has been so manipulated by horticulturists over the years that it's hard to know which species a cultivar belongs to. Although the parent species were red or purple, cultivars come in all colors.

Bougainvillea glabra

Red bougainvillea

Nyctaginaceae family

COLD HARDINESS

Frost-free areas of low zone and warm microclimates of the intermediate zone. Tolerates a few degrees below freezing for a short time, but flowers and leaves are quickly blackened as temperature drops. Lower temperatures and extended hours below freezing will damage the wood, especially new growth.

LANDSCAPE VALUE

- In almost frost-free areas, a large colorful vine to cover banks and shade structures or a large mounding shrub.
- In colder areas, Bougainvillea can be trained as an espalier on warm walls, grown in containers (especially the dwarf forms) or used as a garden perennial. As a perennial, it may be cut to the ground each year due to frost damage. It recovers rapidly in the spring and blooms in the summer.

CULTURAL REQUIREMENTS

- **Exposure:** Full sun; reflected sun and heat. When grown in part shade, a leggy vine results, usually with little bloom.
- **Water:** Tolerates wet conditions, producing a vigorous vine, but at the expense of the flowers. Best results come from a more limited watering schedule, such as every month or two. Bougainvillea is surprisingly drought tolerant; in abandoned landscapes it often continues to bloom spectacularly, even in dry areas.
- **Soil:** Any soil.
- **Propagation:** Cuttings.
- **Maintenance:** Allow to grow wild where space permits or train carefully over support structures. Even grows as a clipped hedge, but at the expense of bloom. In colder areas, remove frost-damaged branches in the spring, but delay this if possible until you see new growth emerge below the frozen branches. When possible, avoid winter pruning of frost-damaged wood because it may shelter surviving wood from later frosts.

POSSIBLE PROBLEMS

- Heavy blooming creates litter as papery bracts* fall and scatter.
- Sharp spikelike thorns complicate pruning and training.
- Dead leaves and branches can be unsightly all winter, though it's best to wait until spring to prune frosted growth.

In frost-free zones, climbs 30 feet (9 m) with support. Equal spread if given room to sprawl. Growth is rapid with good site conditions. Vigorous evergreen vine from South America with dark to medium green 4-inch (10-cm) leaves. Long shoots or vining branches shoot straight in the air, eventually falling over onto neighboring plants or structures, where formidable spines can hook onto the neighbor. The bridge-head is established from which the plants can continue to spread. Produces spectacular color almost continuously in frost-free areas. This color is not from a blossom but actually three bracts* that surround the inconspicuous yellow flower at the center. The bracts are usually shades of red, but some have been developed in orange, yellow and white. Many of the named varieties are hybrids with *B. spectabilis*, while others are *bud sports* of the species. Bud sports are vegetative changes in a bud that later becomes a branch where there is a distinct color change, such as red to orange. Cuttings taken from such a branch will carry the color change. Shrubby dwarf forms are also available.

* *See Glossary*

Bougainvillea spectabilis (B. brasiliensis)

Purple bougainvillea

Nyctaginaceae family

COLD HARDINESS

A little hardier than *B. glabra*, with large-scale uses that extend a little farther into the intermediate zone.

LANDSCAPE VALUE

Same as *B. glabra*, but its greater hardiness extends its practical use beyond the frost-free zones into warmer areas of the intermediate zone.

CULTURAL REQUIREMENTS

Same as *B. glabra* but tolerates cooler situations and blooms well without heat.

POSSIBLE PROBLEMS

Same as *B. glabra*.

To 30 feet (9 m) or more with support. Equal spread if given room to sprawl. Rapid growth. Growth pattern much the same as *B. glabra* but leaves tend to be smaller and shiny on top. The climbing technique is also similar and, if anything, more aggressive. Vertical new growth shoots are more stout and armed with more formidable hooked spikes that help it climb tall trees with spectacular results. The neon purple of the bracts* (see floral description for *B. glabra*) makes it a special color plant. There also are pink and rose cultivars*, yellow fading to rose, even all white, as well as a shrubby form with bronze-red bracts. The bloom season is not as long as *B. glabra*, but it blooms well in cooler summer climates. Sometimes partially deciduous.

* See Glossary

Brachychiton acerifolia (Sterculia acerifolia)

Australian flame tree

Sterculiaceae family

Grows 20 to 30 feet (6 to 9 m) high, rarely up to 50 feet (15 m) in desert regions. Spreads 20 to 30 feet (6 to 9 m). Slow to moderate growth. Upright tree with a stout trunk covered with smooth, mostly green bark. Produces an oval crown of shiny green leaves that may be evergreen or briefly deciduous just before the summer flowering season. The large leaves may be as wide as 10 inches (25.5 cm) and have a palmately* lobed maplelike shape. Only the flowering branches tend to shed leaves prior to the bloom period. Waxy 3/4 inch (2 cm) bell-shaped flowers range in color from clear light red to deep crimson, opening in big clusters at or near the branch tips. For a time after the spent blooms drop, they spread to create a solid red carpet beneath heavily flowering trees. Large brown seed pods fall to the ground at maturity. Native to Australia.

COLD HARDINESS

Low zone and warmest microclimates of intermediate zone.

LANDSCAPE VALUE

- Stunning accent or specimen tree when in flower.
- Dramatic focal point in outdoor living areas.
- Parks, roadways and other public spaces.
- Richly abundant glossy foliage evokes the tropics.

CULTURAL REQUIREMENTS

- **Exposure:** Thrives in intense heat and sunlight, but requires shelter from strong winds.
- **Water:** Soak the root zone of established trees every month or less often during the warm dry season. Water young plants every week during the hot season.
- **Soil:** Deep uniform soil to provide room for tap-root development. Performs well in lawns.
- **Propagation:** Seed.
- **Maintenance:** Fertilize every year or two in late winter to maximize flower production. Low branches can remain or be removed, if you wish, especially to encourage the central leader* of strong plants.

POSSIBLE PROBLEMS

- Trees vary in flowering habit. Some individual trees flower abundantly, while others produce only a light scattering of bloom clusters over the crown.
- Fallen seed pods create litter.
- Subject to Texas root rot*.

Brachychiton australis (Sterculia australis)

Broadleaf flame tree

Sterculiaceae family

COLD HARDINESS

Low zone and warmer areas of the intermediate zone.

LANDSCAPE VALUE

- Sturdy trunk and branch structure plus bold foliage make a handsome statement.
- Useful for parks, plazas, roadsides and large street plantings where space permits.

CULTURAL REQUIREMENTS

- **Exposure:** Full sun but tolerates reflected heat.
- **Water:** Soak the root zone of young developing trees every week or two, less often once established.
- **Soil:** Any soil with good drainage.
- **Propagation:** Seed.
- **Maintenance:** Develops sturdy trunk and branch structure with no pruning. Remove low branches if you wish.

POSSIBLE PROBLEMS

None observed.

About 40 feet (12 m) high, spreading to about 30 feet (10 m). Moderate growth rate. Sturdy large-leafed tree, almost evergreen but goes semideciduous to deciduous when blooming. Leaves are bright green, 4 to 8 inches (10 to 20.5 cm) long and wide, with five to seven lobes. Tubular flowers borne on short racemes* are pinkish, hairy on the outside and not as showy as those of its relative *B. acerifolia*. However, the sturdy spreading form and impressive foliage creates a strong presence in the landscape.

* See Glossary

Brachychiton populneus (Sterculia populneus, Sterculia diversifolia)

Bottle tree

Sterculiaceae family

COLD HARDINESS

Low and intermediate zones.

LANDSCAPE VALUE

- Park and street tree.
- Residential.
- Informal group plantings.
- Background or framing for buildings, privacy or wind screen.
- Shiny leaves that flutter with breezes add further landscape interest.

CULTURAL REQUIREMENTS

- **Exposure:** Full or reflected sun to part shade. Tolerates light to moderate frost.
- **Water:** Thoroughly soak the root zone every couple months.
- **Soil:** Deep well-drained soils.
- **Propagation:** Seed.
- **Maintenance:** Annual fertilization promotes faster growth and better foliage color. Low branches can remain or be removed to expose massive trunk flaring into a bottle shape.

POSSIBLE PROBLEMS

- Highly susceptible to Texas root rot*.
- Iron chlorosis* is an occasional problem.
- Dried woody seed pods may cause litter.
- Pods are filled with an irritating fuzz—don't get it in your eyes!

Grows 30 to 45 feet (9 to 13.5 m) high, spreading to 30 feet (9 m). Slow to moderate growth. Dense evergreen tree introduced from Australia. Narrow and pyramidal in youth, sometimes becoming rounded at maturity. Lustrous bright green leaves, 2 to 3 inches (5 to 7.5 cm) long, give a lush effect. Green to light gray trunk is swollen at the base and decreases rapidly in diameter as it rises. Small, white bell-shaped flowers with pink dots are followed by sculptural woody boat-shaped seed pods in late spring.

Brachychiton rupestris (Sterculia rupestris)

Narrow-leaved bottle tree

Sterculiaceae family

COLD HARDINESS

Low and intermediate zones.

LANDSCAPE VALUE

- Slender, vertical element in the landscape.
- Spidery open foliage reveals the inner structure of the tree.

CULTURAL REQUIREMENTS

- **Exposure:** Full sun; enjoys exposed situations.
- **Water:** Drought resistant, but thoroughly soak the root zone every month or two during the growing season.
- **Soil:** Most soils with good drainage.
- **Propagation:** Seed.
- **Maintenance:** Low maintenance.

POSSIBLE PROBLEMS

None observed, but *Brachychiton* species typically have little resistance to Texas root rot*.

To 30 feet (9 m) high, perhaps higher, spreading to 20 feet (6 m). Slow to moderate growth. Rather open lacy-foliaged tree with a strong central leader*. Straight smooth trunk grows bulbous or swollen with age. Evergreen or briefly deciduous before new foliage comes out. Native to Australia.

* *See Glossary*

Brahea armata (Erythea armata)

Mexican blue palm

Arecaceae (Palmae) family

COLD HARDINESS

Low and intermediate zones and warm microclimates of the high zone.

LANDSCAPE VALUE

- Sturdy and reliable heat- and cold-resistant palm.
- Attractive foliage makes it useful as a specimen or grouped informally or in rows.
- Handsome container plant when young.
- Well-suited to small spaces and residential landscapes where taller palms would be out of scale.

CULTURAL REQUIREMENTS

- **Exposure:** Full sun and intense heat. One of the more frost-resistant palms.
- **Water:** Thoroughly soak the root zone of established trees every month or two. Tolerates brackish water.
- **Soil:** Well-drained sandy soil—not a palm for wet places.
- **Propagation:** Seed.
- **Maintenance:** Considered difficult to transplant as a large tree. Dead brown leaves persist and form a shag around the trunk. Remove for a more trim appearance. Also remove old flowers to eliminate spent fruit-stalk litter. This will definitely improve the general appearance.

POSSIBLE PROBLEMS

None observed.

Grows 25 to 30 feet (7.5 to 9 m) high, spreading 8 to 10 feet (2.5 to 3 m). Slow growth. Young vigorous specimens of this palm from Baja California display a large elegant crown of ice blue fan-shaped leaves. These leaves grow 3 to 5 feet (1 to 1.5 m) across on a stout columnar trunk. At maturity, the foliage crown and individual leaves within it are smaller, which somewhat diminishes the ornamental character of the tree. Hanging clusters of fragrant cream-colored flowers are borne on 15-foot (4.5-m) stems that arch gracefully out and toward the ground. These are followed by dense clusters of large green marblelike fruit 1/2 to 3/4 inch (1 to 2 cm) long, which turn brown at maturity.

Brahea brandegeei (Erythea brandegeei)

San Jose hesper palm

Arecaceae (Palmae) family

COLD HARDINESS

Low zone and mild-winter areas of intermediate zone.

LANDSCAPE VALUE

- Whether planted as a single specimen, in groups or clumps, on golf courses, in parks and other public spaces, its handsome tropical appearance makes it a unique character plant.
- Suitable for large commercial settings and residential landscapes.

CULTURAL REQUIREMENTS

- **Exposure:** Full or reflected sun; moderately frost-tolerant.
- **Water:** Enjoys the moist oasis situation, but shows some drought tolerance. Maintain healthy established trees by thoroughly soaking the root zone every month or two.
- **Soil:** Any soil with fast drainage.
- **Propagation:** Seed (which takes forty to fifty days to germinate).
- **Maintenance:** Prune occasionally to maintain neat appearance of trunk and shag of dead foliage. To maintain without a shag, remove dead leaves below the crown each year.

POSSIBLE PROBLEMS

None observed.

To 40 feet (12 m) high, spreading to 6 feet (2 m) or more. Moderate growth rate. This tall distinctive fan palm from Baja California is rarely seen in the landscape in spite of obvious good traits. Has a slender trunk and a graceful crown of evergreen leaves 3 to 5 feet (1 to 1.5 m) wide. Leaves are dull green on the upper sides and covered with a waxy whitish green powder below. Dead foliage clings to the trunk to form a long-lasting shag or "skirt." Slender leaf petioles* as long as 3 feet (1 m) are armed with sharp curved spines. Arching flower stalks appear in spring but they are short and mostly hidden by the foliage. Puffy oblong fruits 1/2 to 3/4 inch (1 to 2 cm) long have a papery texture and turn a shining brown or yellow color at maturity.

* *See Glossary*

Brahea edulis (Erythea edulis) and Brahea elegans (Erythea elegans)

Guadalupe island palm, Franceschi palm

Arecaceae (Palmae) family

COLD HARDINESS

Low and intermediate zones and warm microclimates of the high zone.

LANDSCAPE VALUE

- Large crown of handsome bright green fronds make this an excellent palm for specimen or group planting in arid or oasis landscapes.
- Effective where space limitations require a palm of small to moderate height, such as home landscape.
- Small container plant.
- Tropical effects.

CULTURAL REQUIREMENTS

- **Exposure:** Full or reflected sun to part shade. Tolerates extremes of heat, cold and aridity. Also particularly tolerant of salt spray near seashore environments.
- **Water:** Thoroughly soak the root zone of established trees every month or two, every week or two during hot, dry months.
- **Soil:** Most soils with good drainage.
- **Propagation:** Seed.
- **Maintenance:** Remove fallen fruit and fruiting stalks in tailored landscapes.

POSSIBLE PROBLEMS

None observed.

Brahea edulis grows 20 to 35 feet (6 to 11 m) high, spreading 8 to 10 feet (2.5 to 3 m). Slow to moderate growth. This *Brahea* species from Guadalupe Island off the Pacific Coast of Mexico resembles *Brahea armata* but is more graceful and slender-trunked. It has larger fan-shaped leaves to 6 feet (2 m) wide which are light green instead of gray blue. Old fronds drop cleanly from the gray trunk, leaving behind the distinct imprint of a leaf scar. Flower stalks 4 to 5 feet (1 to 1.5 m) long and less showy than those of *B. armata* produce edible black fruits 1 inch (2.5 cm) or more in diameter.

B. elegans grows to 4 feet (1 m) high or higher, with equal spread. Slow growth. A small fan palm whose exact place of origin is unknown but is believed to be Sonora in northwestern Mexico. Thin gray-green to green leaves, 18 to 22 inches (46 to 56 cm) across on spiny petioles* 2 feet (61 cm) long, form a large open evergreen crown. Densely flowered bloom stalks grow to a length of 2 to 3 feet (61 cm to 1 m), often extending beyond the foliage. These are erect at first but gradually bend in a graceful curve under the weight of heavy masses of yellow globular fruits 3/4 inch (2 cm) in diameter.

* *See Glossary*

Brahea nitida (Erythea nitida)

Rock palm, Hesper palm

Arecaceae (Palmae) family

COLD HARDINESS

Low zone and warmer areas of the intermediate zone.

LANDSCAPE VALUE

- Tropical effects, especially in limited spaces. It will not bolt for the sky like *Washingtonia robusta* and leave you with nothing but a view of a telephone pole trunk at eye level.
- The old leaves self-clean, meaning they drop from the trunk on their own, eliminating need to groom.
- Possible container plant.

CULTURAL REQUIREMENTS

- **Exposure:** Full sun to part shade.
- **Water:** Quite drought tolerant but thoroughly soak the root zone every week or two to speed up growth.
- **Soil:** Any soil, including most desert and rocky soils.
- **Propagation:** Seed.
- **Maintenance:** Apply nitrogen fertilizer in late spring and again in midsummer for better foliage and faster growth. Needs little attention other than occasional clean-up of fallen leaves. Allow leaves to remain for thatched effect.

POSSIBLE PROBLEMS

None observed except slowness of growth.

To about 30 feet (9 m) high, spreading about 10 feet (3 m). Slow growth. A solitary erect fan palm. Leaves are medium green or sometimes slightly gray, especially below where they are cleft. Petioles* have no teeth along the edges. Old leaves don't last long on the trunks. An attractive small palm, but slow growing and not often seen in cultivation. Native to lower Sonoran Desert and south along the Pacific Coast of Mexico.

Brahea prominans (Erythea prominans)

Magadalena palm, Canyon palm

Arecaceae (Palmae) family

COLD HARDINESS

Low and intermediate zone, where foliage may be browned by cold winter temperatures.

LANDSCAPE VALUE

- Attractive small-scale palm (if you don't mind the wait).
- Excellent for hot, difficult locations.

CULTURAL REQUIREMENTS

- **Exposure:** Reflected sun to part shade.
- **Water:** Drought resistant but extra water in the hot season will speed up growth.
- **Soil:** Most soils. Tolerates salinity.
- **Propagation:** Seed.
- **Maintenance:** Apply nitrogen fertilizer during the warm weather growing season to improve growth rate and appearance. Clean up fallen leaves or allow them to remain for thatched effect.

POSSIBLE PROBLEMS

None observed except slowness of growth.

Grows 10 to 18 feet (3 to 5.5 m) high, spreading 6 to 9 feet (2 to 3 m). Slow growth. Small, slow-growing fan palm with light green foliage. Old leaves may be particularly persistent. A durable palm that is quite drought- and heat-resistant. Native to Sonora and farther south in Mexico.

* See Glossary

Brongniartia alamosana

Alamos pea tree

Fabaceae (Leguminosae) family

COLD HARDINESS
Low zone and warm microclimates of intermediate zone.

LANDSCAPE VALUE
Light and airy large shrub to small tree for patios and tracery patterns in front of plain walls.

CULTURAL REQUIREMENTS
- **Exposure:** Full sun to part shade.
- **Water:** Water every week or two during warm season and every month or two during winter.
- **Soil:** Most soils, but some depth will produce better growth and appearance.
- **Propagation:** Seed.
- **Maintenance:** May need some staking and side pruning to encourage patio-tree form.

POSSIBLE PROBLEMS
None observed.

Grows 8 to 10 feet (2.5 to 3 m) high, spreading 6 to 8 feet (2 to 2.5 m). Moderate growth. Small, round-headed deciduous tree with delicate compound leaves and interesting twiggy branch structure that forms a small canopy. Brownish red pea-shaped flowers scattered throughout the foliage in summer are a decorative addition at close range. Native to northwestern Mexico and on south.

Buddleia marrubifolia

Woolly butterfly bush

Loganiaceae family

COLD HARDINESS
All three zones.

LANDSCAPE VALUE
A unique and colorful shrub that may be used as a single specimen or massed in groups for
- Borders.
- Medians.
- Foundation plantings.
- Parking-lot islands.

CULTURAL REQUIREMENTS
- **Exposure:** Full sun.
- **Water:** Drought tolerant; water every month or two for adequate growth and appearance, but it grows faster with more frequent watering.
- **Soil:** Most soils with good drainage.
- **Propagation:** Cuttings.
- **Maintenance:** Prune occasionally to maintain form.

POSSIBLE PROBLEMS
None observed.

To 5 feet (1.5 m) high, with equal spread. Moderate growth. This evergreen shrub from the Chihuahuan Desert possesses several distinctive qualities. It has a graceful rounded form and dense mass of fuzzy silvery gray, almost-white, leaves. Ball-shaped clusters of tiny orange flowers about 1/2-inch (1-cm) across appear in profusion throughout summer and fall. Native to Mexico.

* See Glossary

Bulbine frutescens
Bulbine
Liliaceae family

COLD HARDINESS
Low and intermediate zones. Tolerates 20°F (-5°C) without damage.

LANDSCAPE VALUE
- Containers and planters.
- In combination with other succulents.
- Rock gardens.
- Border planting.
- Foundation planting.

CULTURAL REQUIREMENTS
- **Exposure:** Full sun to shade but no reflected sun. Best-looking plants grow in open shade.
- **Water:** Endures long periods of drought, but water every week or two for best appearance.
- **Soil:** Any soil.
- **Propagation:** Seed. Use cuttings to achieve a particular color.
- **Maintenance:** Needs periodic grooming to remove old bloom stalks.

POSSIBLE PROBLEMS
Rangy, unkempt character makes it unsuitable for more refined landscapes.

Grows 12- to 18-inch (30.5- to 46-cm) flower stalks. Clumping growth spreads about the same. Moderate growth rate. A tough, evergreen succulent with bright green cylindrical leaves. Small yellow flowers packed on 12- to 18-inch (30.5- to 46-cm) racemes* stand well above the foliage. The growth habit is somewhat leggy. An orange-flowered form called 'Hallmark' is more compact than the yellow-flowered form. Both bloom over long periods of the year. Native to South Africa.

Bursera fagaroides (B. odorata)
White bark tree, Fragrant elephant tree
Burseraceae family

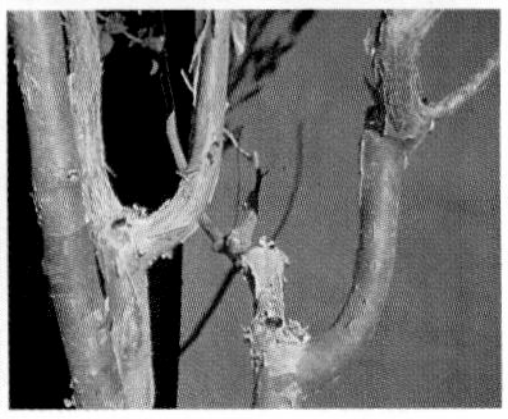

To 12 feet (3.5 m) high or more, spreading 9 to 10 feet (3 m). Slow to moderate growth. A shrub or small tree with attractive smooth bark that peels off in papery sheets. The species is widely distributed throughout southwestern Arizona and along the northwestern coast of Mexico. There are variations in bark color, including pale orange, red and snowy white. The latter is a characteristic of the variety that grows in Baja California, Mexico.

COLD HARDINESS
Low zone. Frost tender. Will recover from frost damage but plant structure is distorted.

LANDSCAPE VALUE
- A most interesting trunk and branch structure, either as a large shrub or small tree, especially where the silhouette can be appreciated.
- Can be maintained for years as a container plant, even in small containers where it will take on bonsai characteristics.
- Combines well with other desert plants, becoming a central point of interest in such compositions.
- Becomes a unique patio tree with time and favorable conditions but produces little shade.

CULTURAL REQUIREMENTS
- **Exposure:** Full sun to reflected sun. Tolerates part shade, but loses some of its structural character because of leggy growth.
- **Water:** Quite drought resistant, but soaking the root zone twice a month during the warm season stimulates new growth and helps maintain a satisfactory appearance.
- **Soil:** Most soils with good drainage.
- **Propagation:** Seed or cuttings.
- **Maintenance:** Prune frost-damaged wood in spring if necessary. Selectively thin and head back to enhance the unique branch structure and trunk.

POSSIBLE PROBLEMS
None observed.

Small, interesting, fragrant compound leaves sparsely cover twigs, creating an open pattern. Inconspicuous flowers and fruit add little interest—the desirable landscape features are the striking silhouette and unique peeling bark.

* See Glossary

Bursera hindsiana

Red elephant tree

Burseraceae family

COLD HARDINESS

Low zone and warm microclimates of the intermediate zone. Tolerates light frost at temperatures around 27°F (-3°C) for short periods. Recovers from lower temperatures but plant structure can be distorted by die-back*.

LANDSCAPE VALUE

- Striking miniature tree or large shrub for planters, against plain walls, or where its silhouette can be appreciated.
- Excellent in water-efficient plantings. Combines well with agaves, yuccas and cacti.
- Can be grown in containers for many years, creating a large bonsai effect.

CULTURAL REQUIREMENTS

- **Exposure:** Full sun; tolerates reflected heat; will grow in part shade but leggy growth usually ruins its interesting silhouette.
- **Water:** Quite drought tolerant but some irrigation may be necessary to prevent leaf drop or to speed up growth and development. Water container plants every week or two during the hot season.
- **Soil:** Most soils with good drainage.
- **Propagation:** Seed or cuttings.
- **Maintenance:** Prune frost-damaged wood in spring if necessary.

POSSIBLE PROBLEMS

None observed.

Grows 9 to 15 feet (3 to 5 m) high, with equal spread. Slow to moderate growth, depending on irrigation frequency. Large shrub or small tree with an interesting heavy trunk. Lower branches are covered with reddish gray bark. Structure is generally open and transparent, presenting a nice silhouette. Dark green compound leaves consist of five to seven leaflets; flowers are inconspicuous. Small orange fruits add some interest at close range. Evergreen, but can be drought deciduous. Native to central Baja California and across the Gulf of California to Sonora, Mexico.

Bursera laxiflora

Torote prieto

Burseraceae family

COLD HARDINESS

Low zone. Withstands only light frost. Recovers in the spring but the plant structure is distorted.

LANDSCAPE VALUE

- Large shrub or small tree adds an interesting touch, especially if placed where the silhouette can be appreciated.
- Patio tree.
- Mix with other desert plants, such as cacti, euphorbias and so forth, for a desert plant composition. Add agaves and certain yuccas for a more tropical mood.

CULTURAL REQUIREMENTS

- **Exposure:** Full sun, including reflected sun, to part shade.
- **Water:** Quite drought resistant. It comes from a region that is typically dry in the winter. Water in winter will help tree become more evergreen. Thoroughly soak the root zone every week or two during the hot season to promote good growth and satisfactory appearance.
- **Soil:** Any soil with good drainage.
- **Propagation:** Seed.
- **Maintenance:** Prune frost-damaged wood in spring if necessary.

POSSIBLE PROBLEMS

Susceptibility to cold damage complicates silhouette development.

To 18 feet (5.5 m) high or higher, depending on the location and local climate. Spreads 9 to 10 feet (3 m). Slow to moderate growth. Tall shrub or, in optimum conditions, a tree with a rounded crown. Semi-evergreen to drought deciduous with dark gray bark that is slightly scaling. Twigs are reddish gray. Pinnate* leaves cover the twigs but not so thickly as to obscure the structure of the tree. Flowers and fruit are small and inconspicuous. Native to central Sonora, south to Sinaloa.

* See Glossary

Bursera microphylla

Little-leaf bursera, Yellow paperbark elephant tree

Burseraceae family

COLD HARDINESS

Low zone.

LANDSCAPE VALUE

- Open form and unique shape of mature specimens add design and interest for patios, large planters, and against plain walls.
- In containers it can take on a bonsai form, not bothered by being root bound for years.

CULTURAL REQUIREMENTS

- **Exposure:** Full sun, including reflected sun, to part shade.
- **Water:** Thoroughly soak the root zone every month or two.
- **Soil:** Any soil with good drainage.
- **Propagation:** Seed.
- **Maintenance:** Prune frost-damaged wood in spring if necessary.

POSSIBLE PROBLEMS

Tender to frost. Cold damage can distort the tree's structure.

Grows 12 to 18 feet (3.5 to 5.5 m) high, with equal spread. Moderate to slow growth, depending on available moisture. An irregular large shrub or small rounded-top tree that develops a picturesque form as it ages. Small bright green compound leaves on cherry red branches and twigs add interest. The trunk and larger branches are showy, with papery, peeling bark that reveals smooth yellow bark beneath. Small flowers and fruit are inconspicuous. Native to southern Arizona and south into Mexico.

Butia capitata

Pindo palm, Jelly palm

Arecaceae (Palmae) family

COLD HARDINESS

Low and intermediate zones and protected locations in the high zone. Hardy to 15°F (-9.5°C).

LANDSCAPE VALUE

- Attractive subject for large containers and for tropical-effects foliage massing. This is valuable in colder regions, where other hardy tropical-appearing plants do not survive.
- Massing and grouping is best effect.
- Grayish green fronds contrast nicely with darker green foliage of other tropicals.

CULTURAL REQUIREMENTS

- **Exposure:** Tolerates most exposures from reflected sun to open shade.
- **Water:** Develops faster with water every week or two but will perform satisfactorily with water every month or two.
- **Soil:** Most soils, but prefers prepared garden soil, which promotes more rapid growth and lush foliage.
- **Propagation:** Seed.
- **Maintenance:** Clean up fruit that drops onto paved areas. Remove old blossoms.

POSSIBLE PROBLEMS

- Slowness of growth.
- Fruit drop could be objectionable.

Grows 10 to 20 feet (3 to 6 m) high, spreading 6 to 8 feet (2 to 2.5 m). A slow-growing palm with unique arching pinnate* fronds, grayish green in color, and a thick, stubby trunk. Old leaf bases persist and form an interesting trunk pattern, so take care to trim them the same length when removing declining leaves. Tiny yellow flowers are followed by large clusters of yellow to red edible fruit, which have a delicious pineapple flavor. Slow to develop, the thick trunk seems out of proportion to the foliage as it ages. One of the world's most hardy palms. Native to Brazil and Argentina.

** See Glossary*

Caesalpinia cacalaco

Cascalote

Fabaceae (Leguminosae) family

COLD HARDINESS

Low zone and protected microclimates of the intermediate zone. Tolerates light frost, but not hardy to intense cold.

LANDSCAPE VALUE

- Attractive foliage, showy flowering and interesting seed pods.
- Specimen or accent, either as a large shrub or small multi- or single-trunk tree.
- Shrub borders, buffers, street medians and other roadway plantings.

CULTURAL REQUIREMENTS

- **Exposure:** Full to reflected sun
- **Water:** Shows moderate drought tolerance once established. Growth is faster and appearance better with thorough irrigation every month or two.
- **Soil:** Well-drained.
- **Propagation:** Seed.
- **Maintenance:** Selectively prune to encourage the desired growth habit. Remove frost-damaged branches and limbs.

POSSIBLE PROBLEMS

- Winter temperatures below 20°F (-4°C) cause unsightly die-back* or loss of plant.
- Frost damage removal in borderline hardiness zones.

To 15 feet (4.5 m) high, spreading 10 to 15 feet (3 to 4.5 m). Slow to moderate growth, depending on soil moisture. Large evergreen shrub or small tree that grows wild in many areas of tropical Mexico. The dense rounded foliage crown is made up of bipinnate* leaves whose leaflets are ½ to 1 inch (1 to 2.5cm) long, rounded or oval, and often notched at the tip. Branches are equipped with stout thorns. In tropical regions, flowering takes place in winter, but it is delayed until spring where winters are cooler. Clear yellow five-petaled flowers about 1 inch (2.5 cm) long open in dense spikes at the branch tips. Conspicuous reddish brown woody seed pods are 4 to 6 inches (10 to 15 cm) long and constricted between the large seeds. The pods remain attached to the plant long after they ripen.

Caesalpinia gilliesii

Yellow bird of paradise

Fabaceae (Leguminosae) family

COLD HARDINESS

Low and intermediate zones and protected microclimates of high zone. May die back to ground in high elevations in severe winters but quickly produces new top growth when weather warms in spring.

LANDSCAPE VALUE

- Unusual and interesting branching pattern and exotic flower display over a long season. Good accent or specimen shrub, equally at home in arid, transitional and lush oasis landscape settings.
- Revegetation and naturalizing.

CULTURAL REQUIREMENTS

- **Exposure:** Full or reflected sun.
- **Water:** Drought tolerant but loses its leaves when severely stressed for moisture. Looks best and flowers most heavily with water every week to every month.
- **Soil:** Well-drained.
- **Propagation:** Seed. Naturalizes freely from volunteer seedlings.
- **Maintenance:** Prune to develop desired growth habit. Remove spent flower clusters to prolong blossoming.

POSSIBLE PROBLEMS

- Ripe seeds are poisonous.
- Reseeds and naturalizes. Must remove unwanted seedlings.

Grows 5 to 10 feet (1.5 to 3 m) high, spreading 4 to 6 feet (1 to 2 m). Rapid growth. Large shrub or small tree from Argentina and Uruguay, but naturalized in Mexico and United States. Cold deciduous over most of its range but evergreen in the warmest areas. Open, irregular branching structure is free of spines and lightly clothed with finely divided foliage. The yellow flowers have showy bright red stamens* 4 to 5 inches (10 to 13 cm) long. They appear in large clusters at the branch tips midspring through late summer. Flat seed pods to 4 inches (10 cm) long burst open when mature, scattering the enclosed seeds over the surrounding area. This process facilitates its spread, making it an outstanding plant for revegetating and naturalizing.

* *See Glossary*

Caesalpinia mexicana

Mexican bird of paradise

Fabaceae (Leguminosae) family

COLD HARDINESS

Low zone and all but the coldest microclimates in the intermediate zone. A tough plant in most respects but severe frost results in die-back*.

LANDSCAPE VALUE

- Effective background when grown as a large shrub.
- Assumes treelike proportions with corrective pruning. Becomes a handsome specimen in this form.
- Flowers add color to the landscape over a long season.

CULTURAL REQUIREMENTS

- **Exposure:** Full sun to part shade.
- **Water:** Water every month or two once established but more often for continuous bloom.
- **Soil:** A wide range of arid-region soils.
- **Propagation:** Seed.
- **Maintenance:** Prune occasionally to develop and maintain the desired form or to remove cold-damaged twigs and branches.

POSSIBLE PROBLEMS

- Ripe seeds are poisonous.
- Some cleanup of the numerous seed pods may be necessary in a highly maintained landscape.

Grows 10 to 15 feet (3 to 4.5 m) high, spreading to 10 feet (3 m). Moderate to rapid growth. Distinctive large shrub or small tree from Mexico. Bipinnately* compound leaves are divided into oblong or rounded leaflets that remain green in mild winters. The branches are spineless. Yellow flowers in 6-inch (15-cm) long clusters bloom throughout the year in warm-winter areas, in spring through fall elsewhere. Seed pods are 2 to 3 inches (5 to 7.5 cm) long.

Caesalpinia platyloba

Palo Colorado

Fabaceae (Leguminosae) family

COLD HARDINESS

Low zone and warm-winter microclimates of the intermediate zone. Marginally frost hardy.

LANDSCAPE VALUE

- Small specimen or accent flowering tree in arid and transition zones.
- Mass plantings.

CULTURAL REQUIREMENTS

- **Exposure:** Full sun.
- **Water:** Thoroughly soak the root zone every month or two throughout the year, more often during the growing season for best landscape performance.
- **Soil:** Most soils with good drainage.
- **Propagation:** Seed.
- **Maintenance:** Prune occasionally for desired form and branching structure.

POSSIBLE PROBLEMS

Clusters of persistent seed pods may be objectionable in manicured landscapes.

Grows 15 to 30 feet (4.5 to 9 m) high, spreading 10 to 20 feet (3 to 6 m). Moderate growth. Small thornless tree with a trunk diameter up to 8 inches (20.5 cm). Native from Chihuahua and Sonora and south at least into the state of Colima, Mexico. Leaves are bipinnately* compound with four to eight pairs of dull green elliptical to oblong leaflets. Leaflets are 3/4 to 2 1/4 inches (2 to 6 cm) long and 3/8 to 1 1/4 inches (1 to 3 cm) wide on each of the four to eight primary leaf divisions *(pinnae)*. All young vegetative parts are covered with a dense mat of fine hairs. Clusters of five-petaled flowers open anytime from spring into late summer, depending on local conditions. The conspicuous reddish brown seed pods are flat and 2 to 4 inches (5 to 10 cm) long by about 1 inch (2.5 cm) wide. They hang in clusters that remain on the tree from midsummer into winter.

** See Glossary*

Caesalpinia pulcherrima

Red bird of paradise

Fabaceae (Leguminosae) family

COLD HARDINESS

Low and intermediate zones.

LANDSCAPE VALUE

- Exotic warm weather accent for arid, transitional and oasis landscapes.
- Informal shrub borders and mass plantings.
- Striking floral display against a plain wall during the warm months.
- Naturalizes to a limited extent on favorable sites.
- Combine with other plants that are attractive during the winter months to disguise its winter dormancy.

CULTURAL REQUIREMENTS

- **Exposure:** Full or reflected sun to part shade.
- **Water:** Drought resistant but water every week or two during the warm season for maximum flowering.
- **Soil:** Most soils with good drainage.
- **Propagation:** Seed.
- **Maintenance:** Stems die back with hard winter frost but plant regrows rapidly once the weather warms in spring. For a denser, more compact plant and heavier flowering, treat like a perennial by pruning the plant back to within a few inches of the ground in late winter. In coldest areas, mulch base of plant over winter to protect plant crown.

POSSIBLE PROBLEMS

- Ripe seeds are poisonous.
- Plant looks ragged in winter.

Grows 4 to 10 feet (1 to 3 m) high, spreading 4 to 6 feet (1 to 2 m). Rapid growth with regular irrigation. Lush tropical-looking shrub native to the West Indies and Mexico and a workhorse color plant in the Southwest United States. Rounded to vase-shaped, with scattered prickles along the stems. Feathery foliage is semi-evergreen in warm winter areas, deciduous elsewhere. During the warmer months, branches are tipped with clusters of dazzling orange-red flowers, each bloom highlighted by long curved red stamens* to 2 1/2 inches (6.5 cm) long. Bean pods 3 to 4 inches (7.5 to 10 cm) long are poisonous. Mature plant size greatly affected by soil moisture and severity of winter cold.

Caesalpinia pumila

Copper caesalpinia

Fabaceae (Leguminosae) family

COLD HARDINESS

Low zone and warm microclimates of the intermediate zone.

LANDSCAPE VALUE

- Shrub group plantings.
- Specimen.
- Open growth habit and appealing shape, foliage texture and flowers look great close to large buildings and on commercial sites.

CULTURAL REQUIREMENTS

- **Exposure:** Full sun.
- **Water:** Withstands considerable drought but needs water every month or two to look attractive when established.
- **Soil:** Most soils with good drainage.
- **Propagation:** Seed.
- **Maintenance:** A low-maintenance shrub that requires only occasional corrective pruning to look its best.

POSSIBLE PROBLEMS

None observed in the landscape, but because seeds of other *Caesalpinia* species are poisonous, its mature seeds are probably also toxic.

Grows 6 to 10 feet (2 to 3 m) high, spreading to 8 feet (2.5 m). Moderate growth. This deciduous shrub is native to central Sonora in Mexico. Slender reddish brown to gray branches are clothed with yellow-green bipinnately* compound foliage 1/4 to 3/4 inch (0.5 cm to 2 cm) long. Leaflets have a papery texture. Small clusters of yellow flowers appear at intervals midsummer into fall. Seed pods are elliptical, 3/4 to 1 1/2 inches (2 to 4 cm) long and reddish in color when mature.

** See Glossary*

Calliandra californica

Baja fairy duster

Fabaceae (Leguminosae) family

COLD HARDINESS

Low zone and warm microclimates of the intermediate zone. Frost tender but recovers rapidly as the weather warms in spring.

LANDSCAPE VALUE

- Delicate, fine-textured shrub with a long and colorful flowering season.
- An exotic color accent or specimen planted singly or in groups.
- Foundation or border plant.

CULTURAL REQUIREMENTS

- **Exposure:** Full sun to part or filtered shade.
- **Water:** Drought tolerant, but water every month or two for continuous flowering and good appearance.
- **Soil:** Adapted to rocky, well-drained soils as well as more fertile types.
- **Propagation:** Seed and probably cuttings.
- **Maintenance:** Prune to remove frost-damaged wood.

POSSIBLE PROBLEMS

Not adapted to normal hard winter frost. Plant in warm protected microclimate to prevent cold-winter damage.

Grows 2 to 5 feet (61 cm to 1.5 m) high, with equal spread. Moderate to rapid growth with regular water. Open, rounded shrub with stiff gray stems and dark green finely cut foliage. Native to Baja California, Mexico. Evergreen in warm winters but killed back to the ground by a hard frost. Plants typically regrow from their roots in spring. Tassel-shaped flower heads are made up mostly of bright red stamens*. Flowers grow about 1 inch (2.5 cm) or less. Flowering is continuous during warm weather, depending on moisture. Blooms are most abundant in spring.

Calliandra eriophylla

Fairy duster, False mesquite

Fabaceae (Leguminosae) family

COLD HARDINESS

All three zones.

LANDSCAPE VALUE

Fairy duster offers drought resistance, limited size and showy flowering habit. It is well suited for planting in groups as a

- Border.
- Informal hedge.
- Filler shrub beneath taller plants.
- Foundation plant.
- Shrubby groundcover.
- Median plant.

CULTURAL REQUIREMENTS

- **Exposure:** Full sun. Withstands both heat and cold.
- **Water:** Water once or twice during long dry spells. More regular watering encourages flowering and foliage retention.
- **Soil:** Grows well in most garden soils but also adapted to fast-draining gravelly or rocky soils.
- **Propagation:** Readily grows from seed. Those with particular flower colors are propagated from cuttings.
- **Maintenance:** Prune back long stems to promote compact habit.

POSSIBLE PROBLEMS

None observed.

Grows 1 to 3 feet (3.5 cm to 1 m) high, spreading 3 to 4 feet (1 m). Moderate growth. Bipinnately* compound leaves less than 1 inch (2½ cm) long create the fine-textured, lacy foliage effect of this low-spreading shrub. Native from West Texas to Southern California and into northern Mexico. Evergreen with adequate moisture but goes deciduous under prolonged dry conditions. Blooms in early spring and at other times if triggered by moisture. White to pink or reddish purple ball-shaped bloom clusters make an exquisite floral display.

* See Glossary

Calliandra hybrid (*C. peninsularis* X *C. eriophylla*)

Red hybrid fairy duster

Fabaceae (Leguminosae) family

COLD HARDINESS
Low and intermediate zones. May be hardy in high zones, but no data available to date.

LANDSCAPE VALUE
- Low-growing, feathery evergreen plant with intermittent bloom.
- Foundation planting.
- Banks and medians.

CULTURAL REQUIREMENTS
- **Exposure:** Sun to part shade.
- **Water:** Undemanding but appreciates water every week to every couple months for good bloom and appearance.
- **Soil:** Grows well in most garden soils but also adapted to fast-draining gravelly or rocky soils.
- **Propagation:** Cuttings.
- **Maintenance:** Prune back long stems to promote compact habit.

POSSIBLE PROBLEMS
Propagation slow because cuttings do not root easily and plants grown from seed are variable because of hybridization.

To 3 feet (1 m) high or higher, with equal spread. Moderate growth rate. Small feathery shrub with puffball flowers that are similar to its red-flowered parent *C. peninsularis* but not as bright red or as cold tender. Apparently, it inherited the cold hardiness of *C. eriophylla*, its other parent.

Calliandra peninsularis

La Paz fairy duster

Fabaceae (Leguminosae) family

COLD HARDINESS
Low zone and warm microclimates in the intermediate zone. Dies back with hard frost but grows out quickly in spring.

LANDSCAPE VALUE
Low-flowering plant for banks, foundation planting, medians and similar situations.

CULTURAL REQUIREMENTS
- **Exposure:** Full sun to part shade.
- **Water:** Drought resistant but needs water once or twice a season for adequate growth and blooming.
- **Soil:** Well-drained.
- **Propagation:** Seed or cuttings, which is sometimes difficult.
- **Maintenance:** Prune back long stems to promote compact habit.

POSSIBLE PROBLEMS
- More open and straggly form than *C. californica*.
- Pods pop or explode, scattering seeds, which makes it difficult to collect them for planting.
- Cuttings do not root readily.

To 6 feet (2 m) high, with equal spread. Moderate growth rate. Rather open-branched shrub with fine feathery leaves. Clusters of red flowers bloom in summer. Less leafy and seems to produce fewer flowers than *C. californica*. Both are being grown in nurseries. At times, it's difficult to tell them apart when young. Native to western Mexico.

* See Glossary

Callistemon citrinus (*C. lanceolatus*)

Lemon bottlebrush

Myrtaceae family

COLD HARDINESS

Low and intermediate zones and warm microclimates of the high zone, where it recovers rapidly from a freeze.

LANDSCAPE VALUE

- Outstanding flowering shrub that lends itself to shaping and pruning into a variety of shapes and forms. Train as tall hedge for screening or as an espalier against large blank walls. Or stake and train as a patio tree.
- Best use is probably large informal shrub planting.

CULTURAL REQUIREMENTS

- **Exposure:** Reflected sun to part shade.
- **Water:** Reasonably drought resistant. Tolerates wetter garden situations except in areas with soils high in calcium carbonate. Performs well on bimonthly irrigation after established, but growth is slower.
- **Soil:** Porous well-drained soil. Avoid wet situations, especially in calcareous* soil and irrigation water. Keep the soil on the dry side in such situations.
- **Propagation:** Cuttings. Can be grown from seed but flowers and plant form may be variable.
- **Maintenance:** Regular trimming and hedging will reduce flowering. This color loss is partially compensated by the regular coppery new-growth spurts stimulated by the shearing.

POSSIBLE PROBLEMS

Chlorosis* is a problem in regions of calcareous* soil and water.

Grows to 15 feet (4.5 m) high, spreading to 10 feet (3 m). Moderate to rapid growth. Large evergreen shrub that can be staked and trained into a 15-foot (4.5-m) patio-size tree. Vivid red 6-inch (15-cm) long bottlebrush-shaped flower clusters are set in narrow bright green leaves 6 inches (15 cm) long. Blooming occurs off and on throughout the year. Showy copper new growth adds additional interest in spring. Variable in size. Cultivars of various colors are sometimes available. Hard seed capsules encircle stems. Native to Australia.

Callistemon phoenicus

Crimson bottlebrush

Myrtaceae family

COLD HARDINESS

Low and intermediate zones and probably warm microclimates of the high zone.

LANDSCAPE VALUE

- Mixed shrubbery planting.
- Its irregular growth habit does not accept more controlled planting treatments as well as its relative *C. citrinus.*
- Outstanding color show in spring.
- Roadsides and medians.

CULTURAL REQUIREMENTS

- **Exposure:** Reflected sun to part shade. Withstands windy, dry situations.
- **Water:** Quite drought resistant. Thoroughly soak the root zone every month or two. Tolerates moist garden situations.
- **Soil:** Most soils with good drainage.
- **Propagation:** Seed or cuttings.
- **Maintenance**: Prune side branches and stake for tree form.

POSSIBLE PROBLEMS

None observed. Chlorosis* does not seem to be as much of a problem as with *C. citrinus.*

Grows 8 feet (2.5 m) high, spreading to 6 feet (2 m). Moderate growth rate. Large, somewhat rangy evergreen shrub from western Australia. Deep crimson bottlebrush flower clusters set amid narrow, leathery gray-green leaves 4 inches (10 cm) long. Bloom period seems to be limited to spring. Flowers contrast handsomely at that time among the gray-green foliage. Mature shrub maintains an open form, with its branch structure always visible.

* *See Glossary*

Callistemon rigidus

Stiff bottlebrush

Myrtaceae family

COLD HARDINESS

Low and intermediate zones.

LANDSCAPE VALUE

- Stiff, rangy character adds interest when planted against walls or where its open craggy pattern can be featured.
- Combines well with other desertlike plants.
- *Not* a plant for screening or shade.

CULTURAL REQUIREMENTS

- **Exposure:** Thrives in full to reflected sun but accepts part shade.
- **Water:** Reasonably drought resistant. Moisten the root zone every week or two during the warm season.
- **Soil:** Any soil.
- **Propagation:** Seed or cuttings.
- **Maintenance:** Little maintenance required.

POSSIBLE PROBLEMS

None observed.

To 20 feet (6 m) high, spreading to 10 feet (3 m). Moderate growth. A large evergreen shrub to a rangy small tree with a see-through character. Stiff, rather sparse sharp-pointed gray-green leaves, sometimes purplish, are widely spaced around the stems. Red bottlebrush flower clusters, 2½ to 4½ inches (6.5 to 11.5 cm) long appear in spring and summer, leaving prominent seed capsules that encircle the stems. Capsules persist for some time and actually add an interesting aspect to the silhouette. Native to Australia.

Landscape Design Example

Calliandra in combination with columnar cactus in Warren Jones's yard.

* See Glossary

Callistemon viminalis

Weeping bottlebrush
Myrtaceae family

COLD HARDINESS

Low zone and warm areas of intermediate zone, where foliage is sometimes damaged by cold.

LANDSCAPE VALUE

- Strong vertical element in the landscape despite its pendulous branches.
- Profuse, spectacular color in season.
- Accent plant.
- Street tree, in parking lots and on medians where location and irrigation are adequate.
- Dwarf cultivars* are useful as space definers, hedges, foundation plantings and borders.

CULTURAL REQUIREMENTS

- **Exposure:** Reflected sun to part shade, such as among taller trees. Avoid windy, dry, stressful locations.
- **Water:** Water every week or two. Will tolerate lawn situations where soil drains well and the soil and water are not high in calcium carbonate. Thorough soakings of the root zone every month or two are adequate, but dwarfs require regular irrigation.
- **Soil:** Appreciates deep, improved soil.
- **Propagation:** Cuttings. Nurseries are offering better selections, and seed-grown plants can be quite variable in appearance. Dwarf selections must be propagated vegetatively.
- **Maintenance:** Staking young trees. Thin excess pendulous branches for best appearance.

POSSIBLE PROBLEMS

- May suffer chlorosis* where soil and water is high in calcium carbonate.
- Wind and frost damage can be a problem when grown in marginal climate areas.

Grows 20 to 30 feet (10 m) high, sometimes taller, spreading to 15 feet (4.5 m). Dwarf cultivars* are much smaller, to 3 feet (1 m) high, with equal spread. Rapid growth. A fast-growing, large evergreen shrub or small to medium tree. Distinctive pendulous branches are covered with long, narrow light green leaves to 6 inches (15 cm) long. Rather open growth with leaves at ends of branches creates a somewhat stringy effect at close range. Bright red bottlebrush flower clusters, 6 inches (15 cm) long, are borne in abundance during late spring and early summer and sporadically throughout the rest of the year. Some dwarf cultivars*, such as 'Captain Cook' and 'Little John,' have a superior form and blood red flowers from fall to spring. The cultivar 'McCaskillii' is more vigorous and an outstanding bloomer. All are native to Australia.

* See Glossary

Calocedrus decurrens

Incense cedar

Cupressaceae family

COLD HARDINESS

All three zones. Tolerates high temperatures of intermediate zone, but heat tolerance untested in the hottest regions of the low zone.

LANDSCAPE VALUE

- Elegant, columnar element.
- Background plant.
- Ultimately a skyline tree.

CULTURAL REQUIREMENTS

- **Exposure:** Withstands shade as a young tree. Full to reflected sun is best.
- **Water:** Thoroughly soak the root zone every month or two. New plants may need water every week or two to stimulate growth, especially in early years.
- **Soil:** Most soils with good drainage.
- **Propagation:** Seed. Possibly cuttings.
- **Maintenance:** Little required.

POSSIBLE PROBLEMS

None observed.

Grows 75 to 90 feet (23 to 27.5 m) high in its native California habitat. Spreads to 20 feet (6 m). Likely to be much smaller in lower arid regions. Slow growth when young, then growth rate accelerates. Can put on as much as 2 feet (61 cm) a year after it's established. This evergreen denizen of the California mountain transition zone has shown surprising adaptation to the lower desert climates, particularly the high summer heat. Develops as a dense, narrow green column, with aromatic foliage arranged in flat layers. Bark is rich, reddish and furrowed at maturity.

Calotropis procera

Sodom apple

Asclepiadaceae family

COLD HARDINESS

Low zone and warm microclimates of the intermediate zone. Frost tender.

LANDSCAPE VALUE

Dramatic large-scale leaves and pods make this Middle Eastern immigrant a potential accent or silhouette against a wall, especially where water for landscaping is limited.

CULTURAL REQUIREMENTS

- **Exposure:** Full sun.
- **Water:** None after plant is established, except to speed growth.
- **Soil:** Any soil.
- **Propagation:** Seed.
- **Maintenance:** Little maintenance.

POSSIBLE PROBLEMS

- All plant parts are poisonous, especially its milky juice. Avoid eye and skin contact.
- Reseeds, but not difficult to eradicate seedlings when they do occur.
- Has become invasive in lower Colorado River Valley and Mexico.

Grows 6 to 9 feet (2 to 3 m) high, spreading to 6 feet (2 m). Moderate to rapid growth, depending on irrigation frequency. A bold-foliaged evergreen shrub with a silvery gray cast. The large scale of the leaves, 6 inches (15 cm) long or more, belie its ability to persist under the worst of hot, dry conditions. Clusters of wavy white blossoms, tinged with lavender, verify its kinship to the milkweed family. Large green balloonlike pods resemble apples from a distance. Close inspection reveals that they are bags of seed, ready to be launched into the air. Widely distributed throughout the Old World deserts. Probably also growing on the site of ancient Sodom and Gomorrah.

Calylophus hartwegii
Calylophus
Onagraceae family

COLD HARDINESS
All three zones. May not remain evergreen in colder winter areas of intermediate or high zone.

LANDSCAPE VALUE
- Informal perennial garden subject.
- Rock gardens.
- Drought-tolerant, meadowlike groundcover.
- Blooms well in containers.

CULTURAL REQUIREMENTS
- **Exposure:** Full sun, reflected heat to part shade.
- **Water:** Quite drought resistant but needs water every week or two during the warm season to stay in bloom.
- **Soil:** Tolerates poor soil as long as it drains well.
- **Propagation:** Seed, cuttings or divisions.
- **Maintenance:** Remove spent flowers and trim foliage lightly to encourage flowering.

POSSIBLE PROBLEMS
Foliage becomes dull and somewhat off-color in colder winter locations. Sometimes becomes deciduous in the cold winters of the high zone.

To $1\frac{1}{2}$ feet (46 cm) high, spreading to 3 feet (1 m). Moderate growth rate. A woody perennial that forms a sprawling clump with narrow evergreen leaves and single butter yellow blooms that resemble night-blooming primrose (to which it is related). Fresh sets of buds open each evening to replace the just-closed flowers that bloomed the night before. The flower show starts in early spring. With periodic trimming to remove some old growth and intermittent water, calylophus flowers throughout most of the warm season.

Campsis radicans (Bignonia radicans)
Common trumpet creeper
Bignoniaceae family

COLD HARDINESS
All three zones.

LANDSCAPE VALUE
- Vine to cover fences and shade structures wherever a deciduous vine is appropriate.
- Showy summer color makes plant almost tropical in appearance.

CULTURAL REQUIREMENTS
- **Exposure:** Full sun, including reflected heat to part shade.
- **Water:** Quite drought resistant. For good bloom and foliage, soak the root zone thoroughly every week or two.
- **Soil:** Most soils that are not extremely alkaline or saline.
- **Propagation:** Can be grown from seed, but cuttings are more logical because it roots easily. Cuttings will also retain the improved qualities of the cultivars*.
- **Maintenance:** Can be trained to grow as a large mounding shrub by periodically cutting back vigorous branch terminals.

POSSIBLE PROBLEMS
None observed except invasiveness in moist situations. Don't use in wet oasis situations.

Grows 30 to 40 feet (9 to 12 m) high, with equal spread, under optimum conditions. Smaller in arid regions. Rapid growth. A vigorous deciduous vine that is self-climbing with aerial rootlets that stick to either wood or masonry. Dark green compound leaves to 2 inches (5 cm) long divide into nine to eleven "teeth." Leaves provide a striking background for the bright orange-red 3-inch (7.5-cm) trumpet-shaped flowers produced in clusters of six to twelve blossoms. The vine will spread over the ground if there is nothing for it to climb, rooting as it spreads if moisture is present. Forms a large freestanding shrub. Native to middle and eastern United States, it was brought to the desert Southwest by early settlers. It exhibited considerable tolerance of heat and drought. Nurseries offer a number of cultivars with superior flowers and color variations, including a true yellow bloom.

* See Glossary

Capparis spinosa and *C. spinosa inermis*

Spiny caper, Spineless caper, Thornless caper

Capparaceae family

COLD HARDINESS
Low and intermediate zones.

LANDSCAPE VALUE
- Tough mounding groundcover for banks and hot exposed locations.
- Foundation plant.
- Flowers are interesting at close range.

CULTURAL REQUIREMENTS
- **Exposure:** Full sun (thrives in heat) to part shade.
- **Water:** Tolerates long periods of drought but needs water once or twice a season to grow and develop.
- **Soil:** Most soils with good drainage.
- **Propagation:** Seed or cuttings.
- **Maintenance:** Little maintenance.

POSSIBLE PROBLEMS
Cuttings are slow to root and seeds are slow to germinate.

Grows 3 to 5 feet (1 to 1.5 m) high, with equal spread. Slow to moderate growth. *C. spinosa* is a somewhat vining, sometimes spiny, deciduous shrub while *C. spinosa* 'Inermis' is evergreen and more shrubby. Both develop into gray-green mounding shrubs and each produce 2-inch (5-cm) white flowers on long stalks with showy purplish lavender stamens*. Buds picked in early stages of development can be pickled to make *capers*, a condiment. Both produce green nonedible egg-shaped fruit with tomatolike seedy pulps.

Cardiospermum halicacabum

Balloon vine, Heartseed

Sapindaceae family

COLD HARDINESS
All three zones as an annual vine. A perennial vine in low and intermediate zones that recovers from light frost.

LANDSCAPE VALUE
- Quick warm-season cover and screening for trellises, chain-link fences and other support structures that accommodate its tendril-climbing growth habit.
- Mature seed capsules make an attractive addition to the summer garden. Also used in dried-flower arrangements.

CULTURAL REQUIREMENTS
- **Exposure:** Full sun to part shade. Well adapted to heat and aridity.
- **Water:** Thoroughly soak the root zone every week or two during the period of active growth.
- **Soil:** Tolerates many soil types, but growth is faster and more lush in improved garden soil.
- **Propagation:** Seed.
- **Maintenance:** Will not climb walls. Use wire or lattice that tendrils can attach to and new growth shoots can twine around.

POSSIBLE PROBLEMS
Hard frost kills the entire plant.

To 10 feet (3 m) high, with equal spread. Rapid growth. Inflated globular seed capsules 1 inch (2.5 cm) in diameter are the most unique feature of this tropical vine. It climbs by means of tendrils. Although an evergreen perennial in warm-winter frost-free regions, it is most widely used as a herbaceous* annual or biennial. The alternating compound leaves with coarsely toothed leaflets are about 4 inches (10 cm) long. Small white flowers to 1/4 inch (.5 cm) long open in clusters throughout the warm months and produce tan-colored balloonlike fruits. Seeds are black and each has a white heart-shaped marking. Native to India, Africa and tropical America. It has naturalized in many other areas, including Florida to Texas in the United States.

* See Glossary

Carissa macrocarpa (C. grandiflora)

Natal plum

Apocynaceae family

COLD HARDINESS

Low zone and warm pockets of the intermediate zone. Recovers rapidly from freezing, but damaged wood must be removed, compromising its form and value for certain landscape uses.

LANDSCAPE VALUE

- Superb shrub for screening, banks, medians and hedging (formal and informal). Accepts shearing well.
- Large containers.

CULTURAL REQUIREMENTS

- **Exposure:** Full sun, including reflected heat to open shade.
- **Water:** Quite drought tolerant, especially after plant is established. Water every week or two during the warm season when plant is young and developing. Soak the root zone every month or two to maintain good foliage color after it fully develops.
- **Soil:** Any soil with good drainage. Tolerates high soil temperatures.
- **Propagation:** Cuttings.
- **Maintenance:** Light pruning of rangy growth will improve thickness. Takes shearing well for formal effects.

POSSIBLE PROBLEMS

- Spines on branches are a hazard when planted too close to paths and walkways.
- When planted in colder areas, frost-damaged foliage remains unsightly until new spring growth begins. Recovers rapidly in spring from a winter freeze, but appearance may be rugged during winter.

Grows 5 to 7 feet (1.5 to 2 m) high, sometimes higher, with equal spread. Moderate to rapid growth, depending on available moisture during the warm season. South African evergreen shrub with an open form that becomes a thickening mound as it matures. Lustrous, leathery bright green 3-inch (7.5-cm) oval leaves tolerate bright sun and harsh exposed locations. Fragrant five-petaled white jasminelike flowers bloom continuously over the warm season. Pink to red edible fruit follow blossoms and, because of continuous bloom, are often present at the same time as flowers. Stout spines along branches and at ends of twigs can discourage trespassers.

Cultivars* have many special uses: *C. m.* 'Boxwood Beauty' is exceptionally compact. It grows up to 2 feet high and makes an excellent small trimmed hedge. *C. m. compacta* 'Fancy' has showy large fruits and bold foliage on a large plant up to 6 feet (2 m) tall. 'Horizontalis,' a trailing and spreading groundcover, grows 1½ to 2 feet (46 to 61 cm) with dense foliage. *C. m.* 'Prostrata' can spread vigorously to 2 feet (46 cm) high, but much wider if given the space. Prune out strong, vertical shoots, which detract from its groundcover form. There are other cultivars with similar special qualities that appear in the nurseries from time to time.

* *See Glossary*

Carnegiea gigantea
Saguaro cactus
Cactaceae family

COLD HARDINESS
Low and intermediate zones. Best adapted to warm south-facing slopes at higher elevations in the intermediate zone.

LANDSCAPE VALUE
- Rugged plant of striking individuality, the saguaro lends a dramatic accent, focal point or silhouette with a strong vertical effect to the arid landscape.
- Often used as the symbol or logo for the state of Arizona.
- Hard wood midribs gathered from dead saguaros have been used for centuries by native people and early anglo settlers for fences, ramadas and ceilings.

CULTURAL REQUIREMENTS
- **Exposure:** Tenacious under hot, dry conditions. Full to reflected sun except in early stages when small plants generally are shaded by nurse shrubs or trees in their native habitat. Most eventually outgrow and dominate their protectors.
- **Water:** A remarkably drought-resistant plant. Irrigation is unnecessary except during prolonged drought in the hottest and driest desert regions.
- **Soil:** Rocky alkaline soils.
- **Propagation:** Seed. Most plants for landscapes are collected from the wild and must have approval tag.
- **Maintenance:** Dusting severed root ends of transplanted saguaros with sulfur may prevent certain root disease problems. Do not plant too deep. If planted in summer, wait two to four weeks after planting before watering. Wait until spring to water if transplanted in winter.

POSSIBLE PROBLEMS
- Bacterial necrosis is the major disease of saguaros.
- Lightning occasionally destroys saguaros during the summer rainy season.
- Heavy rains and strong winds may cause large saguaros to topple, especially when sandy soils become saturated.
- Heavy fruit crop creates some litter beneath the plant.

To 50 feet (15 m) high, spreading to 25 feet (7.5 m). Very slow growth. Arborescent upright cactus native to Arizona and Southern California and Sonora in Mexico. The massive columnar trunk may have as many as fifty branches but more commonly one to five. Both trunk and branches are conspicuously ribbed and armed with stiff straight spines. White flowers (the state flower of Arizona) at the tips of previous years' growth are nocturnal and span about 3 to 4 inches (7.5 to 10 cm). Flowers in the evening hours make a handsome display in late spring. Green oval fruits, 2 1/4 to 2 3/4 inches (5.5 to 7 cm) in diameter, split open on the plant in early summer to reveal bright red to reddish purple pulp that is edible and sweet.

* See Glossary

Carpobrotus chilensis (Mesembryanthemum chilensis)

Chilean ice plant, Pacific coast sea fig

Aizoaceae family

COLD HARDINESS

Low zone and warmer microclimates of the intermediate zone, where it may suffer frost damage during the coldest winters.

LANDSCAPE VALUE

- Flowering groundcover for lower slopes and among rocks and flat areas, but known to slide off steep slopes during heavy rains.
- Erosion control, especially in sandy soils and beachfront situations.
- Fire-retardant strip or to break adjoining, more combustible vegetation.

CULTURAL REQUIREMENTS

- **Exposure:** Full to reflected sun or part shade. Tolerates salty conditions.
- **Water:** Fleshy leaves store water and the plant can stand drought when established, but water every month for best appearance.
- **Soil:** Well-drained soil, preferably of low to medium fertility.
- **Propagation:** Stem sections or cuttings.
- **Maintenance:** Bare spots in mature plantings may require replanting from time to time. It does reseed in its native habitat, but elsewhere replant bare spots with stem sections and cuttings.

POSSIBLE PROBLEMS

- A fungus disease causes die-back*.
- Rabbits eat the plants, especially during drought.
- Aggressive roots compete with roots of trees and shrubs planted in the same area. Plan to water and feed such plants to compensate.
- Does not withstand foot traffic.

To 6 inches (15 cm) or higher, spreading 6 feet (2 m) or more. Rapid growth with adequate water. Creeping perennial evergreen succulent that is native to the Pacific coast, from Oregon to Baja California and Chile. Three-angled fleshy leaves 3 to 4 inches (7.5 to 10 cm) long grow in clusters along prostrate woody stems. Roots develop along the trailing branches as they extend, a valuable trait for binding to sandy soils. Solitary terminal* flowers are slightly fragrant, rosy purple to pinkish and 3 inches (7.5 cm) in diameter. They appear in summer and can be quite showy at times. An attractive, somewhat less coarse succulent than its African relative *C. edulis.*

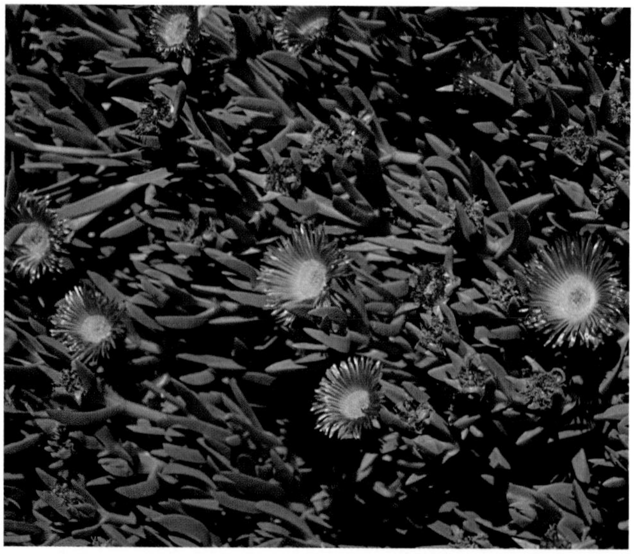

* See Glossary

Carpobrotus edulis (Mesembryanthemum edulis)

Sea fig, Hotentot fig

Aizoaceae family

COLD HARDINESS

Low zone and intermediate zone, where it is sometimes damaged by frost.

LANDSCAPE VALUE

- An attractive, but somewhat coarse, quick-spreading groundcover for disturbed areas, especially sandy places.
- Best near the sea, but makes a reasonable though not particularly long-lived groundcover for interior arid regions, too.

CULTURAL REQUIREMENTS

- **Exposure:** Full sun to part shade.
- **Water:** Leaves have great water-storage capacity but groundcover plantings need water every month or two for good appearance. Requires more water in hot interior regions than near the sea.
- **Soil:** Any soil with drainage (especially in sand) and some depth. Some fertilization in poor soil will maintain vigor and cover.
- **Propagation:** Cuttings (will root soon after planting).
- **Maintenance:** Occasionally refurbish bare spots that occur in mature plantings from time to time.

POSSIBLE PROBLEMS

- Does not tolerate foot traffic and is therefore hard to weed.
- Roots are efficient water- and nutrient-seekers and often starve and stunt adjoining plantings.
- Should not be used as cover for steep slopes. During heavy rains, large areas of groundcover have been known to slide off banks after plants have become heavy with moisture.
- Old plantings may be disfigured by brown bare spots; in some cases a fungus disease is responsible.
- Rabbits will eat the plant in exposed places, especially during dry periods.

Grows 9 to 12 inches (23 to 30.5 cm) high and 6 feet (2 m) wide. A single plant can develop into a large patch, rooting as it spreads. Rapid growth. Evergreen succulent groundcover from Cape Province, South Africa, with thick, juicy three-sided leaves. Single sea-anemonelike flowers in shades of pale yellow to pinkish purple, up to 4 inches (10 cm) in diameter, appear in summer followed by edible but not very tasty fruits. Vigorous spreading by long runners*, which develop long wiry roots from stems as they trail.

* *See Glossary*

CASSIA

The genus *Cassia* is a large clan of leguminous plants that includes many useful and colorful trees and shrubs for arid-region landscapes. At one time, botanists placed many species in the genus *Senna*, then changed them to *Cassia*. Currently, the process is being reversed and many, especially those from the Australian deserts, are moving back to *Senna* classification. We list the old name under *Cassia* and refer to the new classification and description under *Senna*. This seems to be an ongoing move: Many species still listed under *Cassia* will eventually be renamed as *Senna*.

Cassia excelsa

Crown of gold tree

Fabaceae (Leguminosae) family

COLD HARDINESS

Low zone and warm-winter microclimates of the intermediate zone. Mature specimens can endure a brief period of subfreezing temperatures without injury, but young trees are more sensitive to cold and frost.

LANDSCAPE VALUE

Radiant color display when in full bloom. An exceptional flowering accent or specimen tree for

- Residential gardens.
- Golf courses.
- Commercial sites.

CULTURAL REQUIREMENTS

- **Exposure:** Full sun.
- **Water:** Thoroughly soak the root zone every week or two during the period of active growth, every month or two for the rest of the year.
- **Soil:** Most soils with good drainage.
- **Propagation:** Seed.
- **Maintenance:** For continued heavy flowering, prune terminal* branches back to a side bud at the end of the bloom season.

POSSIBLE PROBLEMS

Heavy seed-pod production creates litter in the fall and is not attractive.

Grows 20 to 30 feet (6 to 9 m) high, with equal spread. Moderate to rapid growth with regular irrigation during the growing season. One of the yellow-flowered *Cassia* trees, this species from Argentina retains at least some green foliage throughout the year. The pinnately* compound leaves with ten to twenty pairs of oblong leaflets to 1½ inches (4 cm) long grow on twigs and branchlets covered with soft fine hairs. Clusters of fragrant bright yellow flowers open over a long period but the big show is usually in late summer or early fall. Leathery brown pods that are about 6 inches (15 cm) long and ½ inch (1 cm) in diameter follow as plant matures.

Cassia fistula

Golden shower tree

Fabaceae (Leguminosae) family

COLD HARDINESS

Completely or almost frost-free microclimates in the low and intermediate zones. May be severely damaged or killed by hard frosts.

LANDSCAPE VALUE

- True to its common name, this refined and elegant tree puts on an arresting color display during the late spring or summer bloom season. It serves as a choice flowering accent or specimen tree for residential and commercial landscapes, parks, medians and roadside plantings.
- The handsome foliage also provides dappled shade for patios and other outdoor living areas.

CULTURAL REQUIREMENTS

- **Exposure:** Full sun to part shade. Heat tolerant, but avoid sites exposed to strong drying winds. Not a tree for ocean-front plantings, but endures salt air in inland areas beyond the beach.
- **Water:** Established trees can tolerate periods of drought but perform best with a thorough soaking of the root zone every week or two during the summer growing season. Water every month or two for the remainder of the year.
- **Soil:** Grows well in many soil types.
- **Propagation:** Seed.
- **Maintenance:** Flower buds are produced on one-year-old wood. Prune at the end of the current bloom season to promote heavier flowering the next year.

POSSIBLE PROBLEMS

Seed pods not particularly attractive and may produce litter.

Grows 20 to 30 feet (6 to 9 m) high, spreading 15 to 25 feet (4.5 to 7.5 m). Moderate to rapid growth with enough water. Small to medium-size tree that is evergreen in tropical climates but sheds some or most of its foliage where winters are cooler. The open, oval or rounded canopy is formed by long, slender branches that often weep near the tips. Pinnately* compound leaves 6 to 12 inches (15 to 30.5 cm) long are divided into four to eight pairs of glossy 4-inch (10-cm) long leaflets. The clear yellow fragrant flowers have five petals and open in large hanging clusters 12 to 18 inches (30.5 to 46 cm) long during late spring or summer. These are replaced by black cylindrical bean pods less than 1 inch (2.5 cm) in diameter but as long as 2 feet (61 cm). Young trees bloom at an early age and often produce a scattering of flower clusters the first or second year after they are planted in the landscape. Native to India.

* *See Glossary*

Casuarina cunninghamiana

River she oak, Australian pine
Casuarinaceae family

COLD HARDINESS
Low and intermediate zones.

LANDSCAPE VALUE
- Magnificent skyline silhouette.
- Reforesting tree.
- Single or grove planting.

CULTURAL REQUIREMENTS
- **Exposure:** Full sun. Tolerates exposed situations. Good for brackish saline conditions.
- **Water:** Drought resistant but not quite as drought resistant as *C. stricta*. Thoroughly soak the root zone every month or two.
- **Soil:** Tolerates most soils and performs wet or dry, but needs soil depth.
- **Propagation:** Seed.
- **Maintenance:** Do not plant in small spaces.

POSSIBLE PROBLEMS
- Heavy foliage drop, which makes a thatch under trees, may be objectionable.
- Can be invasive in high-rainfall areas, such as regions in Florida.

Grows 60 to 70 feet (18 to 21.5 m) high, spreading 30 to 35 feet (9 to 11 m). Moderate to rapid growth. Evergreen tree from Australia; tallest of the *Casuarina* clan. Foliage consists of clusters of jointed stems that resemble pine needles. That and little conelike woody fruits give rise to the common name of the entire genus, Australian pine. Certainly the distant view and skyline effect are similar to others of the same genus.

Casuarina equisetifolia

Horsetail tree, Australian pine
Casuarinaceae family

COLD HARDINESS
Low zone and warm microclimates of intermediate zone. Withstands light frost.

LANDSCAPE VALUE
- Windbreak and screen.
- Buffer or barrier plantings.
- Large sheared hedge.
- Street tree.
- Stabilizes sand dunes.

CULTURAL REQUIREMENTS
- **Exposure:** Full or reflected sun to part shade. Grows well in both coastal and arid inland environments. Accepts salt spray.
- **Water:** Drought resistant when established but looks best with soakings of the root zone every month or two.
- **Soil:** Highly tolerant of salty conditions and poor soils, except heavy clay soils. Takes extremes of dry or wet planting sites.
- **Propagation:** Seed.
- **Maintenance:** Prune as needed for a neater appearance in tailored landscapes.

POSSIBLE PROBLEMS
- Damaged by hard frosts.
- Fallen branchlet debris creates considerable litter.
- Aggressive roots compete for water and nutrients and may restrict the growth of nearby plants.
- Under favorable (wet) conditions, may become invasive and displace native vegetation.

Grows 40 to 65 feet (12 to 20 m) high, spreading 20 to 30 feet (6 to 9 m). Rapid growth. This upright to spreading evergreen tree derives its two common names from the almost pine-needlelike leaves, which are actually jointed branchlets. These hang in plumy brushes reminiscent of the horsetail rush, *Equisetum hyemaliae*. The overall effect of the tree canopy is feathery and open. The 1/2- to 3/4-inch (1- to 2-cm) dry fruits look like tiny pine cones. Native to southeast Asia, Australia.

Casuarina stricta
Coast beefwood, She oak
Casuarinaceae family

COLD HARDINESS
Low and intermediate zones.

LANDSCAPE VALUE
- Specimen.
- Parks.
- Buffers.
- Streets and medians.
- Skyline silhouette.
- Large sheared hedge.
- Replant disturbed sites.

CULTURAL REQUIREMENTS
- **Exposure:** Tolerates heat, intense sun and some frost.
- **Water:** Drought resistant. Maintain with water only once or twice during long dry periods. Appearance is significantly improved, however, by soakings of the root zone every month or two.
- **Soil:** Tolerates poor soil.
- **Propagation:** Seed.
- **Maintenance:** Prune as needed for tree health and appearance.

POSSIBLE PROBLEMS
Brittle wood—where prevailing winds are strong, tree canopy will be irregular and contorted because of broken branches.

Grows 25 to 35 feet (7.5 to 11 m) high, spreading 20 to 25 feet (6 to 7.5 m). Rapid growth.Evergreen tree of upright, slender, sometimes irregular form. Native to Australia. Open feathery canopy of fine-textured branchlets is darker green than *C. equisetifolia.* Female trees bear pine-cone-shaped woody fruits to 2½ inches (6.5 cm) long.

Ceiba aesculifolia (C. acuminata)
Silk cotton tree
Bombacaceae family

COLD HARDINESS
Low zone and warm microclimates of intermediate zone.

LANDSCAPE VALUE
- Unique accent and silhouette tree.
- The straight trunk creates a strong vertical element in the landscape.
- The large thorns of the trunk and side branches create an interesting patterned look during the dormant season.

CULTURAL REQUIREMENTS
- **Exposure:** Full sun.
- **Water:** Endures complete drought in winter but needs water every week or two for good development and appearance in summer.
- **Soil:** Any soil with depth and good drainage.
- **Propagation:** Seed.
- **Maintenance:** May need to remove frost-damaged thorny twigs and branches.

POSSIBLE PROBLEMS
Difficult to prune, especially after frost damage in borderline areas.

Grows 40 to 45 feet (12 to 13.5 m) high, spreading 20 to 30 feet (6 to 9 m). Rapid growth. Deciduous tree. Sturdy trunk is armed with interesting thick cone-shaped spines, enough to discourage any cat (or monkey) from climbing up. Late to leaf out. With summer rains it becomes a tropical green column in the thorn-scrub forest that edges the Sonoran Desert of Sonora, Mexico. Blooms in winter with large silky white blossoms among the bare branches. Elongated melonlike fruits filled with cottony airborne brown seeds follow bloom.

* See Glossary

Celtis pallida

Desert hackberry
Ulmaceae family

COLD HARDINESS

All three zones, although leaves will turn brown and drop during cold winters in high zone.

LANDSCAPE VALUE

- Large screening shrub.
- Space definer.
- Barrier plant.
- Takes shaping well and can be trimmed up to make a small patio-size tree.
- Erosion control and revegetation.

CULTURAL REQUIREMENTS

- **Exposure:** Full sun to part shade.
- **Water:** Thoroughly soak the root zone every month or two to ensure good appearance.
- **Soil:** Most soils.
- **Propagation:** Seed. Probably rooted cuttings.
- **Maintenance:** Requires little attention other than pruning when you want a special shape, such as a tree form.

POSSIBLE PROBLEMS

Thorny branches make shaping difficult.

Grows 10 to 16 feet (3 to 5 m) high, spreading 8 to 10 feet (2.5 to 3 m). Moderate growth rate. Thorny evergreen shrub with small dark green leaves. This is usually a dense twiggy plant with foliage to the ground but occasionally grows as a small multistemmed tree. Produces tiny edible orange fruits in fall. These are sweet to the taste and an attraction for birds. Native to the U.S. Southwest and northern Mexico.

Celtis reticulata (C. douglasii)

Western hackberry, Net-leaf hackberry
Ulmaceae family

COLD HARDINESS

Native to intermediate and high zone but will grow well in low zone.

LANDSCAPE VALUE

- Residential or woody plantings in parks and school yards.
- Provides winter sun and summer shade.
- It naturally takes twisting irregular form, which is especially interesting in winter.

CULTURAL REQUIREMENTS

- **Exposure:** Full sun.
- **Water:** Water every week or two. Also performs well with a thorough soaking of the root zone every month or two.
- **Soil:** Deep moist soil.
- **Propagation:** Seed or cuttings.
- **Maintenance:** Stake and prune young trees to develop a better form or a shade tree.

POSSIBLE PROBLEMS

- Erratic growth habit creates training problems, especially when young.
- Reseeds and comes up where not wanted.

Grows 20 to 30 feet (6 to 9 m) high, spreading to 30 feet (9 m). Moderate to rapid growth. A sprawling deciduous tree, sometimes with pendulous branches. Small dark green 2½-inch (6.5-cm) long leaves resemble foliage of the Siberian elm (*Ulmus pumila*). Birds relish the tiny red berries. Nubby protrusions develop on otherwise smooth gray bark. Native to Arizona.

* *See Glossary*

Centaurea cineraria (C. gymnocarpa)

Dusty miller, Cutleaf dusty miller

Asteraceae (Compositae) family

COLD HARDINESS

All three zones.

LANDSCAPE VALUE

- Rich foliage texture and color and compact growth habit make this an excellent bedding plant in transition and oasis irrigation zones.
- Low border or in rock gardens.
- Containers.
- Small area groundcover.

CULTURAL REQUIREMENTS

- **Exposure:** Full sun, high heat and low humidity.
- **Water:** Reasonably drought resistant, but water every week or two. Allow soil to dry somewhat between irrigation.
- **Soil:** Most soils with good drainage.
- **Propagation:** Seed or cuttings.
- **Maintenance:** Because plants tend to become leggy over time, trim back at the end of the bloom season. To create and maintain a uniform low groundcover, set plants close together and trim or shear as needed.

POSSIBLE PROBLEMS

Flowers attract bees.

Grows 1 to 3 feet (30.5 to 1 m) high, with equal spread. Moderate growth rate. Several plants have the common name dusty miller because of their shared characteristic of whitish or silvery foliage. The species described here, a perennial from southern Europe, produces a dense clump of narrow leaves up to 12 inches (30.5 cm) long with rounded lobes. A dense mat of woolly whitish hairs gives the plant a soft, silvery gray appearance. In summer, solitary purple or yellow 1-inch (2.5-cm) flower heads are borne on erect stems. Spreads only about a foot, in contrast to *C. gymnocarpa*, which may spread as much as 3 feet.

C. gymnocarpa (cutleaf dusty miller) has velvety white 8-inch (20.5-cm) leaves that are more fine textured than that of *C. cineraria* and the plant grows dense and shrubby. Violet or purple flower heads about 1½ inches (4 cm) across open in groups of two or three at the tips of leafy stems. Native to Capri.

Cephalophyllum aestonii 'Red Spike' (Cylindrophyllum speciosum)

Red spike ice plant

Aizoaceae family

COLD HARDINESS

Low and intermediate zones. Moderately frost tolerant.

LANDSCAPE VALUE

- Neat, small perennial succulent. Extremely showy during its bloom period.
- Foliage texture provides year-round interest.
- Groundcover in small or narrow spaces, but not effective for erosion control on slopes.
- Containers (often used as an underplanting for larger container plants).

CULTURAL REQUIREMENTS

- **Exposure:** Full sun to part shade.
- **Water:** Drought tolerant, but water every month or two to maintain desired growth and flowering.
- **Soil:** Adapted to most soils.
- **Propagation:** Seed or division of clumps.
- **Maintenance:** Little maintenance except to occasionally add a few new plants. Plant at close intervals if growing a groundcover.

POSSIBLE PROBLEMS

- Rabbits love it.
- Cannot withstand foot traffic, so unsuitable for large areas where weeding without walking on the plant would be impossible.

Grows 3 to 5 inches (7.5 to 13 cm) high, spreading 15 to 18 inches (38 to 46 cm). Slow growth. Dwarf evergreen succulent native to South Africa. A slow-spreading clump of upright, pointed cylindrical leaves are gray-green, sometimes with a reddish cast. In late winter to early spring, brilliant red flowers up to 2 inches (5 cm) across transform the plant into a mound of eye-catching color. Sporadic flowering may occur at other times of the year.

* See Glossary

Ceratonia siliqua
Carob
Fabaceae (Leguminosae) family

COLD HARDINESS
Low and intermediate zones.

LANDSCAPE VALUE
- Street tree.
- Shade tree for wide lawns or parks.
- Hedge or wide screen if allowed to grow as a large shrub.

CULTURAL REQUIREMENTS
- **Exposure:** Full or reflected sun to part shade.
- **Water:** Drought tolerant. Tolerates considerable water stress as an established plant but is at its best with thorough soakings of the root zone every month or two.
- **Soil:** Deep fertile soil. Intolerant of heavy, wet soil types.
- **Propagation:** Seed.
- **Maintenance:** Stake and prune if you want a tree. Selectively thin branches to prevent damage in windy locations.

POSSIBLE PROBLEMS
- Bean pod, flower and foliage drop create considerable litter.
- Large roots near base of trunk buckle nearby pavement in narrow planting spaces.
- Subject to several diseases, including Texas root rot*, verticilium wilt*, sooty canker, crown rot and nematodes*.
- Young trees are frost sensitive.
- Flowers on male trees produce an odor that some find unpleasant.

Grows 30 to 40 feet (9 to 12 m) high, with equal spread. Moderate growth rate. Evergreen tree from the Mediterranean region. Pinnately* compound leaves of the dense, rounded, symmetrical crown are divided into four to ten glossy dark green leaflets up to 2 inches (5 cm) long. In nature, grows as a large multistemmed shrub, but in a landscape, carob is more often trained as a tree with a single trunk. The small clusters of pink-yellow to red flowers on trunks and branches are male or female and occur on separate plants; female trees produce flattened leathery pods 1 inch (2.5 cm) wide and up to 1 foot (30.5 cm) long. Pods are dark brown at maturity and may be ground into a powder for use as a chocolate substitute. The sweet-tasting leathery pods are considered a treat by the children of the Mediterranean area.

* *See Glossary*

CERCIDIUM

Cercidium species include a number of useful desert trees and shrubs. Their common name, palo verde, which translates as "green stick" from Spanish, is an indication of their smooth green bark. Aside from being some of the most drought-tolerant trees on the arid plant palette, they produce an outstanding color show when in bloom, ranging from almost white to deep yellow, depending on the species. The species listed here are all native to the Sonoran and Mojave Deserts, except for *C. praecox glaucum*, which is from Argentina. Some species in the Chihuahuan Desert are small shrubby bushes without landscape potential.

Cercidium floridum floridum (C. torreyanum)

Blue palo verde

Fabaceae (Leguminosae) family

Grows 15 to 30 feet (4.5 to 9 m) high, with equal spread. Slow to moderate growth, depending on water supply. Rounded and low-branched deciduous tree native to the Sonoran and Mojave Deserts of Arizona and southern California in the United States and Sonora, northern Sinaloa and Baja California in Mexico. Dense-growing, spiny twigs, branches and trunks are a distinctive blue-green color; the lower trunk on older trees is gray. Fine-textured foliage is deciduous in dry and cold spells. The tree may be leafless most of the year, but the greenness of twigs and branches give it an evergreen appearance. Masses of fragrant bright yellow pea-shaped flowers literally overlay the entire tree in spring; these give way to 1½- to 3-inch (4- to 7.5-cm) long bean pods that are flat and constricted at intervals.

COLD HARDINESS

Low and intermediate zones and warmer locations in high zone. Moderately frost tolerant.

LANDSCAPE VALUE

- Picturesque beauty and charm when in full bloom.
- Stunning spring color accent or specimen tree for streets and parks.
- Privacy screens, medians and buffer zones.
- Train as a small tree for filtered shade over patios.

CULTURAL REQUIREMENTS

- **Exposure:** A tree of remarkable durability. Withstands great heat and intense reflected sun.
- **Water:** Drought tolerant once established, but being native to desert washes, trees need a thorough soaking of the root zone once or twice during the warm season. Young trees benefit from irrigation every month or two until large enough to serve the intended function. Most tolerant species of palo verde for lawn and other regularly irrigated situations.
- **Soil:** Tolerates alkaline soils but also adapts to lawns.
- **Propagation:** Seed.
- **Maintenance:** To train as a small tree, gradually remove lower branches over a period of several years. It is usually necessary to remove low-growing branches once or twice each year if you want an above-the-head canopy.

POSSIBLE PROBLEMS

- Fallen flowers and bean pods create litter.
- Small thorns on twigs and branches may be a hazard.
- Root borer*, mistletoe and witches' broom caused by gall mites are the most serious pest problems encountered in its native regions.

Cercidium floridum peninsularis

Baja Peninsula palo verde

Fabaceae (Leguminosae) family

COLD HARDINESS

Low and intermediate zones.

LANDSCAPE VALUE

Round-headed patio-size shade tree that holds its leaves.

CULTURAL REQUIREMENTS

- **Exposure:** Full sun. Very heat resistant.
- **Water:** Drought tolerant. Thoroughly soak the root zone once or twice a season.
- **Soil:** Prefers sandy, gravelly soils but will grow in any soil.
- **Propagation:** Seed.
- **Maintenance:** No maintenance except staking and trimming off lower branches to develop a patio-size tree.

POSSIBLE PROBLEMS

Same as blue palo verde (*C. floridum floridum*).

Grows 18 to 25 feet (5.5 to 7.5 m) high, spreading to 20 feet (6 m). Moderate growth rate. Round-headed tree similar to the blue palo verde (*C. floridum floridum*) except it maintains foliage all year. A profusely leafy appearance. Spring flowers are yellow but as yet the tree has failed to produce the complete yellow floral display that the blue palo verde is known for. Blue-green bark and twigs. Native to southern Baja California.

* *See Glossary*

Cercidium microphyllum

Littleleaf palo verde, Foothills palo verde

Fabaceae (Leguminosae) family

COLD HARDINESS

Low and intermediate zone and into high zone. Frost tolerant.

LANDSCAPE VALUE

- Specimen with unique form that can be pruned to expose its attractive structure.
- Background.
- Screen.
- Spring color.
- Dry sites in public, commercial and residential landscapes.

CULTURAL REQUIREMENTS

- **Exposure:** Well-adapted to deserts, withstanding heat and intense sun.
- **Water:** Established trees survive without supplemental water except in low-rainfall regions where water every month or two maintains acceptable appearance and encourages more rapid growth of young landscape specimens. Does not tolerate lawn or other well-watered situations.
- **Soil:** Most soils with good drainage.
- **Propagation:** Seed.
- **Maintenance:** Prune occasionally to remove dead branches, mistletoe and witches' broom or to improve or expose form.

POSSIBLE PROBLEMS

- Heavy seed-pod litter.
- Palo verde root borer*, mistletoe and witches' broom.
- During prolonged drought, tree may shed some of its branches.
- Unirrigated trees grow very slowly.
- Existing native trees on a site may decline or die when nearby plants receive regular irrigation.

Grows 10 to 20 feet (3 to 6 m) high, with equal spread. Slow growth. A small short-trunked deciduous tree with ascending branches and a dense, spreading crown of spiny twigs. Tiny leaflets and smooth bark have the characteristic yellow-green color. Foliage is present only for a short time following rain. In spite of this, the twigs give a year-round green effect. Pale-yellow flowers have a delicate fragrance and appear briefly in mid to late spring following the usual bloom period of *C. floridum*. Bloom is prolific some years, usually following wet winters, but sparse in others. Bean pods 1½ to 3 inches (4 to 7.5 cm) long get narrower between seeds and taper toward both ends. Native to Mojave and Sonoran Deserts of Arizona and Southern California in the United States and deserts of Sonora and Baja California in Mexico.

Cercidium praecox glaucum

Argentine palo brea

Fabaceae (Leguminosae) family

COLD HARDINESS

Low and intermediate zones.

LANDSCAPE VALUE

- Shade tree.
- Median or street tree.
- Specimen or flowering accent.
- Trunk and twig color provide a special note in the landscape.

CULTURAL REQUIREMENTS

- **Exposure:** Full sun, reflected heat to part shade.
- **Water:** Needs no supplemental irrigation in regions of 5 inches (130 mm) or more rainfall. Develops faster and looks better with thorough soaking of the root zone every month or two during the warm season.
- **Soil:** Any soil.
- **Propagation:** Seed.
- **Maintenance:** No maintenance except to trim lower branches and stake to develop a patio-size tree.

POSSIBLE PROBLEMS

None observed.

To 20 feet (6 m) high, with equal spread. Slow to moderate growth, depending on moisture. Medium-size open-structured tree from the Argentine desert closely resembles the palo brea from Sonora, Mexico. Limited observation under cultivation shows it is more distinctly winter-deciduous. The Mexican native remains evergreen under optimum conditions. It is suspected that the Argentine native is completely cold hardy in the intermediate zone, while the Sonoran palo brea is not and has experienced minor to severe damage in freeze years.

* See Glossary

Cercidium praecox praecox

Sonoran palo verde, Palo brea

Fabaceae (Leguminosae) family

COLD HARDINESS

Low zone and protected microclimates of intermediate zone. Sensitive to hard frost, which causes some branch die-back*.

LANDSCAPE VALUE

Same as *Cercidium praecox glaucum.*

CULTURAL REQUIREMENTS

- **Exposure:** Full to reflected sun.
- **Water:** Water every month or two until established and of functional size; then water only during long droughts.
- **Soil:** Adapted to and tolerant of a wide range of soils.
- **Propagation:** Seed.
- **Maintenance:** Prune to maintain tree form and balanced branching structure.

POSSIBLE PROBLEMS

- Seed-pod litter.
- Low-hanging spiny branches are a hazard in foot-traffic areas.
- Young trees vulnerable to rabbit damage.
- Young trees vulnerable to frost damage in some locations.

Grows 15 to 30 feet (4.5 to 9 m) high, spreading 15 to 25 feet (4.5 to 7.5 m). Moderate to rapid growth. A handsome desert tree. Native from Sonora and Baja California in Mexico to Peru and Venezuela. Characterized by a short trunk, long upright, angular branches and a dense rounded canopy of spiny twigs. The lime green color of the bark adds considerable landscape interest. Foliage is slightly larger and more lush than that of *C. floridum* and appears in spring at about the same time as when the golden yellow flowers open. Seed pods are more or less oblong and 2 to 3 inches (5 to 7.5 cm) in length with no constriction between seeds.

Cercidium sonorae (C. microphyllum X C. praecox)

Hybrid Sonoran palo verde

Fabaceae (Leguminosae) family

COLD HARDINESS

Low and intermediate zones. Moderately frost tolerant.

LANDSCAPE VALUE

- Small median tree.
- Specimen or flowering accent.
- Privacy screen or buffer.
- Border for dust and wind control.
- Good patio tree for small properties.

CULTURAL REQUIREMENTS

- **Exposure:** Full to reflected sun.
- **Water:** Low water use once established. Requires water once or twice a season during severe droughts or in low-rainfall regions.
- **Soil:** Grows well in most arid-climate soils.
- **Propagation:** Seed may reproduce the hybrid.
- **Maintenance:** Careful and selective pruning ensures that young trees develop a strong, well-proportioned branching structure.

POSSIBLE PROBLEMS

- Not widely available because of lack of reliable propagation techniques.
- Seed pods create litter.

Grows 10 to 20 feet (3 to 6 m) high, with equal spread. Slow to moderate growth. A natural hybrid palo verde from Sonora, Mexico. The rounded form, dark blue-green bark and abundant display of yellow flowers in midspring make a valuable contribution to the arid landscape. The spiny twigs and branching habit are similar to *C. praecox*, but trunks and twigs are a darker green. As with other palo verdes described, the foliage is cold- and drought-deciduous. Small rounded leaflets emerge in spring at the same time as the flowers. The 1½- to 3-inch (4- to 7.5-cm) long seed pods are more narrow between seeds and taper gradually at each end.

* *See Glossary*

Cercis canadensis mexicana

Mexican redbud

Fabaceae (Leguminosae) family

COLD HARDINESS

All three zones.

LANDSCAPE VALUE

- Evokes a woodsy quality.
- Vibrant purplish spring color and leaves that turn a golden yellow in fall add color interest.

CULTURAL REQUIREMENTS

- **Exposure:** Full sun to part shade.
- **Water:** Drought resistant. Soak the root zone every month or two once established.
- **Soil:** Tolerates poor or rocky soil with good drainage.
- **Propagation:** Seed.
- **Maintenance:** Little required.

POSSIBLE PROBLEMS

Heavy seed production can be unattractive and creates litter.

To 15 feet (4.5 m) high, with equal spread. Slow to moderate growth. Large, attractive deciduous shrub with dark green heart-shaped leaves. Can become a multistemmed small tree under favorable conditions. Small pinkish purple flowers sprout along bare twigs and branches in a colorful display just before new spring leaves appear. Produces abundant brown bean pods. Native to washes* at the edge of the Chihuahuan Desert in Texas and northern Mexico. A purple-leafed form is available.

Note: The *C. canadensis* found in the eastern United States was brought to the desert Southwest by early anglo settlers and seems to do well in urban situations, becoming a much larger tree than *C. c. mexicana.*

Cercis occidentalis

Western redbud

Fabaceae (Leguminosae) family

COLD HARDINESS

All three zones.

LANDSCAPE VALUE

- Attractive single- or multistem patio tree when trimmed up.
- Dry, woodsy plant compositions, especially for spring-flower and fall-foliage color.
- Shade tree in lawns and other wet situations.

CULTURAL REQUIREMENTS

- **Exposure:** Reflected sun to open shade.
- **Water:** Drought resistant. Water every week or two for the first few years to speed its growth and development. Once established, soak the root zone every month or two. If arranged permanently, such as in a lawn, plant will respond to weekly irrigation, even when mature.
- **Soil:** Any soil with good drainage except high alkaline or saline soils.
- **Propagation:** Seed.
- **Maintenance:** Little maintenance. To encourage tree form, prune lower branches and stake.

POSSIBLE PROBLEMS

None observed.

Grows 10 to 20 feet (3 to 6 m) high. Usually grows a clump that spreads 10 to 18 feet (3 to 5.5m), but can grow as a single tree with an 18-foot (5.5-m) spread and no side branches below head height. Moderate growth rate that can be increased with good horticultural practices (extra water, pruning and fertilizing). Interesting small deciduous tree, usually multitrunked from the base. Blossoms in early spring with a display of 1/2-inch (1-cm) wide magenta pea-shaped blossoms that line twigs and even the trunks. Flowers are followed by 3-inch (7.5-cm) blue-green heart-shaped leaves notched at the tip or rounded. Interspersed are newly forming seed pods, also brilliant magenta. This tree can be counted on for year-round interest because its foliage turns light yellow to bright red in fall and the interesting bare-branched structure is festooned with reddish brown seed pods in winter. Native to dry foothills of California, Arizona and Utah below 4,000 feet (1,220 m).

* See Glossary

Cercocarpus betuloides

Birch-leaf mountain mahogany, Mountain ironwood
Rosaceae family

COLD HARDINESS
All three zones but native to high zone. Probably less tolerant of summer heat in intermediate zone and not a good choice for low zone.

LANDSCAPE VALUE
- Massed in a large shrubbery composition.
- Trained into a patio-size tree, single- or multitrunk.
- Grouping multitrunked trees creates an attractive bosque* or woodsy effect.

CULTURAL REQUIREMENTS
- **Exposure:** Full sun to part shade.
- **Water:** Drought resistant once established. Water developing plants every week or two during spring and summer, especially in the low zone.
- **Soil:** Well-drained soil. Not particular otherwise—native to poor soil and rocky slopes.
- **Propagation:** Not much propagation work has been done on *Cercocarpus* species because they have been largely overlooked. Will grow from seed or probably root easily from cuttings.
- **Maintenance:** Little maintenance. Prune lower branches and stake to encourage tree form.

POSSIBLE PROBLEMS
None observed.

Grows 10 to 20 feet (3 to 6 m) high, spreading to 15 feet (4.5 m). Moderate growth rate. Evergreen shrub or small tree native to dry foothills of the West, from south Oregon to northern Baja California and the limited chaparral areas of Arizona. Makes an attractive small tree or shrub with spreading crown and arching open branching stucture. Small wedge-shaped leaves cluster on short spurs. They are leathery, veined, dark green above, pale beneath, and have toothed edges. Like most of its numerous relatives, the fall fruit is especially interesting because of the feathery plumes that persist for some time, adding a sparkle in the sunlight. Flowers are small and inconspicuous.

Cereus peruvianus and *C. peruvianus* 'Monstrosus'

Peruvian apple, Monstrous Peruvian cereus
Cactaceae family

COLD HARDINESS
Low zone and more-protected microclimates of intermediate zone. Hard frost results in stem die-back*.

LANDSCAPE VALUE
- A different and picturesque container plant.
- A specimen or accent.

CULTURAL REQUIREMENTS
- **Exposure:** Full sun or part shade.
- **Water:** Water every month or two. Water container plants only when the soil is thoroughly dry.
- **Soil:** Avoid heavy, slow-draining soils.
- **Propagation:** Seed or cuttings.
- **Maintenance:** No maintenance except possibly removing some branches to enhance a specimen.

POSSIBLE PROBLEMS
Tender to hard frost.

To 20 feet (6 m) or higher, spreading to 15 feet (4.5 m) or more. Slow to moderate growth. Branching, shrubby or treelike cactus native to southeastern South America. The ribbed cylindrical branches are first deep green, becoming gray-green as they mature and reaching a diameter of 4 inches (10 cm). Armed with needle-shaped spines as long as 2 inches (5 cm). White funnel-shaped flowers up to 7 inches (18 cm) long and 5 inches (13 cm) in diameter are faintly fragrant, opening at night during the summer months. The variety 'Monstrosus' (common name monstrous Peruvian cereus) is slower growing and smaller at maturity, to 10 feet (3 m) high. Conspicuous for the bizarre bumps and knobs that cover the stems. It can develop into a unique specimen with considerable interest, but it will often appear deformed and unattractive.

* *See Glossary*

Chamaerops humilis

Mediterranean fan palm

Arecarceae (Palmae) family

COLD HARDINESS

Low and intermediate zones and warm microclimates of the high zone. One of the most cold-hardy palms, it withstands moderate to hard frost.

LANDSCAPE VALUE

- Appealing shrubby palm when young.
- Effective alone or in groups.
- Often placed at the base of taller palms.
- A dependable, attractive container subject.
- A fascinating and unusual multitrunked specimen plant when mature.

CULTURAL REQUIREMENTS

- **Exposure:** Full sun or part shade.
- **Water:** Soaking of the root zone every month or two is adequate for survival of established plants, but more frequent irrigation promotes better foliage and performance, especially in the hottest, driest months.
- **Soil:** Improved garden soil for best results
- **Propagation:** Seeds.
- **Maintenance:** Some removal of unwanted shoots may be necessary to develop the unique character of a specimen.

POSSIBLE PROBLEMS

- Palm-heart rot can occasionally attack but this is rare.
- Thorny petioles* inhibit grooming.

Grows 5 to 15 feet (1.5 to 4.5 m) high, spreading 5 to 20 feet (1.5 to 6 m). Slow growth. Small, compact multistemmed fan palm in youth; at maturity, the green to blue-green fronds cluster in a dense head at the top of each arching trunk. Spiny leaf petioles. Produces clusters of reddish-brown fruit 1/2 inch (1 cm) in diameter. From Mediterranean region, Europe and North Africa.

* See Glossary

Chilopsis linearis arcuata and C. linearis linearis

Western desert willow, Eastern desert willow, Texas or Chihuahuan desert willow

Bignoniaceae family

COLD HARDINESS

All three zones.

LANDSCAPE VALUE

- The graceful willowy character of this small tree along with its profuse and long-lasting bloom period make it a choice addition to the small-tree list.
- Shade tree, street tree.
- In parks, medians, buffer zones and roadside plantings.
- Appealing in group plantings.
- Attracts birds.

CULTURAL REQUIREMENTS

- **Exposure:** Full to reflected sun.
- **Water:** Requires little water, but water every month or two will considerably improve the performance of established plants. Water more often to develop it into a patio-size tree.
- **Soil:** Most soils with good drainage.
- **Propagation:** Seed, cuttings, layering, budding or grafting.
- **Maintenance:** A cold-hardy low-maintenance plant. May require pruning occasionally for shaping and general appearance.

POSSIBLE PROBLEMS

- Some seed-pod litter.
- Volunteer seedlings can be numerous and invasive.
- Less attractive in winter than some other arid landscape trees because of the heavy crop of straw-colored seed capsules that hang on the bare tree all winter; less a problem with the almost-evergreen type and certain other selections.

Grows 6 to 30 feet (2 to 9 m) high, spreading 8 to 30 feet (2.5 to 9 m). Moderate to fast growth, depending on water availability. Small willowlike deciduous tree or large shrub, native to the U.S. Southwest and Mexico. One to several ascending trunks form the base and irregular open form. Slender branches support a canopy of bright green leaves 4 to 12 inches (10 to 30.5 cm) long. The main difference between the two subspecies is that subspecies *arcuata* has drooping curved leaves and subspecies *linearis* has short, wide, straight, erect leaves, giving it a less willowy appearance than its western relative. Terminal clusters of fragrant funnel-shaped flowers 1 to 1½ inches (2.5 to 4 cm) long appear on new growth in shades of pink, lavender and purple as well as white. Flowering peaks in spring continuing into late summer with adequate moisture. Some currently available selections representing both subspecies include 'Regal Purple' (variegated), 'Hope' (white), 'Lucretia Hamilton' (purple), 'Dark Storm' (purple), 'Barranco' (pink) and 'Marfa Late' (pink with double flowers). 'Lois Adams' has full pink clusters and produces few seed pods, a distinct advantage for winter appearance.

A nearly evergreen type belonging to subspecies *linearis* from the Chihuahuan Desert holds its more dense leaves in warm winters but drops them after a hard frost. Blossoms are soft pink-lavender with a deeper center and fewer seed pods than other varieties. Slender straw-colored seed capsules 4 to 12 inches (10 to 30.5 cm) long often persist on all trees throughout winter.

COLD HARDINESS

All three zones.

LANDSCAPE VALUE

- Interesting small tree that can put on an attractive flower show most of the warm season.
- Best under oasis conditions.
- Can be trained into a patio-size tree.
- Flowers and foliage are attractive at close range.

CULTURAL REQUIREMENTS

- **Exposure:** Full sun to part shade.
- **Water:** Tolerates occasional dry periods, but for best landscape performance, soak the root zone every week or two during the warm season. Its bloom and foliage will be more attractive, especially in high heat areas.
- **Soil:** Tolerates most desert soils but responds best to garden conditions.
- **Propagation:** Cuttings.
- **Maintenance:** Prune and train to encourage small tree form.

POSSIBLE PROBLEMS

None observed.

Chitalpa tashkinensis hybrid (*Chilopsis linearis* X *Catalpa bignonioides*)

Chitalpa

Bignoniaceae family

Grows 20 to 30 feet (6 to 9 m) high, with equal spread. Rapid growth under optimum conditions. This hybrid of two American trees was developed by a botanist in Russia, thus the name *C. tashkinensis*. A fast-growing deciduous tree with clusters of large trumpet-shaped flowers that bloom in spring. Bloom size is similar to the blooms of its parent *Catalpa bignonioides*. Pinkish lavender bloom color resembles its other parent, *Chilopsis linearis*. It also inherited some of the latter's desert toughness but requires more water to perform well. The leaves are linear but broader than those of *C. linearis*, creating a more lush effect. Several different selections are available: for example, 'Morning Cloud' (white) and 'Pink Dawn' (pink).

COLD HARDINESS

Low zone and protected microclimates of intermediate zone. Not adapted to extreme cold.

LANDSCAPE VALUE

- Effective as a solitary specimen or horticultural curiosity in large-scale public and commercial landscapes.
- Abundant graceful flowers make a significant fall or winter display.
- Where hard winter frosts are common, this tree may be grown successfully in sheltered courtyards and similar warm microclimates.

CULTURAL REQUIREMENTS

- **Exposure:** Full sun to part shade.
- **Water:** Thoroughly soak the root zone every month or two to promote heavier flowering and winter hardiness; reduce frequency in late summer.
- **Soil:** Most soils with good drainage.
- **Propagation:** Seed.
- **Maintenance:** As tree develops, prune lower side branches to open up view of unique trunk.

POSSIBLE PROBLEMS

Hard frost stops flowering and may damage tender young growth.

Chorisia insignis

White floss silk tree, Palo borracho, Bottle tree

Bombacaceae family

To 50 feet (15 m) high, spreading 30 to 40 feet (9 to 12 m). Moderate growth rate. Large, briefly winter-deciduous tree with a striking appearance derived in part from the swollen flask-shaped trunk. Smooth green bark and stout conical thorns on the younger trunk and branches add to the unusual character of this tree. As the tree matures, the lower trunk turns gray and may lose its thorns. Waxy, palmately* compound leaves make up the open and irregular foliage canopy. Each leaf is divided into five to seven leaflets 2 1/4 to 3 1/4 inches (6 to 8 cm) long. Light creamy yellow flowers 2 to 3 inches (5 to 7.5 cm) long (which look like Easter lily blooms) fade to cream or white as they mature. Flowering can occur at any time from fall into winter, but may be cut short by frost. The fruit is a 5-inch (13-cm) long capsule. Native to South America.

* See Glossary

Chorisia speciosa

Pink floss silk tree
Bombacaceae family

COLD HARDINESS

Low zone and protected microclimates of intermediate zone. Most cold sensitive as a young tree. Mature specimens are hardier, but their flowering season can be cut short by a fall frost.

LANDSCAPE VALUE

- A spectacular flowering tree that makes a color statement unmatched by any other tree species during the fall and winter months.
- In areas where it is marginally cold hardy, floss silk tree may grow best in the warm microclimate of an enclosed courtyard.
- Where winters are frost-free or nearly so, it serves as an impressive accent or specimen for framing or background or as a central feature in large public landscapes.
- Interesting thorn-studded green trunk.

CULTURAL REQUIREMENTS

- **Exposure:** Full sun to part shade.
- **Water:** Soak the root zone every month or two during most of the year, but less often in late summer and fall to encourage more abundant flowering. This will also confer greater cold hardiness where the tree is marginally adapted.
- **Soil:** Fast soil drainage is essential.
- **Propagation:** Seed. Cuttings for selected varieties.
- **Maintenance:** Little maintenance if plant has room to grow.

POSSIBLE PROBLEMS

- Susceptible to cold damage.
- Cleaning up fallen flowers is another maintenance chore.
- Can drop branches in summer. Cause unknown. May be due to brittle branches and weight of summer's leaf growth.
- Most are too large for residential situations, but there are smaller grafted cultivars* available.

Grows 30 to 50 feet (9 to 15 m) high, spreading 30 to 40 feet (9 to 12 m). Rapid growth when young, slowing somewhat as the tree approaches maturity. Large winter-deciduous tree. Bright green bark of the trunk is moderately to densely covered with cone-shaped thorns that are broad at the base and taper to a sharp point. Thorns disappear with age on some trees; on others they persist. Alternate, palmately* compound leaves have lance-shaped leaflets up to 5 inches (13 cm) long that give the tree an oval to rounded canopy shape. The tree often blooms after leaves are shed in fall or in winter, occasionally later. Some bloom while foliage is still on the tree. Flower size and color are variable. The five-petaled blooms may be 2 to 5 inches (5 to 13 cm) across in colors ranging from shell-pink and deep rose-pink to violet-red, shading to yellow or white with brown markings toward the base of the inner surface of the petals. A few named cultivars offer reliable flower color and growth size. The pear-shaped capsules that follow the flowers may be as long as 8 inches (20.5 cm). At maturity, they release seeds densely covered with silky fibers. Native to Argentina and Brazil.

* See Glossary

Chrysactinia mexicana

Domianita daisy

Asteraceae (Compositae) family

COLD HARDINESS

All three zones. Reputed to tolerate temperatures as low as 0°F (-18°C).

LANDSCAPE VALUE

- A colorful low-growing border shrub.
- Mass planting and among large succulents such as agaves, hesperaloes, yuccas and even some cacti.
- In patios and sitting areas where the fragrance of the foliage can be enjoyed at close range.

CULTURAL REQUIREMENTS

- **Exposure:** Full sun, including reflected sun. Can grow in open shade, but becomes leggy and blooms less.
- **Water:** Quite drought resistant once established. Additional watr during bloom season increases flowering.
- **Soil:** Any soil with good drainage.
- **Propagation:** Seed or cuttings.
- **Maintenance:** Encourage more bloom by pruning dead bloom and applying a little extra water, which will get the bloom going again.

POSSIBLE PROBLEMS

Slow growth rate: takes about three years to make a presence in a planting.

Grows 1 to 2 feet (30.5 to 61 cm) high, spreading to 3 feet (1 m). Slow-growing, mounding evergreen shrub with aromatic needlelike leaves. The dark green leaves give off a pleasant aroma when brushed or crushed. An outstanding color producer with a heavy display of 1-inch (2.5 cm) yellow, daisylike blooms that cover the plant from early spring through fall. Flowers grow on 2- to 3-inch (5- to 7.5-cm) stems. There is a slight let-up in blooming during the hottest part of summer, especially in lower elevations. At a glance, domianita somewhat resembles turpentine bush (*Eracameria laricifolia*) but produces color throughout the warm season, while turpentine bush puts on its show only in the fall. Native to West Texas, New Mexico and Mexico.

Cissus incisa

Possum grape, Texas grape ivy

Vitaceae family

COLD HARDINESS

All three zones.

LANDSCAPE VALUE

- Vigorous self-climbing vine on a trellis or fence for summer screening or microclimate modification.
- Attractive when trained to scramble over low walls and boulders.
- Will also cling to and climb rough-surfaced building walls.

CULTURAL REQUIREMENTS

- **Exposure:** Full sun to part shade.
- **Water:** Water every month or two throughout the warm season to encourage best appearance and growth. One or two waterings are usually adequate during the dormant period.
- **Soil:** Wide range of soils.
- **Propagation:** Seed or cuttings.
- **Maintenance:** May need occasional pruning to shape and direct growth.

POSSIBLE PROBLEMS

- Plant can be invasive. Runners* will take root wherever they touch the ground. Reseeds at times.
- Foliage can cause mild dermatitis on some people.

To 20 feet (6 m) high or higher, with equal spread. Can root and spread widely if not restrained. Rapid growth. Deciduous vine with smooth tan or greenish bark on stems. Tendrils may be simple or two-branched. The leaves are fleshy and palmately* divided into three oval- to lance-shaped, coarsely toothed leaflets 3/8 to 2 inches (1 to 5 cm) long by 1 1/4 to 4 inches (3 to 10 cm) wide. Unimportant flowers open in clusters throughout summer. The small rounded berries that follow are black when ripe while the branches that bear them turn red. Native to southern Texas in the United States and south into Mexico.

* *See Glossary*

Cissus trifoliata

Arizona grape ivy, Sonoran desert grape ivy

Vitaceae family

COLD HARDINESS

Adapted to low and intermediate zones, although top growth may be damaged by frost. More intense cold may freeze plant back to the ground, but spring regrowth quickly restores landscape appearance.

LANDSCAPE VALUE

- Fence or trellis for screening and privacy.
- Attractive when allowed to scramble over rocks and boulders.
- A good wall plant if given something to climb on.

CULTURAL REQUIREMENTS

- **Exposure:** Full sun or part shade.
- **Water:** Water once or twice during dry weather to maintain established plants. Growth and foliage cover of young plants is faster with more frequent watering.
- **Soil:** Any soil.
- **Propagation:** Seed or cuttings.
- **Maintenance:** Pruning and training may be necessary to direct and shape growth or to clean up the plant after a hard winter.

POSSIBLE PROBLEMS

- Evergreen in mild winters, but loses its leaves after a hard frost.
- The underground tuber is poisonous if eaten.
- Contact with leaves is said to cause a mild dermatitis similar to that caused by poison ivy in some individuals.
- Can be invasive if not controlled.

To 40 feet (12 m) high, with equal spread. Rapid growth. A sprawling vine, evergreen or deciduous depending on the severity of winter cold. Fleshy dark green leaves to 3 inches (7.5 cm) long and 2 inches (5 cm) wide are three-lobed or palmately* divided into three leaflets. The plant grows from an underground tuber and climbs by means of tendrils that may be simple or two-branched. Clusters of inconspicuous flowers appear from late spring into summer. These are followed by small inedible black berries about 1/4 inch (0.5 cm) in diameter. Native to southern Arizona and Mexico.

Clematis drummondii

Desert clematis vine

Ranunculaceae family

COLD HARDINESS

All three zones.

LANDSCAPE VALUE

Not beautiful, but a valuable and undemanding self-climbing vine to cover fences or trellises for screening in informal garden settings.

CULTURAL REQUIREMENTS

- **Exposure:** Full sun to open shade.
- **Water:** Thoroughly soak the root zone every week to every month (depending on soil moisture) for best appearance. Needs intermittent deep irrigation to perform well.
- **Soil:** Most desert soils with some depth.
- **Propagation:** Seed or cuttings.
- **Maintenance:** Needs wire or other vine-support structure. Not a good plant for masonry. Prune back every year or so.

POSSIBLE PROBLEMS

Because of its vigorous growth, it tends to develop a thick, not particularly attractive mat that you need to prune back or thin out to keep new growth coming.

To 30 feet (9 m) high, with equal spread. Rapid growth. Vigorous evergreen vine climbs over shrubs and trees in its native Sonoran and Chihuahuan Deserts on both the U.S. and Mexican side, making a dense mat of green. Small greenish white flowers are not particularly notable but plumy white filiform* seed in clusters can be quite showy.

** See Glossary*

Clerodendrom indicum (C. inerme)

Tube flower, Indian privet

Verbenaceae family

COLD HARDINESS

Low zone and protected microclimates of intermediate zone. Tolerates light frosts but defoliates at about 28°F (-2°C).

LANDSCAPE VALUE

- Can be used as a sprawling shrub, clipped or hedged into a variety of shapes, trained over fences and shade structures or used as a wide-spreading groundcover.
- It is particularly tolerant of salt wind and sea-front exposure in hot climates.

CULTURAL REQUIREMENTS

- **Exposure:** Reflected sun to part shade.
- **Water:** Water every week or two when plant is young, then thoroughly every month or two when mature. Performs well on brackish water.
- **Soil:** Almost any soil. Tolerates poor drainage and saline situations.
- **Propagation:** Cuttings.
- **Maintenance:** Needs support or shade structures when used as a vine and requires regular trimming when used for topiary and hedging.

POSSIBLE PROBLEMS

- Tends to outgrow allotted space if individual plants are planted too close together.
- Needs frequent pruning when used as a hedge.
- Older hedges become quite woody after a few years of regular trimming.

Will climb with support to over 30 feet (9 m) high. As a vining shrub, spreads 6 to 10 feet (2 to 3 m). As a groundcover it will spread 12 to 15 feet (3.5 to 4.5 m) or more. Extremely rapid growth. Although not particularly drought resistant, this plant can be especially useful in hot arid regions because of its tolerance of extreme heat and salinity. It develops as a vining shrub with lush bright green leaves and small white clusters of jasminelike flowers that bloom throughout the warm season. Grows luxuriantly on brackish water, which many other landscape plants cannot tolerate. Native to India.

* See Glossary

Clytostoma species

Paraguay trumpet vine, lavender trumpet vine
Bignoniaceae family

COLD HARDINESS

Low and intermediate zones, although foliage may be damaged by moderate frost. In high zone it may freeze back but returns rapidly in spring from the hardy, fleshy roots.

LANDSCAPE VALUE

- A real flower show during late spring and most of the summer.
- Covers overhead shade structures better than it covers vertical freestanding support, such as a wire fence—it makes a dense garland at the top, but growth on the lower portion of the fence is leafless.
- Because it climbs by tendrils, provide shade structures that allow it to attach and twine, such as wire or wire fencing.

CULTURAL REQUIREMENTS

- **Exposure:** Full sun, including reflected sun. Will probably accept part shade but would try to climb over whatever provides the shade.
- **Water:** Drought resistant because it is native to a dry winter region where it normally goes deciduous; however, some watering during this period encourages it to remain evergreen. Thoroughly soak the root zone every week or two during the hot season to ensure good growth. The interval between soakings can be extended with mature plants.
- **Soil:** Any soil will work, but good garden soil with some depth is best.
- **Propagation:** Cuttings. Could be grown from seed but cuttings are more practical because they root so readily.
- **Maintenance:** This large plant needs plenty of room to spread.

POSSIBLE PROBLEMS

- Outgrows some locations where space is inadequate.
- In colder regions where the top freezes back each winter, spring pruning can be a problem.

Vining to 30 feet (9 m) high over trees or other vine support, with equal spread. Slow growth at first but rapid after the root system is developed. A wide-ranging vine from Paraguay. Evergreen to deciduous depending on temperatures and water supply. Deciduous in Paraguay's rainless winter but holds its leaves in maintained landscapes with year-round irrigation. Dark green leaves are divided into two leaflets. Abundant small lavender trumpet flowers bloom in late spring and summer. Develops a fleshy underground root system that sparks regrowth after a freeze and extends its drought tolerance.

Note: This attractive vine was collected by Dr. David Palzkill in Paraguay. To date the species has not been determined, although several U.S. Southwest nurseries offer it for sale.

Coccoloba goldmannii

Sonoran sea grape, Desert sea grape
Polygonaceae family

COLD HARDINESS

Low zone and frost-protected locations in intermediate zone.

LANDSCAPE VALUE

- Shade and understory planting.
- Reputed to become a small tree eventually, but under cultivation it has achieved only medium shrub stature.

CULTURAL REQUIREMENTS

- **Exposure:** Partial sun or open to deep shade.
- **Water:** Water every week or two during the hot season, but mature plant tolerates water every month or two, especially during the cool season.
- **Soil:** Improved soil and garden conditions to maintain good foliage.
- **Propagation:** Seed and probably cuttings.
- **Maintenance:** Low maintenance.

POSSIBLE PROBLEMS

Slow to develop.

To 25 feet (7.5 m) high, usually much lower, spreading 6 to 12 feet (2 to 3.5 m). Slow-growing evergreen shrub sometimes grows into a small tree. Has broad roundish leaves that are dark green and leathery, with a reddish cast to new growth. It has not flowered or set fruit under cultivation. Native to Sonora, Mexico.

Landscape Design Example

Groundcover (such as *Carpobrotus chilensis* shown here) can be used to define the edges of a path.

Cocos nucifera

Coconut palm

Arecaceae (Palmae) family

COLD HARDINESS

Subtropical to tropical areas of low zone. Tolerates light frost or brief cold periods but will not succeed in the cool winters of Mediterranean-type climates, even in frost-free locations.

LANDSCAPE VALUE

- One of the most striking plants in tropical flora, beautiful in every respect. Adds drama and character to the landscape through height and elegant form.
- Specimen or accent as a single plant, but best in groups or informal clumps of three or more trees of varying height.
- Bold background or frame plant.
- Skyline silhouette near water features, in large-scale plantings, especially appropriate in seaside gardens and on beaches where roots tolerant of sea water prevent sand erosion. Also tolerates occasional strong storm tides.

CULTURAL REQUIREMENTS

- **Exposure:** Full sun and intense heat.
- **Water:** Coconuts are somewhat tolerant of drought stress but in most landscape situations, water thoroughly every week or two for acceptable growth and appearance. Some plantings in Guaymas, Mexico, are not irrigated and have a good appearance.
- **Soil:** Supremely adapted to brackish soil and wind-blown salt spray but also thrives inland in deep fertile soil.
- **Propagation:** Plant stem end of the whole coconut in sand or soil with plenty of moisture and heat.
- **Maintenance:** To eliminate the hazard of falling coconuts and leaves, remove the stalks of flowers or immature fruit as well as older unsightly leaves on a regular basis.

POSSIBLE PROBLEMS

- Lethal yellowing disease has devastated coconut plantings in many areas. The introduction of resistant hybrids appears to be the most effective control measure at this time.
- Fungi and viruses, as well as nematodes* and various insects, may attack coconut palms. Control measures are seldom necessary in arid-region landscapes.
- Nuts and leaves torn loose in intense storms may be a threat to pedestrians, vehicles and structures.

To 100 feet (30.5 m) high, spreading to 40 feet (12 m). Moderate growth rate. A stately feather-leaf palm thought to have originated somewhere near the Indian Ocean. Widely cultivated in Mexico, where plant is common along tropical, even arid coasts and inland where soil moisture is adequate. The smooth, erect or leaning trunk is swollen at the base, slender above. Evergreen pinnate* leaves 9 to 21 feet (3 to 6.5 m) long with many drooping segments form the graceful feathery crown. Separate male and female flowers borne on the same 3- to 4-foot (1-m) long stalk are replaced by as many as twenty large ovoid fruits 6 to 8 inches (15 to 20.5 cm) wide and 12 inches (30.5 cm) long when full size. Mature coconuts are green, yellow or brown. Inside each nut is a layer of edible fleshy endosperm* and up to 1 quart (1 liter) of "water," which is clear in young fruits, becoming creamy white as they mature. Bears fruit almost year-round.

* See Glossary

Combretum erythrophyllum

Bush willow

Combretaceae family

COLD HARDINESS

Low and intermediate zones.

LANDSCAPE VALUE

- Leafy background planting.
- Tropical effects combinations.
- Can be developed into a patio-size tree.

CULTURAL REQUIREMENTS

- **Exposure:** Full sun, including reflected sun to open shade where understory planting beneath taller trees is appropriate.
- **Water:** Water every week or two for best effects; however, at Boyce Thompson Arboretum in Arizona, it has shown no negative effects from an infrequent irrigation schedule.
- **Soil:** Any soil.
- **Propagation:** Cuttings.
- **Maintenance:** Add landscape interest by pruning excess lower branches to expose multibranch trunks.

POSSIBLE PROBLEMS

None observed except "tacky" look in winter.

To 40 feet (12 m) high, usually shorter, with equal spread. Moderate to rapid growth depending on growing conditions. A small tree, deciduous to semi-evergreen depending on winter temperatures. 3-inch (7.5-cm) leaves, pointed at the tip, are dark green and then turn red in late fall. The leaves persist in the winter in frost-free locations but drop in colder locations. Tends to be bushy and multitrunked, but can be staked and developed into an attractive small tree. Smooth light bark is an attractive close-range feature. Native to South Africa.

Condalia correllii (C. mexicana)

Mexican blue wood

Rhamnaceae family

COLD HARDINESS

All three zones.

LANDSCAPE VALUE

- Screening and barrier potential.
- Mounding shrub from the ground up has a sculptural, coniferlike look.

CULTURAL REQUIREMENTS

- **Exposure:** Full sun to part shade.
- **Water:** Drought tolerant. Thoroughly soak the root zone once or twice during the hot season to speed up growth.
- **Soil:** Grows in poor, gravelly soil, even caliche* (in outcrops), but needs good drainage.
- **Propagation:** Seed or cuttings.
- **Maintenance:** Low maintenance. May need to shape to fit certain landscapes.

POSSIBLE PROBLEMS

- Slow to develop.
- Branches have sharp tips.
- Not readily available from commercial nurseries.

Grows 6 to 10 feet (2 to 3 m) high, spreading 6 feet (2 m) or more. Slow growth. Dense evergreen shrub from southern Arizona and the Mexican states of Chihuahua, Coahuila and Sonora. Zig-zag sharp-tipped twigs are tightly clothed with tiny dark green leaves. Shrubs usually rounded in form and much thicker than most desert shrubs look almost like a shrubby conifer. Blackberries appear in spring or summer, but are not showy. A tough plant that endures hot inhospitable situations, maintaining its deep green fine texture throughout the year.

* *See Glossary*

Condalia globosa

Globosa blue wood

Rhamnaceae family

COLD HARDINESS

Low and intermediate zones; borderline in high zone.

LANDSCAPE VALUE

- Large background shrub for screening.
- Can be trimmed up to make an attractive patio tree.

CULTURAL REQUIREMENTS

- **Exposure:** Full sun, including reflected sun to part shade.
- **Water:** Drought resistant but responds to watering once a week to once a month with faster growth and improved landscape appearance.
- **Soil:** Native to sandy soils. Other types of soils are acceptable as long as drainage is good.
- **Propagation:** Seed or rooted cuttings.
- **Maintenance:** Low maintenance except pruning for patio-tree form.

POSSIBLE PROBLEMS

Thorns make pruning difficult.

To 20 feet (6 m) high, give or take, spreading to 15 feet (4.5 m). Moderate growth rate can be increased with regular irrigation. Large evergreen shrub or small tree with sturdy single or multiple trunk. Small, crisp green leaves thickly cover stiff twiggy branches. Abundant but tiny and inconspicuous blossoms make their presence known by their pleasant fragrance. Small reddish brown berries follow. Berries are also inconspicuous. Native to the U.S. Southwest and northern Mexico.

Convolvulus cneorum

Bush morning glory

Convolulaceae family

COLD HARDINESS

All three zones.

LANDSCAPE VALUE

- Showy, flowery mounding groundcover.
- Foreground plantings.
- Rock gardens.
- Containers.
- A plant for exposed locations.

CULTURAL REQUIREMENTS

- **Exposure:** Full sun to part shade.
- **Water:** Moderately drought resistant. Water every month or two during the summer, allowing the surface to dry in between waterings. Water every week or two during the cool season.
- **Soil:** Needs especially well-drained soil; plant away from soggy situations.
- **Propagation:** Seed.
- **Maintenance:** May need to be pruned back at intervals to promote new growth and prevent leggyness.

POSSIBLE PROBLEMS

Damping off* can be a problem, especially with humid heat such as occurs during the summer rainy season of some arid region climates.

Grows 1 to 2 feet (30.5 to 61cm) high, spreading 3 feet (1 m). Rapid growth. Sprawling shrubby evergreen perennial that makes a silvery mound of soft silky foliage covered with white-tinted pink morning glory blossoms that bloom from late spring to fall. Leaves are about 1 to 2½ inches (2.5 to 6.5 cm) long. Native to southern Europe.

* *See Glossary*

Cordia boissieri

Texas olive, Anacahuita

Boraginaceae family

COLD HARDINESS

Low and intermediate zones and warm microclimates of the high zone. Leaves tender to hard frost, but woody parts are frost hardy.

LANDSCAPE VALUE

- Both the small tree and shrub forms make handsome and interesting specimens that bloom over a long period.
- Patio tree.
- Background and screening.
- On small properties.
- Near buildings, on medians, and along roads.

CULTURAL REQUIREMENTS

- **Exposure:** Full to reflected sun or part shade.
- **Water:** Drought tolerant but water every week or two during the warm season to enhance flowering and growth.
- **Soil:** Adapted to most soils with good drainage.
- **Propagation:** Seeds or cuttings. Seed slow to germinate.
- **Maintenance:** May be pruned to a single- or multistemmed form.

POSSIBLE PROBLEMS

- Fallen flowers and leaves require cleanup in tailored landscapes.
- Frost-killed leaves turn brown and remain on the tree, dropping slowly.

Grows 10 to 25 feet (3 to 7.5 m) high, with equal spread. Moderate to fast growth with adequate water. Small tree or large shrub native to the Rio Grande Valley of Texas and south to Monterey, Mexico. The dense crown of coarse, slightly gray-green foliage is evergreen in mild winters but deciduous when subjected to hard frosts. A profusion of 2½-inch (6.5-cm) wide white flowers with yellow throats in terminal clusters decorate the tree if moisture is present. Flowers bloom spring through fall, concluding only when the weather becomes too cold. The rounded yellow-green fruit resembling green olives is eaten only by birds.

Cordia myxa

Assyrian plum

Boraginaceae family

COLD HARDINESS

Low zone and very warm pockets of intermediate zone. Foliage damaged with light frost and wood is damaged in the mid-20s F (-4°C).

LANDSCAPE VALUE

- Dramatic and bold foliage.
- Tropical effects.
- Patio tree or residential-scale tree.

CULTURAL REQUIREMENTS

- **Exposure:** Full sun to part shade. Tolerates extremely hot reflective locations where other bold-scale foliage would burn.
- **Water:** Drought resistant. Water every week or two. Tolerates brackish water with no apparent distress.
- **Soil:** Any soil; tolerant of salinity.
- **Propagation:** Seed.
- **Maintenance:** Low maintenance. Stake young plants.

POSSIBLE PROBLEMS

- Foliage subject to frost damage.
- Fruit, though small, could be messy after a heavy set.

To 30 feet (9 m) high, with equal spread. Rapid growth if moisture is present. Large shrub or small to medium tree depending on situation and moisture supply. Large evergreen leaves evoke a tropical feeling. Edible fruit and castaway seed responsible for often-seen volunteer trees along roads and urban streets in many Middle Eastern locales where it survives with no support. Native to warm areas of the Middle East.

* *See Glossary*

Cordia parvifolia

Little-leaf cordia

Boraginaceae family

COLD HARDINESS

Low and intermediate zones, and warm locations in high zone. Propagation wood from Chihuahuan populations yields plants that are hardy in all three zones. Not true of populations from western Mexico.

LANDSCAPE VALUE

- Showy flowering accent, planted singly or in groups.
- Foundation, border and boundary plantings.
- Schools, parks, road medians.

CULTURAL REQUIREMENTS

- **Exposure:** Reflected sun to part shade.
- **Water:** Water established plants every month or two, more often when young and to maintain growth and flowering.
- **Soil:** Most soils with good drainage.
- **Propagation:** Seed or cuttings.
- **Maintenance:** Grows with little care when established. Selectively head back longest branches to encourage denser growth.

POSSIBLE PROBLEMS

Evergreen but sparse in winter; foliage may drop completely with prolonged drought or hard frost. Stems are less cold sensitive.

Grows 4 to 8 feet (1 to 2.5 m) high, spreading 4 to 10 feet (1 to 3 m). Rapid growth with water. A native of Chihuahua, Sonora, Baja California and several other spots in Mexico. Open, spreading shrub characterized by arching gray-barked branches and small grayish to olive-green leaves that are oval with toothed margins. Leaves are rough to the touch, 3/8 to 1 1/4 inches (1 to 3 cm) long and evergreen except when subjected to severe frosts or prolonged drought. Snowy white flowers 1 to 1 1/2 inches (2.5 to 4 cm) in diameter appear in small clusters beginning in spring and again at intervals into late fall after a rain or when soil moisture is plentiful.

Cordia sonorae

Sonoran cordia

Boraginaceae family

COLD HARDINESS

Low zone and protected microclimates in the intermediate zone. Tolerant of light frost.

LANDSCAPE VALUE

- Fine small evergreen tree that puts on a floral display in spring.
- Good patio-tree potential.

CULTURAL REQUIREMENTS

- **Exposure:** Full sun to part shade.
- **Water:** Thoroughly soak the root zone every month or two. Needs more water for good bloom and foliage during hot season.
- **Soil:** Most soils with good drainage.
- **Propagation:** Seed.
- **Maintenance:** Low maintenance. Trim for patio-tree form.

POSSIBLE PROBLEMS

Blossoms remain on tree and fade to brown; may be unsightly until they fall.

To 20 feet (6 m) high, spreading 15 feet (4.5 m). Moderate growth rate. Small erect tree with rounded top and evergreen foliage similar to *C. boissieri.* Flowers in dense cymes* are smaller but not as showy because of the number of blossoms in the cluster. Flowering seems to be more limited to spring. White blossoms turn purplish and eventually brown, remaining on the tree. Native to Sonora, Mexico. Flowers are about 2 1/2 inches (6.5 cm) in diameter.

* *See Glossary*

Cortaderia selloana

Pampas grass

Poaceae (Gramineae) family

COLD HARDINESS

All three zones.

LANDSCAPE VALUE

- Unique specimen or accent.
- Background or screen in group plantings on slopes and banks.
- When cut at the proper stage, the feathery plumes make an attractive and long-lasting addition to indoor arrangements.

CULTURAL REQUIREMENTS

- **Exposure:** Adapted to hot arid regions with full to reflected sun or part shade.
- **Water:** Water every week or two during the growing season in hot arid climates, every month or two to maintain plants during the cooler months.
- **Soil:** Tolerates many soil types and performs well in turf areas.
- **Propagation:** Easily propagated by clump divisions or seeds.
- **Maintenance:** Periodic grooming is necessary to remove old foliage and flower stalks. A long-sleeve shirt and gloves are essential for this chore.

POSSIBLE PROBLEMS

- Sharp leaf edges pose a threat to passersby in close-up situations.
- Where growing conditions favor germination of its abundant seed crop, volunteer seedlings can overwhelm nearby native vegetation. This characteristic eliminates pampas grass as a suitable landscape plant in some regions. Check with local horticultural authorities before adding to a planting.

To 15 feet (4.5 m) high, spreading to 10 feet (3 m). Rapid growth with adequate water. One of the largest grasses to find use in the landscape, pampas grass forms a broad clump of graceful arching foliage on short stems. The narrow leaves 1/2 to 3/4 inch (1 to 2 cm) wide and 3 to 6 feet (1 to 2 m) long with small but sharp serrated edges are replaced each growing season from a perennial crown that lives many years. In late summer or early fall, slender flower stalks rise above the foliage adorned in delicate fluffy plumes 1 to 3 feet (30.5 cm to 1 m) long in subtle shades of silvery gray, lavender or pink. Native to Argentina, Brazil and Chile.

Cowania mexicana stansburniana

Cliff rose

Rosaceae family

COLD HARDINESS

Completely hardy in the cold winter microclimates of intermediate and high zone. Will not tolerate low zone or do well in most areas of the intermediate zone.

LANDSCAPE VALUE

- Accent or character plant in street, median and highway plantings.
- Shrub borders.
- Understory plant in naturalistic woodsy settings.

CULTURAL REQUIREMENTS

- **Exposure:** Full sun to part shade.
- **Water:** Established plants survive and grow without irrigation in areas to which they are adapted. Water at two-month intervals to improve performance during long unseasonably dry periods.
- **Soil:** Adapted to a wide range of soils, including poor rocky types, but grows larger and more dense on deep fertile sites.
- **Propagation:** Seed and probably cuttings.
- **Maintenance:** Requires little maintenance once established.

POSSIBLE PROBLEMS

None observed.

Grows 6 to 8 feet (2 to 2.5 m) high, spreading 3 to 6 feet (1 to 2 m). Slow to moderate growth depending on site conditions. Evergreen and shrubby with rigid, erect stems growing in a clump. Cliff Rose has small 1/2-inch (1-cm) leathery leaves that are deeply toothed, wider above the middle and narrowing to a triangular base where they attach to the stems. The solitary flowers that open at the branch tips in spring or summer look like 1/2-inch (1-cm) wide single wild roses with five pale yellow, cream-colored or white petals. After spring and summer bloom, and then in fall, this rugged but rather ordinary-looking high-country shrub is transformed into a silver-gray cloud by the delicate feathery tails attached to the small, dry one-seeded fruits. Native in the higher elevations in arid regions of the western and southwestern United States and northern Mexico.

** See Glossary*

Crescentia alata

Calabash Tree, Cuatztecomate

Bignoniaceae family

COLD HARDINESS

Low zone and protected microclimates of the intermediate zone. Frost tender.

LANDSCAPE VALUE

- Accent with rich, dark foliage, interesting silhouette and broad horizontal character.
- Patio-size tree (if trained).
- Close-range interest because of unusual foliage, branching, flowers and fruit-covered trunk.
- Shade.

CULTURAL REQUIREMENTS

- **Exposure:** Full sun.
- **Water:** Thoroughly soak the root zone every week to every couple months, depending on how quickly the soil dries, to maintain evergreen foliage. Established trees shed their leaves when stressed by drought and are able to survive long dry periods.
- **Soil:** Any soil.
- **Propagation:** Seed.
- **Maintenance:** Needs space. When crowded with other plantings that obscure its silhouette, it loses its value as an accent plant.

POSSIBLE PROBLEMS

Aging flowers sometimes produce an unpleasant odor, though wild trees in Mexico don't seem to have this problem.

Evergreen to deciduous tree, depending on moisture supply, that grows to 20 feet (6 m) high, with equal spread. Moderate growth rate. Pronounced horizontal-branching pattern. Dark green cross-shaped leaves encircle branches, giving them the look of outstretched garlands. The tree has a spidery silhouette. The interesting cannonball- to gourd-shaped fruit has a hard exterior shell about 6 inches (15 cm) in diameter. Once the flesh is removed, it can be dried and used for a cup or container. Fruit sets directly on the main trunk as well as on branches.

Cryptostegia grandiflora

Rubber vine

Asclepiadaceae family

COLD HARDINESS

Low zone and protected microclimates of intermediate zone.

LANDSCAPE VALUE

- Vine to cover large trellises or arbors.
- Mounding shrub on slopes or medians.
- Large colorful flowers and lush foliage.
- Evokes a tropical feeling.

CULTURAL REQUIREMENTS

- **Exposure:** Full to reflected sun to part shade.
- **Water:** Tolerates extended periods of drought once established. Water every week or two during warm season to develop young plants and to keep them attractive.
- **Soil:** Thrives in a wide variety of soils. Tolerates salinity.
- **Propagation:** Seed or cuttings.
- **Maintenance:** Needs room to grow. Design vine support and shade structures to accommodate its climbing-by-twining growth habit. Thin and train on a regular basis.

POSSIBLE PROBLEMS

Rampant growth can become a tangled mass.

Twining vine that grows to 20 feet (6 m) high, with equal spread. Rapid growth with moisture. Large waxy evergreen leaves and big tubular pink to lavender flowers in terminal* clusters. Can become shrubby. Thought to be of Indian origin but has naturalized in many other regions, including the southern edge of the Sonoran Desert in Mexico.

* See Glossary

Cupressus arizonica

Rough-barked Arizona cypress

Cupressaceae family

COLD HARDINESS

All three zones.

LANDSCAPE VALUE

- Screen and windbreak.
- Barrier and space definer.
- Buffer zone planting.
- Forest and woodsy effects in parks and public landscapes.

CULTURAL REQUIREMENTS

- **Exposure:** Tolerant of full sun, heat and wind, especially at middle and higher elevations.
- **Water:** Drought resistant once established. Does well with thorough soakings of the root zone every month or two, more frequently in the hot low and intermediate zones.
- **Soil:** Grows in poor soil as well as more fertile types.
- **Propagation:** Seed, cuttings and grafts.
- **Maintenance:** Low maintenance. Withstands pruning but best to let it take its natural form.

POSSIBLE PROBLEMS

- Red spider mites may bother trees, especially during hot, dry periods.
- Drought-stressed trees are susceptible to the cypress bark beetle, which tunnels into the branch tips in Arizona trees.
- Tends to grow a bit open and unkempt in hot low-desert locations, where it also seems to be more susceptible to the cypress bark beetle.

Evergreen conifer from Arizona that grows 40 to 50 feet (12 to 15 m) high, spreading to 20 feet (6 m). Moderate growth rate. Form of seed-grown plants varies from pyramidal to sometimes rounded. The color of the scale-like foliage ranges from light green to silvery blue. The outer bark is deeply furrowed and remains attached on older trunks and branches. Hard, rounded female cones to 1 inch (2.5 cm) across may persist on the tree for years. Various cultivars* offered in the trade as *C. arizonica* appear to be more correctly identified as belonging to the related species *C. glabra*.

Cupressus glabra

Smooth-barked Arizona cypress

Cupressaceae family

COLD HARDINESS

All three zones.

LANDSCAPE VALUE

- In addition to the uses listed for *C. arizonica*, cultivars* of this species serve as attractive specimens or accents.
- Commercial and residential landscapes.
- Parks.
- Schools.
- Roadway medians.

CULTURAL REQUIREMENTS

- **Exposure:** Tolerant of full sun, heat and wind, especially at middle and higher elevations.
- **Water:** Drought resistant once established. Does well with thorough soakings of the root zone every month or two. Water more frequently in the hottest, driest situations.
- **Soil:** Grows in poor as well as fertile soil.
- **Propagation:** Seed, cuttings and grafts.
- **Maintenance:** Low maintenance.

POSSIBLE PROBLEMS

- Red spider mites.
- Drought-stressed trees in Arizona are susceptible to the cypress bark beetle, which tunnels into the branch tips.
- Form tends to become a bit open and unkempt in low hot-desert locations.

Foliage similar to *C. arizonica*. Plants grown from seed are as variable in form and color as *C. arizonica*. Cultivars such as 'Gareei,' 'Compacta' and 'Pyramidalis' offer uniform color and shape. The bark on older trunks and branches as well as that on smaller stems sheds in flat sheets. The inner cherry red bark is smooth and glossy, a decorative feature for close-up viewing. Pyramidal in youth but when mature, becomes shorter and broader at the top than *C. arizonica*. To 40 feet (12 m) high or higher, spreading to 20 feet (6 m) or more. Moderate to rapid growth.

** See Glossary*

Cupressus sempervirens 'Stricta'

Columnar Italian cypress

Cupressaceae family

COLD HARDINESS

All three zones.

LANDSCAPE VALUE

- Stately, elegant and unique vertical accent or specimen, especially in formal gardens. The scale of the composition and the size of the mature tree must be compatible.
- Tall screen, windbreak or background and in rows along roads and drives.

CULTURAL REQUIREMENTS

- **Exposure:** Full to reflected sun. Withstands intense heat and aridity.
- **Water:** Established plants show moderate drought tolerance and perform well with water every month or two, less often during the cooler months.
- **Soil:** Soils that provide adequate depth and drainage.
- **Propagation:** Cuttings or seed, although seed result in plants of varying growth characteristics.
- **Maintenance:** Too much fertilizer and water result in lush growth that pulls away from the foliage mass and detracts from the appearance of the plant. Prune or tie branches back in place to restore uniformity, but never top the plant or limit its height.

POSSIBLE PROBLEMS

- Spider mites.
- Excessive water or fertilizer encourage unattractive growth.
- Young container-grown nursery stock of this cypress has considerable consumer appeal and it is often used in inappropriate locations without regard for the size, shape or landscape impact of the mature plant.

This well-known evergreen tree grows erect in a narrow, almost perfectly symmetrical tapering column 40 to 60 feet (12 to 18 m) high, spreading 8 to 15 feet (2.5 to 4.5 m). Moderate growth rate. Tiny dark green juniperlike leaves are dense and fine-textured. Neither the inconspicuous flowers nor the hard rounded cones, 1 inch (2.5 cm) in diameter, contribute to the plant's landscape appearance. *C. sempervirens*, the parent species, has spreading horizontal branches and a picturesque open form that give it a quite different look. Native from southern Europe into parts of Asia. Other cultivars* include blue-green and golden foliage types.

Cycas revoluta

Cycad, Sago palm, Japanese fern

Cycadaceae family

COLD HARDINESS

Low and intermediate zones and protected microclimates in the high zone. Foliage will sustain damage but trunk is hardy to below 20°F (-7°C). However, the lush foliage is this plant's best feature, so regular freezing will make its use in cooler regions questionable.

LANDSCAPE VALUE

- Ideal for tropical effects and mini oases, although tolerant of more difficult conditions.
- Planters, containers and pots, large and small.
- Accent in entryway and other points of emphasis.
- Tiny plants have even been used as bonsai, surviving for years in a small pot.
- Tough for such a lush-looking plant: Survives limited dry periods without loss of foliage, which is most unusual and makes it particularly useful in hot arid regions.

CULTURAL REQUIREMENTS

- **Exposure:** Full sun (no reflected sun) to full shade. Best foliage and general development in light shade situations or morning sun.
- **Water:** Water every week or two during the warm season. Little to no water during the cool season.
- **Soil:** Prefers improved garden soil and fertilizer at the start of the warm season. Avoid alkalinity.
- **Propagation:** Seed or by rooting bulblike sprouts taken from trunks of older plants.
- **Maintenance:** Low maintenance. To encourage single-trunk specimen, remove side sprouts. Moderate fertilization when terminal* bud begins to swell for new growth cycle results in attractive, vigorous foliage.

POSSIBLE PROBLEMS

None observed.

Not a palm, regardless of the common name "sago palm." Belongs to an ancient group of plants in the botanical kingdom, the *Cycads*, which preceded flowering plants. *Cycads* produce cones instead of flowers. Female plants bear nut-like seeds for reproduction and male plants produce a cone for pollen production. Other than the variation in cones, there is no difference in their appearance. Older plants do resemble palms after they have developed short, stubby dark brown trunks, about 3 feet (1 m) tall. These trunks are topped with a whorl or head of dark green, glossy finely divided palmlike leaves that also grow to about 3 feet (1 m). In their youthful, trunkless stages, they resemble ferns and supply a visually cooling effect to arid-region landscape plantings where ferns don't grow successfully. This Japanese *Cycad* is a member of the Cycadaceae family, which is represented by different species throughout the warm semitropical and tropical world. Native populations of most *Cycads* are limited in number and many species threatened by over-collecting in the wild are protected by law. *Cycas revoluta*, however, has been a garden and container favorite since Victorian times. Its use will continue because of its tolerance of a wide range of conditions and ease of propagation. It grows up to 10 feet (3 m) high, spreading 3 to 6 feet (1 to 2 m). Sometimes grows multiple trunks. Such specimens have a much wider spread. Slow growth can be increased with fertilizer and good horticultural practices at the beginning of each warm season. This is when growth of new foliage is initiated and may be the only growth spurt of the year.

* *See Glossary*

Dalbergia sissoo

Sissoo tree, Indian teakwood

Fabaceae (Leguminosae) family

COLD HARDINESS

Low zone and warmer areas of the intermediate zone, where foliage is sometimes damaged by frost. The tree recovers quickly in spring.

LANDSCAPE VALUE

- Large shade tree.
- Adds a luxurious bright green mass of foliage to the arid landscape.
- Wide-spreading root system stabilizes erosion-prone stream banks.

CULTURAL REQUIREMENTS

- **Exposure:** Full sun.
- **Water:** Weekly to monthly thorough soakings of the root zone when mature, depending on your microclimate.
- **Soil:** Any soil, but some depth is best.
- **Propagation:** Seed or cutting. Cutting roots quickly.
- **Maintenance:** Some training to limit vigorous growth of young plants. Prune out frost-damaged growth if necessary.

POSSIBLE PROBLEMS

None observed.

Beautiful evergreen to semideciduous tree with a round or more vertical oval-shaped foliage canopy. Grows 30 to 50 feet (9 to 15 m) high or higher. Reputedly reaches 80 feet (24 m) in its native India. Spreads to 30 feet (9 m). Moderate to rapid growth. Medium to light green compound leaves resemble those of the genus *Robinia* but they are thicker. Tiny green-yellow pea-shaped blossoms have no ornamental value. Seeds are borne in small green pea pods, typical of legumes. Seed pods are not noticeable sandwiched among the thick foliage. Hosts nitrogen-fixing bacteria nodules on its roots, which enhances appearance and stimulates growth.

Dalea bicolor argyrea

Silver dalea

Fabaceae (Leguminosae) family

COLD HARDINESS

Low and intermediate zones. Frost hardy.

LANDSCAPE VALUE

- Foundation shrub.
- Border and space definer.
- Buffer zone and median plantings.
- Provides color and interest in fall, when few shrubs are in flower.

CULTURAL REQUIREMENTS

- **Exposure:** Full sun to part shade.
- **Water:** Water established plants every month or two during warm season for acceptable appearance.
- **Soil:** Any soil with good drainage.
- **Propagation:** Seed or cutting.
- **Maintenance:** Requires little care when established. Head back branch tips to create a fuller, more compact growth habit.

POSSIBLE PROBLEMS

None observed in the landscape other than loss of leaves when subject to hard frosts or very dry conditions.

The genus *Dalea* includes a number of little-known species that have great potential as arid-landscape shrubs. Desirable characteristics of silver dalea include the semideciduous silvery white leaves and clusters of small rose-purple flowers that bloom in fall. Grows 3 to 4 feet (1 m) high with equal spread. Moderate growth rate but more rapid with supplemental irrigation. Native to U.S. desert Southwest.

Dalea capitata

Golden dalea

Fabaceae (Leguminosae) family

COLD HARDINESS

All three zones.

LANDSCAPE VALUE

- Low-growing, flowering groundcover for small areas.
- Rock gardens, path edgings and small banks.

CULTURAL REQUIREMENTS

- **Exposure:** Full sun, including reflected sun to open shade.
- **Water:** Drought resistant but for good appearance, growth and bloom, soak the root zone every few weeks to every couple months.
- **Soil:** Most soil with good drainage.
- **Propagation:** Cuttings or seed.
- **Maintenance:** Cut back in winter to generate new spring growth.

POSSIBLE PROBLEMS

Looks scruffy in winter. Cut back to rejuvenate.

Small evergreen shrub with compound leaves. Grows about 1 foot (30.5 cm) high, spreading 3 feet (1 m) or more. Moderate growth rate. Remains low-growing and spreads laterally to cover the ground with its fresh medium green foliage. The plant collected in the Mexican state of Coahuilla was almost passed up by plant collectors—it was so drab in the wild. Under cultivation, however, it revealed its capacity as an excellent desert groundcover. Its abundant golden bloom (unusual color for the *Dalea* clan) is a special bonus in late spring and again in fall: The fall bloom is the showiest. A selection, 'Sierra Gold™,' is for sale in the nursery trade.

Dalea greggii

Trailing indigo bush

Fabaceae (Leguminosae) family

COLD HARDINESS

Low and intermediate zones. Tolerates warm locations in high zone if hardened off* in fall. New growth is sometimes damaged late in the year.

LANDSCAPE VALUE

- One of the best drought-resistant groundcovers.
- Rabbit resistant.

CULTURAL REQUIREMENTS

- **Exposure:** Full sun to part shade.
- **Water:** Every month or two, water mature plantings thoroughly to maintain good appearance. Water young plantings more often. With no water, plant goes dormant and remains undamaged.
- **Soil:** Loose, gravelly well-drained soils instead of tight, heavy clay. Space new plantings 3 to 6 feet (1 to 2 m) apart and well away from walks and paths.
- **Propagation:** Cuttings.
- **Maintenance:** Cut back to renew plants every few years and to prevent build-up of woody growth.

POSSIBLE PROBLEMS

Tolerates little foot traffic. Foot trails and similar damaged spots in mature plantings are slow to fill back in.

One of the few true desert groundcovers and a native of the Chihuahuan Desert, this plant grows about 2 feet (61 cm) high and spreads 6 to 9 feet (2 to 3 m). Roots more as it spreads, especially in a gravelly surface or decomposed granite. Moderate to rapid growth under optimum conditions. Small leaves with tiny pearly gray leaflets create a spreading, undulating cover. Clusters of tiny lavender to purple pea-type flowers bloom in spring to early summer. Flowers are not large enough or profuse enough to put on much of a show.

* *See Glossary*

Dalea lutea
Yellow-flowered dalea bush
Fabaceae (Leguminosae) family

COLD HARDINESS
Low and intermediate zones and probably warm microclimates of high zone, judging from its native origin.

LANDSCAPE VALUE
Low mounding shrub for
- Banks and foundation plantings.
- Space division.
- Rock gardens.
- Medians.

CULTURAL REQUIREMENTS
- **Exposure:** Full sun, including reflected sun, to part shade.
- **Water:** Drought resistant. Soak the root zone every week or two during the warm season to trigger bloom period and maintain a good appearance.
- **Soil:** Any soil with good drainage.
- **Propagation:** Seed or cuttings.
- **Maintenance:** Cut back plants after they flower to rejuvenate them.

POSSIBLE PROBLEMS
None observed.

A mounding evergreen shrub with small grayish green leaves that sometimes drop in drought conditions. Grows at a moderate rate to 3 feet (1 m) high, with equal spread. Blooms after receiving moisture in the warm season. The pea-shaped flowers are yellow, an unusual color for a *Dalea*, which usually produces flowers in lavender and purple shades. Native to Chihuahuan Desert in Mexico.

Dalea pulchra
Bush dalea
Fabaceae (Leguminosae) family

COLD HARDINESS
Low and intermediate zones and warm microclimates of high zone.

LANDSCAPE VALUE
- Specimen, foundation plant or background.
- Borders, medians and buffer zone plantings.

CULTURAL REQUIREMENTS
- **Exposure:** Full sun is best. Becomes open and sparse with too much shade.
- **Water:** Tolerates dry conditions when established, but more attractive with water every month or so.
- **Soil:** Any soil with good drainage.
- **Propagation:** Seed or cuttings.
- **Maintenance:** Low maintenance. Prune out woody growth to rejuvenate old plants if necessary.

POSSIBLE PROBLEMS
None observed.

This beautiful, rugged, upright evergreen shrub grows 4 to 6 feet (1 to 2 m) high and spreads 3 to 5 feet (1 to 1.5 m) wide at a moderate rate. Native to higher elevation desert areas in Arizona and northern Sonora. Small, hairy silvery gray leaves. Numerous small rose-purple flowers on 1/2-inch (1 cm) spikes at the branch tips bloom late winter into spring.

* *See Glossary*

Dalea wislizenii

Wislizenii's dalea

Fabaceae (Leguminosae) family

COLD HARDINESS

Low and intermediate zones, probably warm microclimate of high zone. Moderately frost hardy.

LANDSCAPE VALUE

Border shrub, foundation plant or space definer.

CULTURAL REQUIREMENTS

- **Exposure:** Full sun.
- **Water:** Drought tolerant. Water every month or two.
- **Soil:** Most soils.
- **Propagation:** Seed or cutting.
- **Maintenance:** Prune occasionally for best form and foliage density; otherwise requires little maintenance.

POSSIBLE PROBLEMS

None observed.

Open slender-branched shrub native to Arizona and New Mexico in the United States and to Sonora and Durango in Mexico. Shrub grows 1½ to 4 feet (46 cm to 1 m) high and 3 to 4 feet (1 to 1.5 m) wide at a moderate rate. Leaves are pinnately* compound and composed of nine or more oblong hairy leaflets. They grow about ½ to 1 inch (1 to 2.5 cm) long or longer. Dense ½- to 1-inch (1 to 1.5 cm) wide long spikes of rose-purple flowers open at the branch tips from spring into fall.

Dasylirion acrotriche

Green desert spoon, Green sotol

Agavaceae family

COLD HARDINESS

All three zones.

LANDSCAPE VALUE

- Bold accent plant.
- Combines well with tropical-effects plants.
- Also at home in desert scenes.

CULTURAL REQUIREMENTS

- **Exposure:** Full sun, including reflected sun to part shade.
- **Water:** Drought resistant, but growth increases and general appearance improves with water every two to four weeks during the warm season.
- **Soil:** Any soil with good drainage.
- **Propagation:** Seed.
- **Maintenance:** Remove dead leaves as needed to groom plant.

POSSIBLE PROBLEMS

Saw-toothed leaves could be a hazard near pedestrian-traffic areas.

This green sotol from north central Mexico resembles *D. wheeleri* in all respects except it is bright green instead of gray. Produces spiky yucca-like whorl of leaves to 3 feet (1 m) long and wide. Bloom stalk reaches 10 feet (3 m) or higher. Moderate growth rate. From a landscape point of view, the refreshing green color presents a more tropical effect and less "deserty" mood. Mature plants develop a tall bloom stalk with small greenish flowers and abundant seed from spring into summer. Dry stalks can remain for some time and add landscape interest. Old plants may develop short trunks, adding to the overall visual mass.

* *See Glossary*

Dasylirion longissima

Toothless sotol, Mexican grass tree
Agavaceae family

COLD HARDINESS

Low and intermediate zones and probably all but the coldest areas of high zone.

LANDSCAPE VALUE

- Dramatic accent plant.
- Combines well with palms and other tropical-effects plants.
- Less desertlike appearance than other gray-foliaged sotols but still blends well in desert-plant combinations.

CULTURAL REQUIREMENTS

- **Exposure:** Full sun, reflected heat or open shade.
- **Water:** Drought tolerant. Water only every month or two. No need to water at all in regions receiving 10 inches (255 mm) of annual rainfall. Also no problems if planted in areas that receive water every week or two.
- **Soil:** Any soil with good drainage.
- **Propagation:** Seed.
- **Maintenance:** Low maintenance. If you wish to show off the trunk, remove dry leaves.

POSSIBLE PROBLEMS

None observed, except that slow growth rate can be frustrating.

To 10 feet (3 m) high, spreading 6 to 8 feet (2 to 2.5 m). Slow growth. Narrow dark green leaves, almost round with no teeth along the margins, grow in clumps arranged in whorls around a woody base. Leaves may grow as long as 4 to 5 feet (1 to 1.5 m) and create quite a lush effect. Trunk slowly develops 8 to 10 feet (2.5 to 3 m) tall. Overall width reaches 8 feet (2.5 m). Tightly clustered greenish white flowers are borne on tall narrow spikes in spring and early summer. Does not bloom until it reaches a larger scale; then blooming is an annual event. Old leaves cascade in a dry thatch around the trunk if not removed. Native to Mexico.

Dasylirion texanum

Texas sotol
Agavaceae family

COLD HARDINESS

All three zones.

LANDSCAPE VALUE

- Strong accent or point-of-interest specimen, alone or in groups.
- Dramatic, undemanding container plant.
- Less "deserty" than the more common *D. wheeleri*.
- Blends into tropical-effects planting compositions.

CULTURAL REQUIREMENTS

- **Exposure:** Full sun to light shade.
- **Water:** Water new plantings every week or two to hasten their establishment. Water established plants only once or twice during long dry periods to maintain good appearance.
- **Soil:** Most soils with good drainage.
- **Propagation:** Seed.
- **Maintenance:** Needs little pruning except to remove the flower stalk when it is no longer attractive.

POSSIBLE PROBLEMS

Small but sharp saw teeth along leaf edges pose a danger in pedestrian-traffic areas.

Stiff, narrow green leaves 2 to 3 feet (61 cm to 1 m) long and 1/3 to 1/2 inch (1 cm) wide form a dense, rounded foliage clump. Leaf margins are saw toothed but leaf tips have no sharp point. In late spring and early summer, a single erect flower stalk as tall as 15 feet (4.5 m) bears small creamy white flowers in a slender, densely packed column along the high half of the stem. Overall, grows at a slow to moderate pace to 3 feet (1 m) high and 3 to 5 feet (1 to 1.5 m) wide. Native to Texas and Chihuahua, Mexico.

Dasylirion wheeleri

Desert spoon, Sotol

Agavaceae family

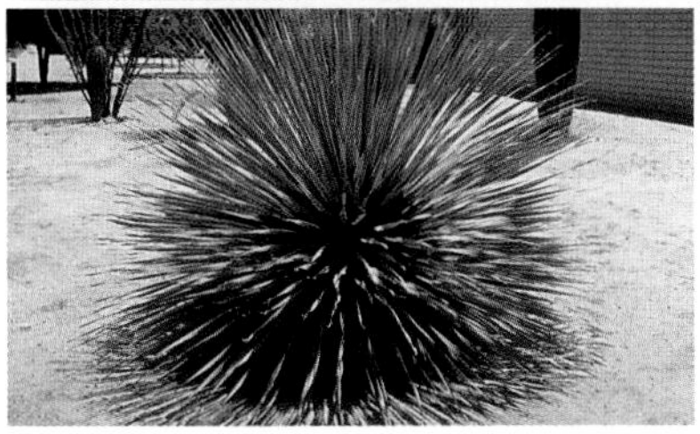

COLD HARDINESS

All three zones; native to the high zone.

LANDSCAPE VALUE

- Desert accent plant.
- Striking silhouette with bold foliage and distinctive floral display and seed stalk.
- Leaf base and petiole* flare out at the trunk to form a spoon shape with the leaf blade as a handle. When dried, these serve a number of decorative uses and are popular with flower arrangers.

CULTURAL REQUIREMENTS

- **Exposure:** Full to reflected sun.
- **Water:** Drought tolerant when established. Water once or twice during the hot season, especially at lower elevations. This will accelerate growth and maintain plant appearance.
- **Soil:** Well-drained gravelly or rocky soil.
- **Propagation:** Seed.
- **Maintenance**: Almost maintenance-free. Prune away the skirt of dried leaves that accumulate on large plants if you wish to expose the interesting trunk.

POSSIBLE PROBLEMS

None observed.

Evergreen succulent that is native to higher elevation desert, grassland and oak woodland regions of Arizona, New Mexico, Texas and northern Mexico. Narrow, linear gray-green leaves to 3 feet (1 m) long have sharp curved thorns along the margin and grow in a crowded rosette* of rounded form that spreads to about 5 feet (1.5 m) wide and slowly grows 3 to 6 feet (1 to 2 m) high. Older specimens develop a short, stout trunk to 3 feet (1 m) tall. Lower dried leaves lie against the trunk and form a tan-colored skirt. From late spring into summer, elongated clusters of creamy white flowers open on erect stems 9 to 15 feet (3 to 4.5 m) tall. The tan seeds that follow make the stalk look like a giant sheaf of grains.

Decatropis bicolor

No common name available

Rutaceae family

COLD HARDINESS

Low and intermediate zones. Probably parts of the high zone, too, judging by the temperatures that occur in its native region in Mexico.

LANDSCAPE VALUE

- Large shrub or small open-form tree.
- Handsome foliage and open structure make an interesting pattern and silhouette against a plain wall and add richness to mixed shrub combinations.
- Coppery color of new growth in spring and fall adds seasonal interest.

CULTURAL REQUIREMENTS

- **Exposure:** Full sun, including reflected sun, to open shade.
- **Water:** Endures periods of drought but a thorough soaking of the root zone every week or two during the warm season helps assure growth and satisfactory appearance.
- **Soil:** Most soils with good drainage. Although native to limestone mountains, it doesn't seem to require calcareous* soil.
- **Propagation:** Seed and probably cuttings. (To date, not enough cutting wood for this purpose.)
- **Maintenance:** Improve irregular growth by staking and guiding growth.

POSSIBLE PROBLEMS

None observed except slowness of growth.

A large, open evergreen shrub or small tree from Mexico. The big glossy and leathery dark green leaves are compound with eight to twelve leaflets. Striking copper color of new growth is a showy aspect of the plant. Bloom is a curious twiggy brown inflorescence* that produces small inconspicuous flowers, which are not a decorative landscape element. Grows up to 10 feet (3 m) high, give or take, with equal spread. Slow to moderate growth.

* See Glossary

Delonix regia

Royal poinciana, Flamboyant, Flame tree, Arbol del fuego
Fabaceae (Leguminosae) family

COLD HARDINESS
Frost-free areas of the low zone.

LANDSCAPE VALUE
- Breathtaking show and startling splash of color during its bloom season.
- Striking accent or specimen.
- Spreading shade tree where space permits.

CULTURAL REQUIREMENTS
- **Exposure:** Full sun. Withstands summer heat. Not tolerant of salt spray.
- **Water:** Water every few weeks during the flowering and growing season. Continue watering into fall to shorten leafless period. Water once or twice during the dormant period if the climate is dry.
- **Soil:** Any soil.
- **Propagation:** Seed, or cuttings of improved varieties for better flowering characteristics.
- **Maintenance:** Tends to start out low-branching. Nip back and clip low branches *gradually* to achieve above-head-height canopy. Heavy set of long woody pads may need clean-up.

POSSIBLE PROBLEMS
- Hard freeze will result in severe die-back* or loss of entire tree.
- Leafless and unattractive for several winter months.
- Soft, brittle wood is easily broken.
- Bean pods create litter.
- Aggressive roots can damage nearby walls and walks.

When royal poinciana is in its winter-deciduous period, the broad spreading crown of the dormant tree has little appeal. This is, however, one of the most lavishly ornamental flowering trees. Native to Madagascar, it is now cultivated in gardens throughout the tropical world. In late spring or early summer, the tree bursts into bloom with huge masses of brilliant crimson to orange orchidlike flowers 3 to 4 inches (7.5 to 10 cm) across. The display is long-lasting and, as it ends, a new crop of feathery fern-like leaves appear. Dangling flat, woody seed pods are as long as 2 feet (61 cm) and are dark brown at maturity. They sometimes persist on the tree for many months. In tropical areas, a second crop of flowers may appear when seed pods of the first bloom cycle are nearly full size, striking in combination. Grows rapidly up to 40 feet (12 m) high and wide.

Dichrostachys cinerea

Dichrostachys, Sickle pod
Fabaceae (Leguminosae) family

COLD HARDINESS
Low zone and warm microclimates of intermediate zone. Damaged at 26° to 28°F (-3°C to -2°C).

LANDSCAPE VALUE
- Screen where width is not a problem.
- Almost constantly in bloom during warm season.
- Branches have small thorns, making it a good barrier plant.
- Considered a good forage plant in its native Sudan.

CULTURAL REQUIREMENTS
- **Exposure:** Full sun to part shade.
- **Water:** Drought resistant but looks best with water every month or two. Tolerates ample water.
- **Soil:** Any soil.
- **Propagation:** Seed.
- **Maintenance:** Though interesting at close range, the tiny thorns can be a hazard. Branches may need pruning and training to minimize this problem.

POSSIBLE PROBLEMS
- Tiny thorns can be a hazard when grooming and pruning.
- Frost tender. May need to remove frost-damaged wood but tree recovers quickly in spring.
- Tends to spread by root sprouts, which can be invasive in more tropical areas.

Large evergreen shrub with feathery acacia-like leaves borne on limber branches. Unusual two-toned pendulous flower spikes hang below the branches, creamy yellow at the tip ranging to lavender-pink at the base. Flowers are not showy at a distance but do add considerable interest at close range. With enough water, it rapidly grows 6 to 12 feet (2 to 3.5 m) high and wide. Native to tropical Africa.

* *See Glossary*

COLD HARDINESS
Low and intermediate zones and warmer microclimates in the high zone. Heavy frost can damage buds, causing a lapse in the flower display.

LANDSCAPE VALUE
- Outstanding low-water-use winter groundcover for natural effects.
- Color display in winter and early spring is a real traffic stopper.
- African daisy can also be planted in low, wide containers for colorful displays on sunny patios.

CULTURAL REQUIREMENTS
- **Exposure:** Full sun, reflected sun to very light shade.
- **Water:** Water every week or two. Brief drying out is not a problem, but regular moisture is necessary for good cover and flowering.
- **Soil:** Any soil, but prefers sandy types.
- **Propagation:** Seed. Best planted in early fall followed by water every week or two if rain doesn't materialize. Applying water in early fall will bring the new plants up with no scarifying of the seeds. Seedlings are often grown in flats for setting out in small garden plots and in pots.
- **Maintenance:** Mow the dry plants after the seed is set in late spring to create a thatch that serves as a dry groundcover through the summer, useful for keeping dust down at the landscape perimeter.

POSSIBLE PROBLEMS
None noted if used in natural landscape situations.

Dimorphotheca sinuata
African daisy, Cape marigold
Asteraceae (Compositae) family

Annual plant with narrow medium green leaves 2 to 3 inches (5 to 7.5 cm) long. Bright orange to yellow daisy flowers 1½ inches (4 cm) in diameter cover the plants in winter and spring in sunny arid regions. They create a colorful annual carpet that reseeds year after year. The flowering ends in late spring when the plants go to seed and die. Depending on the warmth of the season and the moisture supply, blooming can begin in early winter and continue through spring. Once the weather warms, the show begins again. In coastal climates with a pronounced winter rainfall pattern, the species naturalizes, but the bloom will be more of a spring event. Flowers remain closed on cloudy days. There is a white hybrid, but it does not persist. Native to South Africa. Plant grows rapidly to 4 to 12 inches (10 to 30.5 cm) high and wide.

COLD HARDINESS
Low and intermediate zones. Frost tolerant.

LANDSCAPE VALUE
- Rich and exotic palmlike plant.
- Dramatic focal point or accent.
- Natural companion plant with other tropical-effects plants. Especially appealing when nestled at the base of a palm trunk.
- Containers.

CULTURAL REQUIREMENTS
- **Exposure:** Filtered sunlight or morning sun and afternoon shade. Avoid reflected sun and windy locations.
- **Water:** Water every week or two throughout the year. Tolerates brief periods of drought, but needs water weekly in spring and summer. Container-bound plants require weekly water year-round.
- **Soil:** Improved garden soil. Good drainage is essential.
- **Propagation:** Seed and possibly offsets*. It has been given endangered species status to protect native stands, but unfortunately, illegal collection continues. Buy only from a reputable grower.
- **Maintenance:** Little to no maintenance required.

POSSIBLE PROBLEMS
None observed.

Dioon edule
Palma de la virgen, Chestnut dioon
Zamiaceae family

Unique evergreen with a rosette* of palm-like foliage that imparts a tropical ambiance to the landscape. Grows slowly 3 to 6 feet (1 to 2 m) high, 6 to 12 feet (2 to 3.5 m) wide. Young plants are open and fernlike with feathery, flexible grayish blue-green leaves. Mature specimens have more of a palm character. The arching mature leaves are greener, stiff and shiny. They grow 3 to 6 feet (1 to 2 m) long. Eventually a short trunk 6 to 10 inches (15 to 25.5 cm) in diameter forms with a conspicuous cover of dried leaf bases. Plants are male or female. The reproductive parts of both sexes resemble large felt-covered pine cones in the center of the foliage rosette. Native to Mexico.

* See Glossary

Diospyros texana

Texas persimmon

Ebenaceae family

Large shrub to small evergreen tree with rounded contours, dappled silvery gray bark and small satiny smooth leaves that turn dark green and leathery as they mature. Grows to 15 feet (4.5 m) high, with equal spread under optimum conditions. Speed up slow growth with regular water and good care. Flowers are inconspicuous. In summer, however, clusters of purple grapelike fruit appear, which are edible and have some decorative appeal.

COLD HARDINESS

Low and intermediate zones. Probably hardy in most high-zone regions.

LANDSCAPE VALUE

- Round-headed tree for patios.
- Beautiful bark and rich green foliage make it well worth the wait for it to develop.
- Screening if side branches are unpruned and remain near the ground.

CULTURAL REQUIREMENTS

- **Exposure:** Full sun to part shade.
- **Water:** Drought resistant. Tolerates water every month or two, but until desired size is achieved, thoroughly soak the root zone every week or two during the warm season.
- **Soil:** Any soil will do, but reasonable soil depth will speed up its normally slow growth.
- **Propagation:** Grows easily from seed, but probably could grow from cuttings as well.
- **Maintenance:** Apply fertilizer in late winter, just before new spring growth surge. Gradually remove side branches and stake or train to speed growth into a tree form.

POSSIBLE PROBLEMS

Occasional heavy set of fruit can litter adjoining paved spaces.

Landscape Design Example

An accent (such as *Fouquieria splendens*) can be the perfect touch for an entryway.

* See Glossary

Dodonaea viscosa

Hop bush, Hopseed bush

Sapindaceae family

COLD HARDINESS

Quite variable depending on native habitat of plants from which propagation material is taken. Green forms are generally hardy in low and intermediate zones. Bronze-purple form is hardy in low zone and occasionally damaged in intermediate zone. Some forms are native to high zone in Arizona and Mexico.

LANDSCAPE VALUE

- Excellent quick-growing screen.
- The narrow-leaf types are best for shearing into a tall, narrow hedge.
- Topiary or a small tree (with training). The broad-leaf types make the best small trees.
- Adds a bright green touch to the arid landscape.
- Bronze-purple form adds a rich color note in contrast to greens. Leaf color is most intense in winter.

CULTURAL REQUIREMENTS

- **Exposure:** Full sun to part shade.
- **Water:** Drought resistant. Water every month or two (or more often) for good appearance, depending on your particular landscape. Tolerates wetter areas, but chlorosis* may result.
- **Soil:** Any soil with good drainage.
- **Propagation:** Seed or cuttings.
- **Maintenance:** Regular shaping during growing season if used as hedge or topiary.

POSSIBLE PROBLEMS

- Short-lived.
- Vulnerable to strangulation from root girdling. Probably a result of being kept too long in small pots during early propagation.
- Subject to chlorosis*.

Large evergreen shrub (or small tree) that rapidly grows 12 to 15 feet (3.5 to 4.5 m) high and12 feet (3.5 m) wide. Native to many areas of the warmer arid regions of the world, so there are many foliage variations, including a bronze-purple–leafed form: 'Purpurea' from Australia. The green-leafed forms from Arizona and Mexico are hardier to frost. Small blossoms and round seeds turn from green to pinkish lavender, interesting at close range. They are more noticeable on the green-leafed form and resemble hop—thus its common name. The green-leafed form also has varying leaf widths, including a narrow-leaf type from Arizona and a broad-leaf type from Mexico.

* See Glossary

Dorstenia contrajerva

Ground fig

Moraceae family

COLD HARDINESS

Low and intermediate zones and probably high zone because it is dormant in winter.

LANDSCAPE VALUE

- Groundcover for small spaces in a shady oasis-type situation.
- Close-up viewing adjoining an outdoor sitting area or entry garden.
- Combines well with other shade plants.

CULTURAL REQUIREMENTS

- **Exposure:** Filtered sun to deep shade.
- **Water:** Keep moist during the warm season. Accepts completely dry conditions in winter. Will not die out from drought in summer, but might go dormant.
- **Soil:** Improved soil; not tolerant of alkaline soils or saline water or soils.
- **Propagation:** Divisions, or seed if available.
- **Maintenance:** A winter annual, such as viola or Johnny jumpups, can cover bare spots and be removed when spring arrives.

POSSIBLE PROBLEMS

Delicate soft leaves don't tolerate foot traffic or raking.

Attractive, soft fig-leaf-shaped leaves grow 3 to 4 inches (7.5 to 10 cm) long and hug the ground. Plant grows 6 inches (15 cm) high and 3 to 4 feet (1 to 1.5 m) wide or wider at a moderate pace. Strictly herbaceous*, spreading by underground stems. Curious small greenish paddle-shaped flowers are actually open-faced figs among the leaves. They are not decorative but are interesting at close range. Deciduous and generally bare in winter. Native from Sonora south into Mexico.

Drosanthemum floribundum

Rosea ice plant

Aizoaceae family

COLD HARDINESS

Low and intermediate zones.

LANDSCAPE VALUE

- Erosion control on slopes.
- Beds and rock gardens.
- Seasonal floral display is exceptional.

CULTURAL REQUIREMENTS

- **Exposure:** Full sun to part shade.
- **Water:** Every week or two during the warmer months. Every month or two during winter.
- **Soil:** Grows well in many soils of average to poor quality. Not well suited to the intense heat and aridity of some desert climates, preferring instead the milder climate of coastal areas.
- **Propagation:** Seed or cuttings.
- **Maintenance:** Weed carefully—does not withstand foot traffic. Fortunately, mature plants have little problem with weeds.

POSSIBLE PROBLEMS

Does not grow as vigorously or flower as abundantly in inland arid regions as it does in coastal areas.

The fleshy, cylindrical light green leaves of this evergreen groundcover from South Africa are covered with minute glistening bumps. The plant grows as a low dense mat of trailing stems that develop roots as they extend out from its base. Light pink 3/4-inch (2-cm) wide flowers with many stamens* transform the plant into a vivid carpet of color in late spring or early summer. Grows at a moderate pace to 6 inches (15 cm) high and 18 inches (46 cm) wide.

See Glossary

Dyssodia pentachaeta

Golden dyssodia

Asteraceae (Compositae) family

COLD HARDINESS

Low and intermediate zones. Frost hardy.

LANDSCAPE VALUE

- Arid- and transition-zone wildflower carpet.
- In minioasis gardens.
- Lively color contrast during the hottest months of the year.

CULTURAL REQUIREMENTS

- **Exposure:** Full sun.
- **Water:** Anywhere from a week to a couple months between watering from spring into fall maintains vigorous free-flowering plantings and allows them to reseed from year to year. Water every week or two during the growing season for a good seed crop.
- **Soil:** Most soils.
- **Propagation:** Seed, sometimes offered by nurseries as seedling plants.
- **Maintenance:** Requires little attention if in informal plantings.

POSSIBLE PROBLEMS

Short-lived, and behaves as an annual in marginal situations.

Low-growing herbaceous* perennial that grows at a moderate rate to 7 inches (18 cm) high, with equal spread. Shrubby with many branches and bright green lacy leaves 3/8 to 3/4 inch (1 to 2 cm) long. Leaves are deeply cleft into five to seven sharp-pointed, threadlike divisions that are 1/8 to 1/3 inch (.5 to 1 cm) long. Bright yellow flowers that resemble miniature daisies open on slender stems 1 1/4 to 2 3/4 inches (3 to 7 cm) long well above the foliage. Native to New Mexico, Texas and northern Mexico.

Echinocactus grusonii

Golden barrel cactus

Cactaceae family

COLD HARDINESS

Low and intermediate zones. Other *Echinocactus* species are hardy in all three zones.

LANDSCAPE VALUE

- The most "gardenesque" of all the *Echinocactus* and less deserty looking.
- Bold accent.
- Combines well with other cacti and succulents to create striking plant compositions.
- Containers.

CULTURAL REQUIREMENTS

- **Exposure:** Full sun to light shade.
- **Water:** Water every month or two, more frequently during the warm season. Some of the other species require less to no supplemental water.
- **Soil:** Gritty well-drained soil.
- **Propagation:** Seed.
- **Maintenance:** No maintenance.

POSSIBLE PROBLEMS

- Can scorch in reflected-heat situations (*E. grusonii* only).
- Will rot with poor drainage.
- Careless handling can result in scarring and mutilation that will never disappear or grow over.

All members of this genus take the traditional barrel shape and many of the Southwest native species are used in the landscape. *E. grusonii* is perhaps the most striking for its globe-shaped trunk and vertical ribs lined with thick rows of golden spikes, a very interesting pattern and color in the landscape. Other species may have red, pink or plain spines. Flowers appear in a ring, garland-like on the top in spring; fruit follows. Grows slowly to 3 feet (1 m) high (after many years), spreading 2 feet (61 cm).

* *See Glossary*

Ehretia anacua

Sandpaper tree

Boraginaceae family

COLD HARDINESS

All three zones, but the leaves turn brown and are eventually shed after a hard frost.

LANDSCAPE VALUE

- Patio-size tree (with training).
- Can be left bushy with branches to the ground for background or screening.

CULTURAL REQUIREMENTS

- **Exposure:** Full sun to part shade.
- **Water:** Water every week or two to stimulate growth, but thoroughly soak the root zone every month or two when mature.
- **Soil:** Almost any soil.
- **Propagation:** Seed or cuttings.
- **Maintenance:** Prune and shape to develop a patio tree. The resulting specimen more than justifies the time and effort required to do this.

POSSIBLE PROBLEMS

- Some root suckering, but not a real problem.
- Leaves turn brown with hard frost and hang on for a spell before dropping. Not too handsome at this point.

Semi-evergreen tree with rough sandpaper-textured leaves densely arranged. Clusters of small white flowers bloom in spring. These are followed by golden berries that make a striking contrast against the dark green summer foliage. Develops slowly into a sturdy-trunked round-headed tree, but goes through rangy growth spurts earlier in the process. From southern Texas and northern Mexico. Grows 15 to 20 feet (4.5 to 6 m) high or higher, spreading to 15 feet (4.5 m) or more. Moderate growth rate.

Ehretia tinifolia

Bastard cherry tree

Boraginaceae family

COLD HARDINESS

Low zone and warm locations in intermediate zone. (Probably hardier—it has never shown frost damage on the University of Arizona campus.)

LANDSCAPE VALUE

- Street tree.
- An appropriate size for residential situations and general landscape use.
- Because of its considerable landscape potential, this tree deserves more attention.

CULTURAL REQUIREMENTS

- **Exposure:** Full sun to part shade. Tolerates reflected sun situations.
- **Water:** Soak the root zone every week or two during the warm season, less frequently as tree matures.
- **Soil:** Any soil.
- **Propagation:** Seed or cuttings.
- **Maintenance:** Prune as new growth develops to maintain good branching structure and canopy shape.

POSSIBLE PROBLEMS

None observed.

An evergreen shrub or tree that grows vertically to 35 feet (11 m) high, spreading 30 feet (9 m). Native to Mexico and the West Indies. Observed in street tree plantings in the southern Chihuahuan Desert cities from which seed was collected for University of Arizona specimens. Attractive, oblong dark green leathery leaves $4\frac{1}{2}$ inches (11.5 cm) long have pointed tips and look great year-round. Flowers are white, in panicles* to 6 inches (15 cm) long. Fruit are red or purple. Moderate growth rate. Flowers bloom in late spring and fruit follows.

* See Glossary

Elaeagnus angustifolia

Russian olive

Elaeagnaceae family

COLD HARDINESS

All three zones but does not take well to heat in low zone.

LANDSCAPE VALUE

- Windbreaks, background screening and barrier plantings.
- Can be trimmed up into an interesting small tree with a gnarly brown trunk and branches.
- Although a little rough, it can be used as a patio and street tree where choices are limited.
- Medium-size clipped hedge (accepts trimming well).
- The silver gray foliage is an interesting color in the landscape
- Although inconspicuous, flowers are intensely fragrant.

CULTURAL REQUIREMENTS

- **Exposure:** Full sun (including reflected heat in high zone) to part shade. A plant for punishing situations: Endures wind, drought, heat and cold, especially in the high zone.
- **Water:** Weekly to monthly soaking of the root zone for good growth and foliage. Accepts little or none in regions of 12 inches (305 mm) annual rainfall or more, but will probably remain small.
- **Soil:** Most soils, including alkaline.
- **Propagation:** Seed or cuttings.
- **Maintenance:** Tends to be bushy, with low side branches. Stake, prune and train for tree form.

POSSIBLE PROBLEMS

- Short-lived, especially in low zone.
- Wood is somewhat brittle and branches may suffer storm damage.

A small deciduous tree that grows at a moderate rate up to 20 feet (6 m) high, smaller under dry conditions, with equal spread. Regular irrigation will speed up growth. Willow-like leaves are 2 inches (5 cm) long. Angular trunk and branches (sometimes thorny) covered with shredding dark brown bark are especially attractive in winter and contrast nicely with the gray foliage in summer. Fragrant, small greenish yellow flowers appear in early summer, followed by berry-like fruit resembling miniature olives, which are a food source for some birds. Native to dry interior areas of Europe and western Asia.

Encelia californica

Brown-eyed Susan

Asteraceae (Compositae) family

COLD HARDINESS

Low and intermediate zones.

LANDSCAPE VALUE

- Colorful at times.
- Bank cover or foreground shrub.

CULTURAL REQUIREMENTS

- **Exposure:** Full sun to part shade.
- **Water:** Drought resistant. Water every month or two for good appearance, every week or two during the cool season for good growth and flowering.
- **Soil:** Any soil with good drainage.
- **Propagation:** Seed.
- **Maintenance:** Cut back to rejuvenate.

POSSIBLE PROBLEMS

- Tends to look poor in late summer and after a bloom period when it needs grooming.
- Short-lived.

Sprawling green-leafed shrub, covered at times in the cool season with dark-centered yellow daisies about 1 inch (2.5 cm) wide. May bloom several times from fall to spring if conditions are favorable. Evergreen but can be drought deciduous. Native to Southern California and Baja California. Grows 3 to 4 feet (1 m) high and to 6 feet (2 m) wide. Moderate to rapid growth in winter; slow growth in spring; no growth at all in summer.

** See Glossary*

Encelia farinosa
Brittle bush
Asteraceae (Compositae) family

Usually a woody perennial that persists for a number of years if there is enough moisture, but dies out if there is a long rainless period. Then it behaves as an annual, coming back quickly from seed. An attractive gray mounding shrub that grows to 3 feet (1 m) high with equal spread. Foliage is almost white under dry conditions. Bright yellow daisies about 1 inch (2.5 cm) in diameter on long stems above the foliage cover the shrub in spring and at other times. Native to Sonoran and Mojave deserts. Rapid growth, especially after rains. Goes dormant in drought.

COLD HARDINESS
Low zone and warm microclimates in the intermediate zone. New growth that often occurs after winter rain is tipped back by temperatures in the mid-20s F (-4°C).

LANDSCAPE VALUE
- A bright spot of yellow in spring with lesser displays from summer into fall when moisture is available.
- Medians.
- Banks.
- Foundation planting.
- Revegetation.

CULTURAL REQUIREMENTS
- **Exposure:** Full sun.
- **Water:** Drought resistant. Water every month or two for acceptable appearance. Naturalizes and lives without supplemental water, but will die out after a long (6- to 8-month) rainless period. Will go dormant and lose leaves in drought. Blooms only after it receives moisture.
- **Soil:** Any well-drained soil, even rocky.
- **Propagation:** Seed.
- **Maintenance:** Replace old woody plants with young ones. Reseeds readily, so it will usually maintain its presence in an informal planting. Shear off seed heads for good appearance and to induce additional bloom periods.

POSSIBLE PROBLEMS
- A heavy bloom crop is followed by abundant seed production. Seed heads detract from appearance.
- Short-lived

Enchylaena tomentosa
Ruby sheep bush
Chenopodiaceae family

COLD HARDINESS
All three zones.

LANDSCAPE VALUE
- Groundcover for rough, dry situations.
- Suitable for revegetation and erosion-control areas where its tendency to naturalize would not be a problem.

CULTURAL REQUIREMENTS
- **Exposure:** Full sun. Tolerates reflected heat and open shade.
- **Water:** No supplemental water needed in regions receiving 7 to 10 inches (180 to 255 mm) annual rain but water as needed during long dry periods to maintain a satisfactory appearance.
- **Soil:** Grows in almost any soil. Salt tolerant.
- **Propagation:** Seed or cuttings.
- **Maintenance:** Low maintenance. Restrain it from spreading where it's not wanted.

POSSIBLE PROBLEMS
- Will naturalize and may spread into areas where it's not wanted.
- In Queensland, Australia, it was shown to have a potentially toxic level of soluble oxalate, but there were no ill effects noted when sheep heartily grazed on this plant.
- Lacks the refinement needed for well-groomed landscape plantings.

Sprawling gray evergreen shrub with small, almost cylindrical, hairy leaves. Grows rapidly from 1 inch to 3 feet (2.5 cm to 1 m) high, but will climb higher on adjoining shrubs and fences. Spreads 10 feet (3 m) or more. Inconspicuous flowers bloom in early spring and produce small fleshy fruit, green to yellow and then red, which add interest up close but are not abundant enough to make this a useful color plant. Native to Australia.

* See Glossary

Enterlobium cyclocarpum

Monkey's ear tree

Fabaceae (Leguminosae) family

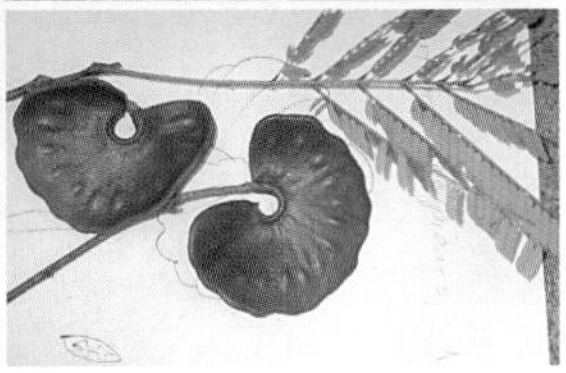

COLD HARDINESS

Low zone and warmer locations in intermediate zone.

LANDSCAPE VALUE

- Bright green spot in a hot landscape.
- Side branches can be trimmed high to create a spacious area of shade for outdoor living and understory planting.

CULTURAL REQUIREMENTS

- **Exposure:** Full sun.
- **Water:** Soak the root zone thoroughly every week or two at first (summer only) and then every month or two at maturity.
- **Soil**: Any soil with depth to develop size and allow plant to live on infrequent irrigation.
- **Propagation:** Seed.
- **Maintenance:** May need to train and remove low branches on young plants.

POSSIBLE PROBLEMS

- Ear pods produce some litter.
- Reseeds abundantly in wetter areas, such as Florida.
- Because of plant size, frosted twigs are difficult to remove after a cold winter.

Great spreading canopy tree with large bright green fine-textured leaves resembling *Jacaranda* or *Delonix*. Smooth gray trunks with eventually fat lateral branches. Flowers unimportant but the glossy dark brown or black seed pods curl around to resemble a human ear. Evergreen to deciduous depending on winter temperatures or drought. Grows 40 to 60 feet (12 to 18 m) high, with equal or even wider spread. Moderate to rapid growth. Native to southern Mexico.

Ephedra viridis

Mormon tea, Joint fir

Ephedraceae family

COLD HARDINESS

All three zones.

LANDSCAPE VALUE

- Adds texture and color effects to arid and transition zone plantings.
- Street-median and highway landscapes.
- Revegetation projects.

CULTURAL REQUIREMENTS

- **Exposure:** Full to reflected sun.
- **Water:** Drought tolerant. Water every month or two to maintain satisfactory plant appearance in hot, low-elevation arid regions. At the higher elevations, water once or twice a season only during long dry spells.
- **Soil:** Most soils with good drainage.
- **Propagation:** Seed or clump divisions.
- **Maintenance:** Requires little maintenance other than occasional thinning out of dead stems and those that detract from the natural symmetry of the plant.

POSSIBLE PROBLEMS

Sensitive to overwatering and poorly drained planting sites.

At first glance it may be difficult to see a relationship between this unusual shrub and a juniper or a pine. It grows 2 to 4 feet (61 cm to 1 m) high and wide as a dense clump of thin, up to 1/8-inch (0.5-cm) diameter stems that are rigidly erect, jointed and bright green or yellow-green. Pairs of tiny, sharp-tipped, scalelike leaves are shed after a brief life on the branches. Close inspection of the small 1/4-inch (.5-cm) "flowers" that open in spring reveals that they are actually unisexual (male or female) cones. Each plant bears cones of one sex or the other, not both. Native to middle- and high-elevation regions of the western and southwestern United States. A medicinal tonic once made from this plant gives it one of its common names. Slow to moderate growth.

* *See Glossary*

Eracameria laricifolia *(Haplopappus laricifolia)*

Turpentine bush

Asteraceae (Compositae) family

COLD HARDINESS

All three zones.

LANDSCAPE VALUE

- Attractive fall-flowering shrub that tolerates difficult hot locations.
- Foreground and foundation plantings.

CULTURAL REQUIREMENTS

- **Exposure:** Full sun.
- **Water:** Drought resistant. Water thoroughly every month or two, especially in late summer, for good foliage and fall bloom.
- **Soil:** Tolerates poor soil.
- **Propagation:** Seed or cuttings.
- **Maintenance:** Little to no maintenance.

POSSIBLE PROBLEMS

- Slow growth limits its usefulness for the impatient grower.
- Seed heads somewhat unattractive after flowering, but only briefly.

Low-mounding evergreen shrub that grows slowly to 3 feet (1 m) high, with equal spread. At a glance, the plant is almost conifer-like with its tiny dark green, almost needle-like, leaves. Puts on a display of tiny yellow flowers in clusters that cover the shrub in mid-fall. The best landscape plant of the genus. Some other species make a colorful fall show of yellow but are weedy-looking the rest of the year. Native to the U.S. Southwest and the Chihuahuan Desert in Mexico.

Erythrina bidwillii

Bidwell's coral tree

Fabaceae (Leguminosae) family

COLD HARDINESS

Low and intermediate zones. Hardened-off* wood is damaged in mid-20s F (-4°C). Can be grown more as a perennial in high zone, where it may gradually develop short trunks after several years.

LANDSCAPE VALUE

- Spectacular flowering plant either as a shrub or small tree for color in the landscape.
- The form of trunks and branches can add interest with proper annual pruning to enhance gnarly growth habit.

CULTURAL REQUIREMENTS

- **Exposure:** Full sun.
- **Water:** Water every week or two. Can perform on less frequent but thorough soakings of the root zone after it is mature.
- **Soil:** Any soil with good drainage.
- **Propagation:** Cuttings. Even branch sections will root.
- **Maintenance:** Needs at least one or more cleanup prunings to remove old bloom stalks for good appearance. Some prefer to keep it shrub size for easy maintenance.

POSSIBLE PROBLEMS

- Vigorous growth produces need to remove spent blossom stalks.
- Thorniness complicates grooming and pruning.

Reputedly a hybrid between *E. crista-galli* and *E. herbacea*, this deciduous to semi-evergreen shrub or small tree is notable for its almost continuous flowering throughout the warm season, producing 3-foot (1-m) long spikes of deep red pea-shaped flowers. Grows rapidly to 20 feet (6 m) high and wide, but only hardens a portion of this growth to become part of its permanent structure each season. The balance dries and sloughs off or needs to be cut back. The stalks of the sterile blossoms dry after each successive bloom spurt. Eventually it becomes a gnarly squat tree with fat branches and trunk.

* *See Glossary*

Erythrina flabelliformis

Arizona coral bean, Chilicote, Sonoran coral tree

Fabaceae (Leguminosae) family

COLD HARDINESS

Low and intermediate zones and warm microclimates of high zone. Performs best on a nearly frost-free planting site, but it can be treated as a perennial in the high zone, where it is also native and where it freezes to the ground most winters.

LANDSCAPE VALUE

- Flowering accent or specimen.
- Unique container plant.
- Foliage is short-lived but takes on attractive yellow-orange fall colors.
- In warm, nearly frost-free areas, it assumes the form of a small tree.

CULTURAL REQUIREMENTS

- **Exposure:** Full to reflected sun.
- **Water:** Drought tolerant but responds well to water every week or two during the warm months.
- **Soil:** Most soils with good drainage.
- **Propagation:** Seed or softwood cuttings.
- **Maintenance:** Can be trained to grow as a small tree. Prune in spring to remove frost-damaged wood.

POSSIBLE PROBLEMS

- Stems are brittle, spiny and frost-sensitive.
- The plant is leafless for a long period.
- Seeds are poisonous but very hard and could pass through a digestive tract without emitting any toxic chemical. To be on the safe side, pods could be removed before ripening to eliminate this hazard.
- Because stems are thorny, use with care in pedestrian-traffic areas.

Small multistemmed deciduous shrub that grows 3 to 30 feet (1 to 9 m) high, and spreads 2 to 8 feet (61 cm to 2.5 m). Native to desert, desert grassland and oak woodland regions of Arizona, New Mexico, Texas and Mexico. Plants collected in the frost-free zones of Mexico become treelike under suitable conditions. Open ascending framework of thick, spiny branches. Gray-green triangular leaflets 1 to 3 inches (2.5 to 7.5 cm) long appear in response to summer rains. Clusters of brilliant red or scarlet tubular flowers, 1 to 2 inches (2.5 to 5 cm) long, bloom in spring on one-year-old stems. The 5- to 10-inch (13- to 25.5-cm) bean pods that follow contain one to several bright red poisonous seeds. Leaves turn a bright gold before dropping in the fall. Slow growth can be sped up with supplemental irrigation.

** See Glossary*

Eschscholzia californica

California poppy

Papaveraceae family

Tap-rooted perennial or annual, a native over the southern half of California. Seeds germinate in fall to produce a mounding rosette* of finely dissected blue-green leaves; in late winter and early spring, leafy flower stems are topped by a 2-inch (5-cm) solitary flower consisting of four satiny petals. Flowers close at night and on cloudy days. Colors in the wild type include a rich intense orange, pale yellow and occasionally white. Garden selections are available in a wide range of colors and single or semidouble types. Grows 8 to 24 inches (20.5 to 61 cm) high and wide at a moderate pace.

COLD HARDINESS

All three zones.

LANDSCAPE VALUE

- Usually treated as an annual in the landscape, but may be perennial in the high zone.
- Most effective when planted in large informal drifts.
- Provides spectacular seasonal color and ground-surface treatment along highways, roads and drives.
- Reseed disturbed areas, around housing developments and similar large projects and in residential landscapes where arid-region plants play a dominant role.

CULTURAL REQUIREMENTS

- **Exposure:** Full sun.
- **Water:** Periodic rainfall or irrigation during the cool growing season is adequate but generally not necessary at other times of the year, except in the high zone to keep this plant a perennial. For dependable spring bloom, water occasionally if fall and winter months are dry.
- **Soil:** Well-drained, even sandy or gravelly, soil.
- **Propagation:** Seed.
- **Maintenance:** In early fall, work up a shallow seed bed and scatter seed by hand at 3 to 4 pounds per acre (3.5 to 4.5 kg per hectare) or about 8 to 11g per 273 sq. ft. Reseeds itself and flowers the following spring if soil moisture is adequate.

POSSIBLE PROBLEMS

No warm season impact on the landscape because it survives this part of its life cycle as seed or as a holdover perennial.

Eschscholzia mexicana

Mexican poppy

Papaveraceae family

Similar in most respects to *E. californica*. Differs in that Mexican poppy is a true annual, somewhat smaller in size—6 to 12 inches (15 to 30.5 cm) high, with equal spread. Also bears most of its orange, yellow or infrequently white flowers on leafless stems. Native to Arizona and southern Utah to Western Texas and northern Mexico.

COLD HARDINESS

All three zones. Frost hardy.

LANDSCAPE VALUE

Same as *E. californica* except it tends to reseed and come back year after year.

CULTURAL REQUIREMENTS

Same as *E. californica.*

POSSIBLE PROBLEMS

Same as *E. californica.*

* *See Glossary*

EUCALYPTUS

Eucalyptus trees and shrubs present a large collection of potential arid-landscape plants. They are not particularly popular in many arid-landscape situations. Possibly, the reason for this is because the first introduced species were not ideal for the region or were much too large and overwhelming for the space where planted. However, there is a new outlook on these Australian natives. Many of the species were collected and tested in southern Arizona, particularly at Boyce Thompson Arboretum in Superior. There are many worthwhile landscape subjects that are not grown in nurseries because of the lack of demand and the potential to quickly become rootbound in containers. Consequently, to use any quantity, it's best to make a contract with a nursery to grow what you need. Most species listed are fast growing. The best trees often develop from small freshly grown plants.

Eucalyptus albens
White box
Myrtaceae family

COLD HARDINESS
Low zone and warmer locations in the intermediate zone.

LANDSCAPE VALUE
- Roadsides.
- Parks.
- Background skyline silhouettes.
- General reforestation projects, especially in the desert.

CULTURAL REQUIREMENTS
- **Exposure:** Full sun, including hot reflected situations.
- **Water:** Drought resistant. Survives on annual rainfall in Tucson, Arizona, when grown in deep soil. Soak the root zone once or twice a year when grown in shallow soil. More often for young plantings.
- **Soil:** Any soil with good drainage.
- **Propagation:** Seed.
- **Maintenance:** Remove dead branches and clean up litter. Prevent maintenance problems by giving it enough space to grow to mature size.

POSSIBLE PROBLEMS
None observed other than the typical eucalyptus litter drop.

Evergreen tree with thick boughs and a canopy of pointed gray-green leaves. Grows rapidly from 30 to 80 feet (9 to 24 m) high, usually shorter in the desert, and 20 to 60 feet (6 to 18 m) wide. The straight trunk and growth eventually fans out to a fairly wide, dense crown that produces good shade. Bark is smooth and light colored, eventually becoming dark and rough on the lower trunk. Small white flowers and fruit are not conspicuous. Native to Australia.

Landscape Design Example

A small lawn space combined with desert plants, such as the *Hesperaloe* accent, create a minioasis in Warren Jones's yard.

* See Glossary

Eucalyptus camaldulensis (E. rostrata)

Red gum, Red river gum

Myrtaceae family

COLD HARDINESS

Low and intermediate zones, but can be damaged in cold winters in the latter. Also planted in high zone where it can be severely damaged, but it recovers rapidly from stumps the next season.

LANDSCAPE VALUE

- This is probably the most planted *Eucalyptus* species worldwide for reforestation, wind breaks and roadside plantings.
- Impressive skyline tree for large areas, but not suitable for residential spaces or garden situations.

CULTURAL REQUIREMENTS

- **Exposure:** Full to reflected sun.
- **Water:** Drought resistant. Survives on little water but will also tolerate wet situations.
- **Soil:** Not picky about soil. Will tolerate lawns, but not soils high in calcium carbonate* where the tree becomes chlorotic* and dies back. This is not a problem when planted in dry situations.
- **Propagation:** Seed. Because of variability within the species, a good seed source is important.
- **Maintenance:** Needs plenty of space away from structures, overhead wires and so on. Do not top or plant where topping or heading back would be necessary. Prune only to improve open silhouette or to remove storm or frost damage.

POSSIBLE PROBLEMS

- Chlorosis* is often severe in wet calcareous* soils.
- This is the tree that gives eucalyptus a bad name in many areas of the southwestern United States because it was planted in the wrong places, such as near residences and in garden landscapes where its mature size and aggressive characteristics created problems.
- Sheds seed capsules, bark and sometimes branches.
- Size can be a hazard during high winds if structures or utilities are nearby.
- Removing freeze-damaged wood can be expensive and a major problem because of branch height.
- Roots are aggressive seekers of water and nutrients, to the detriment of nearby plantings.
- Massive spreading roots will lift curbs and pavement as they increase in diameter.
- Invasive into septic tanks and leaching fields.

Tall, massive tree with a spreading crown under ideal conditions. Grows very rapidly from 80 to 120 feet (24 to 36.5 m) high and 30 to 50 feet (9 to 15 m) wide. May never reach this scale when grown in the dry, shallow soils of some arid regions. Long, slender, green lance-shaped leaves cover the massive crown and cascading side branches when grown under ideal conditions. It maintains a much sparser more open foliage crown in drier situations. Not particularly noticeable small white to yellow flowers are followed by round pea-sized seed capsules. Bark peels annually, revealing smooth gray, tan or even whitish bark on trunk and branches. This is an attractive feature of the species. Native to Australia.

* See Glossary

Eucalyptus campaspe

Silver-topped gimlet

Myrtaceae family

COLD HARDINESS

Low and intermediate zones.

LANDSCAPE VALUE

- Small-scale tree but may be a little too rustic for the typical residential garden scene. Better for the wilder, more natural plantings of hillside groupings, parks, informal roadsides and median plantings.
- When planted in little groves along park trails or walks, the tree's attractive smooth copper bark can be viewed at close range and enrich the walker's experience.

CULTURAL REQUIREMENTS

- **Exposure:** Full sun.
- **Water:** Drought tolerant, even in areas receiving only 7 inches (180 mm) of rain annually. Develops more quickly and looks better with soaking of the root zone from every week to every couple of months, depending on your location.
- **Soil:** Any soil with good drainage.
- **Propagation:** Seed.
- **Maintenance:** Little staking or trimming needed when used in informal natural plantings. Easy to grow.

POSSIBLE PROBLEMS

None observed.

A slender evergreen tree 25 to 35 feet (7.5 to 11 m) high and 20 to 25 feet (6 to 7.5 m) wide. Narrow silver-gray leaves and copper or cinnamon brown bark that is so smooth it appears polished. Flowers and seed capsules appear late winter to spring but are inconspicuous. One of the lesser-known smaller-scale *Eucalyptus*, but it is tough and undemanding. Tolerates dry conditions but also accepts garden environments. Moderate to rapid growth, depending on moisture and general growing conditions. Native to Australia.

Eucalyptus cinerea

Spiral eucalyptus, Ash gum

Myrtaceae family

COLD HARDINESS

Low and intermediate zones and all but the coldest areas of the high zone.

LANDSCAPE VALUE

- Foliage adds interest and blue color in mixed large shrub or small tree compositions.
- The juvenile foliage is prized by flower arrangers and is sold by the florist industry.
- Good for bank planting where the sprawling growth habit is appropriate.

CULTURAL REQUIREMENTS

- **Exposure:** Full sun, including reflected sun.
- **Water:** Soak the root zone every month or two when plant is mature, more often when young or in the hotter low zone.
- **Soil:** Any soil with good drainage.
- **Propagation:** Seed.
- **Maintenance:** Low maintenance.

POSSIBLE PROBLEMS

Rangy, irregular growth habit makes it unsuitable for many situations.

Irregular evergreen tree that grows rapidly from 20 to 50 feet (6 to 15 m) high and 18 to 30 feet (5.5 to 9 m) wide. Unique roundish blue-green juvenile leaves give a spiral illusion. Mature leaves slowly appear in pairs, 1 to 2 inches (2.5 to 5 cm) long. Juvenile leaf type is almost always present regardless of age. Mature specimens tend to be a shapeless mound with no characteristic form associated with the species. Native to Australia.

COLD HARDINESS
Tender in colder microclimates of low and intermediate zones. Can be damaged by temperatures in the mid-20s F (-4°C).

LANDSCAPE VALUE
- One of the most, if not *the* most, beautiful tall silhouette trees for groves and skyline effects in the large landscape.
- Not a tree for the small residential garden or shopping-center medians, but lends itself to larger garden situations and landscapes on hills or along roadsides where it can be allowed to grow unhampered to its full magnificence.
- Does not have aggressive roots, making it an acceptable garden tree that can be planted near paving and garden walls without fear of heaving and cracking.

CULTURAL REQUIREMENTS
- **Exposure:** Full to reflected sun.
- **Water:** Drought resistant, but tolerates the well-watered garden if the soil is right. Water every month or two.
- **Soil:** Most soils with good drainage. Avoid shale or soils high in calcium.
- **Propagation:** Seed.
- **Maintenance:** Requires little pruning and no topping. Self-prunes small side branches as it grows. Because of its rapid growth, young trees need staking for a few years until the trunk attains some size. Permanent structure is not developed until it reaches mature height. This results in the smooth, branchless lower trunk.

POSSIBLE PROBLEMS
- Some problems with chlorosis* in calcareous*, poorly drained soils and in overwatered landscapes.
- Suffers frost damage in colder locations, which can permanently distort the desired structure and silhouette. Because of the tree's size and the importance of its skyline silhouette, frost damage should be considered a major deterrent to its use in colder zones.
- Do not place where it must be topped, because this mutilates its beautiful structure. Unfortunately, this has often been the case in Southern California.

One of the tallest evergreen skyline trees, rapidly growing 70 to 100 feet (21.5 to 30.5 m) high and 20 to 30 feet (6 to 9 m) wide. Usually has a single straight trunk with permanent side branches as much as 20 to 30 feet (6 to 9 m) above ground. Bark is a major landscape feature. It is smooth as skin, pinkish-tan to almost white, and peels once a year to reveal new bark that often has a greenish cast for a short time. Narrow light green leaves are deliciously lemon-scented. Native to Australia.

Eucalyptus citriodora
Lemon-scented gum
Myrtaceae family

* *See Glossary*

Eucalyptus cladocalyx (E. corynocalyx)

Sugar gum

Myrtaceae family

COLD HARDINESS

Low zone and sometimes intermediate zone, where it recovers rapidly after a freeze but never attains the silhouette quality for which it is planted. Somewhat cold tender, suffering leaf damage in mid-20s F (-4°C), branch and structure damage at 20°F (-7°C).

LANDSCAPE VALUE

- Silhouette tree for big spaces, hilltops and the like.
- Fine for wide boulevards, but don't plant where it must be topped to avoid utilities or adjoining structures.

CULTURAL REQUIREMENTS

- **Exposure:** Full to reflected sun.
- **Water:** Tolerates lawn-watering situations, such as next to a golf-course, but it really is a dry-area tree where it will flourish on soakings of the root zone every month or two.
- **Soil:** Any soil with good drainage.
- **Propagation:** Seed.
- **Maintenance:** Needs no pruning except to remove breakage and to preserve its natural open character.

POSSIBLE PROBLEMS

- Structure can be damaged by wind or freezing.
- Roots are invasive, stealing water and nutrients from adjoining plants.

Tall, open evergreen tree, often with a wagon-wheel-spoke branch structure when mature. Grows from 75 to 100 feet (23 to 30.5 m) high, spreading 50 to 70 feet (15 to 21.5 m). *E. cl.* 'Nana' grows 20 to 25 feet (6 to 7.5 m) high and spreads 15 to 20 feet (4.5 to 6 m). All varieties grow rapidly. Lower trunk is generally straight. Foliage is borne in large clumps and puffs, with space in between, creating an attractive silhouette against the sky. Bronze-green leaves vary in shape from oval to elongated. They are shiny and sometimes reddish as they shimmer in sunlight. Small creamy white flowers in 3-inch (7.5-cm) clusters appear June to August, followed by oval-shaped seed capsules. Smooth tan bark peels to show cream-colored patches, resulting in a dappled effect. Native to Australia.

Eucalyptus erythrocorys

Red cap gum

Myrtaceae family

COLD HARDINESS

Low zone and protected microclimates of intermediate zone. Frost tender.

LANDSCAPE VALUE

- Striking large shrub to small tree with foliage and flowers that add interest to almost any landscape.
- The open structure that reveals the smooth white trunks, plus the bold, almost succulent foliage and bright blossoms make this a real showpiece in the smaller garden landscape.

CULTURAL REQUIREMENTS

- **Exposure:** Full sun.
- **Water:** Tolerates lawn situations, but does well on irrigation only every month or two.
- **Soil:** Any soil with good drainage, which is especially important if planted in a lawn.
- **Propagation:** Seed.
- **Maintenance:** Nip back in early stages to encourage multitrunked development. Later, open up to reveal the attractive white trunks.

POSSIBLE PROBLEMS

Nothing major.

Small bush-like tree, generally multitrunked, that grows at a moderate rate from 10 to 30 feet (3 to 9 m) high and 10 to 15 feet (3 to 4.5 m) wide. Lance-shaped leaves 4 to 7 inches (10 to 18 cm) long are bright green, thick and shiny. The trunk is smooth and white. Spectacular blossoms are first covered with a bright red cap that tilts off to free a large 4-inch (10-cm) yellow shaving-brush–like bloom. They are borne in clusters occurring anytime, but most abundantly from fall to spring. Cone-shaped seed capsules also add interest at close range. Native to Australia.

Eucalyptus formanii

Forman's eucalyptus

Myrtaceae family

COLD HARDINESS

Low and intermediate zones and milder locations in the high zone.

LANDSCAPE VALUE

- Informal large shrubby border or screening.
- Hillside plantings, freeway borders or naturalistic planting where space is not an issue.
- Can be trimmed into a gnarly small tree, which might be interesting.

CULTURAL REQUIREMENTS

- **Exposure:** Enjoys full and reflected sun. Tolerates part shade but this results in rangy growth pattern. Withstands windy situations.
- **Water:** Drought tolerant. Thoroughly soak the root zone every month or two. No water when established in areas receiving 8 to 9 inches (205 to 230 mm) of annual rain. This would not be true in shallow soils.
- **Soil:** Any soil with good drainage.
- **Propagation:** Seed.
- **Maintenance:** Low maintenance.

POSSIBLE PROBLEMS

None observed.

Billowy shrub or small tree grows 15 to 30 feet (4.5 to 9 m) high, rarely the taller height, and spreads 15 to 20 feet (4.5 to 6 m). Slow to moderate growth. Light green leaves are 2½ inches (6.5 cm) long and bark is smooth and silvery or sometimes tan. Branch structure is twisted and irregular. Flowers are small, white and not showy, followed by small rounded seed capsules. Native to Australia.

Eucalyptus kruseana

Book-leaf mallee, Kruse's mallee

Myrtaceae family

COLD HARDINESS

Low zone and all but the coldest locations in intermediate zone.

LANDSCAPE VALUE

- Single specimen or in a mass planting on a slope.
- Understory plantings in open shade.
- Dainty shrub with interesting leaves and flowers that wouldn't look out of place in a Japanese garden.

CULTURAL REQUIREMENTS

- **Exposure:** Full sun, including reflected sun to open shade.
- **Water:** Drought resistant. Water every week or two to stimulate good growth and appearance.
- **Soil:** Any soil with good drainage.
- **Propagation:** Seed.
- **Maintenance:** Cut back periodically to stimulate new growth. Prune branches as much as ¼ to ⅓ their length during winter dormant season.

POSSIBLE PROBLEMS

None observed.

Open, angular shrub, sometimes almost a groundcover, that forms a silvery blue mound. Grows to 2¼ feet (68.5 cm) high, with equal spread, at a slow to moderate pace. Tiny round leaves, 1 inch (2.5 cm) long or less, are spaced along the branches. Yellow 1½-inch (4-cm) flowers appear in between when in season, from winter through spring. Seed capsules take the form of showy miniature acorns. Native to Australia.

** See Glossary*

Eucalyptus leucoxylon and *E. leucoxylon rosea*

White ironbark, Pink-flowered ironbark

Myrtaceae family

Form varies within the species, but tree is usually upright, slender and rather open. It grows 20 to 80 feet (6 to 24 m) high and spreads 20 to 40 feet (6 to 12 m). Moderate to rapid growth rate, depending on the situation. More graceful and slender and less massive than some of its relatives, it seldom reaches the towering scale of 80 feet (24 m). Ultimate height and spread are determined by soil depth and available moisture. It sheds bark annually, revealing a satin-smooth white trunk that is sometimes dappled with gray, a most attractive feature of the tree. The 3- to 6-inch (7.5- to 15-cm) long gray-green leaves are sickle-shaped. The tiny white blossoms occur mostly in winter with a scattering of blooms in other seasons. Seed capsules are 3/8 inch (1 cm) wide and bullet-shaped. *E. leucoxylon rosea* has all the same attractive features, but with the added bonus of especially vibrant hot pink blossoms scattered through the gray-green foliage. Free-flowering tree, with its heaviest bloom in winter when there often is little color—a real plus. Native to Australia.

COLD HARDINESS

Low and intermediate zones and warmer locations in high zone. Tolerates temperatures down to 14 to 18°F (-10 to -8°C).

LANDSCAPE VALUE

- Groves and roadside plantings.
- The light, open character, pendulous branches, plus the attractive smooth white bark make it special even at close range, such as along park trails.
- Winter color.

CULTURAL REQUIREMENTS

- **Exposure:** Full sun. Tolerates hot and windy exposures.
- **Water:** Drought resistant. Water every month or two to every week, depending on your location.
- **Soil:** Tolerates heavy to rocky soils.
- **Propagation:** Seed.
- **Maintenance:** Completely undemanding, except cleanup of litter.

POSSIBLE PROBLEMS

Twig and leaf litter, plus the annual bark shedding, can be a problem in the well-groomed landscape setting.

Eucalyptus microtheca

Coolibah, Tiny-capsule eucalyptus

Myrtaceae family

Sometimes bushy multitrunked tree that can also be grown with a single trunk. Seldom upright, even as a single trunk, it tends to lean at an angle in picturesque configurations. Grows at a moderate rate from 35 to 40 feet (11 to 12 m) high, with equal spread. Slender 8-inch (20.5-cm) long leaves are generally silvery gray, which is the preferred selection, although a green type is also available. Small, insignificant creamy white flowers are followed by tiny seed capsules the size of a match head. At first the bark is smooth and light colored on the trunk and smaller branches, but it becomes thicker and grayer on trunks and stouter branches as the tree matures. Native to Australia.

COLD HARDINESS

All three zones. Tolerates temperatures of 5 to 10°F (-15 to -12°C).

LANDSCAPE VALUE

- Clumping or in groves.
- The silvery gray form adds an interesting accent to the landscape.
- Its small size makes it an acceptable tree for more limited spaces.

CULTURAL REQUIREMENTS

- **Exposure:** Full to reflected sun.
- **Water:** Tolerates long periods of drought, but must receive intermittent water to grow and develop. Strangely enough, it also tolerates high-water situations, such as in lawns. Will grow with brackish water high in salts without detrimental effect.
- **Soil:** Any soil, even alkaline soils. This tree's tolerance of hot, dry and saline-soil sites has made it invaluable in the Middle East. In contrast, it grows well and seems to have no chlorosis* problems when planted in lawns.
- **Propagation:** Seed.
- **Maintenance:** Undemanding.

POSSIBLE PROBLEMS

None observed.

* See Glossary

Eucalyptus papuana

Ghost gum

Myrtaceae family

COLD HARDINESS

Low zone and warmer locations in intermediate zone.

LANDSCAPE VALUE

- Acceptable size for in-town locations.
- Grove plantings in parks, along roadsides and urban planting in general.
- Especially well adapted to the desert.
- The silhouette and white bark make it a real attention-getter.

CULTURAL REQUIREMENTS

- **Exposure:** Full to reflected sun.
- **Water:** Drought resistant, but can be used in well-irrigated landscapes also.
- **Soil:** Any soil with good drainage.
- **Propagation:** Seed.
- **Maintenance:** Requires little pruning. Do not top.

POSSIBLE PROBLEMS

None observed.

Varies from a multitrunked, irregularly shaped tree to tall single-trunk specimens with narrow side branches, which is the most common form. From 20 to 60 feet (6 to 18 m) high, spreading 15 to 30 feet (4.5 to 9 m), it grows at a moderate to rapid rate, depending on moisture availability. The beautiful snow white bark and foliage are outstanding. The leathery gray to medium green leaves are 3 to 5 inches (7.5 to 13 cm) long, pointed at the tip, narrow at the apex, and broad midway from 1 to 1½ inches (2.5 to 4 cm) wide. Frost sometimes tints leaves purple. Small white flowers appear in summer. Fruit that follows is inconspicuous. Leaves present a striking configuration, especially when arranged in loose clusters along the branches. A bold effect in general, adding to the overall silhouette. Native to Australia.

Eucalyptus polyanthemos

Silver-dollar gum

Myrtaceae family

COLD HARDINESS

Low and intermediate zones and warmer locations in high zone. Tolerates temperatures of 14 to 18°F (-10 to -8°C) without damage.

LANDSCAPE VALUE

- Acceptable size for the smaller-scale landscape.
- Decorative grayish green foliage adds an interesting color.
- The juvenile round-leaf phase is much admired and cut foliage is used in flower arrangements. This tree is sometimes grown for the florist trade.
- Groves, roadsides and residential areas.

CULTURAL REQUIREMENTS

- **Exposure:** Full and reflected sun.
- **Water:** Water every week or two when tree is young, every month or two when mature. Although it does well in regularly watered situations, it is a drought-resistant species and may not tolerate high-water situations.
- **Soil:** Tolerates a wide variety of soils, but good drainage is preferable and lawn locations are questionable.
- **Propagation:** Seed.
- **Maintenance:** Undemanding tree in general. Prune and shape when young to direct growth. May need to remove dead or broken branches from mature trees.

POSSIBLE PROBLEMS

Few problems other than chlorosis* in some well-watered situations, such as in lawns.

Single- to multitrunked slender tree that grows 20 to 60 feet (6 to 18 m) high and spreads 20 to 40 feet (6 to 12 m) at a moderate to rapid rate, depending on moisture availability. The 2- to 3-inch (5- to 7.5-cm) juvenile leaves are roundish and an attractive gray-green, hence the name "silver dollar." The mature leaves are lance-shaped. The rough, mottled bark is persistent, not peeling annually as so many *Eucalyptus* species do. Creamy white flowers appear in 1-inch (2.5-cm) clusters in spring and summer, but are not showy. Cylindrical cup seed clusters follow. Native to Australia.

* *See Glossary*

Eucalyptus populnea

Poplar box, Poplar leaf gum

Myrtaceae family

COLD HARDINESS

Low zone and all but the coldest locations in intermediate zone. Has tolerated as low as 20°F (-7°C) in the intermediate zone but no information is available on what temperatures inflict real damage.

LANDSCAPE VALUE

In groves or as a single tree along streets, in medians, or in park areas or residential locations.

CULTURAL REQUIREMENTS

- **Exposure:** Full sun. Tolerates reflected heat, such as in parking areas and west facing banks.
- **Water:** Seems drought resistant. Soak the root zone every week or two to speed up its slow development.
- **Soil:** Any soil.
- **Propagation:** Seed.
- **Maintenance:** Low maintenance.

POSSIBLE PROBLEMS

None observed.

Slender in youth but eventually develops a dense roundish crown and a short trunk. Grows 35 to 70 feet (11 to 21.5 m) high, but is typically shorter in the desert. Spreads to 30 feet (9 m) or more. Not a rapid grower like so many of the genus. The round green leaves shimmer in the wind, adding to the poplar-like illusion, justifying both the scientific and common names. Small white flowers are inconspicuous. Roots are not as aggressive as others in the *Eucalyptus* clan. Adjoining mixed plantings show no evidence of competition. Native to Australia.

Eucalyptus robusta

Swamp mahogany

Myrtaceae family

COLD HARDINESS

All three zones.

LANDSCAPE VALUE

- Large shade tree for parks and public places, but not for small spaces.
- Combines well with tropical-effects plants, but not in lawns.

CULTURAL REQUIREMENTS

- **Exposure:** Full sun.
- **Water:** Tolerates wetness but is drought resistant, growing well on thorough soaking of the root zone every month or two.
- **Soil:** Most soils. Tolerates salinity and poor drainage but not lawns in calcareous* soils.
- **Propagation:** Seed.
- **Maintenance:** Needs plenty of room to grow. Restrictive pruning, topping and the like destroy its natural form.

POSSIBLE PROBLEMS

- Such a large heavily foliated tree creates a bit of litter.
- Its tall size makes it more vulnerable to wind damage, requiring corrective pruning and cleanup.

A large round-headed evergreen tree that can grow rapidly up to 80 feet (24 m) high, usually shorter under desert conditions. Spreads to about 70 feet (21.5 m). Densely foliated with shiny, leathery dark green leaves that grow 4 to 7 inches (10 to 18 cm) long. The large leaves, almost tropical in appearance, are unusual for desert-adapted trees. Pink-tinted creamy white flowers are fairly attractive and unusual for a large eucalyptus. They appear any time, but mostly in winter. Bears clusters of cylindrical 3/8 inch (1 cm) seed capsules. Bark is rough, dark reddish brown and stringy. Native to Australia.

* See Glossary

Eucalyptus salmonophloia

Salmon gum

Myrtaceae family

COLD HARDINESS

Low and intermediate zones, but not tested in high zone.

LANDSCAPE VALUE

- Parks.
- Medians or along roadways or trails.
- Natural planting compositions.
- Bark is especially attractive close up.

CULTURAL REQUIREMENTS

- **Exposure:** Full sun.
- **Water:** Drought resistant. Water every week or two during the warm season to encourage more rapid development.
- **Soil:** Most soils.
- **Propagation:** Seed.
- **Maintenance:** Low maintenance.

POSSIBLE PROBLEMS

None observed except possible problems with size if crowded. Plant where it will not be restricted by buildings or other trees.

This handsome tree with glistening dark green leaves and smooth salmon-colored bark has been a slow grower in Arizona plantings. Over time, it can reach 100 feet (30.5 m) high and 40 feet (12 m) wide. The structure is open, revealing glimpses of the attractive bark even up to the top of the tree. Native to Australia.

Eucalyptus sideroxylon and E. sideroxylon rosea

Red ironbark, Pink ironbark

Myrtaceae family

COLD HARDINESS

Low zone and warmer locations in intermediate zone. Withstands temperatures of 20 to 25°F (-7 to -4°C).

LANDSCAPE VALUE

- Dramatic contrast between the dark trunk and the lighter foliage, not to mention the white or pink bloom, make this tree a rich addition to the landscape.
- Roadside and street plantings.
- Large urban situations.
- Screening.
- Single specimen.

CULTURAL REQUIREMENTS

- **Exposure:** Full to reflected sun.
- **Water:** Water established plants every month or two, but keep young plants moist to support rapid growth.
- **Soil:** Most soils with good drainage. Performs better in lighter soils. Do not plant in lawns or wet clay soils.
- **Propagation:** Seed.
- **Maintenance:** Prune to correct tree structure, if necessary.

POSSIBLE PROBLEMS

- Becomes chlorotic* on heavy, poorly drained soils.
- Variation in form sometimes creates problems in planting design.
- Occasional freeze damage can result in pruning costs to remove damaged branches, which also can distort the silhouette.

Quite a variable species. It can be either a slender open tree or dense and squat. Reaches 20 to 80 feet (6 to 24 m) high and spreads 15 to 30 feet (4.5 to 9 m). Moderate to rapid growth, depending on moisture supply. Slim blue-green leaves are sometimes grayish and grow about 4 inches (10 cm) long. Thick furrowed bark ranges in color from dark reddish to almost black. Attractive, tiny fluffy white to pinkish crimson flowers are arranged in pendulous clusters, blooming from fall to spring. Goblet-shaped seed capsules are 3/8 inch (1 cm) wide. Native to Australia.

* *See Glossary*

Eucalyptus spathulata

Narrow-leafed gimlet, Swamp malee

Myrtaceae family

COLD HARDINESS

Low and intermediate zones and warmer locations in high zone. Withstands minimums of 15 to 20°F (-10 to -7°C).

LANDSCAPE VALUE

- Picturesque tree adds a striking note of interest in a landscape setting. The narrow leaves and the small mature tree size contrast with the massive size and heavy foliage found in so many *Eucalyptus* species.
- Patio-size tree or a shorter windbreak.
- Blends well with desert-type landscape plantings, unlike many *Eucalyptus* species.

CULTURAL REQUIREMENTS

- **Exposure:** Full sun. Tolerates reflected sun.
- **Water:** Tolerates drought or wet situations, from water every few months to twice-weekly watered lawns.
- **Soil:** Any soil. Tolerates desert soils and conditions well.
- **Propagation:** Seed.
- **Maintenance:** Undemanding.

POSSIBLE PROBLEMS

None observed.

Small multistem or multitrunk tree with smooth reddish bark and grayish green ribbonlike leaves from 2 to 3 inches (5 to 7.5 cm) long. Grows at a moderate rate from 6 to 20 feet (2 to 6 m) high, with equal spread. Flowers are cream to gold and bloom in summer. Bell-shaped seed capsules are small and unnoticeable to passersby. Native to Australia.

Eucalyptus torquata

Coral gum

Myrtaceae family

COLD HARDINESS

Low and intermediate zones. Withstands minimum temperatures of 17 to 22°F (-8 to -5°C)

LANDSCAPE VALUE

- In small and narrow spaces, including residential areas.
- A spot of bloom color in the landscape at varying times of the year.
- Groves or larger open areas.
- Street or median tree.
- Good as a cut flower.

CULTURAL REQUIREMENTS

- **Exposure:** Reflected sun or part shade when adjoining taller trees.
- **Water:** Reasonably drought resistant. Soak the root zone every week or two.
- **Soil:** Any soil with good drainage.
- **Propagation:** Seed.
- **Maintenance:** Needs little pruning or staking except when planted as a street tree.

POSSIBLE PROBLEMS

None observed except occasional branch breakage after heavy bloom, but this is not a serious concern.

Slender upright tree that grows at a moderate rate from 15 to 20 feet (6 m) high, with equal spread. Light green leaves vary from long and narrow to blunt and round. Rough bark is flaky and dark brown. Japanese-lantern–shaped buds, 3/4 inch (2 cm), precede flowering. These open to beautiful coral red and yellow flowers followed by 1/2-inch (1-cm) long round capsules. Heavy blooming and seed-capsule production sometimes results in shedding of branches. Blooms off and on all year. Native to Australia.

* *See Glossary*

Eucalyptus woodwardii

Lemon-flowered gum

Myrtaceae family

COLD HARDINESS

Low and intermediate zones.

LANDSCAPE VALUE

- Informal plantings, single or in groups.
- Along paths and walks where foliage and flowers can be observed at close range.
- Creates interesting silhouette pattern against large blank walls.

CULTURAL REQUIREMENTS

- **Exposure:** Full sun.
- **Water:** Drought resistant. Soak root zone deeply every month or two.
- **Soil:** Any soil with good drainage.
- **Propagation:** Seed.
- **Maintenance:** Some pruning and shaping of young trees may improve irregular growth habit, but this can be a difficult task.

POSSIBLE PROBLEMS

Informal ungainly growth habit defies training and shaping.

A rangy evergreen tree to 40 feet (12 m) high, usually lower, with an irregular spread from 15 to 25 feet (4.5 to 7.5 m). Moderate, sometimes rapid, growth. Handsome 5-inch (13-cm) long gray leaves and showy large lemon yellow puff flowers are abundant from fall to summer. Definitely not a shade tree but the irregular structure often takes interesting form. No two trees are alike. Native to Australia.

Euphorbia antisyphilitica

Candelaria, Wax plant

Euphorbiaceae family

COLD HARDINESS

All three zones.

LANDSCAPE VALUE

- Cluster of slender upright leafless stems offers a striking contrast with many broadleaf arid-climate plants.
- Combines well with cacti and other popular landscape succulents.
- Accent or character plant.
- Containers.

CULTURAL REQUIREMENTS

- **Exposure:** Full or reflected sun to part shade.
- **Water:** Established plants rarely require irrigation for survival but water once or twice in long dry periods may improve growth and appearance, especially in the low zone.
- **Soil:** Any soil with fast drainage.
- **Propagation:** Clump divisions or seed.
- **Maintenance:** Grows with little care once established.

POSSIBLE PROBLEMS

Milky sap is poisonous, as with all *Euphorbias*.

The slender gray-green cylindrical stems of this succulent shrub exude a milky latex and are covered with a layer of wax that has been put to a variety of commercial uses. The plant consists of a cluster of many erect branched or unbranched stems, 1/4 inch (0.5 cm) in diameter, that are leafless except on new growth where tiny leaves, 1/8 inch (0.5 cm) long, are present for a brief time. New stems that grow from spreading rhizomes* slowly increase the diameter of the clump. Flowering takes place in early to midsummer when small green bell-shaped cups containing several male flowers and one female open along the stems. The native range extends from northeast Mexico into southwest Texas and down into the Chihuahuan Desert of Mexico where it is still being harvested for wax production. Grows slowly to about 3 feet (1 m) high, with equal spread.

* *See Glossary*

Euphorbia dendroides

Mediterranean euphorbia bush
Euphorbiaceae family

COLD HARDINESS

Low and intermediate zones. Probably warmer locations in the high zone, but not tested there yet.

LANDSCAPE VALUE

- A special-interest plant in winter and spring because of foliage and blossoms that peak when many plants are in their off-season.
- Not a total zero in summer when it is deciduous because young coral twigs from last season's growth add color.
- Bank stabilization.
- Informal compositions with succulents, aloes, agaves and so forth.
- Foundation plant.
- Accent plant against blank walls or in large containers.

CULTURAL REQUIREMENTS

- **Exposure:** Full sun, including reflected sun to part shade.
- **Water:** Drought resistant, especially in summer, but must have regular soil moisture for growth and good appearance in winter.
- **Soil:** Tolerates poor rocky soils but good drainage is important.
- **Propagation:** Seed or cuttings.
- **Maintenance:** Low maintenance.

POSSIBLE PROBLEMS

- Toxic milky sap, common to all *Euphorbias.*
- Being summer deciduous, it could be unacceptable in some landscape plant compositions.

Summer-deciduous shrub with coral-colored young branches that add interest during the dry season. Moderate to rapid growth in winter if moisture is present. Normally grows only 3 to 4 feet (1 m), but in areas of side confinement or optimum conditions, it can reach 10 feet (3 m). Usually wider than it is tall. Lush, slightly gray-green lanceolate* leaves appear in the fall on the new-growth stems. Leaves last through winter, turning reddish, and drop in late spring as the hot weather comes on. Winter blooming generally peaks in March, when the mounding shrub can be covered with clusters of greenish yellow flowers 1 inch (2.5 cm) wide. Three-seeded capsules follow but are not showy. Native to Mediterranean shores and islands.

Euphorbia rigida (E. biglandulosa)

South African perennial euphorbia bush
Euphorbiaceae family

COLD HARDINESS

Low and intermediate zones and warmer microclimates of high zone. Quite frost hardy for such a lush-looking plant.

LANDSCAPE VALUE

- Unusual and interesting as a specimen, en masse as a foundation plant in the landscape, or in containers as a conversation piece.
- Winter color.

CULTURAL REQUIREMENTS

- **Exposure:** Full sun or part shade.
- **Water:** Water every month or two. Don't overwater in summer heat. Water just enough to prevent die-back*. Give more water after nights cool down to bring on winter vigor.
- **Soil:** Tolerant of most fast-draining soils.
- **Propagation:** Seed or cuttings.
- **Maintenance:** Prune away old flowering stems as they die back after winter and spring bloom periods.

POSSIBLE PROBLEMS

- Needs grooming following bloom.
- Reseeds in other areas.
- Damping off* can be a problem during summer rainy periods.
- Sap is toxic. Be careful when pruning.

Small, shrubby evergreen perennial to 2 feet (61 cm) high and 3 feet (1 m) wide. Slow to moderate growth. Thick, narrow 1½-inch (4-cm) long pointed leaves are gray-green and arranged spirally around ascending stems. Rounded flower clusters appear in late winter and last into spring. Showy bracts* are chartreuse-yellow, changing to green and tan. When seeds mature, stems die back and are replaced by new growth. Native to South Africa.

* *See Glossary*

Euphorbia tirucalli

Milkbush, Pencil tree

Euphorbiaceae family

COLD HARDINESS
Low zone and warm microclimates of intermediate zone.

LANDSCAPE VALUE
- The upright mass of slender green leafless stems makes this a unique accent plant or focal point in the landscape. The effect is especially dramatic with a simple wall as a background.
- Salt-tolerant and therefore useful near the beach.
- Picturesque, easy-care container plant.

CULTURAL REQUIREMENTS
- **Exposure:** Full sun to part shade.
- **Water:** Water every week or two when plant is young, every month or two when established.
- **Soil:** Most soils.
- **Propagation:** Cuttings.
- **Maintenance:** Other than occasional pruning to balance growth, requires little care.

POSSIBLE PROBLEMS
- Hard freezes cause unsightly die-back* or loss of the plant.
- The milky sap is toxic. Take special care to keep sap out of the eyes when pruning.

Usually seen as a slender, upright succulent shrub or container plant, but has the potential to become treelike in warm frost-free climates. Grows to 30 feet (9 m) high, spreading to 8 feet (2.5 m) at a moderate pace. May grow single- or multitrunked, with a dense irregular crown of light green cylindrical branches, each about the diameter of a pencil. Like many other *Euphorbias*, it has milky sap that flows freely from cut surfaces. The tiny leaves are shed soon after they appear and flowers are insignificant. Native to tropical Africa

Eysenhardtia orthocarpa (E. polystachya)

Kidneywood

Fabaceae (Leguminosae) family

COLD HARDINESS
Low and intermediate zones.

LANDSCAPE VALUE
- Specimen, focal point or background plant with white flower spikes that are pleasant summer accents.
- Shrub borders, naturalistic plantings and as part of an informal enclosing barrier or screen.
- Can be developed into a multitrunk patio tree with training, staking and regular watering.

CULTURAL REQUIREMENTS
- **Exposure:** Full sun or part shade. Grows best in hot, low-elevation arid regions.
- **Water:** Survives with little water once established. Water every month to only a couple times per season during the long growing season. Dry spells result in improved growth and flowering. Water every week or two if you want a small tree.
- **Soil:** Any soil with good drainage.
- **Propagation:** Seed.
- **Maintenance:** Prune occasionally for shape and branching habit.

POSSIBLE PROBLEMS
Pungent foliage odor may be disagreeable to some.

Depending on site conditions, this thornless legume may grow as a semi-evergreen or deciduous shrub or a small tree with a trunk as big as 10 inches (25.5 cm) in diameter. Grows at a moderate rate from 3 to 10 feet (1 to 3 m) high, occasionally to 18 feet (5.5 m). Spreads 3 to 10 feet (1 to 3 m). The pinnately* compound leaves, 2 to 3¼ inches (5 to 8 cm) long, are made up of ten to twenty pairs of narrow oblong leaflets that have a strong resinous odor when bruised or crushed. Small white flowers open in terminal* spikes throughout the summer months. Clusters of flat, slender seed pods, each about ½ inch (1 cm) long, contain a single seed and turn tan or brown as they ripen. Native range extends from southern Arizona and southern New Mexico south into central Mexico. In Mexico, the wood is used as a diuretic for treating various kidney and bladder problems.

* See Glossary

Eysenhardtia texana

Texas kidneywood

Fabaceae (Leguminosae) family

COLD HARDINESS

All three zones.

LANDSCAPE VALUE

Same as *E. orthocarpa*, except it is not suitable to trim into a patio tree.

CULTURAL REQUIREMENTS

Same as *E. orthocarpa*, except more drought resistant.

POSSIBLE PROBLEMS

Same as *E. orthocarpa*.

Very similar to *E. orthocarpa*, but usually smaller and less lush and vigorous. Reaches about 8 feet (2.5 m) high, give or take, with equal spread. Slower growth than *E. orthocarpa*. It definitely would be classed as only a shrub, while *E. orthocarpa* makes a patio-size tree.

Fallugia paradoxa

Apache plume

Rosaceae family

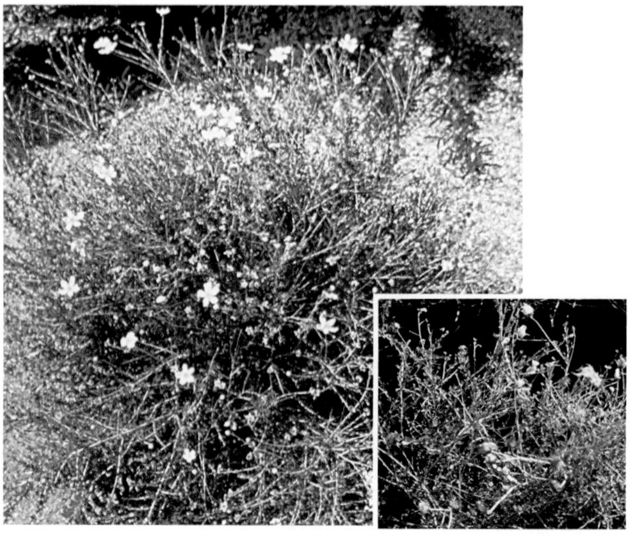

COLD HARDINESS

All three zones.

LANDSCAPE VALUE

- Foundation, background or space definer.
- Erosion control on high disturbed areas.

CULTURAL REQUIREMENTS

- **Exposure:** Full sun in the high zone where it is best adapted; part shade suitable in the intermediate zone and necessary in the low zone.
- **Water:** Water is seldom necessary for established plants in the high zone. In the low and intermediate zones, water every week or two during the warm months, every month or two in winter for satisfactory growth and appearance.
- **Soil:** Most soils with good drainage.
- **Propagation:** Seed.
- **Maintenance:** May need some grooming after seed plumes fade. Plants can look ragged.

POSSIBLE PROBLEMS

None observed.

Several unique characteristics make this evergreen-to-partly-deciduous shrub easy to identify. Mature stems have peeling bark while twigs and smaller branches are covered with gray wool-like material. Leaves 1/2 inch (1 cm) long and 1/4 inch (0.5 cm) wide are divided into three to seven slender lobes, dark green on the upper surface, rust-colored below. Five-petaled white flowers similar to small single roses and about 1 inch (2.5 cm) across open singly or in a group of two or three on a long stalk, in spring and occasionally into late summer. The fruits develop in a cluster as much as 2 1/2 inches (6.5 cm) in diameter. Each fruit has a long tail covered with soft hairs that give it a feathery appearance. Ripening fruit clusters are first greenish, changing to pink or purplish as they mature. Apache plume takes its common name from the resemblance of the feathery fruit clusters to a headdress worn by Apache American Indians. Grows at a moderate rate to 6 feet (2 m) high, spreading to 4 feet (1 m). Native to higher elevation areas of the southwestern United States and Chihuahua, Coahuila and Durango in northern Mexico.

Feijoa sellowiana

Pineapple guava

Myrtaceae family

COLD HARDINESS

All three zones.

LANDSCAPE VALUE

- Background shrub.
- Large hedges, including formally trimmed shapes.
- Small standard trees.
- Espalier for large wall spaces.
- Large containers.
- Can be slow to develop for some of the above uses.
- Blossoms are attractive at close range.

CULTURAL REQUIREMENTS

- **Exposure:** Full sun or reflected sun to part shade.
- **Water:** Every week or two at first and then every month or two after mature.
- **Soil:** Tolerates most soils, but improved garden soil will speed up its rather slow growth.
- **Propagation:** Cuttings (although seed propagation is possible).
- **Maintenance:** Trim and train to achieve several of the forms listed under Landscape Value. Best done in winter.

POSSIBLE PROBLEMS

None observed except slow growth.

Attractive evergreen shrub that grows slowly to moderately, reaching 15 feet (4.5 m) in height with equal spread. Leathery leaves are dark green above and almost white beneath, giving a gray-green effect. Generally a multistem shrub but can be trained into a small tree. The flower is unique with pinkish white succulent petals arranged around a center of tufted red stamens*. It resembles a large apple blossom. Gray-green 3-inch (7.5-cm) egg-shaped fruits ripen in the fall. The flavor resembles that of its more tender tropical namesake, the tropical guava (*Psidium guajava*). In addition, the succulent petals have a sweet, fruity flavor and can be added to salads. There are selected varieties for larger, better quality fruit and fruit production, but for general landscape use, this is not particularly important. Native to South America.

Landscape Design Example

A lush green groundcover (such as *Myoporum parvifolium*) can take the place of a thirsty lawn.

* *See Glossary*

Ferocactus cyclindraceus (F. acanthodes)

Compass barrel cactus

Cactaceae family

COLD HARDINESS

Low and intermediate zones and warmer locations in high zone. Once established this species is moderately frost hardy.

LANDSCAPE VALUE

- A striking and picturesque accent plant of bold form and texture, with a seasonal display of colorful flowers and fruit.
- Often develops with a single stem but multistemmed specimens do occur. The unique form of the latter offers considerable landscape interest.
- Various desert birds and animals eat the ripe fruits of this species.

CULTURAL REQUIREMENTS

- **Exposure:** Full sun to part shade. Remarkably tenacious under extremes of heat, drought and withering sun. Tender plants produced under optimum growing conditions in a shade house often sunburn if abruptly moved to an open sunny location. Acclimate such plants by gradual exposure to higher light intensities and a drier environment.
- **Water:** Among the most drought tolerant of plants. Supplemental irrigation is unnecessary except in extremely dry locations or during unusually prolonged dry periods.
- **Soil:** Tolerates alkaline sandy to rocky soils, but needs good drainage.
- **Propagation:** Seed.
- **Maintenance:** Essentially zero maintenance once established.

POSSIBLE PROBLEMS

- Avoid planting where the sharp-pointed thorns are a threat to passersby.
- Bermuda grass and weeds can invade plantings.
- Wind-blown debris that can accumulate in spines are hard to remove.
- Taller mature plants become top heavy during rains and tip over, which means the end unless they can be replanted, as in a landscape situation.

Large specimens of this desert succulent often lean south or southwest, a trait that inspired its common name. However an occasional plant can be found inclined in a different direction, so this species is not infallible as a compass. Grows slowly from 3 to 5 feet (1 to 1.5 m) high, rarely 8 to 10 feet (2.5 to 3 m). Trunk diameter up to 18 inches (46 cm). Young plants are rounded or globular, becoming more cylindrical as they grow larger and older. The stout ribbed trunk has twenty to thirty ribs and is ringed with clusters of thick spreading spines. The trunk is defended by a formidable array of thorns arranged in closely spaced clusters. From the center of each cluster grows four heavy central spines 2 or more inches (5 cm) long with tips that may be hooked or curved. As many as fifteen to twenty lateral spines or bristles surround the four "centrals" of each cluster. Spine color is variable—yellow, pink, red or brown and sometimes gray toward the base of the plant. In late spring or early summer, several broadly funnel-shaped, many-petaled flowers, 1½ to 2 inches (4 to 5 cm) long, bloom in a circle at the top of the stem. These flowers are yellow to orange with a touch of red. The globular fruits are fleshy and smooth skinned, about ¾ inch (2 cm) across and yellow when mature. Inside each fruit are numerous small, rounded brown or black seeds. This cactus grows native in parts of Arizona, Nevada, southern California and Utah in the United States as well as Baja California and Sonora in Mexico. Although the fruit is edible, the story that barrel cactus contains drinkable water to sustain the desert traveler is pure fiction and has led to the needless destruction of many fine specimens in the wild.

Ferocactus wislizenii

Fishhook barrel cactus

Cactaceae family

COLD HARDINESS

Low and intermediate zones and warmer locations in high zone. Moderately frost hardy.

LANDSCAPE VALUE

- Accent or specimen in succulent compositions.
- Both flowers and fruit have ornamental value.

CULTURAL REQUIREMENTS

Same as *F. cyclindraceus.*

POSSIBLE PROBLEMS

Same as *F. cyclindraceus.*

Usually single-stemmed but occasionally branched from the base, this spiny cactus resembles *F. cyclindraceus* and is ball-shaped to columnar depending on age. It can grow as high as 10 feet (3 m) high. Trunk diameter reaches about 2 feet (61 cm). The twenty to thirty ribs are heavily armed with spines. The four large central spines in each cluster are red-brown or gray; the longest is up to 4 inches (10 cm) and typically hooked at the tip. Numerous fiery orange-red to yellow flowers $2\frac{1}{2}$ inches (6.5 cm) long are grouped at the top of the stem, opening during summer. Rounded, fleshy yellow fruits are about $1\frac{3}{4}$ inches (4.5 cm) long and persist on the plant for some time, extending seasonal interest. Native from Arizona to western Texas and northern Mexico.

Landscape Design Example

The right groundcover (such as *Dimorphotheca sinuata*) can make a wild paradise in your own backyard.

Ficus benjamina

Weeping Chinese banyan
Moraceae family

COLD HARDINESS

Low zone. Warm-winter, and nearly frost-free, microclimates for long-term success as a landscape tree. Frost tender, but in marginal areas damage that results from light frost is soon replaced by growth as temperatures rise in spring.

LANDSCAPE VALUE

- In areas that are frost-free or nearly so, this elegant tropical tree is useful as an oasis shade tree, clipped hedge, large screen, framing tree or specimen.
- Where winters are cooler, it has a place in warm microclimates as a small patio tree or as an accent or focal point in large containers, clipped to a formal shape or with a natural crown shape.

CULTURAL REQUIREMENTS

- **Exposure:** Full to reflected sun or part shade in outdoor areas that are sheltered, although it survives desert heat well. Tolerates sheltered locations near but not directly on the beach, where exposed to salt wind.
- **Water:** Established trees can survive moderately long dry periods, but thoroughly water every week or two, to maintain health and landscape appearance.
- **Soil:** Most soils with good drainage.
- **Propagation:** Cuttings or air layering*.
- **Maintenance:** Choose frost-free planting location or be prepared to prune cold-damaged branches.

POSSIBLE PROBLEMS

- Dense shade and invasive roots make it difficult to grow other plants near large trees.
- Expanding roots may cause pavement to heave and buckle when trees are planted close to walks, drives and other landscape areas.
- Heavy crops of tiny hard figs create ground litter and require cleanup in some landscape situations.

Planted throughout warm-winter regions as an evergreen landscape tree and in most other climate zones as a container plant for both indoor and outdoor use. Grows at a moderate to rapid rate from 30 to 50 feet (9 to 15 m) high, in frost-free areas, with equal spread. The dense spreading foliage canopy is rounded and symmetrical with gracefully drooping outer branches. Glossy, dark green oval to elliptical leaves grow 3 to 5 inches (7.5 to 13 cm) long. In summer, tiny rounded figs about 1/3 inch (1 cm) in diameter are orange to bright red when mature. *F. benjamina* 'Exotica' is more weeping in form. Its slender hanging leaves 3 1/2 to 4 3/4 inches (9 to 12 cm) long have wavy margins and tips that are long and twisted. There is also a slower growing variegated form. Native to India and Asia.

* *See Glossary*

Ficus carica

Edible fig, Common fig

Moraceae family

COLD HARDINESS

Low and intermediate zones and in warm microclimates, or with protective cover, in the high zone. Frost tolerant but a hard freeze will result in moderate to severe die-back*. Plants can survive winter safely in marginal areas with a wrap or enclosed cylinder of dry insulating material such as leaves or straw to protect the above-ground part of the plant.

LANDSCAPE VALUE

- Interplay of bold tropical-looking foliage, twisting irregular trunk and limbs, and smooth gray bark add richness to any landscape.
- Large old specimens cast dense summer shade and have a starkly picturesque character in the winter dormant period.
- Espalier or wall plant.
- Large containers.

CULTURAL REQUIREMENTS

- **Exposure:** Full or reflected sun to part shade. Some varieties are adapted to high heat; others thrive in cooler summer temperatures.
- **Water:** Established trees endure long dry periods, but for satisfactory landscape appearance and fruit production, water every month or two during the growing season to once or twice a season during the dormant period.
- **Soil:** Any soil with good drainage that is not highly alkaline or salty.
- **Propagation:** Cuttings, air layering* or root suckering*.
- **Maintenance:** Prune for optimum fruit production and to maintain desired canopy shape and heights.

POSSIBLE PROBLEMS

- Birds, green June beetles and other insects are attracted to ripening fruit.
- Fallen fruit creates messy litter, especially on paved areas.
- Edible fig is susceptible to Texas root rot*, root knot nematode*, crown gall* and oak root fungus* ('Mission' and 'Kadota' are resistant to the latter).

Young vigorous fig trees may have one or more upright slender stems but old specimens usually display a single short, heavy trunk that is knobby and contorted, with thick spreading branches. The bark is silvery gray and smooth to the touch. This small deciduous tree is native to the Mediterranean region and southwestern Asia. Its large rough-textured leaves are 4 to 10 inches (10 to 25.5 cm) long and as wide, with three to five lobes. The sweet edible fruits may be yellow, green, purple, brown or black when ripe, depending on variety. The two principal crop periods are spring and fall. Grows 15 to 30 feet (4.5 to 9 m) high or higher, with equal spread, at a moderate to rapid pace.

** See Glossary*

Ficus microcarpa (F. retusa)

Indian laurel fig
Moraceae family

COLD HARDINESS

Warm, nearly frost-free microclimates in the low zone. Frost tender.

LANDSCAPE VALUE

- Specimen or shade tree.
- Framing tree for structures.
- In groups in urban parks and other large areas and along roadways.
- Clipped hedge.
- Can be sheared into sculptural shapes.
- Large container plant.

CULTURAL REQUIREMENTS

- **Exposure:** Full sun to part shade. Tolerant of high temperatures and low humidity.
- **Water:** For satisfactory landscape performance, water established trees thoroughly every week or two in hot dry weather and every month or two during cool winter months. Surprisingly, trees in an abandoned landscape planting seem to survive well even though they are no longer watered.
- **Soil:** Gives satisfactory performance in a wide range of soils but best in fertile types.
- **Propagation:** Cuttings or air layering*.
- **Maintenance:** Pruning requirements may be significant or minimal depending on how you plan to use the tree.

POSSIBLE PROBLEMS

- In some areas, it is pest free, but in the western and southeastern United States, the foliage is distorted by a mite that is difficult to control.
- Subject to frost injury.
- Aggressive roots may cause heaving and buckling of nearby paved areas.

The distinctly rounded silhouette of Indian laurel fig is enhanced by long pendulous branches and dense refined foliage. It grows at a moderate rate from 20 to 35 feet (6 to 11 m) high in most warm-winter arid regions, with equal spread. May reach 70 feet (21 m) or higher in tropical climates, with equal spread. Waxy oval elliptical leaves, 2 to 4 inches (5 to 10 cm) long, are at first pale pink or yellow-green, changing to deep green as they reach full size. The slender trunk has smooth gray bark. Will develop aerial roots on trunk and branches in high humidity areas. Native to India and Malaya.

* *See Glossary*

Ficus microcarpa nitida (F. retusa nitida)

Compact Indian laurel fig

Moraceae family

COLD HARDINESS

Same as *F. microcarpa.*

LANDSCAPE VALUE

- Beautifully symmetrical growth habit and rich foliage texture make it ideal for shearing into formal shapes, hedges and topiary specimens in gardens and large containers.
- Also a wonderful avenue or shade tree, in public places and downtown areas where winters are warm and mostly frost free.

CULTURAL REQUIREMENTS

Same as *F. microcarpa.*

POSSIBLE PROBLEMS

Same as *F. microcarpa.*

This tree differs from the parent species in its branching habit, which is strongly ascending to erect. Also, its smooth, glossy bright green leaves to 4 inches (10 cm) long taper to more of a point at both the base and the tip. The foliage canopy is just as dense as that of *F. microcarpa* but more regular and formal in appearance. Size and growth rate are the same as *F. microcarpa.* The cultivar* 'Green Gem' has thick dark green foliage and resistance to mites that distort the leaves.

Ficus pertusa (F. padifolia)

Sonoran strangler fig

Moraceae family

COLD HARDINESS

Low zone and warmest microclimates of intermediate zone. Foliage blackened in high-20s F (-2°C) and wood damage in low-20s F (-6°C).

LANDSCAPE VALUE

- A large tree best for the oasis, it adds a tropical effect and a lush note to the landscape. It can maintain that appearance on much less water than most tropical-effects trees.
- In the more humid air of warm coastal deserts, it may develop aerial banyan-tree–like roots from the branches.
- Could be good in containers because it doesn't collapse with temporary drought.

CULTURAL REQUIREMENTS

- **Exposure:** Full sun to part shade.
- **Water:** Thoroughly soak the root zone every week or two (or perhaps every month, depending on your location).
- **Soil:** Any soil. Can even grow in dry rocky places as long as it can send roots down into moist crevices.
- **Propagation:** Seed or cuttings.
- **Maintenance:** Prune to maintain desired proportions. Cold tender—may need to remove frost-damaged wood.

POSSIBLE PROBLEMS

Cold tenderness and removal of frost-damaged wood.

Large glossy-leaved evergreen tree with smooth light-colored bark. In its native habitat, seeds (passed by birds or bats who have feasted on the tree's figs) often germinate on trunks and branches of host trees and send roots spiraling down the trunk of the host to the ground. These eventually overgrow and crush the host, thus the name "strangler." Growing along intermittent streams of the lower Sonoran Desert makes this species tolerant of occasional droughts. Although well-adapted to high summer heat, it is not a true desert tree. May reach 60 feet (18 m) in height, but is usually smaller, with equal spread. Rapid growth under optimum conditions but will remain small and gnarly under more stressful situations.

* *See Glossary*

Ficus petiolaris palmeri

Palo blanco, Palmer's fig

Moraceae family

COLD HARDINESS

Low zone and warm microclimates of intermediate zone. Frost damaged in mid-20s F (-4C).

LANDSCAPE VALUE

- Handsome foliage and trunks, especially outstanding in rocky situations.
- Great effects for a rocky site. Often found growing down cliffs.
- Makes an interesting bonsai in a container.

CULTURAL REQUIREMENTS

- **Exposure:** Full sun to part shade.
- **Water:** Thoroughly soak the root zone every week to every couple months, depending on how fast the soil dries.
- **Soil:** Any soil with good drainage.
- **Propagation:** Seed or cuttings.
- **Maintenance:** Low maintenance. In spring, remove frost-damaged wood if necessary.

POSSIBLE PROBLEMS

None observed except frost tenderness.

Spreading tree with somewhat heart-shaped glossy leaves and interesting veining, almost white buttressed trunks. Surface roots often snake over rock areas or down cliffs to create a striking effect. Evergreen to almost deciduous during dry periods. This is another desert-edge ficus that survives very dry conditions, but is best in more optimum moisture situations. It is one of the many white-trunked trees called palo blanco in Mexico. Grows 25 to 45 feet (7.5 to 13.5 m) high, with equal spread. Moderate to slow growth rate, depending on available moisture. Native to western Mexico.

Ficus petiolaris petiolaris

Rock fig

Moraceae family

Distinctive evergreen fig whose common name derives from its occurrence on dry slopes, often on the face of cliffs in Sonora and along most of Mexico's western coast and Baja California. Varies in size from a large shrub to a medium-size tree, to 30 feet (9 m) high and wide, depending on growing conditions. Rapid growth with good soil and regular water. May be upright with a single trunk or spreading with numerous stems from the base and flattened twisting roots that extend to a considerable distance over rock surfaces searching for a moist spot or crevices in which to grow. Medium to dark green leaves to 3 inches (7.5 cm) wide are heart-shaped to rounded. Leaf veins are scarlet. The trunk of young container-grown plants may develop an enlarged swollen base; this characteristic is more pronounced and dependable in *F. petiolaris* subspecies *petiolaris* than *palmeri*, which lacks red leaf veins. Neither flowers nor fruit have ornamental value.

COLD HARDINESS

Low zone and warm microclimates of intermediate zone. Frost tender. As a container plant, can be moved to a protected location on frosty nights.

LANDSCAPE VALUE

- Picturesque and unusual specimen in the landscape or in containers.
- Particularly exotic appearance with its heavy, irregularly swollen trunk base.
- Multistemmed plants may be even more unique.

CULTURAL REQUIREMENTS

- **Exposure:** Full sun to part shade.
- **Water:** Established plants can be gradually acclimated to water every month or two, although this results in a sparse foliage canopy. Weekly watering produces a faster-growing, lusher plant.
- **Soil:** Tolerant of many soil types but grows faster in deep improved garden soil.
- **Propagation:** Cuttings root readily, but plants must be grown from seed if you want a bulbous trunk base.
- **Maintenance:** Prune as necessary to control branching structure and form.

POSSIBLE PROBLEMS

Infestations of scale insects or mealy bugs may require control measures in some locations.

* See Glossary

Ficus radulina

Alamos fig

Moraceae family

COLD HARDINESS

Low zone and warmest microclimates of intermediate zone. Foliage burns in the high-20s F (-2°C), followed by young wood, which burns in mid-20s F (-4°C).

LANDSCAPE VALUE

- Dark, cool shade.
- Lush tropical feeling.

CULTURAL REQUIREMENTS

- **Exposure:** Full sun to part shade. Prefers a warm sunny location with moisture somewhere near.
- **Water:** Drought tolerant once established but water every week or two to maintain landscape appearance.
- **Soil:** Any soil.
- **Propagation:** Cuttings. Can be grown from seed.
- **Maintenance:** Prune for patio size, but no matter what form you choose, give it plenty of room to grow.

POSSIBLE PROBLEMS

- Roots may heave pavement.
- Pruning out frost damage when grown in borderline climates can be a pain.

A lush dark green fig with 3-inch (7.5-cm) long laurel-like leaves and plump gray trunk and branches, all with smooth bark. Found growing by seeps and wet spots at the lower edge of the Sonoran Desert and along a creek east of Alamos, Sonora, Mexico. Looks inviting and cool in hot reflective landscapes. Not as truly a desert ficus as the others mentioned in this book. Found where the moisture is assured year-round. Rapidly reaches 40 feet (12 m) in height and spread, under optimum conditions.

Ficus rubiginosa

Rustleaf fig

Moraceae family

COLD HARDINESS

Nearly frost-free locations in low zone, but withstands more cold than many other *Ficus*.

LANDSCAPE VALUE

- Oasis-zone specimen, shade or patio tree.
- Background or large framing park tree.
- Tolerant of salt wind—does well in seafront locations, with some pruning.

CULTURAL REQUIREMENTS

- **Exposure:** Full sun and heat.
- **Water:** Deep irrigation every week or two throughout the warm weather, less often during the cool months.
- **Soil:** Well-drained, fertile soil types are best but also adapted to sandy beachfront planting sites.
- **Propagation:** Seed or cuttings.
- **Maintenance:** Train young plants to develop basic structure.

POSSIBLE PROBLEMS

Develops buttressed roots that can raise pavement or curbs if planted in too tight a position.

The spreading crown of this Australian fig bears a dense cover of leathery 4- to 5-inch (10- to 13-cm) oval-shaped leaves that are dark green above, fuzzy and rust colored on lower surfaces. The tree may be single- or multitrunked. In a humid habitat, this species may develop aerial roots and a banyan growth habit. It produces inedible round warty figs to 1/2 inch (1 cm) on new growth. Grows to 20 feet (6 m) high, rarely to 40 feet (12 m) or even higher. Spreads to 40 feet (12 m) or wider. Moderate growth rate.

* See Glossary

Forchammeria watsonii

Palo jito, Lollipop tree

Capparidaceae family

COLD HARDINESS

Low zone. Appears to tolerate temperatures in mid-20s F (-4°C). From observations in the wild, foliage is damaged at the same temperatures that Ironwood *(Olneya tesota)* foliage is affected by cold.

LANDSCAPE VALUE

While this tree has had little exposure to landscape situations, its dark rich foliage and upright character suggests it would add richness and vertical accent to the water-efficient landscape.

CULTURAL REQUIREMENTS

- **Exposure:** Reflected sun to part shade but best in exposed positions.
- **Water:** Drought resistant. Thoroughly soak the root zone of mature trees every month or two, more often for young trees.
- **Soil:** Needs good drainage and prefers some soil depth.
- **Propagation:** Seed or cuttings.
- **Maintenance:** Slow grower, so plant in permanent location as soon as possible. It seems to languish in containers. Growth is rangy and irregular when young, so stake and train at first.

POSSIBLE PROBLEMS

Particularly difficult to grow in containers, but unimpressive stunted plants seem to take off when planted in the ground.

A tall, usually narrow, evergreen tree that slowly grows 9 to 25 feet (3 to 7.5 m) high and spreads 9 to 12 feet (3 to 3.5 m). Thick masses of long thin leaves create a dark solid note in the desert landscape. In its native Sonoran habitat, the lower growth is often grazed off by cattle, giving the tree a lollipop silhouette; thus the English common name. The density of the conifer-like growth is unique among desert trees, which generally have a more open character.

Forestiera acuminata parvifolia

Desert Olive

Oleaceae family

COLD HARDINESS

All three zones.

LANDSCAPE VALUE

- Background planting or screening.
- Woodsy effect.
- Thicket.

CULTURAL REQUIREMENTS

- **Exposure:** Full sun to part shade.
- **Water:** Quite drought resistant but needs thorough soaking of the root zone every month or two for good growth and appearance.
- **Soil:** Most soils with good drainage.
- **Propagation:** Seed or cuttings.
- **Maintenance:** A little shaping and clipping will increase its density and improve its general appearance.

POSSIBLE PROBLEMS

None observed.

Medium to large twiggy shrub, usually evergreen, that grows 6 to 12 feet (2 to 3.5 m) high and spreads 9 feet (3 m). Moderate growth rate. Small leaves are pointed and purple-black fruit resemble small olives.

Fouquieria columnaris (Idria columnaris)

Boojum tree, Cirio

Fouquieriaceae family

COLD HARDINESS

Low and intermediate zones.

LANDSCAPE VALUE

- Bizarre tree form presents a super accent plant where its silhouette can be displayed, such as against a plain wall (or the sky for large specimens).
- Protected status in its native habitat and very slow growth rate in cultivation make it unlikely to ever become a popular choice for the planned landscape.

CULTURAL REQUIREMENTS

- **Exposure:** Full sun, including reflected sun to part shade.
- **Water:** Completely drought resistant but needs water in winter, its growing season.
- **Soil:** Excellent drainage.
- **Propagation:** Seed. Possible to root twiggy side branches, but they are unable to produce a terminal* bud from which a terminal column emerges. Transplanting old specimens has often proven unsuccessful.
- **Maintenance:** No maintenance.

POSSIBLE PROBLEMS

- Its slowness of growth and sensitivity to poor drainage and overwatering at the wrong time practically rules out any abundant availability for landscaping.
- Damping off* a problem.

Spectacular tall desert tree, usually with a single trunk, that reaches to 60 feet (18 m) in height and spreads 10 to 15 feet (3 to 4.5 m). Very slow growth. Some describe it as resembling an upside down carrot or parsnip. It does have a thick trunk (a woody exterior and pithy interior), wide at the base, tapering to the tip. Many short twiggy side branches extend from the trunk, with a tuft of slightly larger ones at the top. Yellow straw-colored flowers are borne in large panicles* at the summit of the trunk. Deciduous part of the year, usually in summer. The 1/2 to 3/4 inch (1 to 2 cm) grayish green leaves and new growth usually are present only in winter. Native to central Baja California with a small population on the coast of Sonora, Mexico.

Fouquieria diguetii

Diguetii ocotillo

Fouquieriaceae family

COLD HARDINESS

Low zone and protected locations in intermediate zone.

LANDSCAPE VALUE

- Bold accent plant or tree with periods of colorful blooming.
- Barrier planting.
- Train into a small tree or a bonsai in containers.

CULTURAL REQUIREMENTS

- **Exposure:** Full sun.
- **Water:** Water every month or two. Tolerates water every week or two during the warm season.
- **Soil:** Any soil with good drainage.
- **Propagation:** Cuttings.
- **Maintenance:** Train to encourage tree-like structure, using deeper soil and more water.

POSSIBLE PROBLEMS

None observed.

A unique thorny shrub that can develop into a small tree with twisted branches. Growth is more lateral than *F. splendens*, especially when treelike. Reaches 6 to 26 feet (2 to 8 m) in height and spreads 6 to 20 feet (2 to 6 m) at a slow to moderate rate. Red flowers are borne in crowded panicles* at branch tips from late winter to spring. Dark green leaves usually persist if not frosted, but the plant will go drought deciduous under extreme conditions. Native to northwestern Mexico.

** See Glossary*

Fouquieria macdougalii

Tree ocotillo

Fouquieriaceae family

COLD HARDINESS

Low zone and warm microclimates of the intermediate zone, where branches are damaged by moderate frost.

LANDSCAPE VALUE

- Interesting treelike silhouette but not as striking as *F. splendens*.
- Massing or barrier planting.
- Containers.

CULTURAL REQUIREMENTS

- **Exposure:** Full sun to part shade.
- **Water:** Drought resistant but leafs out and grows best with water once or twice during the warm season.
- **Soil:** Most soils with good drainage.
- **Propagation:** Cuttings.
- **Maintenance:** Low maintenance. Shape for tree form.

POSSIBLE PROBLEMS

None observed.

Small spiny tree or a large distinctly treelike shrub with a short thick trunk and side branches. Grows up to 24 feet (7.5 m) high and spreads 12 to 18 feet (3.5 to 5.5 m) at a slow to moderate rate. Smooth yellow-green bark on mature wood is brownish or reddish on young growth. The small green leaves are drought deciduous. Loose clusters of small bright red flowers that seem to hang, fuschia-like, create an airy effect—not like the heavy thick clusters of *F. splendens*. Blooms off and on whenever in leaf. Native to Sonora, Mexico.

Fouquieria splendens

Ocotillo

Fouquieriaceae family

Deciduous shrub that grows 6 to 27 feet (2 to 8 m) high, spreading to 15 feet (4.5 m). Growth rate is moderate with rainfall or irrigation every month or two during the growing season. Many stiff, slender stems rise from a common base at ground level to form an inverted cone. Native to southwestern United States from southern California to New Mexico and Texas, as well as Baja California and Sonora, Mexico. At close range, the gray stems reveal prominent ridges and stout 1-inch (2.5-cm) long spines. Following rainfall in warmer months, dark green rounded leaves 1/2 to 1 inch (1 to 2.5 cm) long emerge rapidly but are short-lived, turning yellow to pink and dropping quickly as the soil dries. After spring and summer rains, bright red tubular flowers, 3/4 to 1 inch (2 to 2.5 cm) long, open in dense spiky clusters that rise to almost 1 foot (30.5 cm) long at the stem tips.

COLD HARDINESS

All three zones. Frost hardy.

LANDSCAPE VALUE

- Stark dramatic silhouette against a plain wall or skyline view.
- Spectacular fiery red flower clusters are especially lavish during the first bloom cycle of spring.
- Effective living fence or barrier planting.
- Desert landscape accent.

CULTURAL REQUIREMENTS

- **Exposure:** Naturally grows in searing heat and full to reflected sun.
- **Water:** No water necessary for survival except in the driest of climates. Regular water can kill the plant.
- **Soil:** Any soil with good drainage. Grows naturally in parched soil.
- **Propagation:** Seed, or plant stem-tip cuttings of any length in spring or summer. Water cuttings occasionally until leaves or new growth appear.
- **Maintenance:** No maintenance after established other than occasional removal of an unwanted stem where space is limited.

POSSIBLE PROBLEMS

Use with care in foot-traffic areas because of spines.

** See Glossary*

Fraxinus greggii and F. gooddingii

Greg ash, Goodding ash

Oleaceae family

COLD HARDINESS

All three zones.

LANDSCAPE VALUE

- Attractive patio-size tree.
- Multistemmed thicket for woodsy effects or background planting.
- Slow-growing jewel worth waiting for.

CULTURAL REQUIREMENTS

- **Exposure:** Full sun to part shade.
- **Water:** Water deeply every month or two when mature. Because of its somewhat slow growth habit, thoroughly soak the root zone more frequently to speed up growth.
- **Soil:** Any soil with good drainage.
- **Propagation:** Seed.
- **Maintenance:** Stake and prune to encourage a patio-tree form.

POSSIBLE PROBLEMS

None observed.

Large shrub or small tree, usually evergreen, that grows at a slow to moderate rate. Reaches 9 to 12 feet (3 to 3.5 m) high and spreads about 9 feet (3 m). Small compound leaves are light green to grayish. The smooth bark is also gray. Develops single or multiple trunks. Becomes a small round-headed tree form with trimming and training. This Chihuahuan Desert native is sometimes linked with goodding ash *(F. gooddingii)*, found in higher elevations of the Arizona desert. For landscape use the species basically perform the same.

Landscape Design Example

Look to nature for the best landscape "design" examples.

* See Glossary

Fraxinus velutina

Arizona ash, Velvet ash, Modesto ash, Rio Grande ash, Fan-tex ash

Oleaceae family

COLD HARDINESS

All three zones.

LANDSCAPE VALUE

- Residential-scale shade tree that moderates intense summer heat and, during leafless period, allows winter sun to warm structures and outdoor living areas.
- Street tree, suitable for parks and other public spaces, school grounds, commercial landscapes.
- Minioasis tree (native habitat near intermittent streams).

CULTURAL REQUIREMENTS

- **Exposure:** Full sun to part shade.
- **Water:** Once established, adapts to thorough soaking of the root zone every month or two during the growing season and once or twice during its dormant period, especially if the season is quite dry.
- **Soil:** Most soils with good drainage.
- **Propagation:** Grows easily from seed but the varieties are best grown from cuttings to avoid unwanted hybrids.
- **Maintenance:** Prune to develop strong, well-proportioned branching structure.

POSSIBLE PROBLEMS

- Subject to Texas root rot*, nematodes*, ash decline, chlorosis*, spider mites and ash flower gall*.
- 'Modesto' sometimes suffers wind damage to its branches.

Rounded, somewhat open and spreading deciduous tree that reaches 30 to 45 feet (9 to 13.5 m) in height, spreading 25 to 45 feet (7.5 to 13.5 m). Moderate to rapid growth rate. Pinnately* compound leaves made up of five to nine medium green leaflets, 3/4 to 2 1/2 inches (2 to 6.5 cm) long, turn bright yellow in fall. Unimportant flowers give way to winged fruit less than 1 inch (2.5 cm) long on female trees. 'Modesto' has a more uniform dense crown of glossy bright green leaves, best for golden fall color. 'Rio Grande' (or 'Fan-tex') develops an attractive oval shape at maturity and the leaflets are larger and darker green than the species in general. This selection also retains its foliage later, sometimes into winter, and leafs out early in spring. It is also more tolerant of desert heat, aridity and alkaline soils. Native from California to Texas and northern Mexico.

* See Glossary

Gaura lindheimeri

Pink gaura

Onagraceae family

COLD HARDINESS
All three zones, but dies back to ground in cold areas.

LANDSCAPE VALUE
- Combined with other desert perennials for summer effects.
- Rock gardens.
- Oasis plantings.
- Planters and containers.
- The pink variety is especially attractive for the above uses. Lacks interest in winter, so combine with plants that have good winter-season appearance.

CULTURAL REQUIREMENTS
- **Exposure:** Full sun to part shade.
- **Water:** Drought resistant but water every week or two during the warm season to produce the June–September flowers.
- **Soil:** Most soils with good drainage, but silty soils are best.
- **Propagation:** Seed or cuttings.
- **Maintenance:** Cut back in winter or early spring to induce new healthy growth.

POSSIBLE PROBLEMS
None observed.

Attractive perennial that grows about 18 inches (46 cm) tall, 12 inches (30.5 cm) wide. Growth is rapid during the warm season when moisture is present. Sprays of mosquitolike flowers are borne on spikes in an open airy display. Flowers typically open white and fade to pink, but there is a pink variety available in nurseries that opens pink from the bud. The cluster of stems rising from the ground are heavily clothed with small green leaves. Stems may be evergreen in milder areas or die back to the ground in colder regions. Blooms last through September if moisture is present. Native to southwestern United States and northern Mexico below 4000 feet (1220 m) on silty soils.

Gazania rigens hybrids

Clumping gazania

Asteraceae (Compositae) family

COLD HARDINESS
All three zones.

LANDSCAPE VALUE
- Groundcover or filler in sunny beds and borders, on level or gently sloping open locations with well-drained soil.
- Colorful edging plant, useful in containers, planting strips and other confined spaces.

CULTURAL REQUIREMENTS
- **Exposure:** Open sunny locations. No heavy shade.
- **Water:** Water thoroughly, but only as necessary for good appearance. Schedule irrigation early enough in day to allow foliage and crowns to dry before nightfall.
- **Soil:** Light soils with good drainage.
- **Propagation:** Seed or divisions.
- **Maintenance:** Refurbish with new plants each winter if using as a groundcover.

POSSIBLE PROBLEMS
Crown and root rots develop in extremely wet soils. Select an appropriate planting site and do not overwater.

Crosses between various *Gazanias* have yielded hybrid clumping types that display flowers in glowing colors with decorative markings. These herbaceous* South African plants form a low, dense, nonspreading mound of foliage, only about 6 to 12 inches (15 to 30.5 cm) high and wide. Growth rate is moderate. Daisylike flowers 2 to 4 inches (5 to 10 cm) across develop on stems 6 to 10 inches (15 to 25.5 cm) long. Flowering is heaviest in spring and fall and scattered throughout the rest of the year. At night and on cloudy days, the flowers of most hybrids close. Nurseries offer some clumping *Gazanias* as started plants in flats or small containers, and others as seeds of named selections in single colors or color mixes.

* *See Glossary*

Gazania rigens leucolaena

Trailing gazania

Asteraceae (Compositae) family

A prostrate, trailing perennial groundcover from South Africa. Grows rapidly 6 to 8 inches (15 to 20.5 cm) high,18 inches (46 cm) wide. Gray-green or green leaves, 4 to 6 inches (10 to 15 cm) long, are the background for daisylike flowers in shades of yellow, orange, white or bronze, 2 to 3 inches (5 to 7.5 cm) in diameter. Blooms profusely in spring and again in fall with a scattering of flowers throughout the summer months. Large-flowered hybrids extend the peak bloom season and show improved resistance to crown rot. Flowers of most types remain closed at night, in heavy shade and on overcast days.

COLD HARDINESS

Low and intermediate zones. In intermediate zone, severe cold may cause considerable winter die-back*.

LANDSCAPE VALUE

- Creates a carpet of foliage that serves as a foreground and herbaceous* filler to help tie larger elements into a unified composition, or as a transition into more arid plant material.
- Untreadable groundcover for controlling erosion on large slopes and banks, as well as on level areas.
- Attractive in hanging containers.

CULTURAL REQUIREMENTS

- **Exposure:** Highly tolerant of intense sun and heat, and low humidity. Grows well in congested urban areas.
- **Water:** Water every month or two to maintain growth and good appearance. Schedule fewer waterings of longer duration, rather than frequent and light waterings.
- **Soil:** Any soil with good drainage.
- **Propagation:** Seed or cuttings.
- **Maintenance:** Thin and replant established plantings each spring if bare spots develop.

POSSIBLE PROBLEMS

Crown rots* caused by rainy weather or overwatering, especially in summer on poorly drained soil. To avoid these diseases, plant *Gazanias* in full sun in well-drained soil. Water only when necessary and early enough in the day so foliage and crown will be dry by sunset.

Geijera parviflora

Australian willow

Rutaceae family

COLD HARDINESS

Low zone and warm microclimates of intermediate zone. Withstands light frost but is damaged at colder temperatures.

LANDSCAPE VALUE

- Screen.
- Medians and streets.
- Single specimen.
- Small patio tree.
- Under utility wires.
- Courtyards or other confined spaces and small properties.

CULTURAL REQUIREMENTS

- **Exposure:** Full to reflected sun.
- **Water:** Water every week to every couple of months. More liberal watering results in faster growth and denser foliage.
- **Soil:** Adapts to a wide range of soils.
- **Propagation:** Seed or cuttings.
- **Maintenance:** Prune as needed to maintain symmetrical growth habit.

POSSIBLE PROBLEMS

None observed.

Large Australian evergreen shrub or small tree, rounded to pyramidal in shape. Grows at a moderate rate from 15 to 25 feet (4.5 to 7.5 m) high, spreading 15 to 20 feet (4.5 to 6 m). Drooping branchlets and pendulous willowy leaves are 3 to 6 inches (7.5 to 15 cm) long. Small creamy flowers in inconspicuous clusters open in spring and fall.

* *See Glossary*

Geoffroea decorticans (Gourleia chilensis)

Chilean palo verde, Chañar

Fabaceae (Leguminosae) family

COLD HARDINESS

Low and intermediate zones.

LANDSCAPE VALUE

- Handsome woodsy tree, especially useful as a bosque.
- Develops into a grove if root sprouts are allowed to grow.
- Produces the first golden flower display of spring.
- Single-trunk tree in confined planting areas within paved spaces or parking areas.

CULTURAL REQUIREMENTS

- **Exposure:** Full sun.
- **Water:** Thoroughly soak the root zone every month or two.
- **Soil:** Most soils with good drainage.
- **Propagation:** Seed or root sprouts.
- **Maintenance:** Needs space to develop but, as mentioned, can be used as a single-trunk tree in confined paved spaces, which controls the invasive root sprouting.

POSSIBLE PROBLEMS

- Sometimes invasive because of root sprouting if planted in the wrong place.
- Thorns can be a hazard.

Semi-evergreen tree with an open irregular structure and striking satiny smooth, dappled green bark. Reaches 20 feet (6 m) in height, spreading 10 to 15 feet (3 to 4.5 m). Moderate growth rate. Usually multi-trunked. Often develops into a little grove because of its root sprouts. Small golden yellow blossoms cover prickly branches in early spring, blooming before *Cercidiums* species. Native to Chile.

* See Glossary

Gleditsia triacanthos (G. triacanthos inermis)

Honey locust, Thornless honey locust

Fabaceae (Leguminosae) family

COLD HARDINESS

All three zones except the more tropical edges of low zone.

LANDSCAPE VALUE

- Residential roadsides and parks where cultivars* of *G. triacanthos inermis* are almost universally used. Not for narrow planting strips between curbs and sidewalks.
- Its hardiness to heat and cold extends its value.
- Excellent in groves and bosques* in large spaces such as parks.
- Creates a woodsy effect and highlights the change of seasons.
- It has become a major urban tree since the demise of the American elm *(Ulmus americana)* to Dutch elm disease. It does equally well in low hot-desert zones where there is a defined winter season.

CULTURAL REQUIREMENTS

- **Exposure:** Full sun. Tolerates reflected heat.
- **Water:** Thoroughly soak the root zone every month or two once mature, but every week to ten days in the warm season to speed growth.
- **Soil:** Most soils, including alkaline, but better in deeper soils.
- **Propagation:** Species can be grown from seed, but *G. triacanthos inermis* cultivars must be propagated vegetatively or grafted on the species root.
- **Maintenance:** Remove low branches, shape and stake when tree is young.

POSSIBLE PROBLEMS

- Thorns of the species limit its landscape value.
- Heavy production of large pods creates litter.
- The late leafing out in spring often leaves areas unshaded when the first hot days of spring arrive.
- Roots and some buttressing at trunk base of mature trees heave paving and curbs if planted in too small a space.

Deciduous tree with straight upright trunk and spreading arching branches. Under optimum conditions, grows rapidly from 30 to 75 feet (9 to 23 m) high, spreading to 50 feet (15 m). Feathery compound leaves split into many oval 3/4- to 1 1/2-inch (2- to 4-cm) long leaflets. Leafs out rather late in spring, but produces a pleasant light shade when it does. Turns a golden yellow in late fall, supplying a touch of autumn color—a rarity in hot arid climates. Leaves disintegrate as they fall, leaving only the midribs to rake up. Inconspicuous flowers are followed by broad brown pods, 12 to 18 inches (30.5 to 46 cm) long and filled with sweetish pulp and hard, roundish seeds. Trunks and branches of the species produce formidable thorns (even the thorns have thorns); it is seldom planted, but *G. triacanthos inermis* varieties and cultivars have fewer thorns. They also produce far fewer pods, which results in less litter. For the most part, they remain smaller, more suitable for residential and street tree planting. Native to midwestern United States.

Cultivars: 'Sunburst' has golden green foliage and an irregular form. 'Moraine' is faster growing, more spreading in form. 'Imperial' is symmetrical with dense leaves and about 35 feet (11 m) at maturity. 'Shademaster' is less spreading and a rapid grower, to 24 feet (7.5 m) high and 16 feet (5 m) wide in about 6 years, eventually reaching 40 to 50 feet (12 to 15 m). Other selections are also available.

* *See Glossary*

Gossypium harknessii

San Carlos hibiscus

Malvaceae family

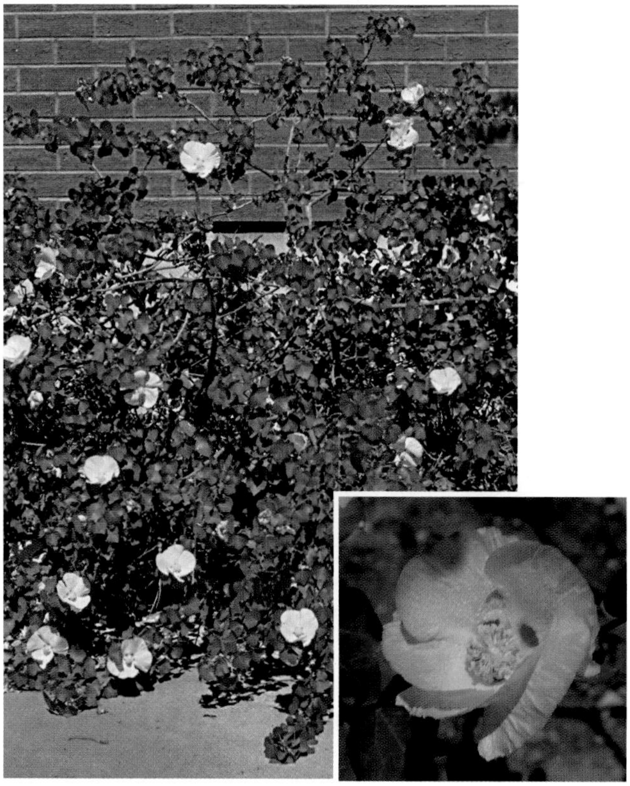

COLD HARDINESS

Low zone and warm locations of intermediate zone. Tolerates light frost but damaged when temperature reaches mid-20s F (-4°C).

LANDSCAPE VALUE

- Flowering shrub for foundation and foreground plantings, especially where salinity is a problem.
- Its lush green foliage looks almost tropical and is drought- and heat-tolerant.

CULTURAL REQUIREMENTS

- **Exposure:** Full sun to part shade.
- **Water:** Drought resistant but looks best with water every week or two during the warm season. Tolerates brackish water.
- **Soil:** Any soil. Grows naturally in sandy, gravelly soil.
- **Propagation:** Seed or cuttings.
- **Maintenance:** Low maintenance.

POSSIBLE PROBLEMS

None observed except tenderness to frost.

Attractive low-growing evergreen shrub, 1½ inches to 3 feet (46 cm to 1 m) high, with equal spread. Grows at a moderate to rapid rate in moist conditions. Leaves are broad, shiny and heart-shaped. Yellow flowers resemble hibiscus blooms. Actually a wild cotton, but it resembles its other mallow* relative the hibiscus. Collected on the shores of the Sea of Cortez at San Carlos, Mexico. It is salt-tolerant and considered almost a halophyte*. Blooms throughout the warm season.

Gossypium thurberi

Wild cotton

Malvaceae family

COLD HARDINESS

All three zones.

LANDSCAPE VALUE

- Not yet fully evaluated but certainly has landscape potential.
- Tropical and lush in the wild, especially during summer rains.
- Summer garden.

CULTURAL REQUIREMENTS

- **Exposure:** Full sun to part shade.
- **Water:** Water every week or two during the warm season, every month or two at other times, to maintain good foliage and flower production.
- **Soil:** Grows in rocky almost soil-less situations.
- **Propagation:** Seed.
- **Maintenance:** Head back fast-growing terminal branches to side buds or branches for a more dense, compact plant.

POSSIBLE PROBLEMS

Looks tacky in winter, during dormant leafless period. Plant with evergreen to disguise.

Upright shrub that grows rapidly during the warm season from 6 to 14 feet (2 to 4 m) high and spreads to 3 feet (1 m). Branch structure is open and leaves have three to five lobes, resembling domesticated cotton plants. Flowers, 1½ to 2½ inches (4 to 5 cm), are creamy white, turning to purple with age, and resemble hibiscus cotton blossoms. Native to Sonoran Desert, from southern Arizona into Mexico.

* See Glossary

Grevillea robusta
Silk oak
Proteaceae family

An impressive vertical-growing evergreen tree that rapidly reaches 60 feet (18 m)—taller in deep soil and optimum conditions, smaller in drier conditions. Spreads 25 feet (7.5 m), more or less, depending on the above conditions. May be briefly semideciduous in spring when it produces large dense flat clusters of showy golden orange flowers. Lush, finely divided ferny leaves (one of its particularly striking features) thickly cover the branches. Leaf drop is heavy in spring and, to a lesser degree, at times of new growth. This will create a leafy mulch if not raked up. Old trees develop a broader picturesque silhouette against the sky. Dark brown furrowed bark. Native to Australia.

COLD HARDINESS
Low zone and warmer locations in intermediate zone. Young trees are more tender; older trees can withstand considerable cold.

LANDSCAPE VALUE
- Tall background tree for roadside use, parks and other larger spaces.
- Showy spring bloom contrasts nicely with *Jacaranda mimosifolia* which often blooms at the same time.
- Foliage adds a rich green note to arid landscapes.

CULTURAL REQUIREMENTS
- **Exposure:** Full sun, including reflected sun and heat.
- **Water:** Water developing trees every week or two for good growth. Mature trees are drought resistant. Maintain by soaking the root zone every month or two.
- **Soil:** Tolerates a wide variety of soils, even heavy clay soil if not overwatered. Tends to become chlorotic* in lawns and in slow-draining soils, especially soils high in calcium carbonate.
- **Propagation:** Seed.
- **Maintenance:** Heavy leaf drop in spring requires considerable cleanup in lawns and near pavement, but it can be left as a mulch elsewhere.

POSSIBLE PROBLEMS
- Wood is brittle and can break in high winds.
- Heavy leaf drop can require high maintenance when planted in inappropriate situations.
- Chlorosis* can be a problem in wetter locations.

Guaiacum angustifolium (Porlieria angustifolium)
Texas guaicum
Zygophyllaceae family

COLD HARDINESS
All three zones.

LANDSCAPE VALUE
- An important addition to the rather short list of dark green shrubs for desert areas.
- Foundation plantings.
- Mixed shrubby borders.
- Medians and even underplantings below tall shade trees.

CULTURAL REQUIREMENTS
- **Exposure:** Full sun to open shade.
- **Water:** Endures prolonged periods of drought, but thoroughly soak the root zone every month to maintain a satisfactory appearance. Water every week or two during the warm season to speed development of new plantings and increase growth.
- **Soil:** Tolerates most desert soils but because of its slow growth, best to use enriched garden soil.
- **Propagation:** Seed or cuttings.
- **Maintenance:** Little maintenance. Slow-release fertilizer will speed up growth.

POSSIBLE PROBLEMS
Slow growth seems to be the only negative aspect of this plant.

A mounding evergreen shrub that slowly reaches 8 to 10 feet (2.5 to 3 m) in height and spread. Thick dark green leaves are compound. The small blue to purple, sometimes white, flowers appear in late spring. They are attractive at close range but fall short of the spectacular show put on by its Sonoran Desert relative, *G. coulteri.* However *G. angustifolium* makes up for this by producing bright orange fruit in clusters—very striking set against the dark green foliage. Native to south Texas and northeast Mexico.

* *See Glossary*

Guaiacum coulteri

Guayacán

Zygophyllaceae family

COLD HARDINESS

Low zone and, with protection, warm-winter microclimates of the intermediate zone. Sensitive to frost.

LANDSCAPE VALUE

Few arid-climate plants can match the rich color of guayacán at full bloom. In warm-winter areas, it serves as an exceptionally beautiful flowering specimen, accent or character shrub or small tree.

CULTURAL REQUIREMENTS

- **Exposure:** Full or reflected sun. Tolerates intense heat.
- **Water:** Withstands long dry periods, but more attractive with thorough soaking of the root zone once or twice during the summer growing season.
- **Soil:** Most soils with good drainage.
- **Propagation:** Seed.
- **Maintenance:** Little maintenance. Slow-release fertilizer will speed up growth.

POSSIBLE PROBLEMS

Intolerant of cold. Severely damaged or killed by repeated hard frosts.

Unmistakable during its bloom season when intensely blue-purple flowers create a startling splash of color. Guayacán is a shrub or small tree native to the deciduous tropical thorn scrub of western Mexico. It grows at a slow to moderate pace (depending on soil moisture) to about 25 feet (7.5 m) high, with equal spread. Because it lacks cold hardiness, mature size is controlled by low winter temperatures. In warm-winter areas of its range, guayacán develops into a small tree, but where winter frosts are more common, it remains a shrub of 6 feet (2 m) or less in height and spread. Dark green pinnately* compound foliage grows tightly along crooked twisting branches. Each leaf consists of three to five pairs of small linear to oval leaflets. Severe dry or cold weather may trigger defoliation. The five-petaled flowers 3/4 to 1 1/4 inches (2 to 3 cm) in diameter open in clusters of three to twelve at the leaf base anytime from spring into midsummer. Curious green or greenish purple fruits 1/4 to 1/2 inch (0.5 cm to 1 cm) long have five angles with five narrow wings.

Haematoxylum brasiletto

Brazilwood

Fabaceae (Leguminosae) family

COLD HARDINESS

Warm frost-protected areas of the low zone and similar locations in intermediate zone. Frost tender but recovers by late spring from light to moderate damage.

LANDSCAPE VALUE

- Picturesque small tree with an impressive floral display.
- Ridged and fluted branches and trunk of larger specimens are unique and interesting.
- Specimen.
- Background or border plantings.
- Where marginally cold hardy, may survive if planted against a warm, south-facing wall.

CULTURAL REQUIREMENTS

- **Exposure:** Hot, sunny, mostly frost-free planting sites.
- **Water:** Established plants can survive long dry periods but will shed their foliage. Water every month or two to maintain appearance.
- **Soil:** Deep well-drained soil.
- **Propagation:** Seed, possibly by cuttings.
- **Maintenance:** Stake and prune to develop a single-stemmed growth habit.

POSSIBLE PROBLEMS

- Stiff 1-inch (2.5 cm) spines limit use in foot-traffic situations.
- Water-stressed trees have a sparse appearance.

The irregular vase-shaped to spreading crown of this large subtropical shrub or small tree is formed by an ascending branch structure. Grows slowly from 7 to 20 feet (2 to 6 m) high, spreading 5 to 20 feet (1.5 to 6 m). Slow growth can be sped up with regular water. It may grow with one to several trunks. Older branches and trunks have gray bark and well-defined bark fissures while the younger stems are smooth, reddish brown and thorny.

The heartwood of brazilwood has a characteristic dark red color. Small leathery leaflets in two to four pairs per compound leaf are 1/4 to 1 inch (0.5 to 2.5 cm) long and drought deciduous. The pale yellow flowers are borne in short loose clusters. Each bloom is 1/4 inch (0.5 cm) long with red edges. Flowers appear in profusion after a significant rain. Native to the west coast of Mexico, south to Colombia and Venezuela.

* *See Glossary*

Hamelia patens

Scarlet bush, Fire bush, Texas flame bush
Rubiaceae family

COLD HARDINESS

Low zone and warm locations in intermediate zone. Damaged by light frost but dies back to the ground when temperatures fall into the low-20s F (-5°C).

LANDSCAPE VALUE

- Scarlet show of flowers throughout the warm season add color accent.
- Combine with other shrubs or in a foundation planting against a warm south or west wall.

CULTURAL REQUIREMENTS

- **Exposure:** Full sun and reflected heat. Tolerates part shade, but the flowers will be much less abundant.
- **Water:** A tough plant that tolerates long periods of drought. To maximize the colorful bloom period, water every week or two during the warm season.
- **Soil:** Most soils will do, but prepared garden soil is best.
- **Propagation:** Softwood cuttings in spring, or seed.
- **Maintenance:** Prune up to develop small tree. Remove cold-damaged growth each spring in colder climates.

POSSIBLE PROBLEMS

Other hardy plants needed to cover the empty space frost-damaged plants leave in the winter garden.

Vigorous shrub that grows rapidly from 3 to 25 feet (1 to 7.5 m) high, with equal spread in frost-free areas with regular water. Gray-green to bright green pubescent* leaves are about 6 inches (15 cm) long. These evergreen leaves are arranged opposite or in whorls. Bright red to orange flowers are abundant throughout the warm season; small dark red to purple fruit follows bloom. In colder areas where it freezes back to the ground each winter, it usually only grows to a 3-foot (1-m) shrub, but in frost-free and protected areas it may become a small tree. Native to Mexico, Central America, and Florida.

Hechtia montana

Sonoran hechtia, Mescalito
Bromeliaceae family

COLD HARDINESS

Low zone (sometimes damaged by frost) and protected microclimates of intermediate zone. Hardy to mid-20s F (-4°C) in intermediate zone.

LANDSCAPE VALUE

- Clumps among rocks and at base of palms.
- Tropical effects.
- Containers.

CULTURAL REQUIREMENTS

- **Exposure:** Full sun or open shade.
- **Water:** Accepts water every week to only once or twice a season.
- **Soil:** Any soil with good drainage.
- **Propagation:** Seed or divisions.
- **Maintenance:** Little to no maintenance required.

POSSIBLE PROBLEMS

Sharp hooked, thorn-edged leaves make weeding difficult.

Ground-hugging bromeliad* that reaches about 1 foot (30.5 cm) high. Gray-green, shiny, prickle-edged succulent leaves in rosettes*. Plants can develop into clumps 3 feet (1 m) or more across. Grows at a moderate rate. Small flowers not colorful but stalks provide vertical accents to low clumps. Native to west coast of Mexico.

** See Glossary*

COLD HARDINESS
All three zones.

LANDSCAPE VALUE
Same as *H. montana.*

CULTURAL REQUIREMENTS
Same as *H. montana.*

POSSIBLE PROBLEMS
Sharp hooked, thorn-edged leaves make weeding difficult.

Almost identical to *H. montana* in appearance but grayer and more cold-tolerant. Reaches 12 to 16 inches (30.5 to 40.5 cm) high, clumping to 3 feet (1 m). Slow to moderate growth. Native to southern Texas and the Chihuahuan Desert.

Hechtia texana

Texas hechtia, False agave
Bromeliaceae family

COLD HARDINESS
Low zone and protected microclimates of intermediate zone.

LANDSCAPE VALUE
- Untreadable groundcover with spring flowers.
- Foundation plant, low border, edging or mass planting.
- Facer for taller plants.
- Planters and other confined spaces.

CULTURAL REQUIREMENTS
- **Exposure:** Full sun.
- **Water:** Tolerates short dry periods. Water every week or two for satisfactory appearance.
- **Soil:** Grows in various soil types but performs best in improved garden soil.
- **Propagation:** Seed.
- **Maintenance:** Prune to remove seed heads before they mature.

POSSIBLE PROBLEMS
- Seed heads are unsightly and produce litter.
- May reseed where unwanted.

A dense spreading mound of silvery gray foliage serves as a background for bright yellow daisylike flowers that bloom late winter into spring. Flowers grow up to 2 inches (5 cm) across and are borne singly on stems well above the foliage mass. Seed heads, which somewhat resemble dandelion seed heads, ripen in a few weeks to release an abundant seed crop. Grows at a moderate to rapid rate to 20 inches (51 cm) high, spreading 4 feet (1 m).

Hertia chirifolia

Hertia daisy
Asteraceae (Compositae) family

* See Glossary

Hesperaloe funifera

Giant hesperaloe

Agavaceae family

COLD HARDINESS

Low and intermediate zones. Withstands moderate to hard frost.

LANDSCAPE VALUE

- The striking foliage, growth habit and flower display of this plant add character and drama to the arid landscape.
- Interesting and unusual accent or specimen.
- Large containers.
- Tropical-effects plant combinations.

CULTURAL REQUIREMENTS

- **Exposure:** Reflected heat and sun.
- **Water:** Drought tolerant. Water every month or two during warm season after plants are established, more often when plants are young.
- **Soil:** Most soils with good drainage.
- **Propagation:** Seed or divisions.
- **Maintenance:** No maintenance other than removal of old flower stalks.

POSSIBLE PROBLEMS

None observed.

Large impressive evergreen succulent from the Chihuahuan Desert in Mexico. Slowly grows to 6 feet (2 m) in height, spreading 8 to 10 feet (2.5 to 3 m). A clump of tough, narrow leaves to 6 feet (2 m) long and 2⅜ inches (6 cm) wide rise from a common base at ground level. Loose fibers are evident along the margins. Greenish white flowers with a trace of purple open in late spring to early summer on 8 foot (2.5 m) stalks.

Hesperaloe nocturna

Night-blooming hesperaloe

Agavaceae family

COLD HARDINESS

Low and intermediate zones.

LANDSCAPE VALUE

- Accent.
- Combine with palms and other tropical-effects plants.
- Containers.

CULTURAL REQUIREMENTS

- **Exposure:** Full sun, including reflected sun and heat to part shade.
- **Water:** Drought tolerant. Water every month or two during warm season after plant is established, more often when plant is young.
- **Soil:** Most soils with good drainage.
- **Propagation:** Seed or divisions.
- **Maintenance:** No maintenance other than removal of old flower stalks.

POSSIBLE PROBLEMS

None observed.

Grows in rosettes* of dull green, narrow strap-like leaves. Produces tall bloom stalks, to 6 feet (2 m), capped with small white flowers that open at night. Not colorful but bloom stalks have dramatic form and silhouette. Blooms in summer. Interesting possibilities for hybridizing with *H. parviflora* to achieve bloom color. Grows at a moderate rate to 3 feet (1 m) high, with equal spread. Native to Sonora, Mexico.

** See Glossary*

Hesperaloe parviflora

Red yucca

Agavaceae family

COLD HARDINESS

Low and intermediate zones and probably warmer locations in high zone. Very frost tolerant.

LANDSCAPE VALUE

- Conspicuous showy flowering habit and interesting foliage make this a valuable accent plant, as a specimen or in groups among rocks and in medians.
- Combines well with many other arid-region plant types.
- Container culture.

CULTURAL REQUIREMENTS

- **Exposure:** Full sun for best flowering but grows in part shade.
- **Water:** Established plants are drought resistant. Water every week or every month during the warm season to stimulate growth and flowering.
- **Soil:** Most soils with good drainage.
- **Propagation:** Seed or division of large clumps.
- **Maintenance:** Remove spent flower stalks; otherwise maintenance-free.

POSSIBLE PROBLEMS

None observed except slow growth.

Evergreen succulent that grows slowly to 3 feet (1 m) high and 4 feet (1 m) wide. Many narrow arching leaves, tough and stiff with marginal threads, spread to form a crowded grasslike clump. In late spring to early summer, long slender spikes of nodding bell-shaped flowers bloom $1\frac{1}{4}$ inches (3 cm) long. These pink to light red blossoms are borne on stalks 3 to 6 feet (1 to 2 m) tall or taller; in milder climates, bloom cycle may repeat in late summer to fall. Native to Texas and adjacent Mexico.

Heteromeles arbutifolia

Toyon, California holly, Christmas berry

Rosaceae family

COLD HARDINESS

All three zones.

LANDSCAPE VALUE

- Valued for colorful fruit, rich foliage character and versatile shrub or tree form.
- Privacy screen, background, informal shrub border, sheared hedge, buffer planting and highway and street median plant.
- Can be pruned into a small multi- or single-stemmed accent or specimen tree.
- Christmas garland and other holiday decorations.
- Performs well in congested urban environments.

CULTURAL REQUIREMENTS

- **Exposure:** Full sun or part shade.
- **Water:** In hot dry areas, water every month or two during summer, more often during the cool season. *Heteromeles* is native to a dry-summer/wet-winter region, but in the desert, supplemental summer moisture is necessary because of the extreme dry heat.
- **Soil:** Any soil with good drainage.
- **Propagation:** Seed or cuttings.
- **Maintenance:** Prune for desired growth habit: shrub or tree. To enhance berry production, head back branch terminals* to side buds to encourage the one-year-old wood on which flower buds develop.

POSSIBLE PROBLEMS

- Mildew or fireblight may occur during wet weather.
- Berry crop not as profuse in regions with summer rains.

A dense evergreen shrub, becoming a small tree in favorable locations, that grows 8 to 25 feet (2.5 to 7.5 m) high, with equal spread. Moderate growth rate. The dark green leathery leaves are 2 to 4 inches (5 to 10 cm) long and 1 to 2 inches (2.5 to 5 cm) wide with prominent veins and strongly toothed margins. In summer, clusters of small white flowers open at the tips of one-year-old branches. These give way to bright red fruit (berries) about $\frac{1}{4}$ inch (0.5 cm) in diameter that persist through the winter if not eaten by birds. 'Macrocarpa' has larger fruit to $\frac{3}{8}$ inch (1 cm) in diameter in bigger clusters. A California native.

** See Glossary*

Hymenoxys acaulis

Angelita daisy

Asteraceae (Compositae) family

COLD HARDINESS

All three zones.

LANDSCAPE VALUE

- A colorful and persistent perennial for more informal desert gardens.
- Planters and containers to show off profuse colorful flowers.

CULTURAL REQUIREMENTS

- **Exposure:** Full sun.
- **Water:** Survives on monthly water but weekly watering during the warm season ensures best bloom and landscape effect.
- **Soil:** Most soils with good drainage.
- **Propagation:** Seed.
- **Maintenance:** Undemanding.

POSSIBLE PROBLEMS

None observed

A bushy compact perennial that grows at a moderate rate about 1 foot (30.5 cm) high, with equal spread. Produces 1-inch (2.5-cm) yellow daisies most of the year with an especially heavy bloom show in spring. Resembles desert marigold *(Baileya multiradiata)* but has green rather than gray foliage and the flowers are deeper yellow. Like *Baileya*, it will naturalize. This tough desert native occurs most often on high and dry mesas and rocky slopes in Arizona, New Mexico, Colorado, Nevada, and Southern California at 4,000 to 7,000 feet (1220 to 2135 m).

Hyptis emoryi

Desert lavender

Lamiaceae (Labiatae) family

COLD HARDINESS

Low zone and warm locations in intermediate zone. Frost tender.

LANDSCAPE VALUE

- Attractive gray leaves contrast with darker foliage in a shrubbery composition.
- Medium-size shrub for general use, especially for reflective-sun locations.
- Foliage and flowers have a nice fragrance.

CULTURAL REQUIREMENTS

- **Exposure:** Full sun. Tolerates reflected sun and heat. Becomes more rangy in part shade.
- **Water:** Drought resistant but water every month or two during hot season for attractive appearance.
- **Soil:** Any soil with good drainage.
- **Propagation:** Seed or cuttings.
- **Maintenance:** Intermittent light pruning helps keep older plants more dense. Remove frost-damaged wood in spring.

POSSIBLE PROBLEMS

None observed.

Compact in early stages but rangy and open with age, this shrub grows 4 to 8 feet (1 to 2.5 m) high, with equal spread. With moisture, the usually moderate growth rate becomes rapid. Leaves are powder gray and aromatic. Small sagelike clusters of pale pink-lavender flower clusters are not particularly showy against this gray foliage. They appear in late spring and after summer rains. Native to dry hot slopes of the low and intermediate zones of the Sonoran Desert.

Ipomoea arborescens

Tree morning glory, Palo blanco

Convolvulaceae family

COLD HARDINESS

Low zone and warm microclimates of intermediate zone. Tender below high-20s F (-2°C).

LANDSCAPE VALUE

- Dramatic tree with bold foliage in summer and bare white trunks, plus a spotting of white flowers over bare branches in winter.
- Reforestation of disturbed sites in warm-winter, nearly frost-free arid regions.

CULTURAL REQUIREMENTS

- **Exposure:** Full sun.
- **Water:** Drought resistant in cool season. Thoroughly soak the root zone every week or two during warm season.
- **Soil:** Most soils with good drainage.
- **Propagation:** Seed or cuttings.
- **Maintenance:** Low maintenance

POSSIBLE PROBLEMS

Very late to leaf out in spring. Geared to arrive with the summer monsoon rains in its native Sonora, Mexico.

Deciduous tree to 36 feet (11 m) tall, spreading to 24 feet (7.5 m). Moderate growth rate at times. Rapid growth with summer moisture. Trunks and branches are stout, bark smooth and whitish. Large green leaves appear in summer and small white morning glory flowers dot the bare branches during the winter dormant season. Twiny growth sometime appears at ends of branches, which identifies its kinship to its many vining relatives. Native to Sonora, Mexico.

Ipomoea fistulosa carnea (I. carnea fistulosa)

Pink bush morning glory, Diez de la mañana

Convolvulaceae family

COLD HARDINESS

Low zone and all but the coldest areas of the intermediate zone. Tender to temperatures in the high-20s F (-2°C) but recovers rapidly in spring.

LANDSCAPE VALUE

- Colorful tropical-effects plant.
- Somewhat weedy but adds interest to informal garden settings when sandwiched in with other bold effects plants.
- A favorite in barrio gardens on both sides of the Mexican–U.S. border.
- Background plantings.

CULTURAL REQUIREMENTS

- **Exposure:** Tolerates some shade but best in full sun or in reflected sun if moisture is adequate.
- **Water:** Reasonably drought resistant. Water every week or two in the warm season to ensure attractive foliage and abundant flowers.
- **Soil:** Any soil.
- **Propagation:** Seed.
- **Maintenance:** Prune selectively to remove old seed clusters and promote more bloom. Replace woody plants with young ones for best effect. Prune back once a year to renew growth. Remove cold-damaged wood, if necessary, as spring growth resumes.

POSSIBLE PROBLEMS

- Soft wood and weedy growth is damaged by wind or frost. Prune selectively for best effect.
- Clusters of seed capsules require seasonal removal for the same reason.

A rangy open shrub that grows rapidly during the warm season from 6 to 8 feet (2 to 2.5 m) high, with equal spread. Thick, soft woody stems are 1/2 inch (1 cm) in diameter. The 6- to 8-inch (15- to 20.5-cm) long triangular leaves taper to a point at the tip from a 3- to 5-inch (7.5- to 13-cm) spread at the base. They are scalloped along the margins. Showy 6-inch (15-cm) morning glory–type blossoms, bright pink with cherry red centers, are borne in clusters at branch tips throughout the warm season. The large clusters of seed capsules that follow bloom produce little interest. Flowers open early in the day but usually close by noon. May stay open longer on cool, moist days, thus the Spanish common name of the plant, which translates to "ten in the morning." This plant is widely distributed in north Africa, Arabia, Mexico and Latin America.

* See Glossary

Ipomoea pes-caprae

Beach morning glory

Convolvulaceae family

COLD HARDINESS

Low zone but has been grown in warm microclimates of intermediate zone. Withstands little frost.

LANDSCAPE VALUE

- Native to beachfronts in the tropical world and semitropical world, this plant is important for control of beach erosion and blowing sand.
- Groundcover in medians and larger areas or over shade structures.

CULTURAL REQUIREMENTS

- **Exposure:** Full sun. Tolerant of salinity.
- **Water:** Can endure long periods of drought because of its succulent nature, but needs water every month or two to perform well. Thrives on brackish water.
- **Soil:** Almost any soil but found naturally in sandy situations.
- **Propagation:** Cuttings.
- **Maintenance:** Trim and guide to fill desired space and train if used to climb.

POSSIBLE PROBLEMS

Rapid spreading growth can be difficult to control and train. Sometimes invades and overwhelms other plantings.

Vigorous, spreading perennial creeper that will climb to considerable height over shade structures, but on flat ground will mound up to 3 feet (1 m). Spreads easily to 30 feet (9 m) or more. Very rapid growth. Stout stems are succulent and contain astringent milky juice. Large deep green fleshy leaves cover the wide stems. Plant forms 30-foot (9-m) wide mats, sometimes even larger, rooting as it goes. Can be trained over vine supports. Large lavender-rose morning-glory blooms appear anytime during the warm season. Evergreen. Native to tropical shores all over.

Jacaranda mimosifolia

Jacaranda

Bignoniaceae family

COLD HARDINESS

Low zone and warm, protected winter microclimates of the intermediate zone. Hard frost causes moderate to severe die-back* of top growth, although trees become somewhat more cold tolerant with age.

LANDSCAPE VALUE

The distinctly tropical aspect, filtered shade and electrifying flower display of jacaranda give it excellent credentials for use as a street tree, shade tree or flowering specimen for parks and commercial sites as well as larger residential properties.

CULTURAL REQUIREMENTS

- **Exposure:** Full sun and summer heat for maximum flowering. Successful in the open landscape if winter frosts are light, but best used in a sheltered courtyard or other protected microhabitat if hard frosts are a common occurrence.
- **Water:** Thoroughly soak the root zone every week or two during the growing season, once or twice during the dormant leafless period.
- **Soil:** Deep well-drained soil.
- **Propagation:** Seed or cuttings.
- **Maintenance:** Prune and (sometimes) stake young trees for good trunk development and branching habit.

POSSIBLE PROBLEMS

Litter of fallen leaves, flowers and seed capsules.

This Brazilian tree grows from 5 to 50 feet (1.5 to 15 m) high, even larger in tropical areas, and spreads 15 to 30 feet (4.5 to 9 m). Moderate to rapid growth. The canopy has a characteristic open, rounded yet irregular shape. It may have one to several trunks. In warm-winter areas, the fine-textured bipinnately* compound foliage persists until late winter. Where frosts are more severe, the tree can be leafless for two or three months.

Trumpetlike lavender blue flowers 2 inches (5 cm) long by 1½ inches (4 cm) wide open in 8-inch (20.5-cm) long clusters any time during the warm months. Peak bloom usually occurs in late spring or early summer. White- and pink-flowered forms are occasionally seen. The woody seed capsules are flat, rounded at the tip and about 2¼ inches (6 cm) across. Fallen blossoms hold their color for some time, creating a lavender blanket on the ground.

* See Glossary

Jaquinia pungens

Jaquinia, San Juanico

Theophrastaceae family

COLD HARDINESS

Low zone and warm microclimates of intermediate zone. Tender to hard frost.

LANDSCAPE VALUE

- Picturesque gnarly tree with handsome foliage.
- Barrier plant or screen if kept shrubby.

CULTURAL REQUIREMENTS

- **Exposure:** Full sun and reflected heat.
- **Water:** Quite drought resistant but water every week or two during the summer to speed growth.
- **Soil:** Any soil.
- **Propagation:** Seed, possibly cuttings.
- **Maintenance:** Train for tree growth habit.

POSSIBLE PROBLEMS

- Slow growth limits its value in many landscape projects but it is well worth the wait.
- Spiny-tipped foliage difficult to work around.

Interesting large shrub, eventually becoming a small tree, that grows very slowly from 9 to 12 feet (3 to 3.5 m) high, sometimes higher, with equal spread. Leaves are small and spine-tipped. Small yellow flowers are followed by rust-colored fruit, adding contrasting color to the dark green hollylike foliage. Light gray bark on mature plants. Native to Sonora.

Jatropha cardiophylla

Limberbush

Euphorbiaceae family

COLD HARDINESS

Low and intermediate zones. Moderately frost hardy.

LANDSCAPE VALUE

- Integrates well with other arid-landscape plants.
- The sudden appearance of the lush foliage that covers the brown succulent stems after summer rain is quite dramatic.
- Its small size is an asset in many situations.
- Often occurs in nature as an understory plant for taller shrubs and small trees.
- An unusual container plant, even when leafless.

CULTURAL REQUIREMENTS

- **Exposure:** Rugged and hardy to severe desert growing environments. Tolerant of most sun exposures.
- **Water:** Quite drought resistant. Water once or twice during the warm season to extend the leafy period. No water during winter.
- **Soil:** Most soils.
- **Propagation:** Division of root sprouts or seed.
- **Maintenance:** Remove small plants that appear along the roots to produce a single shrub under favorable conditions.

POSSIBLE PROBLEMS

- Unwatered plants remain leafless most of the year.
- A planting may spread beyond its allotted space.

A deciduous shrub with an open spreading habit, reddish brown upright, flexible stems and short, stubby spur branches. Grows to 3 feet (1 m) high, spreading 2 to 4 feet (61 cm to 1 m). Slow to moderate growth. Generally leafless for long periods but interesting because of the branch color and thick, almost succulent look. Following summer rains or summer irrigation, glossy dark green heart-shaped leaves appear. These are as wide and long as 1 inch (2.5 cm). They remain until the soil completely dries or when cooler fall temperatures arrive. Flowers and fruit are inconspicuous. Spreads by running rootstocks* and remains as an individual or develops into a small colony of plants of various sizes. Native to Arizona south into central Mexico. A most handsome shrub, especially when viewed in a hot-desert setting.

* See Glossary

Jatropha cinerea

Leafy limberbush

Euphorbiaceae family

COLD HARDINESS

Low zone and warm microclimates of intermediate zone.

LANDSCAPE VALUE

- Produces a green leafy effect, almost poplar-like.
- Plump trunks and branches add interest in winter.

CULTURAL REQUIREMENTS

- **Exposure:** Full sun, including reflected sun, to part shade.
- **Water:** Water every month or two, perhaps every two weeks in summer for good foliage and appearance.
- **Soil:** Well-drained soil.
- **Propagation:** Seed or cuttings.
- **Maintenance:** Prune to shape. Remove frost damaged wood in borderline areas.

POSSIBLE PROBLEMS

Dormant period is long. Remains leafless until late spring.

Large shrub or small tree to 18 feet (5.5 m) or higher, spreading about 12 feet (3.5 m). Moderate growth rate. Bright green leaves cover the tree all the way to the ground. A great green spot in the arid landscape. Winter deciduous. Native to Sonora, Mexico. Flowers are inconspicuous.

Jatropha dioica

Leather stem

Euphorbiaceae family

COLD HARDINESS

All three zones.

LANDSCAPE VALUE

- Container plant.
- Foreground spot in a rock garden where its form can be observed at close range.
- Not particularly deserty in appearance but can be used with small-scale cacti and other succulents.

CULTURAL REQUIREMENTS

- **Exposure:** Reflected sun to open shade.
- **Water:** Quite drought resistant. Water every month or two to keep it healthy and looking good.
- **Soil:** Well-drained soil.
- **Propagation:** Seed or divisions.
- **Maintenance:** Completely undemanding.

POSSIBLE PROBLEMS

None observed.

From southwest Texas and on into the Mexican Chihuahuan Desert, this plant grows at a moderate rate to about 2 to 3 feet (61 cm to 1 m) high and 3 feet (1 m) wide. Forms a clump that can continue to expand. Small-branched plant resembles a succulent. Expands mostly by underground runners* that put up additional upright stems, thus increasing the size of the clump. Small, pointed medium green leaves are widely spaced. The open character in general takes on the quality of a manipulated dwarf tree or bonsai. Flowers are inconspicuous.

* *See Glossary*

Jatropha malacophylla (J. platanifolia)

Sycamore leaf limberbush

Euphorbiaceae family

COLD HARDINESS

Low zone and protected microclimates in intermediate zone.

LANDSCAPE VALUE

Bold form and foliage creates a tropical feeling in summer and bare stems and branches have a dramatic quality in winter, especially if planted against a plain wall.

CULTURAL REQUIREMENTS

- **Exposure:** Full sun to part shade.
- **Water:** Water every month or two, more often in summer.
- **Soil:** Any soil with good drainage.
- **Propagation:** Seed or cuttings.
- **Maintenance:** Prune to shape. Remove frost-damaged wood in borderline areas.

POSSIBLE PROBLEMS

Deciduous for a long period before new growth begins in late spring.

A multistem deciduous shrub that grows at a moderate pace from 9 to 12 feet (3 to 3.5 m) high, 6 to 9 feet (2 to 3 m) wide. Large velvety lobed leaves resemble sycamore leaves. Flowers and fruit are unimportant, but the thick fleshy stems and branches, as well as the leaves, make a strong statement in the landscape. Native to Mexico.

JUNIPER

Junipers, as a group, are common in areas north of arid regions. They may seem out of context with typical arid-region plants, yet their tolerance of heat and ability to grow well with infrequent irrigation warrant their use. There are probably many more varieties of *Juniperus chinensis* that could be included here, but we have selected the ones that are commonly seen doing well in southwestern gardens.

Juniperus chinensis 'Kaizuka' (*J. chinensis* 'Torulosa')

Hollywood juniper, Twisted juniper

Cupressaceae family

COLD HARDINESS
All three zones.

LANDSCAPE VALUE
- Twisted picturesque growth habit and unique texture.
- Accent in mixed plantings or strong focal point when used as a solitary specimen or in groups for oasis and transition compositions. Keep the eventual size of the mature plant in mind.

CULTURAL REQUIREMENTS
- **Exposure:** Full sun. Tolerates part shade, especially in low-elevation arid regions.
- **Water:** Water every week or two throughout the hot season, every month or two during winter.
- **Soil:** Most soils with good drainage.
- **Propagation:** Cuttings.
- **Maintenance:** Keep pruning to a minimum for full dramatic effect of the natural plant silhouette. Never use hedge shears.

POSSIBLE PROBLEMS
- Spider mites.
- Twig borers.
- Aphids.
- Bagworms.
- Juniper blight.

This distinctive-looking conifer derives one of its common names from contorted branches that grow in an irregular upright pattern. Tiny scalelike leaves are closely spaced and snugly clamped against the stems. The flowers and small berrylike blue-gray cones are inconspicuous. Grows at a slow to moderate pace from 15 to 20 feet (4.5 to 6 m) high, 6 to 10 feet (2 to 3 m) wide. Native to China.

Juniperus chinensis pfitzeriana

Pfitzer juniper

Cupressaceae family

COLD HARDINESS
All three zones.

LANDSCAPE VALUE
- The dense fine-textured foliage provides contrast and winter interest and color in mixed shrub borders for the oasis and transition zones.
- Facer shrub against taller leggy plants or a background for lower-growing shrubs and flower borders.
- Informal space definer or enclosing barrier.
- Foundation plantings where mature size is compatible with the scale of the site.

CULTURAL REQUIREMENTS
- **Exposure:** Full sun in intermediate and high zones. Part shade in low zone. Tolerates heat and low humidity of arid climates.
- **Water:** Established plants thrive with water every week or two during the warm months, every month or two during winter.
- **Soil:** Most soils with good drainage.
- **Propagation:** Cuttings.
- **Maintenance:** Head back terminals* to side branches to maintain plant density and form, especially with vigorous young specimens. Never use hedge shears or the plant will lose all of the aesthetic qualities for which it is valued.

POSSIBLE PROBLEMS
- Spider mites.
- Bagworms.
- Aphids.
- Juniper blight.
- Bermuda grass infestation.

This broad, vase-shaped evergreen shrub has branches that spread and angle upward with arching terminals and side branchlets. Averages 6 feet (2 m) in height, 10 feet (3 m) in spread, or even 15 to 20 feet (4.5 to 6 m) under optimum growing conditions. Moderate growth rate. The feathery gray-green foliage is prickly to the touch and aromatic when crushed. Compact forms as well as those with silvery blue or golden foliage are available. Flowers are inconspicuous. Native to China.

* *See Glossary*

Juniperus deppeana pachyphlaea

Alligator juniper
Cupressaceae family

COLD HARDINESS
All three zones.

LANDSCAPE VALUE
- Furrows in the bark that resemble alligator scales along with the dense fine-textured foliage make this a handsome specimen or accent tree.
- Screening, background and median or buffer plantings.

CULTURAL REQUIREMENTS
- **Exposure:** Full sun to part shade. Plants become open and straggly in heavy shade.
- **Water:** In low and intermediate zones, thoroughly soak the root zone of young plants, every week or two during the warm months to ensure survival and faster growth. Water two or three times during winter. In high zone locations, water only during long dry periods.
- **Soil:** Well-drained soil is essential.
- **Propagation:** Seed or cuttings.
- **Maintenance:** When using as a screen or hedge, prune back terminals* to maintain compact form. Don't remove too many branches at one time, especially during hot season.

POSSIBLE PROBLEMS
None observed.

The dense scalelike foliage of this evergreen juniper is green to blue-green, although silvery gray types also occur. Large specimens typically develop a rounded to somewhat irregular form. Can grow 20 to 40 feet (6 to 12 m) high and spread 15 to 30 feet (4.5 to 9 m), but growth is slow. Flowers are inconspicuous. The berrylike cones are hard, round and mealy or resinous. This species is easily recognized by its thick rough bark, which is divided into rectangular alligatorlike plates with deep furrows between. Native to West Texas into Arizona and Mexico.

Juniperus erythrocarpa (J. monosperma)

One-seeded juniper
Cupressaceae family

COLD HARDINESS
All three zones.

LANDSCAPE VALUE
- Background, screening or roadside plantings.
- Older trees are picturesque character plants with sculptural trunks and branches.

CULTURAL REQUIREMENTS
- **Exposure:** Full sun.
- **Water:** Drought tolerant as an established plant in intermediate and high zones. In low zone, thoroughly soak the root zone of young and mature plants every month or two.
- **Soil:** Fast-draining soil.
- **Propagation:** Seed, and probably cuttings.
- **Maintenance:** Prune occasionally to direct and shape growth.

POSSIBLE PROBLEMS
None observed.

This long-lived evergreen grows as a large shrub or small to occasionally medium-size tree of rounded form and open branching habit. Slowly climbs to 50 feet (15 m) high, spreading to 33 feet (10 m). Typically develops with many ascending stems from the ground. On some specimens, several large branches fuse at the base to form a short, knobby flaring trunk up to 3 feet (1 m) across. Fibrous gray outer bark shreds and peels away to show attractive red-brown inner bark. Tiny thickened scalelike leaves are blue-green and occur in pairs. Rounded fruit is soft and juicy, dark blue to coppery in color. Flowers are inconspicuous. Native to U.S. Southwest.

* See Glossary

Justicia californica (Beloperone californica)

Chuparosa

Acanthaceae family

COLD HARDINESS

Low zone and warm microclimates of the intermediate zone.

LANDSCAPE VALUE

- Desert shrub for informal dry landscape situations.
- Bank, foundation and foreground planting.
- Showy spot of color off and on throughout the year.
- Flowers attract hummingbirds.

CULTURAL REQUIREMENTS

- **Exposure:** Full sun.
- **Water:** Quite drought resistant, but water every month or two during the rainless periods for growth and to promote blooming.
- **Soil:** Well-drained soil. Tolerates sandy, rocky conditions.
- **Propagation:** Cuttings and divisions.
- **Maintenance:** Low maintenance.

POSSIBLE PROBLEMS

None observed.

Sprawling shrub to 6 feet (2 m) high, usually lower. Clump spreads 3 to 12 feet (1 to 3.5 m). Moderate growth rate. Native to the gravelly washes* and rocky places in the lower elevations of the Sonoran Desert. Generally leafless except when producing new growth, during the warm season. Somewhat succulent green stems are covered several times a year (if moisture is present) with small red tubular flowers. There is also a yellow-flowered form.

Justicia candicans (Jacobinia ovata, Justicia ovata)

Red Mexican honeysuckle, Red justicia, Red jacobinia

Acanthaceae family

COLD HARDINESS

Low and intermediate zones and some protected microclimates of the high zone where it often freezes to the ground. Recovers quickly in spring even in these cold locations.

LANDSCAPE VALUE

- Does not flower as heavily as some arid species, but with moisture, it provides a splash of red against a background of pleasing green foliage through the long hot months.
- Low borders and foundation plantings
- Planters and containers.
- Facer for taller shrubs.
- Beneath small trees that provide filtered shade.
- Attracts hummingbirds.

CULTURAL REQUIREMENTS

- **Exposure:** Prefers filtered sun to part shade but also grows in full sun.
- **Water:** Water every week or two during spring and summer, less often once cooler fall weather begins.
- **Soil:** Grows best in good garden soil.
- **Propagation:** Seed or cuttings.
- **Maintenance:** Prune frost-damaged plants back in early spring.

POSSIBLE PROBLEMS

None observed.

Upright spreading stems and medium green oval leaves up to 2 inches (5 cm) long combine to form a neat evergreen shrub. Both stems and leaves are covered with short fine hairs. Bright red to orange tubular flowers to 1/2 inch (1 cm) long appear between leaves near the stem tips. These flowers are an attractive display over a long season, depending on available moisture and amount of frost damage sustained during winter. Grows at a moderate pace to 5 feet (1.5 m) high and 3 feet (1 m) wide. Native to southern Arizona and south into Mexico.

* *See Glossary*

Justicia spicigera (J. ghiesbreghtiana)

Mexican honeysuckle

Acanthaceae family

The 3-inch (7.5 cm) oval leaves of this evergreen shrub are fuzzy to the touch because of a covering of soft short hairs. Foliage is dense and the plant form is rounded to upright. Clusters of bright orange to reddish orange two-lipped tubular flowers reach 1½ inches (4 cm) long. They are borne year-round in mild, nearly frost-free, climates and from spring until the first freeze in cooler areas. In all regions flowering is usually most abundant in late spring. Grows rapidly (with abundant water) from 3 to 6 feet (1 to 2 m) high, spreading to 6 feet (2 m). Native from Mexico into South America.

COLD HARDINESS

Low zone and warm microclimates of intermediate zone. Sensitive to hard frosts, which kill stems back to the ground. Recovers quickly in spring.

LANDSCAPE VALUE

- Lush quality that along with the extended, showy flower display, adds a distinct tropical ambiance, particularly in a minioasis.
- Specimen.
- In groups.
- Foundation plant.
- Containers.
- Attracts hummingbirds.

CULTURAL REQUIREMENTS

- **Exposure:** Filtered or dappled shade is best but also tolerates full to reflected sun.
- **Water:** Moderately drought tolerant once established but much more attractive with water every week or two during the warm season, every month or two during the cooler months.
- **Soil:** Well-drained, improved garden soil.
- **Propagation:** Cuttings.
- **Maintenance:** In cool climate areas, prune back frost-damaged plants in early spring in cool-climate areas. Prune plants in warmer regions back to 2 feet (61 cm) in early winter to induce new growth on older stems that have sparse foliage.

POSSIBLE PROBLEMS

Occasional chlorosis*.

Koeberlinia spinosa

Crucifixion thorn

Koeberliniaceae family

COLD HARDINESS

Low and intermediate zones and warm areas of the high zone. Extremely frost hardy.

LANDSCAPE VALUE

- Rugged accent.
- Traffic-stopping barrier.
- Erosion control potential because it tends to grow in thickets.

CULTURAL REQUIREMENTS

- **Exposure:** Full to reflected sun.
- **Water:** Extremely drought tolerant. Irrigation rarely necessary for survival of established plants, except in very low rainfall regions.
- **Soil:** Medium- to light-textured soils.
- **Propagation:** Seed.
- **Maintenance:** Very low maintenance. Use long-handled loppers for any necessary pruning.

POSSIBLE PROBLEMS

Spiny, thorn-tipped branches preclude use in close-up situations.

A rounded, thorny deciduous shrub that grows slowly to 6 feet (2 m) high and wide, rarely as high as 30 feet (9 m). Essentially leafless because the tiny scalelike leaves are short-lived. Rigid, very spiny stems form an intricate branching pattern. Green to yellow-green bark on the young branches becomes gray and flaky on older stems. Small clusters of insignificant white flowers bloom late spring into summer. Shiny black berries, ⅛ inch (0.5 cm) in diameter, ripen in fall. Native from California to Texas and Baja California in Mexico.

** See Glossary*

COLD HARDINESS
All three zones.

LANDSCAPE VALUE
- Summer color *par excellence.*
- Patio-size tree that excels along streets, in parking areas and on medians.
- Small shrub is also useful in medians as well as foundation plantings, space definers and large containers.
- The satiny, smooth bark is especially attractive in close-up situations such as patios, entryways, and public spaces where the plant does not heave pavement and requires a relatively small planting opening.

CULTURAL REQUIREMENTS
- **Exposure:** Full sun, including reflected sun. Must have heat to bloom well.
- **Water:** Quite drought resistant. Thoroughly soak the root zone every month or two. Will tolerate lawn conditions if soil is well-drained and non-alkaline.
- **Soil:** Well-drained soil. Not tolerant of high alkalinity.
- **Propagation:** Usually cuttings, but can be grown from seed.
- **Maintenance:** Fertilize lightly. Some spring pruning is said to increase flowering, but often this is overdone at the expense of the silhouette. Avoid.

POSSIBLE PROBLEMS
- Mildew in cooler summer climates, especially those with high humidity. This distorts the bloom and leaves with a powdery white substance. Spray with fungicide just before it flowers.
- Leaf burn and chlorosis* result from alkaline soil or salty water. Treat by leaching soil and applying iron.

This showy deciduous flowering shrub or small tree, a native to China, has been a prized garden subject throughout the warm temperate and subtropic regions of the world since the time of Marco Polo. Tree forms reach 15 to 20 feet (4.5 to 6 m) in height. Shrub forms grow 3 to 6 feet (1 to 2 m) high. The spread of both tree and shrub forms is the same or slightly smaller than the height. Both grow at a moderate rate.

The plant is root hardy* and can be grown as a perennial even in cold temperate regions. In warmer areas, it is generally used as a patio-size tree for all seasons. In spring, the oval leaves are light green with bright coppery tones, maturing to shiny dark green leaves, 2 to 3 inches (5 to 7.5 cm) long. Mature leaves make an attractive contrast for the spectacular color display of midsummer. The delicate flowers are borne in large clusters and burst into bloom with the first onset of summer heat. Flowering continues until the weather cools in the fall. This, however, is not the end of the show: The leaves can turn a glowing yellow to orange or red before dropping. Clusters of seed capsules that follow and the smooth satiny tan bark add silhouette and interest to the winter landscape.

Cultivars: Cultivars* come in an endless array of brilliant reds, pinks, lavenders, purples, and white. 'Glendora White', a small tree with large showy white flowers. 'Near East,' formerly 'Shell Pink', a large shrub or small tree with shell pink flowers. 'Watermelon Red, a large shrub or small tree with vivid red flowers. Smaller plants include 'Petites,' a dwarf crape myrtle that grows 5 to 7 feet (1.5 to 2 m) high; 'Petite Embers,' a tiny dwarf with rosy red flowers; 'Petite Orchid,' a dwarf with dark orchid flowers; 'Petite Red Imp,' a tiny dwarf with deep red flowers; and 'Petite Snow,' a tiny dwarf with white flowers. Two outstanding new hybrids are 'Majestic Orchid,' a small heavy-stemmed tree with large clusters of orchid-colored flowers, and 'Peppermint Lace,' a medium-size, upright and compact variety with deep red flowers edged in white. The National Arboretum in Washington, DC, has recently developed a group of crape myrtles called 'Indian Tribes.' 'Catawba' is a compact plant with dark purple flowers. 'Cherokee' is upright and spreading with red blooms. 'Seminole' is upright and spreading with medium pink flowers.

* See Glossary

Lagerstroemia indica
Crape myrtle
Lythraceae family

Lampranthus spectabilis

Trailing ice plant
Aizoaceae family

COLD HARDINESS
Low zone and warm-winter microclimates of intermediate zone.

LANDSCAPE VALUE
- Untreadable groundcover or foreground plant with blazing spring color display.
- Rock gardens.
- On low, gently sloping banks and mounds and in other small-scale plantings.
- Containers.

CULTURAL REQUIREMENTS
- **Exposure:** Full sun. Intolerant of heavy shade.
- **Water:** Tolerant of some drought, but looks best with water every week or two. Allow soil to dry between waterings.
- **Soil:** Grows and flowers well in average garden soil but requires good drainage. Intolerant of wet soils.
- **Propagation:** Seed or cuttings.
- **Maintenance:** Periodically groom and replant bare spots.

POSSIBLE PROBLEMS
None observed.

Succulent groundcover with a trailing growth habit. Reaches 6 to 12 inches (15 to 30.5 cm) high and spreads 18 to 24 inches (46 to 61 cm). Grows at a moderate rate. Three-angled fleshy gray-green leaves are arranged in pairs opposite each other. Leaves 3/4 to 1 3/4 inches (2 to 4.5 cm) long make a dense foliage mass on prostrate-branching stems that become somewhat woody as they mature. In spring, this ice plant is transformed into a living tapestry of color as solitary flowers 2 to 2 1/2 inches (5 to 6.5 cm) across in hot glowing shades of red, pink and purple appear in such abundance that leaves and stems are completely hidden. Native to arid subtropical areas of South Africa.

Lantana horrida

Desert lantana, Hierba de cristo
Verbenaceae family

COLD HARDINESS
Low zone and warm microclimates of intermediate zone. At 26°F (-3°C) leaves drop and stems are damaged. Dies back to the ground in the low-20s F (-6°C).

LANDSCAPE VALUE
- Its main value over that of the horticultural *Lantana* varieties is its ability to go dormant during long periods of drought and come back quickly when moisture is again available.
- Loose shrubby cover that can be colorful after rain or irrigation.

CULTURAL REQUIREMENTS
- **Exposure:** Reflected sun to part shade.
- **Water:** Tolerates long periods of drought. Water every month or two for bloom and good appearance.
- **Soil:** Heavy soil.
- **Propagation:** Seed or cuttings.
- **Maintenance:** Regular pruning improves appearance. Remove frost-damaged wood after a cold winter.

POSSIBLE PROBLEMS
Foliage and stems have a rough texture with some prickles and a strong odor.

Rangy evergreen shrub that grows rapidly (with moisture) to 6 feet (2 m) high, with equal spread. Resembles its garden relative *L. camera* but growth is much coarser and wilder. Orange flowers are a bright spot on the Sonoran desert after summer rains. Seeds and black berries that follow flowers attract birds. Native to Sonora and other Mexican deserts.

Lantana species (L. orange)

Trailing lavender, Desert lantana, Texas orange-flowered lantana

Verbenaceae family

COLD HARDINESS

All three zones. Usually freezes to the ground in winter in the high zone.

LANDSCAPE VALUE

- Should have potential for hybridization to develop more drought-tolerant varieties.
- Attracts birds.

CULTURAL REQUIREMENTS

- **Exposure:** Full sun to part shade.
- **Water:** Water every month or two, more frequently during the warm season for more profuse blooming and general appearance.
- **Soil:** Any soil.
- **Propagation:** Cuttings.
- **Maintenance:** Remove frost-damaged wood in early spring.

POSSIBLE PROBLEMS

None observed.

A low-water-demanding prostrate shrub from the Chihuahuan Desert. Grows to 1½ feet (46 cm) high at a moderate rate. Spreads 3 to 4 feet (1 m). It may be a desert form of *L. montevidensis*, which it resembles, but it is not as vigorous or colorful as the *L. montevidensis* in cultivation. It is, however, much more drought resistant. Evergreen unless frosted back in winter. Lavender flowers bloom in spring about 1 to 2 inches (2.5 to 5 cm) in diameter. Small dull green leaves are about an inch long.

Lantana velutina

White lantana

Verbenaceae family

COLD HARDINESS

Low and intermediate zones. Cut down by temperatures in low-20s F (-6°C) but recovers quickly in spring.

LANDSCAPE VALUE

- Mounding shrub mass.
- Foundation plant with a little pruning.

CULTURAL REQUIREMENTS

- **Exposure:** Full sun to part shade.
- **Water:** Thoroughly soak the root zone every week or two during warm season. Tolerates water every month or two, especially during the cool season.
- **Soil:** Well-drained soil.
- **Propagation:** Seed or cuttings.
- **Maintenance:** Prune to shape or to remove frost-damaged wood.

POSSIBLE PROBLEMS

None observed.

Mounding shrub that reaches 3 to 6 feet (1 to 2 m) in height and spread at a moderate growth rate. White flower clusters, typical of *Lantana*, may become pinkish with age. Flowers appear during the warm season, followed by pink berry fruit, which is said to be edible and sweet. Native to the lower edges of the Sonoran Desert south to Panama.

** See Glossary*

Larrea divaricata

Creosote bush, South American creosote bush
Zygophyllaceae family

COLD HARDINESS

All three zones. Tolerates wide range of high and low temperatures.

LANDSCAPE VALUE

- A loose, open desert shrub for background, space definition, buffers and medians, screening or revegetation of disturbed sites.
- Can be trained as a clipped hedge with limited success.

CULTURAL REQUIREMENTS

- **Exposure:** Full or reflected sun and heat to part shade.
- **Water:** An exceptionally drought tolerant plant that responds to occasional irrigation with denser, more rapid growth.
- **Soil:** Most soils with good drainage.
- **Propagation:** Difficult to propagate by seed or vegetative techniques.
- **Maintenance:** Thin the weak growth of old specimens growing on arid sites to emphasize structural character.

POSSIBLE PROBLEMS

- Thought to exude a toxic substance that inhibits growth of nearby seedlings and larger plants.
- At this time, difficult to propagate by seeds or cuttings and grow as container nursery stock.

This *Larrea* grows slowly from 4 to 12 feet (1 to 3.5 m) in height and spread. In overall appearance this and *L. divaricata tridentata* are quite similar. *L. divaricata* leaflets are longer, more slender and less curving. In addition the branchlets have a more conspicuous coating of short, silky white hairs. From a landscape point of view, *L. divaricata* develops as a lusher, fuller plant. In terms of use and culture, these two species of creosote bush may be treated as one. Small bright yellow flowers appear with moisture almost any time of the year but are most abundant in spring. Native from Peru to Argentina.

Larrea divaricata tridentata

Creosote bush, North American creosote bush
Zygophyllaceae family

COLD HARDINESS

All three zones. Tolerates hard frost.

LANDSCAPE VALUE

Same as *L. divaricata.*

CULTURAL REQUIREMENTS

Same as *L. divaricata.*

POSSIBLE PROBLEMS

Same as *L. divaricata.*

A tough evergreen shrub superbly adapted to arid environments. Grows slowly to 4 to 12 feet (1 to 3.5 m) in height and spread. On dry sites in poor soil, it grows straggly, open and vase-shaped with older branches that gradually bend down. With more abundant water, it becomes dense and rounded. Distinctive crescent-shaped leaflets are yellow-green under conditions of heat and drought, darker green and aromatic after rain. Leaflets have a more sticky, lacquered surface coating and less conspicuous veins than *L. divaricata.* Small bright yellow flowers appear with moisture almost any time of the year but are most abundant in spring. These are replaced by round, fuzzy gray seed pods. Native to Sonoran and Mojave Deserts, California to Texas and Mexico.

** See Glossary*

Laurus nobilis

Grecian laurel, Sweet bay

Lauraceae family

COLD HARDINESS

Low and intermediate zones and warmer locations in high zone. Last summer's growth can be damaged by frost in the high zone and sometimes in the intermediate zone. Established plants generally endure temperatures down to 20°F (-7°C) without damage.

LANDSCAPE VALUE

- Background screening.
- Small to medium tree with proper moisture.
- Accepts clipping and shearing well and has long been popular as a clipped hedge, topiary or a small formal tree for decorative tubs and boxes. These practices have been popular since Victorian times for summer terraces and formal gardens in the temperate climates of Europe and North America. Tubbed specimens should be sheltered in greenhouses for the winter.
- Focal point in an herb garden. This is the bay leaf used in cooking.

CULTURAL REQUIREMENTS

- **Exposure:** Full sun. Avoid reflected sun in the low and intermediate zones.
- **Water:** Quite drought resistant. Thoroughly soak the root zone of young plants every week or two to speed the growth. Maintain appearance of mature trees by soaking the root zone every two to three weeks. Tolerates oasis-type irrigation if soil is well drained.
- **Soil:** Any soil with good drainage.
- **Propagation:** Could be propagated from seed but most nursery plants are grown from rooted cuttings.
- **Maintenance:** Needs minimal pruning except to remove frost-damaged wood or to train as a topiary or patio tree. Light applications of nitrogen fertilizer will speed up the slow growth and is necessary for permanent container specimens.

POSSIBLE PROBLEMS

- May need to spray to control scale.
- Reflected sun in low and intermediate zones can sunburn leaves.

Large evergreen shrub or small to medium bushy tree, 15 to 30 feet (4.5 to 9 m) tall, sometimes taller, with equal spread. Grows at a slow to moderate rate. Handsome, aromatic, leathery leaves are 2 to 3 inches (5 to 7.5 cm) long. The leaves densely cover the plant all the way to the ground unless trimmed up. Two foliage variations are available: one more narrow and pointed, and another broader and less pointed at the tip. Few differences have been observed in the landscape performance of these two types or their value as a cooking herb. Can be grown with a single trunk, but multitrunk is more common. Single-trunk specimens tend to continuously produce suckers* at the base. Small yellow flowers bloom in late spring and are followed by 1-inch (2.5-cm) long black or dark purple inedible berries. Native to Greece and Mediterranean region. The laurel leaf crown of ancient Greece was fashioned from *L. nobilis*.

* See Glossary

Lawsonia inermis

Henna plant
Lythraceae family

COLD HARDINESS

Low zone. Not dependable for uses such as hedging in intermediate zone because of its limited hardiness, but you can tuck it into warm pockets in your landscape to add fragrance.

LANDSCAPE VALUE

- Adds wonderful fragrance to a garden.
- Privet-like hedge and other topiary shapes, with trimming.

CULTURAL REQUIREMENTS

- **Exposure:** Full sun to part shade.
- **Water:** Drought resistant. Tolerates water every month or two but needs water every week or two if used for hedging.
- **Soil:** Any soil.
- **Propagation:** Seed or cuttings.
- **Maintenance:** Probably would not bloom if pruned for formal shapes. Light pruning thickens an informal shrub. Requires some grooming, such as removing old bloom and seed clusters to be presentable or regular clipping when used for hedging.

POSSIBLE PROBLEMS

None observed.

Somewhat rangy evergreen shrub that can become almost treelike with training. Generally easy to trim. Grows at a moderate rate, more rapid under garden conditions, and can reach 9 to 18 feet (3 to 5.5 m) high. Reputed to grow even higher, up to 25 feet (7.5 m). Spreads 9 to 15 feet (3 to 4.5 m). Leaves are tiny. Round seed capsules are not decorative. Sprays of whitish green flowers are not showy but add an elusive fragrance to a garden. This plant has been grown since ancient times in the Old World (leaves are source of henna dye). Has naturalized in many places in the New World, including Sonora and Baja California, Mexico.

Leucaena greggii (L. cuspidata)

Yellow popinac
Fabaceae (Leguminosae) family

COLD HARDINESS

Low and intermediate zones. Needs more testing to determine hardiness in high zone.

LANDSCAPE VALUE

- Patio tree with umbrella shape.
- Combined with other tropical-effects plants.
- Seasonal color.

CULTURAL REQUIREMENTS

- **Exposure:** Full sun.
- **Water:** Tolerates lawn conditions but does best with thorough watering every month or two during the warm season. Water young trees more often to speed up somewhat slow development.
- **Soil:** Any soil with good drainage.
- **Propagation:** Seed.
- **Maintenance:** Develops many side branches and horizontal growth. Gradually stake and train to develop a shade tree with a high canopy.

POSSIBLE PROBLEMS

None observed.

As of this writing, not much is known about this showy yellow-flowering tree, but based on its performance at the University of Arizona campus, it has considerable potential. Semideciduous to deciduous, it reaches 30 feet (9 m) in height and spread, growing rapidly at first, then slowing to moderate before it becomes a small tree. Beautiful green, feathery leaves are about 6 inches (15 cm) long. Abundant clusters of large yellow puffball flowers bloom in early summer and often repeat later during the warm season. Bloom is followed by brown seed pods, not unattractive because they are well-hidden by foliage. Also it does not reseed and become a nuisance. Native to Mexico.

* See Glossary

Leucaena leucocephala

White popinac, Guaje

Fabaceae (Leguminosae) family

COLD HARDINESS

Low and intermediate zones, but damaged by frost in the latter.

LANDSCAPE VALUE

- Revegetation, wood lots and reforestation in disturbed areas.
- Acceptable small tree with grooming.
- Forage plant.
- Quick shade in difficult locations.

CULTURAL REQUIREMENTS

- **Exposure:** Full sun to part shade.
- **Water:** Quite drought resistant. Water every month or two for good appearance.
- **Soil:** Any soil.
- **Propagation:** Seed. Grows anywhere it can get a foothold.
- **Maintenance:** Requires regular grooming for good appearance. Remove frost-damaged wood after a cold winter.

POSSIBLE PROBLEMS

- Reseeds everywhere.
- More maintenance required than your average arid-region plant.

Weedy, fast-growing evergreen tree that spreads and invades under suitable conditions and climates. Reaches about 36 feet (11 m) high, 20 feet (6 m) wide. Trees are usually covered with brown pods that can look messy. Small white pincushion flowerheads in spikelike clusters are followed by beanpods 6 to 8 inches (15 to 20.5 cm) long. The twice pinnately compound foliage has twelve to sixteen pairs of small leaflets in the second division. Native to Mexico, Central America, and the West Indies. Now naturalized in many of the world's tropical regions.

Leucaena pulverulenta

Texas lead ball

Fabaceae (Leguminosae) family

COLD HARDINESS

Low and intermediate zones. Probably high zone, but no knowledge of it being planted there as of this writing.

LANDSCAPE VALUE

- Patio tree.
- Could be used as a street tree.
- Quick shade.

CULTURAL REQUIREMENTS

- **Exposure:** Full sun.
- **Water:** Water every week or two until plant is mature. Then water every month or two.
- **Soil:** Any soil with good drainage.
- **Propagation:** Seed.
- **Maintenance:** Low maintenance.

POSSIBLE PROBLEMS

None observed.

Semi-evergreen round-headed tree that grows quickly (with enough water) to 30 feet (9 m) high, with equal spread. Under optimum conditions, it produces good shade but the foliage canopy is naturally open in character. Small yellow puffball flowers. Feathery leaves are 6 to 8 inches (15 to 205 cm) long. Bean pods are brown. Found in Texas south into Mexico.

** See Glossary*

Leucaena retusa

Golden lead ball

Fabaceae (Leguminosae) family

COLD HARDINESS

Low and intermediate zones and warm microclimates of the high zone. Tolerates frost.

LANDSCAPE VALUE

- Courtyard patio or entry garden tree.
- Filtered shade on small properties.

CULTURAL REQUIREMENTS

- **Exposure:** Full sun to part shade.
- **Water:** Can attain moderate drought tolerance but needs water every week or two during the growing season for satisfactory appearance.
- **Soil:** Most soils.
- **Propagation:** Seed.
- **Maintenance:** Selective pruning helps establish a strong well-proportioned branch structure.

POSSIBLE PROBLEMS

Lacks interest during the winter leafless period.

Deciduous tree that grows at a moderate rate 10 to 20 feet (3 to 6 m) high, spreading 15 to 25 feet (4.5 to 7.5 m). Graceful tree with dainty, fine-textured medium green foliage that forms an oval crown. Bark and branches are smooth and gray. Showy yellow puffball flower heads 1/2 inch (1 cm) across appear intermittently from late spring into summer. Flattened papery bean pods 2 to 4 inches (5 to 10 cm) long ripen late summer into fall. Native to the Chihuahuan Desert.

* See Glossary

LEUCOPHYLLUM

Leucophyllum frutescens (Texas ranger or cenizo) could be credited as the first true desert species to be used in designed desert Southwest landscapes. Over the years, the more realistic Xeriscape™ landscaping practice has resulted in the collection, testing and introduction of many more outstanding *Leucophyllum* species that have a variety of foliage types and blossom color. *Leucophyllums* are native to the Chihuahuan Desert and eastern Mexico. All are considerably drought tolerant and most are cold hardy.

Leucophyllum candidum

Cenizo, Violet silverleaf
Scrophulariaceae family

COLD HARDINESS

Low and intermediate zones. Moderate frost tolerance.

LANDSCAPE VALUE

- Adds color and excitement to the landscape during summer, when few plants are in bloom.
- Specimen.
- Foundation plant.
- Massed as a low border, space definer, buffer or median planting.

CULTURAL REQUIREMENTS

- **Exposure:** Full to reflected sun.
- **Water:** Water young plants every week or two until established, then every month or two during hot, dry weather for acceptable growth and bloom.
- **Soil:** Fast-draining soil. Tolerates alkalinity.
- **Propagation:** Softwood cuttings.
- **Maintenance:** Little or no maintenance required for form or density.

POSSIBLE PROBLEMS

Susceptible to Texas root rot*.

Evergreen shrub with a dwarf rounded form that grows at a moderate rate to 3 feet (1 m) high, with equal spread. Silvery gray hairs form a dense mat over the small rounded leaves and lavender flowers. Flowers of the cultivar* 'Thunder Cloud' are an intense purple. 'Silver Cloud' grows larger but blooms less profusely. Both cultivars can bloom in repeat cycles, but the largest, most colorful display occurs in late summer. Native to Texas and Mexico.

Leucophyllum frutescens

Texas ranger, Texas sage
Scrophulariaceae family

COLD HARDINESS

All three zones.

LANDSCAPE VALUE

- Informal space definer or border, privacy screen or background.
- Medians and buffer zones.
- Parks, school grounds.
- Colorful accent.
- Especially suitable as a transition shrub between low- and high-water-use plantings.
- Tolerates shearing into hedges, but this reduces the number of flowers.

CULTURAL REQUIREMENTS

- **Exposure:** Full to reflected sun with intense heat. Tolerates some shade but form becomes more open and rangy.
- **Water:** Drought resistant. Watered every week or two in hot low-elevation locations. Water every month or two in cool higher elevation areas. Overwatering is generally bad for the plant.
- **Soil:** Well-drained, alkaline soil.
- **Propagation:** Cuttings.
- **Maintenance:** Low maintenance. Head back overly vigorous branches for denser foliage and more attractive natural shape. Shear in early spring or after bloom.

POSSIBLE PROBLEMS

Texas root rot*.

Rounded evergreen shrub that grows at a slow to moderate pace 4 to 8 feet (1 to 2.5 m) high, with equal spread. Gray felt-like leaves 1 inch (2.5 cm) long may form a solid or open foliage canopy depending on growing conditions. Masses of bell-shaped rose-purple flowers open intermittently after warm-season rain or irrigation, but its moment of splendor occurs in midsummer when a solid mass of blooms covers the plant. Cultivars* include 'Compacta,' which is 3 feet (1 m) tall and wide, smaller and more compact than the species in general; 'Green Cloud,' which is 8 feet (2.5 m) high and wide, has pale green leaves and large purple flowers; 'White Cloud,' 8 feet (2.5 m) high and wide with gray foliage and profuse large white flowers. Native to Texas and Mexico.

** See Glossary*

Leucophyllum laevigatum

Chihuahuan rain sage

Scrophulariaceae family

COLD HARDINESS

Low and intermediate zones and warmer locations in high zone.

LANDSCAPE VALUE

- Foundation plant.
- Low-growing space definer.
- Banks.
- Shrubbery border.

CULTURAL REQUIREMENTS

- **Exposure:** Reflected sun to light shade.
- **Water:** Quite drought resistant. Needs some moisture to develop and for good appearance during the warm season.
- **Soil:** Average but well-drained soil.
- **Propagation:** Cuttings.
- **Maintenance:** Head back fast-growing branch terminals to encourage dense growth habit.

POSSIBLE PROBLEMS

Seems to have few problems. Occasionally subject to Texas root rot*.

A broad-spreading evergreen shrub, usually as wide as it is tall—up to 5 feet (1.5 m)—sometimes even wider. Branches are upturned at the ends, sometimes giving the plant a flat-topped look. Small leaves are slightly gray but not as silvery as many of the *Leucophyllum* genus. The plant is also a little more open, revealing its structure. Flowers are about 3/4 inch (2 cm) in diameter and a lavender color that produces the illusion of being bluish. They are most profuse during summer, especially during periods of humidity. Native to U.S. Southwest and Mexico.

Leucophyllum langmaniae

Rio Bravo™ sage, Cinnamon sage, Langmanie's sage

Scrophulariaceae family

COLD HARDINESS

Low and intermediate zones, and probably warmer locations in the high zone.

LANDSCAPE VALUE

- Space defining.
- Medians.
- Large foundation planting.
- Mixed shrubbery groupings.
- It can be sheared for a more formal hedging, but flowers will be less abundant.

CULTURAL REQUIREMENTS

- **Exposure:** Reflected sun to part shade.
- **Water:** Quite drought resistant, but soak the root zone every week or two during the summer for good bloom and appearance.
- **Soil:** Any soil with good drainage.
- **Propagation:** Seed or cuttings.
- **Maintenance:** Selectively prune in winter to renew.

POSSIBLE PROBLEMS

None observed—possibly Texas root rot*.

One of the more recent introductions to the outstanding landscape choices from the genus *Leucophyllum*. To all intents and purposes, this is a more lush version of *L. laevigatum*, with greener leaves, giving a fuller foliage mass, and a fine display of lavender violet flowers that bloom with summer moisture. There is a named selection offered as 'Rio Bravo™ sage' that has uniform growth and flowering characteristics. Reaches about 5 feet (1.5 m) in height and width at a moderate pace. Native to the Chihuahuan Desert.

** See Glossary*

Leucophyllum prunosum

Sierra Bouquet™
Scrophulariaceae family

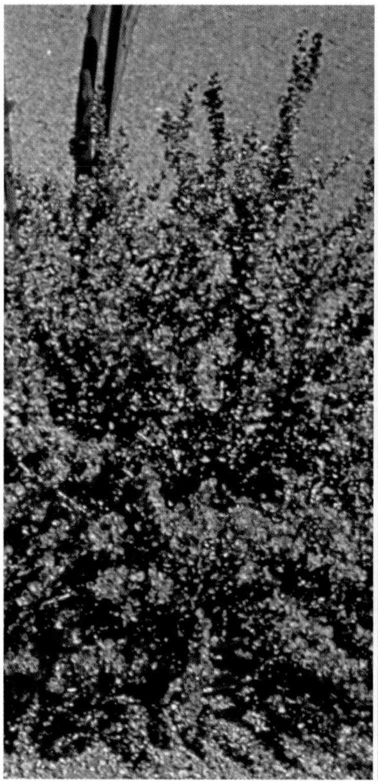

COLD HARDINESS
Low and intermediate zones.

LANDSCAPE VALUE
- Foreground and foundation planting.
- Space definer.
- Medians.
- Hedging or mixed shrubbery groupings.

CULTURAL REQUIREMENTS
- **Exposure:** Reflected sun to part shade.
- **Water:** Quite drought resistant. Soak the root zone every couple weeks for good growth, bloom and appearance.
- **Soil:** Most desert soils with good drainage.
- **Propagation:** Seed or cuttings.
- **Maintenance:** Low maintenance.

POSSIBLE PROBLEMS
None observed.

Another new introduction, this compact shrub grows about 6 feet (2 m) high and wide at a moderate pace. Leaves are whitish gray, more so than *L. frutescens,* which it somewhat resembles, although this foliage is more lush and leaves are larger and rounded at the tip. Flowers are violet-blue and not only eye-catching but also fragrant. A trade-marked variety, 'Sierra Bouquet™,' is offered as a selection for outstanding form and color. Native to U.S. Southwest and Mexico.

Leucophyllum zygophyllum

Blue rain sage, Blue Ranger™
Scrophulariaceae family

COLD HARDINESS
All three zones.

LANDSCAPE VALUE
- Seems to hold its compact growth habit well under cultivation. Fine medium shrub, eventually large but slow to get there. Maintain medium size indefinitely with a little pruning.
- A handsome silver note that contrasts with greener plants.

CULTURAL REQUIREMENTS
- **Exposure:** Full sun to part shade.
- **Water:** Quite drought resistant, but soak the root zone every week or two during the summer for good bloom and appearance and to speed growth.
- **Soil:** Any soil with good drainage.
- **Propagation:** Seed or cuttings.
- **Maintenance:** Little maintenance except some pruning to keep the shrub medium size.

POSSIBLE PROBLEMS
- Slow growth.
- Texas root rot*.

Roundish evergreen shrub that grows slowly to about 3 to 6 feet (1 to 2 m) high, with equal spread. Small dusty green leaves and little blue-violet to purple flowers make a striking contrast with the silvery foliage. May bloom several times during the warm season with the heaviest bloom in midsummer. Native to U.S. Southwest and Mexico.

* *See Glossary*

Lobelia laxiflora

Red Mexican lobelia

Lobeliaceae family

COLD HARDINESS

Low zone and warm areas of the intermediate zone. Foliage frosted when temperatures drop to the high-20s F (-2°C). Recovers quickly in spring.

LANDSCAPE VALUE

- Groundcover with tenacious underground rooting that makes it an excellent plant for banks.
- Flowers and shiny green leaves add color to the garden and give a fresh look to the landscape.
- Borders.
- Containers.

CULTURAL REQUIREMENTS

- **Exposure:** Sun (but not reflected sun) to open shade.
- **Water:** Fairly drought resistant once established because of the somewhat succulent underground stems, especially with some shade. Water young plants every week or two to develop a good cover. Water mature plants every month or two.
- **Soil:** Most soils with good drainage. Fertilization encourages a lush look.
- **Propagation:** Root divisions and cuttings.
- **Maintenance:** Cut back once every year or so to revitalize.

POSSIBLE PROBLEMS

- Tenacious once established and hard to eliminate.
- Can spread into adjacent areas by underground stems.
- Foliage has a strong unpleasant odor.

Shrubby evergreen perennial that grows rapidly to 2 to 3 feet (61 cm to 1 m) high and wide. Red tubular flowers bloom throughout the warm season and are arranged in terminal* racemes*. Makes a thick cover. Narrow lance-shaped leaves are bright green and shining. Native to crevices and rocky slopes in moist areas bordering the Sonoran Desert.

Landscape Design Example

Small shady spot featuring *Cercidium* hybrid.

* *See Glossary*

Lycium brevipes

Mexican wolfberry

Solanaceae family

COLD HARDINESS

Low and intermediate zones.

LANDSCAPE VALUE

- Dense green shrub for banks and space-defining.
- Colorful berry display.

CULTURAL REQUIREMENTS

- **Exposure:** Reflected sun to part shade.
- **Water:** Thoroughly soak the root zone every month or two.
- **Soil:** Any soil with good drainage.
- **Propagation:** Seed or cuttings.
- **Maintenance:** Tolerates pruning.

POSSIBLE PROBLEMS

None observed.

Mounding bright green many-branched shrub that reaches 12 feet (3.5 m) in height and spread at a moderate pace. Leaves are small and somewhat fleshy. Tiny white to lavender flowers are inconspicuous but the small red berries that follow in fall are abundant and can be quite showy. Berries are edible but too small to be worth the trouble; however, birds find them tasty. The most evergreen of the *Lycium* genus and the best for landscape use. Native to northwest Mexico and coastal areas of Southern California.

Lycium fremontii

Fremont thornbush, Fremont wolfberry

Solanaceae family

COLD HARDINESS

Low and intermediate zones.

LANDSCAPE VALUE

- The dense branched canopy serves as an effective screen or barrier and provides wildlife habitat.
- Not particularly attractive when leafless, this tough desert shrub is best in outlying low-traffic areas of the landscape.

CULTURAL REQUIREMENTS

- **Exposure:** Full sun to part shade.
- **Water:** Tolerates long dry periods as an established plant. Water once or twice a season.
- **Soil:** Most soils with good drainage, but appearance is improved with better quality soils.
- **Propagation:** Seed and probably vegetative cuttings.
- **Maintenance:** Low maintenance. Shape if necessary.

POSSIBLE PROBLEMS

Offers little landscape interest during long cold- or drought-induced deciduous periods.

The arching, spreading branches of this drought- and cold-deciduous spiny shrub form a heavy canopy that provides excellent cover for birds. It grows at a moderate rate, 3 to 10 feet (1 to 3 m) high and up to 8 feet (2.5 m) wide. White to pale lavender tubular flowers are $1/2$ inch (1 cm) long. They produce small, oval, bright red fruits that are a favorite food of birds as well as other wildlife. The succulent light green leaves $3/8$ to 1 inch (1 to 2.5 cm) long and $1/4$ to $1/3$ inch (0.5 to 1 cm) wide are spatula shaped, becoming wider from the base toward the pointed or rounded tip. Native to southwestern Arizona and southern California in the United States, Sonora and Baja California in Mexico.

Lysiloma candidum

Baja lysiloma, Palo blanco

Fabaceae (Leguminosae) family

COLD HARDINESS

Almost frost-free areas of low zone.

LANDSCAPE VALUE

- Small patio, entry-garden or shade tree.
- Background.
- Lush tropical-looking foliage, attractive bark and flowers add much to the landscape in frost-free areas.
- Both transition and oasis zones.

CULTURAL REQUIREMENTS

- **Exposure:** Exceedingly tolerant of great heat and intense sunlight but sensitive to frost.
- **Water:** Moderately drought tolerant but looks better and becomes more tree-like with water every week or two.
- **Soil:** Most soils with good drainage.
- **Propagation:** Seed.
- **Maintenance**: Prune to develop single- or multistemmed growth habit.

POSSIBLE PROBLEMS

- Light frost causes foliage to drop.
- More severe cold results in considerable stem die-back*.

Graceful, vase-shaped small to medium-size tree that grows from 10 to 30 feet (3 to 9 m) high and wide at a moderate rate. Evergreen in warm-winter locations. The foliage canopy is dainty and fine-textured. Smooth whitish bark covers branches, except for young stems. During spring, ball-shaped heads of flowers with long white stamens* open in clusters 1/3 to 1 inch (1 to 2.5 cm) long before new foliage emerges. Coppery red seed pods 1 inch (2.5 cm) long are twisted at first, becoming straight as they ripen. Native to the lower Sonoran and Baja California deserts in Mexico.

Lysiloma divaricatum

Mauto, Little-leaf feather tree

Fabaceae (Leguminosae) family

COLD HARDINESS

Low zone and warm microclimates of the intermediate zone. Frost tender.

LANDSCAPE VALUE

- Patio tree.
- Entry garden tree.
- Accent.
- Large background shrub.
- Cold can cut the plant to the ground, but the feathery regrowth is a nice addition to the summer landscape.

CULTURAL REQUIREMENTS

- **Exposure:** Full sun. Intense heat.
- **Water:** Irrigation is a strong growth regulator. A tree results from thoroughly soaking the root zone every week or two. A smaller, more shrubby plant results from less frequent irrigation.
- **Soil:** Most soils with good drainage.
- **Propagation:** Seed.
- **Maintenance:** Basic pruning is necessary to develop the desired form.

POSSIBLE PROBLEMS

None observed.

Delicate ferny-looking foliage, graceful form, and clusters of dainty ball-shaped flowers July through September give this *Lysiloma* considerable landscape potential. Flowers grow 1/3 to 1 1/4 inch (1 to 3 cm) long and have a creamy hue. Grows as a large shrub on dry sites; becomes a tree with adequate soil moisture, barring heavy frost. Usually evergreen, but may go deciduous with moderate frost or long periods of drought. Colder temperatures cause stem die-back*. Reddish brown seed pods are 1/3 to 3/4 inch (1 to 2 cm) long. Can grow as high as 50 feet (15 m) and spread as wide as 40 feet (12 m). Growth rate is rapid with adequate water. Native to Central Sonora, Baja California, Vera Cruz and Oaxaca in Mexico, and also throughout Central America.

* *See Glossary*

Lysiloma watsonii thornberi

Feather tree, Feather bush

Fabaceae (Leguminosae) family

COLD HARDINESS

Low zone and warm locations in intermediate zone. It will only become a tree in warm microclimates. Frost tender.

LANDSCAPE VALUE

- Patio or entry-garden tree.
- Specimen or accent for warm winter areas.
- Valued for the delicate airy foliage and summer floral display.
- Shows potential for medians and park use.
- It freezes to the ground in colder areas, but recovers rapidly in spring to become an attractive feather bush.

CULTURAL REQUIREMENTS

- **Exposure:** Full or reflected sun and heat.
- **Water:** Survives with little water after establishment, but a thorough soaking of the root zone every month or two will improve appearance and speed growth.
- **Soil:** Most soils with good drainage.
- **Propagation:** Seed.
- **Maintenance:** Prune for good branching habit and form. Remove frost-damaged wood each spring in colder areas. Some cleanup of seeds pods may be necessary.

POSSIBLE PROBLEMS

None observed except plant requires more maintenance than most arid-region plants.

Semi-evergreen tree that reaches 15 to 45 feet (4.5 to 13.5 m) in height and spread. Grows rapidly with plenty of water. Characterized by rough gray bark on one or more trunks and the spreading, typically irregular foliage crown. Pinnately* compound leaves consist of fifteen to forty-five pairs of tiny oblong leaflets, which may drop during drought or cold. Small, pale cream-colored flower heads may appear in small numbers during spring. Peak bloom follows summer rain in the native habitat. Dark reddish brown seed pods are linear, $4\frac{1}{2}$ to 8 inches (11.5 to 20.5 cm) long, sometimes longer. Native to Sonora and Sinaloa in Mexico.

Lysiloma watsonii divaricatum

Rincon Mountains feather tree or bush

Fabaceae (Leguminosae) family

COLD HARDINESS

Low zone and warm winter microclimates of intermediate zone. Will grow as a perennial in cold locations. Light frost causes the foliage to drop; hard frost results in substantial die-back* of branches.

LANDSCAPE VALUE

- Small flowering shade tree for patios and entry gardens.
- Medians, buffers, parking-lot islands.
- Golf courses.
- Background or screening.
- Commercial sites, either transition or lush oasis zone.
- Can be treated as a summer foliage perennial in high zone, where it freezes to the ground in colder areas. It recovers rapidly the next season to form an attractive feather bush.

CULTURAL REQUIREMENTS

- **Exposure:** Full sun. Tolerates intense reflected sun and heat.
- **Water:** Drought resistant and survives with widely spaced irrigation; in most arid regions, watering every week or two is necessary for maximum tree size and lush foliage.
- **Soil:** Any soil.
- **Propagation:** Seed.
- **Maintenance:** Prune out cold-damaged wood in late spring after growth resumes.

POSSIBLE PROBLEMS

Seed pods create litter.

Rounded, spreading tree that rapidly grows to 15 feet (4.5 m) in height and spread. Well named for its feathery cloud of foliage, which makes a dense canopy of finely divided bright green leaves. Evergreen in warm winter areas. Short spikes of creamy white ball-shaped flower clusters to $\frac{5}{8}$ inch (1.5 cm) across open in late spring and early summer. Flat seed pods ripen in late summer or fall and are 4 to 8 inches (10 to 20.5 cm) long. They persist on the tree for some time. Native to the Rincon Mountain foothills of southern Arizona. Many authorities believe it is no different from *L. watsonii*, which is found farther south in Mexico. Others claim it is different and should be given a separate classification.

* *See Glossary*

Macfadyena unguis-cati (Doxantha unguis-cati)

Cat's claw vine

Bignoniaceae family

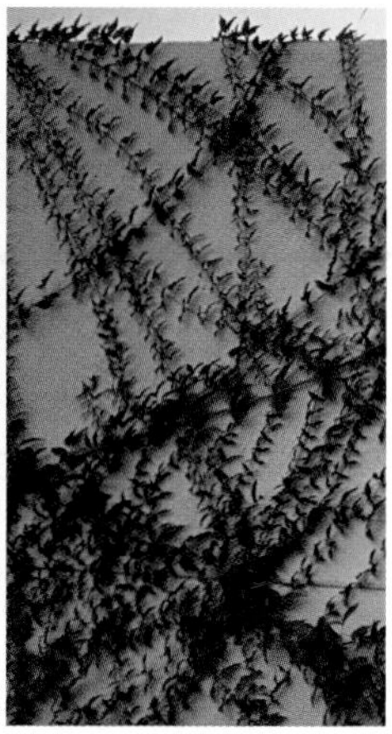

COLD HARDINESS

Low and intermediate zones and, to a limited extent, the high zone. Stems, but not foliage, tolerate moderate to hard frost.

LANDSCAPE VALUE

- Vigorous, high-climbing, self-supporting vine that clings to brick, stone, cement and wood surfaces as well as to fences and tree trunks.
- This is one of the limited number of vines that grow well on hot south- or west-facing masonry walls.
- Although brief, the flowering display is dramatic.

CULTURAL REQUIREMENTS

- **Exposure:** Full to reflected sun and heat to open shade.
- **Water:** Established plants survive with water once or twice a season. Water more often for faster growth, lusher foliage and more abundant flowering.
- **Soil:** Deep fertile soil is best but most well-draining soils are satisfactory.
- **Propagation:** Seed or cuttings.
- **Maintenance:** Tends to concentrate foliage mass in high portion of the plant. Heavily cut back stems from time to time to encourage new growth along lower sections. Horizontal stretches of wire across a wall surface can prevent troublesome pull-away after vine has achieved full coverage.

POSSIBLE PROBLEMS

- Heavy top growth may pull away from support, especially during strong winds.
- Roots are greedy and invasive, often stunting foreground plantings.

Large self-climbing vine with three-part forked and cat's-claw–like tendrils. Young stems form an open, delicate growth pattern that later fills in to become dense and full. Evergreen in mild winters, partly or completely deciduous with hard frost. Grows 20 to 50 feet (6 to 15 m) high, with equal spread. Ultimate height and spread depend on size of structure it can climb on. Growth is slow until established, when it speeds up considerably. Each leaf is divided into two glossy medium green leaflets up to 2 inches (5 cm) long. In spring, bright yellow funnel-shaped flowers 2 inches (5 cm) long and 1¼ inches (3 cm) across in terminal* clusters create a lavish color display. Slender bean pods are 12 to 15 inches (30.5 to 38 cm) long when mature. An underground tuber that stores nutrients and water provides a means of survival over long dry periods. Native to Yucatan in Mexico and from Guatemala to Argentina.

Maclura pomifera

Osage orange

Moraceae family

COLD HARDINESS

All three zones. Tolerates even the coldest locations in high zone.

LANDSCAPE VALUE

- Large windbreak hedge.
- Background plant.
- Trimmed into a shade tree.
- Flower arrangers prize the fruit for form and color in dry arrangements.

CULTURAL REQUIREMENTS

- **Exposure:** Full sun, even reflected situations.
- **Water:** Needs water every week or two to get established but has great drought tolerance when mature.
- **Soil:** Any soil. Tolerates difficult desert types.
- **Propagation:** Seed or cuttings.
- **Maintenance:** Stake and prune when young to develop a proper scaffold for a shade tree.

POSSIBLE PROBLEMS

- Thorny branches may be unpleasant when trimming or hedging.
- Excessive fruit production may be a cleanup problem.

A medium to large deciduous tree that reaches 20 feet (6 m) high or higher under optimum conditions and spreads the same. Growth is rapid with water, slower in dry situations. Growth habit is rather rangy, with loose, spreading thorny branches. Leaves are large, lush, green, 5 inches (13 cm) long and oval- to lance-shaped. Flower clusters offer little landscape interest. Female trees produce an abundant crop of 4-inch (10-cm) bumpy chartreuse-green fruits if a male pollinator tree is near. Fruits are really a hard-pressed ball of seeds that resemble green oranges. A tough, undemanding tree. Native to Arkansas and Texas.

* See Glossary

Malephora crocea

Gray ice plant

Aizoaceae family

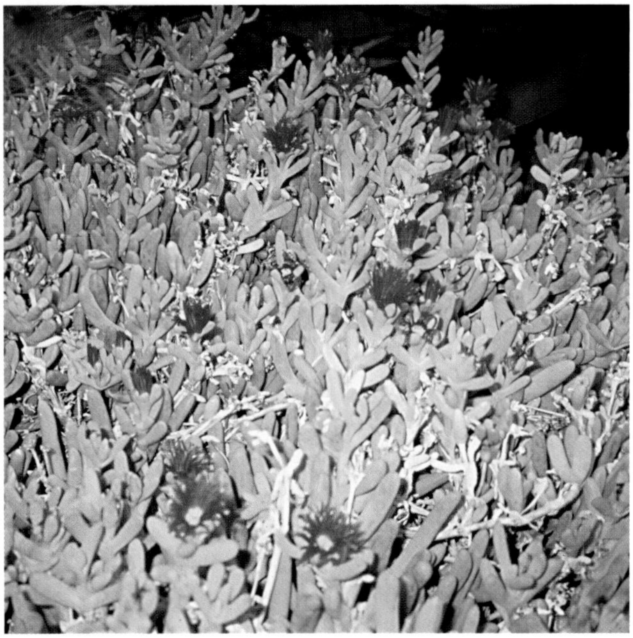

Evergreen perennial succulent that grows at a moderate to rapid rate, reaching 6 to 12 inches (15 to 31 cm) in height and spreading 6 feet (2 m) or more. Trailing stems are grayish brown. Smooth, fleshy gray-green leaves are three-angled, 2 inches (5 cm) long and 1/4 inch (0.5 cm) across. They form a dense mat as the plant grows. Reddish yellow to orange daisylike flowers, 1 1/4 inches (3 cm) in diameter, are most abundant in spring but also bloom throughout the rest of the year. They never appear in solid masses. Native to South Africa.

COLD HARDINESS

Low and intermediate zones plus limited areas of high zone. Moderately frost hardy.

LANDSCAPE VALUE

- Low-growing mat of succulent foliage provides textural interest.
- Flowers add a refreshing touch of color to water-efficient landscapes.
- Trailing groundcover for banks, slopes and beds.
- Residential, commercial and roadside projects.
- Large pots and raised planters.

CULTURAL REQUIREMENTS

- **Exposure:** Full sun to part shade. Tolerates wind and smog. Also fire resistant.
- **Water:** Drought tolerant. Watering every month or two maintains satisfactory appearance. In very hot low-elevation locations, water every week or two in summer to prevent stress and foliage burn.
- **Soil:** Any soil with good drainage.
- **Propagation:** Seed or cuttings.
- **Maintenance:** Pruning may be necessary several times each year to keep a planting within specific boundaries.

POSSIBLE PROBLEMS

- In some situations Bermuda grass may become an invasive weed pest.
- Tolerates little foot traffic, which complicates weeding.

Malephora luteola

Yellow malephora

Aizoaceae family

COLD HARDINESS

Low and intermediate zones. Frost tolerant.

LANDSCAPE VALUE

- Larger foliage and flowers add more lushness than *M. crocea* does.
- Adds color to landscape.

CULTURAL REQUIREMENTS

- **Exposure:** Full sun to part shade.
- **Water:** Tolerant of long dry periods as an established plant. Water once or twice a season to improve landscape performance.
- **Soil:** Grows in most well-drained soils but better quality soils improve appearance.
- **Propagation:** Seeds and probably by vegetative cuttings.
- **Maintenance:** Pruning may be necessary several times each year to keep a planting within specific boundaries.

POSSIBLE PROBLEMS

None observed.

A gray-green trailing succulent that grows at a moderate rate to 1 foot (30.5 cm) high and up to 6 feet (2 m) across. In addition to having larger leaves and flowers, *M. luteola* is a more vigorous grower in general than *M. crocea*. While not a heavy bloomer, the bright yellow flowers add a cheery note to a planting. They appear throughout the growing season, but are more abundant in spring. Native to South Africa.

* See Glossary

Malpighia glabra

Barbados cherry

Malpighiaceae family

COLD HARDINESS

Low and intermediate zones. Parts of high zone when grown from northern populations of the species.

LANDSCAPE VALUE

- Mounding shrub for background and hillside or tall foundation planting.
- Trimmed for hedging.

CULTURAL REQUIREMENTS

- **Exposure:** Full sun to open shade. Tolerates reflected sun.
- **Water:** Quite drought tolerant. May go drought deciduous to survive dry periods with no loss of woody structure. Thoroughly soak the root zone every week or two during the warm season for best appearance.
- **Soil:** Most soils with good drainage.
- **Propagation:** Seed or cuttings.
- **Maintenance:** Undemanding.

POSSIBLE PROBLEMS

Looks drab in winter or when drought deciduous.

A mounding semi-evergreen to deciduous shrub (depending on winter cold) that reaches 10 feet (3 m) in height and spread, at a moderate rate, more rapid with warm season moisture. Dark green lance-shaped leaves are about 4 inches (10 cm) long. Small pink to purple flowers are borne in clusters of three to five, each bloom about 5/8 inch (1.5 cm) across. Flowers are followed by three-seeded 3/8 inch (1 cm) red fruit, sometimes eaten, but not showy enough to be considered a decorative element. Native from Texas to northern South America.

Manihot isoloba

Sonoran manihot, Wild tapioca

Euphorbiaceae family

COLD HARDINESS

Low and intermediate zones and probably warmer locations in high zone. If frozen back to its fleshy underground tubers, it recovers rapidly with warm weather.

LANDSCAPE VALUE

- A filler plant combined with other tropical-effects plants.
- Adds a lush touch without demanding special treatment.

CULTURAL REQUIREMENTS

- **Exposure:** Full sun to open shade.
- **Water:** Fairly drought resistant. Thoroughly soak the root zone every week or two at the beginning of the warm season. Fleshy roots sustain it during dry periods.
- **Soil:** Tolerates a wide variety of soils but rewards good garden treatment with more lush growth.
- **Propagation:** Seed.
- **Maintenance:** Some grooming and clean-up in fall.

POSSIBLE PROBLEMS

- Sometimes reseeds in other areas of garden, but not really invasive.
- Deciduous period leaves a temporary vacant spot in a plant composition.

A many-branched deciduous shrub with milky sap and fleshy young stems. Grows rapidly (with moisture) from 3 to 8 feet (1 to 2.5 m) high, spreading 2 to 5 feet (61 cm to 1.5 m). Leaves are 2 to 5 inches (5 to 13 cm) long and wide, palmately* veined and divided into five to nine lobes that extend to the base of the blade. Insignificant greenish flowers are male or female, both sexes occurring in small terminal* clusters on the same plant. The rounded seed capsules, faintly three-lobed and 3/4 to 1 inch (2 to 2.5 cm) in diameter, develop a wrinkled surface as they dry. A rare native in Sonora and Chihuahua, Mexico.

* See Glossary

Mascagnia lilacina

Lilac orchid vine

Malpighiaceae family

COLD HARDINESS

Low and intermediate zones and warm microclimates of high zone.

LANDSCAPE VALUE

- Garlands at top of vine support or trellis rather than a solid cover, festooned at times with small five-petaled lilac-shade flowers in spring and summer.
- A hardy and tough vine.

CULTURAL REQUIREMENTS

- **Exposure:** Full sun to part shade.
- **Water:** Drought resistant. Thoroughly soak the root zone every month or two during the warm season to encourage flowering and maintain evergreen.
- **Soil:** Most arid-region soils. More drought resistant in deeper soils.
- **Propagation:** Seed or cuttings.
- **Maintenance:** No maintenance if vine has something to climb.

POSSIBLE PROBLEMS

Base of the plant tends to be sparse.

Semideciduous vine that reaches 10 to 15 feet (2 to 4.5 m) high and spreads to 10 feet (3 m) at a moderate to rapid rate. Vine is a twining self-climber that is somewhat more frost hardy than *M. macroptera*. Leaves are about 1½ inches (4 cm). Produces attractive, small purple flowers during the warm season. Native to Mexican deserts.

Mascagnia macroptera

Yellow orchid vine

Malpighiaceae family

COLD HARDINESS

Low zone and protected microclimates of intermediate zone. Sensitive to hard frost.

LANDSCAPE VALUE

Good-looking low-water-use vine with considerable landscape potential.

- Readily climbs a fence or trellis but needs support to grow on walls.
- Useful for screening, covering or softening structural surfaces with pleasing flowers over a long season.

CULTURAL REQUIREMENTS

- **Exposure:** Full sun to part shade.
- **Water:** Drought tolerant when established. Thoroughly soak the root zone every month or two to maintain. Grows faster and larger with more abundant soil moisture.
- **Soil:** Most arid-region soils.
- **Propagation:** Seed or cuttings.
- **Maintenance:** Protect *M. macroptera* from severe frost. Prune as necessary to shape or following hard frost to remove damaged growth.

POSSIBLE PROBLEMS

None observed.

Usually grows as a trailing or twining, climbing woody evergreen vine that reaches 15 to 25 feet (4.5 to 7.5 m). May also grow as an upright shrub to 6 feet (2 m) high with erect smooth-barked stems. In either form, its growth rate is moderate. The vine forms a dense canopy of slender leaves ⅞ to 2 inches (2 to 5 cm) long.

Small yellow five-petaled flowers resemble tiny orchids at a glance. They are borne in clusters intermittently over a long period in warm weather; the first bloom cycle in spring is the largest. Conspicuous fruits in ball-like clusters are a showy lime green and have two large and one small wing. Native throughout most of Mexico.

* *See Glossary*

Maytenus phyllanthoides

Mangle dulce

Celastraceae family

COLD HARDINESS

Low and intermediate zones if plants are propagated from northern populations, such as southern Texas.

LANDSCAPE VALUE

Good large shrub for background and screening, especially where salinity is a problem.

CULTURAL REQUIREMENTS

- **Exposure:** Full sun to part shade.
- **Water:** Thoroughly water every month or two. Will grow well on brackish water.
- **Soil:** Tolerates salinity and heavy, poorly drained soil, but saline conditions are not a requirement.
- **Propagation:** Seed or cuttings.
- **Maintenance:** Remove low growth or allow to remain for multitrunk form.

POSSIBLE PROBLEMS

None observed except slow growth.

Evergreen large shrub or small tree that grows at a slow to moderate pace up to 12 feet (3.5 m) high, with equal spread. Small, leathery light green leaves are rounded. Small red fruits add color to the plant. Notable because of its salt tolerance. Found growing near the ocean along both coasts from Texas and on south and along Baja California, Mexico. It is also found on brackish soils inland.

Medicago arborea

Tree alfalfa

Fabaceae (Leguminosae) family

COLD HARDINESS

All three zones.

LANDSCAPE VALUE

- A nice green touch with cheery yellow blooms that brighten the winter garden scene when many plants are semidormant.
- Foundation planting or mixed medium-size shrubbery borders, combined with species that look good in summer when tree alfalfa can look drab.

CULTURAL REQUIREMENTS

- **Exposure:** Full sun to part shade.
- **Water:** Quite drought resistant. Moisten soil during the cool season.
- **Soil:** Most soils with good drainage.
- **Propagation:** Seed or cuttings.
- **Maintenance:** Low maintenance.

POSSIBLE PROBLEMS

None observed.

A small to medium semideciduous shrub, from 3 to 5 feet (1 to 1.5 m) high and wide, sometimes slightly wider. Grows at a moderate rate. Crisp medium green cloverlike leaves look especially lush during the winter, but they can completely drop in midsummer. This is in response to the rainfall pattern of the plant's native region, the Mediterranean. Small pea-like yellow blossoms highlight the foliage during late winter followed by inconspicuous small pods.

Melaleuca lanceolata

White-flowered melaleuca, Moona bottlebrush

Myrtaceae family

COLD HARDINESS

Low and intermediate zones and probably warmer locations in high zone.

LANDSCAPE VALUE

- Large shrub for mass planting, banks, and background and boundary plantings.
- Medians and other roadside situations.
- Trimmed into a small patio tree.
- Spectacular flower show.

CULTURAL REQUIREMENTS

- **Exposure:** Full sun, including reflected sun to light shade.
- **Water:** Drought resistant. Enhance growth and bloom with water every couple weeks, less in winter.
- **Soil:** Most soils with good drainage.
- **Propagation:** Seed or cuttings.
- **Maintenance:** Lightly prune branches to control growth. Do not shear.

POSSIBLE PROBLEMS

None observed.

Large evergreen shrub, usually about 10 feet (3 m) high, with small dark green needlelike leaves. Grows at a moderate rate, depending on water supply. Clouds of white bottlebrush flowers cover the plant in summer. Each brush of small bloom is 2 to 3 inches (5 to 7.5 cm) wide. Dark bark is rough but not shaggy. Seed vessels are inconspicuous. Native to Australia.

Note: Other *Melaleucas* of this type have been planted in hot arid regions, in particular *M. eliptica* (red flowered), but they are still rarely planted. More should be tried because they represent many useful additions to the landscape.

Melaleuca quinquenervia (M. leucadendra)

Cajeput tree

Myrtaceae family

COLD HARDINESS

Low zone and warm microclimates of intermediate zone.

LANDSCAPE VALUE

- Small to medium tree for streets, commercial and residential plantings, and in parks where it's especially attractive in little groves.
- Tolerates desert heat and salty wind exposure, making it a versatile addition to desert and seafront landscapes.

CULTURAL REQUIREMENTS

- **Exposure:** Full sun to part shade. Not a good understory tree because of its upright growth habit and mature size.
- **Water:** Tolerates wet situations but also performs well with water every month or two.
- **Soil:** Tolerates poor soils.
- **Propagation:** Seed or cuttings.
- **Maintenance:** Little to no upkeep.

POSSIBLE PROBLEMS

None observed other than peeling bark, which could become a slight litter problem if people give in to the temptation to peel it completely off.

Open, vertical-growing evergreen tree that rapidly grows 20 to 40 feet (6 to 12 m) high, or even higher, spreading to about 10 feet (3 m). Growth is slower in drier, stressful situations. Pale green leaves 2 to 4 inches (5 to 10 cm) long sometimes turn purple in winter after light frosts. Young growth is pendulous at first and new leaves have silky hairs, but foliage becomes shiny at maturity. The thick corky bark, which peels off in sheets and is usually white but sometimes light brown, is of special interest. Flowers are yellowish white (sometimes pink or purple) and arranged on 2- to 4-inch (5- to 10-cm) spikes. They bloom in summer and fall. Native to Australia.

* See Glossary

COLD HARDINESS
All three zones.

LANDSCAPE VALUE
- Low-growing untreadable groundcover.
- Good color plant.
- Combined with desert wildflowers.
- In containers.

CULTURAL REQUIREMENTS
- **Exposure:** Full sun to light filtered shade.
- **Water:** Water every week to every couple months during the warm season, depending on how quickly your soil dries. Plants rot if soil stays too wet. Water in winter only during long dry spells.
- **Soil:** Well-drained soil.
- **Propagation:** Seed.
- **Maintenance:** A short-lived perennial that reseeds under favorable conditions. Leggy plants can be cut back in autumn to rejuvenate plant, but you'll need to replace them from time to time. To extend flowering period, remove faded bloom.

POSSIBLE PROBLEMS
Short-lived.

A low-mounding perennial that rapidly grows between 8 inches and 2 feet (20.5 to 61 cm) high and wide. Narrow gray leaves are 1/2 to 3/4 inch (1 to 2 cm) long and 1/4 inch (0.5 cm) wide. Long-lasting white daisies 1 inch (2.5 cm) across have yellow centers and appear intermittently during winters that are nearly frost-free. Blooms more heavily from spring into early fall and only at this time where winter frosts are common. Native to northern Mexico and from Arizona to Texas.

Melampodium leucanthum
Blackfoot daisy
Asteraceae (Compositae) family

Landscape Design Example

On the University of Arizona campus, winter-blooming *Cassias* in combination with bold succulents add close-range interest at the base of a tall palm.

Melia azedarach (M. azedarach 'Umbraculiformis')

Chinaberry tree, Persian lilac tree, Texas umbrella tree

Meliaceae family

COLD HARDINESS

All three zones.

LANDSCAPE VALUE

- A quick-growing medium-size shade tree for the hottest locations, although it does equally well in cool, near-the-coast situations.
- The dark green canopy, with its deep shade beneath, a long-time favorite in the U.S. Desert Southwest, where it has been a popular dooryard tree.
- A spot of golden autumn color in regions with brisk fall night temperatures.
- The chinaberries decorate the bare branches in the winter.
- Older trees become quite picturesque in form.

CULTURAL REQUIREMENTS

- **Exposure:** Full sun. Tolerates reflected heat.
- **Water:** Quite drought-resistant. Thoroughly soak the root zone every three weeks during the warm season, but more often for new trees to develop and less often in winter. Tolerates high-water-use oasis-type areas without problems.
- **Soil:** Most soils with good drainage.
- **Propagation:** Seed or cuttings.
- **Maintenance:** Needs little pruning other than minor shaping and removal of low branches in the beginning to develop the canopy above head height. This is contrary to the widely held concept that it must be headed back to a few main branches each winter. This produces a weak tree and actually shortens its life.

POSSIBLE PROBLEMS

- Heavy crop may produce unwanted litter.
- Heavy pruning subjects tree to heart rot.
- Wood is brittle on old trees.
- Fruit is mildly toxic.

A spreading deciduous tree that grows rapidly (with regular water) 30 to 50 feet (9 to 15 m) in height and spread. Dark green compound leaves are 2 to 3 feet (61 cm to 1 m) long, with many narrow-toothed leaflets 1 to 2 inches (2.5 to 5 cm) long. Loose clusters of lavender flowers, fragrant at night, are attractive at close range, but the soft lavender is a receding color and does not show up at a distance. The small but numerous flowers resemble the color of the true Persian lilac (*Syringa persica*), thus the common name Persian lilac tree. Blooming occurs in late spring. Following bloom, hard green berrylike fruits develop, eventually turning a pale yellow to off-white. These china-hard fruits (slightly poisonous) remain on the tree through fall leaf drop and contribute a minor decorative effect. Birds enjoy the fruit with no ill effects. Native to warm areas of Persia across to China.

Note: *Melia azedarach* 'Umbraculiformis,' Texas umbrella tree, is the same as the above in all respects, with the exception that it naturally takes a more dome-shaped form. This variety is more common in landscapes, although it does not develop the picturesque form of *M. azedarach*.

* See Glossary

Melianthus major

South African honey bush

Melianthaceae family

COLD HARDINESS

Low and intermediate zones.

LANDSCAPE VALUE

- Bold foliage adds an interesting touch to tropical-effects combinations.
- The reddish brown blossom spikes contribute additional drama in late winter.
- Silhouette possibilities with staking.

CULTURAL REQUIREMENTS

- **Exposure:** Full sun to open shade, but reflected sun may be too much in desert situations.
- **Water:** Thoroughly soak the root zone every week or two. Tolerates less frequent watering and some drought.
- **Soil:** Most soil.
- **Propagation:** Seed or cuttings.
- **Maintenance:** Prune back a third of the old canes to the ground in late winter to produce a clumping shrub of lush foliage. Limit growth to four or five strong stems with some staking to encourage vertical growth and a more open silhouette effect. Plant needs grooming at times to remove spent bloom and drying old growth.

POSSIBLE PROBLEMS

Foliage has an unpleasant odor when brushed against.

An upright or sprawling soft-wooded evergreen shrub that can reach 12 to 14 feet (3.5 to 4 m) but is easy to keep much lower. Spreads about 10 feet (3 m). A rapid grower that can produce large compound gray-green leaves up to 1 foot (30.5 cm) long with nine to eleven toothed leaflets under optimum conditions. Will be less lush and slower growing in drier situations. Most new growth springs from the base of the clump but canelike stems will be slightly branched. Reddish brown bloom spikes, about 12 inches (30.5 cm) long, appear in late winter, creating an interesting contrast with the gray-green leaves. Native to South Africa.

Melianthus minor

Dwarf South African honey bush

Melianthaceae family

COLD HARDINESS

Low and intermediate zones.

LANDSCAPE VALUE

- Oasis settings.
- Combines well with *Cycads*, succulents and other bold plants.
- Understory plant in open shade although full sun is its preference.
- Foundation plant, sprawling down a bank or in containers.

CULTURAL REQUIREMENTS

- **Exposure:** Full sun to part shade.
- **Water:** Reasonably drought resistant. Tolerates water every month or two but thoroughly soaking the root zone every week or two will ensure good foliage and appearance.
- **Soil:** Most soils with good drainage.
- **Propagation:** Cuttings, or seed when available.
- **Maintenance:** Remove old bloom stalks.

POSSIBLE PROBLEMS

None observed.

A sprawling soft-wooded evergreen shrub that grows to 3 feet (1 m) tall and 3 to 4 feet (1 m) wide at a moderate to rapid rate. Branches are few. Primary branches originate at the base. Abundant grayish green leaves, 6 to 7 inches (15 to 18 cm) long, are divided into nine to eleven toothed leaflets that create a lush-appearing mound. In more confined spaces, it will develop upright with stems and twigs more visible. Not a prolific bloomer but occasionally produces reddish brown spikes of short, compact flowers in late winter. Native to South Africa.

* See Glossary

Merremia aurea

Yellow morning glory vine

Convolvulaceae family

COLD HARDINESS

Low zone and very protected microclimates of the intermediate zone. Dies back with even light frost but regrows rapidly from the base in spring.

LANDSCAPE VALUE

- Vine of lush tropical appearance and spectacular bloom.
- Good on wire fences.

CULTURAL REQUIREMENTS

- **Exposure:** Full sun.
- **Water:** Water every week or two during the growing season and only once or twice (if at all) during winter, depending on extent of frost damage. More water will speed recovery.
- **Soil:** Fertile garden soil.
- **Propagation:** Seed.
- **Maintenance:** Twining habit requires support if the vine is to be displayed against a solid structural wall.

POSSIBLE PROBLEMS

None observed.

Reliable as a wood vine only in warm winter climates, perennial elsewhere. Vigorous twining evergreen vine that grows about 26 feet (8 m) in every direction, depending on what is available for support. Mostly herbaceous* in cool areas, but woody and drought deciduous in lower frost-free areas, where it grows rapidly, given enough water. A dense mass of leaves are palmately* divided into five leaflets, each 1/2 to 2 inches (1 to 5 cm) long. Bright yellow funnel-shaped (morning glory–like) flowers are 2 inches (5 cm) long and 2 1/2 to 3 inches (6.5 to 7.5 cm) across. Flowers bloom during the warm months if moisture is present, as solitary blooms or borne in clusters. Rounded papery seed capsules contain four brownish black seeds. Native to lower Sonora and arid tropical regions of Baja California, Mexico.

Merremia dissecta

Mile-a-minute vine

Convolvulaceae family

COLD HARDINESS

All three zones. Tolerates light frost but dies back after hard frost.

LANDSCAPE VALUE

Needs a fence or shade structure for most effective use but will clamber over rocks or a bank. Not a plant for refined situations.

CULTURAL REQUIREMENTS

- **Exposure:** Sun to part shade.
- **Water:** Thoroughly soak the root zone every couple weeks to every couple of months (depending on how quickly your soil dries) especially during the warm season.
- **Soil:** Any soil with some depth for fleshy perennial roots.
- **Propagation:** Seed.
- **Maintenance:** Guide and train over fence or shade structure. Clean up after winter.

POSSIBLE PROBLEMS

- Vigorous growth can overwhelm some landscapes.
- Dying back in cold regions reduces its value for screening.
- Not the best winter appearance even in mild winter areas.

Rapid-growing self-climbing vine that grows to 20 feet (6 m) or more in height and spread. Dark green compound leaves and white morning glory–like blossoms densely cover any support. In cold winter areas, the vine dies to the ground after heavy frost but regrows quickly each spring. Remains evergreen in mild winter areas. Native to southern Texas and Mexico.

** See Glossary*

Mimosa dysocarpa

Velvet-pod mimosa

Fabaceae (Leguminosae) family

COLD HARDINESS

All three zones.

LANDSCAPE VALUE

- During the bloom period, unusual and colorful flower spikes add much charm and excitement.
- Combine with plants that divert attention from its appearance when it isn't blooming.

CULTURAL REQUIREMENTS

- **Exposure:** Full sun to part shade.
- **Water:** Water every month or two during the growing season for a larger shrub and more profuse flowering, especially in the low zone.
- **Soil:** Most soils with good drainage.
- **Propagation:** Seed.
- **Maintenance:** Head back long stems early in the growing season to improve plant form. At this time also remove dead or weak stems.

POSSIBLE PROBLEMS

- Looks a bit straggly and unkempt except during the bloom period.
- Prickly stems unpleasant to work around.

Open, spreading and irregular shrub that grows at a moderate rate 1 1/2 to 6 1/2 feet (46 cm to 2 m) high and wide. Goes deciduous or dies back to the ground in its native habitat at 3500 to 6500 feet (1050 to 1950 m) in Arizona, Texas and northern Mexico. Hairy twigs are five-angled and armed with curved yellowish roselike prickles. Small pinkish purple flowers crowded on slender spikes 1 to 4 inches (2.5 to 10 cm) long appear in mid to late summer. Hairy bean pods 1 to 2 1/2 inches (2.5 to 6.5 cm) long and 1/4 inch (0.5 cm) wide are constricted between the seeds.

Mulhenbergia capillaris

Pink mulhy

Poaceae (Gramineae) family

COLD HARDINESS

All three zones.

LANDSCAPE VALUE

A handsome grass clump at any season, but a real traffic-stopper in late summer and fall because of the spectacular color of its plumes (hot pink). Especially striking when planted where back-lit by the fall sun.

CULTURAL REQUIREMENTS

- **Exposure:** Full sun, including reflected sun to part shade.
- **Water:** Drought tolerant but watering every week or two in summer will ensure a good color display at the end of the season.
- **Soil:** Most soils, but appreciates good garden treatment, especially in summer.
- **Propagation:** Seed or divisions.
- **Maintenance:** There is a short period in winter when you need to groom the plant and remove old blooms and growth.

POSSIBLE PROBLEMS

None observed.

A lush green clump of grass that, with good maintenance, rapidly reaches 3 to 4 feet (1 m) in height, with equal spread. This perennial puts on a showy display of large delicate misty pink plumes in late summer. The display lasts well into the fall and completely covers the foliage. Evergreen in frost-free locations, turning tan with frost. A native of southern Texas and northern Mexico. A selection ('Regal Mist™') is offered.

* See Glossary

Mulhenbergia dumosa

Bamboo mulhy

Poaceae (Gramineae) family

COLD HARDINESS

Low and intermediate zones. Probably would succeed in many areas of the high zone. Hardy to moderate frost.

LANDSCAPE VALUE

- Billowy, graceful fine-textured foliage makes this an eye-catching small specimen or accent grass.
- Can be massed as a foundation plant.
- Its color, form and texture provide a pleasing contrast with other low-water-use plants.
- Adaptable to container culture.

CULTURAL REQUIREMENTS

- **Exposure:** Full sun to part shade.
- **Water:** Needs water every couple weeks to every couple months to look attractive as an established plant. It tolerates, but turns brown during long periods of drought, and greens up when moisture becomes available again.
- **Soil:** Grows in many arid-climate soils.
- **Propagation:** Seed or clump divisions.
- **Maintenance:** Thin out if high portions freeze or if the plant grows too large. Periodically remove dry old growth to maintain good appearance.

POSSIBLE PROBLEMS

None observed.

Dense perennial clump-forming grass that rapidly grows 3 to 6 feet (1 to 2 m) in height, with equal spread. Abundant stems are stout and woody. Narrow, curving leaf blades are up to 4 3/4 inches (12 cm) long. The plant is green with moisture but turns brown if very dry. Looks tan in spring as it flowers in clusters on woody stems and produces seed. Native to southern Arizona, and Sonora, Mexico.

Muhlenbergia emersleyi

Bull grass

Poaceae (Gramineae) family

COLD HARDINESS

Low and intermediate zones and warm-winter microclimates of high zone.

LANDSCAPE VALUE

- A bold grass that adds strong textural interest and ambiance in transition and arid zones of the landscape.
- Revegetation and erosion control.

CULTURAL REQUIREMENTS

- **Exposure:** Full sun. Tolerates light shade.
- **Water:** Water every week or two through the heat of summer, every month or two during the cooler months.
- **Soil:** Most soils with good drainage.
- **Propagation:** Seed or clump divisions.
- **Maintenance:** Cut back old clumps to ground level to stimulate fresh attractive new growth.

POSSIBLE PROBLEMS

None observed.

This perennial grass grows at a moderate rate as a large dense mound of evergreen foliage, 5 feet (1.5 m) in height, with equal spread. The leaf stems are erect and hairless, flattened and broader toward the sheath or leaf base. Delicate loose flower spikes open on stems as much as 16 inches (40.5 cm) above the foliage mass in fall. The native range extends from the U.S. Southwest to Panama.

** See Glossary*

Muhlenbergia rigens

Deer grass

Poaceae (Gramineae) family

COLD HARDINESS

All three zones. Foliage is evergreen in warm-winter microclimates of low zone. In intermediate and high zones, leaves may turn brown with cold winter temperatures but roots and base of the plant are hardy.

LANDSCAPE VALUE

- Accent and contrast, either as a single specimen or in mass plantings.
- In oasis, transition and arid zones of the landscape.

CULTURAL REQUIREMENTS

- **Exposure:** Full sun to part shade.
- **Water:** Water established plants every month or two during the warm months. More frequent watering results in a bigger, more lush plant. Water once or twice during the winter season is sufficient for good appearance.
- **Soil:** Most soils with good drainage.
- **Propagation:** Seed or clump divisions.
- **Maintenance:** Prune back old clumps close to the base of the plant for attractive renewal growth.

POSSIBLE PROBLEMS

None observed.

Semi-evergreen perennial grass that grows rapidly to 4 feet (1 m) high, with equal spread. Its crowded slender foliage gives the plant a dense mounding growth habit. In summer, inconspicuous brown flowers open in spikes 5 inches (13 cm) long or longer on thin stalks to 6 feet (2 m) tall. Native range covers parts of California, Arizona, New Mexico, Texas and northern Mexico.

Myoporum parvifolium

Trailing myoporum

Myoporaceae family

COLD HARDINESS

Low zone and warmer microclimates of intermediate zone. Moderately frost tolerant.

LANDSCAPE VALUE

- Dense, neat, lush-looking groundcover for slopes, banks and mounds as well as open level areas.
- Effective among boulders.

CULTURAL REQUIREMENTS

- **Exposure:** Full sun to part shade.
- **Water:** Water every week or two during summer to maintain density and vigorous growth, less frequently in winter.
- **Soil:** Good quality well-draining soil. Not adapted to heavy, wet soil types.
- **Propagation:** Cuttings.
- **Maintenance:** Provide adequate growing space.

POSSIBLE PROBLEMS

None observed.

Low mat-forming evergreen groundcover that rapidly spreads to about 9 feet (3 m) and grows 3 to 6 inches (7.5 to 15 cm) high. Spreads by long trailing stems that root as they grow. Medium green leaves are bright and about 1/2 to 1 inch (1 to 2.5 cm) long. White flowers, 1/2 inch (1 cm) across, open in spring; berries that follow are purple. Native to Australia.

** See Glossary*

Myrtus communis (M. communis 'Compacta')

True myrtle, Roman myrtle, Compact Roman myrtle

Myrtaceae family

COLD HARDINESS
All three zones. Frost hardy.

LANDSCAPE VALUE
- Large hedge, clipped or unclipped, privacy screen, background or space definer where there is ample space.
- Handsome specimen tree with pruning to reveal the beautiful natural branching habit.
- 'Compacta': low formal hedge, edging, space definer or in containers.

CULTURAL REQUIREMENTS
- **Exposure:** Full to reflected sun or part shade. Avoid heavy shade.
- **Water:** Water every month or two when mature to maintain satisfactory landscape appearance, but more often when getting established and growing to desired size.
- **Soil:** Garden soils with good drainage. Avoid soggy soils.
- **Propagation:** Cuttings best to maintain uniform characteristics. Seed possible.
- **Maintenance:** Easy to grow and reliable.

POSSIBLE PROBLEMS
Overwatering results in chlorotic* leaves.

Dense rounded evergreen shrub that grows 5 to 7 feet (1.5 to 2 m) high and spreads 4 to 6 feet (1 to 2 m). Unclipped plants eventually become small trees 15 feet (4.5 m) high and wide. Grows at a moderate rate. Shiny dark green leaves are oval or lance-shaped, to 2 inches (5 cm) long and aromatic when crushed. Fragrant white or pinkish flowers $\frac{3}{4}$ inch (2 cm) in diameter bloom spring through summer. Blue-black fruits grow to $\frac{1}{2}$ inch (1 cm) long. Cultivars* include 'Compacta,' which is dwarf and dense with small leaves. Grows slowly to 3 feet (1 m) tall and wide. Native to the Mediterranean region and southwestern Europe.

Myrtus communis 'Boetica'

Twisted myrtle

Myrtaceae family

COLD HARDINESS
All three zones.

LANDSCAPE VALUE
- Large evergreen shrub that can be pruned into a multi-stemmed, twisted small tree.
- Not a good choice for clipped hedging for which other varieties are so often used, but a good plant where its silhouette can be appreciated.
- It can take on Bonsai characteristics in containers.

CULTURAL REQUIREMENTS
- **Exposure:** Full sun to part shade.
- **Water:** Water every week or two when plant is young, every month or two once mature.
- **Soil:** Most soils with good drainage, but garden soil is best.
- **Propagation:** Cuttings.
- **Maintenance:** Needs some grooming to maintain silhouette.

POSSIBLE PROBLEMS
None observed.

Though a variety of the species *M. communis*, the unique character of 'Boetica' warrants a separate description. Small, aromatic dark green leaves are borne on twisty branches. The entire shrub takes on an interesting gnarled form. Bark is light tan when mature. Small white star-like flowers bloom in clusters spring through summer, followed by purple-black fruit. This description would apply to many of the other *M. communis* cultivars* long grown in the nursery industry, but this variety is not as common and is especially suited to the desert environment. Grows at a moderate rate from 9 to 12 feet (3 to 3.5 m) high or higher, with equal spread.

** See Glossary*

Nerium oleander

Oleander

Apocynaceae family

COLD HARDINESS

Low zone and, depending on variety, intermediate zone. 'Little Red,' for example, is quite frost tolerant, whereas 'Petite Pink' and 'Petite Salmon' may show significant injury following a hard frost. Choose varieties that are adapted to local winters.

LANDSCAPE VALUE

- Shrub background or border.
- Space definer, privacy screen, windbreak.
- Foundation plant.
- Small tree.
- Flowering specimen or accent plant.
- Highway and street median plantings.
- Containers and tubs.

CULTURAL REQUIREMENTS

- **Exposure:** Blooms best in full sun. Tolerates part shade. Withstands great heat and moderate to hard frost, depending on variety. Tolerant of smog and salty seashore conditions, but not well adapted to cool foggy climates.
- **Water:** Drought resistant. Survives long dry periods, although considerable leaf drop may occur. Thoroughly soak the root zone every month or two to ensure excellent landscape performance. Water more often during the hottest season to ensure good blooming.
- **Soil:** Performs well in a wide range of soil conditions.
- **Propagation:** Cuttings.
- **Maintenance:** To control size and form, prune in early spring.

POSSIBLE PROBLEMS

- Bacterial gall*, scale insects, leaf spot diseases, witches' broom, yellow oleander aphid.
- Oleander scorch, a viral disease spread by pruning clippers, has become a problem in Southern California.
- Spent blooms of double-flowered varieties remain on plant and turn brown.
- Aggressive roots may stunt adjoining plantings.
- All parts of the plant are toxic.

An evergreen shrub or tree native to the Mediterranean region and Asia, widely cultivated in warm climates as a versatile, undemanding landscape plant. Grows rapidly with adequate soil moisture from 3 to 20 feet (1 to 6 m) high and 3 to 12 feet (1 to 3.5 m) wide, depending on variety. Many selections have been made over the years on the basis of flower and plant-size characteristics. The typical tree is single- or multitrunked with a rounded spreading crown. Foliage on trees and shrubs is dense, thick and leathery and medium to deep green. At least one variegated type has creamy yellow leaf margins. Depending on variety, the leaves may be 3 to 12 inches (7.5 to 30.5 cm) long and linear to lance-shaped with smooth margins. They grow in pairs or, more commonly, in whorls. Terminal* clusters of funnel-shaped flowers, 2 to 3 inches (5 to 7.5 cm) across, range in color from white, yellow, many shades of pink, salmon and red. They grow as single or double blooms and are sometimes fragrant. Flowering takes place throughout the warm months, but the spring bloom crop may be the most abundant, putting on a tremendous flower show. There are some smaller types: 'Mrs. Roeding' is salmon pink, has narrower leaves and grows only 6 feet (2 m) tall. 'Petite pink' and 'Petite Salmon' can be only 4 to 5 feet (1 to 1.5 m) or shorter but are less hardy than more popular varieties. All parts of the plant are toxic to humans and animals, as is the smoke from burning oleander wood.

** See Glossary*

Nicotiana glauca

Tree tobacco

Solanaceae family

COLD HARDINESS

Low zone and warm microclimates of the intermediate zone. Withstands light to moderate frost.

LANDSCAPE VALUE

- Revegetation of disturbed areas.
- Quick, temporary shade or visual screen.
- Open areas and dry sites.
- Sometimes tamed for gardens to attract hummingbirds.

CULTURAL REQUIREMENTS

- **Exposure:** Full to reflected sun or part shade.
- **Water:** Drought tolerant. For garden use, water every month or two during hot, dry weather to improve appearance.
- **Soil:** Grows in many soil types, including sandy and gravelly.
- **Propagation:** Seed.
- **Maintenance:** Low maintenance.

POSSIBLE PROBLEMS

- Not an especially neat or refined plant; tends to be straggly and unsightly in stressful situations.
- Volunteer seedlings may require removal.
- Leaves and stems reported to be poisonous.

Thick bluish-green leaves 1½ to 6 inches (4 to 15 cm) long and 3 inches (7.5 cm) wide make up the open, often irregular crown of this small tree or large shrub. Foliage is poisonous and sheds with severe frost- or drought-stress. New growth is covered with a white powdery pubescence. Through spring and summer, loose clusters of tubular yellow flowers open at the branch tips. These tubular flowers, 1½ to 2 inches (4 to 5 cm) long, are attractive to hummingbirds. Native to Bolivia and Argentina, naturalized from California to Texas and in Mexico. Rapidly grows 10 to 30 feet (3 to 9 m) high and 10 feet (3 m) wide.

Nolina bigelovii bigelovii

Bigelow nolina

Agavaceae family

COLD HARDINESS

All three zones.

LANDSCAPE VALUE

- Dramatic accent plant.
- Makes an interesting pattern against plain walls or the sky.

CULTURAL REQUIREMENTS

- **Exposure:** Full sun to shade.
- **Water:** Drought resistant. Water every month or two in low zone, less often in higher zones.
- **Soil:** Most soils with good drainage.
- **Propagation:** Seed.
- **Maintenance:** Low maintenance.

POSSIBLE PROBLEMS

None observed.

The trunk of this *Nolina* reaches about 3 feet (1 m) high. Leaves add about 3 or 4 more feet (1 m) to height and grow in a large rosette*. Spreads about 3 feet (1 m) as well. Narrow gray-green leaves have blunt tips. Old leaves hang like thatch on the trunk. Creamy green blossoms on 4-foot (1-m) stalks are not colorful but add silhouette interest. They bloom from spring through summer. Native to southwestern United States.

Note: *N. parryi,* Parry Nolina, is identified by some authorities as a subspecies of *N. bigelovii.* Either way, from a landscape point of view, the use and requirements are similar.

* *See Glossary*

Nolina longifolia

Mexican grass tree

Agavaceae family

COLD HARDINESS

Low and intermediate zones. Probably high zone.

LANDSCAPE VALUE

- Bold accent plant.
- Combines well with other dramatic plants.
- Greenness provides a tropical feel.
- Combines well with palms and yuccas.
- Container plant.

CULTURAL REQUIREMENTS

- **Exposure:** Full sun to open shade.
- **Water:** Quite drought resistant once established. Soak the root zone every week or two during the warm season to speed growth.
- **Soil:** Most soils with good drainage.
- **Propagation:** Seed.
- **Maintenance:** Low maintenance.

POSSIBLE PROBLEMS

Slow growth limits the availability of this good landscape plant.

This plant spreads 3 to 9 feet (1 to 3 m) at a slow to moderate pace. Trunks grow 6 to 10 feet (2 to 3 m), plus at least another 3 feet (1 m) of foliage. Wiry, bright green grasslike leaves are arranged in whorls on trunks, which sometimes have side branches. For a number of years, the plant will be only a foliage clump. Later, trunks begin to develop. Flowers and stalks resemble those of other *Nolinas*, which have some silhouette value. Native from the U.S. Southwest throughout northern Mexico.

Nolina matapensis

Tree bear grass

Agavaceae family

COLD HARDINESS

Low and intermediate zones where it tolerates considerable frost with no damage. Probably will tolerate warmer locations in high zone. It appears to be quite hardy.

LANDSCAPE VALUE

- Unique accent plant.
- Dramatic silhouette against the sky.

CULTURAL REQUIREMENTS

- **Exposure:** Full sun to part shade.
- **Water:** Drought resistant. Thoroughly soak the root zone every week or two during the warm season to speed growth.
- **Soil:** Most soils with good drainage.
- **Propagation:** Seed. Old plants do transplant readily.
- **Maintenance:** Low maintenance.

POSSIBLE PROBLEMS

Slowness to develop may prevent this outstanding landscape plant from becoming readily available.

Unusual tree with a heavy trunk and many slim branches. Grows at a moderate rate, from 9 to 26 feet (3 to 8 m) high and 10 feet (3 m) wide, but it is slow to develop trunk and branches. Each branch is topped with a whorl of flat, gray-green straplike leaves, which are sometimes 9 feet (3 m) long. Blossoms and flower stalks resemble other *Nolina* species but are less noticeable in contrast with the arborescent form.

** See Glossary*

Nolina microcarpa

Bear grass

Agavaceae family

COLD HARDINESS

All three zones.

LANDSCAPE VALUE

- Grassy accent plant.
- Adds interest to planters.
- Banks and medians.
- Rock gardens.

CULTURAL REQUIREMENTS

- **Exposure:** Full sun to open shade. Tolerates exposed situations.
- **Water:** Drought resistant. Thoroughly soak the root zone every month or two.
- **Soil:** Any soil.
- **Propagation:** Divisions or seed.
- **Maintenance:** Low maintenance.

POSSIBLE PROBLEMS

Tends to be too shaggy for refined situations.

Bold clumps of grasslike leaves spread into clumps 6 feet (2 m) or more across. Grows up to 3 feet (1 m) high. Somewhat slow to develop in early stages. The margins have minute teeth and are arranged in a series of rosettes* that grow from underground stems. Branching cluster of pale green to white flowers appear in spring. Blossom stalks generally extend well above foliage, adding interest but not much color—off-white to greenish. Native to U.S. Southwest and northern Mexico.

Nolina recurvata (Beaucarnea recurvata)

Pony tail palm, Bottle palm

Agavaceae family

COLD HARDINESS

Outdoor planting in the low zone and warm locations in intermediate zone; container planting anywhere—move to protected location in cold-winter microclimates.

LANDSCAPE VALUE

- Great, long-lived container plant (container limits size).
- Unique, picturesque, tropical-appearing silhouette tree.

CULTURAL REQUIREMENTS

- **Exposure:** Full or reflected sun to open shade.
- **Water:** Tolerates periods of drought, but best with thorough soakings of the root zone every week to every couple of months, depending on your location.
- **Soil:** Most soils with good drainage, especially when container-grown. Tolerates being root-bound for years.
- **Propagation:** Seed.
- **Maintenance:** Low maintenance.

POSSIBLE PROBLEMS

None observed.

Grass tree that grows 12 to 15 feet (3.5 to 4.5 m) tall, sometimes taller, and spreads 9 to 12 feet (3 to 3.5 m). Slow to moderate growth rate, depending on location and growing conditions. Narrow bright green leaves up to 3 feet (1 m) long grow in dense, moplike, weeping clusters at the tips of slender upright branches. One to several trunks rise from a bulbous base. This bottlelike bulbous base can completely fill the top of a container and in the ground can measure several feet across. Mature outdoor specimens produce clusters of inconspicuous, small white flowers during the warm season. Native to Mexico.

* *See Glossary*

Oenothera berlandieri (O. speciosa childsii)

Mexican evening primrose

Onagraceae family

COLD HARDINESS

All three zones. Moderately frost tolerant. Recovers quickly in spring even when killed back to the ground.

LANDSCAPE VALUE

- Spring color and interest.
- At the base of boulders, beneath the filtered shade of desert trees and in wildflower plantings.
- Borders along walks, paths and garden walls and near patios and other outdoor living areas.
- Groundcover on slopes and in median or buffer plantings where its sparse summer and winter appearance causes no objection.

CULTURAL REQUIREMENTS

- **Exposure:** Full to reflected sun or light shade.
- **Water:** Tolerates dry conditions but stays green and flowers over a longer period if watered every week or two in spring and summer, every month or two in winter.
- **Soil:** Remarkably adapted to a range of soils but at its best in good garden soil.
- **Propagation:** Root division. Runners.
- **Maintenance:** Cut back to near ground in early spring and again after spring bloom for best performance. May also require cutting back to control aggressive spreading growth.

POSSIBLE PROBLEMS

- Somewhat straggly appearance in summer and winter.
- Invasive habit makes it difficult to confine.

A fast-growing, sometimes invasive perennial that reaches 8 to 12 inches (20.5 to 30.5 cm) in height, 3 feet (1 m) in spread. Evergreen to drought- or cold-deciduous, this herbaceous* plant spreads by rhizomes* to form a low open cover. Leaves are 1 to 3 inches (2.5 to 7.5 cm) long and 1/2 inch (1 cm) wide. Bell-shaped flowers are white to rosy pink and 1 1/2 inches (4 cm) across. Blooms most abundantly in spring but also scattered through summer and fall with ample soil moisture. This plant typically has a semi-dormant period in summer as well as winter. In areas of cold winters, it dies back to the ground or is treated as an annual. Native to Texas and Mexico.

Oenothera caespitosa

White or evening primrose

Onagraceae family

COLD HARDINESS

All three zones. Evergreen in the low zone and warm-winter areas of intermediate zone. Deciduous where winters are more severe. The plant crown is cold hardy. Although the foliage may die back to the ground after a hard freeze, spring regrowth is rapid.

LANDSCAPE VALUE

- Seasonal flower display and dense foliage rosette* make a pleasing contrast with other arid-adapted plants.
- Seasonal color.
- For maximum landscape effect, place where its blooms will be viewed up close during the evening and into early morning.

CULTURAL REQUIREMENTS

- **Exposure:** Full sun.
- **Water:** Water every week or two during the period of active growth, every month or two just once or twice a season during dry winters.
- **Soil:** Fast-draining soil.
- **Propagation:** Seed or clump divisions.
- **Maintenance:** Low maintenance. Cut back cold-damaged foliage.

POSSIBLE PROBLEMS

Lacks winter interest when the foliage is killed by cold temperatures. In this case, cut dead foliage back to ground level.

Evergreen (except in cold-winter areas) that reaches about 8 to 12 inches (20.5 to 30.5 cm) in height and spreads to 2 feet (61 cm). Moderate to rapid growth rate, depending on soil moisture. This perennial primrose develops a thick tap root and a low-mounding clump of hairy leaves that are narrowly lance-shaped and 1 to 4 inches (2.5 to 10 cm) long by 3/4 inch (2 cm) wide. Solitary fragrant flowers 3 to 4 inches (7.5 to 10 cm) across are white when they open in early evening. By midmorning of the following day, the four petals turn pink, droop and finally shrivel on the stem. Flowering may occur throughout the warm season but is heaviest in spring and early summer. The fruit is a slender leathery capsule 1/2 to 3/4 inch (1 to 2 cm) long. White evening primrose and its several subspecies are native to large areas of the western United States.

** See Glossary*

Oenothera stubbei (O. drummondii)

Chihuahuan primrose

Onagraceae family

COLD HARDINESS

Low and intermediate zones.

LANDSCAPE VALUE

- The special landscape appeal of this primrose lies in its heavy carpet of dark green leaves and the showy yellow flowers that remain open at night, a peak-use period for many arid climate landscapes.
- Groundcover for control of soil erosion.

CULTURAL REQUIREMENTS

- **Exposure:** Full sun to part shade.
- **Water:** Established plants may survive long dry periods but in such weakened and unattractive conditions that they contribute little to the landscape. For best performance, water every week or two during the warm months, every month or two during winter. It will maintain a solid cover only with regular irrigation. Too little water and the clumps will separate, leaving bare space in between.
- **Soil:** Most soils with good drainage.
- **Propagation:** Offset* plants that develop along the runners*.
- **Maintenance:** Low maintenance.

POSSIBLE PROBLEMS

- Foliage is an irresistible delicacy for hungry rabbits.
- Plant may spread into areas where it is not wanted.

Evergreen herbaceous* perennial that reaches 5 inches (13 cm) in height and spreads 3 to 4 feet (1 m), with enough moisture. Spreads by runners* that take root and produce new plants as they grow and form clumps. Grows rapidly with regular water. Under favorable circumstances, plant colonies develop into a dense low mass of dark green vegetation. During the evening hours, solitary yellow four-petaled flowers 2 to 3 inches (5 to 7.5 cm) in diameter open on erect stems several inches above the foliage. Bloom is intermittent throughout the year but heaviest in spring. Native to northeastern Mexico.

Note: This plant has been misidentified as *O. drummondii* and, under this scientific name, was once sold as Baja primrose.

* See Glossary

Olea europaea
Olive
Oleaceae family

COLD HARDINESS
Low and intermediate zones and warm microclimates of high zone.

LANDSCAPE VALUE
- Medium shade tree.
- Patio or courtyard.
- Street, median, espalier.
- Large planters or containers.
- Parks.
- Massed for visual or wind screen.

CULTURAL REQUIREMENTS
- **Exposure:** Full to reflected sun or part shade.
- **Water:** Thoroughly soak the root zone every month or two from late spring through early fall. Water only once or twice, or not at all, during winter, depending on local climate.
- **Soil:** Most nonsaline soils with good drainage, but deep fertile soil is best.
- **Propagation:** Cuttings.
- **Maintenance:** Selectively prune and, in some cases, stake to produce the desired single- or multitrunked form. Apply growth-regulator sprays or thin out flowering stems during bloom period to eliminate or reduce fruit crop. Prune out basal sprouts regularly.

POSSIBLE PROBLEMS
- Verticillium wilt*, crown gall*, Texas root rot*, nematodes* and scale insects.
- Heavy pollen production of fruiting selections contribute to human allergy problems.
- Very sensitive to improperly applied herbicides.
- Fallen fruit creates considerable litter and temporarily stains paved surfaces.

This tough drought-resistant evergreen tree still holds its place as an important shade tree for arid regions. It grows at a slow to moderate rate, from 20 to 30 feet (6 to 9 m) high, with equal spread. Slender gray-green leaves to 3 inches (7.5 cm) long form the dense rounded crown. One to several smooth gray trunks become heavy, knotted and picturesquely contorted with age. In spring, tiny cream-colored flowers appear in axillary* clusters. Fleshy fruits are 1½ inches (4 cm) long and turn from green to black as they mature in fall. Native to the Mediterranean region. Various cultivars* have been selected, mostly for fruiting characteristics or for not producing pollen or fruit. The cultivar 'Swan Hill' does not produce airborne pollen and sets no fruit (important where allergies or fruit litter are a concern) and it is also verticillium-wilt resistant. 'Oblonga' is wilt-resistant also.

* See Glossary

Olneya tesota

Ironwood tree, Palo fierro, Tesota

Fabaceae (Leguminosae) family

COLD HARDINESS

Low zone and warm-winter microclimates of intermediate zone. Frost tender at times in intermediate zone.

LANDSCAPE VALUE

- Screening.
- Background.
- Shade.
- Spring color.
- Buffer plantings.
- Thorny barrier.
- Specimen.

CULTURAL REQUIREMENTS

- **Exposure:** Full to reflected sun. Performs well under harsh conditions. Best adapted to regions where winters are warm enough for citrus to grow.
- **Water:** Survives even severe droughts once established. Thoroughly soak the root zone every week to once or twice a season during summer to promote faster growth. Test soil for dryness to determine frequency in your particular location.
- **Soil:** Most soils with good drainage.
- **Propagation:** Seed. Scarify to aid germination.
- **Maintenance:** Prune over a period of several years to develop a shade tree.

POSSIBLE PROBLEMS

- Thorns limit use in pedestrian-traffic areas.
- Fallen leaves, flowers and seed pods create some litter.

Round topped and thorny evergreen tree that grows slowly from 15 to 30 feet (4.5 to 9 m) high and 15 to 25 feet (4.5 to 7.5 m) wide. Single- or multitrunked. The fine-textured gray-green foliage is generally shed just before bloom but may also drop as a result of hard frost or long drought. Bears masses of 1/2-inch (1-cm) wide lavender-pink blossoms in late spring. Mature seed pods are dark brown, hairy and 2 inches (5 cm) long. Twigs and young branches have needlelike thorns. Native to the Sonoran desert of the United States and Mexico.

* See Glossary

OPUNTIA

Opuntia, the prickly pear and cholla cactus genus and our largest cactus genus, is one of the most diverse in form, most abundant in species and most widely distributed geographically (Canada to the tropics) of any of the Cactaceae family. The species most useful for landscaping come from the deserts of the southwestern United States and northern Mexico. Many of them have dramatic form, are decorative and serve other useful functions in landscape design. The species in this book represent the range of distinctly different forms and functions, but there are many more species that could be chosen for similar uses. Those described as *prickly* or *cactus pear* have pad-shaped segments and large blossoms and fruit, usually showy and often edible. The prickly pear is useful for a variety of design functions in arid regions.

The *chollas* have less-showy flowers and noncolorful, inedible fruit. They are more heavily armed with stout spines that resemble sausage segments. These species are sometimes used in landscaping for their interesting structures, form and color of the spines.

Opuntia acicularis

Bristly prickly pear, Red-flowered prickly pear
Cactaceae family

COLD HARDINESS
All three zones.

LANDSCAPE VALUE
- Accent.
- Dominant center of interest in desert-plant compositions.
- Barrier.
- Foundation.
- Large containers away from foot traffic.

CULTURAL REQUIREMENTS
- **Exposure:** Full sun and reflected heat. Will take shade but color of plant will become bland and then new growth can become distorted.
- **Water:** Will survive on annual rainfall in most arid climates but supplemental water off and on during the warm season will speed up growth and development.
- **Soil:** Any soil with good drainage.
- **Propagation:** Rooting pads. Could be grown from seed but this is more time and energy consuming.
- **Maintenance:** Use tongs, not gloves, to handle plant parts.

POSSIBLE PROBLEMS
Difficult to handle pads for propagation and transplantation.

Large pads are medium green and dotted with prominent, full clusters of rusty brown glochids*. While the glochids represent a formidable armament, they are decorative with an interesting color in contrast with the green color of the pads. Spring bloom adds more color to this showy prickly pear with a display of large reddish orange flowers. These are bright enough to even be visible from a distance. Grows about 3 feet (1 m) at a moderate pace. Spreads the same but can form a larger patch or clump. Native to parts of the Chihuahuan Desert, southern Texas, and northeastern Mexico.

Opuntia basilaris

Beaver tail cactus, Beaver tail prickly pear
Cactaceae family

COLD HARDINESS
Low and intermediate zones and often into high zone.

LANDSCAPE VALUE
- Low barrier.
- Naturalizing in desert areas to which it is adapted.
- Accent or focal point.

CULTURAL REQUIREMENTS
- **Exposure:** Full sun and hot-desert environments with drying winds.
- **Water:** Watering once or twice a season during prolonged droughts may enhance plant growth and flowering but irrigation is seldom necessary for survival.
- **Soil:** Any soil with good drainage, including poor sterile types.
- **Propagation:** Pad (stem) cuttings.
- **Maintenance:** Use tongs, not gloves, to handle plant parts.

POSSIBLE PROBLEMS
Cochineal* scale infestations may become heavy enough to require control measures.

Beavers may not be common in the native habitat of this cactus, but its flattened oval stems, or pads, resemble the tail of that animal. Reaches about 1 foot (30.5 cm) high and spreads to 4 feet (1 m). Grows at a moderate pace. Densely covered with fine hair, like glochids*, the pads are blue-gray, occasionally with a red or purplish tint, and grow from 3 to as much as 8 inches (7.5 to 20.5 cm) long and 4 to 6 inches (10 to 15 cm) wide. New growth originates mostly from lower areas of existing stems and near the plant base to give this *Opuntia* its characteristic low-spreading form. Although thornless, beaver tail prickly pear is well protected by tiny barbed bristles that grow in crowded clumps called *areoles** on the pad surface. Once lodged in the skin, these are painful and difficult to remove. From spring into early summer, flowers 4 to 6 inches (10 to 15 cm) across and intensely rose-purple to pink open on the high edge of pads. When mature, the oval to rounded 2-inch (5-cm) long fruit is dry. Native to areas in Arizona, Utah, Nevada and California as well as Sonora and Baja California in Mexico.

* *See Glossary*

Opuntia bigelovii

Teddy bear cholla

Cactaceae family

COLD HARDINESS

Low and intermediate zones and probably warmer locations in high zone.

LANDSCAPE VALUE

An eye-catching centerpiece for a cactus and succulent garden or a barrier planting with an absolute no-trespassing guarantee.

CULTURAL REQUIREMENTS

- **Exposure:** Full sun, reflected heat.
- **Water:** No irrigation in regions receiving 3 to 4 inches (75 to 100 mm) annual rainfall. Water only once after planting.
- **Soil:** Grows among rocks or in any soil with good drainage.
- **Propagation:** Roots form from easily detached segments. Plant where it will remain permanently. Lobes will root on surface but best to bury stem end for assured rooting in chosen location because they can be moved around by wind. Warm season is the best time to propagate.
- **Maintenance:** Use tongs, not gloves, to handle plant parts.

POSSIBLE PROBLEMS

Barbed spine-covered segments easily break off and attach to the unsuspecting passerby. Do not plant near pedestrian traffic.

The most handsome and appealing of the cholla tribe and without a doubt the most wicked. This upright cactus on a sturdy straight trunk is covered with persistent old spines that turn a sooty brown or black, a striking contrast to younger growth on top that bears a dense interlocking array of light yellow spines. Strangely enough these light-colored spines give the illusion of softness, thus the name "Teddy bear." Flowers are inconspicuous. High terminal* joints are easily detached by unfortunate passing animals or humans, who carry them to new locations before successfully removing them. Joints then take root where discarded and a new colony is born. Grows at a slow to moderate pace from 3 to 6 feet (1 to 2 m) high and 3 feet (1 m) wide. Native to northern Mexico and Arizona, Nevada, and California.

Landscape Design Example

A colorful succulent mix at Boyce Thompson Southwest Arboretum.

* See Glossary

Opuntia engelmannii (O. phaecantha major disacta)

Engelmann's upright prickly pear

Cactaceae family

COLD HARDINESS

All three zones.

LANDSCAPE VALUE

- Barrier, banks and foundations.
- Foreground plant for other large desert succulent planting compositions.
- The flowering is showy and an abundant fruit set is colorful and edible, lasting most of the summer or until devoured by birds and rodents.

CULTURAL REQUIREMENTS

- **Exposure:** Reflected sun to part shade.
- **Water:** No supplemental water in regions receiving 3 inches (75 mm) or more annual rainfall.
- **Soil:** Any soil with good drainage.
- **Propagation:** Roots easily from pads or even smaller chunks of the plant, which send out roots if just laid on top of the ground. Can be grown from seed.
- **Maintenance:** Use tongs to handle plant parts.

POSSIBLE PROBLEMS

- Can be invasive as every discarded piece can start a new plant. Birds eat the fruit and seeds pass through their digestive system unharmed, thus spreading seed to new locations. Plant has naturalized into the Mediterranean region and become a pest in Australian grazing lands.
- Prickly pears are not only covered with spines, but they are also well protected by polka-dot tufts of short, soft-looking, almost silky little spines called *glochids**. These will attach to skin on contact, work through clothing or gloves.
- Fruits also are dotted with rosettes* of glochids and are generally disarmed by brushing with rolled pieces of paper.
- Subject to cochineal* scale; heavy infestations can be an unsightly problem.

Large shrubby plant that reaches 4 to 6 feet (1 to 2 m) high and spreads 4 to 15 feet (1 to 4.5 m), or even more (forms large clumps). Growth rate is moderate. New growth is usually limited to one spurt in spring each year. Dusty green pad-shaped segments are up to 12 inches (30.5 cm) long. Showy green-yellow to orange flowers are about 3 inches (7.5 cm) and appear midspring. Abundant egg-shaped red fruit appear in summer and are decorative and edible. Short brown glochids occasionally have a long spine. Native to U.S. desert Southwest and into Mexico.

** See Glossary*

Opuntia ficus-indica

India fig, Tuna cactus

Cactaceae family

COLD HARDINESS

Low zone and protected microclimates of intermediate zone. Sometimes seen in warmer locations in high zone, too. Tender to hard frost.

LANDSCAPE VALUE

- Striking silhouette plant.
- Informal space-definer screen or barrier.
- Large container plant.
- Colorful flowers.
- Edible fruit.

CULTURAL REQUIREMENTS

- **Exposure:** Full to reflected sun.
- **Water:** Water every month or two during the warm season, rarely, if at all, in winter.
- **Soil:** Most soils with good drainage.
- **Propagation:** Cuttings. A large many-segmented branch cut from mature plants will root in new locations, saving growing time for more instant effects.
- **Maintenance**: May require occasional shaping for control or removal of frost-damaged segments. Otherwise almost maintenance free.

POSSIBLE PROBLEMS

- Cochineal* scale is an occasional problem.
- Discarded pads will root where they fall, making disposal of prunings a problem.

Evergreen succulent that slowly grows shrubby or even tree-like on favored sites, up to about 15 feet (4.5 m) high and 10 feet (3 m) wide. Smooth green pads are 12 to 20 inches (30.5 to 51 cm) long. They are usually free of spines but may have scattered small clusters of bristles (glochids*). Attractive cup-shaped flowers are yellow to orange, numerous in late spring and early summer, usually about 3 to 5 inches (7.5 to 13 cm) across. The rounded, fleshy fruit armed with small, sharp bristles are 2 to 3½ inches (5 to 9 cm) long and turn from yellow to red or purplish red when ripe. These are edible and harvested by man as well as various birds and animals. Native habitat unknown; cultivated in many subtropical and tropical regions.

Opuntia fulgida

Chainfruit cholla

Cactaceae family

COLD HARDINESS

All three zones.

LANDSCAPE VALUE

A dramatic background cholla and barrier plant, but plant away from foot traffic.

CULTURAL REQUIREMENTS

- **Exposure:** Full sun to open shade.
- **Water:** No irrigation required in regions receiving 5 inches (130 mm) annual rainfall.
- **Soil:** Most soils with good drainage.
- **Propagation:** Cuttings.
- **Maintenance:** Use tongs, not gloves, to handle plant.

POSSIBLE PROBLEMS

- A difficult species to handle because of spines.
- Spiny segments break loose and can blow around. Keep well away from paths.
- Blowing litter, paper, leaves and such can lodge in plantings and are difficult to remove.

A sturdy treelike cholla that grows at a slow to moderate pace up to 12 feet (3.5 m) high and 6 feet (2 m) wide. Usually develops a distinct well-defined trunk with numerous sausage-link spiny branches. Spines are straw-colored and formidable (the favorite habitat for the Arizona cactus wren, which nests in it). Flowers are whitish pink, 1 inch (2.5 cm) across and not showy. They bloom midspring. Small green fruit usually remain on plant, blooming from last year's fruit to form drooping chains of fruit. If broken off, fruit will take root where they fall and start a new plant. Native to U.S. desert Southwest and into Mexico.

* *See Glossary*

Opuntia lindheimeri forma linguiformis

Cow's tongue prickly pear

Cactaceae family

COLD HARDINESS

All three zones.

LANDSCAPE VALUE

- Strong vertical thrust of pads create a more exciting, strong statement for accent planting.
- Foundation, banks, medians.

CULTURAL REQUIREMENTS

- **Exposure:** Full or reflected sun. Tolerates open shade, but growth will become leggy and floppy.
- **Water:** No irrigation in regions receiving 3 to 4 inches (75 to 100 mm) annual rainfall. Water once or twice during prolonged drought to stimulate new growth and plumpness of existing pads as well as encourage flowering and decorative fruit production.
- **Soil:** Any soil, from sand to clay, with good drainage.
- **Propagation:** Cutting.
- **Maintenance:** Use tongs, not gloves, to handle plant parts.

POSSIBLE PROBLEMS

- Occasional Cochineal* scale infestations can require control measures.
- Weeding and removal of wind-blown litter in a large clump is often difficult.

The elongated pads of this cactus taper almost to a point from a broad base, which is unusual. This departure from the common Texas prickly pear occurred in only one spot in nature (in Texas) and has since disappeared entirely in the wild. However, this bizarre form has so attracted cactus fanciers that it is now commonly seen in Southwest cactus gardens and desert landscapes in general, thanks to its ease of propagation by cutting. Probably there are more plants in existence now then there ever were in the wild. Flowers and fruit are similar to other prickly pears. Grows at a moderate pace to about 6 feet (2 m) high, usually less. Spreads about 6 feet (2 m) but can spread indefinitely as the outer pads root and extend the clump.

Opuntia microdasys

Bunny ears

Cactaceae family

COLD HARDINESS

Low and intermediate zones.

LANDSCAPE VALUE

- Picturesque shape, interesting texture and a showy display of summer flowers make bunny ears a worthy accent or specimen succulent in the arid landscape.
- Grows well in containers and remains much smaller than field-grown plants.

CULTURAL REQUIREMENTS

- **Exposure:** Full to reflected sun. Tolerates intense heat and aridity.
- **Water:** Established plants survive without irrigation. During long dry periods a fresh and lively appearance can be maintained with water once or twice a season.
- **Soil:** Most desert soils with good drainage.
- **Propagation:** Cuttings.
- **Maintenance:** Needs little care other than occasional shaping to direct growth.

POSSIBLE PROBLEMS

Cochineal* scale.

Low-growing cactus that rapidly reaches 2 to 3 feet (61 cm to 1 m) high and 4 to 5 feet (1 to 1.5 m) wide. Small ear-shaped young pads growing along the flat high edge of mature pads, up to 6 inches (15 cm) across, give this species a rabbitlike profile and its common name. Conspicuous tufts of yellow to light brown barbed bristles grow in a closely spaced orderly arrangement over the pad surfaces. Although harmless looking compared to the long thorns of some cacti, these bristles are easily detached and painful to remove once embedded in human skin. Creamy yellow flowers, 1½ to 2 inches (4 to 5 cm) in diameter, open in summer and are replaced by red globe-shaped fruit. 'Albaspina' has white bristles and the variety 'Rufidula' (red bunny ears) has reddish bristles. Native to Texas and northern Mexico.

** See Glossary*

Opuntia phaecantha (O. phaecantha major, O. mojavensis)

Sprawling Engelmann prickly pear

Cactaceae family

Spreading, spiny succulent with branches composed of paddle-shaped segments, radiating in all directions to create an impressive clump. Grows at a moderate pace, but new growth is usually limited to one spurt in spring each year. Averages 3 feet (1 m) in height but can spread as much as 9 to 10 feet (3 m). In midspring, arrays of buds appear on the edges of the highest pads. These buds develop into showy blossoms, yellow flushed with red. The flowers are about 2½ to 3½ inches (6.5 to 9 cm) across and are followed by wine red, elongated oval-shaped fruits, which are edible and tasty (used for jams and jellies), as well as decorative. *O. phaecantha major* is the *Opuntia* most think of when referring to prickly pears. Native to U.S. desert Southwest and into Mexico.

COLD HARDINESS

All three zones.

LANDSCAPE VALUE

- Sprawling barrier planting.
- Banks.
- Foundation plant for other desert succulent planting compositions.
- Flowers are showy and abundant red fruit is colorful and edible, lasting most of the summer or until devoured by birds or rodents.

CULTURAL REQUIREMENTS

- **Exposure:** Reflected sun to part shade.
- **Water:** No supplemental water is needed in regions receiving 5 inches (130 mm) or more of annual rain.
- **Soil:** Any soil with good drainage.
- **Propagation:** Roots easily from pads or even smaller chunks of the plant, which will literally send out roots if just laid on top the ground. Can be grown from seed.
- **Maintenance:** Use tongs to handle plant parts.

POSSIBLE PROBLEMS

- Can be invasive because every discarded piece can start a new plant. Birds eat the fruit and seeds pass through their digestive system, spreading seed to new locations. Plant has naturalized into the Mediterranean region and become a pest in Australian grazing lands.
- Prickly pears are not just covered with longer spines, but they are also well protected by polka-dot tufts of short, soft-looking, almost silky little spines called *glochids**. These will attach to skin on contact, work through clothing or gloves.
- Fruits also are dotted with rosettes* of glochids and are generally disarmed by brushing with rolled pieces of paper.
- Cochineal* scale can be disfiguring.

Opuntia versicolor

Staghorn cholla

Cactaceae family

A large cholla-type *Opuntia*, sometimes treelike, with a stout main trunk and a spreading crown of dark green to purplish sausage-like branches. Grows at a slow to moderate rate from 3 to 12 feet (1 to 3.5 m) high and 3 to 9 feet (1 to 3 m) wide. Less spiny than other chollas. Spring flowers are smaller (1 inch [2.5 cm]) than prickly-pear blossoms but unique in that plants in the same colony will vary in color. Blossoms can be lime green, yellow, orange, red, bronze or purple. Summer fruit is green and not interesting.

COLD HARDINESS

All three zones.

LANDSCAPE VALUE

- Large plant with good silhouette and interesting trunk and branch structure.
- Unusual flower colors vary from plant to plant if used in a colony. Mix by taking cuttings during spring flowering.
- Barrier or background plant.

CULTURAL REQUIREMENTS

- **Exposure:** Full sun.
- **Water:** No water in regions receiving 5 inches (130 mm) of annual rain.
- **Soil:** Any soil with good drainage.
- **Propagation:** Best grown from cuttings, preferably taken in spring or summer. Large plants can be easily transplanted bare root*. Leave dry after initial watering.
- **Maintenance:** Use tongs to handle plant parts.

POSSIBLE PROBLEMS

None observed.

* *See Glossary*

Opuntia violaceae santa rita

Purple-pad prickly pear, Purple prickly pear, Santa Rita prickly pear
Cactaceae family

COLD HARDINESS
Low and intermediate zones and into high zone. Moderately frost tolerant.

LANDSCAPE VALUE
- Colorful specimen or accent for dry sites.
- Showy contrast of yellow flowers on purple pads.

CULTURAL REQUIREMENTS
- **Exposure:** Full to reflected sun.
- **Water:** Quite drought tolerant. Water only to increase growth and size or once or twice during long dry periods in the warm season.
- **Soil:** Most soils with good drainage, including sandy or gravelly soils.
- **Propagation:** Rooting sections or cuttings.
- **Maintenance:** Use tongs to handle plant parts.

POSSIBLE PROBLEMS
Susceptible to cochineal* scale.

Low-growing evergreen succulent that develops a short trunk as it matures. Slowly reaches 2 to 5 feet (61 cm to 1.5 m) in height, with equal spread. The flat, rounded pads grow to 8 inches (20.5 cm) long. Pads of young plants turn red-purple when stressed by drought or cold; older specimens retain the distinctive purplish color year-round. Pads may or may not develop slender spines in the closely spaced clusters of yellowish bristles (glochids*) and grayish wool. Lemon yellow flowers 3 inches (7.5 cm) across open in spring. Oblong purple fruit is 1 inch (2.5 cm) long and 1/2 inch (1 cm) wide and ripens in summer Native from Arizona into Texas.

Osteomeles anthyllidifolia

Osteomeles
Rosaceae family

COLD HARDINESS
All three zones.

LANDSCAPE VALUE
- Background shrub.
- When planted in groups, develops into a mounding mass of fine-textured foliage.

CULTURAL REQUIREMENTS
- **Exposure:** Reflected sun to part shade.
- **Water:** Thoroughly soak the root zone every month or two.
- **Soil:** Most soils with good drainage.
- **Propagation:** Seed or cuttings.
- **Maintenance:** Low maintenance. May need shaping to fit site.

POSSIBLE PROBLEMS
None observed.

Attractive evergreen shrub that grows at a moderate pace from 6 to 8 feet (2 to 2.5 m) high and wide. Small pinnately* compound leaves are grayish and grow densely. Shrub is covered in spring with tiny white flowers that have a slight pinkish cast. Buds are pink. Native to China.

* *See Glossary*

Osteospermum fruticosum

Trailing African daisy

Asteraceae (Compositae) family

COLD HARDINESS

Low zone and warm-winter microclimates of intermediate zone. Moderately frost tolerant.

LANDSCAPE VALUE

- Untreadable groundcover for banks and flat areas.
- Early spring color.
- Planters, containers, hanging baskets.

CULTURAL REQUIREMENTS

- **Exposure:** Full sun to part shade. Best in a cool Mediterranean-type climate but adapts fairly well to hot-desert locations. Also grows in coastal environments.
- **Water:** Water every week or two, but keep an eye on soil moisture. Excessively wet soil conditions result in plant losses.
- **Soil:** Prefers well-drained garden soil but adapts to poor sandy soils.
- **Propagation:** Seed or cuttings.
- **Maintenance:** Prune back in late winter if leggy. Pinch stem tips anytime to encourage branching. Replant bare spots spring or fall.

POSSIBLE PROBLEMS

As plantings mature, unsightly bare spots appear and require replanting.

Low-spreading evergreen perennial that grows at a moderate to rapid rate from 6 to 12 inches (15 to 30.5 cm) high and 2 to 4 feet (61 cm to 1 m) wide. Long horizontal runners* root as they grow over moist soil. Light green fleshy leaves form a dense cover that is hidden in late winter or spring by a lavish display of light purple daisylike flowers 2 inches (5 cm) across. Deep purple varieties are available as well as white hybrids. The latter are slightly less cold hardy. Native to South Africa.

Pachycereus marginatus (Stenocereus marginatus)

Mexican fence

Cactaceae family

COLD HARDINESS

Low zone and warm microclimates of intermediate zone.

LANDSCAPE VALUE

- Accent, specimen or character plant in arid tropical settings.
- Within its native range it has often been planted to make a living fence or space divider.

CULTURAL REQUIREMENTS

- **Exposure:** Full to reflected sun.
- **Water:** Water once or twice a season during prolonged periods of hot dry weather in low-elevation arid landscapes.
- **Soil:** Most soils with good drainage.
- **Propagation:** Seed or stem-tip sections.
- **Maintenance:** Essentially maintenance free.

POSSIBLE PROBLEMS

New growth sometimes damaged by insects deforming the stem.

This unique and handsome columnar cactus grows at a slow to moderate pace up to 25 feet (7.5 m) high and 12 feet (3.5 m) wide. May grow as a single erect stem or branch treelike along the trunk or from the base of the plant. The smooth green stems have five to seven ribs and grow to a diameter of about 5 inches (13 cm) with sharp spines to 3/8 inch (1 cm) long. Tubular flowers with petals that are pink or red on the outside and whitish within occur singly or in pairs. They average about 2 inches (5 cm) long and occur midspring. The rounded fruit about 1 1/2 inches (4 cm) in diameter turns orange and bursts open when ripe to show yellowish to red flesh and many black seeds. This plant is sometimes called "organ pipe cactus" but should not be confused with *Stenocereus thurberi*, the organ pipe cactus of the Sonoran Desert. Native to central and southern Mexico.

* *See Glossary*

Pachypodium lamerei

Madagascar palm

Apocynaceae family

COLD HARDINESS

Low zone and warm microclimates in intermediate zone. Will tolerate only the lightest frosts.

LANDSCAPE VALUE

- Containers and large pots.
- In compositions with other bold succulents and eye-catching plants.
- Great silhouette possibilities.

CULTURAL REQUIREMENTS

- **Exposure:** Full sun, reflected heat to open shade
- **Water:** Tolerates brief periods of complete drying out in containers with no apparent stress, but needs water every week or two during the hot season for good foliage. Water less in winter, when it can go completely dry for several weeks at a time, especially when grown in borderline cool climates.
- **Soil:** Most soils with good drainage.
- **Propagation:** Seed or cuttings from secondary trunks and branches, when obtainable.
- **Maintenance:** No maintenance.

POSSIBLE PROBLEMS

None observed.

Succulent shrub that grows 3 to 12 feet (1 to 3.5 m) tall, often even taller. Cluster of trunks can spread 6 feet (2 m). Growth rate is moderate—slower when root bound and faster when planted in the ground. Single trunk or cluster of trunks are thick and thorny, gray-brown and upright. Side branches encircled with bright green straplike leaves that remotely resemble a palm, but this shrub has no relation to that family. Flowers are white and rarely seen. Native to Madagascar.

Paliurus spina-cristi (Ziziphus spina-cristi)

Christ thorn, Sider, Naba

Rhamnaceae family

COLD HARDINESS

Low and intermediate zones. Because of its wide regional distribution, hardiness varies, depending on origin of seed.

LANDSCAPE VALUE

- All-purpose medium shade tree, from parks to residential locations.
- Can be kept shrubby for large barrier planting or screening.
- Especially useful in areas with saline soil and poor quality water.

CULTURAL REQUIREMENTS

- **Exposure:** Full sun to part shade. Tolerates extreme heat and reflected sun.
- **Water:** Quite drought resistant. Thoroughly soak the root zone every month or two to ensure good appearance.
- **Soil:** Most soils.
- **Propagation:** Seed.
- **Maintenance:** Train young plants for suitable tree scaffold if desired.

POSSIBLE PROBLEMS

- Thorniness makes pruning and training difficult.
- Cost of removing volunteer seedlings that sprout in unwanted locations.

A broad-headed, thorny evergreen tree under favorable conditions, but usually just a large shrub. Grows at a moderate to rapid rate, depending on moisture supply, reaching 30 feet (9 m) in height, 25 feet (7.5 m) in spread. Small simple leaves have three midribs instead of one. Inconspicuous green-yellow spring flowers produce edible reddish fruit in summer. The small datelike fruit is nibbled on by passersby who discard the seed in new locations, where it readily germinates and grows into a new shrub or tree, often in seemingly hostile locations. These volunteers are a common sight in many Middle Eastern cities, contributing greenness and shade. A worthwhile tree when cared for and in a proper location. Native to warm areas of the Old World.

* See Glossary

PALMS

Worldwide there are more than two hundred genera of palms. This is in contrast with many other important plant groups, such as *Acacia*, *Agave*, *Bauhinia* and *Quercus* (oak), each of which has many species with a single genus. Despite their differences, all palm genera have certain characteristics in common that place them in the family Arecaceae (Palmae). From a landscape point of view, the distinctive form and look of palms make them a special design element, one that's hard to overlook.

Palms belong to the *monocotyledon* (monocots) subdivision of plants, which includes such familiar kinds as bamboo and other grasses, lilies, banana, and orchids and bromeliads. Woody trees, shrubs, vines and many other landscape plants are *dicotolydons* (dicots). These two subdivisions of the plant kingdom are distinguished by the number of first leaves (*cotyledons*) to develop from a germinating seed. Dicots have two or more seed leaves, as in a sprouting bean, and monocots have one seedling leaf, as in a germinating corn kernel.

Another difference between woody dicot plants and monocots like palms is that the former have bark and a cambium layer that gives rise to the tissues that transport water and nutrients throughout the plant. Woody dicots also produce distinct growth rings as the stem or trunk increases in diameter and develops a hard central cylinder. Monocots, on the other hand, have a pulpy, spongy center with an epidermis and vertical bundles of hard fibers arranged in a protective outer ring.

A dicot tree can be killed by a girdling cut through the cambium layer around the trunk. The same act to a palm might weaken it structurally and provide an entry court for disease organisms but would not be directly fatal to the plant. Trees like mesquite and acacia (dicots) produce terminal* buds at the tips of all their branches, but palms have one principal point of growth activity, the terminal bud at the center of the foliage crown.

Palms also have a different landscape appearance from most other plant groups. The trunk (or trunks in the case of multistemmed palms) is topped with a luxuriant head of foliage. This head grows upward from the terminal bud, often rapidly in youth, then slower as the palm approaches maturity. A few palm species branch from the trunk well above ground, but they are very rare.

Palms grow primarily in the tropics and subtropics with a few hardy species that survive in pockets along the lower edge or in the protected microclimates of the intermediate zone. Because of their unique form, often great height, and bold foliage, palms are dramatic landscape elements. To many people, especially in the temperate regions, palms represent a symbol of places with a more benevolent climate and a better place to live. This no doubt explains the heavy use of palms in resort areas and borderline climate zones such as Las Vegas, Nevada, and the French Riviera.

Palms are often inappropriately used in the landscape. New residents from the north often rush out to the nursery and purchase an attractive little Mexican fan palm or Canary Island date palm for their patio. Within a few years, however, the rapidly growing fan palm will be well above roof height and the only part visible from the patio will be the trunk, which can resemble a telephone pole. The date palm would soon take up all available space with long fronds springing from a massive trunk that resembles a huge pineapple.

The tall and massive palms have their place in large open spaces such as parks, around large buildings, in resorts, along wide avenues or where their unique patterns and silhouettes against the sky can be appreciated. The tall-growing Mexican fan palm (*Washingtonia robusta*) and the more massive date palms (*Phoenix canariensis* and *Phoenix dactylifera*) are especially appropriate for these uses.

Palms suitable for hot, dry landscapes come mostly from desert oases around the world. While most revel in the heat, palms can not be treated as drought-tolerant plants. Old palm trees may survive for years without irrigation, but gradually their luxuriant foliage will get smaller and then they will lose their picturesque beauty. Most palms, except for a few, need their root zone soaked every week or two to look well and belong in the minioasis part of the landscape design.

The palm family is one of the most unique and interesting groups of plants available for landscape use in the warm arid regions—they are the symbol of the oasis.

Palm genera covered in this book:

Acoelorraphe
Brahea
Butia
Chamaerops
Cocos
Phoenix
Sabal
Syagrus
Washingtonia

Parkinsonia aculeata

Mexican palo verde
Fabaceae (Leguminosae) family

COLD HARDINESS

Low and intermediate zones. Sometimes spreads into high zone. Less frost tolerant than other palo verdes.

LANDSCAPE VALUE

- Graceful and airy, yet tough and drought-resistant tree that provides light filtered shade.
- Accent or specimen tree valued for the bright yellow flower display in spring.
- Leaf midribs create almost constant litter or attractive mulch depending on situation.

CULTURAL REQUIREMENTS

- **Exposure:** Grows well under adverse conditions, especially as a young tree. Endures intense light and great heat and aridity.
- **Water:** Capable of surviving long dry periods as an established tree. For better landscape performance, soak the root zone every week to every couple of months, depending on your microclimate.
- **Soil:** Tolerates poor desert soils, but in good soil, growth is more rapid and luxuriant and foliage is more persistent foliage.
- **Propagation:** Seed.
- **Maintenance:** Low maintenance. Stake young trees and train for particular branching habit.

POSSIBLE PROBLEMS

- Susceptible to palo verde gall mites* and mistletoe, which disfigure growth.
- Trees are also attacked by palo verde root borer*.
- Generally not a long-lived tree.
- Foliage and bean-pod litter can clog drains and may require considerable cleanup where mulch is not wanted.
- Volunteer seedlings can be a costly nuisance where they are not wanted.
- Spiny growth discourages use in high pedestrian-traffic areas unless tree is trimmed above head height.

Semi-deciduous tree native or escaped from cultivation in southwestern United States, Mexico, West Indies, South America. Grows quickly from 15 to 35 feet (4.5 to 11 m) high, with equal spread. Smooth green bark on spiny twigs and branches becomes gray-brown and flaking only on lower trunk and large branches of older plants. The rounded, open fine-textured crown is made up mostly of leaf midribs that are slender, drooping and 6 to 9 inches (15 to 23 cm) long. Tiny leaflets that appear along the midribs are short-lived. They are shed under dry or cold conditions so that the tree is semi-leafless most of the year, except for the persistent midrib, which looks like a silky pine needle. The midribs may also fall in extreme drought or cold, but even then the green bark and twigs give the illusion of an evergreen tree. In late spring and occasionally during summer, loose showy flower clusters 2 to 7 inches (5 to 18 cm) long decorate the tree. Each flower has four yellow petals, one spotted red that turns completely red as it ages. Seed pods 2 to 6 inches (5 to 15 cm) long and constricted between the seeds ripen in summer.

* *See Glossary*

COLD HARDINESS
Evidence accumulated thus far indicates hardiness in low and intermediate zones, perhaps into high zone.

LANDSCAPE VALUE
- Shade.
- Specimen or color accent.
- Park.
- Buffer.
- Street or median.
- Good size for patios (and doesn't shed midribs, a habit that makes its *Parkinsonia* relatives poor patio trees).
- Resistant to major insect and disease pests.

CULTURAL REQUIREMENTS
- **Exposure:** Full to reflected sun.
- **Water:** Thoroughly soak the root zone of an established tree once or twice during long dry periods. Water young, developing trees more often, especially in summer.
- **Soil:** Most soils with good drainage.
- **Propagation:** Cutting only to maintain true form. Use greenwood cuttings under mist with bottom heat for best results.
- **Maintenance:** Low maintenance once established.

POSSIBLE PROBLEMS
Difficult to propagate and therefore not yet widely available. However, promising results have been achieved with new techniques (see Cultural Requirements above). Lack of availability should not be a long-term problem.

A hybrid palo verde whose parents include *P. aculeata, C. microphyllum* and *C. Floridum*. The resulting hybrid combines a number of highly desirable landscape traits: rapid, thornless growth; strong upright branching structure that requires little pruning or staking; large showy yellow flowers whose lavish color display lasts for a month or more; insignificant litter and few if any serious pest problems. This natural hybrid occurred near Tucson, Arizona, and was presented to the horticultural world by Dr. Mark Dimmit of the Arizona-Sonora Desert Museum. Grows 20 to 30 feet (6 to 9 m) high, with equal spread.

Parkinsonia aculeata X Cercidium floridum and C. microphyllum hybrid

Desert Museum hybrid palo verde, Parkincidium palo verde

Fabaceae (Leguminosae) family

* See Glossary

Passiflora foetida longipedunculata

Mulege, Passion vine

Passifloraceae family

COLD HARDINESS

Low zone. Can freeze back to ground in heavy frost and in intermediate zone, but it recovers quickly in spring.

LANDSCAPE VALUE

- Self-climbing.
- A delicate tracery for vine supports or over rocks.

CULTURAL REQUIREMENTS

- **Exposure:** Reflected sun to part shade.
- **Water:** Quite drought resistant. Thoroughly soak the root zone every month or two.
- **Soil:** Any soil with good drainage. Tolerates rocky, sandy conditions.
- **Propagation:** Seed.
- **Maintenance**: Head back some branches to control vigorous growth.

POSSIBLE PROBLEMS

Foliage has an unpleasant odor when bruised.

An attractive little gray-green evergreen vine that can sprawl 10 feet (3 m) in any direction, although it is usually smaller. Its moderate growth rate becomes rapid with regular moisture. Leaves are velvety and flowers are white to lavender, typical of *Passiflora.* Blooms throughout the warm season. Native to hot, rocky, sandy places in Baja California, so it has great tolerance for stressful situations.

Pedilanthus macrocarpus

Devil's backbone, Candelilla

Euphorbiaceae family

COLD HARDINESS

Low zone and warm microclimates of intermediate zone. Moderately frost tolerant.

LANDSCAPE VALUE

- Cluster of slender, upright stems offer unique plant form and texture.
- Small specimen or accent shrub.
- Interesting in containers.
- The red floral display along bare stems adds seasonal interest in late spring and sometimes in summer after rain.

CULTURAL REQUIREMENTS

- **Exposure:** Endures full sun and hot, dry difficult sites.
- **Water:** Quite drought tolerant. Established plants typically perform well without irrigation. During extreme drought, water once or twice a season. During the hot season, container plants grow best with water every week or two.
- **Soil:** Adapted to most sandy, rocky arid soils.
- **Propagation:** Clump divisions or cuttings.
- **Maintenance:** Essentially maintenance-free.

POSSIBLE PROBLEMS

Will damp-off* in containers with poor drainage.

Gray-green succulent shrub that grows slowly to 3 feet (1 m) high or higher and 2 feet (61 cm) wide or wider. Grows as a clump of erect forking stems and has the white milky juice characteristic of this family. Tiny leaves appear briefly on new growth and are shed soon after they emerge under dry conditions. As a result, the plant is leafless most of the year. Red "flowers" are actually slipper-shaped structures that each contain a tiny female flower and several male flowers. The blooms are 1 1/4 inches (3 cm) long and are striking at close range against the plump stems. They appear late spring into summer. Native to Mexico.

* *See Glossary*

Pelisiphonia brachysiphon (Macrosiphonia brachysiphon)

Rock trumpet

Apocynaceae family

COLD HARDINESS

Low and intermediate zones and into high zone, where it freezes back in winter but recovers quickly in spring.

LANDSCAPE VALUE

- A promising small shrub for borders, foundations and rock gardens.
- Its delicate quality and fragrance make it an especially appropriate choice for patios and intimate spaces.

CULTURAL REQUIREMENTS

- **Exposure:** Full sun to open shade.
- **Water:** Quite drought resistant as far as survival is concerned, but to encourage bloom and maintain a satisfactory appearance, thoroughly soak the root zone every week or two during the warm season.
- **Soil:** Most soils with good drainage.
- **Propagation:** Seed or cuttings.
- **Maintenance:** Cut back in winter.

POSSIBLE PROBLEMS

None observed, but plant is new to cultivation.

Attractive little evergreen shrub that grows to about 14 inches (35.5 cm) high and 2 inches (5 cm) wide in favorable situations. Growth rate is moderate and completely dependent on moisture supply. Leaves are small, green and slightly grayish. Fragrant white trumpet-shaped flowers, 1 inch (2.5 cm) long, are abundant when moisture is present during the warm season. Native to rocky foothills of the Arizona intermediate zone.

Pennisetum setaceum (P. setaceum 'Cupreum')

Fountain grass, Red fountain grass

Poaceae (Gramineae) family

COLD HARDINESS

All three zones. Buds at the clump base and roots are cold hardy.

LANDSCAPE VALUE

- Eye-catching ornamental grass.
- Color, form and texture are a pleasing contrast with other plant types as well as natural and structural surface materials.
- Accent.
- Foundation.
- In borders or road medians.
- Erosion control in arid or transition irrigation zones. Because of its invasive tendency, carefully study its use for erosion control and revegetation. 'Cupreum,' for example, is the choice for general landscaping, but it only propagates vegetatively and would be impractical for large-scale revegetation.
- Used in cut flower arrangements.

CULTURAL REQUIREMENTS

- **Exposure:** Full to reflected sun or part shade.
- **Water:** May survive under fairly arid conditions but is much more vigorous and looks better with water every month or two during the growing season, none during the winter dormant period.
- **Soil:** Most soils.
- **Propagation:** Clump divisions or seed. *P. setaceum* 'Cupreum' only by division.
- **Maintenance:** Cut back old foliage anytime after it dies in fall or winter.

POSSIBLE PROBLEMS

- Reseeds profusely and can be invasive where soil moisture is adequate; for example, where surface runoff collects.
- Dead winter foliage is a fire hazard unless removed.
- Winter appearance of the plant is not especially attractive.

Perennial grass from Africa that grows quickly to 3 to 4 feet (1 m) in height and spread. Slender, curving medium green leaves up to 2 feet (61 cm) long grow on strong hollow stems in a dense billowy clump. Pinkish purple, bristly flower spikes 12 inches (30.5 cm) or more in length open in great numbers throughout summer and fall. Frost-killed foliage gives the plant its tan winter color. 'Cupreum' has reddish foliage and coppery seed heads. It also grows taller and has wider leaves than the parent species and does not reseed. Less common cultivars* are 'Atrosanguineum,' with purple spikes and foliage, and 'Rubrum,' with rose-pink leaves and plumes.

* *See Glossary*

Penstemon species

Desert beard tongue, Desert penstemon
Scrophulariaceae family

COLD HARDINESS

Low and intermediate zones or all three zones, depending on species. Tolerates moderate to severe frost depending on species.

LANDSCAPE VALUE

- Delightful flower display provides seasonal interest in arid or transitional areas of the landscape.
- Residential plantings.
- Entry gardens.
- Perennial borders.
- Tucked in beside boulders, along dry steam beds and garden paths.
- Street medians.
- Commercial landscapes.
- Anywhere there is a need for a splash of vivid color.

CULTURAL REQUIREMENTS

- **Exposure:** Full sun. Plants grow somewhat sprawly in partial or filtered shade.
- **Water:** Water every month or two during the growing season. Harvested surface runoff may supply all of the supplemental water needed the rest of the year.
- **Soil:** Adapts to sandy or gravelly soils but not heavy wet soils.
- **Propagation:** Seed or, in some species, by division.
- **Maintenance:** After seeds have been dispersed, prune bloom stalks to a basal clump of leaves.

POSSIBLE PROBLEMS

Lives three to four years but long drought may kill it sooner.

Penstemon, such as those associated with gardens of the temperate zones, are few and far between when choosing species suited to the warm, dry regions. However, there are exceptions and these along with species native to the desert Southwest produce wonderful color in season and require little water and maintenance. These evergreen herbaceous* perennials (may be annual in long, dry periods) develop a clump of basal leaves and one to many upright flower stalks. Leaves lower on the plant have petioles* and are larger than those that grow on the erect bloom stalks. Leaves on the flower stalks are without petioles, grow in pairs at the nodes* and are clasping or appear to be joined at their common base. Flower clusters are slender, vertical and 4 to 20 inches (10 to 51 cm) long. The two-lipped tubular flowers vary in color according to species and appear mostly in spring, continuing into summer in a few cases. Height and spread varies among species, but all grow at a moderate rate.

Note: The general comments above apply to all of the following Penstemon species unless noted otherwise.

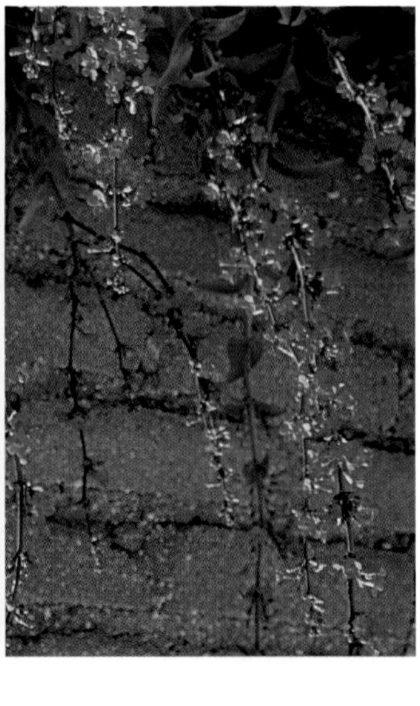

* *See Glossary*

Penstemon barbatus

Scarlet penstemon

Scrophulariaceae family

COLD HARDINESS

All three zones.

LANDSCAPE VALUE

- Brilliant display of flowers late spring into midsummer, depending on elevation.
- Attracts hummingbirds.

CULTURAL REQUIREMENTS

- **Exposure:** Full to reflected sun or part shade.
- **Water:** Water once or twice in summer to continue the flower show.
- **Soil:** Well-drained soil.
- **Propagation:** Seed.
- **Maintenance:** Remove old bloom stalks after seed has fallen.

POSSIBLE PROBLEMS

None observed.

This cold-hardy shrub grows at a moderate pace up to 6 feet (2 m) high and spreads 3 feet (1 m) wide or wider. Basal* leaves are oblong to oval. Flower stalks bear clusters of red two-lipped blooms to 1 inch (2.5 cm) long in early summer. The lower lip typically curves downward, the upper lip projects forward. Native from Utah into Mexico.

Penstemon eatonii

Eaton's penstemon, Firecracker penstemon

Scrophulariaceae family

COLD HARDINESS

Low and intermediate zones and into high zone.

LANDSCAPE VALUE

Attractive year-round bright green foliage is a special landscape attribute for off-season appearance.

CULTURAL REQUIREMENTS

- **Exposure:** Full sun to reflected sun and part shade.
- **Water:** Water once or twice during long summer dry spells.
- **Soil:** Most soils will do but deep soil is best.
- **Propagation:** Seed.
- **Maintenance:** Remove old blooms to stimulate more blooming unless you are collecting seed.

POSSIBLE PROBLEMS

None observed.

This shrub grows at a moderate rate from 1 to 3 feet (30.5 cm to 1 m) high and wide. Thick, bright green foliage composed of lance-shaped lower leaves that have long stems and are broadest at the tip, narrowing toward the base. Excellent all-year foliage. Distinct red or red-purple markings are on the flower stalks. Scarlet flowers are 1¼ inches (3 cm) long, narrow and funnel-shaped and inconspicuously two-lipped. Blooms late winter into summer. Native to Sonoran, Mojave and Colorado River Deserts.

* See Glossary

Penstemon parryi

Parry's penstemon, Desert penstemon
Scrophulariaceae family

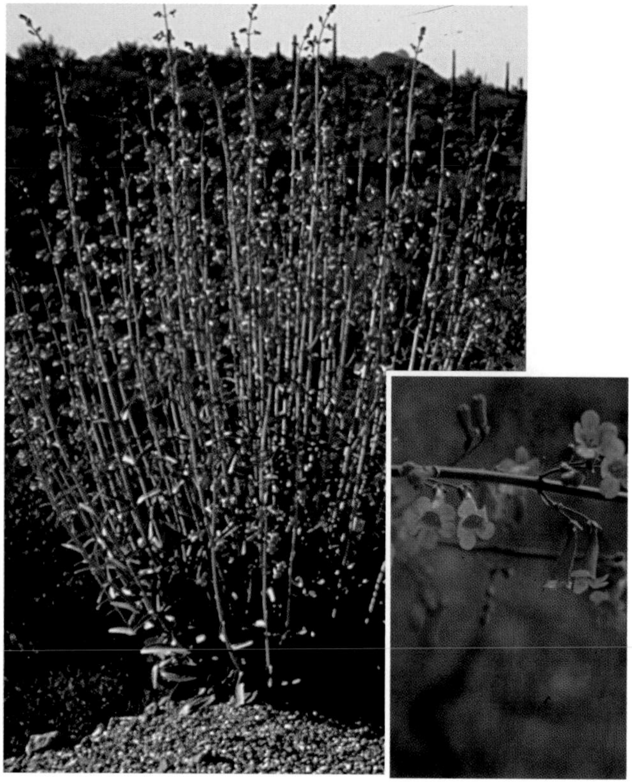

COLD HARDINESS
All three zones.

LANDSCAPE VALUE
- Showy color display midspring.
- Extremely tall with optimum conditions.

CULTURAL REQUIREMENTS
- **Exposure:** Full sun to part shade. Survives and blooms as a smaller plant in difficult situations.
- **Water:** Thoroughly soak the root zone every month or two during hot periods and keep soil constantly moist for best bloom from winter to midspring. Needs intermittent summer rain or moisture to survive as a perennial.
- **Soil:** Improved deep soil for best results.
- **Propagation:** Seed.
- **Maintenance:** Cut back old bloom stalks and groom after bloom.

POSSIBLE PROBLEMS
None observed.

Single- or multistemmed, this *Penstemon* species grows to about 4 feet (1 m) high and 2 to 3 feet (51 cm to 1 m) wide. Growth is rapid in winter and spring. Lower leaves are mostly narrow, lance-shaped and leathery. They do not turn black when dried out. Broadly funnel-shaped flowers are 3/4 inch (2 cm) long and rose to rose-magenta. In spring, they open in slender upright clusters. Native to central Arizona into Sonora, Mexico.

Penstemon pseudospectabilis

Canyon penstemon
Scrophulariaceae family

COLD HARDINESS
All three zones.

LANDSCAPE VALUE
Spectacular spring color display.

CULTURAL REQUIREMENTS
- **Exposure:** Full sun to part shade.
- **Water:** Water every week or two in absence of summer rain to remain perennial; otherwise it will be an annual that germinates with fall or winter moisture.
- **Soil:** Some depth.
- **Propagation:** Seed.
- **Maintenance:** Remove old blooms.

POSSIBLE PROBLEMS
Dies out during periods of drought.

Upright stems grow rapidly when moisture is present, from 2 to 3 feet (61 cm to 1 m) or more in height and spread. A clump of leathery basal* leaves at the base of stems have sharp pointed teeth along the leaf margins. Leaves on the flower stalks grow in pairs at the nodes* and are stemless and disc-shaped. Rose-pink to purple flowers 1 inch (2.5 cm) long bloom in long slender clusters during spring. Native to Sonoran and Mojave Deserts.

* *See Glossary*

Penstemon superbus

Superb penstemon

Scrophulariaceae family

COLD HARDINESS
All three zones. Best in high zone.

LANDSCAPE VALUE
- Perennial garden background plant.
- Color plant.

CULTURAL REQUIREMENTS
- **Exposure:** Full sun to part shade.
- **Water:** Water every week or two in spring and into summer to support bloom, but every month or two after blooming.
- **Soil:** Most soils with good drainage.
- **Propagation:** Seed.
- **Maintenance:** Groom and remove old bloom stalks for good appearance.

POSSIBLE PROBLEMS
Short-lived as a perennial.

Good growing conditions allow this species to become a large, showy clump with numerous flower stalks. Reaches an average of 4 feet (1 m) in height and spread, growing rapidly in spring. Large oval lower leaves turn black when they dry. Deep red to scarlet flowers are almost 1 inch (2.5 cm) long, narrow and funnel-shaped. They open in clusters in spring (or summer in higher elevations).

Pentzia incana

Karroo bush

Asteraceae (Compositae) family

COLD HARDINESS
Low and intermediate zones and protected microclimates of the high zone. Tolerates considerable frost.

LANDSCAPE VALUE
- Groundcover for small areas.
- In small groupings, a facer for taller shrubs, a foundation plant, an informal border or an edging plant.
- In arid-tolerant mix of plants to revegetate disturbed areas.

CULTURAL REQUIREMENTS
- **Exposure**: Full sun is preferable but also grows in filtered shade.
- **Water:** Quite drought resistant once established. Water every month or two to promote good color and growth.
- **Soil:** Most soils with good drainage. Best performance in average garden soil.
- **Propagation:** Seed or cuttings.
- **Maintenance:** Low maintenance.

POSSIBLE PROBLEMS
Naturalizes by seedlings under favorable conditions. This may be undesirable in tailored landscape settings.

Uniform, compact and attractive little evergreen shrub from the Karroo Desert in South Africa. Grows at a moderate pace from 6 to 12 inches (15 to 30.5 cm) high and 2 to 3 feet (61 cm to 1 m) wide. Forms a dense low mound of minute light green fine-textured leaves. Tiny yellow button flowers are most abundant in spring, then continue into fall. May bloom year-round in favored locations.

** See Glossary*

Perovskia atriplicifolia 'Blue Spire'

Russian sage

Lamaiaceae (Labiatae) family

COLD HARDINESS

All three zones.

LANDSCAPE VALUE

- Adds a soft blue haze to desert plantings in the summer.
- Long bloom period.
- Combines with other plants with winter interest to cover its dormant nonpresence in the cold season.
- Foliage has a pleasant aromatic "sagey" smell when brushed against.

CULTURAL REQUIREMENTS

- **Exposure:** Full sun to reflected sun.
- **Water:** Quite drought resistant. Water every week or two to maintain blooming. Little supplemental irrigation is needed in winter.
- **Soil:** Most soils with good drainage.
- **Propagation:** Cuttings. Seed is also an option, but characteristics may vary.
- **Maintenance:** Remove old blooms.

POSSIBLE PROBLEMS

Drab in winter.

Woody, multistem, grayish plant that grows at a moderate pace to about 3 feet (1 m) high and wide. Rather open in character. Gray-green leaves are finely cut on lower part of plant but are merely toothed on the upper part. Leaves are an average of 3 inches (7.5 cm) long. Multibranched spikelike clusters bear small blue-lavender flowers, which creates a blue misty effect above the plant. Blooming is continuous throughout the warm season, especially if spent bloom is occasionally removed. Loves the heat of summer, dormant in winter. Native to Pakistan, Turkistan and eastern Iran.

Landscape Design Example

Grouping of container plants with a bench creates a natural small living space.

* See Glossary

Phoenix canariensis

Canary Island date palm

Arecaceae (Palmae) family

COLD HARDINESS

Low zone and all but the coldest areas of the intermediate zone. Sometimes seen in high zone where it regularly sustains leaf burn from cold. Slow recovery leaves cold-damaged palms unattractive most of the time. Moderately frost hardy.

LANDSCAPE VALUE

- An impressive palm, large in all dimensions and for this reason best used along wide roadways, in large public spaces such as parks, and in large commercial and residential landscapes. Small gardens or streets do not provide adequate growing space.
- A good pot or tub specimen when young, but eventually must be planted in the ground.
- Fruit attracts birds.

CULTURAL REQUIREMENTS

- **Exposure:** Full or reflected sun to part shade.
- **Water:** Withstands considerable drought. Thoroughly soak the root zone every month or two for long-term health and good appearance; more frequent watering promotes faster growth.
- **Soil:** Most soils will do, but deep, well-drained, moderately fertile types are best.
- **Propagation:** Seed.
- **Maintenance:** Periodically prune and groom foliage crown and trunk.

POSSIBLE PROBLEMS

- Abundant fruit creates litter.
- Maintaining trunk in neat, attractive condition is labor-intensive and often costly.
- Recovers slowly from cold injury.
- Susceptible to bud rot* and root-knot nematode*; dry rot of leaf bases and trunk may be an unsightly problem.
- The giant palm borer* may become a significant pest in weak or stressed palms, especially those transplanted as large old specimens.

Pinnate* or feather leaf palm from the Canary Islands that slowly grows 40 to 60 feet (12 to 18 m) tall and spreads 20 to 40 feet (6 to 12 m). There are male and female trees. The trunk is stout, up to 4 feet (1 m) in diameter. Some of this considerable girth results from old leaf bases that persist for many years and give the trunk a pineapple-like appearance. The dense fountain-shaped crown contains as many as two hundred evergreen leaves. These are glossy, deep green, 15 to 20 feet (4.5 to 6 m) long and armed with sharp spines along the lower stems. Branching brushlike flower stalks are 6 feet (2 m) long and bear tiny cream blossoms from spring into summer. The female trees bear heavy masses of orange-colored fruits in fall, each about a 1/2 inch (1 cm) in diameter.

* *See Glossary*

Phoenix dactylifera

Date palm

Arecaceae (Palmae) family

COLD HARDINESS

Low and intermediate zones and warmer locations in high zone. Hardier than *P. canariensis.*

LANDSCAPE VALUE

- Classic symbol of the desert oasis.
- Also appropriate in drier landscape settings as a specimen or bold accent and in groups for shade.
- Stiff formal appearance can be contrasted by allowing two or three selected side shoots to grow to maturity, creating an impressive giant multistem specimen.
- Singles planted in rows along roadways and wide pedestrian walkways have a dramatic impact.
- Effective in large spaces such as golf courses as well as near tall buildings.

CULTURAL REQUIREMENTS

- **Exposure:** Thrives under harsh conditions of great heat and aridity and intense full or reflected sun. Fruiting may be reduced or eliminated in more humid areas near the sea, in cool summer deserts or in cold-winter areas.
- **Water:** Established date palms can survive long periods of hot, dry weather without irrigation, but thoroughly soaking the root zone every week or two encourages high-quality appearance. Reduce irrigation by as much as 50 percent during the cooler months. Water every week or two throughout the year for fruit production.
- **Soil:** Deep sandy loam soils are ideal but performs well on other well-drained types. Tolerates moderately saline conditions.
- **Propagation:** Superior varieties for fruit or form are propagated by offsets*. May be grown from seed but that is a long, slow process with no assurance of fruit quality or whether plant will be male or female.
- **Maintenance:** Prune off old leaves to maintain appearance and neatness of the crown and trunk. Remove expanding flower clusters and unsightly older leaves in one operation to eliminate most of the litter.

POSSIBLE PROBLEMS

- Deep planting to achieve uniform height of palms in rows may result in high losses if the soil is poorly drained.
- Various diseases such as heart rot, bud rot and root-knot nematode* have been recorded.
- Ripening fruit is subject to attack by birds, insects and diseases.
- Fallen fruit creates considerable litter under female trees.
- Pruning and grooming tall trees can be expensive.
- Spiked leaflets at base of fronds are a hazard at time of removal and a danger that affects disposal choices.
- The giant palm borer* may become a significant pest in weak or stressed palms, especially those transplanted as large old specimens.

This palm, cultivated by man for more than 5000 years, is believed to have originated in western Asia and northern Africa. It grows at a slow to moderate pace up to 100 feet (30.5 m) tall, spreading about 30 feet (9 m). A slender trunk typically suckers* near the base. With age, the suckering habit declines and eventually ceases altogether. Old leaf bases remain on the trunk for a long time, but eventually these decay and fall away, if not removed. The remaining scars form a neat geometric pattern. Stiff, sharp-pointed pinnate* leaves are 10 to 20 feet (3 to 6 m) long and waxy gray to blue-green. They ascend in the central part of the crown, gradually angling down in the lower and outer crown area. Very sharp spine-tipped leaflets arm the lower part of the fronds. Life span of individual leaves is generally 3 to 7 years. Date palms are male or female. If pollinated, females produce large clusters of cylindrical orange to brown fruits (dates), 1 to 3 inches (2.5 to 7.5 cm) long and sweet and edible when ripe.

* *See Glossary*

Phoenix roebelenii

Pigmy date palm

Arecaceae (Palmae) family

COLD HARDINESS

Mainly for the low zone but sometimes seen doing well in the microclimates of architectural spaces in intermediate zone. Foliage will brown in the mid-20s F (-4°C), but grows back rapidly in spring.

LANDSCAPE VALUE

- Containers or planters in architectural spaces.
- Grouped with other bold foliage plants for tropical effects or minioasis.

CULTURAL REQUIREMENTS

- **Exposure:** Full sun to complete shade, but not for dark interior spaces. Generally, it was thought of as a shade-only plant, but that has not been the case in hot locations of southern Arizona.
- **Water:** Water every week or two. If containers occasionally dry out, little damage occurs.
- **Soil:** Most soils will do but will respond with more lush foliage and faster trunk development in improved garden soil.
- **Propagation:** Seed or divisions, if available.
- **Maintenance:** Requires little more than occasional grooming to remove old leaves, spent blooms and fruit clusters.

POSSIBLE PROBLEMS

None observed.

Handsome, dwarf palm from Laos that eventually grows to about 6 feet (2 m) tall. A single trunk with a head of foliage spreads about 3 feet (1 m), but multitrunk clumps produce a wider spread, depending on the number of heads. Trunks are exceedingly slow to develop, but new foliage grows at a moderate rate. Shiny, curved bright green leaves are arranged in the typical *Phoenix* pinnate* fashion. The clusters of tiny dates born on female trees and the blossoms in general are of no design importance.

* See Glossary

PINE

Pines seem to belong to the mountains and colder regions. However, a number of species native to the Mediterranean region and arid edges of desert locales are particularly well suited to warm, dry climates. These species offer choices where large trees are appropriate. They tolerate considerable heat and periods of drought. They can be the most substantial elements of arid-region landscapes.

Pinus canariensis

Canary Island pine

Pinaceae family

A tall, tiered candelabralike pyramid with open space between each whorl of branches. This pine grows rapidly, with moisture, from 50 to 80 feet (15 to 24 m) tall, shorter in the desert. It spreads about 30 feet (9 m). It is quite narrow in relation to its height in youth but broadens with age. Silhouette in youth is unique, eventually filling in and becoming almost round-topped and more solid with age. Silky 9- to 12-inch (23- to 30.5-cm) needles are borne in bundles of three. These are bluish when young, turning dark green when mature, and are a special attraction. A sturdy, straight vertical element in the landscape. Native to the Canary Islands.

COLD HARDINESS

Low and intermediate zones. Occasionally seen in warmer locations in high zone. Not a good choice where cold damage occurs often.

LANDSCAPE VALUE

- A marvelous tall background tree with a special silhouette against the sky.
- A strong single vertical accent plant.
- Formal alleys and framing views.
- The long silky needles add a lush, almost tropical feeling to the landscape.

CULTURAL REQUIREMENTS

- **Exposure:** Full sun, including reflected heat and temporary shade when young, but will bolt for the overhead sun regardless of the overstory shade.
- **Water:** More drought tolerant than its lush appearance suggests, but for best results in hot regions use in moist situations where you can thoroughly soak the root zone every week to every month or two.
- **Soil:** Most soils with good drainage.
- **Propagation:** Seed.
- **Maintenance:** Prune out bushy twigs inside the tree to alleviate needle drop. Pruning to open up the interior is often practiced in California, but is not necessary.

POSSIBLE PROBLEMS

- Needle drop is heavy, often hanging upon twigs and branches in the interior of the tree—unattractive at close range.
- Needles sustain frost damage at 20°F (-6.5°C). Usually just the tip half is browned, but it is often a year before they drop and are replaced, a problem in borderline areas.
- Not for small-scale or residential landscapes.

Pinus edulis

Piñon, Nut pine

Pinaceae family

Slow-growing picturesque evergreen tree that grows 10 to 20 feet (3 to 6 m) high and spreads 8 to 16 feet (2.5 to 5 m). Crown is dense and oval to broadly pyramidal when young, spreading to become dome-shaped or irregular and flat-crowned when mature. The trunk is frequently bent or crooked and divided to form two or more leaders*. Stiff yellowish to dark green needles 3/4 to 1 1/2 inches (2 to 4 cm) long grow in bundles of two. Small rounded female cones 1 to 2 inches (2.5 to 5 cm) across yield sweet edible nuts, which are a prized food supplement harvested by Native Americans in fall. Native to areas from Oklahoma, Wyoming, Texas to California and northern Mexico.

COLD HARDINESS

Intermediate and high zones. Marginal in low zone.

LANDSCAPE VALUE

- Small-scale accent or specimen conifer.
- Develops character with age.
- Useful where space is limited.
- Containers.
- Compatible with oriental landscape themes.

CULTURAL REQUIREMENTS

- **Exposure:** Full sun to part shade at the lower elevations.
- **Water:** May require no supplemental irrigation in the high zone after it achieves effective landscape size, but water every week to every couple months at the lower elevations.
- **Soil:** Most soils with good drainage, but not highly alkaline, salty soils.
- **Propagation:** Seed.
- **Maintenance:** Prune and in some cases stake young trees to develop and maintain a symmetrical form.

POSSIBLE PROBLEMS

- Very slow-growing.
- Not at its best in low hot-desert locations.

* See Glossary

Pinus eldarica

Elder pine, Afghan pine

Pinaceae family

Dense, symmetrical and cone-shaped evergreen tree that rapidly grows 30 to 50 feet (9 to 15 m) high and 15 to 25 feet (4.5 to 7.5 m) wide. Needles are medium green, 4 to 6 inches (10 to 15 cm) long, two per bundle. Cones are 5 to 6 inches (13 to 15 cm) long. Closely resembles *P. brutia* and, according to some authorities, is an ecotype* of this species. Native to southern Russia, Afghanistan and Pakistan.

COLD HARDINESS

Does well in all but the hottest microclimates of low zone. Reasonably hardy in the intermediate zone and most areas of high zone.

LANDSCAPE VALUE

- Dependable, fast-growing specimen or accent for low-water-use landscapes.
- Versatility makes this pine useful as a windbreak, screen or large-space definer.
- Woodsy effects.
- Golf courses, parks, school grounds, commercial sites.
- Parking-lot islands, medians.
- Commercial Christmas-tree crop.

CULTURAL REQUIREMENTS

- **Exposure:** Full sun to part shade. Remarkably durable desert pine. Endures extremes of heat and cold.
- **Water:** Quite drought resistant. Water every week to every couple months in the low zone and warmer microclimates of the intermediate zone.
- **Soil:** Any soil but heavy wet types.
- **Propagation:** Seed.
- **Maintenance:** Requires little routine maintenance.

POSSIBLE PROBLEMS

- Constantly wet soils result in chlorotic* foliage.
- Woolly aphids occasionally attack.
- Susceptible in some areas to a rust disease.

Pinus halepensis

Aleppo pine

Pinaceae family

Evergreen tree from the Mediterranean region that grows at a moderate to rapid pace from 30 to 60 feet (9 to 18 m) high and 20 to 40 feet (6 to 12 m) wide. Columnar to oval in youth. Round-topped, irregularly open and billowy with age. Medium green to yellowish green needles are 2 to 4 inches (5 to 10 cm) long, two per bundle. Cones that ripen in fall are oval to oblong, 3 inches (7.5 cm) long, and usually not abundant until the tree is fifteen to twenty-five years old. Cones remaining on branches after opening and dropping seed add close-up interest.

COLD HARDINESS

Low and intermediate zones and sometimes locations in high zone. Mature trees tolerate severe frost; young specimens are more sensitive.

LANDSCAPE VALUE

- Large-scale evergreen tree for shade, screen, windbreak or skyline effects in parks and other large spaces.
- Woodsy effect in mass plantings.
- Interior of mature trees is free of debris and attractive.
- Fallen needles can make a pleasing organic mulch or groundcover.
- Mature tree evolves into many picturesque shapes, adding much to skyline silhouette.

CULTURAL REQUIREMENTS

- **Exposure:** Full to reflected sun and heat.
- **Water:** Water every month to once or twice a season, depending on your microclimate.
- **Soil:** Useful in poor soils. Grows well in coastal situations. Most drought resistant in good-quality landscape soils.
- **Propagation:** Seed.
- **Maintenance:** Prune at the "candle" stage (before new growth opens up to reveal needles) to control size, shape or density of young trees.

POSSIBLE PROBLEMS

- Roots enclosed in the same nursery container too long will stunt tree's growth and make it short-lived.
- Aleppo pine blight in the southwestern United States causes unsightly effect of small dead boughs scattered through some trees in winter, but affected trees generally outgrow this condition in summer.

* *See Glossary*

Pinus monophylla
Single-leaf piñon pine
Pinaceae family

COLD HARDINESS
All three zones.

LANDSCAPE VALUE
Small rugged specimen for informal or naturalistic mid- and high-elevation landscapes.

CULTURAL REQUIREMENTS
- **Exposure:** Full to reflected sun.
- **Water:** Established plants require irrigation only during long dry periods but appearance and growth may be improved by thoroughly soaking the root zone every month or two, especially in low and intermediate zones.
- **Soil:** Most soils with good drainage.
- **Propagation:** Seed.
- **Maintenance:** Prune occasionally for form. Otherwise requires little care.

POSSIBLE PROBLEMS
Does not perform well in low, very hot desert locations.

Small slow-growing evergreen tree that reaches 10 to 25 feet (3 to 7.5 m) in height and spreads 10 to 15 feet (3 to 4.5 m). The slender upright crown of young plants spreads to become broad and dome-shaped at maturity. Stiff gray-green cylindrical needles 3/4 to 1 1/2 inches (2 to 4 cm) long are borne singly. Small 1 1/2-inch (4-cm) long cones bear edible seed. Native to Utah, Arizona, Nevada and California in the United States, Baja California in Mexico.

Pinus pinea
Italian stone pine
Pinaceae family

COLD HARDINESS
Low and intermediate zones and warmer locations in high zone. Cold-hardiness increases with age.

LANDSCAPE VALUE
- Imposing specimen, shade or skyline tree suited for use in parks, along broad streets and avenues, and other public places where there is ample space.
- Grows naturally in dry coastal and mountain locations.
- Attractive at all ages but use where the massive character of the mature tree is appropriate.

CULTURAL REQUIREMENTS
- **Exposure:** Full to reflected sun.
- **Water:** Water young trees every week or two. Thoroughly soak the root zone of mature specimens every month or two.
- **Soil:** Most average landscape soils are acceptable.
- **Propagation:** Seed.
- **Maintenance:** Prune occasionally to direct growth or control shape and raise canopy height.

POSSIBLE PROBLEMS
Mature size is not in scale with most residential landscapes and other situations where space is limited.

Large evergreen tree from southern Europe and Near East. Grows at a moderate rate but is slow to become a full-scale skyline tree. Reaches 40 to 60 feet (12 to 18 m) in height and spreads 30 to 50 feet (9 to 15 m). The juvenile form is rounded, bushy and low-branched, becoming umbrella-shaped as the tree grows larger. Removal of low branches encourages high growth so the broad and flat-topped or dome-shaped appearance is achieved. Vivid green to gray-green needles are stiff, 3 to 7 inches (7.5 to 18 cm) long, two per bundle. Oval brown cones are 6 inches (15 cm) long and yield edible seeds, the pignolia nut of southern Europe.

* See Glossary

Pinus roxburghii

Chir pine, Indian longleaf pine

Pinaceae family

COLD HARDINESS

All three zones. Withstands hard frost.

LANDSCAPE VALUE

- At once a striking, graceful and bold-textured pine for specimen or accent use where space is adequate for the mature size of this tree.
- Suitable for both woodsy background and transitional zones.

CULTURAL REQUIREMENTS

- **Exposure:** Full or reflected sun in intermediate and high zones.
- **Water:** Thoroughly soak the root zone every week or two until effective landscape size is reached, then water every month or two.
- **Soil:** A wide range of landscape soils are acceptable.
- **Propagation:** Seed.
- **Maintenance:** Requires little maintenance other than occasional pruning for shape.

POSSIBLE PROBLEMS

Too large at maturity for many planting sites.

Large evergreen tree from the Himalayas. Grows at a moderate to rapid rate from 60 to 80 feet (18 to 24 m) high, occasionally climbing as high as 150 feet (46 m). Spreads about 30 to 40 feet (9 to 12 m). Dense and pyramidal when young, it gradually assumes a broader rounded shape in age. Slender drooping needles are light green, up to 12 inches (30.5 cm) long in bundles of three. Cones are 4 to 7 inches (10 to 18 cm) in length.

Piscidia mollis

Gray Sonoran pea tree, Fish poison tree, Gray-leaf pea tree

Fabaceae (Leguminosae) family

COLD HARDINESS

Low zone and warmer locations in the intermediate zone.

LANDSCAPE VALUE

- Can be developed into an interesting patio tree.
- Large gray-green foliage and pink flowers create close-range interest.

CULTURAL REQUIREMENTS

- **Exposure:** Reflected sun to part shade.
- **Water:** Quite drought resistant. Water every week or two during summer to develop a small tree. Water once or twice a season the rest of the year to maintain an acceptable appearance.
- **Soil:** Most soils.
- **Propagation:** Seed.
- **Maintenance:** Undemanding.

POSSIBLE PROBLEMS

- Late winter and spring foliage take on a "tired look." New leaves don't come out until late spring.
- A slow grower.

Rounded large shrub or small tree that grows 10 to 20 feet (3 to 6 m) high, with equal spread, at a slow to moderate rate, depending on summer watering. Large compound leaves are velvety gray and usually evergreen. Clusters of small pink pea-shaped flowers in summer are not particularly showy. Pods follow and hang on into winter. The general attractive aspect of the tree is the unique dense head of gray foliage. Native to Sonora, Mexico.

* See Glossary

Pistacia atlantica

Mount Atlas pistacia, Mount Atlas mastic tree

Anacardiaceae family

COLD HARDINESS

All three zones.

LANDSCAPE VALUE

- Handsome large tree for shade, parks and other public spaces.
- Roadsides or medians—where there is adequate space for the mature tree.

CULTURAL REQUIREMENTS

- **Exposure:** Full sun.
- **Water:** The established tree tolerates considerable drought stress. Thoroughly soak the root zone every month or two during the warm season for best specimens.
- **Soil:** Most soils with good drainage.
- **Propagation:** Seed.
- **Maintenance:** Young trees need pruning and in some cases staking to establish good form. Well-adapted to desert growing conditions; requires little care as an established tree.

POSSIBLE PROBLEMS

Susceptible to Texas root rot* and verticilium wilt*.

Large deciduous tree from the Mediterranean region, Canary Islands and Pakistan. Reaches 45 to 60 feet (13.5 to 18 m) in height and spread at a slow to moderate rate. At maturity the crown is dense and rounded. Each leaf is pinnately* divided into seven to eleven shiny deep green leaflets 2 inches (5 cm) long. No fall color, but foliage remains green into late autumn where winters are cold and is almost evergreen in warm-winter areas. Female trees bear small clusters of tiny greenish white flowers in early summer, followed by fruit about 1/3 inch (1 cm), pinkish at first and then dark blue in autumn. Fruit set only happens when male trees are also present in the area.

Pistacia lentiscus

Mastic tree, Evergreen pistacia

Anacardiaceae family

COLD HARDINESS

Low and intermediate zones and all but the coldest microclimates of high zone.

LANDSCAPE VALUE

- Dense attractive evergreen foliage makes this species a useful background or screen for informal settings.
- Can also be trained to grow as an interesting small specimen tree or a more symmetrical patio tree.
- Fits well in transitional areas between lush oasis and arid landscape zones.

CULTURAL REQUIREMENTS

- **Exposure:** Full sun.
- **Water:** Thoroughly soak the root zone of established plants every month or two. Water young plants more often.
- **Soil:** Tolerant of moderately salty soils.
- **Propagation:** Seed or cuttings.
- **Maintenance:** Train and prune to develop a tree.

POSSIBLE PROBLEMS

None observed.

Large shrub or small tree whose form is irregular, spreading and low-branched. Slowly grows 15 to 25 feet (4.5 to 7.5 m) high, spreading 20 to 30 feet (6 to 9 m). The evergreen's pinnately* compound leaves are made up of three to five pairs of glossy green 1-inch (2.5-cm) leaflets with winged petioles*. Leaf buds are whitish. Female plants may produce unimportant flowers and red to black fruit if a male pollinator is in the vicinity, although flowering is uncommon in some areas. Native to Mediterranean region.

** See Glossary*

Pithecellobium dulce

Guamúchil, Manila tamarind
Fabaceae (Leguminosae) family

COLD HARDINESS

Dependable only in almost frost-free areas of the low zone.

LANDSCAPE VALUE

- A tough, fast-growing tree for shade, windbreaks.
- Buffer zones and highway plantings.
- Erosion control and reforestation.
- Salt-tolerant and useful near the beach and saltwater estuaries.
- When pruned as a hedge, it makes a thorny, almost-impenetrable plant barrier.

CULTURAL REQUIREMENTS

- **Exposure:** Full sun or shade. Salt-tolerant.
- **Water:** Tolerates long dry spells as an established tree. Water once or twice during the dry season.
- **Soil:** Grows lush and luxuriant in fertile soils with abundant moisture, but adapts to poor-quality soils and acid to alkaline conditions.
- **Propagation:** Seed or cuttings.
- **Maintenance:** Clean-up of seeds and guidance to control growth.

POSSIBLE PROBLEMS

- High winds can cause considerable damage to the crown.
- Fallen seed pods create ground litter.
- An aggressive invader of native flora. It is classed as a pest in Hawaii.
- The sap contains an irritant that causes an allergic skin reaction in some people. This may limit its use as a shade tree.

Throughout the vast subtropical and tropical regions of the world where guamúchil has become established, it is most often seen as a tree with a rounded spreading crown of nearly evergreen foliage. In areas of limited rainfall it may grow no larger than a shrub. On average, it reaches about 50 feet (15 m) in height, with equal spread, at a rapid rate given adequate soil moisture. Guamúchil foliage is bipinnately* compound and each leaf has just two pairs of oval to oblong leaflets 3/4 to 2 inches (2 to 5 cm) long. One or two sharp upward-pointing spines grow from the base of the leaf, although some trees are thornless. White to pale cream puffball flowers appear in drooping clusters to 15 inches (38 cm) long anytime from winter into late spring. The fruit is 4 to 6 inches (10 to 15 cm) long and a twisted, coiled bean pod is constricted between the seeds. When mature, the pod splits lengthwise to show shiny black seeds embedded in fleshy pulp that may be white, pink or bright red. The pulp is edible, slightly sweet and acidic. People eat the sweet pulp and spit out the seed, thus the spread of the species. The young pods are also eaten as a prepared dish. Original habitat was Mexico and Central America. Many almost treeless settlements along the northern Gulf of California in Mexico now have shade because of the arrival of Guamúchil, which has naturalized.

** See Glossary*

Pithecellobium flexicaule

Texas ebony

Fabaceae (Leguminosae) family

COLD HARDINESS

Low and intermediate zones. Tolerates moderate to severe frost as a mature tree but goes deciduous. Young plants are more cold-sensitive.

LANDSCAPE VALUE

- Distinctive branching pattern, rich dark-green foliage and showy flowers are qualities that make Texas ebony a striking specimen, accent or patio tree in arid or transitional zones.
- Planted in groups or rows, it serves as a thorny barrier or screen.
- Median and buffer zone plantings.

CULTURAL REQUIREMENTS

- **Exposure:** Full or reflected sun to part shade.
- **Water:** Thoroughly soak the root zone every week to every couple months, depending on desired growth and ultimate mature size as a shrub or tree.
- **Soil:** Most arid-landscape soils are acceptable.
- **Propagation:** Seed.
- **Maintenance:** Pruning encourages desirable tree branching structure.

POSSIBLE PROBLEMS

- Because of thorns, use with care in foot-traffic areas.
- Slow to reach effective landscape size.

Small to medium-size thorny evergreen tree that slowly grows 15 to 30 feet (4.5 to 9 m) high and spreads 15 to 20 feet (4.5 to 6 m). Canopy is dense, spreading and low-branched. Bipinnately* compound leaves are divided into three to five pairs of shiny dark green leaflets 1/2 inch (1 cm) long. Creamy yellow 1 1/2-inch (4-cm) long flower spikes are fragrant and open spring into early summer. Thick, woody, sickle-shaped seed pods to 6 inches (15 cm) long remain on the tree for some time. Native to southern Texas and adjoining Mexico.

Pithecellobium leucospermum (P. undulatum)

Palo pinto

Fabaceae (Leguminosae) family

COLD HARDINESS

Low zone and warm microclimates of intermediate zone. Frost tender. Hard frost causes severe die-back* of top growth.

LANDSCAPE VALUE

- Screening and background.
- Highway and street-median plantings.
- Parks.
- Under utility wires.
- Commercial landscapes.
- Small patio shade tree.
- Ferny green foliage and undulating branches add an interesting note to a mixed planting.

CULTURAL REQUIREMENTS

- **Exposure**: Full sun to part shade.
- **Water:** Drought tolerant, but looks best with thorough soaking of the root zone once or twice during dry periods.
- **Soil:** Most soils with good drainage.
- **Propagation:** Seed.
- **Maintenance:** Prune to shape and develop shrub or tree growth habit.

POSSIBLE PROBLEMS

None observed.

A shrub or small tree of rounded form with graceful undulating branches. Grows at a moderate pace from 15 to 20 feet (4.5 to 6 m) high, with equal spread. Bipinnate* leaves are divided into pairs of oblong secondary leaflets 1/4 to 3/4 inch (0.5 to 2 cm) long. Mature bark is brownish gray and smooth. Curved slender pods 4 to 10 inches (10 to 25.5 cm) long with wavy margins contain pale green seeds. White pin-cushion flowerheads that open along branches in spring are not particularly showy. The native range in Mexico extends from Sonora and Baja California south to Colima.

* See Glossary

Pithecellobium mexicanum

Mexican ebony

Fabaceae (Leguminosae) family

COLD HARDINESS

All three zones.

LANDSCAPE VALUE

- A patio-size tree.
- Handsome dark gray trunk and branch structure for background planting and bosque* effects.

CULTURAL REQUIREMENTS

- **Exposure:** Full sun, including reflected-heat situations.
- **Water:** Drought resistant. Thoroughly soak the root zone every month or two for satisfactory growth and good landscape effect. Water more often if soil is shallow.
- **Soil:** Most soils will do, including gravelly wash* types, but depth is desirable. Grows larger in deeper, more moist soils. Struggles in shallow situations such as in caliche* or hardpan.
- **Propagation:** Seed.
- **Maintenance:** Stake and prune when plant is young to develop a tree.

POSSIBLE PROBLEMS

Hooked thorns a problem for pruning and training in youth—not a problem after branch structure is above head height.

A deciduous tree of substantial proportions with a strong, upright trunk. Reaches 45 feet (13.5 m) tall under optimum conditions but is usually much shorter. Spreads to 30 feet (9 m) but usually less. Growth rate is moderate, but can be rapid under moist conditions during the warm season. Small bipinnately* compound grayish green leaves are borne on prickly twigs, creating a delicate tracery and an open shade. Small puffball clusters of slightly fragrant white flowers occur in midspring. Trees of considerable size are found along washes in northern Sonora, Mexico, and south.

Pithecellobium pallens

Tenaza

Fabaceae (Leguminosae) family

COLD HARDINESS

Low zone and the intermediate zone, where there is occasional frost damage to young plants. Mature plants are much hardier.

LANDSCAPE VALUE

- Tall background planting.
- Patio tree.
- Medians.
- Residential-scale street tree.
- Especially showy when in bloom.

CULTURAL REQUIREMENTS

- **Exposure:** Full sun, including reflected sun, to part shade.
- **Water:** Quite drought resistant. Thoroughly soak the root zone every week or two for good foliage and bloom.
- **Soil:** Any soil.
- **Propagation:** Seed.
- **Maintenance:** Stake and prune to train into a tree—single- or multitrunk. Tendency to vertical growth makes this process easier.

POSSIBLE PROBLEMS

The small prickles on young plants complicate pruning and training in the early development stages.

Evergreen gray-barked shrub or tree that grows at a moderate rate from 10 to 30 feet (3 to 9 m) high and 8 to 12 feet (2.5 to 3.5 m) wide. Feathery compound leaves are 1½ inches (4 cm) long and medium green. Small white puffball flowers cover the tree in late spring and early summer or when moisture is present; it can bloom more than once a year. Two-inch (5-cm) brown pods follow blooming and are not unattractive. Tiny prickles arm branches and twigs when young but are not abundant on mature plants. Native to southernmost Texas and northeast Mexico.

* See Glossary

Pittosporum phillyraeoides

Willow pittosporum

Pittosporaceae family

COLD HARDINESS

Low and intermediate zones, and milder microclimates of high zone. Some branch die-back* may occur following severe frost.

LANDSCAPE VALUE

- The appeal of this plant lies in its fine-textured willowy foliage and graceful weeping habit, along with the fragrant flowers and colorful autumn fruit display. Its special charm and character make it a valuable small specimen or accent tree, useful in entry gardens, courtyards and other small spaces.
- Can develop into a small attractive grove or bosque* if root sprouts are encouraged.
- Beside pools and other water features.
- Against large plain structural walls.
- Medians.

CULTURAL REQUIREMENTS

- **Exposure:** Full or reflected sun to part shade.
- **Water:** Thoroughly soak the root zone of young trees every week or two, every month or two once established.
- **Soil:** Soils ranging from light to heavy.
- **Propagation:** Seed or root sprouts.
- **Maintenance:** Young trees may need staking and pruning for form and branching pattern.

POSSIBLE PROBLEMS

- Tends to root-sprout and spread laterally, which may not be desirable in some situations.
- Subject to Texas root rot*.

Small evergreen tree that grows at a moderate rate from 15 to 20 feet (4.5 to 6 m) high and 10 to 15 feet (3 to 4.5 m) wide. May have one to several gray-barked trunks, which are slender and upright. Narrow ribbon-like leaves are light green, 4 inches (10 cm) long and hang from drooping branchlets to form an open airy foliage canopy. In spring, fragrant yellow flowers open singly or in small axillary clusters. Each bloom is tiny, about 1/3 inch (1 cm) in diameter. The orange-yellow heart-shaped seed capsules are about 3/4 inch (2 cm) in diameter. In late summer or early fall, they split open in two to four sections to show bright orange seeds. A less weeping type is sometimes seen, but it is not as attractive. The weeping form root-sprouts to develop a bosque* effect, but the nonweeping type does not do this. Native to Australia.

Plumbago auriculata (P. capensis)

Cape plumbago

Plumbaginaceae family

COLD HARDINESS

Low and intermediate zones, with some damage in mid-20s F (-4°C). Can be grown in the high zone if treated as a perennial. In colder regions, frost damage produces an unattractive winter appearance, but it recovers rapidly in the spring. Leaves blacken in frosty situations.

LANDSCAPE VALUE

- Vibrant blue color.
- A variety of forms are also available, such as a sprawling bank cover, where its toughness and tolerance of difficult situations are distinct assets.
- Climbs well over fences and other vine supports, but does not work well on overhead trellises.
- Clipped into formal hedges and other shapes, but at the expense of bloom.

CULTURAL REQUIREMENTS

- **Exposure:** Full sun, including reflected sun, to part shade.
- **Water:** Quite drought resistant.Thoroughly soak the root zone every week or two for good appearance during the warm season.
- **Soil:** Any soil with good drainage.
- **Propagation:** Cutting, to ensure deeper blues.
- **Maintenance:** Remove frost-damaged wood each spring in colder areas. Train and control when using as a vine.

POSSIBLE PROBLEMS

- Looks tacky in the cool season, even without frost.
- Spent bloom attaches to clothing and pets by small prickles at the base of the old blossom.
- In wet, poorly drained soil, foliage may become chlorotic*.

Semi-evergreen vining shrub sprawls about 10 feet (3 m) high and wide, even taller if it has something to climb. Rapid growth with moisture. Light to medium green leaves are 1 to 2 inches (2.5 to 5 cm) long. Winter appearance can be drab. Phloxlike clusters of tubular flowers, 1 inch (2.5 cm) wide, bloom late spring to late summer and add that rare true-blue color to a planting. Buy plants in bloom, because there is a wide range of intensity of blue and deep blue selections available. There is also a white-flowered form that somehow lacks a gleaming white quality. *Plumbago*, if left to grow naturally, forms a thick cluster of stems with sprawling side growth. If something is nearby, such as a tree or structure, it will climb into or over it even though it has no tendrils or rootlets to facilitate the climb. Native to South Africa.

** See Glossary*

Plumbago scandens

White desert plumbago

Plumbaginaceae family

COLD HARDINESS

Low and intermediate zones and probably warm microclimates of high zone.

LANDSCAPE VALUE

Mostly inconspicuous in the wild, but with a little special treatment can be developed into a groundcover for sunny and shady situations.

CULTURAL REQUIREMENTS

- **Exposure:** Full sun to open shade. One of the few Sonoran Desert plants that does well in shade.
- **Water:** Quite drought resistant. Thoroughly soak the root zone every week or two during the warm season when using as a landscape subject.
- **Soil:** Most soils.
- **Propagation:** Seed or cuttings.
- **Maintenance:** Undemanding.

POSSIBLE PROBLEMS

None observed.

A rambling, half-vining evergreen shrub that grows rapidly (with moisture) to 3 feet high and wide or even more under optimum conditions. Small, tubular white flowers bloom in terminal* clusters. Flowering is sparse and sporadic, but under optimum conditions, it can be quite showy. Usually seen under shrubs or small trees in the wild where it will climb over them for support, yet sometimes is a groundcover under taller shrubs and trees. Native to southern Arizona and into Mexico on south.

Plumeria obtusa

Singapore plumeria

Apocynaceae family

Tropical evergreen large shrub or small tree that grows at a moderate rate to 24 feet (7.5 m) high and about 20 feet (6 m) wide. Glossy dark green leaves are spatula shaped and 6 to 7 inches (15 to 18 cm) long. They are rounded or notched or they taper suddenly at the tip. Waxy, sweetly scented flowers up to 3 inches (7.5 cm) across have a slender snowy white tube to 3/4 inch (2 cm) long that expands abruptly into five white petals. Fragrance is often strongest during the evening hours. Blooms repeatedly during the warm season. May begin flowering when 1 to 1 1/2 feet (30.5 to 46 cm) tall from a rooted tip cutting or air layer. Several varieties are used in the landscape, including 'Bahamas' and 'Greater Antilles.' How the common name 'Singapore' became attached is hard to say, but it refers to the pure white selection used as a small tree in Hawaii. Native to Hispaniola, Cuba and Yucatan.

COLD HARDINESS

Frost-free areas of the low zone and warm, protected microclimates of intermediate zone. Works as a container plant in the high zone if moved to protected area in winter. Sensitive to even a light frost.

LANDSCAPE VALUE

- Exotic foliage, exquisitely fragrant, showy flowers make this a perfect small flowering tropical accent or specimen.
- Patio tree.
- Singly or in groups as part of a shrub border.
- Containers.
- Tolerance of salt air makes it useful in plantings near the beach.
- Adds color, fragrance and lush foliage to warm-winter arid landscapes. It remains green year-round.

CULTURAL REQUIREMENTS

- **Exposure:** Full sun to afternoon shade in the low desert. Grows well at the sea shore. Container plants must be moved to a protected spot on frosty nights.
- **Water:** Water every week or two during the warm summer growing season, every month or two during the winter.
- **Soil:** Rich well-drained garden soil.
- **Propagation:** Seed, cuttings or air layering*.
- **Maintenance:** Do not fertilize late in the year.

POSSIBLE PROBLEMS

Serious insect or disease problems are uncommon in arid climate landscapes although scale* insects, mites and several diseases are reported in moister tropical areas.

* See Glossary

COLD HARDINESS
Frost-free areas of the low zone or in very protected microclimates of intermediate zone. Damaged by light frost.

LANDSCAPE VALUE
- Exotic foliage, exquisitely fragrant, showy flowers make this a perfect small flowering tropical accent or specimen.
- Patio tree.
- Singly or in groups as part of a shrub border.
- Silhouette against plain walls.
- Containers.
- Adds color, fragrance and lush foliage in summer to warm-winter arid landscapes. It remains green year-round.
- *P. rubra acuminata's* high resistance to salt air makes it a dependable beach-front plant.

CULTURAL REQUIREMENTS
- **Exposure:** Full sun to afternoon shade in the low desert. Container plants must be moved to a protected spot on frosty nights.
- **Water:** Water every week or two during the growing season but only once or twice a season during the dormant period. Overwatered plants often develop rot problems in winter.
- **Soil:** Best landscape plants are grown in rich well-drained garden soil. Grows well at the seashore.
- **Propagation:** Seed, cuttings or air layering*.
- **Maintenance:** Low maintenance. Prune young trees to develop good branching proportion and structure.

POSSIBLE PROBLEMS
- Serious insect or disease problems are uncommon in arid-climate landscapes although scale* insects, mites and several diseases are reported in moister tropical areas.
- Plants are leafless and somewhat ungainly from late fall until the weather warms in spring.

Tropical deciduous large shrub or small tree that grows at a moderate rate to 25 feet (7.5 m) high and 20 feet (6 m) wide. Oval to oblong leaves are pointed and up to 20 inches (51 cm) long. They remain green on the plant until they are shed in winter or early spring. Through summer and fall, loose clusters of fragrant flowers, 2 to 4½ inches (5 to 11.5 cm) in diameter, open at the tips of swollen branches. Petals can be white, yellow flushed with pink, or shades of pink, rose or red, usually with a yellow throat. May begin flowering when 1 to 1½ feet (30.5 cm to 46 cm) tall from a rooted tip cutting or air layer. Fruit pods grow up to 1 foot (30.5 cm) long. *P. rubra acutifolia* flowers are white with yellow centers and especially fragrant. *P. rubra acuminata* is the pure white type found growing in canyons and washes* of the lower Sonoran Desert. It is smaller and not particularly fragrant, but quite drought resistant. Native from Mexico south to Panama.

Plumeria rubra acuminata and *P. rubra acutifolia*
Plumeria, Nosegay plumeria
Apocynaceae family

* *See Glossary*

Podranea ricasoliana

Pink trumpet vine
Bignoniaceae family

COLD HARDINESS

Low and intermediate zones.

LANDSCAPE VALUE

- Adds a special touch of color and grace when cascading from a trellis, over walls, raised planters and over doorways.
- A low sprawling shrub.
- Quick shade; screening; sun glare, heat and wind protection.

CULTURAL REQUIREMENTS

- **Exposure:** Full or reflected sun and heat.
- **Water:** Water every week or two during the growing season, once or twice a season during winter.
- **Soil:** Improved garden soil with good drainage is best.
- **Propagation:** Cuttings.
- **Maintenance:** May require annual pruning because the plant can frost back to the ground. Pruning is also necessary from time to time to maintain form and vigor, even in frost-free areas. It resprouts from surviving wood or from below the ground in spring and blooms the same season. Will not grow on a flat wall surface unless given support. Stems must be tied to or woven through a trellis or fence.

POSSIBLE PROBLEMS

- Nematodes*, scale* insects, mites and caterpillars.
- Can be invasive. Runners and branches will root wherever they touch moist soil.

Sprawling, evergreen vine from South Africa. With abundant water, sunshine and heat, will grow rapidly to 20 feet (6 m) in any direction. Glossy deep green foliage is pinnately* compound. Three to five pairs of 2-inch (5-cm) long leaflets have toothed margins. Loose trusses of trumpet-shaped lavender-pink flowers are red-veined on the inner surface; individual blossoms, 2 inches (5 cm) long and 2 to 3 inches (5 to 7.5 cm) wide, appear at the tips of new growth almost year-round in the warmest areas, late spring through fall where winters are frosty. Slender seed pods up to 1 foot (30.5 cm) long split in half when ripe.

Portulacaria afra

African jade plant, Elephant's food
Portulacaceae family

COLD HARDINESS

Low zone and sheltered warm-winter microclimates of intermediate zone. Sensitive to frost and needs protection in marginal areas. Best used in a warm, almost frost-free microclimate.

LANDSCAPE VALUE

- Distinctive branching habit and texture make this a strong accent or specimen.
- Excellent in containers and planters.
- In mild-winter microclimates it can be planted closely spaced in groups and the prostrate variety can serve as a groundcover.
- Where it achieves its full growth potential, it provides background and screening and adds interest to shrub plantings.

CULTURAL REQUIREMENTS

- **Exposure:** Full sun to full shade. Tolerant of heat and low humidity.
- **Water:** Water every week to every couple months in hot dry weather, less frequently in winter.
- **Soil:** Most soils with good drainage.
- **Propagation:** Cuttings.
- **Maintenance:** Head back fast-growing branch terminals to a side branch for more dense, compact plant appearance

POSSIBLE PROBLEMS

None observed.

This shrubby succulent grows irregularly at a moderate to rapid pace to 10 feet (3 m) high and 8 to 10 feet (2.5 to 3 m) wide. Somewhat resembles the jade plant. Although both are native to South Africa they are unrelated. The thick fleshy stems of elephant's food are brown to purple-brown in color, and its glossy, juicy leaves are 1/2 inch (1 cm) long, oval in shape and grow in pairs. Flowering is a rare event in the United States, but when it occurs, the plant produces many clusters of tiny pink flowers. Various selections include smaller, larger, prostrate and variegated-leaf types.

* See Glossary

Prosopis alba

Argentine mesquite

Fabaceae (Leguminosae) family

COLD HARDINESS

Low and intermediate zones and warm microclimates of high zone.

LANDSCAPE VALUE

A handsome tree, uniquely adapted to arid habitats where it is an appropriate choice for many landscape uses:

- Shade.
- Street median or highway.
- Buffer-zone plantings.
- Privacy screen or windbreak.
- Parks and commercial sites.
- Flowers attract bees that produce the highly esteemed mesquite honey.

CULTURAL REQUIREMENTS

- **Exposure:** Full or reflected sun. Thrives in great heat and aridity
- **Water:** Drought tolerant. Looks best with a soaking of the root zone once or twice during prolonged dry periods.
- **Soil:** Most soils with good drainage.
- **Propagation:** Seed. Some selections, such as 'Colorado,' must be cutting-grown or grafted.
- **Maintenance:** Prune to develop a strong, well-balanced branch framework. Thinning the crown of young, fast-growing trees reduces wind resistance and the danger of blow-over.

POSSIBLE PROBLEMS

- Dark-colored sap drips from pruning wounds and bark injuries of some trees. The sap leaves difficult-to-remove stains and spots on masonry and metal surfaces.
- Sometimes affected by mistletoe or witches' broom.
- Insect damage is usually cosmetic.
- Young trees require rabbit-proof fencing for several years because rabbits will chew bark and girdle.
- Leaf-footed plant bugs, palo verde webbers, leafhoppers and psyllids are occasional pests.
- Mesquite roots are invasive and can cause problems in leaky sewer and drainage lines. However, shade plants that grow beneath the tree seem to thrive with no indication of competition from these roots over the years.
- Fallen seed pods create litter beneath the tree, but this litter improves the soil environment for understory plant growth.
- Flowers release pollen to which some people are allergic. However, this mesquite does not flower as abundantly as most native species. In addition, mesquite pollen is heavy and settles out of the air close to the source.
- In pedestrian-traffic areas, place thorny trees with care.

Generally small to medium-size tree with a short erect trunk and vertical branching habit, but under optimum conditions it can grow quite large. Averages 20 to 40 feet (6 to 12 m) in height and spread. Rapid growth with regular water. The dense, lacy crown of foliage is nearly evergreen, especially following mild winters when old leaves persist until spring growth emerges. Bipinnately* compound leaves are made up of delicate dark green leaflets 1/4 to 1/3 inch (0.5 to 1 cm) long. Leaflets grow in pairs, twenty-five to fifty per leaf and more closely spaced than those of *P. chilensis*.

Some trees have sharp spines on young branches, but nurseries offer a thornless type often called "Chilean mesquite." The name is only partially correct because it is a form of *P. alba* from the Chilean side of the Andes Mountains but is not *P. chilensis*. Compact spikes of small greenish white to cream-colored flowers, 2 to 3 inches (5 to 7.5 cm) long, open in spring. The slender strongly curved or ring-shaped seed pods to 8 inches (20.5 cm) long ripen in late summer. As with other mesquites, the flowers of this species attract bees and are a source of excellent honey. The seed pod and its contents are edible, including the sugary material surrounding the seeds. Native range extends through arid regions of Argentina, Bolivia, Chile and Paraguay. 'Colorado' is a thornless, cold-tolerant clone.

* See Glossary

Prosopis chilensis

Chilean mesquite

Fabaceae (Leguminosae) family

COLD HARDINESS

Low and intermediate zones. Can be grown in warm microclimates of high zone.

LANDSCAPE VALUE

- Shade.
- Street or highway planting.
- Specimen.
- Privacy screening or windbreak.
- Parks and other public spaces.

CULTURAL REQUIREMENTS

- **Exposure:** Full or reflected sun.
- **Water:** Irrigation can be an effective tool for regulating growth rate, controlling plant size and establishing a well-anchored root system. Trees watered abundantly at the base of the trunk develop a lush, dense foliage canopy, but lack a sturdy root system. In strong winds, young trees are easily blown over. Avoid the problem by applying water in a zone at the perimeter of the canopy (the dripline) and beyond. Established trees perform well with a thorough soaking of the root zone every month or two during prolonged dry periods.
- **Soil:** Most soils with good drainage.
- **Propagation:** Seed or cutting for special selections. Carefully select seed to get the form you desire. A thornless form of *P. alba* from a population found growing in Chile, is also sold as Chilean mesquite, thus the common name in the trade.
- **Maintenance:** Trim lowest branches above head height to avoid contact with thorns.

POSSIBLE PROBLEMS

Same as *P. alba*.

Evergreen or semideciduous small to medium-size tree that grows to 30 feet (9 m) high, with equal spread. It branches freely close to the ground to form a wide-spreading rounded crown. Elegant ferny foliage, fast growth and rugged character that delivers good landscape performance under harsh desert conditions account for the popularity of this mesquite. Trees may be trained into single- or multitrunked specimens with rough, scaly, nearly black bark at maturity. Thorniness is a variable characteristic; some trees are armed with hard spines up to 2 inches (5 cm) long, but cutting-grown thornless clones are available. To complicate matters, small-thorned types (which are mostly hybrids) may be offered as Chilean mesquite or hybrid South American mesquite. The twisting knotty branches of the true Chilean mesquite are flexible and arch slightly at the tips. Linear leaflets 3/8 to 2 inches (1 to 5 cm) long grow in widely spaced pairs on each primary division of the leaf, giving the impression of a lighter, more open foliage than that of the Argentine or hybrid South American mesquite. Chilean mesquite can be leafless or evergreen in winter, depending on the severity of cold, but it is generally more dependably evergreen than other South American species. Clusters of curved or nearly straight seed pods develop from the drooping 2- to 4-inch (5- to 10-cm) yellowish green catkins that open in spring. Seed pods are 5 to 7 inches (13 to 18 cm) long. Grows as a native in Chile, eastern Argentina and on the Pacific Coast of Peru. It is now naturalized in Hawaii and other warm-climate regions throughout the world.

* See Glossary

Prosopis glandulosa glandulosa

Texas honey mesquite

Fabaceae (Leguminosae) family

COLD HARDINESS

All three zones.

LANDSCAPE VALUE

- A mesquite of graceful form and handsome, almost tropical summer foliage.
- As a shade tree, it provides shelter from the hot summer sun and then, after shedding leaves in fall, allows winter sun to make outdoor living areas warmer and more useful.
- Patio.
- Street or median.
- Park.

CULTURAL REQUIREMENTS

- **Exposure:** Full or reflected sun to part shade.
- **Water:** Drought tolerant when fully established but develops into a larger, more attractive tree with a thorough soaking of the root zone every month or two during the warm season.
- **Soil:** Most soils with good drainage and some depth.
- **Propagation:** Seed.
- **Maintenance:** Prune and stake young trees as necessary to develop regular tree form and branching habit.

POSSIBLE PROBLEMS

Same as *P. alba.*

Spiny deciduous tree that grows at a moderate rate (rapid with regular water) from 15 to 30 feet (4.5 to 9 m) in height and spread. Can be single- or multitrunked with an open spreading growth habit and branches that often droop toward the tips. Shiny bright green foliage resembles that of the California pepper tree *(Schinus molle).* Leaves are bipinnately* compound, with six to fifteen pairs of secondary leaflets per leaf. The leaflets are large, linear and 1 to 2 inches (2.5 to 5 cm) long (occasionally $2\frac{1}{2}$ inches [6.5 cm]) Leaflets are spaced about $\frac{3}{8}$ to $\frac{3}{4}$ inch (1 to 2 cm) apart. In spring, drooping tassels of creamy white flowers appear. Seed pods 3 to 9 inches (7.5 to 23 cm) long, almost straight, ripen in late summer. Native throughout the southwestern United States, as well as Kansas, Oklahoma, Texas and into Mexico.

Prosopis glandulosa torreyana

Western honey mesquite

Fabaceae (Leguminosae) family

COLD HARDINESS

Low and intermediate zones and warm-winter microclimates of high zone.

LANDSCAPE VALUE

- Climate control.
- Screening.
- Roadway planting.
- Wildlife habitat and reforestation.
- Leafless winter appearance has an interesting architectural quality and allows the winter sun to warm outdoor living areas when trimmed into a patio tree.

CULTURAL REQUIREMENTS

- **Exposure:** Full to reflected sun.
- **Water:** In some areas well-established trees survive just with rainfall especially if this amount is supplemented by surface runoff from nearby paved areas, rooftops, etc. In drier regions thorough soaking of the root zone every month or two during the growing season to once or twice a season when the tree is leafless promotes satisfactory growth and appearance.
- **Soil:** Grows in many arid climate soils but is larger and more lush in deep fertile types.
- **Propagation:** Seed or cuttings.
- **Maintenance:** May need training and staking to develop good branching structure.

POSSIBLE PROBLEMS

Same as *P. alba.*

This deciduous to semi-evergreen (in its lowest range) mesquite grows rapidly from 15 to 30 feet (4.5 to 9 m) high and 20 to 40 feet (6 to 12 m) wide. One to several short trunks have dark brown or black bark that becomes fissured and scaly with age. On difficult sites, western honey mesquite never attains treelike proportions, surviving instead as a shrub. The tree canopy is typically broad and spreading, with branches weeping slightly toward the tips. The ferny green leaflets of this variety are a little smaller than those of Texas mesquite (*P. glandulosa glandulosa*), but from a landscape point of view, the important difference is the foliage color. Western honey mesquite is a darker green, lacking the brightness of the Texas mesquite. The flowers and seed pods are not different though. Native to parts of several southwestern states from New Mexico to California. It occurs in Mexico from Baja California to Sinaloa and also in Chihuahua.

* *See Glossary*

Prosopis nigra

Black mesquite

Fabaceae (Leguminosae) family

COLD HARDINESS

All three zones.

LANDSCAPE VALUE

- A shade tree for residential and street or avenue planting.
- A bosque* effect when planted as a multitrunk tree, for parks and larger properties.
- A single-trunk specimen.

CULTURAL REQUIREMENTS

- **Exposure:** Full sun, including reflected heat.
- **Water:** Quite drought resistant. Thoroughly soak the root zone every month or two during the warm season to develop a tree and maintain a satisfactory appearance. Water once or twice during the winter months.
- **Soil:** Any soil, from Xeriscape™ conditions to garden and lawn locations.
- **Propagation:** Seed.
- **Maintenance:** Needs pruning and staking when young to develop into desired tree form—single- or multitrunk.

POSSIBLE PROBLEMS

Same as *P. alba.*

A vigorous evergreen tree that grows rapidly 20 to 30 feet (6 to 9 m) high and wide—even larger under optimum conditions. Bark is dark gray to blackish. Deep green compound leaves are ferny with short, tightly packed leaflets. This seems to be the chief difference between it and its South American relative *P. alba,* which it resembles in most other ways. The trees observed on the University of Arizona campus had fewer stout thorns in youth than the average *P. alba,* but this too is variable within the species as there are thornless forms of *P. alba.*

Prosopis pubescens

Screwbean mesquite, Tornillo

Fabaceae (Leguminosae) family

Deciduous, spiny large shrub or small tree that grows at a slow to moderate rate up to 30 feet (9 m) high, with equal spread. Multi- or single-trunked. Bark on older branches and trunk peels in thin stringy flakes. The foliage canopy is vase-shaped, open and spreading. Fine lacy leaves are bipinnately* compound, composed of five to nine pairs of oblong to elliptical leaflets, each $3/8$ to $7/8$ inch (1 to 2 cm) long, sparsely covered on both sides with gray hairs. Slender white spines to $3/4$ inch (2 cm) long grow in pairs.

COLD HARDINESS

All three zones.

LANDSCAPE VALUE

- Tree form provides light filtered shade during the growing season.
- Medians, buffer zone plantings, parks, confined space and small properties.
- Pods add interest at close range and are prized for decoration in dry flower arrangements.

CULTURAL REQUIREMENTS

- **Exposure:** Full or reflected sun to part shade. Hardy to heat as well as cold.
- **Water:** Drought tolerant once established. Survives but grows rather slowly without irrigation on favorable sites. Water every week to every couple months produces a better landscape tree.
- **Soil:** Most soils with good drainage.
- **Propagation:** Seed.
- **Maintenance:** For the first several years, prune lightly and frequently, pinching back unwanted side branches to encourage faster development of tree form.

POSSIBLE PROBLEMS

Same as *P. alba.*

Hanging cylindrical flower spikes 1 to 2 inches (2.5 to 5 cm) long produce unusual seed pods that are tightly coiled in a spiral curl $3/4$ to $1\frac{1}{2}$ inches (2 to 4 cm) long. Native to the Sonoran and Chihuahuan Deserts in Arizona, Texas and Mexico. Also found in the Mojave Desert.

* *See Glossary*

Prosopis velutina

Velvet mesquite

Fabaceae (Leguminosae) family

COLD HARDINESS

All three zones.

LANDSCAPE VALUE

- Open filtered summer shade for patios, residential areas, parks.
- Twigs are nubbed at joints, adding interest to the winter silhouette.
- Wild trees often display a picturesque gnarled and twisting branching pattern. Interesting structural plant for arid or transitional zones.
- Does well in lawn areas.

CULTURAL REQUIREMENTS

- **Exposure:** Full to reflected sun or part shade.
- **Water:** Tolerates considerable drought once established. Thoroughly soak the root zone every month or two during the warm season.
- **Soil:** Tolerates a wide range of arid soil types, but the deeper the better.
- **Propagation:** Seed.
- **Maintenance:** Prune young trees to assist good branching structure.

POSSIBLE PROBLEMS

Same as *P. alba*.

Deciduous, usually spiny mesquite that grows at a moderate rate (rapid with regular water, slow with none). Reaches 30 feet (9 m) in height and spread. Shrubby on dry difficult sites, becoming a medium-size tree on deep uniform soils with more moisture. Trees are single- or multitrunked with rough bark. They branch close to the ground and become less thorny with age. Soft gray-green fine-textured leaflets are oblong, $1/3$ to $1/2$ inch (1 cm) long, with fourteen to thirty pairs per bipinnately* compound leaf. Short gray hairs cover almost all younger parts of the plant. Yellow catkinlike flower clusters hang from branches in spring. Each bloom is about 2 to 3 inches (5 to 7.5 cm) long. Beaked seed pods as long as 9 inches (23 cm) ripen in late summer. Native from southeastern Arizona into Mexico and western Texas.

Prunus serotina capuli and *P. serotina virens*

Western Mexican chokecherry, Eastern Mexican chokecherry, Southwestern Mexican chokecherry

Rosaceae family

COLD HARDINESS

All three zones. Best in high zone.

LANDSCAPE VALUE

- Patios.
- Bosques*.
- Woodsy plantings in cooler, morning-sun situations.
- Adds a lush green touch in summer and allows for winter sun when deciduous.
- Understory tree.

CULTURAL REQUIREMENTS

- **Exposure:** Full sun to open shade but not reflected sun. May look stressed in reflected sun.
- **Water:** Thoroughly soak the root zone every week or two, less often when tree is mature.
- **Soil:** Appreciates garden situations but tolerates desert soils as long as they are not extremely alkaline.
- **Propagation:** Seed.
- **Maintenance:** Low maintenance.

POSSIBLE PROBLEMS

Same as *P. alba*.

Small to medium-size deciduous tree that grows up to 30 feet (9 m) high and wide, under optimum conditions. On average, it is much shorter. Its growth rate is moderate to rapid, depending on available moisture. Dark green leaves, $2\frac{1}{2}$ to $4\frac{1}{2}$ inches (6.5 to 11.5 cm) long, are shiny above with pointy tips. Leaves may be semi-evergreen depending on moisture and winter temperatures. There is little difference between the subspecies as far as their landscape value, except that *P. serotina capuli* has broader leaves and seems to have a thicker foliage mass, presenting a more luxuriant landscape statement. Spring flowers are small and white, followed by tiny purple-black cherries—edible but mostly pit and hardly worth the trouble. Native to northern Mexico and mountains farther south. The subspecies overlap in both the eastern and western sides of the country.

* *See Glossary*

Psilostrophe cooperi

Paper flower, Yellow paper daisy

Helenieae family

COLD HARDINESS

Low and intermediate zones. Moderately frost tolerant.

LANDSCAPE VALUE

- Provides color over a long season, even year-round under favorable conditions.
- Combines well with many low-water-use shrubs and trees.
- Naturalizing in arid and transition zones or in seed mixes to revegetate disturbed areas.
- Wildflower plantings.

CULTURAL REQUIREMENTS

- **Exposure:** Full or reflected sun to light shade.
- **Water:** Drought resistant. Rainfall is adequate to satisfy water requirements in some arid locations but water every month or two in the hottest low-elevation areas.
- **Soil:** Most arid landscape soils with good drainage.
- **Propagation:** Seed.
- **Maintenance:** Rugged and undemanding. No maintenance required other than occasional removal of unattractive mature plants in close viewing situations.

POSSIBLE PROBLEMS

Not for refined or tailored landscapes. Plants become somewhat open and straggly as they age.

Dwarfish clump-forming perennial that grows an average of 8 to 20 inches (20.5 to 51 cm) in height and spread. Its moderate growth rate is faster during dry seasons with occasional irrigation. Plant is shrubby, with few to many stems covered with white woolly hairs. Stems are woody near the base. Alternating linear to lance-shaped leaves are ¾ to 2 inches (2 to 5 cm) long. The leaves are covered with matted, woolly hairs when young, greener and less hairy with age. Showy bright yellow flowers at the branch tips turn papery and hold their color as they dry; blooms persist over an extended period. Native to the Sonoran Desert, Arizona, and Mojave Deserts of the western United States and Mexico.

Psorothamnus spinosus *(Dalea spinosa)*

Smoketree

Fabaceae (Leguminosae) family

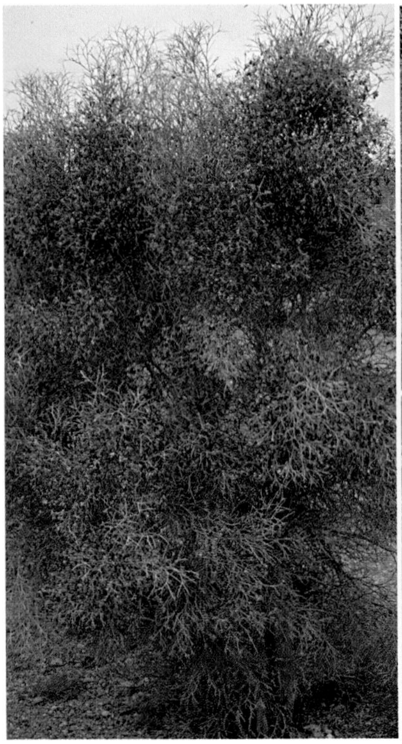

COLD HARDINESS

Low zone and the more frost-free microclimates of intermediate zone.

LANDSCAPE VALUE

- The silvery, smoky gray character and spectacular floral effects make this unique plant an excellent accent or specimen.
- As a foundation plant it provides a beautiful tracery against structural walls.
- Background or boundary plant.

CULTURAL REQUIREMENTS

- **Exposure:** Full or reflected sun. Adapted only where hard freezes are uncommon.
- **Water:** Native to desert washes*, so watering once or twice during long dry periods assures landscape performance.
- **Soil:** Sandy, gravelly or rocky soils.
- **Propagation:** Seed.
- **Maintenance:** Requires little care once established.

POSSIBLE PROBLEMS

Short-lived and temperamental at times.

Small deciduous tree or large shrub that grows at a slow to moderate rate from 10 to 20 feet (3 to 6 m) high and 10 to 15 feet (3 to 4.5 m) wide. Ascending primary branches and a compact, intricate network of silvery gray, smoky-looking branches and slender thorn-tipped twigs give the plant an oval form. Small hairy white leaves are short-lived, being shed before flowering in late spring when masses of fragrant deep violet-purple, pea-shaped flowers in clusters ½ to 1½ inches (1.5 to 4 cm) long cover the plant. Native to southeastern California, southwestern Arizona, southern Mojave Desert, Northern Sonora and Baja California.

* *See Glossary*

Punica granatum and *P. granatum* 'Nana'

Pomegranate, Dwarf pomegranate

Punicaceae family

COLD HARDINESS

All three zones.

LANDSCAPE VALUE

- Lovely flowering specimen as a small tree or large shrub.
- Fruit and fall foliage are decorative.
- Clipped or unclipped hedge.
- Cool-season deciduous screen, windbreak or barrier planting.
- Dwarf selections in containers.
- Seasonal interest provided by bronzy young growth of some types.

CULTURAL REQUIREMENTS

- **Exposure:** Full desert sun and intense heat.
- **Water:** Moderately drought tolerant as an established plant. Thoroughly soak the root zone every week to every month or two, depending on your microclimate. With frequent watering, it grows larger, more lush and provides more fruit.
- **Soil:** Endures most alkaline desert soil types.
- **Propagation:** Seed, layers or hardwood cuttings for selected cultivars*.
- **Maintenance:** Growing it as a tree often requires frequent pruning during the growing season to eliminate suckers* at the base of the trunk. In late winter, prune out weak, twiggy growth and crossing or interfering branches.

POSSIBLE PROBLEMS

- Limited landscape appeal during winter leafless period.
- Fruit may be damaged in some areas by leaf-footed plant bug*.
- Injured fruit splits and attracts other insects and birds that feed on the exposed pulp. Plant bug chemical controls are effective.

A large, deciduous shrub or small tree, multi- or single-stemmed that grows rapidly (with regular water) to 12 to 20 feet (3.5 to 6 m) high and 10 to 15 feet (3 to 4.5 m) wide. This tenacious plant is vase-shaped, with a rounded top and branches. Sometimes is spiny. Glossy deep green leaves are oblong to lance-shaped, up to 3 inches (7.5 cm) long and turn clear yellow in fall. Fiery red flowers have crinkly petals. Each bloom is 1 to 2 inches (2.5 to 5 cm) in diameter. Flowers open singly or in clusters during spring. Cultivar flower characteristics vary from creamy to orange, pink to red and variegated, single or double. Both fruiting and nonfruiting selections are available. Fruiting types produce thick-skinned, rounded apple-size fruits 2½ to 5 inches (6.5 to 13 cm) across. These are filled with tightly packed seeds covered with pink to red sweet juicy pulp. 'Wonderful' is the most common fruiting selection. 'Chico' and 'Nana' are compact dwarf types easily maintained at 2 to 3 feet (61 cm to 1 m) tall. Their fruit is decorative but not edible. Native range extends from Southeast Europe into southern Asia.

** See Glossary*

Puya chilensis
Chilean bromeliad
Bromeliaceae family

COLD HARDINESS
Low and intermediate zones.

LANDSCAPE VALUE
- Container plant.
- Rock garden with other succulents.
- Banks and foreground plantings.
- Flowering is a garden event with unusual color and form.

CULTURAL REQUIREMENTS
- **Exposure:** Full sun to part shade.
- **Water:** Quite drought resistant. Thoroughly soak the root zone every month or two.
- **Soil:** Any soil.
- **Propagation:** Seed or divisions.
- **Maintenance:** Low maintenance.

POSSIBLE PROBLEMS
Difficult to weed because of the spiky, prickly-edged foliage.

Succulent grows at a slow to moderate rate to about 3 feet (1 m) in height and spread. The bloom stalk is much taller. Clumps of sword-like gray-green leaves form a rosette*. Leaves have sharp tips and spined edges. As plant develops, offsets* can become quite a mound. In midspring, unusual 1/2-inch (1.5-cm) metallic blue-green, bell-shaped flowers hang on vertical stalks that resemble asparagus shoots at first. *Puyas* don't have much of a track record in the hot-desert regions, but other species would probably be successful, especially the spectacular *Puya berteroniana* with its 6-foot (2-m) flower stalks. Native to Chile.

* See Glossary

QUERCUS

Many people are surprised to see oaks thriving in the desert urban landscapes. A few years ago they were a rare occurrence. Somehow these sturdy trees were associated with the temperate zone. However if one were to examine the flora of the high edges of the Sonoran and Chihuahuan Deserts, one would find numerous species of oaks, sometimes actually straying into the high zone. They do look different from species that are deciduous and have large leaves. The ones in arid climates are evergreen and, with a few exceptions, the foliage resembles that of the holly. The eight species described in this book can be found thriving in all three zones. Some, such as *Quercus virginiana* and some of its cultivars, have become very popular for street and avenue planting in the United States Southwest. Perhaps the first oaks planted here were cork oaks (*Quercus suber*), during World War I. The bark was the only source of cork in the States at that time and because it is native only to southern Europe and north Africa, close to the shores of the Mediterranean, there was concern that the supply would be cut off. The few survivors of these plantings in southern Arizona are great spreading trees and impressive landscape specimens.

Quercus agrifolia
California coast live oak
Fagaceae family

A round-headed evergreen tree that becomes wide-spreading with age, to 30 to 40 feet (10 to 12 m), usually wider than tall. It reaches 20 to 60 feet (6 to 18 m) high and grows slowly, faster in winter and spring with extra water. Crinkly, slightly glossy holly-like leaves are 1 to 3 inches (2.5 to 7.5 cm) long and smooth. Bark is dark gray, thick and fire resistant, which explains its survival in the regularly fire-ravaged chaparral belt of southern California. Even though dubbed "coast live oak," it also inhabits the hot interior slopes and valleys of the coastal range's desert edge in southern California and northern Baja California, Mexico.

COLD HARDINESS
Intermediate and high zones. Low zone may be too hot. No known examples there.

LANDSCAPE VALUE
- Shade tree that is not too large for residential and/or street and park plantings.
- Tolerates clipping as a large trimmed hedge.

CULTURAL REQUIREMENTS
- **Exposure:** Full sun.
- **Water:** Tolerates weekly water in the cool season but thoroughly soak the root zone every month or two throughout the year to maintain a healthy mature specimen. Young developing trees will grow faster with weekly water in winter and spring, tapering off when the heat of summer arrives.
- **Soil:** Most soils with good drainage.
- **Propagation:** Seed (acorns). Acorns lose viability quickly, so gather and sprout them soon after they drop.
- **Maintenance:** Gradual removal of low side branches to develop it for overhead shade. On rare instances, it can be hit by oak moth caterpillars and requires spraying.

POSSIBLE PROBLEMS
Being native to a region with winter rain and no summer rain, this oak presents special irrigation concerns. In the hot-desert summers, it will need some supplemental water. On the contrary, in its cooler native habitat, it receives no natural precipitation during the summer months so summer irrigation should be light.

Quercus buckleyi (Q. texanum)
Texas hill country red oak
Fagaceae family

A deciduous shade tree that grows at a moderate to rapid rate, depending on soil moisture. Grows 30 feet (9 m) high and wide, up to 50 to 60 feet (15 to 18 m) in its native region, but it does not usually get this large in desert or arid-region landscapes. The dense rounded canopy of bright green sharply lobed leaves turns brilliant scarlet in late fall, persisting into early winter, an outstanding feature that is unusual for trees adapted to warm arid regions. *Q. buckleyi* 'Redrock,' a superior selection offered in Arizona, can be grown with a single or multiple trunk, which looks less stiff in a natural setting. Native to Texas hill country.

COLD HARDINESS
All three zones.

LANDSCAPE VALUE
- Patios and residential areas.
- Parks, parking lots, city streets and roadsides.
- Shade in summer, warmth in winter.
- Brilliant fall color.

CULTURAL REQUIREMENTS
- **Exposure:** Full sun and reflected heat to part shade
- **Water:** Thoroughly soak the root zone every week or two until established, less often in winter. Irrigation intervals can be lengthened as tree matures and becomes quite drought resistant.
- **Soil:** Many types of soil, including alkaline and those high in calcium (native to limestone region).
- **Propagation:** Seed (acorns). Acorns lose viability quickly, so gather and sprout them soon after they drop.
- **Maintenance:** Little pruning or maintenance once it reaches the point when lowest branches are above head height.

POSSIBLE PROBLEMS
Leaf litter in winter.

** See Glossary*

Quercus emoryi

Emory oak

Fagaceae family

COLD HARDINESS

All three zones.

LANDSCAPE VALUE

- Handsome shade tree.
- Parks.
- Commercial landscapes.
- Residential landscapes where there is ample space.

CULTURAL REQUIREMENTS

- **Exposure:** Full sun.
- **Water:** Drought tolerant but needs thorough soaking of the root zone every week or two in low zone and once or twice a season in intermediate and high zones if rainfall is more abundant.
- **Soil:** Most soils with good drainage.
- **Propagation:** Seed (acorns). Acorns lose viability quickly, so gather and sprout them soon after they drop.
- **Maintenance:** Requires only routine pruning for structure and form.

POSSIBLE PROBLEMS

- Slow to reach functional size.
- Fallen acorns may require cleanup in some locations. (Acorns are used for food in northern Mexico, but they must be fresh. They lose viability quickly.)

Evergreen shrub to medium-size tree, depending on site characteristics. Grows slowly to about 50 feet (15 m) high and 40 feet (12 m) wide. Good quality soil and regular water will speed up growth. In the tree form, the single trunk may reach a diameter of $2\frac{1}{2}$ feet (76 cm), with thick, black rough-textured bark. The dense rounded crown is made up of slender red twigs with brownish buds $\frac{1}{3}$ inch (1 cm) long. The oval leaves are $2\frac{1}{2}$ inches (6.5 cm) or, rarely, 4 inches (10 cm) long, leathery and glossy. They have toothed or smooth edges and turn bronzy gold and drop just before new growth emerges in late spring. Oblong acorns grow to $\frac{1}{2}$ to $\frac{3}{4}$ inch (1 to 2 cm) long and are edible. The enclosing cup covers half or less of the nut. Native to Texas, west into Arizona and south into northern Mexico.

Quercus ilex

Holly oak, Holm oak, Italian live oak

Fagaceae family

COLD HARDINESS

All three zones. With severe prolonged cold, young trees may show some die-back* and mature specimens may lose the current crop of leaves.

LANDSCAPE VALUE

- Refined and elegant tree for residential landscapes, parks, golf courses and streets.
- Can be sheared to form a tall hedge, screen or topiary shape.
- Seashore landscapes.

CULTURAL REQUIREMENTS

- **Exposure:** Intense sunlight with high heat and low humidity. Salt tolerant. Endures adverse urban environments.
- **Water:** Thoroughly soak the root zone every month or two to maintain established trees. Somewhat drought tolerant, but stressed trees are smaller and grow slower. Performs well as a lawn tree with irrigation based on turf requirements.
- **Soil:** Most soils with good drainage, including poorer gravelly types as long as depth is adequate.
- **Propagation:** Seed (acorns). Acorns lose viability quickly, so gather and sprout them soon after they drop.
- **Maintenance:** Shear to create hedge, screen or topiary.

POSSIBLE PROBLEMS

Fallen acorn cleanup.

This oak from the Mediterranean region grows at a moderate rate from 30 to 60 feet (9 to 18 m) high, with equal spread. Growth rate is faster with optimum soil and water conditions. Often pyramidal in form as a young tree, with a symmetrical dome-shaped to rounded crown at maturity. The bark is smooth except on the trunks of large trees where it becomes cracked and fissured. The dense evergreen foliage consists of leathery leaves that are variable in size and shape, but typically oval to lance-shaped and 1 to 3 inches (2.5 to 7.5 cm) long by $\frac{1}{2}$ to 1 inch (1 to 2.5 cm) wide. Leaf margins may be smooth or serrated with spines and pointed tips. Bears some likeness to holly (*Ilex*) foliage. The undersides of the leaves are covered with a dense mat of gray to yellowish fine hairs. Mature acorns are 1 to $1\frac{1}{2}$ inches (2.5 to 4 cm) long in a cup that encloses about half of the fruit.

* *See Glossary*

Quercus oblongifolia

Mexican blue oak

Fagaceae family

Small semi-evergreen oak that grows slowly from 16 to 26 feet (5 to 8 m) in height and spread. Trunk and primary branches are covered with rough dark gray bark. Foliage canopy is dense and spreading. Light blue-gray leaves are paler beneath, 1 1/4 to 3 inches (3 to 7.5 cm) long, 1/4 to 1/3 inch (0.5 to 1 cm) wide, and usually rounded at both ends or heart-shaped at the base. Smooth entire margins are sometimes scalloped on young shoots or slightly rolled toward the lower side. Small acorns have a short, sharp point at the tip. A hemispherical cup covered with fuzzy golden brown hairs encloses about one-third of the acorn. Leaves drop in spring before new growth begins. Native to New Mexico west into Arizona in the United States and Chihuahua and Sonora in Mexico.

COLD HARDINESS

All three zones.

LANDSCAPE VALUE

- Landscape potential is based on the distinctive crown of blue-gray foliage.
- A small, slow-growing shade or specimen tree on small properties and other sites where growing space is limited.
- In groups as a screen or background along roadways.

CULTURAL REQUIREMENTS

- **Exposure:** Full sun.
- **Water:** Tolerates dry periods but thorough soaking of the root zone every week or two is essential in low-elevation deserts, less often or not at all for mature established trees at higher, cooler, more moist elevations.
- **Soil:** Most arid-region soils of average quality are suitable.
- **Propagation:** Seed (acorns). Acorns lose viability quickly, so gather and sprout them soon after they drop.
- **Maintenance:** Requires no special care.

POSSIBLE PROBLEMS

None observed, except slow growth.

Quercus suber

Cork oak

Fagaceae family

Evergreen tree that grows at a moderate rate from 30 to 60 feet (9 to 18 m) high, with equal spread. Thick, furrowed and crinkled bark is a source of cork, which can be cut from the trunk without injuring the tree about every eight years. Spreading rounded crown of oval leaves to 3 inches (7.5 cm) long. Leaves have long, toothed margins and are dark green above, covered with gray hairs below. Leaves are shed in spring as new growth appears. A third to a half of the acorn is enclosed by a cup. One of the best oaks for low- and intermediate-zone desert regions. Native to southern Europe and northern Africa.

COLD HARDINESS

Low and intermediate zones. Has sustained serious damage in the high zone.

LANDSCAPE VALUE

- Unique bark gives distinctive ornamental character.
- Shade.
- Streets or parks.
- Large-scale commercial and residential landscapes and public spaces.

CULTURAL REQUIREMENTS

- **Exposure:** Reflected sun and heat.
- **Water:** As an established tree shows significant drought resistance. Thoroughly soak the root zone every couple weeks to every month or two.
- **Soil:** Deep good-quality soil for best growth and appearance. Well-adapted to desert areas.
- **Propagation:** Seed (acorns). Acorns lose viability quickly, so gather and sprout them soon after they drop.
- **Maintenance:** Low maintenance.

POSSIBLE PROBLEMS

- High soil alkalinity may induce iron chlorosis*.
- The bark is sometimes cut up and vandalized when planted in public places.

* *See Glossary*

Quercus turbinellia

Desert scrub oak

Fagaceae family

COLD HARDINESS

All three zones.

LANDSCAPE VALUE

- Roadside planting.
- Buffer zones.
- Reforestation of disturbed sites.
- Dense screen, informal hedge or border.
- A small patio tree, with training.
- It is especially useful where taller trees would interfere with the view from above, as in a terraced residential area on a slope or hill.

CULTURAL REQUIREMENTS

- **Exposure:** Full sun at 3500 to 6000 feet (1070 to 1830 m) but afternoon shade is better in hot low-desert climates.
- **Water:** At the higher elevations—established plants may survive without irrigation except during long drought periods. In hotter, drier low-elevation regions, water every week or two for satisfactory landscape performance.
- **Soil:** Most soils with good drainage, including poor rocky types.
- **Propagation:** Seed (acorns). Acorns lose viability quickly, so gather and sprout them soon after they drop.
- **Maintenance:** Essentially maintenance-free except for occasional pruning to control form or branching structure or to train into patio tree.

POSSIBLE PROBLEMS

None observed, except slow growth.

Dense rounded evergreen shrub or small tree that slowly grows 4 to 10 feet (1 to 3 m) high and 10 feet (3 m) wide. Bark on mature stems is scaly and light colored. The gray-green oval to rounded leaves are 1 to 1½ inches (2.5 to 4 cm) long by ½ to 1 inch (0.5 to 2.5 cm) wide. Toothed margins and leathery texture give the leaves some resemblance to foliage of the American holly (*Ilex*). The slender cylindrical acorns are ¾ to 1 inch (2 to 2.5 cm) long and about ¼ inch (1 cm) in diameter. Native to high reaches of the desert chaparral and desert grasslands in several western U.S. states.

Landscape Design Example

Arizona-Sonora Desert Museum demo garden: a mass planting with nice contrast between *Stachys coccinea* and *Calliandra*.

* See Glossary

Quercus virginiana

Southern live oak

Fagaceae family

COLD HARDINESS

All three zones.

LANDSCAPE VALUE

- Superior, durable and versatile landscape tree for residential and commercial sites.
- Specimen or shade tree in parks, golf courses, large-scale buffer zones, school grounds, along streets and highways and in public places where space permits.

CULTURAL REQUIREMENTS

- **Exposure:** Full or reflected sun and heat.
- **Water:** Maintains good appearance through moderately long dry periods. Thoroughly soak the root zone every couple weeks to every month or two for best growth and development. Trees will be smaller in arid regions on lower irrigation programs than their counterparts in wetter regions.
- **Soil:** Deep, uniform soil. Adapts to rocky, alkaline, even moderately salty soils and poor drainage, especially the 'Heritage' selection.
- **Propagation:** Seed (acorns). Acorns lose viability quickly, so gather and sprout them soon after they drop.
- **Maintenance:** Prune young trees during the early years to encourage good branching structure.

POSSIBLE PROBLEMS

May shed part of or all foliage where winters are very cold.

Evergreen tree from 40 to 60 feet (12 to 18 m) high, less in the desert, and 40 to 80 feet (12 to 24 m) wide or wider, also less in the desert. Grows rapidly with regular water. The dense and spreading foliage crown is made up of leathery elliptical to oblong leaves that are shiny and dark green above, covered with short whitish hairs below. The leaves are smooth-margined, to 5 inches (13 cm) long. Branches eventually grow quite thick, noted for their strong wood. Acorns are about a quarter covered by the enclosing cup, typically borne in clusters of three to five. The best tree of this species for the desert comes from the populations at the western edge of the *Q. virginiana* range in Texas. A selection, 'Heritage Oak™,' has good heat and drought tolerance, is fast-growing and has lush foliage, especially for arid-region landscape use. It has performed well in southern Arizona and in the Las Vegas area of Nevada. However, there are large old trees of unknown origin growing in the Imperial Valley of California, as well as in Phoenix and Tucson, Arizona. This indicates that the species can generally tolerate the desert. Native to the southern United States, from Virginia to Florida and across to Texas as well as northern Mexico.

Randia echinocarpa

Spiny-fruited randia, Papache

Rubiaceae family

COLD HARDINESS

Low and intermediate zones and warm microclimates of high zone, if propagated from northern populations.

LANDSCAPE VALUE

- Thorny barrier.
- Specimen or character plant.
- Flowering adds fragrance to the garden.

CULTURAL REQUIREMENTS

- **Exposure:** Full sun to part shade.
- **Water:** Established plants are highly tolerant of dry conditions. During prolonged drought periods, water once or twice to maintain appearance.
- **Soil:** Most soils.
- **Propagation:** Seed and probably cuttings.
- **Maintenance:** Little maintenance. May need to shape.

POSSIBLE PROBLEMS

Thorns make placement an important consideration in pedestrian-traffic areas.

A shrub or small tree to 20 ft (6 m) high and 12 feet (3.5 m) wide that is evergreen in mild winters but defoliates following hard freezes. The growth habit is upright and open and the growth rate moderate. Thick, spreading branch terminals* are tipped with four spines 1/2 to 1 1/4 inches (1 to 3 cm) long. Clusters of oppositely arranged oval leaves are about 1 1/4 to 3 1/4 inches (3 to 8 cm) long. The fragrant tubular white flowers that appear at the branch ends in midsummer are male or female, from 1/2 to 2 inches (1 to 5 cm) long with lobes that open out in the form of a five-pointed star. The rounded fruits 2 to 4 inches (5 to 10 cm) in diameter are covered with thick tapering projections called *tubercules* and contain edible black pulp. Native from the Texas border south into Mexico as far as the states of Guerrero and Vera Cruz.

Rhus choriophylla

Chihuahuan leather-leaf sumac

Anacardiaceae family

COLD HARDINESS

All three zones.

LANDSCAPE VALUE

- Large background or screening plant.
- Small drought-resistant tree if trimmed.

CULTURAL REQUIREMENTS

- **Exposure:** Reflected sun to part shade.
- **Water:** Drought resistant. Thoroughly soak the root zone every month or two after established. Water every week or two to speed up growth.
- **Soil:** Most soils with good drainage.
- **Propagation:** Seed or cuttings.
- **Maintenance:** Stake and train for patio-size tree but no maintenance for shrub.

POSSIBLE PROBLEMS

Difficult to propagate.

Large spreading evergreen shrub that grows at a moderate rate from 12 to 18 feet (3.5 to 5.5 m) high, and equal spread. Bright green compound leaves have thick and waxy leaflets with rounded tips. Tiny off-white flowers in dense clusters are not of landscape interest nor are the small berry-like fruits. However, the dense foliage of this shrub is not to be missed in an arid setting. Native to Arizona and New Mexico in the United States, Sonora and Baja California in Mexico.

* *See Glossary*

Rhus kearneyi

Kearney's sumac

Anacardiaceae family

COLD HARDINESS

Low and intermediate zones. Not yet tried in the high zone.

LANDSCAPE VALUE

- This newcomer will be most useful as a foundation plant, for medians, and in mixed shrubbery plantings in general.
- Its compact growth habit and leaf size suggest that it will function well as clipped or unclipped hedging.

CULTURAL REQUIREMENTS

- **Exposure:** Full sun to part shade.
- **Water:** Very drought resistant but water every week or two during the spring growing season, and every month or two during summer.
- **Soil:** Should tolerate most desert soils considering it is found growing on rocky cliffs in its limited range in the wild. Good drainage is important.
- **Propagation:** Cuttings. Seed when available.
- **Maintenance:** No maintenance.

POSSIBLE PROBLEMS

None observed.

A rare evergreen sumac found in a limited area of the Tinajas Atlas Range in southwestern Arizona. Grows at a slow to moderate rate from 4 to 5 feet (1 to 1.5 m) tall, with equal spread, taller and wider under optimum conditions. A mounding rich green shrub with leathery, somewhat shiny leaves. Leaves are a little smaller than those of *R. ovata,* which it resembles. It has not flowered yet and, being new in cultivation, many things about it are still unknown. However, it is a most promising candidate for the short list of rich green desert-tolerant shrubs, especially coming from a low elevation and a hot region with little rainfall.

Rhus lancea

African sumac

Anacardiaceae family

Evergreen tree that grows 15 to 30 feet (4.5 to 9 m) high and 15 to 35 feet (4.5 to 11 m) wide at a moderate to rapid rate, depending on soil characteristics and water availability. One to several trunks have rough, orange to reddish brown bark. Round-headed foliage canopy is fine-textured and dense in youth, becoming more open and airy with age. Shiny medium green leaves are palmately compound*, divided into three slender leaflets 2 to 5 inches (5 to 13 cm) long. Tiny greenish yellow flowers in clusters add light fragrance to the garden in winter. The pea-sized fruits are cream or yellow to reddish on female trees. The fruits are of minimal decorative value. Native to South Africa.

COLD HARDINESS

Low and intermediate zones. Moderately frost hardy.

LANDSCAPE VALUE

- Small shade or street tree, suitable for patios, parks, downtown areas.
- Screen or background.
- Large clipped or unclipped hedge.
- Single- or multistemmed specimen, often with twisting, curved primary branches that have sculptural quality in old trees.
- Shelter and food for wildlife.

CULTURAL REQUIREMENTS

- **Exposure:** Full or reflected sun to part shade.
- **Water:** Withstands considerable drought when established. Thoroughly soak the root zone every month or two for a better landscape tree. Water even more often for lusher growth.
- **Soil:** Most soils with good drainage.
- **Propagation:** Seed.
- **Maintenance:** Prune and stake if necessary for the desired number of trunks and canopy height. Basal suckers may require control.

POSSIBLE PROBLEMS

- Pot-bound (girdling) roots result in stunted growth or death of plants held in the same nursery container too long.
- Volunteer seedlings can be a weedy nuisance. May be mildly invasive in wash* areas.
- Fallen fruit on paved surfaces may require cleanup.
- Chlorosis* is a common indicator of poor soil drainage.
- Moderately susceptible to Texas root rot*, scale insects, cicada and sapsucker woodpecker damage.
- Somewhat brittle and subject to breakage in wind.
- Pollen causes allergic reactions with some people.

** See Glossary*

Rhus microphylla

Little-leaf desert sumac

Anacardiaceae family

COLD HARDINESS

All three zones.

LANDSCAPE VALUE

- Informal shrub border.
- Foundation plant.
- Clipped hedge where its bare winter appearance is not objectionable or can be masked by compatible evergreen species.
- Shelter and food to birds and small animals.

CULTURAL REQUIREMENTS

- **Exposure:** Full or reflected sun.
- **Water:** Once established, this tough arid-adapted plant may require water only in extended drought periods for basic survival. However, growth and landscape appearance can be enhanced by watering once or twice during the dry months of the year, especially in the low zone.
- **Soil:** Most soils with good drainage.
- **Propagation:** Seed and probably cuttings.
- **Maintenance:** Pruning needs are minimal if the plant is allowed to follow its natural growth habit, but more training and pruning are necessary to develop a small tree or formal hedge.

POSSIBLE PROBLEMS

The leafless winter appearance may be undesirable for some landscape applications.

Throughout its native range in the desert foothills of the southwestern United States and northern Mexico, little-leaf desert sumac grows as a large dense shrub or small tree (on favored sites) to 8 feet (2.5 m) high or, rarely, as high as 15 feet (4.5 m) as a small tree. Spreads to 12 feet (3.5 m). Growth rate is moderate. The alternating pinnately* compound leaves with five to nine leaflets about $1/2$ inch (1 cm) long by $1/4$ inch (0.5 cm) wide are shed at the onset of winter. Some of the branchlets are spine-tipped. In spring, before new foliage appears, clusters of small white flowers open along and at the ends of the branches. Tiny oval fruits no more than $1/4$ inch (0.5 cm) in diameter are hairy and orange or red at maturity. Fruit appears in early summer.

Rhus ovata

Sugar bush

Anacardiaceae family

COLD HARDINESS

All three zones.

LANDSCAPE VALUE

- The rich green color and bold texture of this chaparral-belt shrub make a distinct and refreshing contrast with many other arid-landscape species.
- Handsome specimen.
- In groups for screening and background effects.
- Parks, medians.
- Hillside cover and buffer plantings.
- Has been trained into a small tree with some success.

CULTURAL REQUIREMENTS

- **Exposure:** Full or reflected sun to part shade.
- **Water:** Thoroughly soak the root zone of young plants every month or two. Once or twice a season for established plants. It is especially important to allow soil to dry between water applications in summer.
- **Soil:** Most soils with good drainage.
- **Propagation:** Seed or cuttings. Plant in winter to lessen damping-off* problems with new plants.
- **Maintenance:** Requires minimal pruning except to train a large shrub as a small tree.

POSSIBLE PROBLEMS

- Excessively wet soils during periods of high temperatures encourage damping-off fungi that can quickly kill even large plants. Practice fall and winter planting to alleviate this problem with new plants.
- Difficult to hold container stock in nurseries over summer.

Dense and rounded evergreen shrub that becomes treelike under favorable conditions. Grows at a moderate rate to 15 feet (4.5 m) high, with equal spread. Smooth, leathery dark green leaves are oval, 2 to 3 inches (5 to 7.5 cm) long, folded upward along the midrib and pointed at the tip. Dense clusters of small pink buds give rise to white flowers in spring. The pulp and secretion of the small hairy red fruit are sweet although fruiting is not common in the landscape. Native to dry rocky mountain slopes and washes* of Arizona, Southern California, and Baja California in Mexico.

* See Glossary

Rhus trilobata
Squaw bush
Anacardiaceae family

COLD HARDINESS
All three zones.

LANDSCAPE VALUE
- Woodsy or naturalized situations, but not for the tailored garden.
- Its undemanding nature makes it useful for revegetation.

CULTURAL REQUIREMENTS
- **Exposure:** Full sun to open shade.
- **Water:** Very drought resistant, but regular soakings of the root zone during the warm season will ensure good landscape performance.
- **Soil:** Tolerates most soils.
- **Propagation:** Seed or cuttings.
- **Maintenance:** Little maintenance.

POSSIBLE PROBLEMS
None observed.

Open-branched, deciduous shrub that grows at a moderate rate from 3 to 5 feet (1 to 1.5 m) high, with equal spread. Stems are grayish and bright green compound leaves have three leaflets. The greenish yellow flowers that appear in spring are not showy, nor are the slightly acidic fruits that follow. These are sometimes gathered by native people for seasoning. Native to a wide range from southeast Oregon, eastern California, Nevada, Utah and New Mexico in the United States and into northern Baja California, Durango and Jalisco in Mexico.

Rhus virens
Huachuca sumac
Anacardiaceae family

COLD HARDINESS
All three zones.

LANDSCAPE VALUE
- Background shrub.
- Understory plant in open shade, an uncommon tolerance among desert shrubs.

CULTURAL REQUIREMENTS
- **Exposure:** Full sun to part shade.
- **Water:** Thoroughly soak the root zone every week or two, every month or two after establishment.
- **Soil:** Most soils with good drainage.
- **Propagation:** Seed. Cuttings more difficult but possible.
- **Maintenance:** Little maintenance.

POSSIBLE PROBLEMS
Difficult to propagate.

Similar to *R. choriophylla* but smaller, to 12 feet (3.5 m) in height and spread. Growth rate is moderate. Compound leaves are a darker green and have pointed leaflets. Good foliage mass. Little white flowers in clusters are followed by small hard berrylike fruit. Often grows as an understory shrub in its native habitat. Native to Southeastern Arizona, New Mexico, Texas and northern Mexico.

* *See Glossary*

Robinia neomexicana

New Mexico locust

Fabaceae (Leguminosae) family

COLD HARDINESS

All three zones. Best adapted to intermediate and high zones.

LANDSCAPE VALUE

- Specimen tree.
- Large shrubby groups as a barrier, for background, as a space-definer or border, and for naturalizing.

CULTURAL REQUIREMENTS

- **Exposure:** Full sun.
- **Water:** Water every month or two during the growing season, especially in the low and intermediate zones, little or none during the dormant period.
- **Soil:** Any soil.
- **Propagation:** Seed or cuttings.
- **Maintenance:** Requires little care as an established plant other than occasional selective pruning for shape and branching structure.

POSSIBLE PROBLEMS

- Leafless for a long period in winter.
- Quite prickly, making close contact unpleasant and a problem for the gardener when pruning.

Thorny deciduous shrub of rounded form that sometimes develops into a small tree in favored situations. Reaches 6 feet (2 m) in height, 30 feet (9 m) under optimum conditions. Spreads to 6 feet (2 m), 20 feet (6 m) under optimum conditions. Grows at a moderate rate. Pinnately* compound leaves bear elliptical or lance-shaped leaflets up to 1 1/2 inches (4 cm) long. Drooping hairy 6-inch (15-cm) flower clusters are rose-colored and open in late spring and on into summer, depending on elevation. Elongated seed pods are 4 inches (10 cm) long when ripe in summer and fall. Native to Arizona and New Mexico.

Romneya coulteri

Matilija poppy, Fried-egg plant

Papaveraceae family

COLD HARDINESS

All three zones.

LANDSCAPE VALUE

- Background in an informal or woodsy planting.
- Underground runners* function as a slope stabilizer.
- Highly valued as a cut flower.

CULTURAL REQUIREMENTS

- **Exposure:** Full sun or open shade.
- **Water:** Water every week or two during the cool season and every month or two in late summer.
- **Soil:** Most soils with good drainage. Drainage is especially important when water and soil are alkaline.
- **Propagation:** Digging root sprouts. Tricky to grow from seed. Burning pine needles on top of nursery flat after seed has been covered reputedly helps assure germination.
- **Maintenance:** Treat as a perennial color plant, although it is actually a woody shrub. Cut back severely in early fall to encourage winter/spring growth.

POSSIBLE PROBLEMS

- Can be invasive.
- Looks tacky when out of bloom.
- Difficult to establish in lower zones.
- Needs a foreground planting to cover its semidormant or cut-back period.

Spectacular semi-evergreen plant that rapidly grows to 9 feet (3 m) in height and spread, even larger under favorable conditions. Deeply cut gray leaves are 4 to 6 inches (10 to 15 cm) long and widely spaced along the vertical, usually unbranched stems. Large white poppy flowers grow singly to about 9 inches (23 cm). Each has five to six crepe-textured white petals arranged about a mass of egg-yolk yellow stamens*. Sometimes called the "fried-egg plant" because of this. The plant is showy when in bloom and cherished for its spring flower show. Clumps and spreads by underground runners*. Native to southern California and Baja California's chaparral belt.

* See Glossary

Rosemarinus officinalis

Rosemary

Lamiaceae (Labiatae) family

COLD HARDINESS

All three zones.

LANDSCAPE VALUE

- Foundation plant.
- Border.
- Clipped or unclipped hedge.
- Transition-zone plant.
- Culinary herb.

CULTURAL REQUIREMENTS

- **Exposure:** Survives in dry difficult environments with full or reflected sun and heat. Tolerates seaside conditions of wind and salt mist.
- **Water:** Water every month or two or more often during the growing season, half as often during cool weather. Over-watered plants make unattractive wild growth and are vulnerable to damping-off* fungi.
- **Soil:** Most soils with good drainage.
- **Propagation:** Cuttings.
- **Maintenance:** Head back and thin branches periodically to keep plants full and attractive. Reduce size of old straggly plants in late winter or replace.

POSSIBLE PROBLEMS

- Older plants tend to become woody and open. Prune heavily or pull out.
- Flowers attract bees, so this is probably not a good plant to use near swimming pools.

Evergreen shrub that grows 3 to 6 feet (1 to 2 m) high and 3 to 8 feet (1 to 2.5 m) wide. Growth rate is moderate with regular water. Dense, semi-upright shrub has many branches. Aromatic, needle-like leathery leaves are dark green above, almost white beneath. They grow about 1/2 to 1 1/2 inches (1 to 4 cm) long. Small clusters of 1/2-inch (1-cm) lavender-blue flowers appear intermittently throughout the year, most abundant in winter and spring, especially in warm-winter areas. Native to the Mediterranean region, Asia Minor and North Africa.

Rosemarinus officinalis 'Prostratus'

Prostrate rosemary, Trailing rosemary

Lamiaceae (Labiatae) family

COLD HARDINESS

All three zones.

LANDSCAPE VALUE

- Ground- or bank-cover.
- Erosion control.
- Facer for taller shrubs or flower beds or borders.
- In raised planters and containers, cascades over the edge and down several feet or more.

CULTURAL REQUIREMENTS

- **Exposure:** Survives in dry difficult environments with full or reflected sun and heat. Also adapted to light shade. Tolerates seaside conditions of wind and salt mist.
- **Water:** Water every month or two or more often during the growing season, half as often during cool weather. Over-watered plants make unattractive wild growth and are vulnerable to damping-off* fungi.
- **Soil:** Most soils with good drainage.
- **Propagation:** Cuttings.
- **Maintenance:** Head back and thin branches periodically to keep plants full and attractive. Reduce size of old straggly plants in late winter or replace.

POSSIBLE PROBLEMS

Same as *R. officinalis.*

Trailing growth habit and light blue flowers characterize this one of several cultivars* that are low-growing shrubs or ground-hugging mats. 'Prostratus' grows at a moderate rate from 2 to 3 feet (61 cm to 1 m) high. Spreads 4 to 8 feet (1 to 2.5 m). Other cultivars: 'Collingwood Ingram' grows up to 2 1/2 feet (76 cm) high and has vivid blue-violet flowers. 'Huntington Blue' is dwarfish, only 1 1/2 feet (46 cm) tall, with blue flowers. 'Lockwood de Forest' is dense and vigorous, similar to 'Prostratus' but with lighter colored flowers and foliage.

** See Glossary*

Ruellia brittoniana and *R. brittoniana* 'Katie'

Mexican barrio ruellia

Acanthaceae family

COLD HARDINESS

Low and intermediate zones and sheltered gardens in the high zone. Foliage blackened by light frost but plant recovers and regrows even after a hard frost.

LANDSCAPE VALUE

- Contributes to the lush feeling of a minioasis.
- Adds blooms continuously unless stopped by the frost.
- 'Katie' is compact and more suitable for refined garden planting situations.
- 'Katie' is also attractive in pots.

CULTURAL REQUIREMENTS

- **Exposure:** Full sun to part shade. Loves heat if moisture is adequate.
- **Water:** Water every week or two. Survives prolonged periods of drought but becomes unattractive and contributes nothing to the landscape.
- **Soil:** Tolerates a variety of soils but prepared soil is best.
- **Propagation:** Division or cuttings.
- **Maintenance:** Cut back in later winter to remove frost damage and renew growth.

POSSIBLE PROBLEMS

- Looks unattractive when frosted in cold winter areas. Less attractive even in frost-free situations in winter.
- The species is somewhat rangy and can spread into other adjoining areas. 'Katie' tends not to naturalize.

Shrubby perennial that develops into a lush 3-foot (1-m) clump with narrow leaves. Rapid grower, vigorous during the warm season. A prodigous bloomer with 2-inch (5-cm) blue flowers present throughout most of the warm season. Spreads and naturalizes. Often found in barrio gardens. 'Katie' is a compact version of the above but more controlled and refined. Native to Mexico and naturalized in many areas of the southern and southwestern United States.

Ruellia californica

Sonoran Desert ruellia

Acanthaceae family

COLD HARDINESS

Low zone and warm microclimates of intermediate zone. Tolerates light frost but disfigured or killed to the ground by hard frost. In marginal locations, the microclimate of a southern exposure next to a building may provide adequate frost protection most winters. Spring regrowth of frost-damaged plants is rapid.

LANDSCAPE VALUE

- Distinctive color shrub for arid or transition zones.
- Specimen.
- Foundation or border shrub.
- Clipped hedge or space definer.

CULTURAL REQUIREMENTS

- **Exposure:** Full to reflected sun, part shade.
- **Water:** Drought resistant but needs water every week or two during establishment. Water every month or two thereafter for better growth and flowering.
- **Soil:** Most soils.
- **Propagation:** Seed or cuttings.
- **Maintenance:** Remove frost-damaged wood after the weather warms in spring.

POSSIBLE PROBLEMS

None observed.

Evergreen shrub with many branches that grows slowly to moderately from 2 to 4½ feet (61 cm to 1.5 m) in height and spread. Dense, rounded foliage consists of light green oval to lance-shaped leaves ⅓ to 1¼ inches (1 to 3 cm) long. Leaves are hairy on both surfaces, sometimes becoming hairless with age. Flowers are purple, pink or deep violet, funnel-shaped, 1¾ to 2¼ inches (4.5 to 6 cm) long and slightly fragrant. Blooms year-round except where winters are frosty, most abundantly in summer if soil moisture is adequate. Inconspicuous fruits. Native to the lower Sonoran Desert of Mexico.

* *See Glossary*

Ruellia peninsularis
Baja ruellia
Acanthaceae family

COLD HARDINESS
Low zone and warm microclimates of intermediate zone.

LANDSCAPE VALUE
Same as *R. californica*.

CULTURAL REQUIREMENTS
Same as *R. californica*.

POSSIBLE PROBLEMS
None observed.

Dense compact evergreen shrub very similar to *R. californica* in general appearance and flowering characteristics. Grows at a slow to moderate rate from 2 to 4½ feet (61 cm to 1.5 m) in height and spread. Bark on lower, older sections of stems is gray or whitish. Leaves are grayish green and hairless. Flowers are blue to purple. Native to southern Baja California as well as the lower Sonoran Desert on the mainland of Mexico.

Russelia equisetiformis
Coral fountain
Scrophulariaceae family

COLD HARDINESS
Low zone and warm microclimates of intermediate zone. Damaged or cut to the ground by freezing temperatures but recovers quickly in spring.

LANDSCAPE VALUE
- A bright spot of red and green cascading from planters or containers.
- Foundation planting.
- Tropical effects.
- Tied up on supports, vinelike.

CULTURAL REQUIREMENTS
- **Exposure:** Full sun and reflected heat to part shade.
- **Water:** Water every week or two during the warm season but every month or two once established.
- **Soil:** Garden soil with good drainage.
- **Propagation:** Cuttings taken in spring.
- **Maintenance:** Fertilize on a regular basis year-round.

POSSIBLE PROBLEMS
None observed.

Fountain-like shrubby perennial from 3 to 6 feet (1 to 2 m) high and to 4 feet (1 m) wide. Grows at a moderate to rapid rate. Bright green angular stems are almost leafless. When present, leaves are tiny and scalelike. Vivid red tubular flowers ¾ to 1 inch (2 to 2.5 cm) long are scattered along the green stems, blooming almost continuously during the warm season. This cultivated form has turned out to be more tolerant of stressful arid conditions than expected and has performed surprisingly well in arid gardens. Native to Mexico.

* See Glossary

Russelia polyedra

Wild coral fountain

Scrophulariaceae family

COLD HARDINESS

Low zone and warm microclimates of intermediate zone. Frost tender.

LANDSCAPE VALUE

Same as *R. equisetiformis*, but more drought resistant.

CULTURAL REQUIREMENTS

- **Exposure:** Full sun to part shade.
- **Water:** Water every week or two in summer.
- **Soil:** Most soils with good drainage.
- **Propagation:** Cuttings.
- **Maintenance:** Prune at ground level stems that become unsightly after flowering. This encourages faster growth of new flowering shoots.

POSSIBLE PROBLEMS

None observed.

This species ranges 18 inches to 3 feet (46 cm to 1 m) high, with equal spread, larger in favored locations. Grows at a moderate rate, rapid in favorable situations. Has most of the desirable qualities of *R. equisetiformis* but is smaller and certainly more drought resistant. Native to regions with six-month rainless (in cool season) periods. Small firecracker red flowers bloom during the warm season when water is available. Native from the lower reaches of the Sonoran Desert to other points in Mexico.

Sabal uresana

Sonoran palmetto

Arecaceae (Palmae) family

COLD HARDINESS

Low and intermediate zones and warm microclimates of high zone.

LANDSCAPE VALUE

- Handsome palm as a single specimen or in groves.
- Dramatic skyline silhouette or vertical accent.
- In parks, along roads and drives.
- Rich character plant for tropical-oasis effect near entrances, in courtyards for large buildings and in residential landscapes.
- Compatible with many tropical-appearing arid region plants.

CULTURAL REQUIREMENTS

- **Exposure:** Full or reflected sun to part shade. Well-adapted to hot dry climates.
- **Water:** Shows drought-tolerance once established. Survives with water every month or two, but watering every week or two will promote faster growth and earlier maturity.
- **Soil:** Lush and vigorous in fertile deep soil. Drainage is not an issue. Tolerates sandy and rocky types as well.
- **Propagation:** Seed, but slow to germinate.
- **Maintenance:** A hardy low-maintenance palm of excellent landscape potential.

POSSIBLE PROBLEMS

Slow germination and development can be a problem for nursery propagators.

Desert-adapted palm native to canyons, beachfronts and table lands of Mexico's lower Sonoran Desert. Grows slowly to moderately to 33 feet (10 m) high and spreads to 20 feet (6 m). Dense rounded foliage crown. Blue leaf blades covered with a white bloom are 3 to 6 feet (1 to 2 m) across and divided palmately* into many segments. The leaf petiole* extends into and through the frond as a distinct midrib, arched strongly downward, twisting the leaf in a shape characteristic of the genus. Leaf stalks, or petioles, 6 to 10 feet (2 to 3 m) long are concave above and eventually drop off as old leaves die, leaving faint scars on the trunk. The many-flowered inflorescence* develops in spring, horizontal at first then drooping toward the ground, followed by small, glossy light brown fruit.

* See Glossary

SALVIAS

Salvias (sages) are well represented in arid regions. They are a useful group of shrubs. Many are low enough for groundcover planting. A large number have colorful blooms in season. All give off a pungent aroma. Some *Salvias* are used as herbs in cooking.

Salvia chamaedryoides
Blue Chihuahuan sage
Lamiaceae (Labiatae) family

COLD HARDINESS
All three zones. Tolerates severe frost.

LANDSCAPE VALUE
- Low perennial border-type plant that adds a touch of light blue to the landscape.
- Low foundation plantings.
- Edging and groundcover for small areas.

CULTURAL REQUIREMENTS
- **Exposure:** Full sun but not exposed to stressful situations.
- **Water:** Drought tolerant, but enjoys a garden environment with water every week or two during the warm season, even more often in low zones to prolong blooming and maintain appearance.
- **Soil:** Needs good well-drained soil.
- **Propagation:** Seed or cuttings.
- **Maintenance:** Cut back old bloom stems.

POSSIBLE PROBLEMS
- Short-lived .
- Somewhat temperamental and erratic in performance.

Small evergreen shrub that grows at a moderate rate to 2 feet (61 cm) in height, with equal spread. Leaves are gray green and flowers are blue, blooming from summer into fall. Both are small. Native to the higher zones of the Chihuahuan Desert.

Salvia clevelandii
Cleveland sage
Lamiaceae (Labiatae) family

COLD HARDINESS
All three zones.

LANDSCAPE VALUE
- Foundation or bank planting in dry, sunny situations.
- Produces a striking display of blue over a long period.

CULTURAL REQUIREMENTS
- **Exposure:** Full sun to part shade.
- **Water:** Water once or twice during summer dormant season. Water every week or two, but just often enough to keep leaves from curling during winter and spring. In the cooler weather this may not be more often than every ten days or so. The point is to keep it vigorous and growing toward the spectacular spring flowering. Allow soil to dry out between waterings in the hot season.
- **Soil:** Well-drained, gritty soil is best, but tolerates most soil types with good drainage.
- **Propagation:** Seed or perhaps cuttings
- **Maintenance**: Cut back old bloom stems in summer.

POSSIBLE PROBLEMS
- Looks seedy after blooming and dies out during the hot season, especially when summer rain occurs.
- Scent of leaves can be overwhelming at close range or when pruning the plant.

Rounded, mounding evergreen shrub that grows at a moderate to rapid rate from 2 to 4 feet (61 cm to 1 m) high, with equal spread. More woody than most *Salvias*. Aromatic gray-green leaves to 1 1/4 inches (3 cm) long are rounded with prominent veins and hairy undersides. Produces abundant blue 3/4-inch (2-cm) flowers arranged on tall upright branches, mostly spring into summer. Native to San Diego County, California.

* *See Glossary*

Salvia dorrii

Mojave sage

Lamiaceae (Labiatae) family

COLD HARDINESS
All three zones.

LANDSCAPE VALUE
- Nice spring and early summer color for wild-type perennial borders where it can be combined with other perennial shrubs of similar informal character and different blooming times.
- The blue-purple contrasts nicely with some of the desert *Penstemons.*
- Rock gardens.

CULTURAL REQUIREMENTS
- **Exposure:** Full or reflected sun.
- **Water:** Drought resistant. Water every week or two from late winter to midspring to produce good blooms. Water less often in summer and fall.
- **Soil:** Most soils with good drainage.
- **Propagation:** Seed or cuttings.
- **Maintenance:** Remove spent bloom stalks.

POSSIBLE PROBLEMS
None observed.

Sprawling evergreen shrub that grows up to 3 feet (1 m) or more in height and spread at a moderate rate. Small leaves are silvery. Bold clusters of 1/2-inch (1.5-cm) blue-purple flowers appear in late spring. Geared for the winter and spring rains of the Mojave Desert, this species is at its best in late winter to early summer and drab-looking in late summer and fall. Native to California's Mojave Desert.

Salvia farinacea

Mealy cup sage

Lamiaceae (Labiatae) family

COLD HARDINESS
All three zones, except in coldest areas of high zone, where it may behave as an annual.

LANDSCAPE VALUE
- A bedding plant for the traditional garden or the desert garden where the blue selections make the most impact.
- Containers.
- A perennial border subject also of interest for the gray-green woolly textured mound of foliage it adds to the landscape when not in bloom.

CULTURAL REQUIREMENTS
- **Exposure:** Full sun to part shade. Dormant in winter, but needs warmth to start growing in spring.
- **Water:** Withstands periods of drought, but needs water every week or two in hot season to bloom well.
- **Soil:** Performs best in improved garden soil with good drainage.
- **Propagation:** Seed or cuttings.
- **Maintenance:** Replace annually in cold areas.

POSSIBLE PROBLEMS
None observed.

A herbaceous* perennial that performs as an annual in cold-winter areas. Grows at a rapid rate during the warm season. Gray-green leaves covered with a mat of short woolly hairs are 1 1/2 to 4 inches (4 to 10 cm) long. Small dark blue or violet-blue to white flowers (numerous cultivars*) bloom in summer and fall. The plant has been much manipulated by horticulturists and selections are generally 12 inches (30.5 cm) tall, but wild types can be 3 feet (1 m) tall and wide. Native to Texas and Mexico.

* *See Glossary*

Salvia greggii

Red Chihuahuan sage

Lamiaceae (Labiatae) family

Small, tough evergreen shrub with many upright stems. Grows at a moderate pace to 3 feet (1 m) in height and spread. Leaves are oblong to spatula-shaped, 1/2 to 1 1/4 inches (1 to 3 cm) long. Valued chiefly for the terminal* flower spikes, each from 2 to 6 inches (5 to 15 cm) long. Individual flowers are about 1 inch (2.5 cm) long, the lower lip larger and showier than the upper. They bloom in early spring through late fall. Commonly bright red to reddish purple. Other selections have flowers that are dark red, pink, purplish, coral or white. Native to the Chihuahuan Desert of Texas, New Mexico and Mexico.

COLD HARDINESS

All three zones.

LANDSCAPE VALUE

Has particular value for landscape use because of low-mounding evergreen character. Useful for foundation planting, as a foreground plant and dependable color producer as it blooms off and on after the main display in spring and especially because there are the varied color selections now offered by the nursery trade.

CULTURAL REQUIREMENTS

- **Exposure:** Full or reflected sun to part shade.
- **Water:** Very drought resistant but needs water every week or two during warm season to stimulate new growth and bloom.
- **Soil:** Any soil with good drainage, except heavy clays.
- **Propagation:** Seed or cuttings. Color selections must be propagated vegetatively.
- **Maintenance:** Cut back in winter to keep it from getting woody and rangy, and also to stimulate fresh new growth and abundant bloom. Prune back after heavy bloom to maintain best appearance.

POSSIBLE PROBLEMS

May have poor appearance at times, especially after heavy bloom and during seeding period.

Salvia leucantha

Purple Mexican bush sage

Lamiaceae (Labiatae) family

Rounded, shrubby evergreen perennial 2 to 6 feet (61 cm to 2 m) high and 3 to 6 feet (1 to 2 m) wide. Grows rapidly in spring and into summer with abundant moisture. Soft, crinkly gray-green leaves are 3/4 to 2 1/2 inches (2 to 6.5 cm) long. Graceful arching stems tipped with velvety purplish spikes and ball-shaped buds produce white tubular flowers to 3/4 inch (2 cm) long in clusters, mostly summer into fall. Native to Mexico.

COLD HARDINESS

All three zones. In colder locations, the bloom period may be shortened. Regrows rapidly from hardy roots in spring.

LANDSCAPE VALUE

- Informal shrub border.
- Foundation plant.
- Perennial border flower.

CULTURAL REQUIREMENTS

- **Exposure:** Full sun to part shade. Open places.
- **Water:** Water every week or two year-round. Extra water in spring and early summer stimulates new growth for the late summer and fall blooming. Not very drought resistant. Survives dry periods, but regular water is necessary for good appearance.
- **Soil:** Most soils with good drainage. Responds to improved garden soil.
- **Propagation:** Cuttings or divisions of old clumps.
- **Maintenance:** Pruning after bloom improves appearance. Next year's flowers bloom only on new growth. Often freezes back, but cut to the ground in winter regardless of condition.

POSSIBLE PROBLEMS

- Somewhat rangy in appearance.
- No winter presence, leaving a gap in mixed planting. Tuck in among all-year plants.

** See Glossary*

Salvia leucophylla
Purple sage
Lamiaceae (Labiatae) family

COLD HARDINESS
Low and intermediate zones.

LANDSCAPE VALUE
- Good foliage value, a showy floral display and dependable performance in low-water-use landscapes.
- Slope and bank plantings.
- Color accent in shrub and perennial borders.

CULTURAL REQUIREMENTS
- **Exposure:** Part shade or afternoon shade in hot desert environments.
- **Water:** Irrigation is usually necessary for satisfactory landscape appearance, but at intervals that allow some drying of the soil, especially in summer.
- **Soil:** Most soils with good drainage.
- **Propagation:** Seed or cuttings.
- **Maintenance:** Cut back after winter, before new growth begins.

POSSIBLE PROBLEMS
Vulnerable to fungus problems brought on by heavy summer watering.

This shrubby *Salvia* grows 2 to 5 feet (61 cm to 1.5 m) high and spreads to 6 feet (2 m) at a moderate rate. It forms a spreading mound of evergreen foliage. The slender gray-green to silvery gray leaves 3/4 to 2 1/2 inches (2 to 6.5 cm) long grow in pairs along the stems. Rose-purple tubular flowers about 3/4 inch (2 cm) long are two-lipped and open in crowded ball-shaped clusters, spaced at intervals on long spikes during late spring and early summer. Native to southern and central California.

Salvia microphylla
Red bush sage
Lamiaceae (Labiatae) family

COLD HARDINESS
Low and intermediate zones and mild-winter microclimates of high zone. Frost hardy.

LANDSCAPE VALUE
- Showy red bloom spikes over a long season give this *Salvia* a place as a flowering accent in transition- and oasis-zone border areas, street medians and other low-water-use compositions.
- Flowers attract hummingbirds.

CULTURAL REQUIREMENTS
- **Exposure:** Full sun. Tolerates heat and aridity.
- **Water:** Water every week or two through fall into spring, every month or two in summer.
- **Soil:** Most soils with good drainage.
- **Propagation:** Seed or cuttings.
- **Maintenance:** Prune for a more compact growth habit and to remove spent flower spikes.

POSSIBLE PROBLEMS
Sensitive to overwatering during summer when growth is inactive.

Shrubby, open and spreading, this *Salvia* grows at a moderate rate from 3 to 4 feet (1 m) high, with equal spread. Herbaceous* stems arise from a woody base. The aromatic leaves are oppositely arranged and triangular to elliptic. They have serrated margins and grow about 1/2 to 3/4 inch (1 to 2 cm) long. In spring and fall, tubular 2-lipped flowers about 1 inch (2.5 cm) long and red to deep scarlet open in 4- to 8-inch (10- to 20.5-cm) long spikes. Cultivars* such as 'Sierra Madre' and 'Red storm' offer improved form and flower color options. Native to Chihuahua, Mexico.

* *See Glossary*

Sambucus mexicana

Mexican elderberry

Caprifoliaceae family

COLD HARDINESS
All three zones. Frost tolerant.

LANDSCAPE VALUE
- Fresh green foliage is a bright spot of summerlike green in midwinter and in natural and minimum-maintenance locations. Flower and fruit display also add seasonal interest.
- Windbreak, screen, buffer.
- Fruit attracts birds.

CULTURAL REQUIREMENTS
- **Exposure:** Full sun to part shade.
- **Water:** Tolerates long periods of drought during the warm season. Water every couple weeks to every couple months, depending on your microclimate, to maintain foliage, especially in winter, spring and summer. Periodic irrigation moderates and shortens the late-summer loss of foliage.
- **Soil:** Deep fertile soil.
- **Propagation:** Seed or cuttings.
- **Maintenance:** Prune in fall before new growth is produced.

POSSIBLE PROBLEMS
- Late summer foliage drop and fruit litter.
- Wood is very brittle.
- Invasive in favored locations.
- Not a plant for refined landscapes because of the rather unkempt look of trees that are not groomed regularly and the late-summer period of sparse foliage.

Deciduous to semi-evergreen large shrub, or occasionally a tree where growing conditions are adequate. Grows rapidly from 10 to 30 feet (3 to 9 m) high and 8 to 20 feet (2.5 to 6 m) wide. Dense, rounded to irregular and straggly. The pinnately* compound leaves are divided into five to seven leathery, succulent-looking bright green leaflets. These leaflets are oval to oblong in shape and 1 to 2½ inches (2.5 to 6.5 cm) long. New growth emerges in early winter. Most or all leaves drop in late summer; defoliation is intensified by drought stress. Tiny yellowish white flowers bloom from spring through summer in showy flat-topped clusters 2 to 6 inches (5 cm to 15 cm) across. Juicy blue-black berries are used for making jelly and wine. Native to Arizona, California, Texas and northern Mexico.

Santolina chamaecyparissus

Lavender cotton

Asteraceae (Compositae) family

COLD HARDINESS
All three zones.

LANDSCAPE VALUE
- Low border or edging.
- Facer for taller shrubs.
- Groundcover where space is limited.
- Tolerates shearing into low formal shapes.
- Beside boulders in rock gardens.

CULTURAL REQUIREMENTS
- **Exposure:** Full to reflected sun.
- **Water:** Moderately drought tolerant. Water every couple of weeks to every month.
- **Soil:** Most soils with good drainage.
- **Propagation:** Cuttings.
- **Maintenance:** Head back periodically to prevent woody, straggly condition. Remove flower buds before they open to extend dense foliage effect; however, plants eventually become woody and ragged and need replacement.

POSSIBLE PROBLEMS
Tends to become woody and open with age.

Dense mounding evergreen sub-shrub from 1 to 2 feet (30.5 to 61 cm) tall and 2 to 3 feet (61 cm to 1 m) wide. Grows at a moderate rate. Aromatic silvery gray leaves, up to 1½ inches (4 cm) long, are divided pinnately* into slender leaflets. In summer, solitary bright yellow buttonlike flower heads open on slender stems well above the foliage mass. Blooms are compact, globular and ½ inch (1 cm) across. Native to Spain and North Africa.

* *See Glossary*

Santolina virens

Green-leaved lavender cotton, Green santolina

Asteraceae (Compositae) family

COLD HARDINESS

All three zones. Moderately frost tolerant.

LANDSCAPE VALUE

- The fresh green mound contributes a welcome note in the arid landscape.
- Low border or edging.
- Facer for taller shrubs.
- Groundcover where space is limited.
- Tolerates shearing into low formal shapes.
- Beside boulders in rock gardens.

CULTURAL REQUIREMENTS

Same as *Santolina chamaecyparissus.*

POSSIBLE PROBLEMS

Same as *Santolina chamaecyparissus.*

Small evergreen sub-shrub of dense and rounded form. Grows at a moderate rate from1 to 2 feet (30.5 to 61 cm) high and 1½ to 2½ feet (46 to 76 cm) wide. Delicate fine-textured foliage is bright green, aromatic, linear and 1 to 2 inches (2.5 to 5 cm) long. Small buttonlike creamy yellow flower heads up to ¾ inch (2 cm) in diameter open in spring. Native to the Mediterranean region.

Sapindus saponaria drummondii

Western soapberry tree

Sapindaceae family

COLD HARDINESS

All three zones.

LANDSCAPE VALUE

- Patio-size tree.
- A bosque* or woodsy effect. In such situations trees will become taller and more slender.
- Understory planting with taller trees.
- Naturalizes in favorable situations.

CULTURAL REQUIREMENTS

- **Exposure:** Full sun to open shade.
- **Water:** Quite drought resistant. Thoroughly soak the root zone every month or two during the warm season for good foliage and growth.
- **Soil:** Most soils.
- **Propagation:** Second-growth saplings can be easily transplanted during dormant season. Also propagated from seed.
- **Maintenance:** Low maintenance.

POSSIBLE PROBLEMS

- The seed is reported to be poisonous, but this is probably not a hazard because of its hardness.
- Slow to become a tree.
- Its tendency to sprout sapling trees around mature specimens may not be desirable in some situations. Of course this doesn't occur when planted in paved spaces or lawn areas. This sprouting of saplings is an asset when going for a bosque effect.

A small, round-headed deciduous tree that grows at a slow to moderate rate as high as 40 feet (12 m) but usually much smaller. Spreads as much as 30 feet (9 m), but usually develops more of a thicket or bosque than its evergreen counterpart, *S. saponaria saponaria.* Tends to develop attractive thickets when planted in a natural area and allowed to spread. Planted as a single specimen, it can be shaped and trained into a fine shade tree for small spaces. Native from Arizona to Texas.

* See Glossary

Sapindus saponaria saponaria

Evergreen soapberry

Sapindaceae family

COLD HARDINESS

Low zone and warm microclimates in intermediate zone. Tolerates light frost but damaged by hard freezes.

LANDSCAPE VALUE

- Neat foliage and rounded head make it a good patio tree.
- Tropical-effects planting compositions.

CULTURAL REQUIREMENTS

- **Exposure:** Partial shade or sun and reflected heat.
- **Water:** Water every couple weeks to every month, less during the cool season, more during the warm season for faster growth and good foliage.
- **Soil:** Most soils with good drainage. Grows naturally in rocky dry-water-course locations in low elevations.
- **Propagation:** Seed.
- **Maintenance:** Low maintenance.

POSSIBLE PROBLEMS

- Slow to develop.
- Reputed poisonous seed is probably too hard to be a hazard.

Round-headed evergreen tree with a broad dense crown of light green compound leaves. Bark is gray. Grows at a slow to moderate rate up to 40 feet (12 m) high and wide, although usually much smaller. Small greenish white flowers in clusters are followed by transparent round, hard fruit (reputed to be poisonous). Both fruit and flowers add some interest to the tree in late summer to fall. Native throughout most of Mexico.

Schinus molle

California pepper tree

Anacardiaceae family

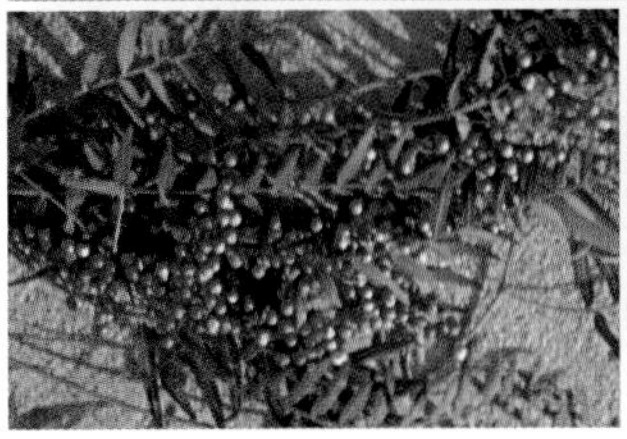

COLD HARDINESS

Low and intermediate zones and mild-winter microclimates of high zone.

LANDSCAPE VALUE

- Attractive specimen tree for shade, roadsides or parks.
- Screening or background in outlying or transitional areas.

CULTURAL REQUIREMENTS

- **Exposure:** Full to reflected sun and heat. Survives under adverse desert conditions.
- **Water:** Remarkably drought tolerant once established but performs best with water every month or two. Overwatering results in chlorosis* or rapid, weak growth, almost always followed by severe branch breakage.
- **Soil:** Any soil.
- **Propagation:** Seed.
- **Maintenance:** Selective pruning and training of young trees is important. Trees that are cut back to the ground every six to ten years make handsome multistemmed small specimens. Regrowth from a healthy root system is rapid. Inspect trees several times each year for damaged branches and growth defects.

POSSIBLE PROBLEMS

- Very susceptible to Texas root rot*.
- Wood heart rot often invades trunk or branches after wind breakage injuries.
- Root-knot nematode* and iron chlorosis* can be a problem.
- Brittle wood predisposes tree to storm damage.
- Leaf, twig and branchlet litter.
- Shallow, invasive roots may lift paved areas and crack walls.

Evergreen tree that grows rapidly from 30 to 40 feet (9 to 12 m) high and 25 to 45 feet (7.5 to 13.5 m) wide. Large trees have coarse, flaking orange-brown bark and sometimes develop picturesque twisting trunks and primary branches. Admired for its graceful weeping habit and pendulous pinnately* compound foliage. Each leaf is 6 to 12 inches (15 to 30.5 cm) long and divided into fifteen to forty or more lacy, linear leaflets as long as 2½ inches (6.5 cm). Leaves give off a distinct peppery odor when crushed. The terminal* clusters of tiny yellowish white flowers on female trees develop into rose-colored berries in fall and winter. Native to Peru but naturalized in Mexico and southern California.

* See Glossary

Schinus teribinthifolius

Brazilian pepper tree

Anacardiaceae family

Evergreen large shrub or small short-trunked tree that reaches 15 to 30 feet (4.5 to 9 m) in height and spread. Grows at a moderate to rapid rate. Single- or multitrunked with crossing, contorted, sometimes interwoven branches. Develops a low spreading canopy at maturity. Dark green shiny foliage is pinnately* compound. Five to thirteen oblong leaflets 2 1/2 inches (6.5 cm) long make up each leaf. In spring, clusters of inconspicuous cream to chartreuse flowers bloom. On female trees these give way to bright red berrylike fruits in late summer. Fruit persists on the tree through fall and into winter. Native to Brazil.

COLD HARDINESS

Low zone and warm microclimates of intermediate zone.

LANDSCAPE VALUE

- A small tree of unusual landscape character that is enhanced by an impressive display of ornamental fruit on female trees throughout fall and winter.
- Dense foliage canopy creates heavy shade.
- Small specimen or patio tree.
- Screening.
- Golf courses or parks.
- Tolerates seaside conditions if sheltered from direct saltwater spray.

CULTURAL REQUIREMENTS

- **Exposure:** Full to reflected sun. A good performer in arid environments.
- **Water:** Water every week to every couple months when fully established, depending on aridity of site and summer heat.
- **Soil:** Most soils with good drainage.
- **Propagation:** Seed.
- **Maintenance:** Prune and stake young trees to develop single-trunked specimens with above-head-height canopy.

POSSIBLE PROBLEMS

- Susceptible to Texas root rot* and verticilium wilt*
- Somewhat brittle wood is vulnerable to storm damage.
- Produces litter that may require cleanup in highly maintained landscapes.
- Invasive in humid climates, such as Florida.

Schizolobium parahybum

Palo de picho

Fabaceae (Leguminosae) family

In the warm humid areas of southern Mexico where this tree grows as a native, it develops a rounded open crown on an erect trunk as wide as 3 feet (1 m). It grows rapidly up to 100 feet (30.5 m) or more in height and spread, less in arid regions. The evergreen bipinnate* leaves average 12 to 20 inches (30.5 to 51 cm) in length. They may grow even longer, to 3 feet (1 m), on young vigorous trees, but not in the desert. Each leaf consists of seven to eleven pairs of primary leaflets that are further divided into seven to twenty pairs of secondary leaflets, linear in shape with smooth margins. The fragrant yellow flowers 3/4 inch (2 cm) long have five petals and develop in large terminal* clusters. At maturity, the seed pod is about 4 3/4 inches (12 cm) long and 2 inches (5 cm) wide with a conspicuous pattern of net veination on its flattened surfaces. The single dark brown seed within is 1/3 inch (1 cm) in diameter. Although this tree is native to a more humid climate, it has shown remarkable tolerance to the low humidity of the desert.

COLD HARDINESS

Low zone and possibly warm-winter microclimates of intermediate zone. It has not sustained frost damage at the University of Arizona campus where it grows in a warm spot in the intermediate zone.

LANDSCAPE VALUE

- Lush tropical appearance and majestic proportions.
- Shade.
- Framing or background use in large oasis landscapes.
- Central feature or point of emphasis in commercial developments, parks and other public spaces. (It grows too large, however, for small residential landscapes.)

CULTURAL REQUIREMENTS

- **Exposure:** Full sun.
- **Water:** In most arid landscapes, thoroughly soak the root zone every week or two to maintain tree health and appearance. It has proven to be more drought tolerant than expected, considering its place of origin.
- **Soil:** Average to good quality soil
- **Propagation:** Seed.
- **Maintenance:** Stake and guide young trees.

POSSIBLE PROBLEMS

None observed as of this writing.

* See Glossary

Senecio cineraria
Dusty miller
Asteraceae (Compositae) family

COLD HARDINESS
All three zones. Survives moderate frost.

LANDSCAPE VALUE
- Handsome white foliage makes a long-lasting color display and rich contrast with other plants in beds and borders.
- Equally effective in landscapes to be viewed at night.
- Attractive in containers.
- Bloom provides a splash of yellow, but the foliage color is the main contribution to the landscape.

CULTURAL REQUIREMENTS
- **Exposure:** Full sun. Heat tolerant. Adapted to seashore conditions.
- **Water:** Water young plants every week or two, mature plants every month or two.
- **Soil:** Grows in heavy or alkaline soil as well as better quality garden soils.
- **Propagation:** Seed or cuttings.
- **Maintenance:** Remove flowers as they form if the plant is grown exclusively for foliage or after they fade to keep blooming plants neat. Head back periodically to maintain compact growth.

POSSIBLE PROBLEMS
Becomes leggy if not pruned at intervals.

Evergreen shrubby perennial that grows at a moderate rate from 1 1/2 to 2 1/2 feet (46 to 76 cm) high and wide. Grows a dense, mounding foliage mass. Silvery white woolly leaves are pinnately* cut with slender, oblong round-tipped segments. Yellow to cream-colored flower heads 1 1/2 inches (4 cm) in diameter are produced practically year-round, most abundantly in summer. Native to the Mediterranean region.

Senecio salignus
Willow groundsell
Asteraceae (Compositae) family

COLD HARDINESS
All three zones. Native to a high-desert climate and often blooms throughout periods of subfreezing nights.

LANDSCAPE VALUE
- Foreground or understory planting.
- Woodsy effects.
- Contributes year-round rich deep green and dependable splash of yellow bloom to brighten the late-winter landscape regardless of cold.
- Adds to the short list of drought-tolerant plants that will grow well under trees and in other shady situations.

CULTURAL REQUIREMENTS
- **Exposure:** Tolerates full sun but ideal under taller trees or on north and east exposures.
- **Water:** Water every week or two during the hottest weather. Do not let it become bone-dry during the hot season, especially in the low zone.
- **Soil:** Does best in good garden-type soil but performs reasonably well in gravelly alluvial soil.
- **Propagation:** Seed or cuttings.
- **Maintenance:** Remove seed heads after bloom.

POSSIBLE PROBLEMS
Seed heads following bloom period are unattractive and are best sheared off before maturing.

Woody evergreen shrub that grows at a moderate to rapid rate from 6 to 7 feet (2 m) high and wide, although usually smaller. Glossy dark green leaves are paler on their undersides. Abundant clusters of small yellow daisies open in late winter and are followed by masses of airborne seed. Narrow leaves can vary between the Sonoran and Chihuahuan Desert forms, the latter being much more narrow. No other difference is noticeable.

* *See Glossary*

SENNA

Senna is the new grouping for many of our low-water-use landscape shrubs formerly listed under *Cassia*. See *Cassia* for more information.

Senna aphylla

Argentine desert senna

Fabaceae (Leguminosae) family

COLD HARDINESS

All three zones.

LANDSCAPE VALUE

Revegetating or naturalizing in desert settings.

CULTURAL REQUIREMENTS

- **Exposure:** Full sun, including reflected sun. Will tolerate part shade but becomes more rangy and blooms less.
- **Water:** Quite drought tolerant. Thoroughly soak the root zone every month or two.
- **Soil:** Most soils with good drainage.
- **Propagation:** Seed.
- **Maintenance:** Low maintenance.

POSSIBLE PROBLEMS

- Tends to reseed in adjoining areas.
- Too rangy for the more "gardenesque" landscapes.

Somewhat open leafless shrub that grows at a moderate to rapid rate from 3 to 6 feet (1 to 2 m) high and 6 to 9 feet (2 to 3 m) wide. Size and growth rate depend on available moisture. Green broomlike stems in youth thicken with age. Puts on a show during the warm season with an abundant display of bright yellow blooms. Although nearly leafless, mature plant becomes quite a solid mound. Native to Argentina.

Senna artemisioides (Cassia artemisioides)

Feathery senna

Fabaceae (Leguminosae) family

COLD HARDINESS

Low zone and warmer microclimates of intermediate zone.

LANDSCAPE VALUE

- Foundation plant.
- Specimen.
- Clipped or unclipped hedge.
- Winter and spring color.
- Border shrub.
- Transition zones where space is limited.
- Medians, buffer zones.
- School grounds.
- Well-suited to both residential and commercial properties.

CULTURAL REQUIREMENTS

- **Exposure:** Full or reflected sun to part shade.
- **Water:** Water once or twice a season is adequate for survival of established plants but appearance improves substantially with water every week or two.
- **Soil:** Most soils with good drainage.
- **Propagation:** Seed or cuttings.
- **Maintenance:** Prune after flowering to eliminate heavy seed crop or to remove frost-damaged wood at the end of winter.

POSSIBLE PROBLEMS

- Frost can eliminate winter bloom.
- Texas root rot*.

Upright, rounded evergreen shrub that grows rapidly (with regular water) from 3 to 5 feet (1 to 1.5 m) in height and spread. Gray pinnately* compound leaves are divided into slender needlelike leaflets, which gives a dense but feathery foliage effect. From late winter into early spring, and sometimes again in fall, fragrant yellow flowers to 3/4 inch (2 cm) diameter appear in clusters of three to eight along the branches. The 3-inch (7.5-cm) long brown papery seed pods are often unsightly because they are so numerous. Native to Australia.

** See Glossary*

Senna artemisioides circinata

Autumn-flowering senna

Fabaceae (Leguminosae) family

COLD HARDINESS

Low zone and warm microclimates of intermediate zone.

LANDSCAPE VALUE

- Striking accent shrub in water-conservative gardens.
- Background, screen, space-definer, buffer.
- In mass plantings such as parks, school grounds and commercial projects.

CULTURAL REQUIREMENTS

- **Exposure:** Full or reflected sun to part shade.
- **Water:** Water every couple weeks to every month or two depending on how quickly your soil dries between waterings.
- **Soil:** Most soils with good drainage.
- **Propagation:** Seed or cuttings.
- **Maintenance:** Prune occasionally to emphasize natural growth habit.

POSSIBLE PROBLEMS

Sensitive to frost in colder locations.

A graceful evergreen *Senna* that reaches 7 feet (2 m) in height and spread at a moderate to rapid rate. Rounded in shape with a semiweeping habit and fine-textured gray-green foliage composed of leaflets to 1 inch (2.5 cm) long. Attractive tiny yellow flowers bloom late winter into late spring or summer and are replaced by interesting coiled seed pods.

Senna artemisioides filifolia (Cassia nemophila)

Desert senna, Green feathery senna

Fabaceae (Leguminosae) family

This evergreen *Senna* grows to 6 feet (2 m) in height and spread, rapidly with regular irrigation and moderately with less frequent watering. The finely divided leaves consist of one or two pairs of narrow green leaflets an inch (2.5 cm) or more in length. The green rather than gray leaf color and greater cold resistance are the primary differences between this plant and *S. artemisioides*. Small clusters of yellow five-petaled flowers about 3/4 inch (2 cm) in diameter are so abundant from late winter into spring that the shrub becomes a fragrant golden ball of color. The resulting crop of slender seed pods, 3 to 4 inches (7.5 to 10 cm) long, is usually so heavy it requires removal for satisfactory landscape appearance. Native to Australia.

COLD HARDINESS

Low zone and all but the coldest locations in the intermediate zone. More cold hardy than the parent species.

LANDSCAPE VALUE

Delicate, refined foliage and free-flowering habit make this a choice transition- or oasis-zone shrub for

- Borders.
- Specimen or accent use.
- Foundation plantings.

CULTURAL REQUIREMENTS

- **Exposure:** Tolerates great heat and full to reflected sun.
- **Water:** Established plants perform well with water every couple months to once or twice a season, depending on local climate and soil conditions.
- **Soil:** Performs well on many arid climate soils including light sandy types.
- **Propagation:** Seed or cuttings.
- **Maintenance:** Head back flowering branches at the end of the bloom cycle to eliminate unslightly seed pods and to stimulate new growth that will flower the following year.

POSSIBLE PROBLEMS

Bees are regular visitors to plants in flower.

Senna artemisioides petiolaris (Cassia phyllodinea)

Silver senna

Fabaceae (Leguminosae) family

COLD HARDINESS

Low zone and warm microclimates of intermediate zone. Frost sensitive.

LANDSCAPE VALUE

- Screen, background or space-divider with a long flowering season.
- Malls, shopping plazas, parks, buffer zones, medians.

CULTURAL REQUIREMENTS

- **Exposure:** Well adapted to intense sunlight and hot dry environments.
- **Water:** Quite drought resistant but appearance is enhanced by water once or twice a season.
- **Soil:** Most soils with good drainage.
- **Propagation:** Seed or cuttings.
- **Maintenance:** Prune after seed pods form.

POSSIBLE PROBLEMS

None observed.

A good-looking heat- and drought-tolerant Australian desert shrub that grows 4 to 6 feet (1 to 2 m) in height and spread at a moderate to rapid rate, depending on water supply. Slender, curving silvery gray leaflets impart an open, airy foliage effect. Leaves are 1 to 2 inches (2.5 to 5 cm) long. Yellow flowers, 3/4 inch (2 cm), may appear as early as October or November. They add color and liveliness from December into spring in warm-winter areas.

Senna artemisioides sturtii (Cassia sturtii)

Sturt senna

Fabaceae (Leguminosae) family

COLD HARDINESS

Low zone and warm microclimates of intermediate zone.

LANDSCAPE VALUE

- Color plant.
- Space definer.
- Foundation plant.

CULTURAL REQUIREMENTS

- **Exposure:** Full sun to light shade.
- **Water:** Drought resistant. Thoroughly soak the root zone every month or two.
- **Soil:** Well-drained soil.
- **Propagation:** Seed or cuttings.
- **Maintenance:** Benefits from a light pruning to remove seed pods after blooming.

POSSIBLE PROBLEMS

Probably subject to Texas root rot*.

Gray-green compact shrub that grows 3 to 6 feet (1 to 2 m) high and spreads 3 to 4 feet (1 m) at a moderate rate. Similar to *S. artemisioides* except that it blooms over a longer period of time and is generally neater in appearance. Flowers are yellow. Native to Australia.

* *See Glossary*

Senna atomaria (Cassia emarginata)

Palo zorillo

Fabaceae (Leguminosae) family

COLD HARDINESS
Low zone and warm microclimates of intermediate zone. Frost tender.

LANDSCAPE VALUE
- Specimen or accent.
- Shade.

CULTURAL REQUIREMENTS
- **Exposure:** Full sun.
- **Water:** Thorough soaking of the root zone every month or two for established plants, more often for young developing plants.
- **Soil:** Best performance on deep good-quality soil.
- **Propagation:** Seed.
- **Maintenance:** Prune to develop strong, well-balanced branching structure.

POSSIBLE PROBLEMS
None observed.

An evergreen (but drought-deciduous) *Senna* that matures as a medium-to-large round-topped tree on the most-favored sites, much smaller elsewhere. Grows at a moderate rate as high as 65 feet (20 m). Spreads 15 to 25 feet (4.5 to 7.5 m), sometimes as wide as 40 feet (12 m). Single or multiple trunks are from 2¾ to 6 inches (7 to 15 cm) in diameter. Bark on trunk and large branches is gray; hairs densely cover twigs. Pinnately* compound leaves grow to 4 inches (10 cm) long with two to five pairs of leaflets that vary in shape from oval to oblong or rounded. The last or outer pair of leaflets is always the largest. Leaflets are 1 to 3 inches (2.5 to 7.5 cm) wide and 2 to 6 inches (5 to 15 cm) long and are covered with tiny soft hairs on the underside. Clusters of a few small yellowish green to orange-yellow blooms appear throughout the year in warm-winter regions. In other areas, flowering may occur in late winter or spring, usually when the tree is leafless or nearly so. Petals are marked with brown veins. Slender seed pods are up to 1 foot (30.5 cm) long. Native from Mexico into South America and also the West Indies.

Senna corymbosa (Cassia corymbosa)

Flowery senna

Fabaceae (Leguminosae) family

COLD HARDINESS
Low and intermediate zones.

LANDSCAPE VALUE
Large background shrub with intermittent color display during warm season.

CULTURAL REQUIREMENTS
- **Exposure:** Full sun to part shade.
- **Water:** Water every week or two during the warm season, every month or two once established.
- **Soil:** Most soils with good drainage.
- **Propagation:** Seed.
- **Maintenance:** Occasionally nip back to thicken rangy growth habit and at times to remove an excessive set of seed pods.

POSSIBLE PROBLEMS
- Tends to outgrow its position. Can get top-heavy and tip over, especially in part shade.
- Reseeds and could become invasive.
- Texas root rot*.

Large, somewhat rangy evergreen shrub that grows rapidly to 10 feet (3 m) high and 10 to 12 feet (3 to 3.5 m) wide. Dark green compound leaves have six leaflets, each abut 1 to 2 inches (2.5 to 5 cm) long. Small bright yellow flowers in rounded clusters bloom from spring to fall. Native to Argentina.

* See Glossary

Senna covesii (Cassia covesii)

Desert senna, Green feathery senna

Fabaceae (Leguminosae) family

COLD HARDINESS

All three zones.

LANDSCAPE VALUE

- Potential as a temporary plant for revegetation seed mixes.
- It produces nice color and naturalizes on desert sites.

CULTURAL REQUIREMENTS

- **Exposure:** Full sun. Tolerates exposed situations and blowing sand.
- **Water:** Needs water every month or two in the warm season to bloom and remain a perennial; otherwise it behaves like an annual.
- **Soil:** Most soils with good drainage.
- **Propagation:** Seed.
- **Maintenance:** Remove spent plants to favor new seedlings.

POSSIBLE PROBLEMS

Can look weedy after blooming.

Small shrubby perennial that grows to 3 feet (1 m) high and wide at a moderate to rapid rate, depending on available moisture. Comes and goes depending on rainfall or supplied moisture. Compound leaves are gray-green. Attractive terminal* clusters of typical yellow *Senna* flowers bloom in summer and fall with moisture.

Senna didymobotrya (Cassia didymobotrya, C. nairobensis)

Nirobe senna

Fabaceae (Leguminosae) family

COLD HARDINESS

Low zone and protected microclimates of intermediate zone. Frost tender but recovers quickly.

LANDSCAPE VALUE

- Medium to large flowering shrub.
- The rangy form suggests mixing in with more presentable shrubs where showy blooms can be appreciated without featuring the shrub's open and leggy aspects.
- Most attractive in mild-winter/cool-summer arid regions, looking somewhat unhappy in the hot-summer climates. Best in coastal deserts.

CULTURAL REQUIREMENTS

- **Exposure:** Full sun.
- **Water:** Drought resistant but needs water every week or two during the hot season for an acceptable performance.
- **Soil:** Most soils with good drainage.
- **Propagation:** Seed.
- **Maintenance:** Cut back periodically to thicken growth, encourage more bloom and remove any excess set of brown pods.

POSSIBLE PROBLEMS

- Prolific seed producer. Large brown pods are not attractive.
- Can be invasive.
- Large leaves wilt midday in hot weather, giving the shrub a stressed look.

Fast-growing evergreen shrub that reaches 8 feet (2.5 m) in height and spreads 8 to 10 feet (2.5 to 3 m). Growth habit is open and leaves are lush green and compound, each leaflet about 2 inches (5 cm) long. Blooms off and on all year if not stopped by frost. Big yellow flowers, 1½ (4 cm) in diameter, on 8- to 10-inch (20.5- to 25.5-cm) spikes are followed by large flat brown pods. Native to east Africa.

* *See Glossary*

Senna lindheimeriana (Cassia lindheimeriana)

Lindheimer senna, Velvet-leaf senna

Fabaceae (Leguminosae) family

Bushy upright perennial shrub that reaches 3 feet (1 m) in height and 2 feet (61 cm) in spread. Moderate growth rate becomes rapid with supplemental water. Herbaceous* stems are somewhat woody toward the base. The alternate pinnately* compound foliage is covered with soft fine hairs. Each leaf is 6 inches (15 cm) long and consists of four to eight pairs of oblong to oval leaflets about 1 inch (2.5 cm) long with no terminal* leaflet. Yellow flowers with five petals about 1 inch (2.5 cm) across open in clusters at the stem tips throughout summer. Seed pods bearing short fine hairs grow to 2 inches (5 cm) long. Native to parts of Texas, New Mexico and Arizona in the United States, Chihuahua and Tamaulipas in northern Mexico.

COLD HARDINESS

Low and intermediate zones. Frost tolerant. Severe cold may kill top growth but regrowth is fast when the weather warms.

LANDSCAPE VALUE

Bright yellow warm-weather color and distinctive foliage texture add interest and accent in

- Arid- and transition-zone borders.
- Natural or wild gardens.
- Revegetation projects.

CULTURAL REQUIREMENTS

- **Exposure:** Full sun.
- **Water:** Water every couple weeks to every couple months during summer, once or twice a season or not at all during winter.
- **Soil:** Most soils with good drainage.
- **Propagation:** Seed and probably cuttings as well.
- **Maintenance:** Requires little care other than occasional pruning to shape.

POSSIBLE PROBLEMS

None observed.

Senna pallida (Cassia biflora)

Two-flowered senna

Fabaceae (Leguminosae) family

COLD HARDINESS

Low zone and warm microclimates of intermediate zone. Frost tender.

LANDSCAPE VALUE

- Specimen or group planting.
- Near large buildings, in parks, buffers and medians.
- Appealing flowers.

CULTURAL REQUIREMENTS

- **Exposure:** Full sun. Adapted to difficult site conditions of intense light, heat and drought.
- **Water:** Low-water-use, but looks best at maturity with soaking of the root zone every month or two.
- **Soil:** Most soils with good drainage.
- **Propagation:** Seed or cuttings.
- **Maintenance:** Prune as necessary for desired form.

POSSIBLE PROBLEMS

None observed.

Evergreen *Senna* with the form of a large shrub or small tree. Grows at a moderate rate to 15 feet (4.5 m) high and 8 to 10 feet (2.5 to 3 m) wide. Sparse open canopy. Green pinnately* compound leaves are divided into four to ten pairs of slender, blunt-tipped leaflets $3/8$ to $3/4$ inch (1 to 2 cm) long. Bright yellow, brown-veined flowers usually occur in pairs throughout summer. Dark brown seed pods are linear, compressed and $2\frac{1}{2}$ to 6 inches (6.5 to 15 cm) long. Native to Mexico, South America and the West Indies.

** See Glossary*

Senna splendida (Cassia splendida)

Golden wonder senna, Autumn senna

Fabaceae (Leguminosae) family

COLD HARDINESS
Low and intermediate zones. Borderline in high zone.

LANDSCAPE VALUE
- Background shrub for late-season color.
- Informal situations (not for refined garden situations).
- Roadsides.

CULTURAL REQUIREMENTS
- **Exposure:** Full sun to part shade.
- **Water:** Thoroughly soak the root zone every couple weeks to every month or two.
- **Soil:** Well-drained soil.
- **Propagation:** Seed.
- **Maintenance:** Cut back after it blooms to remove heavy set of seed pods.

POSSIBLE PROBLEMS
- Heavy seed-pod production can be unattractive.
- Reseeds in garden conditions.

Large, rather open evergreen shrub that grows rapidly from 9 to 12 feet (3 to 3.5 m) high and 6 to 10 feet (2 to 3 m) wide. Bright yellow flowers, 1 1/2 inches (4 cm) wide, cluster at branch tips from late summer into fall. There is now some confusion because several similar-appearing shrubs listed under several different names have been in Arizona and California gardens for many years. All have bright green leaves, but their growth habits differ. A showy bloom period is followed by heavy seed pod production. Native to Brazil.

Senna wislizenii (Cassia wislizenii)

Shrubby senna

Fabaceae (Leguminosae) family

COLD HARDINESS
Low and intermediate zones and warm microclimates of high zone.

LANDSCAPE VALUE
A shrub with distinctive seasonal charm for use as a background, summer color or accent plant.

CULTURAL REQUIREMENTS
- **Exposure:** Full sun.
- **Water:** Endures considerable water-stress but appearance is much improved with water once or twice during dry periods of the warm season.
- **Soil:** Any soil with good drainage.
- **Propagation:** Seed.
- **Maintenance:** Prune occasionally to maintain form.

POSSIBLE PROBLEMS
During the winter-deciduous period it loses much of its landscape appeal.

A tough winter-deciduous, drought-resistant *Senna* that grows 5 to 8 feet (1.5 to 2.5 m) high and spreads 5 to 10 feet (1.5 to 3 m). Growth rate is moderate with supplemental irrigation. Branches are rigid and upright. Form is rounded. Bright green pinnately* compound leaves have two to three pairs of leaflets 5/8 to 1 1/4 inches (1.5 to 3 cm) long. Conspicuous terminal* clusters of yellow flowers make a handsome display from early summer into fall if soil moisture is adequate. Narrow, linear dark brown to black seed pods are 4 inches (10 cm) long. Native from southern Arizona into Texas in the United States, Sonora and Chihuahua in Mexico.

* See Glossary

Serjania palmeri

Serjania vine, Snake-tooth vine
Sapindaceae family

COLD HARDINESS

Low zone and warm microclimates of intermediate zone. Foliage nipped in light frost and growth is cut back drastically by a hard frost. Recovers rapidly in spring.

LANDSCAPE VALUE

- Bold tropical-appearing vine to cover arbors, fences and other vine supports.
- Makes a quick, dense cover.

CULTURAL REQUIREMENTS

- **Exposure:** Full sun to part shade.
- **Water:** Water every month or two, more often during the hot season.
- **Soil:** Some depth for fleshy roots and to increase drought resistance
- **Propagation:** Cuttings.
- **Maintenance:** Climbs by tendrils and needs appropriate vine support to facilitate this characteristic. Will climb into adjoining shrubs and trees.

POSSIBLE PROBLEMS

Vigorous growth can be overwhelming in some situations.

Big clambering vine that will rapidly climb on a support to 30 feet (9 m) or more. Large deep green leaves are pinnately* compound and stems are somewhat succulent. Flowers are of no decorative importance. A vigorous plant. Evergreen if not cut back by frost.

Landscape Design Example

A young planting of *Verbena peruviana*.

* See Glossary

Sesuvium verrucosum

Sonoran ice plant

Aizoaceae family

Prostrate succulent groundcover that grows rapidly to 3 inches (7.5 cm) high, spreading 1 to 3 feet (30.5 cm to 1 m). Forms a dense network of trailing, branching stems and oval leaves 1/4 to 1 1/4 inches (0.5 to 3 cm) long and up to 3/8 inch (1 cm) wide. Tiny rounded crystalline projections give the high leaf surface a warty texture. The flowering season is long, at least from early spring into fall—later in subtropical climates. During this period, small pink flowers with many stamens* are scattered among the branches. Widely distributed from tropical America through Mexico and north into the United States as far as central California, Texas and Kansas.

COLD HARDINESS

Low and intermediate zones and warm-winter microclimates of high zone.

LANDSCAPE VALUE

Not as showy as many other well known succulent groundcovers, but useful in certain difficult situations, such as salty beachfront plantings and harsh desert locations where it can prevent soil erosion and provide a low-spreading mat of greenery.

CULTURAL REQUIREMENTS

- **Exposure:** Withstands extremes of heat, sun exposure and aridity.
- **Water:** Although not required for survival, water once or twice during long dry periods results in a fuller, more uniform planting.
- **Soil:** Tolerant of poor soil conditions and very salt resistant.
- **Propagation:** Seed or cuttings.
- **Maintenance:** Edge to control side growth.

POSSIBLE PROBLEMS

Large plantings are difficult to weed because they do not tolerate foot traffic.

Setcreasea pallida

Setcreasea, Purple heart plant

Commelinaceae family

Sprawling herbaceous* perennial with erect young growth. Grows rapidly to 16 inches (40.5 cm) high, spreading 2 to 4 feet (61 cm to 1 m). Succulent clasping leaves 4 to 7 inches (10 to 18 cm) long and about 1 inch (2.5 cm) wide grow in pairs on fleshy stems. Leaf color varies from green to the rich purple violet of the well-known selection 'Purple Heart.' The small three-petaled flowers that appear throughout summer may be pink, lavender or purple. Native to Mexico.

COLD HARDINESS

Low and intermediate zones, but often damaged by frost in the intermediate zone. A hard winter frost may kill top growth back to the ground. Recovery is rapid, however, as the weather warms in spring.

LANDSCAPE VALUE

- Groundcover in a minioasis setting for mostly frost-free microclimates.
- Bedding plant.
- Outdoor or indoor container plant.

CULTURAL REQUIREMENTS

- **Exposure:** Although bright sunlight stimulates intense leaf color, filtered shade may be best in the low desert.
- **Water:** Water every week or two for fast growth and lush appearance, less often for established plantings.
- **Soil:** Performs best in good garden soil, but tolerates poor soil as well.
- **Propagation:** Cuttings.
- **Maintenance:** Prune back fast-growing runners to maintain a dense compact foliage mass.

POSSIBLE PROBLEMS

Brittle growth does not withstand foot traffic.

** See Glossary*

Simmondsia chinensis

Jojoba, Goatnut

Simmondaceae (Buxaceae) family

COLD HARDINESS

Low and intermediate zones and warm microclimates of high zone.

LANDSCAPE VALUE

- Mass plantings.
- Space-definer.
- Hedge (can be clipped).
- Some low-sprawling, even prostrate growth habits have been found.
- Jojoba is a particularly dense grower for a desert shrub.

CULTURAL REQUIREMENTS

- **Exposure:** Full sun, reflected heat.
- **Water:** Thoroughly soak the root zone every month or two when plant is young. Established plants need no irrigation in desert regions with annual rainfall of 5 inches (130 mm). This is not true when planted in a hedge or a large shrubbery grouping, where the strongest plants take the moisture from the weaker, resulting in gaps in the planting. In this case, water every month or two is necessary.
- **Soil:** Any soil with good drainage.
- **Propagation:** Seed or cuttings. The latter technique is essential when you want a selected growth habit.
- **Maintenance:** Low maintenance. Clip for hedge form, if desired.

POSSIBLE PROBLEMS

Plants are slow to develop.

Gray shrub with rigid knotty branches, leathery evergreen leaves 1 to 2 inches (2.5 to 5 cm) and inconspicuous flowers. Grows at a slow to moderate rate, depending on moisture, up to 6 feet (2 m) high and wide, sometimes larger. Male and female flowers often bloom on different shrubs, so the famed jojoba nut or seed occurs only if plants of both sexes are present. Commercial interest in the seed has led to collections of plants from all areas of its range and has resulted in selections with a wide variety of foliage size and growth habits. Native to Southern California, Arizona and Mexico.

Solanum hindsianum

Blue solanum shrub

Solanaceae family

COLD HARDINESS

Warm, nearly frost-free, areas of low zone, or warm urban microclimates of intermediate zone. Very frost tender. Frost exposure results in severe die-back* or loss of plant. Avoid cold locations.

LANDSCAPE VALUE

- Colorful desert shrub, with interesting foliage and showy flowers over a long season.
- Border shrub.
- Specimen or accent.
- Foundation plant.
- Median and buffer plantings.
- In arid or transitional zones.

CULTURAL REQUIREMENTS

- **Exposure:** Highly tolerant of intense sun, heat and aridity.
- **Water:** Established plants endure long dry periods without irrigation but lose much foliage and flower little or not at all. Water every couple weeks to every month for denser foliage and heavier flowering.
- **Soil:** Tolerates most soils, including poor sandy or rocky soils.
- **Propagation:** Seed or cuttings.
- **Maintenance:** Head back branch terminals* to an outside bud for a spreading, compact canopy.

POSSIBLE PROBLEMS

None observed.

Evergreen shrub from Mexico's Sonoran Desert that grows 3 to 10 feet (1 to 3 m) high and spreads 1½ to 6 feet (46 cm to 2 m). Growth is rapid with adequate irrigation or rainfall. Form is open and ascending. Branching starts near the base. Spines occur at wide intervals along the stems. Oval to oblong or rounded leaves are ¾ to 2½ inches (2 to 6.5 cm) long, densely covered with light gray to tan feltlike hairs. Solitary blue to purple flowers are 1 to 2 inches (2.5 to 5 cm) across and five-lobed. A dark stripe runs from the tip of each lobe to the center of the flower. Blooms appear year-round in warm winter areas with adequate moisture. Smooth, rounded pale green berries ⅜ to ¾ inch (1 to 2 cm) in diameter show a darker green stripe. Fruiting takes place fall into late spring.

* See Glossary

Sophora arizonica

Arizona mescal bean, Arizona sophora

Fabaceae (Leguminosae) family

COLD HARDINESS
All three zones.

LANDSCAPE VALUE
- Specimen shrub.
- Spring color.
- Space definer.
- Unclipped hedge, foundation or border shrub.

CULTURAL REQUIREMENTS
- **Exposure:** Full or reflected sun to part shade.
- **Water:** Drought tolerant but growth and flowering enhanced by soaking of the root zone every week or two during hot dry season, every month or two through the cooler months.
- **Soil:** Endures dry, rocky alkaline soils, but fast drainage is essential.
- **Propagation:** Seed or, less often, softwood cuttings.
- **Maintenance:** Low maintenance once established.

POSSIBLE PROBLEMS
- Slow growing.
- Over-watered plants are very susceptible to root rot.
- Seed and foliage reputed to be poisonous.
- A species-specific caterpillar sometimes defoliates plant in late spring.

Dense, rounded, multistemmed evergreen shrub that grows very slowly from 3 to 10 feet (1 to 3 m) high and wide. Thornless. Dark gray-green leathery foliage is pinnately* compound with five to nine leaflets, $\frac{1}{2}$ to 1 inch (1 to 2.5 cm) long per leaf. Showy bloom in terminal* clusters of purple to lavender flowers, each 1 to $1\frac{1}{4}$ inches (2.5 to 3 cm) long, opens in spring. Tan-colored seed pods are 4 to 7 inches (10 to 18 cm) long, constricted between seeds and pointed at the tip. Seed pods persist on the plant for three or more months. Dull red seeds approximately $\frac{3}{8}$ inch (1 cm) long are presumed poisonous. Native to Arizona.

Sophora secundiflora

Texas mountain laurel, Mescal bean

Fabaceae (Leguminosae) family

COLD HARDINESS
All three zones.

LANDSCAPE VALUE
- Excellent year-round foliage and colorful fragrant early-spring flower display.
- Handsome border shrub, screen or espalier.
- Medians, buffer zones, parking-lot islands.
- Entry gardens and courtyards.
- Dramatic small specimen, accent or patio tree.

CULTURAL REQUIREMENTS
- **Exposure:** Full or reflected sun to part shade.
- **Water:** Thoroughly soak the root zone every month or two, more often during warm season to speed summer growth.
- **Soil:** Tolerates poor alkaline soils but best in deep, good quality soil.
- **Propagation:** Seed. Select largest nursery stock available to partially offset slow growth.
- **Maintenance:** Gradually raise foliage canopy by removing a few lower branches each year to encourage tree form. Remove immature pods if concerned about the poisonous seed.

POSSIBLE PROBLEMS
- Occasional attack by leaf-eating caterpillars.
- Poisonous seeds.
- Slow growth.
- Flowers attract bumble bees.
- Occasional problems with iron chlorosis* and salt injury.

Large evergreen shrub or small tree from 15 to 25 feet (4.5 to 7.5 m) high and 5 to 15 feet (1.5 to 4.5 m) wide. Grows very slowly at first, but speeds up after plant is established. Single- or multitrunked with ascending branches and a vase-shaped crown. Glossy dark green leaves are pinnately* compound and 4 to 6 inches (10 to 15 cm) long. Each leaf has seven to nine leaflets 1 to 2 inches (2.5 to 5 cm) long. Fragrant wisterialike violet-blue flowers open from late winter into spring in drooping terminal* clusters 4 to 8 inches (10 to 20.5 cm) long. The hard tan to silvery gray seed pods 1 to 8 inches (2.5 to 20.5 cm) long ripen in late summer or fall. Pods contain $\frac{1}{2}$ inch (1 cm) bright orange-red poisonous seeds. The seed is so hard that a child could probably ingest and pass the seed with no effect from the poison. Native from Texas and New Mexico to northern Mexico.

** See Glossary*

Sophora tomentosa

Silverbush, Shore sophora

Fabaceae (Leguminosae) family

COLD HARDINESS

Low zone and warmest areas of intermediate zone.

LANDSCAPE VALUE

- Large shrub for background and general shrubby plantings, adding a silver-gray touch for contrast with other greens.
- Especially useful in seafront plantings, tolerating salt, wind and even inundation by storm tides.
- Also has proved tolerant of desert conditions—heat, saline soils and drought.
- Small tree with intensive training.

CULTURAL REQUIREMENTS

- **Exposure:** Full sun to part shade. Endures reflected heat.
- **Water:** Drought resistant. Thoroughly soak the root zone every month or two during the hot season once established. Water more often to speed growth and maintain best landscape effect.
- **Soil:** Most soils, including highly saline.
- **Propagation:** Seed.
- **Maintenance:** No maintenance.

POSSIBLE PROBLEMS

Seeds may be poisonous, as with other *Sophoras*.

Tall, upright shrub to small tree that grows slowly to moderately up to 15 feet (4.5 m) high but usually shorter. Spreads 6 to 10 feet (2 to 3 m). Velvety silvery gray compound leaves have nine pairs of leaflets 1 to 2 inches (2.5 to 5 cm) long. Pale yellow flowers in loose racemes* 6 inches (15 cm) long are followed by typical *Sophora* bean pods. The silver foliage is the most showy aspect of the shrub. The soft yellow flowers that appear in late spring don't stand out against the silver. Native to seashores of Old World tropics, but found in the New World, too. Considered a halophyte* by some.

Sphaeralcea ambigua

Globe mallow

Malvaceae family

COLD HARDINESS

Low and intermediate zones and milder locations in the high zone.

LANDSCAPE VALUE

- Desert perennial garden.
- Colorful foundation planting.
- Revegetation.
- Containers.

CULTURAL REQUIREMENTS

- **Exposure:** Full sun.
- **Water:** Quite drought resistant. Water once or twice a season to stimulate more bloom and good foliage.
- **Soil:** These plants grow on a variety of desert soils, generally with good drainage but not necessarily. In clay soil, allow to be almost dry before watering again.
- **Propagation:** Seed. Can be grown from cuttings to preserve color or leaf type selections.
- **Maintenance:** Groom after bloom falls.

POSSIBLE PROBLEMS

- May look rough and sparse when stressed or after heavy bloom.
- Short-lived.

Plants with the same common name globe mallow are a large, mostly perennial group of colorful flowering plants that contribute much to the Sonoran and Chihuahuan Desert scene. There are numerous species that have potential landscape value. *S. ambigua* and its varieties are perhaps the most typical and will serve here to identify the qualities that characterize this group. In general, these plants are loose and shrubby and grow at a moderate rate to 3 feet (1 m) in height and spread. Gray-green to almost white leaves are deeply lobed. Small typical mallow blossoms (sometimes referred to as "wild hollyhocks") in a variety of colors (red, orange, rose, pink and white) are arranged along upright stems among the gray leaves. The landscape effect of this contrast is striking. A big flower show occurs in spring but some bloom can be seen almost any month in the year. Selection for flower color and foliage types has been done in some quarters but this is only a small step toward utilizing the great potential this group of plants has for selection and plant breeding.

* *See Glossary*

Stachys coccinea

Texas betony, Scarlet betony

Lamiaceae (Labiatae) family

COLD HARDINESS
Low and intermediate zones. Frost hardy.

LANDSCAPE VALUE
- Mass plantings in shady garden spots and near patios where its long and colorful bloom season can be appreciated up close.
- Maybe in sheltered entries, planters and other small-scale or confined spaces and outdoor living areas.

CULTURAL REQUIREMENTS
- **Exposure:** Partial shade.
- **Water:** Water every week or two during the growing season to maintain a moist soil environment, every month or two in winter.
- **Soil:** Good quality garden soil.
- **Propagation:** Seed or cuttings.
- **Maintenance:** Prune out individual flower spikes as they finish blooming or remove them all in one operation during the winter dormant season.

POSSIBLE PROBLEMS
None observed.

This small mounding evergreen herb grows at a moderate rate from 1 to 2 feet (30.5 to 61 cm) in height and spread. The green four-angled stems are erect or nearly so and the pointed oval-shaped leaves are 3/4 to 3 inches (2 to 7.5 cm) long and 1/4 to 1 3/4 inches (0.5 to 4.5 cm) wide. Leaves have rounded or sharp teeth along the margins. During the bloom season, which extends from spring into fall, bright red two-lipped flowers, often in groups of three, open on 4- to 6-inch (10- to 15-cm) spikes. Native in moist, shaded canyon habitats of Arizona, New Mexico, Texas in the United States and to the southern half of Baja California in Mexico.

Stenocereus thurberi (Lemaireocereus thurberi)

Organ pipe cactus

Cactaceae family

COLD HARDINESS
Low zone and warm-winter microclimates of intermediate zone. Cold- and frost-sensitive. If winter frost kills the stem tips, new branches may grow from healthy tissue just below the damaged area. This somewhat deforms the typical silhouette.

LANDSCAPE VALUE
This cactus is protected by the Arizona Native Plant Law and not commonly available in effective landscape sizes. However, even seedlings or small cutting-grown plants will, in time, become strong accent or specimen plants that enhance the beauty of arid landscape compositions.

CULTURAL REQUIREMENTS
- **Exposure:** Full sun.
- **Water:** Water once or twice a season during long periods of hot dry weather.
- **Soil:** Most soils with good drainage. Intolerant of poorly drained soils.
- **Propagation:** Seed or rooting.
- **Maintenance:** No maintenance.

POSSIBLE PROBLEMS
None observed.

A cactus of distinctive appearance that grows slowly to 20 feet (6 m) high and 12 feet (3.5 m) wide. Large old plants may have thirty or more erect columnar stems that originate from a common point at ground level and grow in a clump. The cluster of vertical branches of differing heights resemble a pipe organ and give this cactus its common name. Stems are up to 6 inches (15 cm) in diameter and, in cross section, have twelve to nineteen rounded lobes 3/8 to 7/8 inch (1 to 2 cm) high, one for each of the supporting ribs. Closely spaced spines 1/2 to 1 inch (1 to 2.5 cm) long are black, shading to gray on older growth. Funnel-shaped flowers are as long as 3 inches (7.5 cm), have recurved* outer petals and are mostly white with a delicate touch of pink to reddish purple. They open at night and close the following morning. They appear at the tip and along the high 12-inch (30.5-cm) stem in mid- to late spring. Rounded waxy fruit up to 3 inches (7.5 cm) in diameter is green, shading to red at maturity. Eventually the fruit splits open to show the sweet, edible bright red pulp and small black seeds within. Native range includes southwestern Arizona in the United States, in Baja California and the state of Sonora and south on the mainland of Mexico.

* See Glossary

Syagrus romanzoffianum (Arecastrum romanzoffianum)

Queen palm

Arecaceae (Palmae) family

A straight-trunked palm up to 50 feet (15 m) high, spreading 15 feet (4.5 m). Grows at a moderate rate, rapid with regular feeding*. A tropical-effects tree that often looks out of place in a truly desert setting. Bright green feathery fronds. The trunk is smooth and attractive, bearing ringlike scars left by former leaves (which are not self-cleaning). Small creamy to yellow blooms borne during the warm season on a triangular brush are followed by 1-inch (2.5-cm) orange fruits. A sweet pulp covers a hard, tiny coconutlike pit. The orange pulp is little more than a fleshy skin but is sweet to the taste. The blossom bud emerges from a 2- to 3-foot (61-cm to 1-m) woody boat-shaped sheath coveted by flower arrangers. Native to Brazil.

COLD HARDINESS

Low zone and warm microclimates of intermediate zone. Fronds damaged in mid-20s F (-4°C) but trees have recovered from below 20°F (- 7°C).

LANDSCAPE VALUE

- This palm only looks appropriate in minioasis settings, urban courtyards and similar situations, even though its cultural requirements are not too different from other more "deserty" palms, such as *Washingtonia robusta*.
- The smooth-ringed trunk, blossoming habit and fruit clusters make it attractive for intimate spaces.
- Blends well with other tropical-effects plants.

CULTURAL REQUIREMENTS

- **Exposure:** Full sun. Tolerates reflected heat. Will grow in open shade when young but bolts for the sunny sky. Best in less wind-prone positions because feathery foliage is damaged by high winds.
- **Water:** Water young plants every week or two. Thoroughly soak the root zone of established plants every month or two. Tolerates wet areas in a mini-oasis situation but good drainage is advisable.
- **Soil:** Tolerates most soils with good drainage but appreciates enriched garden soil.
- **Propagation:** Seed.
- **Maintenance:** Responds to fertilizing with more rapid growth.

POSSIBLE PROBLEMS

- Young trees can become chlorotic* and stunted for unknown reasons.
- Fronds can brown in cold years and must be removed.
- Slow to revegetate, particularly after a freeze year.
- Spider mite a problem in some regions.

Tabebuia chrysantha

Primavera amapa, Yellow-flowered amapa

Bignoniaceae family

Dry-season-deciduous tropical tree to 100 feet (30.5 m) high and 60 feet (18 m) wide. Young trees grow rapidly, slowing down to a moderate rate with age. Oval to rounded crown and light gray bark that is rough and flaking on old specimens. The opposite palmately* compound light green leaves 4 to 7 inches (10 to 18 cm) long are comprised of five oval- to lance-shaped leaflets. Foliage is shed during fall and winter, followed by flowering, which occurs from midwinter into spring. Yellow trumpet-shaped blooms $2\frac{1}{4}$ to $2\frac{3}{4}$ inches (6 to 7 cm) long open in large crowded clusters at the branch tips. Within its native range, which extends from Mexico into South America, this tree may have two flowering cycles, the first the heaviest and a few weeks later a second display that is lighter and of shorter duration. The slender hanging seed capsules are tapered at both ends and as long as 1 foot (30.5 cm). New leaves emerge toward the end of the bloom season.

COLD HARDINESS

Warm-winter areas that are frost-free or nearly so of low zone. Sometimes succeeds in warm urban microclimates of intermediate zone. Hard frost may cause extensive die-back* or death of the tree.

LANDSCAPE VALUE

- During its bloom period this stately handsome tree becomes a huge bouquet of rich yellow flowers. As they fall from the branch tips, spent blossoms lay down a thick golden carpet over the ground below.
- Shade tree in parks and residential gardens as well as in roadway plantings.

CULTURAL REQUIREMENTS

- **Exposure**: Full sun.
- **Water:** Thoroughly soak the root zone every week or two during the growing season. During the leafless period watering once or twice a season maintains tree health.
- **Soil:** Most soils, but reaches its full growth and flowering potential in deep fertile types.
- **Propagation:** Seed.
- **Maintenance:** Fast-growing young trees may need pruning to develop good branching structure.

POSSIBLE PROBLEMS

None observed.

* See Glossary

Tabebuia impetiginosa (T. palmeri) and *Tabebuia chrysotricha*

Lavender trumpet tree, Pink-flowered amapa,
Golden trumpet tree
Bignoniaceae family

COLD HARDINESS

Low zone and mild microclimates of intermediate zone. Twig and wood damage occurs when temperatures reach mid- to low-20s F (-4°C to -6°C). Frost tender.

LANDSCAPE VALUE

- *T. impetiginosa* provides handsome summer shade with an outstanding midspring lavender-pink flower show.
- *T. chrysotricha* has lush foliage, golden flowers, and a tropical look in summer.

CULTURAL REQUIREMENTS

- **Exposure:** Full sun.
- **Water:** Low water needs in winter. Thoroughly soak the root zone every couple weeks during summer to assure good growth and development. More moisture in winter can extend green leafy period up to time of blooming.
- **Soil:** Often found growing on rocky hillsides but prefers deeper soils for good root development.
- **Propagation:** Seed.
- **Maintenance:** Stake and trim when plant is young to develop a good tree trim.

POSSIBLE PROBLEMS

Lateness to leaf out in spring can mean no shade when daily temperatures first get high.

Tabebuia impetiginosa is an open-branched, semideciduous to deciduous umbrella-shaped tree. Grows at a moderate rate from 15 to 60 feet (4.5 to 18 m) high, spreading to 50 feet (15 m), usually smaller in desert regions. Ultimate size determined by available moisture. It puts on a show of pink to lavender clusters of tubular flowers before the palmately* compound leaves appear. The latter appear with the advent of rains or applied soil moisture. Native from the northern Sonoran Desert where it endures six rainless winter months on south into central and northern South America.

T. chrysotricha is a small to medium-size semideciduous tree up to 25 feet (7.5 m) high and wide with a spreading crown. Grows at a moderate rate. Flowering is a stunning show of golden yellow trumpets, each 3 to 4 inches (7.5 to 10 cm) long, in large clusters. Palmately* compound leaves drop before bloom and emerge after blossoming is through. Leaflets are about 2 to 4 inches (5 to 10 cm) long and covered with fuzz on underside. Some years, the tree holds its leaves throughout winter.

* *See Glossary*

Tagetes lucida

Mexican tarragon (Santa Maria), Anise marigold

Asteraceae (Compositae) family

COLD HARDINESS

Low and intermediate zones. Top growth is frost sensitive but the plant recovers from the roots with the return of warm temperatures in spring.

LANDSCAPE VALUE

While the flower display is not as showy as that of some marigolds, the interesting aromatic foliage of this species gives it a place as a point of interest or accent in arid landscapes.

CULTURAL REQUIREMENTS

- **Exposure:** Full sun to part shade.
- **Water:** Water every week or two during spring and summer, every month or two during the cooler months.
- **Soil:** Average garden soils.
- **Propagation:** Seed.
- **Maintenance:** Low maintenance.

POSSIBLE PROBLEMS

Foliage and stems killed by winter frost are not replaced until the weather warms in spring.

In its native habitat, which includes parts of Mexico and Central America, this marigold species is a perennial, but under cultivation it may be treated as an annual. It rapidly grows to about 3 feet (1 m) high and 2 feet (61 cm) wide. Produces one to several erect unbranched stems and narrowly elliptical or lance-shaped dark green leaves 1½ to 3½ inches (4 to 9 cm) long by ¼ to ⅜ inch (0.5 to 1 cm) wide in an opposite arrangement. The leaves are dotted with many tiny round glands and have an intense aniselike fragrance. Small yellow flowers about ⅜ inch (1 cm) across open in terminal* clusters in fall. In Mexican markets the plant is sold fresh or dry and has both culinary and medicinal uses.

Tagetes palmeri (T. lemmonii)

Mount Lemmon marigold, Mountain marigold

Asteraceae (Compositae) family

COLD HARDINESS

All three zones. Hard frost will cut it back to the ground, but it regrows quickly in the spring.

LANDSCAPE VALUE

Showy late summer and fall color.

CULTURAL REQUIREMENTS

- **Exposure:** Reflected sun to part shade. A vigorous plant that tolerates extreme heat.
- **Water:** Fairly drought resistant. Water every week or two during the warm season. Can withstand long periods of drought in cool season.
- **Soil:** Well-drained, nonalkaline soil.
- **Propagation:** Seed or divisions.
- **Maintenance:** Cut back after heavy bloom.

POSSIBLE PROBLEMS

- Can look unattractive when going to seed and in winter.
- Some dislike the strong aromatic odor, which is only noticeable when brushed against.
- Short-lived.

Shrubby perennial marigold from 3 to 6 feet (1 to 2 m) high and wide. Grows at a moderate to rapid rate, depending on moisture supply during the warm season. Size of the mature plant varies from one part of its range to another. Typically is spreading and multistemmed with aromatic pinnately* compound leaves 2 to 3 inches (5 to 7.5 cm) long. Yellow daisylike flower heads 1 inch (2.5 cm) across bloom on tall, slender stems throughout the year but primarily from winter to spring. Native to Arizona and northern Mexico.

* *See Glossary*

Tamarix aphylla (T. articulata)

Evergreen tamarisk, Athel tree

Tamaricaceae family

COLD HARDINESS

All three zones. Freezes back every few years in the high zone but recovers rapidly in spring.

LANDSCAPE VALUE

- Admirably adapted to harsh desert conditions, this rugged tree has certain drawbacks that make it best suited for use in outlying low-maintenance areas.
- Shade tree.
- Screen for wind, dust, blowing sand and for visual control.
- Soil stabilization.
- Revegetation.
- May be sheared into a dense hedge 4 to 10 feet (1 to 3 m) tall or taller.
- May have a place in close-up situations where soil conditions and water scarcity make it difficult or impossible to grow other trees.

CULTURAL REQUIREMENTS

- **Exposure:** Full to reflected sun and heat. Tolerates strong drying winds.
- **Water:** Achieves great drought-tolerance as an established tree, but appearance is significantly enhanced by water once or twice a season.
- **Soil:** Survives in poor salty or alkaline soil types where little else will grow, but more lush and vigorous in good quality soil.
- **Propagation:** Insert branch sections 1/2 to 3/4 inch (1 to 2 cm) in diameter and 10 inches (25.5 cm) long into the soil to half their length. Keep moist until established. Even large tree branches will root in place if buried deep with only a few inches of top growth above ground.
- **Maintenance:** Prune periodically to maintain tree health and to reduce the hazard of falling branches.

POSSIBLE PROBLEMS

- Invasive roots make nearby gardening all but impossible and represent a danger to underground pipes, leach fields, building foundations and paved areas.
- Leaf litter is high in salinity, which also affects nearby gardens.
- Fallen branches are a year-round problem in intensively maintained landscapes.
- Brittle branches are prone to storm damage.
- Old trees can shed heavy limbs and therefore are a hazard around structures.
- Does not reseed, but branches and twigs washed down by floods will root when buried and become established in stream beds.

Round-topped to irregular evergreen tree that grows rapidly (with adequate water) from 30 to 50 feet (9 to 15 m) high, spreading 25 to 50 feet (7.5 to 15 m). Trunk and large branches are covered with coarse, deeply furrowed reddish brown bark. Gray-green jointed branchlets somewhat resemble pine needles. The true leaves are reduced to tiny scalelike appendages at the branchlet joints. Delicate white to pinkish flower plumes up to 2 1/2 inches (6.5 cm) long open in late summer on current season's growth. Does not reseed as does its infamous relative salt cedar (*T. chinensis, T. parvifolia* and so forth). Native to North Africa and the eastern Mediterranean region.

Tamarix chinensis

Salt cedar

Tamaricaceae family

COLD HARDINESS

All three zones.

LANDSCAPE VALUE

- Somewhat weedy in character, but has an airy grace and an attractive flower display over a long season. Color selections for deeper pink are available.
- Soil stabilization and revegetation, especially on poor, alkaline or salty soils.
- Screening or background.
- Properly pruned plants make showy specimen shrubs.
- Its bad reputation in the desert Southwest has all but eliminated it from consideration as a landscape plant there. However, it is widely dispersed already, and there are situations of high alkalinity or salinity where salt cedar might be justifiably used. The color selections offered in midwestern nursery catalogs are certainly superior to the naturalized plants and should be used where appropriate.

CULTURAL REQUIREMENTS

- **Exposure:** Well-acclimated to severe desert conditions of full to reflected sun and heat and dry air.
- **Water:** Highly drought resistant. May survive with nothing more than rainfall in some areas but is a better landscape plant with water every couple weeks to every month.
- **Soil:** Tolerates dry, shallow, saline soils but responds dramatically to better quality, moist soil.
- **Propagation:** Propagates readily by 1/2-inch (1-cm) diameter cuttings inserted into the soil and kept damp until established.
- **Maintenance:** For best landscape performance with summer-flowering types, cut back to the ground each year in early spring. This results in a well-shaped shrub 6 feet to 15 feet (2 m to 4.5 m) tall and abundant flowering from spring into fall. Spring-blooming types are larger shrubs and small trees and need little pruning except to shape.

POSSIBLE PROBLEMS

Invasive roots and spreading growth habit. The latter is mostly a problem along waterways in agricultural areas, especially in the arid Southwest. Salt cedar has even invaded the Grand Canyon.

Deciduous multistemmed shrub or small tree that grows rapidly from 6 to 20 feet (2 to 6 m) high and 4 to 10 feet (1 to 3 m) wide. Has naturalized in the southwestern United States where aggressive spreading habit along the banks of streams, rivers and irrigation ditches has earned it the reputation of being a weedy pest. Slender brown to black trunks and branches form a narrow upright or rounded crown, eventually becoming sprawling and irregular if left unpruned. Lacy, light blue-green leaves are small and scalelike, with salt-secreting glands on the jointed branchlets. Delicate flower clusters, mostly at the tips of current growth, bloom from late spring through summer in colors ranging from white to pink (most common) and deep purple. Native to eastern Asia.

Note: *T. africana, T. chinesis, T. parvifolia* and *T. pentandra* are among the many species of deciduous *Tamarix* collectively referred to by the common name salt cedar, a complex hybrid that has invaded the waterways of the Southwest. There is much confusion in the nursery industry over the various species, but from a landscape point of view, there is little difference except varied bloom time and flower color. Midwestern catalogs offer deep-pink flowering selections of unknown origin.

A large specimen of *T. chinensis* at Boyce Thompson Arboretum, growing near the banks of Queen Creek in Superior, Arizona, has never reseeded in the garden or along the creek. It produces a lovely show of soft pink flowers each spring. It is produced by cuttings only.

Tecoma alata

Orange bells, Orange-flowered tecoma
Bignoniaceae family

COLD HARDINESS

Endures light to medium frost of low and intermediate zones, but will be cut back to the ground in a major freeze. Recovers rapidly in spring.

LANDSCAPE VALUE

- A large background shrub for color in a mixed-shrub border.
- Combines well with tropical-effects plants in a minioasis setting.

CULTURAL REQUIREMENTS

- **Exposure:** Full sun, including reflected sun to part shade.
- **Water:** Reasonably drought resistant. Thoroughly soak the root zone every week or two during the warm season.
- **Soil:** Most soils, but responds to garden conditions with more luxuriant growth and bloom.
- **Propagation:** Green wood cuttings.
- **Maintenance:** Occasionally nip back and groom to thicken growth and improve general appearance. Remove cold-damaged wood.

POSSIBLE PROBLEMS

Excessive set of seed pods can be unattractive at times.

Erect fast-growing evergreen shrub to 8 feet (2.5 m) tall and 4 to 5 feet (1 to 1.5 m) wide. Bright green compound leaves have eleven to seventeen leaflets and funnel-shaped orange flowers 2 inches (5 cm) long bloom during the warm season. Plant tends to be tall and rather leggy, and flowers, while colorful, can't match the display put on by its relative *T. stans*. *Tecoma* 'Orange Jubilee' is apparently a selection of *T. alata*, while others say it's a hybrid of *T. stans* and *Tecomaria capensis*. Native to South America.

Tecoma garrocha

Argentine tecoma
Bignoniaceae family

COLD HARDINESS

Low and intermediate zones. Cut back by hard frosts but recovery is rapid in spring.

LANDSCAPE VALUE

A color-producing desert shrub for the transitional zone or the more lush areas of the garden. It looks at home in both situations.

CULTURAL REQUIREMENTS

- **Exposure:** Full sun, including reflected sun to part shade.
- **Water:** Water every couple weeks to every month or two.
- **Soil:** Most soils.
- **Propagation:** Seed or softwood cuttings.
- **Maintenance:** Self-sufficient. Occasionally cut back to thicken new growth and remove heavy sets of seed pods. Remove cold-damaged wood when necessary.

POSSIBLE PROBLEMS

None observed.

Medium evergreen shrub to 5 feet (1.5 m) high and wide or even larger. Grows at a moderate rate, rapid under optimum conditions. Compound leaves have seven to eleven leaflets with serrated margins. Tubular salmon to orange flowers bloom during the warm season and are 2 inches (5 cm) long and followed by abundant clusters of seed pods. The seed pods are about 4 inches (10 cm) long. Character of the shrub is open and somewhat woody in appearance. Native to Argentina.

* See Glossary

Tecoma stans angustata

Narrow-leaf yellow bells, Narrow-leaf yellow trumpet bush
Bignoniaceae family

COLD HARDINESS

Low zone and warm microclimates of intermediate zone as well as thermal belts of high zone where it is native in Arizona and Texas. Survives colder zones where there is more abundant rainfall. For year-round appearance, plant where winters are mostly frost-free or in a warm microclimate protected from frost. In marginal locations, combine with more cold hardy evergreen plants that will mask frost damage until regrowth occurs. A south or west wall with a wide roof overhang provides considerable protection. Although not that cold hardy, new top growth develops quickly from the base in spring, even faster with generous irrigation and fertilization.

LANDSCAPE VALUE

- Outstanding warm-season color shrub with showy flowers and fresh green foliage.
- Specimen.
- Border.
- Foundation or background.
- Roadway medians and buffer zone plantings.
- Makes a pleasing contrast with many gray-green arid-landscape plants.
- Flowers attract hummingbirds.

CULTURAL REQUIREMENTS

- **Exposure:** Full sun to part shade.
- **Water:** Somewhat drought resistant as an established plant but is more attractive and flowers more freely with water every week or two during the warm season. Plants that shed most or all of their foliage in response to cold weather need little or no irrigation until spring.
- **Soil:** Fairly tolerant of varying soil conditions.
- **Propagation:** Seed or cuttings.
- **Maintenance:** Flowers bloom on current season's growth, so thin and head back in early spring to enhance flowering. This is also the time to remove frost-damaged wood. Remove faded blooms and immature seed pods to extend bloom period.

POSSIBLE PROBLEMS

Tends to look tacky because of the abundant seed pods after a bloom spurt. These should be removed for good landscape appearance and to encourage further flowering.

Fast-growing shrub that is medium to large and evergreen in warm-winter areas but killed back part or all the way to the ground by hard frost. Reaches 4 to 10 feet (1 to 3 m) in height and spreads 3 to 8 feet (1 to 2.5 m). Medium green pinnately* compound leaves have seven to thirteen leaflets, deeply toothed along the margin, no more than 1/2 inch (1 cm) wide. Bright yellow trumpet-shaped flowers up to 2 inches (5 cm) long are borne in terminal* clusters off and on midspring into late fall. Flowers are lightly fragrant and attractive to hummingbirds. Seed pods are narrow, cylindrical and 2 3/4 to 8 inches (7 to 20.5 cm) long. It regularly freezes back in winter, but recovers rapidly in spring. Behaves like a woody perennial and blooms each season. Native from Arizona to Texas and adjoining Mexico. Originated in the high-desert zones in Arizona where there is adequate rainfall to support it.

* See Glossary

Tecoma stans stans (Stenolobium stans stans)

Mexican yellow bells

Bignoniaceae family

COLD HARDINESS

Warm-winter areas of low zone. Can freeze to the ground but grows back rapidly and blooms in intermediate zone and limited areas of high zone. Used as a perennial in high zone where it generally freezes to the ground each winter. Because it lacks cold hardiness, it is not a good choice where hard winter frosts are the rule.

LANDSCAPE VALUE

- Summer color in colder zones, but in frost-free areas it becomes a small tropical-appearing tree with lush evergreen foliage and nearly year-round bloom.
- Flowering tree for entry gardens, patios, courtyards, street medians, golf courses, screening and background.
- Under utility wires.

CULTURAL REQUIREMENTS

- **Exposure:** Full or reflected sun to part shade.
- **Water:** Water every week or two during summer to realize full flowering and landscape potential, although established plants are moderately drought tolerant.
- **Soil:** Performs best in fertile well-drained garden soil.
- **Propagation:** Seed or cuttings.
- **Maintenance:** Prune to remove damaged wood when frosted or to shape and direct growth into a small tree.

POSSIBLE PROBLEMS

None observed.

Subtropical evergreen large shrub or small tree that grows quickly as high as 25 feet (7.5 m), spreading 10 to 20 feet (3 to 6 m). In frost-free regions, it usually grows with a single erect trunk, slim ascending branches and an oval to rounded foliage crown. In colder zones it becomes a thick, multistem shrub. The bright-green leaves are similar to those of *T. stans angustata* but differ in that they are divided into three to nine, most commonly five to seven, lance-shaped leaflets, which are wider, as much as 1 inch (2.5 cm) across, with less deeply-cut margins. Flowers are similar to but slightly larger than those of *T. stans angustata*. Blooms throughout the warm season. Native to Mexico and the West Indies.

Tecomaria capensis

Cape honeysuckle

Bignoniaceae family

COLD HARDINESS

Low zone and warm-winter microclimates of intermediate zone. Light winter frost causes blackened branch tips and foliage injury; moderate to severe stem die-back* follows hard frost, but spring recovery is rapid.

LANDSCAPE VALUE

- Whether trained as a vine, shrub or espalier, vibrant orange blooms that appear over a long season, in addition to the attractive foliage, add color and excitement to the landscape.
- Tolerance of salt air extends its usefulness to seaside plantings.

CULTURAL REQUIREMENTS

- **Exposure:** Full sun to part shade. Tolerates heat and aridity.
- **Water:** Water every week or two until established. Thoroughly soak the root zone of mature plants every month or two.
- **Soil:** Best flowering occurs in fertile well-drained soils.
- **Propagation:** Cuttings.
- **Maintenance:** Pruning and tying to a support are necessary to develop as a vine. Heavy pruning is usually required to maintain a shrub growth habit.

POSSIBLE PROBLEMS

None observed.

This South African plant grows rapidly from 20 to 30 feet (6 to 9 m) when trained as a rambling vine with support, up to 6 feet (2 m) high and 5 feet (1.5 m) wide when trained as a shrub. Produces terminal* clusters of bright orange tubular flowers to 2 inches (5 cm) long from fall into spring unless set back by frosty temperatures. Glossy dark green leaves are pinnately* divided and up to 6 inches (15 cm) long. They serve as a dramatic foliage background. The natural sprawling growth habit becomes more vinelike with the support of a trellis, pergola or other support. If disciplined by periodic hard pruning, a large shrub results.

* See Glossary

Terminalia arjuna

Beddome, Sudan almond

Combretaceae family

Vertical-growing evergreen tree that grows about 30 to 40 feet (9 to 12 m) tall. Reputed to reach 80 feet (24 m) in its native India. Spreads from 20 to 30 feet (6 to 9 m) in arid regions or more under optimum conditions. Moderate growth rate can become rapid under optimum conditions. Dark green, oblong leaves are pointed at the top and narrow suddenly at the base. Leaves are about 6 inches (15 cm) long. Smooth, light-colored bark bears greenish white flowers on short panicles*. Fruit is dark brown and narrowly five-winged. Foliage and branch structure have a crisp, fresh quality, a nice addition to the tree palette for hot regions.

Note: Sudan almond is probably not a valid common name, but trees growing in the desert Southwest were propagated from a seed collected in Sudan, thus the local common name.

COLD HARDINESS

Low zone and very warm microclimates of the intermediate zone. Tolerates light frost, but foliage browns when temperatures are low.

LANDSCAPE VALUE

- A promising addition to the list of overstory trees.
- Patio tree.
- May be useful for parks and larger situations

CULTURAL REQUIREMENTS

- **Exposure:** Full sun, including reflected sun. Will tolerate part shade.
- **Water**: Has grown well with weekly soaking of the root zone during the warm season. Enjoys "mini-oasis" situations but seems to have a certain amount of drought tolerance also.
- **Soil:** As of this writing, no apparent special soil requirements. Grows in a variety of desert soils.
- **Propagation:** Seed. Probably will root by cuttings also.
- **Maintenance:** Stake and train when plant is young to develop tree form.

POSSIBLE PROBLEMS

None observed.

Terminalia catappa

Tropical almond

Combretaceae family

A tropical evergreen to subdeciduous tree that grows rapidly from 30 to 50 feet (9 to 15 m) high and 15 to 25 feet (4.5 to 7.5 m) wide. Easy to recognize by the horizontal branches that develop in distinct whorls at intervals along the upright trunk and the large oval leaves 6 to 12 inches (15 to 30.5 cm) long that grow at the branch tips. Drought or cool temperatures induce red, orange and yellow fall leaf colors and varying amounts of defoliation. Under severe stress, the tree may shed most of its leaves. In favorable tropical environments, trees retain their crowns of leathery deep green foliage most or all of the year. Terminal* spikes of insignificant yellowish green flowers appear in cycles throughout the year, or mostly in spring depending on climate factors. Almond-shaped fruits to 2½ inches (6.5 cm) long change from green to reddish purple or dull yellow at maturity. Although edible, the fruit is not particularly tasty. Native to the East Indies and Malaysia.

COLD HARDINESS

Frost-free areas of low zone.

LANDSCAPE VALUE

- Shiny bold-textured foliage that is highly salt resistant makes this a valuable tree for frontline seashore landscapes in tropical and subtropical climates.
- Street or avenue tree.
- Shade.
- Background or framing.

CULTURAL REQUIREMENTS

- **Exposure:** Full to reflected sun and intense heat.
- **Water:** Established trees are drought resistant and able to survive dry periods of several months, especially in humid microclimates near the sea. For acceptable year-round landscape appearance, thoroughly soak the root zone every month or two during dry spells.
- **Soil:** Tolerates a wide range of soil conditions, including those found in sandy, salty beachfront locations, but landscape performance is enhanced on better quality planting sites.
- **Propagation:** Seed.
- **Maintenance:** No maintenance.

POSSIBLE PROBLEMS

A heavy fruit crop creates considerable ground litter.

* See Glossary

Teucrium fruticans

Bush germander

Lamiaceae (Labiatae) family

COLD HARDINESS

All three zones.

LANDSCAPE VALUE

- Screening.
- Background.
- Space definer.
- Informal flowering hedge.
- Border or foundation shrub.

CULTURAL REQUIREMENTS

- **Exposure:** Full sun.
- **Water:** Water every couple weeks to every month. Allow the soil to dry moderately between waterings. Does not tolerate overwatering.
- **Soil:** Most soils with good drainage. Grows in poor, sandy or rocky soils.
- **Propagation:** Cuttings
- **Maintenance:** To maintain good form and density, selectively thin and head back stems in late winter.

POSSIBLE PROBLEMS

None observed.

Evergreen rounded shrub that grows at a moderate rate from 4 to 8 feet (1 to 2.5 m) high, with equal spread. White hairy twigs are four-angled, a typical feature of the mint family. Oval to lance-shaped leaves up to 1 1/4 inches (3 cm) long are oppositely arranged. Leaves are gray-green and smooth above and covered with whitish hairs below. Blue or lilac-colored flowers to 1 inch (2.5 cm) long have long stamens* that extend beyond the flower. Blooms appear in terminal* clusters throughout the year. Native to the Mediterranean region.

Thevetia peruviana (T. neriifolia)

Yellow oleander, Lucky nut, Be-still tree

Apocynaceae family

COLD HARDINESS

Low zone, with care to avoid cold spots, and frost-protected sites of the intermediate zone. If hard winter freezes are common, mulch the base of the trunk and treat the plant as a perennial that flowers each summer from new top growth. Cold winters result in injury ranging from defoliation to loss of all unprotected top growth. However, even when plants are killed to the ground, regrowth from the base may flower the following summer.

LANDSCAPE VALUE

- Colorful exotic flowers over a long season and dense refined foliage are the chief virtues.
- When not limited by winter cold, it can be trained as a handsome small tree for roadsides or medians.
- Tropical-effects flowering accent, specimen or patio tree.
- As a shrub: privacy screen, background, hedge.

CULTURAL REQUIREMENTS

- **Exposure:** Full to reflected sun.
- **Water:** Thoroughly soak the root zone every week or two throughout the year, less often in winter.
- **Soil:** Good quality soils.
- **Propagation:** Seed.
- **Maintenance:** Requires some pruning and training to establish and maintain tree growth habit.

POSSIBLE PROBLEMS

Poisonous if eaten.

In locations where winter frosts are light and infrequent, develops quickly as a medium to large evergreen shrub to 8 feet (2.5 m) high or higher, or as a tree to 25 feet (7.5 m) high in frost-free areas. Spreads from 8 to 20 feet (2.5 to 6 m), depending on climate and training procedures. Foliage is dense, glossy and dark green. The linear-shaped leaves 3 to 6 inches (7.5 to 15 cm) long by 1/2 inch (1.5 cm) wide typically have a rolled margin. Yellow or peach-colored flowers, 2 to 3 inches (5 to 7.5 cm) in diameter, open in clusters at the branch tips mostly from early summer into fall or year-round in warm-winter regions. 'Alba' is a white-flowered selection. Angular-shaped fruits about 1 inch (2.5 cm) in diameter change from red to black at maturity. All parts of this plant are considered highly toxic, including the white milky sap that oozes from cut surfaces. Native to tropical America.

* See Glossary

Thevetia thevetioides

Giant thevetia

Apocynaceae family

COLD HARDINESS

Low zone and warm microclimates of intermediate zone.

LANDSCAPE VALUE

- Large shrub or patio-size tree.
- Color producer over a long period.
- Silhouette against a plain wall or overhead against the sky.
- Open shade as a patio tree.

CULTURAL REQUIREMENTS

- **Exposure:** Full sun, reflected sun to open shade.
- **Water:** A weekly soaking of the root zone during the hot season produces the best results, but will tolerate longer dry periods especially in winter. Native to winter-dry and summer-rain regions of Mexico.
- **Soil:** Most soils with good drainage. Prefers good garden soil.
- **Propagation:** Seed or cuttings.
- **Maintenance:** Shape and guide young plants.

POSSIBLE PROBLEMS

Bloom drop is attractive at first because they hold their color for several days after falling, but this presents a cleanup problem. Hard fruit also can create litter.

Fast growing, rather open evergreen large shrub or small tree to 12 feet (3.5 m) high and wide or larger. Dark green leaves resemble oleander leaves but have corrugated edges and a more open growth pattern. Clusters of bright yellow 4-inch (10 cm) flowers put on a show late spring to late fall. Large round fruit follows and is hard, green at first, turning black at maturity. Native to Mexico.

Tipuana tipu

Tipu tree, Pride of Bolivia

Fabaceae (Leguminosae) family

COLD HARDINESS

Low zone and warm-winter microclimates of intermediate zone. Moderately frost tolerant, becoming more so with age.

LANDSCAPE VALUE

- An amazing profusion of showy flowers in summer is perhaps the greatest asset.
- Shade tree in oasis and transition zones of residential landscapes as well as in park and roadside plantings.

CULTURAL REQUIREMENTS

- **Exposure:** Full sun. Endures heat and low humidity.
- **Water:** Moderately drought tolerant as an established plant. Thoroughly soak the root zone every month or two during the growing season, but only once or twice during winter.
- **Soil:** Deep, well-drained soil.
- **Propagation:** Seed.
- **Maintenance:** Prune to develop a head-high crown and the desired branching structure.

POSSIBLE PROBLEMS

In some landscape situations, the carpet of fallen flowers creates a litter problem.

The rounded and open foliage canopy of this subtropical tree is usually wider than it is tall. Tree grows at a rapid rate 25 to 40 feet (7.5 to 12 m) high or higher, 30 to 60 feet (9 to 18 m) wide or wider. Its pinnately* compound leaves have six to eleven pairs of oval leaflets to 1½ inches (4 cm) long by ¾ inch (2 cm) wide. The tree is briefly winter-deciduous or semideciduous in most areas where it is adapted. During its summer bloom period, the branches are heavy with sprays of golden yellow or apricot-colored pealike flowers. The fruit is a winged pod to 2½ inches (6.5 cm) long. Native to South Brazil and Bolivia.

* See Glossary

Tithonia fruticosa

Mexican sunflower shrub

Asteraceae (Compositae) family

COLD HARDINESS

Low zone. A cut-back perennial in the intermediate zone. Frost tender. Bloom and new growth damaged by light frost and can look tacky in winter even without frost, especially if seed heads are not removed.

LANDSCAPE VALUE

Colorful flowering shrub throughout the warm season.

CULTURAL REQUIREMENTS

- **Exposure:** Sunny protected location.
- **Water:** Water every week or two for continued bloom.
- **Soil:** Deep enough for rooting and moisture storage.
- **Propagation:** Seed and divisions of clump.
- **Maintenance:** Remove old bloom for best appearance and to assure more continuous flowering. Cut back cold-damaged growth at end of winter for rapid regrowth. Remove seed heads.

POSSIBLE PROBLEMS

Soft, hollow stems break easily in storms.

Large shrub, 9 to 12 feet (3 to 3.5 m) high and wide. Grows rapidly. Stems are thick but brittle. Large 3- to 4-inch (7.5- to 10-cm) leaves are velvety and orange-yellow sunflowers are 4 inches (10 cm) in diameter and consistently in bloom throughout the warm season. Soft growth and big flowers give it the effect of a giant perennial rather than a true shrub.

Ugnadia speciosa

Mexican buckeye

Sapindaceae family

COLD HARDINESS

All three zones.

LANDSCAPE VALUE

- Large shrub but can be trained into a patio-size tree.
- Lush summer foliage, good for spring color and yellow fall-foliage color. Should be used more for its seasonal value.

CULTURAL REQUIREMENTS

- **Exposure:** Full reflected sun to part shade.
- **Water:** Thoroughly soak the root zone every month or two, more frequently during the warm season.
- **Soil:** Tolerates poor soil but needs good drainage.
- **Propagation:** Seed.
- **Maintenance:** Stake and guide young plants to develop tree form.

POSSIBLE PROBLEMS

Seed is mildly poisonous.

Deciduous rose-pink spring-flowering shrub or small tree 8 to 12 feet (2.5 to 3.5 m) high and wide, taller under optimum conditions. Moderate growth rate. Large light green leaves turn yellow in fall. Resembles the buckeye (*Aesculus*), but it is not related.

* *See Glossary*

Ulmus pumila

Siberian elm

Ulmaceae family

COLD HARDINESS

All three zones. Best in intermediate and high zones.

LANDSCAPE VALUE

- Much-maligned and held in contempt as a landscape tree in temperate moist-climate regions, Siberian elm may nevertheless be the tree of choice for shade and shelter functions in certain arid cold-winter areas where few other species can survive.
- Windbreak and erosion control where climate and soil factors rule out trees with more desirable characteristics and fewer problems.

CULTURAL REQUIREMENTS

- **Exposure:** Full sun to part shade. Endures heat and extremes of cold, aridity and wind if minimum water needs are met.
- **Water:** Established trees tolerate arid conditions but severe drought causes considerable die-back* of the branches. Thoroughly soak the root zone every month or two during the growing season. Water once or twice during the dormant season if very dry. Water young trees more frequently to achieve effective landscape size in a shorter time. The more water available, the larger and more lush the tree.
- **Soil:** Most soils. In some mid- and high-elevation arid regions that are devoid of native trees, Siberian elm may be seen growing in washes*, ravines and roadside ditches that supply a little extra soil moisture.
- **Propagation:** Seed or cuttings.
- **Maintenance:** Prune for a stronger framework of branches to prevent storm damage and maintain a walk-under canopy height for shade trees.

POSSIBLE PROBLEMS

- Resistant to Dutch elm disease and phloem necrosis, which are major diseases of certain other elm species, but it is highly susceptible to Texas root rot* and slime flux, a bacterial disease that causes fermenting sap to ooze and drip from any bark opening.
- It is also host to root-knot nematodes* and various insects that feed on the foliage.
- Generates considerable ground litter.
- Its brittle wood is vulnerable to heavy damage in wind and ice storms.
- The invasive roots can create problems in sewer lines and may make it difficult to cultivate less aggressive garden plants nearby.
- Fast-growing volunteer seedlings often appear where they are least appreciated, for example at the base of other plants, entwined in chain-link fences and scattered in groundcover beds.

In its typical form, develops an upright spreading crown from several large ascending branches. Grows rapidly from 30 to 50 feet (9 to 15 m) high and 20 to 40 feet (6 to 12 m) wide. The slender light gray branch terminals* are flexible and pendulous. Tough deciduous tree survives as a shrub in dry difficult locations. The medium green elliptical leaves 3/4 to 3 inches (2 to 7.5 cm) long have toothed margins and grow in an alternate arrangement. In early spring, the tree bears clusters of inconspicuous flowers followed by an abundant crop of 1/2 inch (1 cm) long winged fruits called *samaras.* Several improved hybrids and cultivars* have been developed for landscape use. Native to Eastern Siberia and Northern China.

* See Glossary

Vallesia baileyana

Vallesia

Apocynaceae family

COLD HARDINESS

Low zone and warm-winter microclimates of intermediate zone. Not adapted to areas where hard winter frost is a common occurrence.

LANDSCAPE VALUE

- Background or space definer.
- Understory.
- The waxy white berries provide close-range interest.
- The flowers add fragrance.

CULTURAL REQUIREMENTS

- **Exposure:** Full to reflected sun and heat.
- **Water:** Very drought resistant when established, much fuller and larger with soaking of the root zone every month or two.
- **Soil:** Performance in various landscape soils is unevaluated. Grows well as a native in the dry, sandy, rocky, alkaline soils of Mexico's lower Sonoran Desert.
- **Propagation:** Seed or cuttings.
- **Maintenance:** Needs little pruning except to remove frost-damaged wood in cold years.

POSSIBLE PROBLEMS

None observed.

Evergreen shrub or small tree 6 to 8 feet (2 to 2.5 m) high and 5 to 7 feet (1.5 to 2 m) wide. Moderate to rapid growth rate with water. Upright ascending primary branches and a dense oval form. Glossy dark green leaves are oblong to lance-shaped, 2¼ to 3½ inches (6 to 9 cm) long. Clusters of eight to twenty small fragrant white flowers open in spring at the tips of new growth. Whitish, translucent juicy berries appear in summer. Native to the southern edge of the Sonoran Desert in northwest Mexico.

Vallesia glabra

Smooth vallesia

Apocynaceae family

COLD HARDINESS

Low zone and warm-winter microclimates of intermediate zone. Not adapted to areas where hard winter frost is a common occurrence.

LANDSCAPE VALUE

- Tough arid-adapted plant with attractive foliage and decorative white fruits.
- Background, screen, specimen, border shrub or small multistemmed tree.

CULTURAL REQUIREMENTS

- **Exposure:** Full to reflected sun and heat.
- **Water:** Quite drought resistant when established. Thoroughly soak the root zone every month or two for much fuller and larger growth.
- **Soil:** Performance in various landscape soils is unevaluated. Grows well as a native in the dry, sandy, rocky, alkaline soils of Mexico's lower Sonoran Desert.
- **Propagation:** Seed or cuttings.
- **Maintenance:** No maintenance.

POSSIBLE PROBLEMS

None observed.

Evergreen large shrub (or, rarely, a small tree) that grows at a moderate to rapid rate with water. Reaches 10 to 20 feet (3 to 6 m) in height and 8 to 15 feet (2.5 to 4.5 m) in spread. Upright to oval form with slender branches. Narrow, leathery lance-shaped leaves are 1 to 2¾ inches (2.5 to 7 cm) long. Small inconspicuous flowers are most abundant fall through midspring, scattered throughout the rest of the year. Whitish fruits that follow bloom are fleshy and translucent. Native from Mexico to South America, the West Indies, and Southern Florida.

** See Glossary*

Vauquelinia californica auciflora

Arizona rosewood

Rosaceae family

COLD HARDINESS

All three zones.

LANDSCAPE VALUE

A versatile rugged plant whose rich foliage and ornamental character make it an excellent choice for a variety of landscape uses:

- Specimen or accent shrub.
- Background, screen, informal hedge, barrier or boundary in transition-zone locations.
- Street or highway medians.
- Buffer zones.
- May also be trained into a small patio or specimen tree.

CULTURAL REQUIREMENTS

- **Exposure:** Full or reflected sun to part shade.
- **Water:** Endures long dry periods as an established plant, especially in the intermediate and high zones. Needs water every couple weeks to every month to achieve most attractive landscape character.
- **Soil:** Best suited to deep, well-drained soils but tolerates rocky alkaline locations as well.
- **Propagation:** Cuttings. Also seed, but plants produced by seed vary considerably in appearance.
- **Maintenance:** Prune to develop tree form if that is desired. Vigorous growth of terminals* may require heading back to maintain dense compact form.

POSSIBLE PROBLEMS

- Spider mites, aphids and powdery mildew.
- Young plants may be somewhat slow to establish.

Large evergreen shrub or small tree with one to several trunks, 10 to 25 feet (3 to 7.5 m) high and 5 to 15 feet (1.5 to 4.5 m) wide. Grows at a moderate to rapid rate, depending on water supply. The form and texture are similar to oleander. It lacks oleander's colorful flowering effects but is more cold hardy. Dense to open and oval to rounded in outline with ascending, sometimes twisted branches. Leathery leaves up to 4 inches (10 cm) long are dark green above, covered with tiny light gray hairs below. They are narrow and linear to lance-shaped, usually with serrated margins. Small white flowers in dense flat clusters 2 to 3 inches (5 to 7.5 cm) across open at the tips of branches in late spring. Unimportant woody seed capsules remain on the plant throughout winter. Native to southern Arizona in the United States, Baja California and the northern mainland of Mexico.

* See Glossary

Vauquelinia corymbosa angustifolia

Chihuahuan rosewood

Rosaceae family

COLD HARDINESS

All three zones.

LANDSCAPE VALUE

A versatile rugged plant whose rich foliage and ornamental character make it an excellent choice for a variety of landscape uses:

- Specimen or accent shrub.
- Background, screen, informal hedge, barrier or boundary in transition-zone locations.
- Street or highway medians.
- Buffer zones.
- May also be trained into a small patio or specimen tree.
- The vertical growth habit makes it useful as a tall hedge in a narrow planting strip.

CULTURAL REQUIREMENTS

- **Exposure:** Full or reflected sun to part shade.
- **Water:** Thoroughly soak the root zone every month or two, every week or two during the hottest periods, especially when young and developing. Endures long dry periods as an established plant, especially in the intermediate and high zones.
- **Soil:** Best suited to deep well-drained soils but tolerates rocky locations and alkaline soil as well.
- **Propagation:** Seed or cuttings. Plants produced by seed vary considerably in appearance.
- **Maintenance:** Prune to develop tree form. Vigorous growth of terminals* may require heading back to maintain dense compact form.

POSSIBLE PROBLEMS

Tends to be leggy when young, but fairly trouble-free otherwise.

Attractive evergreen large shrub or small tree with one to several trunks. Grows 10 to 25 feet (3 m to 7.5 m) high and 5 to 15 feet (1.5 to 4.5 m) wide. Growth rate is moderate with moisture, slow under dry conditions. Dense to open and oval to rounded in outline. Ascending, sometimes twisted branches. Leathery leaves to 6 inches (15 cm) long are dark green above, covered with tiny light-gray hairs below, narrow and linear to lance-shaped, usually with serrated margins. Small white flowers in dense flat clusters 2 to 3 inches (5 to 7.5 cm) across open at the tips of branches in late spring. Flowers are not particularly showy. Unimportant brown, woody seed capsules remain on the plant throughout winter. Similar to *V. californica auciflora*, differing mainly in the fine-textured foliage effect created by its slender almost thread-like leaves. It is also less susceptible to spider mites. Resembles oleander but lacks the colorful bloom. Because it is more cold hardy than oleander, it can be used for similar purposes in high-elevation landscapes. Native to Texas and northern Mexico.

* See Glossary

Verbena gooddingii

Goodding verbena

Verbenaceae family

COLD HARDINESS

All three zones.

LANDSCAPE VALUE

Attractive addition to a mix of desert perennials or short-term groundcover.

CULTURAL REQUIREMENTS

- **Exposure**: Full sun.
- **Water:** Water every few weeks for good bloom and appearance.
- **Soil:** Well-drained soil.
- **Propagation:** Seed or cuttings.
- **Maintenance:** Short-lived. Replace from time to time.

POSSIBLE PROBLEMS

- Life span is variable.
- Can look tacky after period of heavy bloom.

Perennial though short-lived groundcover that grows at a moderate rate (rapid with regular moisture) to 18 inches (46 cm) high and 3 feet (1 m) wide. Makes an attractive mound of small finely cut leaves covered with short spikes of tiny pink-lavender flowers. Blooms throughout spring and summer if moisture is present. Reseeds readily. Native to U.S. desert Southwest.

Verbena peruviana and Peruvian hybrids

Peruvian verbena

Verbenaceae family

COLD HARDINESS

All three zones.

LANDSCAPE VALUE

Colorful groundcover or border plant.

CULTURAL REQUIREMENTS

- **Exposure:** Full sun to part shade.
- **Water:** Water every month or two once established, every week or two during the warm season.
- **Soil:** Most soils with good drainage.
- **Propagation:** Seed or cuttings (hybrids from cuttings only).
- **Maintenance:** Plant 2 feet (61 cm) apart for cover during one season. Refurbish bare spots every year.

POSSIBLE PROBLEMS

Not a long-lived groundcover. Hybrids have an even shorter life span.

Tough perennial ground-hugging mat to 1 inch (2.5 cm) high and 3 feet (1 m) wide. Growth rate is moderate to rapid under optimum conditions. Small dark green leaves bear clusters of small brick red flowers that bloom off and on during the warm season. There are many hybrids in a variety of colors—whites, pinks, reds and purples. They do not have the toughness or grow as flat or wide as the parent species. Native to South America.

Verbena pulchella gracilior (V. tenuisecta)

Moss verbena

Verbenaceae family

COLD HARDINESS

Low and intermediate zones. Cold winters cause planted areas to look bare for two or more months but spring regrowth is rapid with irrigation.

LANDSCAPE VALUE

- Untreadable groundcover makes a fine-textured low carpet of purple over a long season with adequate soil moisture.
- Especially colorful for transitional zones.
- Combines well with wild flowers and other groundcovers of similar growth habit.
- Erosion control on slopes and banks.
- Both residential and commercial landscapes.
- Medians and buffer zones.

CULTURAL REQUIREMENTS

- **Exposure:** Full to reflected sun.
- **Water:** Moderately drought tolerant as an established plant but satisfactory landscape performance is dependent on water every couple weeks to every month.
- **Soil:** Grows well in a wide range of sandy to rocky, alkaline, arid-region soils if water is available and the soil contains little organic matter.
- **Propagation:** Seed or cuttings.
- **Maintenance:** Prune back frost-damaged plants in late winter. Naturalizes readily even if existing plants are lost over winter. A fresh vigorous stand can be established from seedlings by periodic irrigation of the site.

POSSIBLE PROBLEMS

None observed.

Evergreen flat-growing perennial 6 to 12 inches (15 to 30.5 cm) high and 2 to 5 feet (61 cm to 1.5 m) wide. Grows rapidly with regular water. Dark green leaves 1-inch (2.5 cm) long are divided into three parts, finely and pinnately* cut. Small flower clusters are blue to purple or violet (sometimes pink or white) and bloom from late winter into fall in warm low-desert locations. Flowers are most abundant in spring on drier sites. Native to South America.

Verbena rigida

Sandpaper verbena

Verbenaceae family

COLD HARDINESS

Low and intermediate zones.

LANDSCAPE VALUE

- Startling splash of color over a long season.
- Banks and slopes.
- Street medians and parking-lot islands.
- Planters.
- Massed in naturalistic plantings.
- Transition plant for larger plants.

CULTURAL REQUIREMENTS

- **Exposure:** Full sun.
- **Water:** Drought tolerant as an established plant. Thoroughly soak the root zone every week or two during the growing season, every month or two or just once or twice during the inactive period.
- **Soil:** Most soils with good drainage.
- **Propagation:** Seed or cuttings. Reseeds itself naturally in favorable locations.
- **Maintenance:** Heavy spring pruning to near the soil line results in vigorous regrowth. Prune back after successive bloom cycles to encourage continued flowering and more compact form.

POSSIBLE PROBLEMS

A short-lived groundcover.

This evergreen perennial grows rapidly (with regular water) from 10 inches to 2 feet (25.5 to 61 cm) high and 3 to 4 feet (1 m) wide. Erect or ascending four-angled stems assume a bushy growth habit where conditions are favorable. The dark green deeply toothed leaves 2 to 4 inches (5 to 10 cm) long clasp the branches in pairs and have a rough surface texture. From summer into fall, cylindrical clusters of deep purple flowers, 1-inch (2.5 cm) wide, appear on stiff upright stems. The bloom clusters often develop in groups of three. Native to southern Brazil and Argentina, naturalized in the United States from North Carolina and Florida west to Texas.

* *See Glossary*

Viguiera deltoidea
Golden eye
Asteraceae (Compositae) family

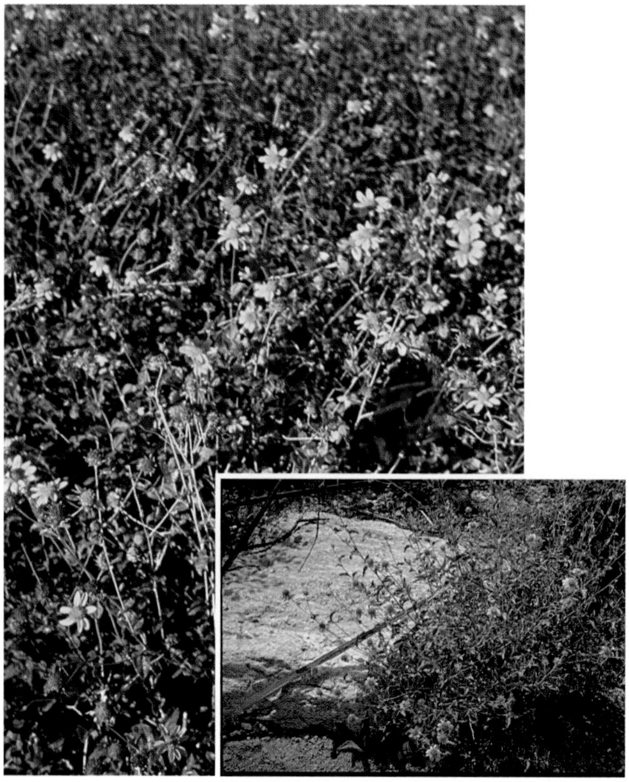

COLD HARDINESS
Low and intermediate zones.

LANDSCAPE VALUE
- Outstanding small shrub in foundation plantings where the flowers are bright seasonal accents.
- Edging or facer shrub.
- Low transition-zone plant, useful for small home grounds near patios or pools, urban street medians and roadside plantings.

CULTURAL REQUIREMENTS
- **Exposure:** Full sun and reflected heat.
- **Water:** Water every month or two during the warm season.
- **Soil:** Most soils with good drainage.
- **Propagation:** Seed or cuttings.
- **Maintenance:** Cut back straggly plants after bloom season for more compact growth.

POSSIBLE PROBLEMS
None observed.

Sprawling evergreen shrub to 3 feet (1 m) high and wide, or larger. Moderate growth rate. The leaves are triangular and wider at the base, variable in size but usually 1/2 to 1 inch (1 to 2.5 cm) long and 3/8 to 3/4 inch (1 to 2 cm) across with toothed margins. Dense hairs on both surfaces of the leaves give them a rough texture. Conspicuous small yellow daisylike flower heads appear singly or in clusters at the tips of the slender stems in spring. Native to parts of Arizona, California and Nevada in the United States and Baja California and Sonora in Mexico.

Vitex agnus-castus
Chaste tree, Monk's pepper tree
Verbenaceae family

Grows as a large shrub or a single- or multistemmed small tree 10 to 25 feet (3 to 7.5 m) high, with equal spread. Rapid growth with regular water. The rounded crown is spreading and low-branched. Winter-deciduous, palmately* compound leaves are divided into five to seven lance-shaped to elliptical leaflets. Leaves are aromatic, 2 to 6 inches (5 to 15 cm) long, medium to dark green above, grayish and hairy on the underside. Small blue or lavender-blue flowers open in 7-inch (18-cm) spikes during summer with an occasional light repeat cycle in fall. Flowers of

COLD HARDINESS
All three zones.

LANDSCAPE VALUE
- Outstanding summer-color shrub or small tree.
- Border.
- Summer screen.
- Road medians.
- Transitional or oasis zones.
- Small specimen or patio tree, often develops an interesting gnarly trunk with age.

CULTURAL REQUIREMENTS
- **Exposure:** Flowering most abundant and colorful with full sun and high summer heat.
- **Water:** Moderately drought tolerant. Water every couple weeks to every month during the growing season, but only once or twice during the dormant period.
- **Soil:** Grows and blooms well in many arid-climate soils. More lush in rich fertile soils but flowering is reduced.
- **Propagation:** Seed or cuttings. Cuttings are best to ensure a good shade of blue bloom. There are many washed-out off-white and dull lavender-flowering individuals.
- **Maintenance:** Prune to develop as a small tree and to maintain a well-groomed look.

POSSIBLE PROBLEMS
- The leafless plant offers little winter interest.
- Old trees seem overly twiggy with last summer's dry blossom stalks persisting.

'Rosea' are pink; those of 'Alba' are white. Small rounded seeds in dry capsules appear in fall and winter and have a peppery smell when bruised. Native to southern Europe.

* *See Glossary*

Vitex trifolia (V. lucens and V. trifolia simplicifolia)

Evergreen chaste tree

Verbenaceae family

COLD HARDINESS

Low zone and protected microclimates of intermediate zone. Hard frost results in unsightly damage in colder areas but regrowth is rapid as the weather warms in spring.

LANDSCAPE VALUE

- Excellent foliage character and attractive flowers over a long season.
- Background, screening, informal shrub borders.
- Roadsides.
- Facer shrub in front of larger leggy plants.
- Flowering specimen or accent.
- Requires shearing for hedging or topiary uses, a popular use for this shrub in Mexico.
- *V. trifolia simplicifolia* has groundcover potential.

CULTURAL REQUIREMENTS

- **Exposure:** Full sun to part shade. Performs well in arid climates.
- **Water:** Tolerates some drought stress but best appearance is achieved with thorough soaking of the root zone every month or two in the growing season to once or twice in winter.
- **Soil:** Grows in a wide range of soil types.
- **Propagation:** Seed or cuttings.
- **Maintenance:** Prune for desired growth form.

POSSIBLE PROBLEMS

None observed.

Fast-growing, spreading shrub or small shrubby tree. Reaches 10 to 20 feet (3 to 6 m) in height, 15 to 25 feet (4.5 to 7.5 m) in spread and is often broader than it is tall. Branches close to the ground unless pruned to higher canopy level. The oppositely arranged leaves are palmately* compound with one to three elliptical or lance-shaped leaflets that are wider above the middle, up to 3 inches (7.5 cm) long, covered with white hairs beneath and darker above. The small blue to purple funnel-shaped flowers appear in terminal* clusters to 9 inches (23 cm) long intermittently from spring into summer. Native to Asia and Australia. The cultivar* 'Variegata' has variegated leaves and *V. t. simplicifolia* has a prostrate wide-spreading growth habit, rounded leaves and 1-inch (2.5-cm) long clusters of blue flowers.

Washingtonia filifera

California fan palm

Arecaceae (Palmae) family

COLD HARDINESS

All three zones. One of the hardiest palms and the most cold-tolerant of the *Washingtonias*. Foliage can be damaged in the high zone during cold winters, but it recovers in spring.

LANDSCAPE VALUE

Stately roadside plantings or other large-scale landscapes, but rather stiff and out of scale for residences.

CULTURAL REQUIREMENTS

- **Exposure:** Will start in part shade but eventually its head will be in full sun; loves heat and doesn't do as well in cool coastal regions.
- **Water:** Truly an oasis palm and needs water every week or two to grow well. Mature specimens seem to be quite drought resistant and survive with thorough watering every month or two.
- **Soil:** Most soils.
- **Propagation:** Seed. Collect only from pure stands because it hybridizes with *W. robusta* if any are near. Seed gathered in urban areas is not dependable.
- **Maintenance:** Needs plenty of room and considerable grooming if you wish to keep the trunk clear of thatch. Otherwise, little maintenance except to remove old bloom stalks, old leaf bases and occasional sweep-up of a heavy fruit drop.

POSSIBLE PROBLEMS

Giant palm borer*, but this insect does not appear to be a major problem in native stands.

Stout-trunked palm to 45 feet (13.5 m) tall or taller, spreading 10 to 15 feet (3 to 4.5 m). Grows rapidly in heat if moisture is constant, slowly in cool-summer regions. Large head consists of light green fan-shaped leaves on long, sometimes toothed petioles*. Old leaves hang down on the trunk unless removed, forming a rather handsome straw-colored thatch. Flower stalks protrude well out of the foliage with crowded, waxy off-white flowers. Female trees produce a heavy crop of little blue-black berries from late spring into summer. These are edible but mostly seed and only worth the trouble to birds. Native to desert oases of Southern California and Arizona in the United States, and Baja California in Mexico.

* *See Glossary*

Washingtonia robusta

Mexican fan palm

Arecaceae (Palmae) family

COLD HARDINESS

Low and intermediate zones and warm microclimates of high zone where fronds will turn brown with hard frost. This can also happen in the intermediate zone, but new foliage regrows so fast in the spring that this may not be too objectionable. Hard freezes that may occur every thirty to forty years have been known to kill mature specimens in South Texas.

LANDSCAPE VALUE

- This is probably the most planted palm in the subtropics of both hemispheres.
- A much-used species for tropical effects and instant landscaping.
- Old trees sway gracefully and lean; not stiff like *W. filifera*.
- Tall older trees planted in clumps, over or along avenues, produce outstanding silhouettes and skyline effects.

CULTURAL REQUIREMENTS

- **Exposure:** Will start in full shade but soon would grow through any canopy tree into open sun. Best in hot-summer regions. Becomes stunted with head out of proportion to trunk in cool-summer areas such as San Francisco or Mexico City.
- **Water:** Another desert (Sonoran) oasis palm that likes water if it is available. Tolerates considerable drought when established, but at the expense of the growth and the lushness of the foliage. Thoroughly soak the root zone every week to every month for good appearance.
- **Soil:** Most soils.
- **Propagation:** Grown from seed but collect from sources not exposed to hybridization.
- **Maintenance:** Old leaf thatch can be left on for a time but eventually it will slough off at the top, giving the appearance of a molting chicken. Then the only choice for good appearance is to skin the trunk clean all the way to the ground. Once this is done however, subsequent old leaf thatch at the top will self-clean. Remove dead leaves for appearance and safety.

POSSIBLE PROBLEMS

- Grooming is a major problem after trees are taller.
- Dead leaves may fall to the ground, creating a hazard to pedestrians.

Slender-trunked palm to 75 feet (23 m) tall, spreading 10 feet (3 m). Grows rapidly when young, adding up to 6 feet (2 m) per year with ample moisture and hot summers. Growth rate tapers off rapidly as tree gets older—mature trees add only inches per year. Cooler summers and drought will slow growth. Lush bright green fan-shaped leaves grow on long reddish brown, sometimes toothed petioles*. The trunk at the base swells to three times greater diameter than the high trunk. Taller specimens often shed old dry thatch. The thatch will remain in wind-protected places but it is not as handsome as thatch on *W. filifera*. Flowering stems protrude beyond the foliage. Tiny cream blossoms appear late spring into summer and can be followed by quantities of blue-black seed. Native to northwest Mexico.

* *See Glossary*

Wedelia trilobata

Wedelia, Yellow dots

Asteraceae (Compositae) family

COLD HARDINESS

Low zone and warm-winter microclimates of intermediate zone. Killed back to the ground by frost but recovers as the weather warms in spring. When planted deeper in beds, more underground parts can recover from a hard freeze.

LANDSCAPE VALUE

- Bright yellow flowers over a long season.
- Forms a low horizontal foliage mass that unifies mixed plantings of trees and shrubs.
- Large beds or flat areas.
- Erosion control on banks and slopes.
- Trailing over the sides of large raised planters, too aggressively for small, sharply defined areas.
- Grows well at the seashore.

CULTURAL REQUIREMENTS

- **Exposure:** Full sun to deep shade. As shade increases flowering is reduced. Tolerates intense heat.
- **Water:** Water every month or two. Tolerates short dry periods if gradually hardened by increasing intervals between watering.
- **Soil:** Most soils with good drainage, including sandy types.
- **Propagation:** Cuttings and stem sections that have already rooted.
- **Maintenance:** Shear back to near ground level if growth becomes top heavy, loose and open. Grows so rapidly with rich soil and abundant moisture that regular trimming may be necessary to contain a planting within its boundaries and to maintain dense compact growth.

POSSIBLE PROBLEMS

None observed.

Dense, fast-growing evergreen perennial groundcover that is intolerant of foot traffic. Grows to 18 inches (46 cm) high, spreading to 6 feet (2 m) or more. Creeping runner*-like stems root at nodes* as they grow. Glossy dark green leaves are oblong, three-lobed or toothed and up to 5 inches (13 cm) long. Leaves are hairy, but less conspicuously so than the stems. Yellow daisylike flowers to 1 inch (2.5 cm) across open at foliage level or up to 6 inches (15 cm) above, often heaviest in spring and summer, but year-round in warm-winter areas. This is not a particularly water-efficient plant but it is heat tolerant and a lush green, even in the most reflective situations, which justifies its inclusion here. It is valuable as a minioasis plant. Native to Central and South America, escaped from cultivation in southern Florida.

* *See Glossary*

YUCCA

Yuccas contribute many dramatic accents to the design-plant palette. There is a large list to choose from, ranging from the very hardy desert species to others that create a more tropical feel. All are extremely drought tolerant, even the more tropical-appearing species, and most are quite cold hardy. Mature plants usually blossom annually with a copious display of waxy white bells. The inflorescence varies from a tight cluster of blooms to a treelike arrangement up to 10 feet (3 m), as is the case with the coastal species *Y. whipplei* (Our Lord's candle). *Yuccas* also range in size from ground-hugging clumps to arborescent species, such as *Y. brevifolia* (Joshua tree). The narrow leaves are usually stiff and tipped with sharp spikes, yet a few species have limber, broader leaves with soft tips. The species that have sharp tips should be planted away from passing foot traffic. Smaller species lend themselves to container and planter culture. Some species, such as *Y. gloriosa* and *Y. elephantipes*, can even be used as interior plants in bright locations. All *Yuccas* have a symbiotic relationship with a moth species that pollinates the fragrant white blossoms at night while simultaneously laying eggs. These eggs hatch as the flowers fade and the larva feed on the fruit, always leaving enough seed to perpetuate the species. Bats also serve as pollinators.

Yucca aloifolia

Spanish bayonet

Agavaceae family

COLD HARDINESS

All three zones.

LANDSCAPE VALUE

- Specimen, accent or silhouette plant in arid or lush tropical landscape settings.
- In mass plantings, it serves as a barrier to control pedestrian traffic.
- May also function as a large landscape shrub.
- Foundation.
- Containers.
- Salt tolerant—grows well on sand dunes at the seashore.

CULTURAL REQUIREMENTS

- **Exposure:** Full or reflected sun to part shade.
- **Water:** Drought resistant but during long dry periods, foliage on the lower trunk is prone to scorch. Water established plants every month or two or more frequently in drier areas.
- **Soil:** Adapted to many well-draining soils from sandy to heavy types.
- **Propagation:** Stem cuttings or seed. Because it needs room to spread, avoid planting near walks or drives.
- **Maintenance:** Requires little maintenance other than removal of spent flower stalks. In close-up situations, remove the vicious terminal* spike from new leaves as they elongate.

POSSIBLE PROBLEMS

- Agave weevil* and spider mites are pests in the southwestern United States.
- Spikes are hazardous to pedestrian traffic.

Grows slowly up to 10 feet (3 m) high or higher, spreading to 5 feet (1.5 m) or more. One to several thick upright trunks angle upward and out in a spreading clump. Trunks are often branched at ground level. Stiff, sword-shaped medium to dark green leaves, 1½ to 2½ feet (46 to 76 cm) long and 2 inches (5 cm) wide, have a sharp terminal* spine. The closely spaced leaves turn reddish purple during cold winters. Flower stalks at the tips of stems grow to 2 feet (61 cm) long and in late spring or summer are densely covered with white flowers that often have a purple blush. Blooms are 3 inches (7.5 cm) in diameter. Fruits follow bloom and are fleshy capsules 5 inches (13 cm) long. They are dry at maturity in summer. Cultivars* with leaves striped in various colors are available. Native to southeastern United States, the Caribbean and Yucatan, Mexico.

Yucca baccata, (Y. arizonica, Y. thornberi)

Banana yucca, Datil yucca

Agavaceae family

COLD HARDINESS

All three zones.

LANDSCAPE VALUE

- Low-growing accent or specimen.
- Distinctive foliage, flowers and fruit.
- Picturesque growth habit.

CULTURAL REQUIREMENTS

- **Exposure:** Withstands intense sunlight and great heat.
- **Water:** Very drought resistant. Watering once or twice a season in the low zone would probably enhance landscape appearance.
- **Soil:** Most sandy to rocky alkaline soils that drain well.
- **Propagation:** Seed.
- **Maintenance:** No maintenance.

POSSIBLE PROBLEMS

None observed. Landscape usage has been too limited thus far to identify specific pest problems.

Grows slowly to 3 feet (1 m) high and 5 feet (1.5 m) wide. Forms clumps and develops as a stemless rosette* or with two to six trunks sprawling or lying on the ground. Stiff, erect sharp-pointed leaves are light blue-green to yellow-green, 1 to 1¾ inches (2.5 to 4.5 cm) wide at the middle and 2 feet (61 cm) long. Older leaves are fibrous along margins of the high half of their length. Bloom stalks 2 feet (61 cm) long appear spring into summer and produce dense masses of white to creamy bell-shaped flowers 2 to 6 inches (5 to 15 cm) long. The fleshy green to purple bananalike fruits 4½ to 6½ inches (11.5 to 16.5 cm) long are edible and once served as a common food source for Indians of the southwestern United States. Native to Arizona, California, Colorado, New Mexico, Texas and Mexico.

* See Glossary

Yucca brevifolia brevifolia

Joshua tree

Agavaceae family

COLD HARDINESS

All three zones.

LANDSCAPE VALUE

- A large accent, specimen or silhouette plant of picturesque and often dramatic form.
- Tan-colored dead foliage gives trunk and branches an interesting shaggy appearance.
- Corky bark on large old specimens is another unique characteristic.
- *Y. b. jaegeriana* is a better choice for planting sites where space is limited.

CULTURAL REQUIREMENTS

- **Exposure:** Full to reflected sun.
- **Water:** Quite drought resistant. Water once or twice a season in very dry low-elevation locations. Overwatering may kill plants or result in rapid unbranched vertical growth that lacks the unique character and appeal of this species.
- **Soil:** Most soils with good drainage. Not compatible with ordinary garden conditions.
- **Propagation:** Seed.
- **Maintenance:** No maintenance.

POSSIBLE PROBLEMS

Established specimens of any size can be difficult to transplant.

Grows slowly from 15 to 30 feet (4.5 to 9 m) high and to 30 feet (9 m) wide. These arborescent *Yuccas* develop a distinct trunk 1½ to almost 3 feet (46 cm to 1 m) across and branches that terminate in clusters of short, spine-tipped gray-green leaves 8 to 14 inches (20.5 to 35.5 cm) long and as wide as ½ inch (1 cm). Old specimens develop a rounded crown. Old leaves persist on the trunk and branches for some time, eventually falling away to reveal rough corky bark below. Thick, fleshy greenish white flowers to 1 inch (2.5 cm) long or longer are borne in dense clusters 1 foot (30.5 cm) long from late winter into spring. Native to Arizona, California and Nevada.

Yucca brevifolia jaegeriana

Dwarf Joshua tree

Agavaceae family

COLD HARDINESS

All three zones.

LANDSCAPE VALUE

- A large accent, specimen or silhouette plant of picturesque and often dramatic form.
- Tan-colored dead foliage gives trunk and branches an interesting shaggy appearance.
- Corky bark on large old specimens is another unique characteristic.

CULTURAL REQUIREMENTS

- **Exposure:** Full to reflected sun. Will tolerate some shade.
- **Water:** Quite drought resistant. Water once or twice a season in very dry low-elevation locations. Overwatering may kill plants or result in rapid unbranched vertical growth that lacks the unique character and appeal of this species.
- **Soil:** Most soils with good drainage. Not compatible with ordinary garden conditions.
- **Propagation:** Seed. Wild collected plants (tagged to ensure that they were legally obtained) are usually available in the desert Southwest.
- **Maintenance:** No maintenance.

POSSIBLE PROBLEMS

Established specimens of any size can be difficult to transplant.

Grows slowly from 15 to 20 feet (4.5 to 6 m) high and to 15 feet (4.5 m) wide. This arborescent *Yucca* develops a distinct trunk to almost 2 feet (61 cm) across and branches that terminate in clusters of short, narrow spine-tipped gray-green leaves 6 to 12 inches (15 to 30.5 mm) long. Old specimens develop a rounded crown. Dead leaves persist on the trunk and branches for some time, eventually falling away to reveal rough corky bark below. Thick, fleshy greenish white flowers to 1 inch (2.5 cm) long or longer are borne in dense clusters, late winter into spring. Found in the more northern and eastern parts of Arizona, California, Nevada and Utah.

* See Glossary

Yucca carnerosa

Giant dagger tree

Agavaceae family

COLD HARDINESS

All three zones.

LANDSCAPE VALUE

- One of the most dramatic of the *Yuccas*, especially good for accents at entrances and other points of emphasis.
- Large green crown of swords and single trunk give it a palmlike quality.
- Combines well with topical-effects plants as well as desert-plant compositions.

CULTURAL REQUIREMENTS

- **Exposure:** Full sun, including reflected sun. Will tolerate part shade.
- **Water:** Very drought resistant, needing no supplemental water in most areas. Benefits in growth and improved general appearance with water once or twice during the summer.
- **Soil:** Most soils with good drainage.
- **Propagation:** Seed, but most plants used in landscapes have been collected in the wild. They transplant best in the warm season.
- **Maintenance:** Old leaves can stay as thatch or be removed to reveal sturdy trunk.

POSSIBLE PROBLEMS

Plants gathered in the wild do not have a particularly good survival rate.

Grows slowly up to 10 feet (3 m), but water during the summer will speed up the growth. Usually partially thatched with old leaves on a single, sturdy upright trunk. The foliage crown consists of stiff green swords 3 to 4 feet (1 m) long and tipped with a large sharp point. Occasionally they will branch or grow multiple trunks, but that is the exception. The fragrant white blossoms 2 to 3 inches (5 to 7.5 cm) wide borne in clusters put on the typical *Yucca* display in spring. This is followed by fleshy green fruits filled with flat black seeds that are released when the fruit capsule matures, dries and opens. Fruits are usually 1 to 2 inches (2.5 to 5 cm) in diameter. The dry cluster of capsules remain on the plant and add interest for some time after the flowering. Native to the Chihuahuan Desert.

Yucca elata

Soaptree yucca

Agavaceae family

COLD HARDINESS

All three zones.

LANDSCAPE VALUE

- Graceful form and attractive flowers make this a striking desert silhouette or accent plant.
- Dry bloom stalks and dry split-open tan-colored fruit are popular with flower arrangers.

CULTURAL REQUIREMENTS

- **Exposure:** Full to reflected sun.
- **Water:** Tolerates long dry periods, but water once or twice a season in low-elevation landscapes.
- **Soil:** Grows best in a deep well-drained soil.
- **Propagation:** Cuttings.
- **Maintenance:** Old leaves can stay as thatch or be removed to reveal sturdy trunk.

POSSIBLE PROBLEMS

Leaves have sharp tips, so do not place too close to pedestrian walkways or other well-traveled areas.

Evergreen perennial succulent that grows slowly from 6 to 20 feet (2 to 6 m) high and up to 8 feet (2.5 m) wide. Grows with one upright trunk or several in a cluster. Individual stems often have two or three branches. Pale green leaves are flexible, sharp-pointed, up to 4 feet (1 m) long and 1/8 to 1/2 inch (0.5 to 1 cm) wide, with fine threadlike fibers along the white margins. Live foliage grows in dense clusters near the stem tips. Tan-colored dead leaves remain attached to the trunk and bend down to form a dense shag. The tall erect flower stalk is topped by an open 1 1/2- to 3-foot (46-cm to 1-m) long spike of white bell-shaped blossoms that appear in late spring. Tan-colored fruits 1 1/2 to 3 inches (4 to 7.5 cm) long split open when mature. Native to Arizona, Texas, New Mexico and northern Mexico.

** See Glossary*

Yucca elephantipes

Spineless yucca, Giant yucca
Agavaceae family

COLD HARDINESS
Low zone and all but the coldest areas of intermediate zone. Fairly frost tolerant.

LANDSCAPE VALUE
A very handsome and distinctive accent, specimen or character plant, noted for its tropical aspect. Because of its potential size, not an appropriate choice for small spaces.

CULTURAL REQUIREMENTS
- **Exposure:** Full sun (but not reflecting) to part shade.
- **Water:** Quite drought resistant, but best landscape performance will be obtained with water every week or two in summer, every month or two in the cooler months.
- **Soil:** Develops its best appearance in good garden soils. Withstands moderately salty conditions near the beach.
- **Propagation:** Cuttings.
- **Maintenance:** Old leaves can stay as thatch or be removed to reveal sturdy trunk.

POSSIBLE PROBLEMS
None observed.

Tropical-looking *Yucca* that grows at a moderate to rapid rate up to to 30 feet (9 m) high and to 8 feet (2.5 m) wide. Shiny bright green leaves grow in rosettes*. The leaves are swordlike and flexible, as long as 4 feet (1 m) and as wide as 3 inches (7.5 cm). Although the margins are rough, the leaf tip is soft and harmless. With age, this species develops a swollen base and numerous thick, rough-barked trunks, including some that branch. In spring, heavy clusters of creamy white flowers open on tall stalks, 3 to 6 feet (4.5 to 6 m). The fruit capsules ripen to a purple-black color in summer. Native to Mexico and Central America.

Yucca faxoniana

Faxon yucca
Agavaceae family

COLD HARDINESS
All three zones.

LANDSCAPE VALUE
- Excels as an ambiance creator, silhouette, character plant, central feature or focal point in arid landscapes.
- Street median and highway plantings.
- Out of scale in confined spaces and small properties.

CULTURAL REQUIREMENTS
- **Exposure:** Full to reflected sun. Tolerates both heat and cold.
- **Water:** Once established, survives with little or no supplemental water. However, during extended periods of hot dry weather, watering once or twice ensures good appearance and growth.
- **Soil:** Most soils with good drainage.
- **Propagation:** Seed.
- **Maintenance:** Old leaves can stay as thatch or be removed to reveal sturdy trunk.

POSSIBLE PROBLEMS
Spine-tipped leaves may be a hazard in high-traffic areas.

A large, imposing *Yucca* to 15 feet (4.5 m) high and 10 feet (3 m) wide. Growth rate is slow to moderate. Produces a rosette* of stiff, ascending sharp-tipped leaves 2½ feet (76 cm) long and 2 inches (5 cm) wide on a stout trunk to 1 foot (30.5 cm) in diameter. Hanging dead leaves clothe the trunk with a protective thatch layer. In spring or early summer, ivory white flowers about 3 inches (7.5 cm) wide open in dense clusters on an erect bloom stalk 3 to 4 feet (1 m) tall. Native range extends from Texas into Mexico.

* See Glossary

Yucca glauca (Y. angustifolia)

Narrow-leaf yucca, High-plains yucca

Agavaceae family

COLD HARDINESS

All three zones.

LANDSCAPE VALUE

- Foreground planting with palms or taller *Yuccas*.
- Planters or containers.

CULTURAL REQUIREMENTS

- **Exposure:** Full sun to part shade.
- **Water:** Thrives on water every month or two when no significant rainfall has occurred over an extended period.
- **Soil:** Any soil with good drainage.
- **Propagation:** Seed. Gathered wild plants are sometimes available.
- **Maintenance:** Old leaves can stay as thatch or be removed to reveal sturdy trunk.

POSSIBLE PROBLEMS

- Damping off* may be a serious disease problem if the plant is overwatered or drainage is poor.
- Aphids sometimes damage bloom spikes.

Grows at a moderate rate to 3 feet (1 m) high and wide or larger. Generally forms a clump of narrow, slightly grayed green leaves but old plants will on occasion develop short trunks. Flower stalks are 3 feet (1 m) tall and tightly packed, with white lilylike blooms that appear in midspring. Some plants make a big clump, others remain a single specimen. Native from Texas north into the Midwest.

Yucca gloriosa

Spanish dagger

Agavaceae family

COLD HARDINESS

Low and intermediate zones and warm microclimates of high zone. Plants damaged by hard frosts are slow to regain attractive condition.

LANDSCAPE VALUE

- Exotic bold-textured green foliage and a dramatic growth habit give this *Yucca* a distinct tropical personality. When combined with lush foliage plant types, it helps create the atmosphere or mood of the tropics in outdoor living areas, entry gardens, commercial and public landscapes.
- As a strong point of emphasis, specimen or character plant, Spanish dagger is unsurpassed.
- Young plants make good container subjects.

CULTURAL REQUIREMENTS

- **Exposure:** Full sun or part shade, but not reflected sun. Intense reflected sun may cause trunk and foliage sunburn.
- **Water:** Drought tolerant. Thoroughly soak the root zone every week or two to maintain growth and appearance.
- **Soil:** Best in good-quality, fast-draining soil.
- **Propagation:** Seed, clump divisions or stem cuttings.
- **Maintenance:** Old leaves can stay as thatch or be removed to reveal sturdy trunk.

POSSIBLE PROBLEMS

None observed.

Grows at a slow to moderate rate up to 10 feet (3 m) high or higher and to 8 feet (2.5 m) wide. The fleshy soft-pointed leaves grow 2 to 3 feet (61 cm to 1 m) long by 2 inches (5 cm) wide and cluster in a dense rosette*. These plants often produce several erect stems that become thick and woody with age. In late summer, white bell-shaped flowers open on a crowded vertical spike to 3 feet (1 m) tall. A variegated form is available. Native to the Southeastern United States from North Carolina into Florida.

** See Glossary*

Yucca recurvifolia (Y. pendula)

Pendulous yucca

Agavaceae family

COLD HARDINESS

All three zones.

LANDSCAPE VALUE

- Most appropriate in transitional or oasis garden settings where its lush tropical look makes it a dramatic accent or specimen.
- Foundation.
- Containers.

CULTURAL REQUIREMENTS

- **Exposure:** Full sun to deep shade.
- **Water:** Develops some drought resistance as an established plant but performs best with water every week or two during the warm months, every month or two during the cool season.
- **Soil:** Most soils with good drainage.
- **Propagation:** Seed, root divisions, or stem cuttings.
- **Maintenance:** Remove dead lower leaves as they appear and flower stalks when blooms have faded. Head back old unkempt-looking plants to within 1 foot (30.5 cm) of the ground in late winter or early spring to induce resprouting and attractive new growth.

POSSIBLE PROBLEMS

- Spider mites.
- Aphids.
- Agave weevil*.

Grows at a moderate pace to 6 feet (2 m) high and wide or even larger. Develops a single upright trunk that is usually unbranched, but old specimens and those that have been cut back for renewal may develop one or more side branches or multiple trunks. Foliage is dense and gray-green with a bluish cast. Each flexible sword-shaped leaf has a soft tip at the point, grows 2 to 3 feet (61 cm to 1 m) long, 2 to 3 inches (5 to 7.5 cm) wide, and curves in an arc toward the ground when mature. Flower stalks 3 to 5 feet (1 to 1.5 m) tall bear an open 2-foot (61-cm) long cluster of large white flowers in late spring or early summer. Native to southeastern United States.

Yucca rigida

Blue yucca

Agavaceae family

COLD HARDINESS

Low and intermediate zones and protected microclimates of high zone

LANDSCAPE VALUE

Dramatic landscape form and foliage texture. The soft blue color of the leaves confers an even more unique appearance that suits this desert succulent well for use as a silhouette, accent or specimen.

CULTURAL REQUIREMENTS

- **Exposure:** Full sun.
- **Water:** Tolerant of arid conditions. Water once or twice during long periods of hot dry weather may help maintain appearance but is seldom necessary for survival of established plants.
- **Soil:** Most soils with good drainage.
- **Propagation:** Seed.
- **Maintenance:** Old leaves can stay as thatch or be removed to reveal sturdy trunk.

POSSIBLE PROBLEMS

Place where the spiny leaves pose no threat to pedestrians.

The columnar trunk of this *Yucca* grows at a slow to moderate rate up to 12 feet (3.5 m) high or higher. Spreads 5 feet (1.5 m). May branch lightly as the plant achieves age and stature. Each stem is topped by a spreading rosette* of stiff, spine-tipped blue-gray leaves about 2 feet (61 cm) long and 1 1/4 inches (3 cm) wide. As the lower foliage dies, it hangs down and lies close to the trunk to form a long-lasting tan-colored thatch. In spring or early summer, a cluster of creamy white flowers 1 1/2 to 2 1/2 inches (4 to 6.5 cm) long open on a short stalk that grows from the center of the rosette. Woody seed capsules 2 inches (5 cm) long persist long after releasing the small black seeds they contain, around fall. Native to the Chihuahuan Desert of Mexico.

* See Glossary

Yucca rostrata (Y. thompsonsiana)

Chihuahuan desert tree yucca

Agavaceae family

COLD HARDINESS

All three zones.

LANDSCAPE VALUE

- Large dramatic *Yucca* for accent and silhouette against walls or sky.
- Central element in compositions with other desert plants.

CULTURAL REQUIREMENTS

- **Exposure:** Full sun. Tolerates relected heat but also will take open shade when planted on north side of large buildings.
- **Water:** Quite drought resistant but moisture speeds up growth when applied during warm season.
- **Soil:** Most soils with good drainage.
- **Propagation:** Seed, although most specimens found in the landscape have come from the wild. Large specimens can be transplanted without difficulty.
- **Maintenance:** Old leaves can stay as thatch or be removed to reveal sturdy trunk.

POSSIBLE PROBLEMS

None other than slow growth.

Slow-growing aborescent *Yucca* to 12 feet (3.5 m) high or higher and to 9 feet (3 m) wide or wider. Branched tree with narrow, sharp-tipped, 2-foot (61-cm) long leaves. Massive trunk is covered with a soft gray fuzz, the remnant of old leaf bases. White flowers in clusters 2 feet (61 cm) long borne on 2-foot (61-cm) stalks appear in late spring. Native from the Big Bend area of southern Texas south into the Chihuahuan Desert in Mexico.

Yucca schidigera (Y. mohavensis)

Mojave yucca

Agavaceae family

COLD HARDINESS

All three zones.

LANDSCAPE VALUE

- Accent plant among boulders and in desert-plant compositions.
- Combined with palms and other tropical-effect plants.

CULTURAL REQUIREMENTS

- **Exposure**: Full sun to part shade.
- **Water:** Quite drought resistant. Needs little supplemental irrigation, but water every couple weeks to every month will speed up its growth.
- **Soil:** Most soils with good drainage.
- **Propagation:** Seed.
- **Maintenance:** Old leaves can stay as thatch or be removed to reveal sturdy trunk.

POSSIBLE PROBLEMS

- Slow to develop into a landscape specimen.
- Sharp-tipped leaves may be hazard in foot-traffic areas.

This short trunked *Yucca* grows slowly from 3 to 12 feet (1 to 3.5 m) high, usually 3 to 4 feet (1 m). Spreads 3 feet (1 m). Can be a multistem clump, which creates a broader specimen. Forms rosettes* of medium green sharp-tipped leaves as long as 3 feet (1 m). Dry spent leaves hang down, forming a thatch on the trunk. This can eventually fall away on older specimens. Purple-tinted white flowers in dense clusters are an annual spring event followed by fleshy green fruit. Native to the Mojave Desert and parts of the Sonoran Desert.

** See Glossary*

Yucca schottii

Mountain yucca, Hoary yucca, Schott's yucca

Agavaceae family

Grows at a slow to moderate pace from 6 to 15 feet (2 to 4.5 m) high, spreading 3 to 4 feet (1 m). Usually grows a single erect trunk although multitrunked or slightly branched specimens occasionally occur. The sharp-pointed gray-green leaves 1½ to 3 feet (46 cm to 1 m) long and as wide as 2 inches (5 cm) grow in a dense terminal* rosette*. The leaf margins are smooth or they separate into fine fibers. Lower dead leaves may persist on the trunk for several years. Anytime from spring into midsummer, heavy clusters of white bell-shaped flowers to 1½ inches (4 cm) long open in heavy clusters just above the foliage. At maturity, the fleshy fruits are 4 to 4¾ inches (10 to 12 cm) long and 1½ to 2 inches (4 to 5 cm) in diameter. The dark flattened seeds they contain have a rough or wrinkled surface. Native from southern Arizona and New Mexico in the United States to Sonora and Chihuahua in Mexico.

COLD HARDINESS

All three zones.

LANDSCAPE VALUE

- Bold foliage texture and an erect growth habit give this *Yucca* its distinctive ornamental character.
- Accent, specimen or silhouette plant of striking individuality for arid landscapes.

CULTURAL REQUIREMENTS

- **Exposure:** Full sun to open shade.
- **Water:** Survives on natural rainfall in many areas but thorough watering once or twice a season is recommended for satisfactory landscape performance in lower zones.
- **Soil:** Most soils with good drainage.
- **Propagation:** Seed.
- **Maintenance:** Requires little care other than removal of lower dead leaves if desired.

POSSIBLE PROBLEMS

Sharp-tipped leaves restrict its use in some locations.

Yucca torreyi

Torrey yucca

Agavaceae family

COLD HARDINESS

All three zones.

LANDSCAPE VALUE

- Accent clump for dramatic effects at entrances, path intersections, or as a key part of a desert-plant composition.
- With grooming, part of groupings with palms and other tropical-effects plants.

CULTURAL REQUIREMENTS

- **Exposure:** Reflected sun to part shade.
- **Water:** No water in regions receiving 3 to 5 inches (75 to 130 mm) annual precipitation, but will develop faster with water every month or two. Will tolerate wetter situations when combined with more thirsty plants in a composition.
- **Soil:** Most soils with good drainage.
- **Propagation:** Seed or divisions.
- **Maintenance:** No maintenance.

POSSIBLE PROBLEMS

None observed.

A large clumping *Yucca* that grows at a slow to moderate rate from 3 to 15 feet (1 to 4.5 m) high, spreading 3 to 9 feet (1 to 3 m). Spike-tipped leaves 3 feet (1 m) long form rosettes* on short trunks. Trunks can slowly elongate to three or four leaning trunks, as with *Y. baccata*, which this species resembles. Abundant succulent white flowers on terminal* spikes appear in the spring followed by fleshy seed capsules. Native to New Mexico and Texas and on south into northern Mexico.

* *See Glossary*

Yucca vallida

Tree yucca, Datillo

Agavaceae family

COLD HARDINESS

Low zone and warm-winter microclimates of intermediate zone. Severe cold may cause serious damage or loss of the plant.

LANDSCAPE VALUE

- The picturesque form and texture give it a rugged and appealing landscape character.
- Striking accent, specimen or silhouette plant.

CULTURAL REQUIREMENTS

- **Exposure:** Full sun.
- **Water:** Very drought resistant. Irrigation is unnecessary except during exceptionally long periods of hot dry weather.
- **Soil:** Most soils with good drainage.
- **Propagation:** Seed.
- **Maintenance:** No maintenance.

POSSIBLE PROBLEMS

Spiny leaf tips are hazardous in high foot-traffic locations.

Grows at a slow to moderate rate from 10 to 20 feet (3 to 6 m) high, spreading 5 to 10 feet (1.5 to 3 m). May be branched or unbranched and grows with one to several trunks that reach a diameter of 18 inches (46 cm) or more in old specimens. The spreading yellow green leaves are stiff, smooth, spine-tipped and as long as 13 inches (33 cm) and as wide as 1 inch (2.5 cm). Drooping dead leaves form a coarse brown or grayish thatch that extends from the lower live foliage down along the trunk for about 3 to 6 feet (1 to 2 m). In spring, a branching erect flower stalk 1 to 2 feet (30.5 to 61 cm) high bears bell-shaped creamy white flowers that have a dill-like odor. The fleshy oblong fruits appear after bloom and eventually dry and turn black in late summer. Native to Baja California, Mexico.

Yucca whipplei

Our Lord's candle

Agavaceae family

COLD HARDINESS

All three zones.

LANDSCAPE VALUE

- Specimen or accent that is spectacular while flowering.
- Closely spaced rosettes* form an effective barrier.

CULTURAL REQUIREMENTS

- **Exposure:** Full to reflected sun or part shade.
- **Water:** Endures long dry periods at the expense of lower leaves, which turn brown and die while remaining foliage fades to a light green color. Water every month or two during the warm season, only once or twice during the cooler months.
- **Soil:** Grows in most well-drained arid-climate soils.
- **Propagation:** Seed or offsets*.
- **Maintenance:** No maintenance.

POSSIBLE PROBLEMS

- Individual foliage rosettes die after flowering but are replaced by seed or regrowth from the underground stem, depending on the variety.
- Spiny tips and rasping margins of the leaves restrict use in some landscape settings.

Grows at a slow to moderate rate to 3 feet (1 m) high and to 6 feet (2 m) wide. Trunkless above ground, but has a subterranean stem or stems branching below ground or at ground level. Closely packed, broad rosettes consist of slender, rigid gray-green leaves that are needle-pointed, with fine sharp teeth along the margins. Individual leaves are to 1 to 2 feet (30.5 to 61 cm) long and 3/8 to 3/4 inch (1 to 2 cm) wide. Nodding bell-shaped flowers in spring are fragrant, creamy white and often flushed with purple. They bloom in an open, branching cluster 3 to 6 feet (1 to 2 m) long. The erect flower stalk grows as tall as 6 to 12 feet (2 to 3.5 m), especially on single-trunk plants and on Y. *whipplei whipplei*. The lower rosette dies after flowering occurs. *Y. whipplei crespitosa*, a smaller growing desert variety, forms new foliage rosettes each year from below ground. *Y. whipplei eremica* grows with several to many plants in a clump. These bloom and fruit repeatedly for many years before dying. Green fruit capsules, about 2 inches (5 cm) long, split open when dry. Native to southern California in the United States and neighboring Baja California in Mexico.

* See Glossary

Zauschneria californica

Hummingbird trumpet bush

Onagraceae family

COLD HARDINESS

All three zones. Rhizomes* are cold hardy and the next season's growth may start in late winter. Dies back to the ground in cold winters.

LANDSCAPE VALUE

- Provides a spectacular warm-season display of scarlet flowers under favorable conditions.
- Groundcover or bank plant in small informal areas.
- Containers or raised planters.
- Flowers attract hummingbirds.

CULTURAL REQUIREMENTS

- **Exposure:** Filtered sun to part shade. Becomes more compact in full sun. Tolerates heat and low humidity.
- **Water:** Water every few weeks.
- **Soil:** Grows faster and blooms more heavily in fertile garden soil.
- **Propagation:** Seed, cuttings, or divisions of clumps in late winter.
- **Maintenance:** Pinch growing terminals* for lower, more dense growth. Can be pruned back after flowering for neater appearance. Cut back to the ground each year in late winter to restore dense vigorous growth and more profuse flowering.

POSSIBLE PROBLEMS

Invasive in favored locations.

Herbaceous* perennial 1 to 2 feet (30.5 to 61 cm) high and wide. Somewhat slow to establish, but grows faster with water. Upright stems are woody at the base, usually many-branched, growing from spreading rhizomes*. Gray-green linear leaves 2 inches (5 cm) long mostly alternate on the high stem. They are hairy, but not densely so. Lateral veins are seldom evident. The leaves often turn reddish in fall but are evergreen in warm-winter climates. Brilliant red trumpet-shaped flowers 1 to 1¾ inches (2.5 to 4.5 cm) long appear early summer into late fall on terminal* spikes. They are often most numerous in late summer and early fall. Low-growing and white-flowered forms have been introduced. Native to California and Arizona in the United States, northern Baja California in Mexico.

Zauschneria californica latifolia

California fuchsia

Onagraceae family

COLD HARDINESS

All three zones.

LANDSCAPE VALUE

Same as *Z. californica.*

CULTURAL REQUIREMENTS

Same as *Z. californica*, except requires more water.

POSSIBLE PROBLEMS

- Not the best survivor in desert environments and less tolerant than *Z. californica*. In addition, it needs more water to look well and bloom.
- Leaves a vacant spot in plantings during winter.

Distinguished from *Z. californica* by its lower growth. Also is completely herbaceous* rather than woody at the base stems. Grows to 6 inches (15 cm) high and 3 feet (1 m) wide. Moderate to rapid growth once established. Leaves are wider than *Z. californica*, have clearly visible lateral veins and are oppositely arranged. Flowers are identical. Although top growth is killed each winter, this plant is more cold hardy than *Z. californica*, occurring as a native from southern Oregon to northern California, southwestern New Mexico and Nevada in the United States, and northern Sonora in Mexico.

** See Glossary*

Zinnia acerosa

Desert zinnia

Asteraceae (Compositae) family

COLD HARDINESS

Low and intermediate zones. Moderately frost hardy, but lush-bloom stage can be damaged by a late frost.

LANDSCAPE VALUE

- The landscape potential of this small perennial zinnia lies in its compact rounded form, long bloom season and ability to grow in harsh arid environments with a minimum of care.
- Where plants are numerous, they serve as a somewhat open groundcover or understory plant and help reduce soil erosion and airborne dust.
- Suited to informal arid and transition zones, wildflower borders, disturbed areas, highway medians, buffer zone plantings and revegetation seed mixes.

CULTURAL REQUIREMENTS

- **Exposure:** Full to reflected sun.
- **Water:** Survives long dry periods but blooms only with rain or supplemental irrigation. The plant becomes completely dormant during long periods of drought and does not resume growth until moisture returns. Water every couple months.
- **Soil:** Tolerant of most arid-region soils.
- **Propagation:** Seed.
- **Maintenance:** Cut back old straggly plants to renew top growth.

POSSIBLE PROBLEMS

None observed.

Small herbaceous* perennial that grows 4 to 10 inches (10 to 25.5 cm) high and wide at a slow rate (moderate with water). Has many branches and is mounding or flat-topped with slender gray stems. The small leaves are hairy and needle-shaped. Within each small bloom cluster are five to seven white to pale yellow ray flowers, each marked with prominent green veins on the underside. Flowering is intermittent from early spring through fall when moisture is present. Native range covers parts of southern Arizona, Texas and northern Mexico.

Zinnia grandiflora

Rocky mountain zinnia, Plains zinnia

Asteraceae (Compositae) family

COLD HARDINESS

All three zones. May be marginal in hottest microclimates of low zone.

LANDSCAPE VALUE

- Color in foreground plantings.
- Massed as a semigroundcover or perennial border.
- Containers.

CULTURAL REQUIREMENTS

- **Exposure:** Full sun. Tolerates light shade.
- **Water:** Tolerates periods of drought but needs water every week or two during hot season to produce its summer display of color.
- **Soil:** Loose well-drained soil.
- **Propagation:** Seed or cuttings.
- **Maintenance:** Low maintenance.

POSSIBLE PROBLEMS

None observed.

Low-spreading evergreen sub-shrub that grows at a moderate rate to 1 foot (31 cm) high and wide. Bright green foliage. Small zinnia-like yellow daisies bloom in clusters. Showy little mounds of color in landscape, especially in mass plantings, in summer and fall. Varies in seasonal appearance depending on available moisture. Summer is best season for good appearance. Native to the Rocky Mountains on south in higher elevations of Mexico.

* See Glossary

Ziziphus jujuba

Jujuba, Chinese date

Rhamnaceae family

COLD HARDINESS

All three zones.

LANDSCAPE VALUE

- Although not widely planted, this tough low-maintenance tree has much to offer: glossy green foliage that takes on attractive fall color before leaf drop, picturesque branching habit, interesting bark texture, edible fruit and striking winter silhouette.
- Shade.
- Specimen.
- Fruit tree.
- May also become a woodsy grove if sprouts are allowed to grow.

CULTURAL REQUIREMENTS

- **Exposure:** Full to reflected sun and heat.
- **Water:** Survives with little water after establishment. Thoroughly soak the root zone every month or two for a larger tree and more abundant fruit.
- **Soil:** Tolerant of poor alkaline soils, but grows best on deep well-drained soils.
- **Propagation:** Seed, root suckers or cuttings. Improved cultivars* are grafted on seedling understock.
- **Maintenance:** Prune for single- or multitrunked form. Remove basal* and root suckers* as necessary.

POSSIBLE PROBLEMS

- Texas root rot*.
- Fallen fruit creates litter.
- Unwanted suckers require removal.

Small to medium-size deciduous tree of rounded to irregular form that grows at a slow to moderate pace from 20 to 40 feet (6 to 12 m) high and 15 to 30 feet (4.5 to 9 m) wide. Single- or multistemmed, it has rough, shaggy, peeling bark on older branches and trunks. Suckers from the roots often develop to form a clump or grove. The branching pattern is ascending in lower portions of the crown, weeping above. Young vigorous stems have spines that may be straight or curved, 1/4 to 1/2 inch (0.5 to 1 cm) long. Stout, knobby twigs grow in a zigzag pattern and give rise to shiny bright green leaves 1 to 2 inches (2.5 to 5 cm) long, oval to oblong or lance-shaped with serrated margins. The foliage turns yellow in autumn before dropping from the tree. Insignificant greenish white flowers open singly or in clusters in spring. Fleshy date-shaped fruits are first green, then reddish brown and 1 to 1 1/2 inches (2.5 to 4 cm) long when mature in late summer or fall. Edible and sweet, these are eaten fresh or dried and in a variety of prepared foods. A thornless cultivar*, 'Inermis,' and improved fruiting types, 'Li' and 'Lang,' are available. Native to China and eastern Europe.

* See Glossary

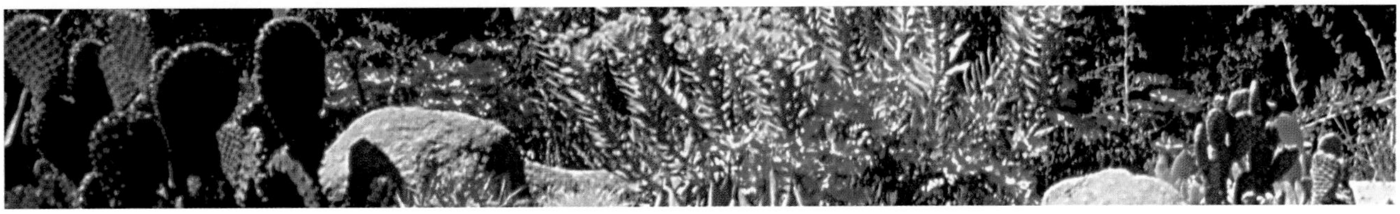

GLOSSARY

Aeration. Exchange of gases between the soil and the atmosphere. Loosen the soil to improve aeration with hand tools, various machines designed for this purpose and, in some cases, with soil amendments.

Aerial root. A root that grows above ground.

Agave weevil. See Appendix B, page 353.

Air layering. See *layering.*

Alkaline soil. Alkaline soil is nonacidic (with a pH higher than 7.0). Also called *sweet soil.*

Aloe mite. See Appendix B, page 353.

Alternate (leaf arrangement). Individual leaves grow at different, alternating points on the stem.

Annual. Plants that live one year or less, often just one growing season, from seed germination to flowering and seed set followed by death of the plant.

Apical. At the tip of a branch.

Arborescent. Resembling a tree in characteristics, growth habit, structure or appearance.

Areole. Small sunken or raised area on the stems of cacti from which spines and glochids grow.

Axil. The angle between a leaf petiole and the stem to which it is attached.

Axillary. Situated in or growing from an axil.

Bacterial necrosis. The death of a localized plant part caused by bacteria.

Bare-root. Plants with all soil removed from roots. Most nursery stock is sold in containers, but some succulents are still sold this way.

Basal. Related to or arising from the base of the plant or plant part.

Biennial. Plants that live two years from seed, usually making vegetative growth the first year then flowering and setting seed in the second year after which the plant dies.

Bigeneric. A hybrid of two different genera.

Biological pest control. Non-pesticide pest control program that relies on natural checks and balances, such as introducing pest predators or parasites.

Bipinnate. See Appendix A, page 352.

Bone meal. Bone that is finely ground and added to soil to boost the soil's nitrogen and phosphorous content.

Bosque. Informal tree planting that has as its theme a small woodland setting. The more or less continuous overhead canopy creates a pattern of dappled sun and shade below.

Bract. Modified leaf, sometimes highly colored, at the base of a flower or flower cluster.

Broadcast. To scatter seed by hand rather than sow in rows.

Bulb. Refers to true bulbs (a bud surrounded by fleshy leaves) as well as other bulblike plant parts, such as tubers, corms and rhizomes. Each bulb stores all the nutrients a plant needs and are therefore useful for propagation.

Bulbil. Small bulblike structures that develop on aboveground stems, often at the base of leaves or on flower stalks. Under favorable conditions bulbils fall to the ground, root and grow into plants of the same species that bore them. This is a convenient way to propagate these plants.

Bulblet. Similar to a bulbil except it forms specifically at the base of a mature bulb.

Calcareous. Containing calcium carbonate.

Caliche. A deposit of calcium carbonate beneath the surface of soil that creates an impervious layer. Common to the U.S. Southwest. Also called *hardpan.*

Calyx tube. The lowest part of a flower, a tube formed by the fusion of green and usually leaflike sepals.

Chlorosis (chlorotic). Lack of chlorophyll, which gives a plant its pigment. Leaves develop a blanched, yellowish look although leaf veins may remain green.

Clay soil. Made up of tiny closely packed particles. Little or no large pore space for free movement of air and water often results in poor drainage and aeration.

Cochineal. See Appendix B, page 353.

Cold hardy. Plants that tolerate repeated exposures to air temperatures in the range of 15 to 18°F(-10 to -8°C).

Compound leaf. See Appendix A, page 352.

Corm. The swollen base of a stem that is found underground and used for propagation.

Crown. The place where roots and shoots join, connecting the aboveground and underground parts of a plant. Also refers to branches and foliage of a tree.

Cultivar. A cultivated variety of plant, created by humans.

Cutting. A leaf, stem or root that can be used to propagate a plant.

Cyme. A flower head whose central flowers open first. Usually flat or domed.

Damping off. Soil-borne fungus diseases favored by wet soils, humidity and crowded plantings.

Deciduous. A plant that sheds all of its leaves periodically either in response to water stress or to the shorter days and lower temperatures of fall and winter.

Desertification. The process of becoming a desert, often due to mismanagement of the environment or climate changes.

Die-back. When parts of a plant die, often "back" to the ground. May be a symptom of cold damage, poorly drained soil, drought stress, salt injury or insect or disease.

Division. Dividing a plant into two or more parts to propagate.

Dormant. Similar to hibernation for animals. Plants that are dormant are in a resting state, usually during a particular season as a shield against weather extremes. Some "die" to the roots, only to regrow from buds at the base of the plant when the dormant period is over.

Drip line. The outermost edge of a plant, such as the farthest a tree's foliage spreads, where rainwater would drip to the ground. Often used as a reference point for irrigating and fertilizing plants.

Drought. A time interval, usually months, seasons or years in length during which rainfall amounts are significantly below normal for an area.

Drought tolerant, drought resistant. These terms are interchangeable and refer to plants that evade or tolerate extended periods of water stress through various modifications of leaves, stems, roots, physiological processes and life cycles. Some but not all of the plants in this category are also adapted to environmental conditions of high temperatures and intense sunlight.

Ecotype. Comparable to a subspecies, an ecotype survives as a distinct subdivision of a species through isolation and environmental selection.

Endosperm. Part of the seed that provides its nutrients.

Evapotranspiration. The combined amount of water that *transpires* through (or vaporizes from) a plant and that evaporates from the soil the plant grows in. Used as a guide for a plant's water needs.

Eucalyptus long-nosed borer. See Appendix B, page 353.

Eucalyptus redgum lerp psyllid. See Appendix B, page 353.

Evergreen. Broad-leaved and narrow-leaved plants, including many conifers, that have live foliage throughout the year.

Family. Group of genera (or just one genus) that share similar floral patterns.

Feed. Fertilize.

Fertilizer. A substance added to soil that provides plants with more nutrients.

Filiform. Shaped like a filament.

Floret. A small flower that is part of a compound flower head.

Flower spike. A flower head with a central stem.

Frost hardy. Refers to plants that tolerate several hours of subfreezing temperatures in the range of 25 to 28°F (-4 to -2°C).

Gall. A swollen growth on a leaf, stem or root usually caused by fungus, bacteria, virus, nematode or insect.

Genus (genera). The genus and species together form the scientific name of a plant. A genus may contain one or several different species that share enough characteristics to be grouped into a genus (just as a family contains one genus or several genera that share floral characteristics).

Giant palm borer. See Appendix B, page 354.

Glochid. Tiny barbed bristles that commonly grow in tufts on the areoles of cacti.

Grafting. The process of joining a stem or bud with the stem or root of a different plant.

Ground layering. See *layering.*

Groundcover. A plant that naturally grows low and spreads wide, providing a "carpet" on the ground.

Halophyte. Salt-tolerant plant

Hardening off. Gradual adjustment of a plant to colder temperatures or of an indoor plant to the outdoors. Usually facilitated by exposing a plant to cold temperatures for longer and longer periods of time, keeping it inside or at least protected in between these intervals.

Hardy. Describes a plant that can withstand prolonged exposure to cold temperatures and frost. Also refers to a tough, vigorous plant that is resistant to pests and diseases. See *Cold hardy.*

Heading back. Pruning by cutting a growing shoot down to its bud or removing an older branch completely or down to a twig.

Herbaceous. Not woody, having soft stem tissue and often a brief lifespan, sometimes one year or less, after which the plant or at least its aboveground growth dies back to the ground. However, there are other nonwoody plants that maintain almost a shrublike form for many years.

Hybrid. The offspring of parent plants of different species, subspecies, varieties, cultivars or genera, but not different families.

Inflorescence. Same as a flower head—the arrangement of flowers on the stem.

Lanceolate. See Appendix A, page 352.

Layering. Propagation by encouraging a stem to root while it is still attached to the parent plant. This can be done by burying part of the stem until it roots, called *ground layering.* Or, to propagate from a stem further above ground, you can make an incision in the outer stem layer and wrap it in a bag of damp sphagnum moss. When roots develop in the moss, you cut and plant the stem and its new roots in a new location. This is called *air layering.*

Leader. Stem or trunk that is large and more vigorous.

Mallow. A genus of herbs with showy flowers, disk-shaped fruit and palmately lobed or dissected leaves. May be used to describe these characteristics in a plant not technically in the *Mallow* genus.

Mulches. A protective covering over soil made of loose material, such as bark, saw dust, rocks, leaves or straw. Also used for aesthetic purposes.

Nematode. Any of a group of parasitic worms, cylindrical in shape and capable of living in soil and water as well as animals and plants.

Node. Point on a stem where one or more leaves are attached.

Oak root fungus. See Appendix B, page 354.

Offset (or offshoot). Small plants that develop at the base of and attached to a mature plant. Once separated from the parent offsets grow on their own and are useful for propagating those species that produce them.

Opposite. See Appendix A, page 352.

Organic materials. May refer to soil amendments, mulches or fertilizers derived from plant or animal residues.

Palmate. See Appendix A, page 352.

Panicles. Loose flower clusters that form roughly pyramidal shapes.

Perennial. Plants that live more than two years. Topgrowth may be evergreen or deciduous or may die back to the plant base during some period of time to be replaced by new stems and leaves in the next growing season.

Petiole. The stalk of a leaf.

Phyllode. Flattened leaf stalk which functions as and replaces the leaf blade.

Pinching. Removing a shoot tip by actually pinching it off. Encourages bushy growth.

Pinnate. See Appendix A, page 352.

Pubescent. Covered with fine short hairs.

Raceme. A cluster of flowers that each bloom on small stalks that stem from a central stalk.

Recurved. Curved backward, usually referring to leaves or flower petals.

Rhizome. Horizontal, often swollen underground stem with nodes and buds that give rise to aboveground stems and leaves. Sometimes the rhizome will grow along the surface of the ground with only half buried in the soil, rooting into the soil as it grows and produces foliage at the tip or along the upper side.

Rootball. Clump of roots and the surrounding soil when removed from a container.

Root hardy. A plant whose roots can survive extreme conditions, allowing a plant to renew itself after aboveground growth dies.

Root stock. Root or root system from which the aboveground part of a grafted or budded plant grows.

Rosette. Whorl of closely spaced leaves that often develops at ground level.

Runner. A horizontal stem that grows along the ground. Runners of some species produce leaves and roots.

Seed heads. Pods or clusters of seeds.

Spatulate. See Appendix A, page 352.

Species. A subdivision of *genus* that indicates plants with genetic similarities.

Sphagnum moss. Moss native to bogs that can be used to line hanging baskets or to propagate by *air layering.* The peat derived from decomposed sphagnum moss has many horticultural uses.

Stamen. The flower part that bears pollen, usually consisting of a slender stalk called the filament and the anther which produces pollen.

Succulent. Fleshy juicy plant or plant organs (leaves, stems or roots) that store water as part of a strategy for surviving dry periods.

Sucker. An extra shoot that grows from the roots and often weakens the plant.

Tap root. A usually large root that penetrates deeper into the soil than other roots from the same plant. Many plants lack a tap root and instead produce a fibrous system of roots that radiate out from near the base of the plant.

Terminal. The growing tip or top bud or flower on a stem.

Texas root rot. See Appendix B, page 354.

Thinning. Removing selected individual stems. The objective may be to open the interior of the plant to more sunlight or to allow freer movement of air through the foliage canopy or both. After thinning, the natural form of the plant should remain unchanged.

Umbel. A cluster of flowers in which individual flower stems grow from the same point and reach about the same height.

Variegated. Plant parts, usually leaves, with irregular shaped areas of two or more colors.

Vermiculite. A soil amendment composed of mica that improves drainage.

Verticilium wilt. See Appendix B, page 354.

Wadi. The name applied to mostly dry river beds in the Middle East. See also *Wash.*

Wash. The general term applied to dry river beds in the U.S. Southwest.

Water stress. Dehydration of plant tissue that occurs when water loss by transpiration from leaves and stems is greater than water absorption by the roots. Such an imbalance can be caused by different factors but in arid landscapes a shortage or deficit of plant-available soil moisture is often responsible. Plant responses vary from changes in leaf appearance and wilting of young tender growth to leaf scorch, defoliation, stunting and die-back of stems and branches and finally death of the entire plant depending on the intensity and duration of the stress.

Whorled. See Appendix A, page 352.

Xeriscape™. The patented term for low-water-use landscapes.

Xerophyte. A plant that can live under extremely dry conditions.

APPENDIX A

LEAF ARRANGEMENT

alternate

opposite

whorled

COMMON LEAF SHAPES

Simple

linear

oblong

elliptic

ovate

lanceolate

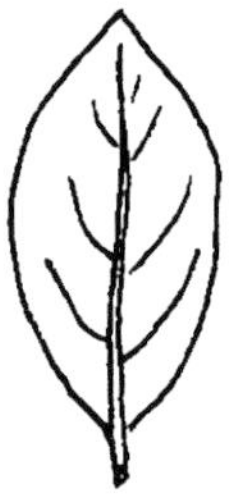

spatulate

Compound Leaves

palmately compound

pinnately compound

bipinnately compound

COMMON LEAF MARGINS

entire

toothed

palmately lobed

pinnately lobed

APPENDIX B

INSECT PESTS AND DISEASES OF WIDESPREAD CONCERN

Agave weevil. This insect poses a serious threat to many of the Agave species planted in the landscape. Adult weevils are dull black and about an inch long. They have a curved beak or snout with chewing mouthparts at the tip. Since they are unable to fly, they walk about over the host Agave, feeding as they go. The damage they cause is negligible but the larvae that hatch from eggs deposited by females in feeding holes eat their way into tender inner parts of the plant. This usually is followed by a bacterial infection that transforms the interior of the plant to a foul-smelling decaying mass of tissue. Agaves thus affected exhibit drooping, shrivelled and off-color leaves and the entire plant may tilt to one side.

At this stage, nothing can be done to save the plant. Larvae pupate within the remains of the Agave and emerge as adults the following year. Control consists of removing the entire plant, including the underground base of the crown, to destroy larvae and pupae that become the next generation of adults. Removal of weevil-infested plants must be done consistently and on an area-wide basis for best results.

Aloe mite (*Eriophyes aloinsis*). A pest that infests certain aloe species, causing discoloration of leaves and deformed new growth and blossoms. Usually not a major problem, but distorted bloom stalks (and occasionally entire plant) will need to be removed from the site and discarded.

Cochineal. White cottony masses on the pads of prickly pear and canes of cholla cactus identify infestations of Cochineal scale. Beneath the crust of waxy material lie bright red soft-bodied female scale insects. Wingless and legless, the adult females are attached to the surface of the cactus from which they suck plant juices with their beaks. The tiny winged male Cochineal is rarely seen by the casual observer.

Heavy infestations of Cochineal are unsightly and can kill affected pads and canes. Several chemical controls are effective but pruning out badly infested parts of the cactus and removing the rest of the scale with a forceful stream of water from a garden hose is the preferred technique.

Eucalyptus long-nosed borer (*Phoracantha semipunctata*). For a long time, the genus *Eucalyptus* has been pest-free in the U.S. Pacific Southwest. This ended with the accidental introduction of the eucalyptus long-nosed borer (or beetle) from Australia in 1984, without the introduction of this pest's natural predators to keep it in check. The beetle larva eats trails under the bark, in the cambium layer, and can girdle the tree, causing branch dieback or even death. Drought-stressed trees are most susceptible. Well-watered trees will actually drown the larva with the flow of sap into the wound.

Recently, the natural enemies of the beetle have been imported, which will eventually help control the pest. The eucalyptus is a mainstay in arid-land forest projects because it can withstand long periods of drought. Even when drought stressed, the tree can resume normal growth when the rains eventually come. These are the areas where the beetle is a major problem, seriously damaging old groves. Some *Eucalyptus* species are resistant, but not much is known about them.

Eucalyptus redgum lerp psyllid (*Glycaspis brimblecombei*). At the writing of this book, another pest has been found infesting eucalyptus trees in urban California. This psyllid is native to Australia and is expected to spread to most areas of California and beyond, where susceptible species of *Eucalyptus* are grown.

Psyllids are insects that suck plant juice. During its larval stage, this psyllid forms a protective covering called a lerp, which resembles armored scales but is actually composed of crystallized honeydew that develops into small white hemispherical caps about 1/8 inch in diameter and height. The larva underneath each lerp is yellow or brownish. The adult lerp psyllids are light green insects, about 1/8 inch long, with orangish and yellow blotches and clear wings.

Females lay eggs on succulent leaves and young shoots. Its numbers therefore increase following new growth, but all of the psyllid life stages can occur on both new and mature leaves.

Psyllids damage the plant by sucking plant juices and secreting honeydew. This liquid sticks to leaf surfaces and eventually a sooty mold covers it. Large psyllid populations can cause severe leaf drop, leaving a sticky mess on the sidewalk or pavement below, weakening the tree and making it more vulnerable to wood-boring pests.

Eucalyptus species affected include *E. camaldulensis*, *E. rudis*, *E. globulus*, *E. diversicolor* and *E. sideroxylon*. Chemical controls are currently being researched. Dr. Don Dahlsten of UC Berkeley is seeking a natural enemy of the lerp in Australia and so far the best candidate is a parasitic wasp. But you don't need to wait until the wasp is introduced in your region to prevent the lerp from thriving. The best cultural control is species diversity, the only sure way to manage pests in the long term, but you can also keep the following in mind:

1. Do not remove infected branches. You can't possibly remove them all and the ensuing new growth will provide more food for the lerp.
2. Don't fertilize or overwater. Water deeply but infrequently from the dripline out during dry periods only. Do not water near the trunk.

Giant palm borer (*Dinapate wrighti*). A pest of growing importance, the larva of this large beetle may infest palms especially of the genera *Phoenix* and *Washingtonia* in the western and southwestern U.S. Healthy palms of most species appear resistant but considerable damage has been noted in large old date palms recently transplanted from commercial date groves into commercial and residential landscapes. Affected palms are often stressed by improper transplanting techniques or inadequate post-planting care. A giant palm borer problem can be avoided by following careful digging, transporting and planting procedures and good maintenance practices. Because heavy pruning of the foliage crown at transplanting time may make large palms more vulnerable to this borer, do not remove live fronds above the horizontal level of the crown.

Oak root fungus (*Armillaria*). This fungus can be a problem in high deserts where some native oaks exist (it doesn't affect plants in the hotter low zone where the soil is warmer). The results are similar to those of Texas root rot, except an oak with oak root fungus doesn't always die. Instead it may experience stunted growth and a general lack of vigor. Plants of other species surrounding the oak, however, may be infected and killed.

The best prevention is to keep water away from the inner area surrounding the tree trunk. Irrigate only under the dripline. Also take care to grow only landscape plants with known resistance in close proximity to the roots of the oak.

Texas root rot (*Phymatotrichum omnivorum*). This soil-borne fungus is lethal to more than 2000 plant species including many that are used in the landscape, mostly at elevations below 3500 ft. (1067 m.) in the U.S. Southwest. Rapid foliage wilt followed by collapse and death of infected plants are symptoms most often observed from June into October. Dead leaves typically remain attached to the stems. Roots decay quickly and white to cream-colored spore mats may develop on the soil surface especially after summer rains.

Verticilium wilt (*Verticilium dahliae*). A soil-borne fungus, *Verticilium dahliae* is the causal agent of the disease, verticilium wilt. It is spread by infested soil or by cuttings infected with the fungus. Several hundred woody and herbaceous plants are susceptible to this disease, which invades, then blocks and destroys xylem tissues that conduct water in the plant.

The first symptoms may be the sudden wilt of foliage on one branch or one side of the plant during warm weather. Wilting leaves turn yellow, then brown, and may persist on the plant or be shed progressively from the base of the affected stem toward the tip. Discoloration and dark streaks are sometimes visible in young xylem just under the bark of infected branches, but other diseases cause similar symptoms and a laboratory analysis is necessary for positive identification of the problem.

At present there is no known cure once this fungus invades a susceptible host. Plants that are not seriously affected often recover. Thorough irrigation at regular intervals and application of nitrogen fertilizers may improve the chances for recovery. Dead and dying plants should be removed and replaced with resistant species.

INDEX

Note: scientific names of plants are *italicized*

B

C

D

E

F

G

H

I

J

K

L

M

S

T